INSIDE SHAREPOINT® 2007
ADMINISTRATION

STEVE CARAVAJAL
TODD KLINDT
SHANE YOUNG

Charles River Media
A part of Course Technology, Cengage Learning

COURSE TECHNOLOGY
CENGAGE Learning™

Australia, Brazil, Japan, Korea, Mexico, Singapore, Spain, United Kingdom, United States

COURSE TECHNOLOGY
CENGAGE Learning

Inside SharePoint® 2007 Administration

Steve Caravajal
Todd Klindt
Shane Young

**Publisher and General Manager,
Course Technology PTR:**
Stacy L. Hiquet

Associate Director of Marketing:
Sarah Panella

Content Project Manager:
Jessica McNavich

Marketing Manager: Mark Hughes

Acquisitions Editor: Mitzi Koontz

Project Editor and Copy Editor:
Marta Justak

Technical Reviewer: Raveen Rajavarma

CRM Editorial Services Coordinator:
Jennifer Blaney

Interior Layout: Jill Flores

Cover Designer: Mike Tanamachi

CD-ROM Producer: Brandon Penticuff

Indexer: Kevin Broccoli

Proofreader: Michael Beady

For product information and technology assistance, contact us at
Cengage Learning Customer & Sales Support, 1-800-354-9706

For permission to use material from this text or product, submit all requests online at **cengage.com/permissions**
Further permissions questions can be emailed to
permissionrequest@cengage.com

Microsoft® Office SharePoint® 2007 and Microsoft® SQL Server® are registered trademarks of Microsoft Corporation in the United States and other countries. Microsoft® Windows Server® is a trademark of Microsoft Corporation in the United States and other countries. All other trademarks are the property of their respective owners.

Library of Congress Control Number: 2008929241

ISBN-13: 978-1-58450-601-0

ISBN-10: 1-58450-601-6

Course Technology
25 Thomson Place
Boston, MA 02210
USA

Cengage Learning is a leading provider of customized learning solutions with office locations around the globe, including Singapore, the United Kingdom, Australia, Mexico, Brazil, and Japan. Locate your local office at: **international.cengage.com/region**

Cengage Learning products are represented in Canada by Nelson Education, Ltd.

For your lifelong learning solutions, visit **courseptr.com**

Visit our corporate website at **cengage.com**

Printed in Canada
1 2 3 4 5 6 7 11 10 09

Dedication

To Rosemary, my wife and companion for more than 30 years, thanks for always being there.
—*Steve Caravajal*

To my lovely wife, Jill. I could not have done this without her love and support. Thanks, Babe.
—*Todd Klindt*

This book is lovingly dedicated to my entire family, especially my Mom and Dad. I truly appreciate the amount of patience you all have for me, especially when I am traveling the globe chasing my dreams or hiding in my office working on another book. Without all of you, none of this is possible.
—*Shane Young*

Acknowledgments

First and foremost, I want to thank my wife, Rosemary, who is a source of inspiration and encouragement. A special thanks to Shane and Todd. It has been great working with you guys and learning more cool stuff. (So when are we going to write another one?) For Raveen Rajavarma, our technical editor and very good friend, thank you very much for all your work. You not only edited the book, but many times your insight improved the overall value as well. Last but not least, our editors, Marta Justak and Jennifer Blaney, thanks for keeping us on the straight and narrow. I know many times you felt like it was herding cats…and it probably was. *Steve Caravajal*

First, I want to thank my lovely wife, Jill. Without her support and understanding, I would have never been able to finish this book with my sanity intact. I also need to thank my beautiful daughter, Lily. She is a constant source of amusement and enjoyment. Next, I want to thank my fellow authors, Shane and Steve. I've learned so much from both of you. Thanks also go out to Darrin Bishop for his help with the PowerShell chapter. I would also like to thank Jennifer Blaney and Marta Justak for putting up with my inability to meet a publishing deadline. You both have the patience of a saint. Finally, I would like to thank our technical editor, Raveen Rajavarma. He kept me honest, and this book is better and more correct, thanks to his attention to detail. *Todd Klindt*

First things first. Thank you to my beautiful wife, Nicola. She is currently writing her own book for SharePoint Information Workers and the fact that she didn't kill me as we both worked through insane deadlines is nothing short of a miracle. You are awesome!

Once again I also need to thank my dogs, Tyson, and Pugsley. They don't get the attention they deserve during these writing cycles, yet every night Pugsley will sleep at my feet while I burn the midnight oil. Tyson…well he is a traitor when it comes to bedtime and will go get in bed with anyone who will let him, but that is okay, I still love him, too.

To my team at SharePoint911, you are all rock stars! Your hard work and dedication for everything from taking my client load to proofreading content makes this all possible. I am excited at the possibilities that lie in front of us.

To my fellow authors—you two are too much. You guys are some of the best friends a guy could ask for, and you are kind of smart. ;) It was a privilege for me to co-author a book with you guys.

To Ted, Polly, and the rest of the Ted Pattison Group—thank you. This book was written largely based on my SPA401: Professional SharePoint Administration class, which I never would have written had it not been for you.

To the team from Cengage Learning, I extend my gratitude. Jennifer and Marta, you have been wonderful to work with throughout this process. The fact you could put up with Todd, Steve, and my shenanigans is just amazing.

To our technical editor, Raveen, I say muchas gracias. Your dedication to fixing all of my technical indiscretions was outstanding. I don't know how you managed to find all of those little details I left out, but you did. You must be a smart little cookie.

I love you little Sparky! *Shane Young*

About the Authors

Steve Caravajal is a principal architect with the Microsoft Corporation. He has been architecting, deploying, and customizing SharePoint solutions for over eight years. Steve has 20+ years experience in technology and product development, consulting and training. He holds a B.S. degree in chemistry and mathematics and a doctoral degree in chemistry and computer science. Steve has also written and managed the development of numerous enterprise software applications in C++, Java, and .NET. He currently lives in Cincinnati, Ohio, with his wife Rosemary.

Todd Klindt has been a professional computer nerd since 1995, focusing primarily on Windows. He has been using SharePoint since curiosity got the best of him when he saw it on the Office XP CD and wondered what it was. Since then he has been active in the SharePoint community, and was awarded the MVP award for Windows SharePoint Services in 2006. He has written books and magazine articles. He has also presented at several technical conferences, including TechEd in the United States and Europe, the Microsoft SharePoint conference, and various other user groups. He is currently a technical consultant for Solanite Consulting, Inc.

When he's not exercising his geekiness or traveling around spreading the good work about SharePoint, he enjoys spending time with his lovely wife, Jill and his daughter, Lily.

Shane Young, owner of SharePoint911, has over 12 years experience architecting and administering large-scale server farms using Microsoft enterprise technologies. For the past three years, he has been working exclusively with SharePoint Products and Technologies as a consultant and trainer for http://www.sharepoint911.com. Shane has been recognized by Microsoft as an authority on SharePoint and is among an elite group of Microsoft Office SharePoint Server 2007 MVPs. He has architected SharePoint solutions for clients ranging from 20 to 50,000 users. Shane is a renowned speaker at national and international SharePoint conferences. He is also the author of The Ted Pattison Group's course SPA401: Professional SharePoint Server 2007 Administration. Shane also maintains a popular SharePoint focused blog http://msmvps.com/blogs/shane that contains a lot of beneficial technical information about SharePoint administration.

Contents

Introduction   xv

1   SharePoint 2007 Components and Services   1

    Introduction   1

    Choosing a Version   2

      WSS   2

      MOSS   5

    Supporting Technologies   11

      Windows Server   11

      SQL Server   12

      Email Server   13

    Upgrading Options   14

2   Architecture and Capacity Planning   17

    Introduction   17

    Planning for SharePoint Software Boundaries   18

      Other Software Limits   21

    Planning for Hardware Throughput   22

      Network Considerations   23

      32 Bit Versus 64 Bit   23

      Virtualization Considerations   27

    Planning for SQL Limits   30

SharePoint Scaling Options   32
Use SharePoint Server Roles to Scale   32
Which Should You Use?   42

3   Installation and Configuration   49
Introduction   49
Installing SharePoint   50
Basic Install   51
Advanced Installs   52
WSS-Only Option   54
Choosing the Proper Install Accounts   54
Two Versus Many   54
Kerberos or NTLM   57
Configuration Wizard   60
SharePoint Central Administration   61
Operations   62
Application Management   63
Shared Service Providers   64
One or Many SSPs?   65
Another Advantage of SSPs   66
How to Set Security   66
Web Applications   68
Site Collections   69
Install Microsoft Office SharePoint Server 2007   72
Installing on Additional Servers   74
Avoiding DCOM Errors   75
Starting the Services   76
Configuring Outgoing Email   79
Enable Usage Analysis Processing   79

Creating Your First Shared Services Provider 80
Creating Your First User Web Application 83
Slipstreaming Service Pack 1 84
The Infrastructure Update 85

4   Securing and Managing Site Content 87
Introduction 87
Site and Content Authorization 88
Security Architecture and Components 88
Permission Management 114
Web Application Authorization 124
Policy Management 125

5   Command Line Administration with STSADM 129
Introduction 129
An Overview of STSADM 130
Common Operations 135
Working with Sites 135
Backup and Disaster Recovery with STSADM 149
Advanced Management 159
Solution Management 159
Feature Management 161
Template Management 162
Content Database Management 162
Managed Paths and Zones 167
Web Application Management 168
Things You Can Only Do in STSADM 170
Working with Properties 170
Other STSADM-Only Operations 174
Extending STSADM 175

6   SharePoint Navigation and Governance   177

    Introduction   177

    Navigation   178

        Global Bread Crumbs   179

        Global Navigation   180

        Quick Launch   181

        Current Bread Crumb   183

        Security Trimming   183

        WSS Navigation   183

        MOSS Navigation   187

    IT Governance   191

        Controlling Downtime   192

        Managing Growth   193

        Usage   195

        Quotas   197

        Managing Third-Party Code   198

        Control Site Proliferation   198

        Security and Site Auditing for SharePoint   199

        Communication   200

        More Governance Resources   200

7   Managing Site Customization: Templates, Features,
    and Solution Packages   201

    Introduction   201

    Site Creation and Customization   202

        Customized and Uncustomized Pages   203

    Custom Site Templates   204

        Template Composition   204

        Site Definition Dependency   205

        Saving a Template   205

        Global Use of the Template   208

Site Definition 209

Definition Folder Hierarchy 209

Definition Description and Registration 211

Definition Configuration 214

Custom Site Templates Versus Custom Site Definitions 215

Features 217

Feature Folder Hierarchy 217

Feature Description and Feature.xml 217

Feature Dependency 220

Feature Deployment 221

Creating a New Feature 222

Solution Packages 223

Key Points 223

8 Configuring and Managing Enterprise Search 227

Introduction 227

Shared Service Provider Architecture 228

Index Server Role 229

Query Server Role 236

Database Server Role 238

Web Server Role 239

Search Administration and Management 239

Farm-Level Administration 240

SSP-Level Administration 245

9 Personalization and People Search 273

Introduction 273

User Profiles 274

Profile Management and Configuration 275

People Search 287

Search Center 288

My Sites   296
   My Site Creation   297
   Using My Sites   299

10 Configuring Internet-Accessible Web Sites   305
   Introduction   305
   User Authentication   307
      Anonymous Access   307
      Secure Access   312
   Extranet and Intranet Scenario   313
      Creating the SQL Database   313
      Creating and Configuring the Web Applications   314
   Alternate Access Mapping   319

11 Optimizing SharePoint Performance   321
   Introduction   321
   IIS   322
      The Web Application   322
      Application Pools   327
      IIS Compression   332
   SQL Server   336
      The Databases   336
      Database Don'ts   341
      Maintaining the Databases   341
   Software Boundaries   344
   Cache   344
      Output Caching   345
      Object Caching   346
      Binary Large Object Cache   347

Other Performance "Gotchas" 347
   Backups and Indexing 347
   Slow Page Loads 348
   Networking Issues 350
   End to End 351

12 High Availability, Backups, and Disaster Recovery 353
   Introduction 353
   Content Recovery 354
      First Defense, Versioning 354
      Second Defense, Recycle Bin 358
   Backup and Disaster Recovery 376
      What Are You Backing Up? 376
      How Will You Back It All Up? 383
   High Availability 403
      Web Front Ends 403
      Application Servers 403
      Database Servers 404

13 SharePoint with Windows Server 2008 and SQL Server 2008 407
   Introduction 407
   Windows Server 2008 408
      Management Improvements 408
      Security Improvements 440
      Performance 442
      Other Changes in Windows Server 2008 443
      What if I Have Windows Server 2003? 443
      Windows Server 2008 Resources 444
   SQL Server 2008 444
      Management 444
      Transparent Data Encryption 448

14   Administrating SharePoint 2007 with PowerShell   453

    Introduction to PowerShell   453

    Installing PowerShell   454

    PowerShell Commands   456

        Cmdlets   456

        Functions   457

        Scripts   457

        Native   458

    Using PowerShell Cmdlets   458

    PowerShell Scripts   460

    PowerShell and SharePoint   463

        PowerShell Setup for SharePoint   464

        Working with the Farm   465

        Working with Web Applications   468

        Working with Sites   470

        Working with Webs   475

        Working with Solutions   477

        Working with Features   480

Index   485

Introduction

Build it, and they will come. That is the scary part about this SharePoint phenomenon. What often starts as a simple pilot or proof of concept quickly snowballs into a business critical application, and you are left wondering what to do. And because SharePoint just happened, often you find yourself as the administrator of the servers along with the one hundred other things you do every day. Don't fret—you are not alone in this assignment.

The proper care and feeding of your SharePoint servers is paramount in a successful deployment. No matter how easy SharePoint is for the users or what cool whiz-bang features the developers have created, none of this will matter if the server doesn't run. But at the end of the day, you don't want the server to just limp along, you want it to perform like a champ.

This book is being published two years after the release of SharePoint for a reason—it took that long to work out all of the details. This book is a collection of two years of blood, sweat, and tears and the knowledge contained within wasn't available two years ago. Inside this cover, you'll find the most up-to-date guide available on everything you need to know to be a professional SharePoint administrator.

WHAT YOU'LL FIND IN THIS BOOK

This book was written completely for you, the IT guy, from the view of three other IT guys. In the pages that follow, you will find all of the details necessary to administer SharePoint—everything from detailed real-world installation instructions and proper backup procedures to performance optimizations and scripting help that will keep your farm humming. This book is based 100 percent on tried-and-true experience from actual SharePoint administrators and not just theoretical knowledge based on ideas.

WHO THIS BOOK IS FOR

While this book was written with a focus on the IT guy, that doesn't mean others wouldn't benefit from reading this book. IT managers could review this book for guidance on planning their deployments and the various options available to them throughout the project. All developers would benefit greatly from this book. As SharePoint is the platform on which they are building their solutions, understanding how it works out of the box and where the hooks are for extending the product can greatly enhance their end results.

HOW THIS BOOK IS ORGANIZED

This book is set up in the logical progression for a new deployment, starting with understanding the foundation and architecture and ending with backups and disaster recovery. While each chapter stands on its own, optimally you would start at the beginning and work through the chapters in order. All instructions for accomplishing specific tasks are contained within the text of the various chapters and include numbered steps.

Below you will find a brief overview of each chapter.

Chapter 1, "SharePoint 2007 Components and Services": This chapter is designed to help get you up to speed on the things necessary before you even think about installing SharePoint. The different versions available and the supporting technologies that go into SharePoint are the focus.

Chapter 2, "Architecture and Capacity Planning": This chapter provides guidance on planning your deployment. Items such as software and hardware boundaries and how they play into scaling SharePoint are covered. Server infrastructure is the focus.

Chapter 3, "Installation and Configuration": If it's time to install SharePoint, then this is the chapter for you. Guidance on doing the install and how to make sense of all of the required accounts is the center of this chapter. It rounds out with creating your first Shared Services Provider and Web application for your users to access.

Chapter 4, "Securing and Managing Site Content": Security is the name of the game for this chapter. User authorization is covered for everything from the entire Web application down to the item level.

Chapter 5, "Command Line Administration with STSADM": While SharePoint has a GUI for most administration tasks, some things are better left to the command line. In this chapter, the stsadm.exe tool will be covered from top to bottom.

Chapter 6, "SharePoint Navigation and Governance": This two-part chapter first exposes you to the power of navigation customization with the out-of-the-box tools. Then it concludes with IT governance and how it can help to make sure that you have a successful deployment.

Chapter 7, "Managing Site Customization: Templates, Features, and Solution Packages": This chapter will help you control all of the customization options available to SharePoint. Custom code from the developers opens up great possibilities for the platform, but there is a right way and a wrong way to deploy their changes; this chapter covers both.

Chapter 8, "Configuring and Managing Enterprise Search": Everyone loves SharePoint Search, and this chapter covers it all. Whether you are looking for how to deploy and configure Search or how to use Advanced Search and custom properties, you can find it all here.

Chapter 9, "Personalization and People Search": Social networking is a popular topic these days, and this chapter shows you how SharePoint can get you started. Importing profiles, exposing that information on personal sites, and searching for that information is the focus of this chapter.

Chapter 10, "Configuring Internet-Accessible Web Sites": If you want to expose SharePoint to the outside world, this is your chapter. Extranet and Internet sites are covered, along with the various authentication options you have when deploying these sites.

Chapter 11, "Optimizing SharePoint Performance": SharePoint performance makes the difference between happy and unhappy users. This chapter tries to help you find your way through the maze of optimizing performance with a focus on IIS and SQL Server administration for SharePoint administrators.

Chapter 12, "High Availability, Backups, and Disaster Recovery": This chapter will discuss how to maximize the uptime of your SharePoint and how to be prepared if a failure does occur. Backup and recovery is at the top of every good administrator's list.

Chapter 13, "SharePoint with Windows Server 2008 and SQL Server 2008": Windows 2008 and SQL 2008 are quickly becoming the new guys in the datacenter. This chapter makes sure you know how they will play with SharePoint so you will be prepared.

Chapter 14, "Administrating SharePoint 2007 with PowerShell": This chapter focuses on automating your SharePoint tasks with PowerShell. Starting with the basics for installing PowerShell to the creation of your own custom scripts, this chapter will have you up to speed on this tool.

ABOUT THE CD-ROM

The CD-ROM for *Inside SharePoint 2007 Administration* includes selected scripts from the book and software demos from Idera, iDevFactory, Quest Software, and SharePoint Solutions.

CD FOLDERS

You'll find the following two folders on the CD-ROM.

Selected Scripts—Selected scripts from the book are included from Chapters 5, 12, 13, and 14.

Software Demos—The following SharePoint 2007 Administration software demos have been included:

- **Idera Point Admin Toolset.** Idera Point Admin Toolset consists of a set of highly useful tools that can make your daily administration and troubleshooting tasks simple, easy, and quick.
- **iDevFactory Universal SharePoint Manager v2007™.** Universal SharePoint Manager v2007™ enables enterprises to administer and manage their SharePoint environments and focus on the key areas of burden. Universal SharePoint Manager v2007™ features turn SharePoint administration and support tasks from days into hours and hours into minutes.
- **SharePoint Solutions Alert Manager 2007** (14-day trial version). Alert Manager 2007 provides SharePoint 2007 administrators with the ability to manage alerts for users quickly and easily. For every list in the site collection where Alert Manager 2007 is installed, a Manage Alert template for this list link is added. For every Web in the site collection where Alert Manager 2007 is installed, a Manage Alerts link is added. Through Alert Manager 2007 SharePoint 2007, administrators can maximize the business value of the SharePoint alerting engine.
- **Quest Software Site Administrator.** Quest Site Administrator for SharePoint provides tools to understand and manage your entire SharePoint environment, giving IT much-needed visibility into all SharePoint servers, site collections, and sites. You can utilize the over 30 out-of-the-box reports available, build custom reports, and set built-in global policy settings to help you reduce the risk and avoid poor network performance, server storage issues, security breaches, support backlogs, and nonconformance to information compliance guidelines.
- **Quest Recovery Manager for SharePoint.** This provides granular recovery of anything in the backup of your SharePoint content database—individual documents, lists, document libraries, sites, and workspaces. It restores all information stored in the databases, including alerts, permissions, metadata, and custom

views. To simplify the recovery process, it also provides a convenient way to search, locate, and preview any item from across multiple database backups before restoring it. Best of all, you can leverage the backups you already have; no proprietary platforms and no site- or item-level backups required.

SYSTEM REQUIREMENTS

Selected Scripts

- Chapter 5 requires SharePoint 2007.
- Chapter 12 requires SharePoint 2007 and SQL 2005 or later.
- Chapter 13 requires SQL 2008 or later.
- Chapter 14 requires PowerShell 1.0 or later.

Idera Point Admin Toolset

The Point Admin Toolset requires Windows SharePoint Services 3.0 or Microsoft Office SharePoint Server (MOSS) 2007. The Idera Point Admin Management Service can be installed on any Web Front-end in the SharePoint farm. Currently, only the English language versions of SharePoint are supported. The toolset client also requires .NET Framework 2.0, 3.0, or 3.5.

iDevFactory Universal SharePoint Manager v2007™

System Requirements: MOSS 07 or WSS v3

SharePoint Solutions Alert Manager 2007

System Requirements: Windows SharePoint Services version 3.0 or MOSS 2007 compatible

Quest Site Administrator

System Requirements:

Platform	For Site Administrator console: Intel® Pentium® 1GHz processor (x86, x64) or equivalent
	For Site Administrator database and reporting server: Intel® Pentium® 2GHz processor (x86, x64) or equivalent; two or more processors recommended
Memory	For Site Administrator console: 512MB of RAM
	For Site Administrator database and reporting server: 1GB of RAM (4GB recommended)
Disk Space	For Site Administrator console: ~ 100MB of available hard disk space for install; 200–300MB of available hard disk space for logs
	For Site Administrator database and reporting server: disk space depends on the SharePoint content data base size
	1–5GB of available hard disk space for temporary tables
Operating System	One of the following:
	Windows Server 2003 SP1 or higher (recommended)
	Windows XP SP2 or higher
	Windows 2003 64-bit
Additional Software	Microsoft .Net Framework 2.0
	Microsoft Internet Explorer 6.0 or higher
	One of the following:
	Microsoft SQL Server 2005 SP1 (remote or local)
	Microsoft SQL Server 2005 Express SP1 or higher (remote or local)
	Microsoft SQL Reporting Services 2005 SP1 (remote or local)

Quest Recovery Manager

System Requirements:

Platform	Intel x86 (500MHz or higher)
Operating System	Either of the following:
	Microsoft Windows 2003 SP1
	Microsoft Windows XP SP2
Additional Software & Services	Microsoft .NET Framework 3.0
	Site Administrator for SharePoint 1.6 or later (recommended)
	Windows PowerShell 1.0 downloadable from http://www.microsoft.com/windowsserver2003/ technologies/management/powershell/ default.mspx (required for PowerShell Cmdlets)

SharePoint Server

Software & Services	Either of the following:
	Windows SharePoint Services v.2
	SharePoint Portal Server 2003
	Windows SharePoint Services v.3
	Microsoft Office SharePoint Server 2007

SharePoint Backend SQL Server

Platform	Intel x86 /x64
Memory	Minimum 512MB; 2GB of RAM recommended

1 SharePoint 2007 Components and Services

In This Chapter

- Introduction
- Choosing a Version
- Supporting Technologies
- Upgrading Options

INTRODUCTION

In this chapter, you will discover everything you need to know to get started with SharePoint. Understanding the different versions you can use is a key first step. Primarily this comes down to one question: Windows SharePoint Services v3 (WSS) or Microsoft Office SharePoint Server 2007 (MOSS)?

No matter which version you choose, there are other server requirements you will need to look into, such as SQL servers and email servers. SharePoint stores almost everything in the database and if you fail to get that piece right you cannot have a successful deployment.

At the end of the chapter, a quick review of the upgrade options is in order. Understanding the current road from v2 to v3 (this version) can shed some light on likely scenarios for v3 to v4. Nothing official has come from Microsoft on this topic, so just call it a hunch.

The goal of this chapter is to make sure you have a good understanding of the platform as a whole and the baseline decisions that are made before you even consider planning your install. If you are a seasoned pro, this chapter will serve to make sure all of those things you had to "just figure out" were correct.

CHOOSING A VERSION

Most people consider this to be a simple battle of WSS versus MOSS, or as they equate it: free versus pay. While it may seem that simple, it is just one of many questions to consider. Really, in this equation, you need to weigh WSS, MOSS Standard, MOSS Enterprise, MOSS for Internet, Forms Server, Search Server 2008 Express, and finally Search Server 2008. Yikes! That simple question has just gotten a whole lot harder. Each product has its own strengths and places where it is best suited to be used. So make sure that you read up on everything before you make a choice because there are a couple of surprises.

WSS

This product provides the foundation that all of the other versions are built on. Often referred to as the "free" product, this one has no additional license fees to use. It is licensed via your Windows Server. If a user has a client access license (CAL) to access the Windows Server that is running WSS, then he is covered to access all the SharePoint content on the box. Typically, in a corporate environment, all users already have CALs to access the Windows Servers so there is no additional expense in deploying WSS. However, if you want to open up your WSS site to partners and customers all over the world, then you can take a look at the Windows External Connector License (http://www.microsoft.com/windowsserver2003/howtobuy/licensing/extconnector.mspx). This license allows unlimited nonemployee access to your Windows Server, which would include the WSS sites hosted on that server.

Licensing Advice

Throughout this chapter you will receive pieces of general license guidance and considerations for SharePoint. The information here is provided only to point you in the right direction. You should contact Microsoft Licensing or your software reseller for official information for your scenario. As you probably already know, licensing is a very complicated topic that requires way more legalese than could ever be included in a simple admin book. Also, while you are reviewing licensing, don't forget about SQL, Active Directory, and possibly even email servers. There are lots of pieces to this puzzle, so good luck.

For more extensive information on the licensing of SharePoint check out http://office.microsoft.com/en-us/sharepointserver/FX101865111033.aspx.

WSS is the foundation upon which everything in SharePoint is built. It handles the following information:

- Storage
- Web presentation
- Authorization and user management
- APIs and Web services
- Hooks into the Windows Workflow Foundation
- Collaborative tools and features

Because this laundry list of core functionality was built as a platform, it is highly extensible and underscores why SharePoint is quickly becoming the platform of choice on which to build .NET applications. Developers can take the core platform and easily snap in their own functionality. The most readily noticeable functionality to the casual observer is a SharePoint site and its associated lists and Web parts.

There are three main types of sites included with WSS: Team Sites (collaboration), Meeting Workspaces, and Web 2.0 sites (see Figure 1.1). Each has its own features that make it unique, but overall they are all very similar. General navigation, functionality, search, and storage are consistent from one site to the other, allowing users to quickly become familiar, regardless of the template.

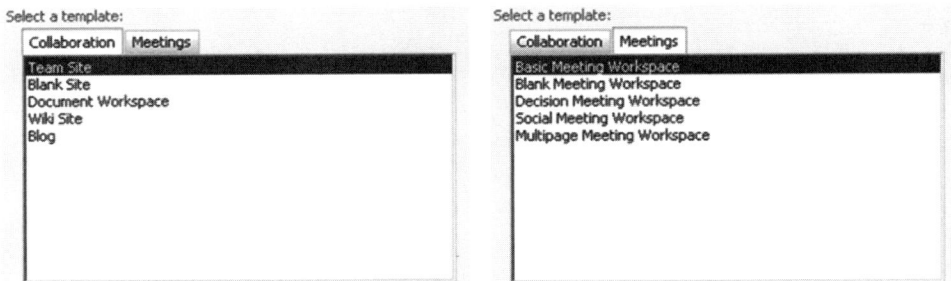

FIGURE 1.1
The site templates available for a WSS-only farm.

The Team Site templates are primarily geared to getting things done. There are not lots of pretty bells and whistles or fancy controlled publishing features to slow things down. Get in, get your information, maybe add some information, and get out. The Team Site, Blank Site, and Document Workspace are all built on this same principle. While it is possible to take one of these templates and enable something like document versioning or workflows, by default they are all off.

The Meetings templates consisting of Basic Meeting Workspace, Blank Meeting Workspace, Decision Meeting Workspace, Social Meeting Workspace, and Multi-page Meeting Workspace are meant to facilitate a meeting quickly. Each has unique default settings, but overall they use the same interface that maximizes screen real estate and uses a tab navigation interface to move from page to page. Like Team Sites, they are quick to edit and get content on the site for working together.

If Web 2.0 is on your agenda for SharePoint, then be sure to check out the Blog and Wiki Site templates. Corporate blogging is becoming very mainstream for everything from executives trying to push their thoughts down from the ivory tower to small teams tracking information from shift to shift. You can enable comments on the blogs to get feedback from your readers, which is a great way to vet ideas without going through formal publishing and review processes. Wiki Sites are ideal when you want to take the whiteboard approach. Having multiple contributors making updates and expanding the information can make for some great documentation. Want to try out a Wiki? As you do your SharePoint project, use a Wiki to track and plan the project. Keep notes on decisions made and steps taken during the multiple phases. Then you have a living, breathing document that can be referenced by your boss when you win the lottery.

Some of the WSS fan-favorite functionality includes a built-in two-stage recycle bin, major and minor versions on documents, security-trimmed user interface, quick branding through themes, all lists being RSS enabled, and the seamless integration with Microsoft Office 2007.

MOSS

Looking to do more than just collaborate with SharePoint? MOSS is probably your answer. This product takes everything WSS and extends it to new heights for you. Lots of new functionality is added, such as a publishing infrastructure, aggregation and personalization Web parts, enterprise search, and about a thousand other cool things. But with this great functionality comes a price tag. MOSS is licensed per server, and each user needs a client access license. Something else that is fun with MOSS is that while there is only one server license, there are two different CALs. There is a standard CAL and an enterprise CAL, and if you want enterprise functionality, you will need to purchase both. Many companies will purchase these CALs bundled with the Office client CALs to reduce costs.

MOSS Standard

The standard edition of MOSS is quite powerful and feature rich. The first major enhancement it brings to the table is a set of scalable and reusable centrally managed services called the *Shared Services Provider* or SSP. The SSP allows you to set up and maintain services such as search or profiles from one location and then consume that from many different SharePoint sites or even farms. It is covered extensively in Chapter 3, "Installation and Configuration."

Some of its core features are the following:

- Several new site templates
- User profiles, social networking, and My Sites
- Rollup Web parts for aggregating info across sites in the collection
- Enterprise search
- Publishing features
- Built-in workflows

In addition to the templates provided by WSS, MOSS adds even more, as shown in Figure 1.2.

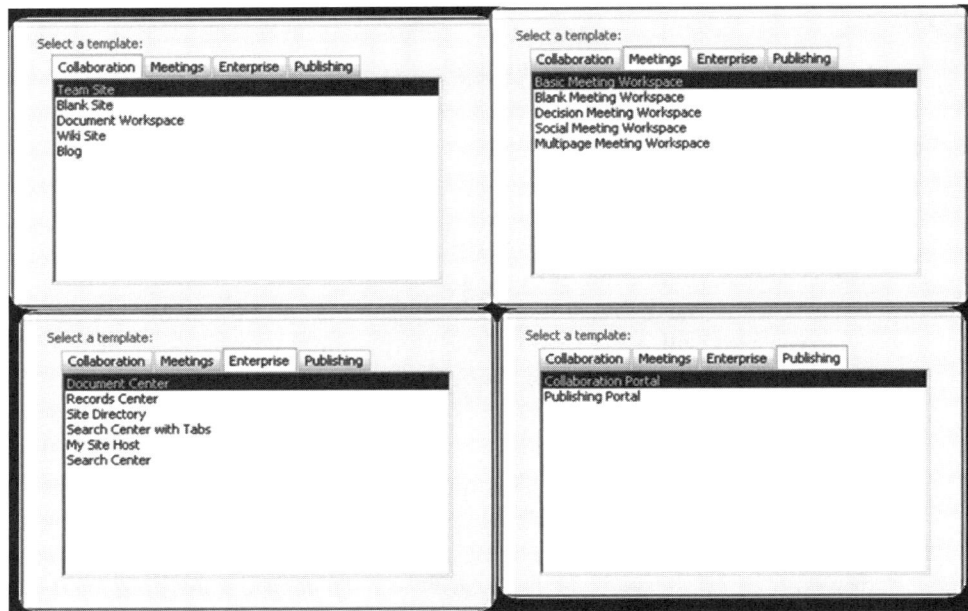

FIGURE 1.2
The site templates available for a MOSS standard farm.

The Collaboration and Meetings tabs are identical to WSS. The Enterprise tab, which you should be careful not to confuse with the Enterprise version of the product, and the Publishing tab are unique to MOSS.

On the Enterprise tab, you will find core sites with extended functionality. The Document Center is a team site with additional functionality enabled for managing documents. This includes the automatic addition of the tree view control on the home page, and in the document library the options for required checkout and major/minor versions are enabled.

The Records Center is used as a repository for storing and managing records. The idea is that you can configure a Records Center to accept copies of incoming documents and then route them to the appropriate storage location and apply policies to them as necessary. Because it allows you to set things such as audit trails or retention periods, it should really help with those legal compliance issues faced by many businesses today. Or even setting a hold on a document and allowing you to keep a snapshot of the doc the way you presented it could be very important for documents submitted in court. The Records Center adds so many additional features that you are encouraged to go online for a complete overview and demo at http://office.microsoft.com/en-us/help/HA102045611033.aspx.

The Site Directory is put into place to do one thing, help you organize your subsites. This template creates a special list that captures metadata about each site as it is created, allowing users to browse all sites later based on that metadata. Some new features for the Site Directory are its ability to control whether it creates subsites or site collections, and to have it automatically collect data for any site in the current site collection.

The Search Center and Search Center with Tabs are unique for searching. MOSS and Search Server have 11 search Web parts available out of the box, and the Search Center is ready to use them. The sky is the limit in creating custom search solutions, and they are covered extensively in Chapter 8, "Configuring and Managing Enterprise Search."

The My Site Host is not used very often. When you define an SSP, you must specify where My Sites will be hosted, and at this location, SharePoint will automatically create a site collection using this template. The site collection then handles the display of users' common My Site information and creation of their My Site the first time they visit. You should only use this template in special circumstances, for example, in creating a new My Site host because the previous one was unrecoverable. This template is only available when creating a new site collection. If you are creating a subsite in a site collection, then you will have the additional option of the Personalization Site. This is the template used to create each user's My Site automatically by SharePoint and generally should not be used. For more information on My Sites see Chapter 9, "Personalization and People Search."

The Publishing tab only contains two sites when you are creating a site collection: Collaboration Portal and Publishing Portal. These two are unique in the use of the publishing features. These features do several things, but the most drastic is the changing of the SharePoint pages to objects in a document library called *Pages*. With the items located in the Pages library, you then gain the ability to use versions, check-in/out, and even apply workflow for approving edits to your content pages. This capability opens doors for true content management scenarios. Perhaps you are hosting your public site on SharePoint? You could allow the marketing team to check out the home page and make several rounds of edits. Once they are happy with it, they could submit the page for approval, which could start a workflow that routed the page to the VP and then the CEO for approval before going live on the site. Sounds like a complicated scenario to configure? The Publishing Portal does that out of the box.

There are two primary differences between the Collaboration Portal and the Publishing Portal. The Collaboration Portal has several subsites predefined so you can hit the ground running, but the Publishing Portal is very bare bones. The other difference is that the Collaboration Portal is not set up with a workflow for approving new pages, while the Publishing Portal is set up that way.

If you come to the Publishing tab to create a subsite while in a publishing site collection, you will see three different options: Publishing Site, Publishing Site with Workflow, and News Site. These templates have the same publishing functionality, allowing you to expand your site collection with subsites with the content controls preconfigured.

When you add up all of these features, building out your corporate intranet or even your public Web site becomes a very real possibility. And this is where you really start to see ROI unifying on one platform. Think about it—how many shops have three different platforms doing the same thing? Maybe SharePoint for the intranet, Cold Fusion for the public Web site, and PHP for the extranet. While the techies of the world understand the nuances of this and the justification, to the bean counters of the world this makes no sense. Three sets of skills to maintain, three sets of hardware, and three sets of software to build Web sites doesn't really add up. This is where the MOSS story becomes very compelling. Bring all three of those sites onto one platform and make the bean counters happy.

MOSS Enterprise

Wow—if Standard does all of that, what can Enterprise possibly add? It can add the following items:

- InfoPath forms that can be filled out via a browser and are simple enough to create and publish so that a power user can do it
- Interactive Excel workbooks tied in with key performance indicators (KPIs) creating dynamic dashboards
- Connections to your line of business data that not only allow you to view it and repurpose it but also to search it

Taking advantage of the power of InfoPath 2007, MOSS Enterprise includes Forms Services functionality. InfoPath is a WYSIWIG editor for creating electronic forms. These forms natively create XML files to store the information gathered from the form, but they can easily be configured to send the information to a database. The challenge is that these forms require InfoPath 2007 to input data also. While it may be possible to guarantee that everyone in your company has InfoPath on their desktops for filling out these forms (though this is usually not the case), it is *not* possible to require partners, vendors, or customers to have InfoPath to fill out your forms. This is where Forms Services comes into play.

With Forms Services, it is possible for you to create the form on your desktop using InfoPath and then publish that form to the SharePoint form library. The form will then be converted to a Web-based form that can be filled out using nothing more than a browser, removing all requirements for end users to have InfoPath. Tie in a SharePoint workflow to the completed form, and you can create a very powerful business solution with little effort.

The next major addition is the Excel Calculation Service or Excel Services. This service allows the publishing of an Excel 2007 workbook to a SharePoint site for display. Not only do you get display, but you also have the ability to enable input of data for calculation using Excel formulas, interaction with Pivot Tables and Charts, and even data refreshes from external content sources. Imagine taking that workbook today that takes 20 minutes to open because of the external data requests and having that compiled by the server on a schedule. Then users could just browse to a page on the SharePoint site and see the data—no more waiting.

Enterprise brings one additional site template to the table, which is the Report Center. This template works in tandem with Excel Services to create rich dashboards. These dashboards can be built using Excel Web Access Web parts or KPI Web parts, which allow multiple data sources for their metrics, and even tie in with SQL Reporting and Analysis services. If your goal is to start getting reporting online, then look to MOSS Enterprise to be the hub of your information.

Businesses today thrive on the business systems and the key data that plays a role in every decision. Systems such as PeopleSoft, Siebel, SAP, and even just simple databases for customer relationship management (CRM) systems are just a few of these systems. For many companies, a primary challenge is that even though they have these systems with these invaluable details, the information lives on an island, meaning there is no method for reuse of that data in other systems. That is where the Business Data Catalog or BDC comes into play.

With the BDC, MOSS Enterprise can connect to these systems. Once connected, this data can be displayed, searched, and even reused with SharePoint. For example, you could have an existing SQL database for your CRM where all details about your customers' lives reside, such as address and order history. Let's say that you are using a SharePoint document library for storage of the customer proposals. Using the BDC, it is possible to configure the document library to add a metadata column that looks up a customer number from the BDC. Now when a sales rep is looking in the document library, she can quickly look at the document and tell which customer it belongs to. She can also click on the customer number and have it display the customer's record from the BDC, saving her from having to go open the CRM application for additional info. Finally, the menu can also have a custom action added that allows the sales rep to launch the CRM and make changes to the record, if necessary.

MOSS Enterprise also provides additional filtering Web parts. These Web parts can filter based on query strings, current logged-in users, input from page, current date, and several others. Allowing for custom solutions to be created with no code are just some of the out-of-the-box configurations.

Microsoft Office Forms Server 2007

Quite possibly after reading all of the features that MOSS Enterprise makes available, the only one that interests you is the Forms piece. If that is the case, you are in luck, because you can purchase Forms Server as a stand-alone product. The product is licensed per server and with user CALs. If you are looking to use the forms in an extranet/Internet scenario, you can also buy an unlimited, nonemployee access license for those scenarios that is licensed per server. For more information on the stand-alone product, look at http://office.microsoft.com/en-us/formsserver/FX100490391033.aspx.

MOSS for Internet Sites

MOSS also allows you to purchase a license for those external scenarios, and it is called Office SharePoint Server 2007 for Internet Server or MOSS FIS. This license allows for unlimited, nonemployee access to your MOSS server. It does not cover employees; they will still need their own CALs. MOSS FIS does include all of the functionality of MOSS Enterprise, and it is actually the same install—it just has a different product key, but does not have any different capabilities. This license is great because now you can open up the power of MOSS Enterprise to the whole world if you like. Unfortunately, there is no version of MOSS Standard for the Internet.

Search Server 2008

There is another free option. Take everything WSS and add MOSS Standard's search engine and capabilities, and you have arrived at Search Server. As long as you do not need high availability in your server farm, you can use Search Server Express for free (licensed the same as WSS). What this means is that if you are currently planning on deploying or already running WSS on a single server, then there is no reason not to upgrade to Search Server 2008 Express. You get all of the WSS functionality, plus a greatly enhanced search engine. Some of the features include the following:

- The Search Center templates and the associated search Web parts
- The ability to add external content sources such as file shares, other Web sites, or Exchange public folders
- Comprehensive administration dashboards with scheduling and tuning capabilities
- Complete search reporting
- Federated search connections, allowing you to have queries ran against your index and other open search-compliant search engines at the same time.

For a complete overview of all of the power of Search, see Chapter 8.

Essentially, what Microsoft has done is they've taken MOSS Standard and removed all of the functionality except for Search and made it available as a separate product. There is no reason if you are currently running a single WSS server that you shouldn't upgrade to Search Server Express. If you need your WSS farm to have high availability, then you will need to consider purchasing regular Search Server 2008 to add the functionality. One thing to note is that neither version of Search Server allows for the indexing of the BDC. For additional information or to download a copy of Search Server, check out http://www.microsoft.com/Enterprisesearch/default.aspx.

A Few More Thoughts on Choosing a Version

For many people, this process can be a very daunting task. Luckily, there is a 180-day trial of all of the versions so you can take them for a test drive, as well as a comprehensive feature comparison that is available for download at http://office.microsoft.com/en-us/sharepointserver/HA101978031033.aspx.

You will also notice from time to time some references to MOSS 2007 for Search Standard and Enterprise. These were early products that have been replaced by Search Server and should be ignored.

SUPPORTING TECHNOLOGIES

SharePoint is ultimately just an application and can only be as good as the platforms it is built on top of and its supporting infrastructure. Identifying these pieces and their prerequisites is the key to any good deployment.

WINDOWS SERVER

SharePoint is installed on top of either Windows Server 2003 (W2k3) or 2008 (W2k8). While the SharePoint functionality and install is very similar on either platform, there are some differences in the prerequisites.

W2k3 SP1 or later is supported, although it is recommended, as with most servers, that you run the latest service pack and hot fixes. If you have deployed W2k3 R2, SharePoint also supports that. You can even deploy WSS v3 on top of Small Business Server 2003. With any of these operating systems, you will need to install the Windows components for Internet Information Services (IIS) with common files, Simple Mail Transfer Protocol (SMTP), and the World Wide Web service. Additionally, you will need to install .NET Framework 3.0; service pack 1 is recommended. As SharePoint ships with both a 32- and 64-bit edition, you can run either Windows 32 bit or Windows 64 bit as your platform.

32 Bit Versus 64 Bit?

This is becoming a very common question today. If you are buying new hardware and setting up a new SharePoint farm, which processor architecture should you use? It depends, of course. Start with some important things to help you in your decision.

The current SharePoint version, v3 or 2007, is the last one that will be available on the 32-bit platform, meaning that future versions of SharePoint will only be available on 64 bit. While there is currently no official information on what upgrade scenarios there will be for the next version, it is safe to assume that upgrading from v3 64 bit to v4 64 bit will have to be less complicated than upgrading from v3 32 bit to v4 64 bit due to the need to change the OS. This is a very compelling reason to go 64 bit today.

Plus, 64-bit Windows also has better large memory support. If you are going to run more than 4GB of RAM in your SharePoint servers, you will be well served by 64 bit.

The downside to running 64 bit today is that not all third-party components support it. For example, when SharePoint first shipped, there was no ifilter (see Chapter 8 for more information) for indexing PDFs, so you had to run 32-bit Index servers. This problem has been taken care of, but there could be additional issues. So before you commit to a 64-bit farm, be sure that any supporting components you may want to run support 64 bit.

You will also need to determine on which edition of W2k3 to deploy. All editions, including Web, are supported. But the Web edition, due to its two GB of RAM maximum, often will not work for SharePoint.

W2k8 is also a possibility for running SharePoint, but the key point is that you must install SharePoint service pack 1. This requires either slipstreaming the bits (as covered in Chapter 3) or downloading updated media that has SP1 pre-installed. Deploying SharePoint on W2k8 and all of the differences involved is covered in Chapter 13, "SharePoint with Windows Server 2008 and SQL Server 2008."

If you are deploying SharePoint in any type of farm (multiserver) scenario, Active Directory is required. Farms will not function in an NT4 domain.

SQL Server

Almost everything you do or store in SharePoint is written to the SQL server, making it a very key component in your farm. When you upload a document to SharePoint, it is stored in a database; when you create a new site, it is stored in the database; when you add list items, they are stored in the database—literally everything that you do while interacting with a SharePoint site is stored in the database. For this reason, making sure that the database tier is solid is crucial.

For the database engine, there are currently five different options for hosting the database.

- **SQL Server 2000.** With service pack 3a or later installed, any version is supported.
- **SQL Server 2005.** With service pack 1 or later installed, any version is supported.
- **SQL Server 2008.** RTM should be supported for SharePoint with SP1. More details in Chapter 13.
- **SQL Express 2005.** If you choose to do a basic install of MOSS, this will be automatically installed for you.
- **Windows Internal Database.** If you choose to do a basic install of WSS, this will be automatically installed for you.

For SQL Servers 2000, 2005, and 2008, it makes no difference which one you use from the perspective of SharePoint, as SharePoint functions equally well in all versions. However, there are definitely advantages to the later versions for features, such as fault tolerance, Reporting Services, and so on. SQL Express is limited to 4GB database sizes, which makes it a challenge to use in a production environment. Windows Internal Database has no storage limits, but it does have a very limited set of management functionality.

Email Server

SharePoint has capabilities to both send and receive email. Outgoing email is used to send alerts and notifications to users and administrators. Incoming email allows SharePoint to receive email and then route the message or the attachments to the appropriate SharePoint list for storage.

Alerts are great because they let a user subscribe to a SharePoint list or library and be notified when changes occur. So instead of looking at the calendar every day for new events, the user could choose to get alerted of changes immediately, daily, or weekly. These alerts can be administered by the user or by a site administrator with the appropriate rights.

To configure outgoing email, you only need to specify the SMTP server, the email address the email comes from, the reply-address, and the character set. Specifically, the SMTP server needs to be configured to allow your SharePoint servers to relay off it anonymously. Of course, you will also need to make sure that port 25 is open between your SharePoint servers and the SMTP server. Typically, this is not an issue, but there are cases where the antivirus client on the SharePoint server has disabled port 25 outbound. If email notifications are not going out, this is often the first place to check.

Incoming email is slightly more complicated. In these scenarios, you need to configure the email server to route the messages to the IIS SMTP engine running on the SharePoint server. SMTP should route the messages to an email drop folder. A SharePoint timer job will then periodically check this folder and grab any email messages. These messages will be routed to the appropriate SharePoint list or library based on the address the email was sent to.

While incoming email does not require Microsoft Exchange Server, there is added functionality if you are using Exchange. In an Exchange environment, you can allow list owners to add incoming email functionality and automatically generate an email address, thus reducing the administrative burden of setting up email accounts. For more information on incoming email and for guidance on configuring it, see http://www.toddklindt.com/blog/Lists/Posts/Post.aspx?ID=31.

UPGRADING OPTIONS

If you are currently running v2 or just want some baseline information on how the upgrade process works (which should provide some clues for v3 to v4), then read on. There are three primary methods for upgrading: in place, gradual, and database migration. Each one has its uses and should be reviewed. Also, before attempting any of the upgrade methods, you should be certain you have good backups and have tested your restore procedures. Many companies do not confirm their restore procedures until it is too late.

The in-place upgrade allows you to do a simple install of v3 on top of v2. Then the upgrade process will run and reuse all of your existing databases and upgrade them to v3. This is meant to be your next, next, finish method of upgrading. As a general rule, you should never use this method. The reason is because you only get one chance. You start the upgrade process; it takes your entire environment offline and begins upgrading. If for any reason any part fails or has an error, the entire upgrade is lost. The only way to recover at this point is to restore v2 from backups and start over. This method should only be considered for a small environment with zero customizations and even then only if you have solid backups. For additional information on this method, check out http://technet2.microsoft.com/Office/en-us/library/bff35d1d-af83-45ae-a4d0-30f7cee8630c1033.mspx?mfr=true.

The gradual upgrade is a very popular method due to its flexibility. With this method, you install v3 alongside v2 on the same server. Then you can upgrade one to all site collections at a time. This allows you to have a mixed environment during the upgrade process. After you upgrade a site collection, if you are unhappy with the results, you can revert back to the v2 version of the site. This is because this upgrade creates a new v3 database and as content is upgraded, it is re-created in that database. Your v2 databases are not disturbed, and this is what allows you to simply revert back. Another nice thing is that your v2 content is continuously available at a secondary URL even after the upgrade, so comparing versions is no problem.

For more details on this method, check out http://technet2.microsoft.com/Office/en-us/library/0c0e7bb9-8a81-4007-824b-688e8eba23ff1033.mspx?mfr=true.

Using the database migration method, you build a brand new v3 farm on new hardware. Then you back up your v2 database and restore it to your v3 SQL Server. Then by attaching a new Web application, SharePoint will automatically upgrade everything for you. The biggest challenge with this method is that there are several small steps in the process, but overall it is the fastest method for upgrading your actual data. If you are using this method, consider making the switch over to 64-bit hardware. For more information, look at http://technet2.microsoft.com/Office/en-us/library/b6580f87-40b4-4768-b589-6ba54013f7e41033.mspx?mfr=true.

These are your primary upgrade methods. For more resources on upgrading, check www.sharepointupgrade.com for guidance and tricks for the upgrade. This site tries to pull together the best of the Web upgrade information into one location.

When planning how difficult your upgrade will be, there are several factors to consider:

- Number of unghosted pages
- Number of custom site definitions in use
- Amount of data

The best tool for gathering these metrics for you is prescan. It can either be downloaded directly from Microsoft at http://www.microsoft.com/Downloads/details.aspx?familyid=E8A00B1F-6F45-42CD-8E56-E62C20FEB2F1&displaylang=en, or it is included with any v3 install of SharePoint. This tool will generate log files that will list a lot of critical information for planning your upgrade. It will also highlight any errors that would cause your upgrade to fail. It is highly recommended that you run prescan early and often and solve all issues it highlights before proceeding with the upgrade.

2 Architecture and Capacity Planning

In This Chapter

- Introduction
- Planning for SharePoint Software Boundaries
- Planning for Hardware Throughput
- Planning for SQL Limits
- SharePoint Scaling Options

INTRODUCTION

There are as many different SharePoint installations as there are grains of sand on the beach. SharePoint 2007 is very flexible in the way you can install and configure it. In this chapter, we will cover the options you have when installing and configuring SharePoint 2007 and how to determine which options are best for you.

Before you can decide how you want to design your SharePoint farm, you need to know what limitations you may face. In this chapter, we will cover three boundaries to keep in mind: SharePoint software boundaries, hardware boundaries, and boundaries around SQL Server.

PLANNING FOR SHAREPOINT SOFTWARE BOUNDARIES

SharePoint 2007 can support an incredible amount of data; however, it does have some boundaries that you need to be aware of. Some of these limits are hard limits that should be taken very seriously; some of them are just guidelines and if you exceed them, keep an eye on your farm's performance. As with any guidance you get, please take these guidelines with a grain of salt. Keep your real-world experience in mind when evaluating these guidelines. Some may not apply to your environment. In most cases, as you approach the boundaries, performance begins to suffer. The key is to balance your performance needs with usability. Weigh the performance against the usability and effort needed to break things. This is one case where you should have an idea of what kind of performance your users expect. One tool you can use is a Service Level Agreement (SLA), which we will cover later in this chapter. If you have quantifiable performance metrics to meet, you can use that, along with these guidelines to plan your farm and your taxonomy. If you find that you cannot get acceptable performance or get below a specific limit, you may need to redesign your farm or split parts of it out.

We will start with the smallest SharePoint object, which is the list item. Tests and experience have shown that SharePoint's performance starts to suffer once you get close to 2,000 items in a single view. That could be 2,000 contacts in a contact list, 2,000 documents in a document library, or 2,000 users in a user list. After you go above 2,000, SharePoint has trouble displaying all of the items, and it starts taking longer and longer amounts of time to deal with those items. Because of the size of the list, adding a single item could take a minute because in the background SharePoint has to compare the new item to every existing item to make sure the new one is unique. The official word from Microsoft is that lists can contain more than 2,000 items, but you should not display more than 2,000 at a time. At that point, generating the page becomes cumbersome for SharePoint and rendering it starts to become very slow for your Web browser. Microsoft's suggestion is either to put the items into folders, with no folder having more than 2,000 items, or to create views to the library and make sure that no view shows more than 2,000 items. While using views does work, it is not a complete fix. Even if you alter all the default views, someone else that does not know the size of the list could easily create a new view that showed all items. We generally use folders, or find a way to use more than one list. The proper use of folders is a great way to scale.

You can also use indexed columns to speed up views of lists or libraries. Indexing a column gives SharePoint a heads up that you are going to be filtering or sorting a specific column or columns. It then creates indexes for the columns selected and stores them in the content database. Any views you create based on indexed columns will respond more quickly. This allows you to increase the number of items in a list without incurring quite as much of a performance penalty. Let's walk through indexing a column.

Open up a list or library and go to its settings by clicking the Settings menu, as shown in Figure 2.1.

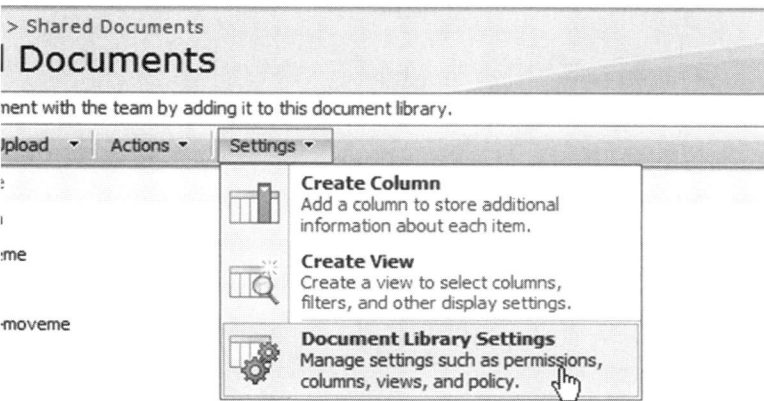

FIGURE 2.1
Document Library Settings.

Under Columns, click Indexed columns to get to the list of indexed columns.

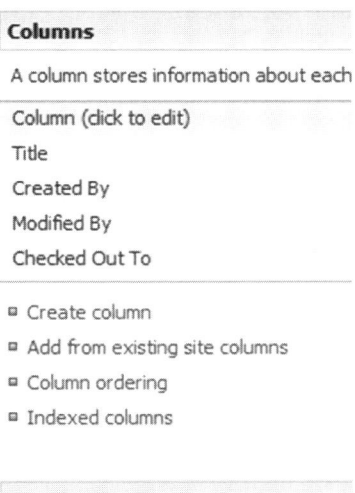

FIGURE 2.2
Indexed columns link.

After you click the link in Figure 2.2, you will see a list of the columns in the list or library. Choose the column you want to sort or filter. In Figure 2.3, we have selected the Created By Column.

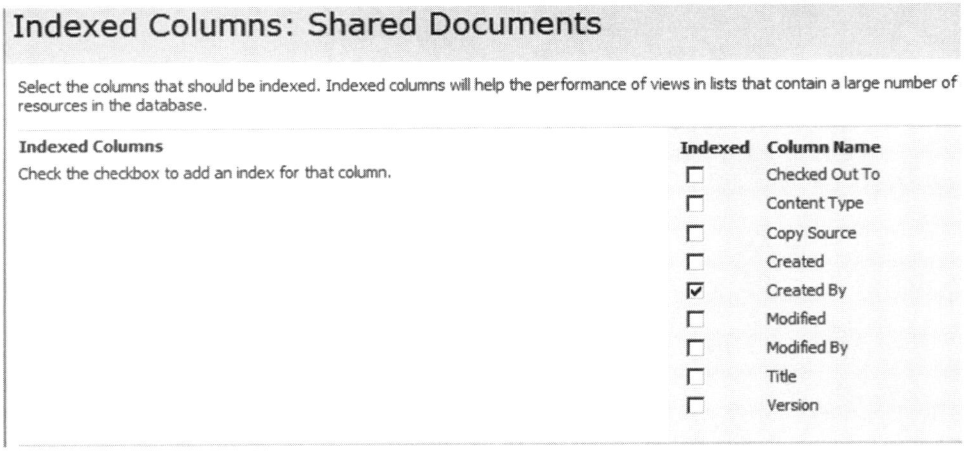

FIGURE 2.3
Select the Created By Column.

After you have the column selected, click OK. Now you need to create a view that uses the column. Scroll to the bottom of the page and click Create View. For this example, we will use a view based on the Standard View, as shown in Figure 2.4.

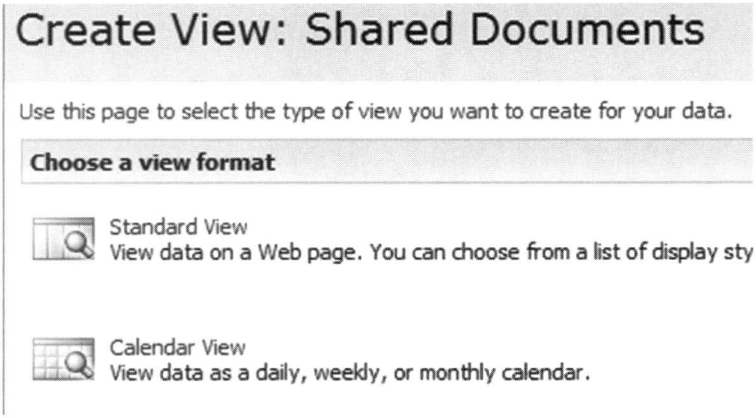

FIGURE 2.4
Use a Standard View.

Type **MyDocs** for the View Name. Scroll down to the Filter section and click the Indexed Column under Show items only when the following is true. Notice the column has (indexed) after it.

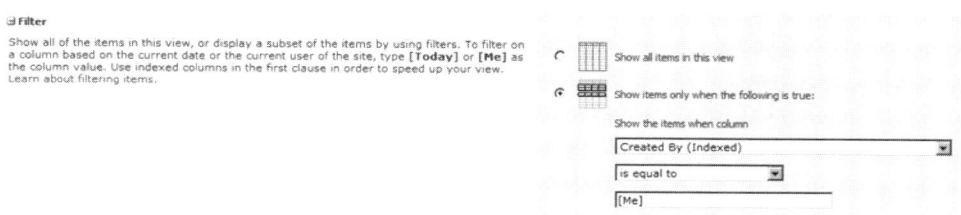

FIGURE 2.5
Select the Indexed Column.

Fill out the rest of the filter to match Figure 2.5 by putting [Me] in the filter value. Click OK to complete the view. Now you have a view that will show you only the documents created by the current user that will scale for large libraries or lists. Using these types of views off Indexed columns and making them the default view for a list or library is one way to scale above the 2,000 item limit.

OTHER SOFTWARE LIMITS

List items are not the only objects that you should keep in mind when scaling SharePoint 2007. Microsoft has a white paper, "Plan for software boundaries," that gives some guidance on different objects in SharePoint 2007 and how you should scale them. The following are some of the key objects and how you should scale them. You can read the entire white paper at http://technet.microsoft.com/en-us/library/cc262787.aspx.

- **Site Collection.** This is your primary unit of scale with SharePoint. The theoretical limit is 150,000 site collections per Web application and 50,000 per content database. The limit depends on the performance of your database server and the network bandwidth between the database server and your SharePoint farm. If you want to scale farther or increase performance, add database servers and spread your content databases across them. The scaling limit is determined by your performance requirements.
- **Subsites.** The recommended subsite limit is 2,000 per level. This limit is based on the 2,000 items per view limit. You can nest subsites to increase the number of them in a site collection.
- **Items.** Performance begins to suffer when the number of items per view is greater than 2,000. This limit is a presentation issue, so it applies to any group

of items that you manage in the Web UI. This could be subsites in a site collection, users in a group, or documents in a library. Techniques such as indexing, folders, and views can be used to mitigate the performance issues. Microsoft has a white paper that offers guidance on how to deal with large lists entitled, "Working with large lists in Office SharePoint Server 2007." It can be downloaded at http://technet.microsoft.com/en-us/library/cc262813.aspx.

- **Document.** Documents also have the item limitation listed previously. In the case of documents and list items, you can have more than 2,000 in a single library by using folders and nesting them.
- **Document Size.** The default upload size in SharePoint is set to 50MB. You can configure this to up to 2GB in Central Administration. As you increase the file size, the upload and download speeds decrease. To support larger uploads, you may need to increase timeouts in your web.config file. The network bandwidth between your database server and your WFEs will impact this limit as well.
- **List.** Lists are another casualty of the 2,000-item limit. Because of the interface used to manage lists in a site, your performance will suffer as the number of lists approaches 2,000.
- **Field Type.** As the number of field types per lists approaches 256, performance starts to degrade in list views.
- **Column.** As with most limits, the number of columns per list or library is not a hard limit, just a recommendation for where performance starts to suffer. In the case of columns, performance begins to suffer at 2,000 columns per document library and 4,096 columns per list.
- **Web Part.** The number of Web parts you can put on a page is dependent on how long it takes the page to load. With simple Web parts, page-loading times start to degrade at around 50. The more complicated the Web parts are, the fewer it will take to affect page-load time.
- **Managed Path.** Every incoming request to SharePoint is evaluated against the list of managed paths, so the fewer managed paths, the better the performance is. The guidance is to limit the number to 20. Again, this is a soft limit. If you want to use more managed paths, test their performance in a test environment.

PLANNING FOR HARDWARE THROUGHPUT

Planning for what the software can do is only half the battle. The software can only do its work if it has the hardware resources necessary to do it. In this section, we will cover some of the more common hardware aspects to consider.

Network Considerations

Of all the hardware considerations, this one is the easiest. Unfortunately, it is also often overlooked. The machines in your SharePoint farm are in constant communication, so they need a good pipe to talk over. In this day and age, we consider a gigabit Ethernet connection essential for all interfarm communication. Considering how common and inexpensive gigabit cards are these days, it just does not make sense *not* to use it. On more than one occasion, we have seen the performance of a farm be increased simply by replacing 100MB cards and switches with a gigabit backbone. This cuts down on the time-intensive operations (such as indexing), and it also makes processes like loading up large lists for users go more quickly, too. For the cost, it is one of the easiest things you can do to improve performance.

You may also want to consider dual-homing your SharePoint servers, especially your WFEs. Keeping your user traffic from competing with your backend traffic can allow your farm to support more users on the same hardware.

32 Bit Versus 64 Bit

Another question facing SharePoint administrators is whether to use the 32-bit or 64-bit versions. Both Windows SharePoint Services and Microsoft Office SharePoint Services offer fully functional 64-bit versions. The question is whether you should use them or not. Granted, 64 bit is a new frontier in Windows computing, and all the kinks are not completely ironed out yet. Plus, 32-bit Windows is comfortable and feels safe. That being said, unless you have a compelling business need, any new SharePoint installations should be 64 bit. SharePoint 2007 is the last version that will offer a 32-bit version. If you plan on upgrading to the next version of SharePoint when it is released, having your environment already at 64 bit makes the upgrade one step easier. If you think this is not significant, ask any Exchange administrators how their upgrades from Exchange 2003 to Exchange 2007 went. Exchange 2003 was only available in 32 bit and Exchange 2007 only at 64 bit. Upgrades required purchase of all new equipment, and 32-bit installations of SharePoint 2007 will face similar hurdles when upgrade time comes around.

Besides an easier upgrade path, what does a 64-bit installation get you? Performance, performance, performance. The biggest performance benefit is increased memory support. In general, 32-bit operating systems can only address 4GB of RAM, without special techniques like PAE. Depending on your hardware, you may only see 3.5GB of that due to memory being used for memory mapping. Of the memory the OS can see, it can only make 2GB of that available to applications. While Windows supports the /3GB switch that expands the memory available to applications to 3GB, SharePoint does not support the /3GB switch. Finally, once memory usage in Application Pools in 32-bit Windows gets around 800MB to 1GB, the Application Pools start to become unstable. SharePoint does not support Web gardens, so you cannot use those to get around the memory limitation. By comparison, 64-bit Windows supports 2TB of RAM, with the limit supported by 64 bits being even higher. This allows for more RAM available to applications individually, and also allows for more memory available to all the applications on the machine. This means better support for scaling with more Web applications. It also means more documents can be indexed at a time. More available memory has several benefits for SharePoint.

What's PAE?

PAE is an acronym for Physical Address Extension. It is a feature of x86-based Windows 2003 that allows access to memory above 4GB for certain applications. PAE was only available in the Enterprise and Datacenter versions of Windows Server 2003 and only worked for applications that were specifically compiled to use it. If an application was written to support PAE, it could access up to 64GB of RAM by extending the addressable memory space from 32 to 36 bits. In the background, the OS would swap memory pages around to make the magic happen. Because of this, it did not perform as well as the native support that 64 bit offers.

Expanded memory support is not the only advantage to using 64-bit environments. CPUs also get to stretch their legs a little more. The 32-bit environment supports machines with multiple CPUs, but moving to 64 bit allows you to scale to more CPUs. You also get better bang for buck for those CPUs when you scale. As you add CPUs, the return is not linear, because each CPU adds less and less computing power to the machine until eventually you hit a plateau. The 64-bit environments scale better, and the performance you lose for additional CPU is less. Also, 64-bit Windows also support more CPUs. Windows 2008 Standard supports four CPUs in both 32-bit and 64-bit versions, and Enterprise supports eight CPUs for both as well. Once you get to the Datacenter version of Windows, the 32-bit version only supports 32 CPUs, whereas 64 bit supports 64 CPUs. SharePoint does support installation on Windows 2008 Datacenter Edition, so those extra CPUs can be used to scale. That 64-bit wide pipe also allows faster communication between the CPU and the cache, allowing you to take better advantage of it.

With the upgrade and performance advantages, it is our recommendation that all of the servers in your farm should be 64 bit, unless there is a compelling reason for them to remain 32 bit. To be fair, there are a few reasons where it makes sense to stick with a 32-bit OS and 32-bit SharePoint. The biggest reason is third-party software. In order for your 64-bit environment to be successful, all of the third-party software you have installed must ideally be 64 bit, or at least run in a 64-bit environment. From an OS perspective, make sure that your antivirus software, backup software, and any management software you use will work with 64-bit Windows. After you have your OS dependencies figured out, it is time to look at any SharePoint software you might be using. This includes any Web Parts, Solutions, or iFilters you may be using. As you evaluate your third-party software and their 64-bit support, keep your topology in mind and which machines in your farm they impact. If all of your iFilters are 64 bit, but you have a Web Part that does not work well in a 64-bit environment, you may have a 64-bit Index server while keeping your WFEs at 32 bit. Later in this chapter, we will cover how you can mix and match 32-bit and 64-bit machines in your farm.

Adobe PDF iFilter and the 64-Bit Blues

One glaring omission from the 64-bit landscape is a PDF iFilter from Adobe. The only iFilter they produce is 32 bit only. This causes problems for SharePoint administrators who want to move their Index server to 64 bit. The iFilter being 32 bit only means that your Index server must be 32 bit, which is unfortunate, as your Index server is a hardworking machine and can really take advantage of that extra RAM or CPUs. Recently, Adobe released a white paper on how to install their 32-bit iFilter on a 64-bit OS, but it is a kludge. It requires using thunking to load the 32-bit DLL in the 64-bit system. There are a couple of reasons why we do not recommend this approach. You pay a huge performance penalty when using thunking. Your Index box is one of your most highly taxed boxes, and in large environments, you cannot afford the performance penalty that is associated with thunking. Second, the Adobe PDF iFilter along with only being 32 bit, is also single-threaded. Because of the way the Index loads DLLs for the documents, it is breaking apart; if a single-threaded DLL is loaded, it locks out any other instances of itself being loaded. This means that regardless of how much RAM you have, or how many CPUs you have, you can only index a single PDF file at a time.

Don't worry, though, as there is another, better option. Another company, Foxit, has made a PDF iFilter that addresses these issues. It is both multithreaded and native 64 bit. Unlike Adobe's iFilter, though, it is not free, although the licensing is very reasonable. The Foxit PDF performs very well, and it is well respected. If you have a need to index many PDF files, consider the Foxit iFilter. You will not regret it.

The other reason to install a 32-bit environment is if you are doing a gradual upgrade from SharePoint 2003, either Windows SharePoint Services v2 or SharePoint Portal Server 2003. SharePoint 2003 only ran in 32-bit environments. Since a gradual upgrade requires that SharePoint 2003 and SharePoint 2007 be installed on the same machine, it must be 32 bit. However, this is only required for as long as the upgrade is in process. Once the upgrade is completed, and the SharePoint 2003 bits have been uninstalled, you can reinstall the WFE as 64 bit.

If none of the preceding issues are keeping you from upgrading to 64 bit, you should do so. If your hardware was manufactured after 2004 or so, it likely supports 64-bit Windows, and therefore 64-bit SharePoint. Check with your hardware manufacturer to be sure. As we stated before, verify that any software you run on your servers has 64-bit versions. As you plan to move your servers from 32 bit to 64 bit, we recommend upgrading your servers in this order:

- SQL server
- Index server
- WFEs
- Other application server

Nearly everything SharePoint does touches your SQL servers, and SQL Server can make good use of more RAM and CPU. This makes it a natural choice to be upgraded first. While the process requires careful planning and testing, it is not complicated. Two things make this upgrade go smoothly. First, the database format used by 32-bit SQL Server can be upgraded seamlessly by 64-bit SQL Server. This means that you do not need to do anything to them when you upgrade. If they are located on a SAN or NAS device, or even attached directly, you can detach them from your 32-bit SQL Server and simply attach them to your 64-bit SQL Server. There are no additional steps. You can also restore backups made in 32-bit SQL Server to 64-bit SQL Server. That is another easy way to upgrade your databases. Whichever way works best for you will still go very smoothly. The other aspect that makes this upgrade easy is that SharePoint does not care about the SQL server it is talking to. All it cares about is the SQL server name and instance, and the database name. If you choose to upgrade your SQL server to 64 bit, and you give it the same name as the 32-bit server it is replacing, there is nothing to do in SharePoint. The architecture behind it does not matter to SharePoint. All you need to do is power down all the SharePoint servers in your farm before you upgrade your SQL server. Once the 64-bit SQL Server is online, power your SharePoint servers up, and they will connect automatically. The ease of this operation and the payback you get make it a very good candidate for your first 64-bit server.

After your SQL servers are 64 bit, the next machine you should consider upgrading is your Index server. After the SQL server, your Index server is the hardest working server in your farm. The process of crawling your content sources, indexing all the documents, and creating the index files and databases is very memory, CPU, and I/O intense. It also can take advantage of the additional RAM support that a 64-bit environment offers. As we mentioned before, verify that any iFilters you use have 64-bit versions.

To Mix or Not to Mix?

A SQL Server technically is not part of your SharePoint farm (this topic does get debated), as it does not have SharePoint installed on it. Your Index server is. Should you be concerned if one member of your farm is 64 bit while the rest are 32 bit? You should not. Microsoft fully supports mixed architecture in your farm. However, you should consider keeping all members of the same tier at the same architecture when you can. If there are any differences between the 32-bit and 64-bit versions of third-party software, that would make for an inconsistent end user experience. The performance difference between 32-bit and 64-bit boxes would also cause issues if your WFEs were load balanced. Because of this, try to keep machines in the same tier at the same architecture if you can. Of course, while you are upgrading them, they will be mixed for a while, and that is okay.

After your database servers and Index servers are 64 bit, it is time to look at upgrading your WFEs. As mentioned in the sidebar, your goal should be to get them all to 64 bit eventually. You do not want to install new WFEs as 64 bit, but rather leave your existing ones at 32 bit. If you do, plan to retire your 32-bit WFEs sooner rather than later. After you have verified that all of your third-party software has 64-bit versions, the upgrade is easy. First, remove the 32-bit WFE from your farm. You can do this in Central Admin or by uninstalling SharePoint from the server. If the server was a member of a load-balancing group, remove it so that end user requests are not sent to it. After the machine is out of your farm, install the 64-bit OS and SharePoint on it and join it back into your farm. Adding a 64-bit server is exactly the same as adding a 32-bit WFE. After all of your WFEs are running at 64 bit, upgrade any remaining application servers you may have. If you have broken out your Query or Excel Calculation Services roles, this is the time you would upgrade them.

Congratulations, all of your servers are now running at 64 bits, and you are well positioned for your upgrade to the next version of SharePoint.

VIRTUALIZATION CONSIDERATIONS

Virtualization has become a hot topic lately. In the last few years, it has come of age as a technology to be taken seriously in a production environment. If you are designing a new SharePoint installation or adding to an existing one, the question of whether you should use virtualization is not one to be taken lightly. In this section, we will discuss virtualization and how it figures into your SharePoint topology.

Before we go any farther, we need to discuss Microsoft's official position on virtualization. KB article 897615 specifies that Microsoft support will only support Microsoft virtualization technology. If you have Premier level support, Microsoft will use "commercially reasonable efforts" to support your farm. No guarantees. If you do not have Premier support from Microsoft, they will not support third-party virtualization at all. If you need support for your issue, you will have to reproduce it on Microsoft virtualization technology or on bare hardware. We do not mention this to suggest that any of the third-party virtualization technologies are inferior, because they are not. In some organizations, it is very important to stay in a supported configuration, and we only mention this for those organizations. It is also important to mention that all of Microsoft's virtualization software is free with the appropriate licenses for Windows. VMware also make their VMware Player, VMware Server, and VMware ESX Server 3i available as free downloads.

Is Hyper-V Supported?

At the time this chapter was written, Microsoft did not officially support Hyper-V in production environments. However, support for Hyper-V is expected, so please check with Microsoft Support if you plan on using Hyper-V. By the time you read this chapter, it will likely be supported.

What About VMware?

Not to be ignored, VMware, Microsoft's main competitor in the virtualization space, has published a white paper outlining their experience in virtualizing SharePoint. They found that a SharePoint environment virtualized on VMware's ESX server outperformed a pure hardware environment by four percent. You may think that is a modest improvement, and you would be correct. It becomes more impressive when you find that it was done with fewer servers, and it used 26 percent of the power that the physical farm did—1017 watts as opposed to 3952 watts. This adds up to serious savings to your company both in hardware costs and ongoing power and cooling costs. From a more practical standpoint, the virtualized environment used only six power cords, as opposed to 22 needed in the physical. You can read all about the environment VMware used at http://virtualgeek.typepad.com/virtual_geek/2008/07/virtualizing-sh.html.

Now that you know that virtualizing SharePoint is supported, how should you use it? As we look at SharePoint topology, we think of three environments: Development, Test, and Production. We will cover these as they pertain to virtualization.

Development Environment

Virtualization is a great fit for development environments. We almost insist on it, actually. Performance demands are not nearly as great in development environments, so any penalty for virtualization is negligible. Having a virtualized dev environment gives each developer his own sandbox to play in. They can do IIS resets whenever they would like, and there is no worry that their code is stepping on someone else's code. They also have the ability to roll their environment back to a previous version if there is a problem, or they can start from a completely clean environment if they would like. All of this can be done quickly and without involving IT. This keeps requests down for developers running Server operating systems as their desktop OS.

There are many virtualization products, and nearly all of them can be used in the development environment. It could be each developer running his own copy of Virtual PC on his desktop, or a centralized server running Hyper-V and each developer given his own images to run. Which to use is determined mainly on how tightly your organization wants to control virtualized environments.

Test Environment

After your developers have finished their work in their development environment, it should be moved to a test environment to be tested. Virtualization is also a great fit for this environment. Like development, the performance demands on test are not as great as production, so lower-end hardware and virtualization can be used. For your tests to be valid, you should have many people using the environment. If it does not perform as well as production, it will serve as a good "worst case" to set expectations. If you virtualize your test environment, you have the flexibility to roll back versions, which is good for testing different versions. You can also use this environment to test the latest OS, SharePoint, or application patches to see what effect they will have. Having a good, flexible test environment reduces the chance that you will be tempted to test things in production, which is never a good idea.

Production Environment

The final step from Development to Test is Production. This is where all that hard work pays off. Should you virtualize production? This is a hotly debated topic. It basically comes down to your environment and how much you are already leveraging virtualization technologies. As mentioned earlier, Microsoft will only support its own virtualization, or make a best effort to support third-party virtualization software if you have paid for Premier support. If you do choose to virtualize your servers, we recommend doing it in this order:

- Query (if they are separate)
- WFE
- Application servers (Index, Excel Calculation Services, and so on)
- SQL servers

This is essentially a list of the roles in ascending order of CPU and I/O usage. Both SQL and Index servers are very CPU and I/O intensive, so if you virtualize either of them, be sure to scale accordingly and test to verify the performance is acceptable. Query servers and WFEs are decent candidates for virtualization. When virtualizing production environments, you will probably want to consider only the big virtualization products like Microsoft's Virtual Server, Hyper-V, or VMware's ESX server. They will offer the best performance and the best management tools.

Disaster Recovery Environments

The final type of SharePoint you may want to virtualize is a disaster recovery environment. This is another great candidate for virtualization. Depending on the type of disaster recovery plan you have in place, and what type of software you are using, you may find yourself needing to restore databases or site collections to retrieve individual items. In this case, it is very handy to have a virtual environment handy. You can restore your database into your virtual environment, pull out whatever data you need, and move just that piece back into production. As long as all of the software is the same, and at the same versions, backups from production will restore just fine. For more information on disaster recovery, please see Chapter 12, "High Availability, Backups, and Disaster Recovery."

PLANNING FOR SQL LIMITS

When planning your SharePoint environment, you need to figure in your SQL hardware limits. SQL is the backbone of SharePoint, so you will need to size it correctly for SharePoint. I/O is the main bottleneck for large SQL environments. There are many ways to test and measure I/O performance. We recommend reading Microsoft's "Predeployment I/O Best Practices" white paper at http://www.microsoft.com/technet/prodtechnol/sql/bestpractice/pdpliobp.mspx. This gives excellent guidance on how to test your SQL I/O. We will cover some of the basic I/O tweaking techniques in this chapter.

Your first consideration to scale SQL is where to put different databases and logs files. Databases should be placed on fast disks in the following order:

- SQL TempDB database and logs
- SharePoint Config database and logs
- SharePoint Content database log files
- SharePoint Search database and logs
- SharePoint Content database files
- Other databases

RAID 10 is the ideal level to use for high performance and should be considered for the top three or four database types listed previously. RAID5 is suitable for primarily read operations, like the Search and Content databases.

When designing your SharePoint architecture, you should plan for your Content databases to never grow larger than 100GB. This is not a SQL limit; SQL Server can handle very large databases. It is more guidance that comes from a few years of experience with SharePoint. Certain SharePoint functions result in large row and table scans in SQL. As database sizes grow, the chance of table or database locks when these functions run will increase. This is one of those soft boundaries that you should use as guidance; it is not a hard limit. Since your databases should not be larger than 100GB, and a site collection must exist entirely in a single content database, you should also plan for no site collection to grow larger than 100GB. You should also consider your backup and restore times, as well as your SLA when you plan site collection and database size. If your SLA says you must recover data for users within four hours, but you have a 100GB database that takes five hours to restore, you need to either increase your SLA or make your site collections and content databases smaller.

If you do choose to use large databases, you can use filegroups to improve their performance. You will need to put the data files on different disks, and the number of data files should be less than or equal to the number of cores in your SQL server. The SharePoint backup tool cannot restore to multiple files. This will likely not be a problem, because if your environment warrants SQL filegroups, then you are probably not using the SharePoint backup tool.

We also recommend presizing your data files and log files, rather than using autogrow. Autogrow is a very slow process, and it can negatively impact your SQL server's performance, so it should not be done when end users are using SharePoint. If you grow databases on the fly as you need them, it will also increase the chance that your database and transaction log files will become fragmented on the file system of your SQL server. If these files are fragmented, it can cause severe performance problems. Steps should be taken to keep your database files contiguous. We recommend pre-growing your databases and logs to contain one year's worth of growth. Not only will this keep your databases from getting fragmented, but it will also make it easier for you to budget for drive space and hardware purchases. Many environments have a long budget and acquisition process. Knowing your churn rate and database needs ahead of time keeps these needs from sneaking up on you. There are many ways to determine your churn rate. This can be done by monitoring the size of your backups or using commands like STSADM –o enumsites.

Size Matters

One SQL management technique we cannot stress enough is that you should not shrink your SQL databases. As IT pros, it is common to try to keep things orderly, like defragmenting file systems. You may be tempted to shrink databases that have significant white space in them. In most situations, that is a bad idea. If you shrink your databases, you force them to grow when more content is added, which will happen. Databases grow—it is what they do. When they grow, you incur a performance penalty, and you increase the likelihood they will become fragmented on the SQL file system. The only instances where shrinking databases make sense are if you are removing site collections from them. This may be happening as you move site collections from one database to another, or if you are deleting site collections en masse, like during a gradual upgrade. Otherwise, give your databases breathing room. They will thank you for it.

As your WFEs are the window to your SQL databases, the number of WFEs has a direct impact on your SQL server's sizing. Performance tests show that in collaboration environments, as would be a typical intranet environment, five WFEs can saturate a single SQL server. However, in read-only environments, such as Internet facing sites, it can take up to eight WFEs to saturate a single SQL server. You should also try to have at least one SQL core per WFE. If you need more than five WFEs in your environment, add more SQL servers on the back end. SharePoint supports keeping your content databases on multiple SQL servers.

SHAREPOINT SCALING OPTIONS

As you are planning your SharePoint architecture, it is important to know all the options you have. In this section, we will cover the different ways that SharePoint scales both in server roles and farm scaling.

USE SHAREPOINT SERVER ROLES TO SCALE

SharePoint uses server roles to scale and provide flexibility in architecture. Here we will cover each of the roles and their scaling considerations.

Web Front Ends (WFE)

These are the outward faces of your farm. Servers that have the WFE role are servers that serve up Web pages to end users. They require very little in the way of local drive space. You should estimate 4GB for the Windows OS, a Pagefile equal to the amount of RAM, 1.3GB for SharePoint install files, plus enough space for all Solutions and

Features. In a typical collaboration environment, these machines are used for both read and write operations. Scale seems to plateau once you get five WFEs for each SQL server—at that point the WFE tier is no longer the bottleneck. In a Publishing environment where traffic is largely read-only, WFEs scale to seven or eight per SQL server before the plateau. When multiple WFEs are used, some sort of load balancing software or hardware must be used. The Network Load Balancing Service (NLBS) included with Windows can be used, or you can use a higher-end hardware device from companies like Cisco or F5.

Application Servers

There are several roles that fall under the umbrella of Application servers: Query, Index, Excel Services, and Document Conversion. Each has different purposes and scaling implications.

Query servers handle end user search requests. In most environments, this role is on the same machines as the WFE role. This reduces network traffic when queries are run and provides redundancy for the role. Servers with the query role have the same drive space requirements as WFE machines, with the added requirement of needing 2.8x the size of the index file. When scaling Query servers, performance plateaus around seven. When multiple Query servers are used, SharePoint load balances them automatically, and it requires no additional configuration.

Index servers crawl content sources and break the documents up into searchable words, and they only exist in MOSS environments. There really are not many scaling considerations for Index servers, as you can only have one per Shared Service Provider and only one index file per server. You do need to consider the size of your index file, which unfortunately is tough to estimate. Its size is based heavily on the type of content being indexed. Some guidance says the index file can be as large as 30 percent of the size of the content being indexed, also known as the corpus. Usually, this is much lower, between 5 percent and 10 percent. Because of the way the index file is created, you need 4x the size of the index file available in free space on the Index server. Microsoft has tested indexing 50 million documents, but this is not a limit. When designing this box, add CPUs to decrease the amount of time needed for crawls and add more RAM to increase the number of documents that can be indexed in parallel.

Excel Calculation Services (ECS) servers also only exist in MOSS, and they are used to render Excel content in Web pages. This can be offloaded to discrete servers, but most organizations run this on their WFE servers. Like the Query role, this role is automatically load balanced by SharePoint. There is no limit to the number of ECS servers you can have. Information on sizing ECS servers is scant, as not very many organizations are making heavy use of it. This is not because it does not work—rather, it works very well. Making use of ECS requires a change in how organizations use Excel, and that change has been slow in coming.

Document Conversion Services are used to convert documents to HTML so that they can be read in Web browsers without client software. They scale by adding additional servers. When additional servers are added, they must have the same document conversion software installed on them, and you must run the Document Conversion Load Balancer service to balance the load. It is not done automatically. Like ECS, this is not widely used, so metrics for scale are tough to come by.

While not SharePoint servers, you need to scale your SQL servers as well. They scale in many ways. You can have multiple SQL servers to house your data. Adding SQL servers provides support for more WFEs. You can also add CPUs and RAM to your SQL servers to improve their performance. You can also scale SQL out by adding spindles to improve the I/O.

Topologies

Now that you are familiar with the different roles SharePoint has, let's see the different topologies that we can use for SharePoint to meet the needs of different environments.

If you used SPS 2003 you are familiar with the different SharePoint topologies like small farm and medium farm. SharePoint 2007 uses some of the same topologies, but they are not rigidly enforced like they were in SPS 2003. The first one we will look at is a single server.

Figure 2.6 shows a single server install. In this configuration everything runs on one box, including SQL. This environment offers no redundancy or fault tolerance. It is probably not suitable for most production environments.

MOSS
WFE
Index
Query
Excel

FIGURE 2.6
A single server install.

Don't Do a Basic Install, or Else!

When looking at single server installs, it's tempting to do a Basic install. Regardless of how strong the temptation is, resist it. Why such venomous opposition to a Basic install? There are several reasons why Basic installs are bad. First, they automatically install a named instance of SQL Embedded for WSS or SQL Express for MOSS, regardless of whether SQL already exists on the box or not. Both versions of SQL are limited, and the way it is installed in Basic makes it very difficult to break out. You can upgrade SQL Express to SQL Standard or Enterprise, but that does not undo all the problems with Basic. Even if you upgrade SQL, SharePoint is configured to throttle itself when installed as Basic, since it knows its underlying SQL is single threaded. Upgrading SQL does not remove that limitation. Finally, when you do a Basic install, all of your service accounts are configured as built-in accounts like Local System instead of regular Windows accounts. This makes assigning permissions difficult, and these accounts' permissions have been changed with patches to the .NET Framework to cover security issues. There are instances where Basic installs quit working after specific .NET patches were applied.

If you can't do a Basic install, what are your options? My advice is to install SQL Express, which is a free install, along with its Management suite. Then install SharePoint (either WSS or MOSS) and do an Advanced > Complete install. *Do not* do an Advanced > Stand-Alone install. It is exactly the same as a Basic install. If you use this method, you get to assign all the service accounts manually, and if you choose to split SharePoint off, or upgrade SQL you can, and you will get the full benefits of it.

Server Types

When installing SharePoint, you have several options. After the previous sidebar, you know that both Basic install and Advanced > Stand-Alone install are bad ideas. What about the remaining two options: Complete and Web Front End? In 99 percent of installs, Complete is the correct option. It installs all the bits for all the different SharePoint roles, but does not turn any of the roles on. This gives you maximum flexibility in your farm. Should you need to move roles around, the bits are already installed, and you just turn them on. As machines age and are retired, this flexibility can be used to make the transitions easy. The only time when a Web Front End install makes sense is in highly secure environments. It reduces the attack vector of a machine, and it reduces the chance that some service is turned on unintentionally. If you do a Web Front End install on a box, and later want to add other roles, you must reinstall SharePoint. There is no easy way to install the other functionality.

If a single server is too small for you, consider the topology in Figure 2.7, a small farm.

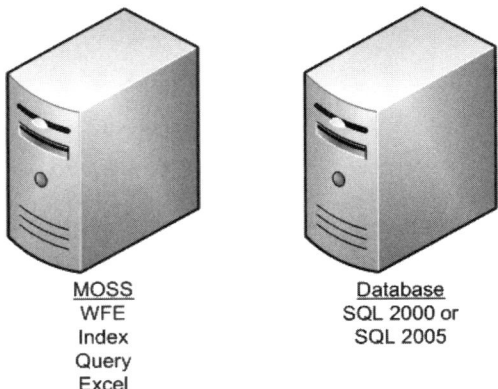

MOSS
WFE
Index
Query
Excel

Database
SQL 2000 or
SQL 2005

FIGURE 2.7
A small farm.

In this farm, we have added a second server. We have broken out the database role to its own server. All of the SharePoint functionality is still running on a single server. This arrangement gives better performance, but it still does not offer any re-dundancy or fault tolerance.

The next step up is a medium farm. You can see in Figure 2.8 that we have jumped from two servers to five. This is the smallest configuration that offers any re-dundancy. First, we have added a second SQL and clustered it for high availability. We have added a second machine for redundant WFE, Query, and Excel roles. We also introduced a load-balancing device for the WFE boxes. Finally, we have added a dedicated Index box. The configuration has a couple of elements that require ex-planation. Why haven't we added a second Index server? SharePoint is limited to a single Index server per Shared Service Provider, so there is no way to offer redun-dancy. The impact of this is not as bad as it sounds. If an Index server crashes, there is no interruption in end user performance since the index file is continuously prop-agated to the Query servers when the Index server is running. Since Query servers handle search requests, they will continue to be able to do searches. However, new content will not be discoverable in Search until the Index server is rebuilt and a full crawl is completed, or the index file and Search database are successfully restored. You may also wonder why Index has to be on its own box—for example, why not have it run on one of the WFEs? This is because of a bug in SharePoint. If the Index server also has the Query role, it will not copy the index file to any other Query servers. In a medium farm this means if a user's search request was handled by the Query server that is not running the Index role, there would not be any results since it would not have an index file. So why not have the Query role on one WFE and the Index role on the other? In that case, if the one WFE that had the Query role were to fail, there would be no backup and users could not search. The fifth box is necessary.

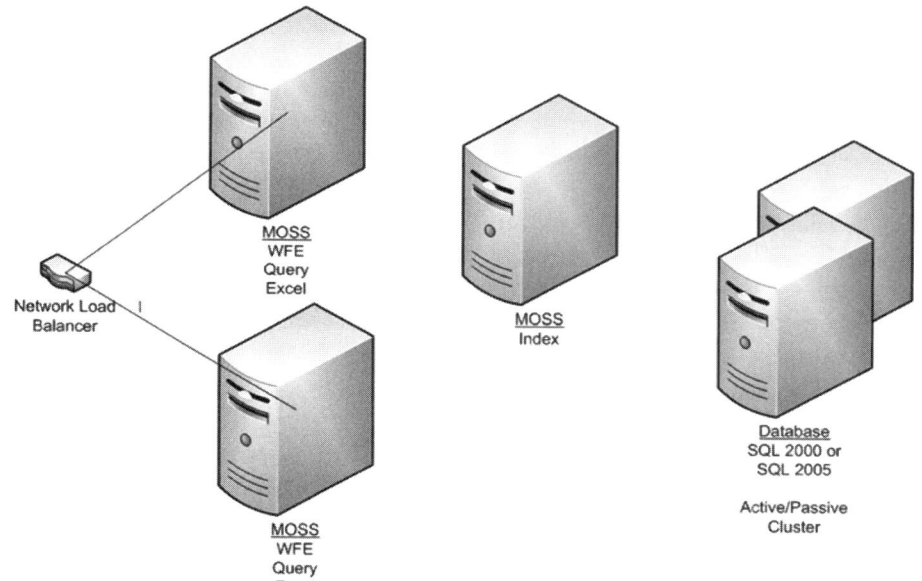

FIGURE 2.8
A medium farm.

To improve performance, you can install the WFE role on the Index server and have it crawl itself. If you do not do this, when the Index server does its crawls, it will hit the load balancer and use one of the WFEs that end users use. Not only does this compete against end users for WFE time, but it also increases network traffic. To relieve some of this pressure, you can enable the WFE role on the Index server, but do not add it to your load balancer.

SharePoint allows you to choose which WFE should be crawled if you want to specify one. We have found a few problems that are associated with using that. In Figure 2.9, you can see the default setting, which is "Use all web front end computers for crawling." If you leave the default, your Index server will simply use DNS to resolve the content URL. This setting assumes you have a content URL that is a

Fully Qualified Domain Name (FQDN) and not a machine name. It also assumes your WFEs are load balanced behind that FQDN. The default setting hits the FQDN and lets the load balancer decide which WFE gets the traffic. If you do not want to do any optimizing, or choose a specific server, this works fine. If you do want to specify which WFE to use, like the Index server itself, you may be tempted to choose the "Use a dedicated web front computer for crawling" and select it from the drop-down.

This option has a couple of significant issues, which is why we don't recommend it. It accomplishes this by creating an entry in the Index server's HOSTS file (normally found in c:\windows\system32\drivers\etc) that maps the FQDN that is being crawled to the IP address of the WFE you selected. Seems harmless enough, but it is not. It always chooses the first IP address it finds for the server. If your WFE has two NICs, it may choose the wrong one, and there is no way to fix it. If you edit the HOSTS file yourself, a Timer Job will fix it the next it runs. Also, if your Content Source URL is not a FQDN, but the machine name of the first WFE you created, and you choose a different WFE for crawling, you can no longer contact the first WFE from the Index server. Confused yet? This happens most often in upgrades. SharePoint was not as finicky about URLs in the 2003 product. Most SharePoint farms had an internal URL of http://server1, where server1 was the name of the first machine SharePoint was installed on. Then a DNS record was created for the FQDN and pointed at the server1, or a load balancer. When you do an upgrade, that URL stays with the farm, and gets added automatically by the SSP as a content source. This means the SSP will be trying to crawl http://server1. Now imagine you chose a different WFE for the crawling, like Server2. SharePoint will create an entry in the Index server's HOSTS file for server1 and assign it server2's IP address. Things really get complicated if server1 has the Query role and the Index server tries to copy the index file to it. It cannot do so, because it resolves to server2's IP address. Because of these issues, we suggest doing it manually.

Central Administration > Operations > Services on Server > Office SharePoint Server Search Service Settings

Configure Office SharePoint Server Search Service Settings on server stockholm

Use this page to configure Office SharePoint Server Search Service Settings.

Warning: this page is not encrypted for secure communication. User names, passwords, and any other information will be sent in clear text. For more information, contact your administrator.

Query and Indexing Use this option to specify if you want to use this server for search queries or indexing or both.	☑ Use this server for indexing content ☑ Use this server for serving search queries
Contact E-mail Address Specify an e-mail address that external site administrators can contact if problems arise when their site is being crawled. This setting applies to all servers in the farm.	E-mail Address: `admin@stockholm` Example: someone@example.com

Farm Search Service Account
The search service will run using this account. Setting or changing this account affects all index and query servers in the server farm.
 	
The farm search service account must not be a built-in account for security reasons and for it to access the database and content index. Examples of built-in accounts are Local Service and Network Service.
	User name
	`stockholm\spadmin`
	Password
	`                    `

Index Server Default File Location The search index will be located at this path by default on this server. For index servers, you can specify a different path when you create a Shared Services Provider. To change this index file location for an existing Shared Services Provider, use the command stsadm.exe -o editssp.	Default index file location: `C:\Program Files\Microsoft Office Serve`
Indexer Performance Indexing information can place a large load on the local SQL Server database and might slow down the responsiveness of the local SharePoint sites. However, reducing the maximum allowed indexing activity will slow down the speed at which items are indexed, and therefore might cause search results to be outdated. Use information about the local server load to select the appropriate indexer performance level.	○ Reduced ◉ Partly reduced ○ Maximum
Web Front End And Crawling Use this option to specify a dedicated web front end for crawling. Crawling through a dedicated web front end will reduce the impact of crawling on the other web front ends in the farm. If your index server is not running other shared services, it is recommended to enable the web front end role on this computer and use it as the dedicated web front end for crawling. If your index server is also running the Excel Calculation service or other shared services, select no dedicated web front end for crawling. Otherwise, these services may not work as expected.	◉ Use all web front end computers for crawling ○ Use a dedicated web front end computer for crawling `stockholm ▼`

FIGURE 2.9
Choose a WFE for crawling.

To do this manually, leave the setting to its default, which is "Use all web front end computers for crawling." Then go into the HOSTS file on the Index server and make an entry for the FQDN and point it at the IP address of the WFE you want to use. By doing this, you can specify the correct IP address, and you will not accidentally break communication between two members of your farm. Figure 2.10 shows how your HOSTS file would look if the FQDN for your farm was http://sharepoint.example.com and the IP address of the WFE you wanted to specify for crawling was 192.168.100.5.

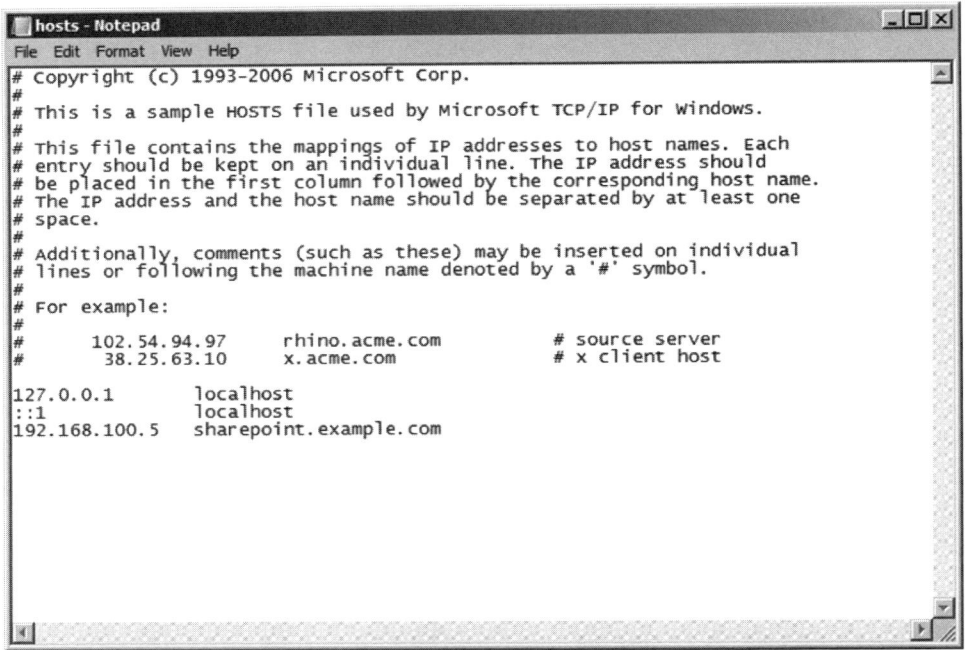

FIGURE 2.10
Manually edit the HOSTS file to specify a WFE.

Figure 2.11 shows a possible large farm. Unlike SPS 2003, MOSS does not have rigid farm topologies. The configuration in Figure 2.9 is not necessarily a recommended topology, but it gives us some examples to discuss. We will start with the Index server. Instead of having the Index server crawl itself, we have given it its own WFE to crawl. This keeps index traffic off the same boxes that handle user traffic, but the Index server does not have to split duty either. It can spend all its resources on indexing files.

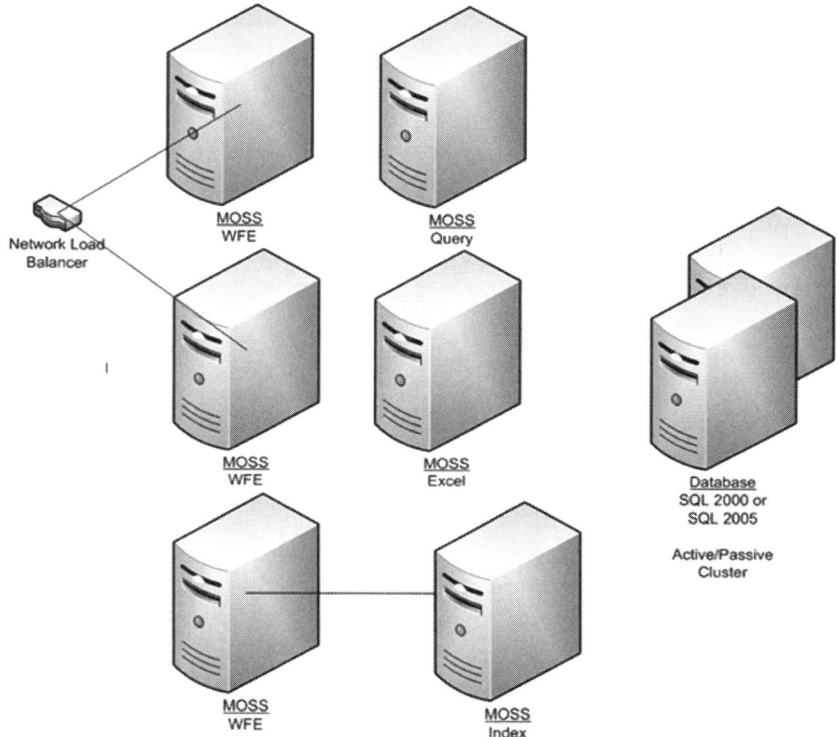

FIGURE 2.11
A possible large farm.

This large farm also has the Query and Excel roles split out onto their own boxes. This might be necessary if your organization makes heavy use of Excel Calculation Services or Search. More servers could be added to this role, if traffic required it.

We did not add any additional WFEs to the load-balanced group, but we could have added up to three more WFEs before starting to lose any benefit until more SQL servers are added.

Using the previous guidance, you should be able to design a topology that meets your needs.

Farm Roles

SharePoint can also use farms to scale out. To make sure we are clear, a farm is de-fined as all SharePoint servers pointing to the same configuration database. When scaling with farms, this means you will have multiple configuration databases that may or may not be on separate SQL servers.

The first way you can use farms in is an Authoring and Publishing configuration. This is used mainly when using SharePoint to publish information to read-only environments such as the Internet. Content is created in the Authoring farm, which has standard read-write usage patterns. After the content is generated in the Authoring farm, it is pushed to the Publishing farm via Content Deployment, which is functionality included with SharePoint. The Publishing farm is read-only, so its demands are not quite as high. WFEs can support more users than they would be able to in the Authoring farm. The design might also be used to distribute content to geographically dispersed offices. This would allow remote offices fast access to content created at other offices.

Another multi-farm scenario is one we covered earlier in this chapter: Dev-Test-Production. In this arrangement, software development is done in one or more Development farms. This could be something as simple as a single server farm running in a Virtual PC on a developer's desk, or something as elaborate as a several server environment. This farm is a good candidate for virtualization. After development is finished, functionality is evaluated in the Test farm. This should be a closer copy to production. Ideally, it would have the same number of servers, and should be running all of the same software. In this farm business, users, not IT, will test the software. This gives them the chance to kick the tires without impacting the production environment.

After the software has been developed and tested thoroughly, it can be moved to the Production farm. Unfortunately SharePoint does not have any tools built in to facilitate the move between farms. This can be done manually or with third-party tools. You may be able to use Content Deployment or other backup/recovery methods to move your content and solutions around.

A twist on using farms to scale is to have multiple SSP farms. This is normally used to meet very specific purposes like hosting My Sites in geographically dispersed locations or a centralized Search environment for multiple farms.

These are just a few examples of how you can use SharePoint farms as a way to scale. You may be able to use these techniques differently in your own environment.

WHICH SHOULD YOU USE?

All those options can be overwhelming. Which ones are right for you? That is the million dollar question. In the next section, we will cover things you should consider when deciding how to scale your environment.

Usage Considerations

The whole reason your farm exists is to serve end users, so they should be your first consideration. Knowing their expectations goes a long way in helping you design your farm. We recommend getting with your business owners, or other power users and agreeing on a Service Level Agreement. In the SLA, you will want to map out what they find to be acceptable performance. You will want to measure this in numbers of requests per second or how long specific tasks take to complete. This can be simple like how long it takes for a site's home page to come up, or how long it takes to resolve a username when it is added to a site. Here are a few activities to consider:

- Browse to home page
- Browse to document library
- Create a subweb
- Create a list
- Add a user to a site
- Upload a 1MB file
- Download a 1MB file

These are just a few examples. It is important to engage your users to find out what operations they execute, and which ones are most important to them. After all the metrics are defined, it is much easier to answer questions such as "Why is Share-Point slow?" If your metrics are already defined, you have something more objective to use as a data point then "feels slow."

When writing your SLA, you will also want to address downtime and recovery times. These two factors will help you determine how much redundancy your system needs and how to size databases and site collections. If your end users require recovered data be available within four hours of request, then you need to make sure your backup environment can restore your largest database and make the data available in that timeframe. If not, then you will need smaller databases or a different disaster recovery plan. The downtime requirements in the SLA will also help you decide whether you need redundant WFEs or SQL servers. If your users need a highly available system, you may need additional WFEs or SQL servers for fault tolerance.

Traffic Types

To properly size your servers, you also need to know what kind of content they will serve. The type of traffic basically breaks down to two different types: Collaboration and Publishing. Collaboration traffic is your typical internal traffic. The users will likely be authenticated. This adds burden to the WFE in two ways. It requires talking to an Active Directory Domain Controller, which takes time. Security trimming also takes time and resources. The traffic is commonly both read and write. Write traffic takes more of a toll on the SQL servers and cannot be cached on WFEs, like read traffic can. Because of the additional overhead, when scaling for collaboration traffic the SQL server becomes saturated at around five WFEs. Additional WFEs do not improve performance, as the SQL server is the bottleneck.

Publishing traffic is much easier traffic. It is commonly traffic from Internet users. This means it is likely anonymous and read-only. Anonymous users do not present the overhead of Active Directory authentication, and since their traffic is primarily read-only, it can be very successfully cached. It presents a much smaller burden on the back-end database server. You can usually keep eight WFEs busy with one SQL server.

Microsoft has two white papers that outline the characteristics of each kind of traffic. The "Estimate performance and capacity requirements for portal collaboration environments" white paper can be found at http://technet.microsoft.com/en-us/library/cc263100.aspx and the "Estimate performance and capacity requirements for Internet environments" white paper is at http://technet.microsoft.com/en-us/library/cc262405.aspx.

Once you know the specifics of your environment, you can plug this information into a sizing tool to get an idea of what your farm should look like. Microsoft has been kind enough to release a free SharePoint sizing tool for this purpose. It is part of the System Center suite, though you do not actually need to purchase System Center to use it. First, you will need to download the System Center Capacity Planner 2007 from http://www.microsoft.com/downloads/details.aspx?FamilyId=E754F35D-59DB-4BC4-8386-E83E66A16FAD&displaylang=en. After you have installed that, download the SharePoint Capacity Planning Tool from http://www.microsoft.com/downloads/thankyou.aspx?familyId=dbee0227-d4f7-48f8-85f0-e71493b2fd87&displayLang=en#. The installation is the common wizard-based install; just click Next until it is finished. After the install is finished, start the tool up from the Start menu, as shown in Figure 2.12.

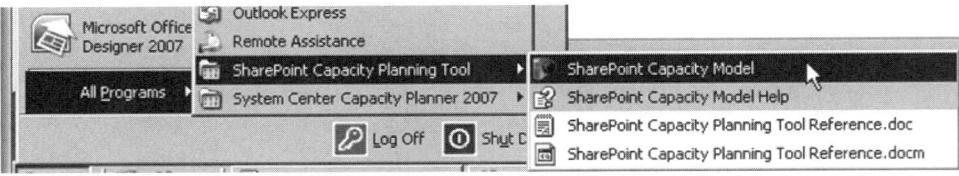

FIGURE 2.12
Starting the Capacity Planning Tool.

You can see from the picture that the install includes Help files and documentation to help you model your environment. After looking them over, fire up the planner and make a simple model. Your first task is to choose the product you will be modeling. In Figure 2.13, we selected Windows SharePoint Service 3.0. Then click Create a new Capacity Model. In the next screen, you create your farm and enter some details about it. Figure 2.14 shows our Farm named Chapter2. We clicked Add SharePoint (WSS) Farm Name, added 100 users, set the farm to Intranet only, and set their client profiles to Average Collaboration.

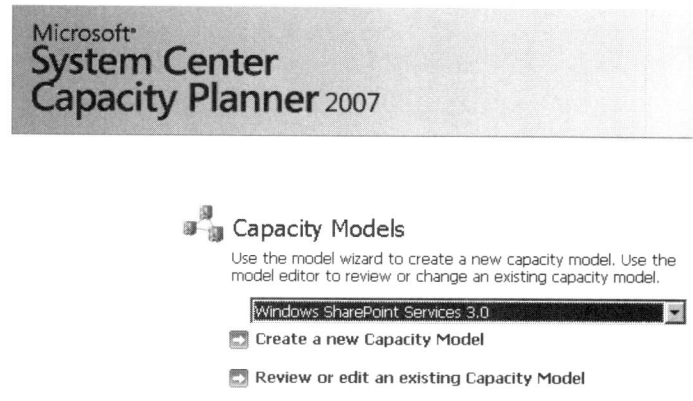

FIGURE 2.13
The Home screen.

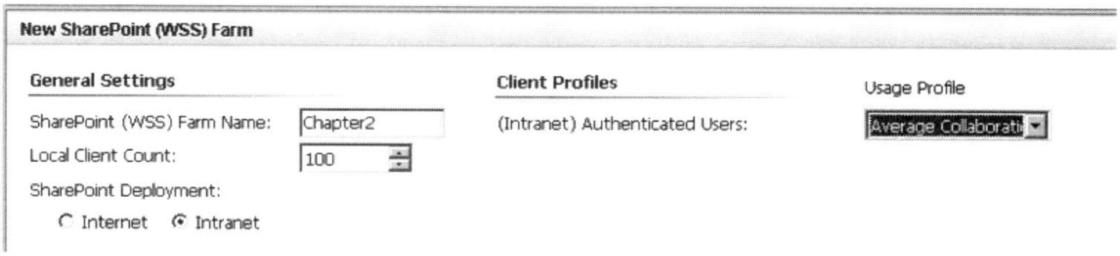

FIGURE 2.14
Farm information.

Click OK and Next. The next screen allows you to add a branch office if you have one. For this chapter, we will not add one. Click Next to go to the Network screen. If you had a branch office, you would configure their links here. The next screen lets you choose the type of servers and disks you will be using. You can add more choices with the Hardware Editor when you are not configuring a farm. Click Next. This screen lets you select whether you need high availability and how much data you will have. Notice there is a limit of 2TB of data. For our demonstration, we estimated that we would have 500GB of content. Click Next to get to the Model Summary. It will look similar to Figure 2.15.

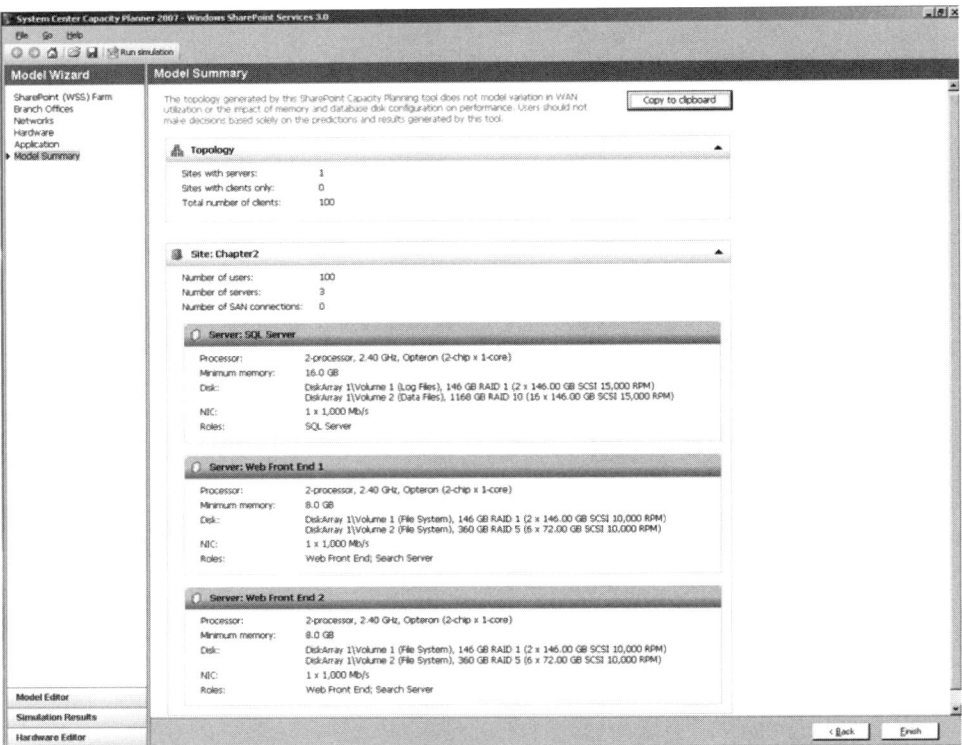

FIGURE 2.15
The Model Summary.

This is a pretty basic summary, but it is a good starting spot. You can hit Back and tweak settings and come back to the Summary. You can also get usage summaries by clicking Run simulation in the toolbar. The tool will churn some and give you a Results Summary screen. This provides usage information about various portions of your farm. Once you have read over the Summary, click Model Editor in the left nav. This will generate a Visio diagram of the network designed. You will have to double-click each office to get the detailed view. Figure 2.16 shows the view of the simple WSS farm we modeled.

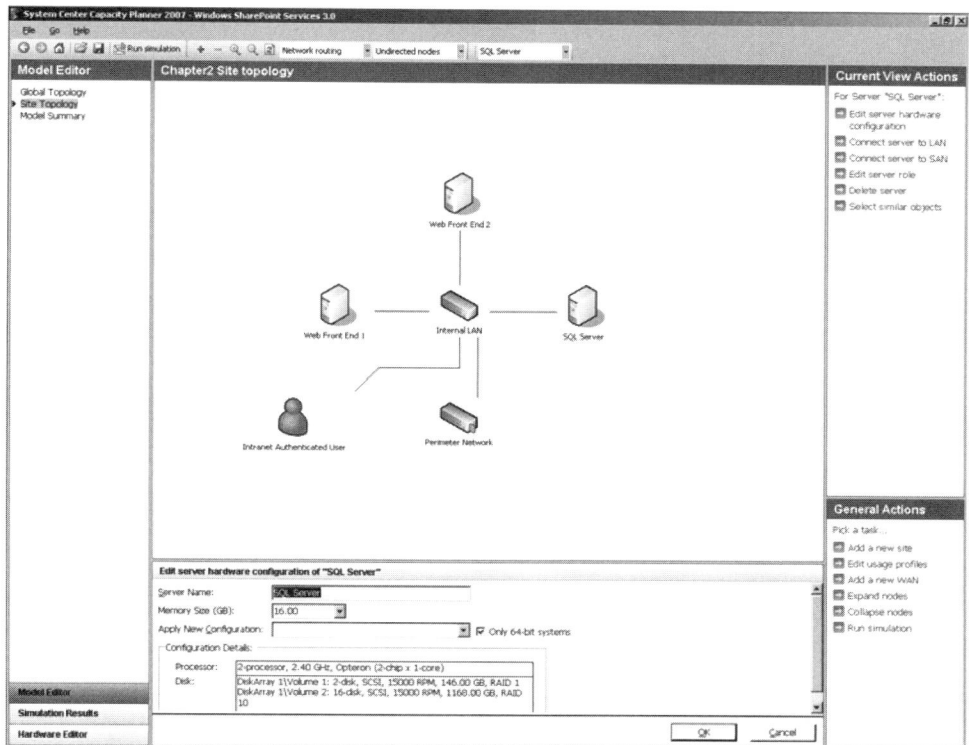

FIGURE 2.16
Model topology.

If you click any of the items in the drawing, you can drill into the specifics of it. In Figure 2.16, you can see the SQL server has 16GB of RAM, which you can change if you would like. You have the option of exporting this diagram out to Visio. To do so, click File in the menu bar, followed by Export, and then Visio Topology Report. Doing this and exporting the summary to Excel make great foundations for reports.

As with any sizing tools, only use this for guidance. You need to exercise a lot of common sense when using automatic tools like this. It does have a couple of limitations. As we mentioned earlier, it only allows for 2TB of content. It also does not allow you to specify any external content that will be indexed. Because of some of these limitations, you will likely need to build on the results this gives you. It does give you a good starting point, though.

HP has also released a SharePoint sizing tool. You can download it at http://h71019.www7.hp.com/ActiveAnswers/cache/548230-0-0-0-121.html. It is similar to Microsoft's tool. If you use HP hardware, it is worth checking out.

3 Installation and Configuration

In This Chapter

- Introduction
- Installing SharePoint
- Choosing the Proper Install Accounts
- Kerberos or NTLM
- Configuration Wizard
- SharePoint Central Administration
- Shared Services Providers
- Web Applications
- Site Collections
- Installation Guides

INTRODUCTION

In this chapter, you will dig into what it takes to get SharePoint up and running. But you will need to install SharePoint before you can administer it. Unfortunately, Microsoft has spoiled many administrators with the capability to do next, next, finish and have a product up and running. While this could be the case with SharePoint, the results are less than ideal. Even after extensive planning, SharePoint still requires a great deal of steps that need to be followed in order to build a reliable platform.

Once the platform is installed and the proper services are running, then you need to build out some initial sites before you can turn things over to the project manager. All Web applications (the Web sites the users will go to) are required to be associated with one Shared Services Provider (SSP). An SSP is a set of reusable services that are centrally managed. You'll find more details later in the chapter.

Finally, with the server configuration out of the way and the first SSP available, you will need to create a user Web application and a site collection. The site collection will have a root site created in it, which gives your users somewhere to go to start using SharePoint.

That is enough setting the stage—let's dive in headfirst and see if we can get SharePoint up and running.

INSTALLING SHAREPOINT

Whether you are installing Windows SharePoint Services v3 (WSS) or Microsoft Office SharePoint Server 2007 (MOSS), the core concepts are the same, with slight variance for each. You can choose one of three options: basic install, advanced single-server install, or advanced multiserver install.

Be careful with the screen shown in Figure 3.1. If you click Basic, then the install starts right away. There is no going back. If you choose Advanced, there are additional choices so you can still turn back.

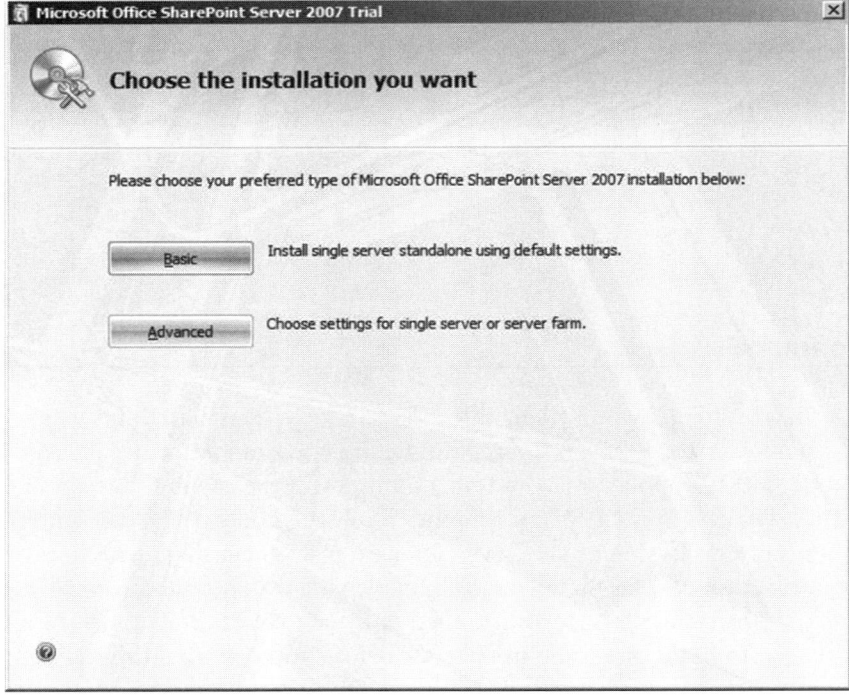

FIGURE 3.1
Choose the installation you want. Odds are good that you want Advanced.

Basic Install

This is SharePoint in its most simplistic form. The idea of the Basic install is the traditional next, next, finish. When you click finish, SharePoint will automatically be installed for you along with some form of SQL Express. Then the product will be automatically configured. All of the necessary services and databases will be created, and you will be ready to start using SharePoint. To some people this may sound ideal.

The problem lies in the details. The first problem comes from the simple SQL server that has been installed. If you are doing a WSS install, then a copy of the Windows Internal Database engine has been installed and configured. This version does not have any database size limitations, but it is not meant to manage large databases either. It does not include any management tools other than command line use of osql.exe. SQL optimization is also not readily available with the use of SQL Management Studio and remote connections are not allowed.

If you deploy MOSS using the Basic option, you will automatically get a copy of SQL Express 2005. Above and beyond the problems mentioned previously, there is a storage limit. Each database cannot exceed 4GB of storage. There are very few MOSS installs where this is an acceptable boundary. If you do choose to use this setup, there is a management tool you can download that will make your life "slightly" easier. You can get the tool from http://msdn.microsoft.com/en-us/library/ms365247.aspx.

Along with the use of SQL Express, Basic installs have one other challenge to overcome. Because all of the services are configured automatically for you, SharePoint will run the services under local system and network services' built-in accounts. This will cause another level of heartache every time Windows or .NET hotfixes introduce changes to security. It will also cause errors in the event logs and general chaos when trying to use third-party applications or customization with SharePoint.

Accidental deployment of SharePoint using the basic setup is a common issue. Many admins will perform a Basic install without realizing the ramifications until it is too late. For many, the fact that they are not able to store more than 4GB of content in one database is the first red flag. At this point, many admins are tempted to just install SQL Server 2005 over the top of their current SQL engine. While this *does* overcome the storage boundaries, it may have long-term repercussions. For one, updating SQL Server does not change your service accounts to use actual accounts. A second issue is that SharePoint will forever know it is a Basic install. There have been occasions when various patches and even the upgrade paths from v2 to v3 were different for Basic installs versus Advanced installs. If you accidentally deployed using Basic, you should back up your environment and start over from scratch. This is the only way to be sure you are in a good, stable state.

Most of the unstable, buggy installs of SharePoint that have been encountered in the wild are Basic installs. Due to the install's reliance on network service accounts and local systems, every .NET or security hotfix has the potential of wreaking havoc on your SharePoint install.

Hopefully, you will feel convinced that you should never use this setup except for the most simple of deployments. Even developers should be discouraged from developing against this environment due to the awkwardness of not using typical AD (Active Directory) accounts for the various services. If you do choose to go this route, then proceed with caution.

Advanced Installs

Circle this whole section right now. If you have taken the time to purchase and read this book, it is all but guaranteed that this is the route you want to go. In the Advanced install, you get to make all of your own decisions. And best of all, you will connect to a real SQL server (SQL Express or WID are not real SQL servers in our book) for hosting all of your databases. The Advanced install is broken into two methods: single server and farm, with there being a few differences if SQL Server is installed on the local SharePoint server versus on a remote machine.

The simplest difference between the two involves the capability to scale. In the previous chapter, you learned about SharePoint topologies and how they can be used to scale from a couple of users to hundreds of thousands of users. One of the advantages of scaling capabilities is the simple idea that you can grow as you go. The only time growth can be challenging is when you need to separate SharePoint from one server to two. In that case, you will be moving the database off the SharePoint server. While this is a difficult process, it is possible to do. However, we recommend that you start with SharePoint and SQL Server on separate boxes from each other if you anticipate the need to grow your farm later.

In Figure 3.2, you can see that after choosing Advanced, you have three options.

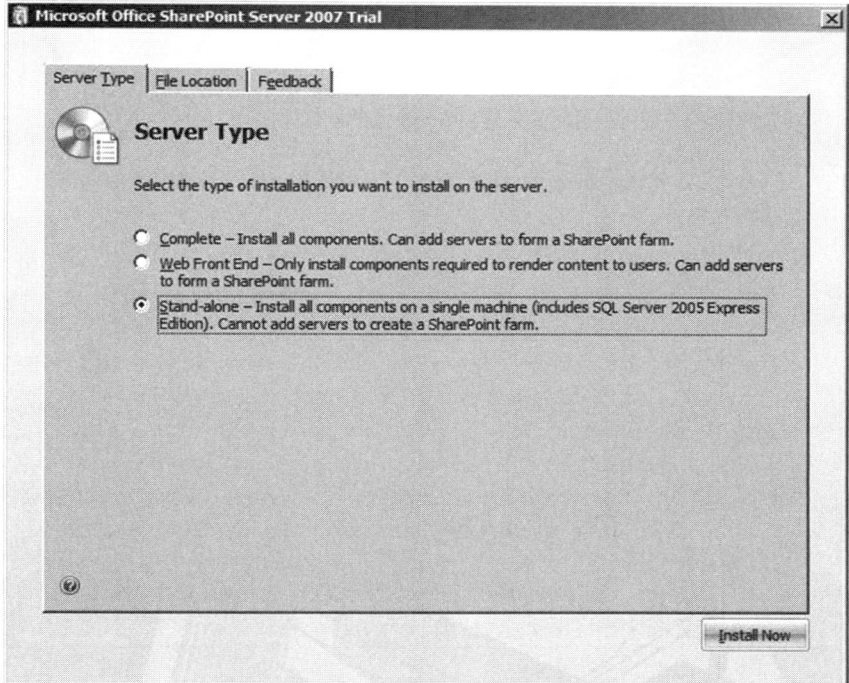

FIGURE 3.2
Server Type options.

- **Complete.** This is the option that is chosen 99 percent of the time. With this option, all of the SharePoint bits are installed on this server. This means that as you configure this server, it can serve any of the various roles (WFE, Index, Query, or Excel). The various bits are not activated until you assign the server that role. Also, you can easily add or remove servers from the farm as necessary.
- **Web Front End.** With this setting, only the bits required to have the server act as WFE are installed on the server. This limits the server from serving other roles in the future. This option should only be used in cases where you are installing a dedicated server in the DMZ and will never need the flexibility of changing roles. For internal deployments, even if the server will only be serving as a WFE, this option should be avoided due to the lack of flexibility in your farm topology in the future. A perfect example is upgrade scenarios. In many cases, companies find themselves attempting to reallocate hardware and condense farms during transition periods. WFE-only servers provide little help in these situations. As with the complete option cited earlier, adding or removing these servers from the farm is possible.

■ **Stand-alone.** Those guys at Microsoft are sneaky. This is the default setting when you first come to this screen, and if you read the fine print, you know what is coming. This does the exact same thing as Basic install. Yikes! Read the "Basic Install" section if you need a refresher why *not* to choose this option.

WSS-Only Option

WSS does bring one unique option to the table. It can be installed in a mode called Active Directory account creation mode. In this configuration, instead of using existing Active Directory accounts, you can configure SharePoint to point at a specific OU (organizational unit) within AD. Then every time you add users to a site, they have an account created in this OU, based on their email address. The downside to this mode is that you cannot add users' existing AD accounts. So, in an internal deployment, new users would have separate accounts for SharePoint than their normal AD logins. Most users do not appreciate additional username/passwords to remember. This option is generally only used in hosted SharePoint scenarios.

CHOOSING THE PROPER INSTALL ACCOUNTS

When an admin first sits down and starts looking into doing an install of Share-Point, the admin may be startled by the sheer number of accounts required. In a standard least-privileged install, nine accounts are the norm. The other end of the spectrum is a minimal account install where only two accounts are required. In this section, we will discuss the pros and cons of both methods, look at a happy medium, and figure out what each of these accounts is really doing.

Two Versus Many

It really boils down to process isolation (greatest security) versus ease of administration (least security)—two polar opposites for two totally different worlds. But life would be no fun without choices, so there is a third method. This is called the practical method. Let's take a look at the choices.

For complete process isolation, you will run under what is called least-privileged administration. In this environment, each SharePoint process runs as a separate account, with each of these accounts only having the bare minimum rights that it needs. The goal being that if any account is compromised (or less drastic, locked out), then it only affects the process that account is assigned to. The downside to this method is that from time to time administration can be cumbersome. Not only do you have to maintain separate usernames and passwords, but also because each account has minimal permission, administration can be painful. An example is activating a Web application feature, where typically you would log into Central Admin with your SharePoint admin account. But in a least-privileged install, this account would not have the rights to activate the feature. At that point, you have to elevate the account's rights, activate the feature, and then demote the account again. Not hard, just extra work.

For the part-time administrator just trying to get SharePoint up and running for a purely internal environment, we have a much simpler method. We use two accounts. One SharePoint admin account that runs everything except search, and then we configure a dedicated search account. That is all. While this method is less than perfect, it does make things work nicely and smoothly.

Now for the rest of the world, the practical or hybrid method is always on the table. In this method, we will still use unique accounts, but in places where overlap makes sense, we will go that route. This method still has some of the headaches of least privileged, but some job security is good.

To help make these options make a little more sense, take a look at the following various accounts. Included also is an example account name. This is just a suggestion and will be used at the end of the chapter in the step-by-step install.

- **SharePoint Admin Account** (domain\sp_admin). This is the account with which you will log in to the Windows Server and actually perform the install and run Configuration Wizard. This should be a domain user account and must be a local administrator of all servers that SharePoint is installed on. It is important that you do the install using this account and not as a personal administrator account. The reason is that this account is given special rights, and in extreme problem solving, this account is sometimes the only account that can successfully run Configuration Wizard and detach from a broken farm. It is also recommended that you perform all service pack and hotfix installations for SharePoint using this account. Finally, this account will also need to have a SQL Login and be granted the roles of dbcreator and securityadmin before you begin installation. This will be done on the SQL server itself.
- **SharePoint Farm Account** (domain\sp_farm). This account is specified when running Configuration Wizard for the first time. SharePoint will then configure this account as the Application Pool identity for Central Admin and the service login account for the Windows SharePoint Services Timer Service. This account only needs to be created as a domain user account. SharePoint will automatically configure this account with the SQL roles of dbcreator and securityadmin, along with setting this account as database owner (dbo) of all SharePoint databases.

- **MOSS Search Account** (domain\sp_search). This is the account you will specify for the Office SharePoint Search Service in Central Admin. This account only needs to be configured as a domain user. SharePoint will then grant this account the ability to read the config database and both SSP databases. Additionally, full control is granted to the location of the physical index file and the propagation folder on the query servers.

  This account is also automatically set up as the default content access account. This means that, by default, the search index process will use this account to crawl content, and profile imports from Active Directory will be done with these credentials. You may change this after you create your SSP. Until then, this account is also granted full-read access to all SharePoint content databases. It is very important that this account is *not* given any additional permissions (such as being made an administrator). If this happens, improper content will be indexed, such as unpublished items and versions.

- **WSS Search Account** (domain\sp_wsssearch). This is the account you will specify for the Windows SharePoint Search Service to run under. This account only needs to be configured as a domain user. SharePoint will then grant this account the ability to read the config database and the SharePoint Admin Content database. It will be set as dbo for WSS Search Database, which is created when you start the service and specify this account.

- **WSS Crawl Account** (domain\sp_wsscrawl). This is the account you will specify as the default content access account for the Windows SharePoint Search Service to use. This account only needs to be configured as a domain user. SharePoint will then grant this account full read access to all Web applications.

- **SSP Application Pool Account** (domain\sp_sspapppool). This is the account you will specify as the identity for the SSP Application Pool. This account only needs to be configured as a domain user. SharePoint will then grant this account read access to the config database and the SharePoint Admin Content database. This account will be set as dbo for both of the SSP databases.

- **SSP Service Account** (domain\sp_sspservice). This is the account you will specify as the identity for the SSP service to run under when you create an SSP. This account only needs to be configured as a domain user. This account is given the same permissions as the SSP Application Pool Account.

- **All Application Pool Accounts** (domain\sp_webname). This is the account you will specify as the identity when you are specifying a new Application Pool. This account only needs to be configured as a domain user. SharePoint will then grant this account read access to the config database and the SharePoint Admin Content database. This account will be set as the dbo of all content databases associated with the Application Pool along with all search databases for those Web apps. Additional read and write access is granted to all associated SSP databases.

As you can see, there are quite a few accounts that SharePoint will ask for. If you have chosen to do a least-privileged install, then you will use each and every one of those accounts just as specified earlier. If you have chosen to do the super simple, "let's get this thing up and running" method, then you can simply use sp_admin for all of the various accounts except for Search. Then instead of specifying a separate account for MOSS Search Account, WSS Search Account, and WSS Crawl Account, you would use one account, typically sp_search. That is it—you are up and running.

But what if you are interested in the practical method? In this setup, you will still use several accounts, but you will also reuse accounts where it makes sense. The suggestion would be to use sp_admin and sp_farm, as described earlier. Then, for each Application Pool, use a separate account as appropriate. In most environments, the WSS Search Service is used only for indexing the help system. If this is the case, then using sp_search for MOSS Search, WSS Search, and WSS Crawl makes complete sense. Finally, the SSP App Pool Account and the SSP Service are set with the same permissions. Having two separate accounts doesn't really accomplish anything, so just use one, sp_sspservice. Now you have reduced the number of accounts while not really compromising isolation.

KERBEROS OR **NTLM**

The assumption is that anyone reading this book is familiar with NTLM authentication. We have been using this since NT was in its infancy, and for most of us, this authentication has become second nature. The short version is that it is a challenge response form of authentication.

There is a faster, more secure alternative to NTLM that most of us tend to ignore. This is Kerberos authentication, which was introduced with Windows 2000. Typically, even though most domains are capable of supporting it, applications such as SharePoint have fallen back on old faithful, NTLM. Why? Because Kerberos authentication is very challenging to configure and maintain properly. There are lots of rules, such as server time being in sync, delegation being allowed, and service principal names (SPN) to name a few. For most scenarios, the pain far exceeds the rewards of slightly faster and more secure authentication.

Then why would you ever set up SharePoint to use Kerberos? It really boils down to one answer: avoiding the double-hop problem. The double-hop problem best exposes itself when speaking of Excel Services and data connections.

For example, you create an Excel 2007 workbook with a pivot table that is fed from a database connection to SQL Server. The database connection is set to pass the current user's credentials to SQL Server when refreshing the data.

You then publish this workbook to Excel Services hosted within SharePoint and render the pivot table through the Excel Web Access Web part. Users using either NTLM or Kerberos authentication can see the pivot table with no issues.

Then the user clicks Refresh data connection. With NTLM, you are greeted with an access denied message. But when you properly configure Kerberos, your table is updated with fresh data. This has just demonstrated the double-hop problem.

There is one hop of authentication between the user and the Excel Web part. Then when the user says to refresh the data, the Excel Web part tries to authenticate on behalf of the user with the SQL server. NTLM was designed not to allow this to work. With Kerberos and the proper configuration, this is no problem.

While there are many facets to Kerberos, there are two primary stumbling blocks when configuring it with SharePoint, which are setting up the proper SPNs and allowing delegation between the servers and the accounts.

SPNs are mapping between a service, a server name, and an account that are used by the key distribution center to issue the proper tickets for delegation. To create SPNs, you can either create them manually by using an AD editing tool (not recommended), or you can use a Windows 2003 Support tool called SetSPN.exe available at http://support.microsoft.com/?kbid=832769. So, for example, if we wanted to do so for a Web application running at http://portal.company.com in an Application Pool using the identity domain\sp_portalapppool, we would create an SPN like so:

```
Setspn.exe —A http/portal.company.com domain\sp_portalapppool
```

After creating that SPN, we would then go into AD Users and Computers on the domain controller and configure the account sp_portalapppool for delegation, as shown in Figure 3.3.

If you were to check other accounts, you would see they do not have the Delegation tab, because it only appears for accounts with an SPN defined.

Seems simple enough but with SharePoint, there are always challenges— primarily figuring out what SPNs to create and what machines to set up delegation for. Here is a typical example:

- FQDN is domain.local.
- Netbios domain name is domain.
- Central Admin is hosted at http://server:5555 running in an App Pool with an identity of domain\sp_farm.
- SSP is hosted at http://ssp, running in an App Pool with an identity of domain\sp_sspapppool.
- The portal Web application where you need Kerberos is at http://portal, running in an App Pool with an identity of domain\sp_portalapppool.

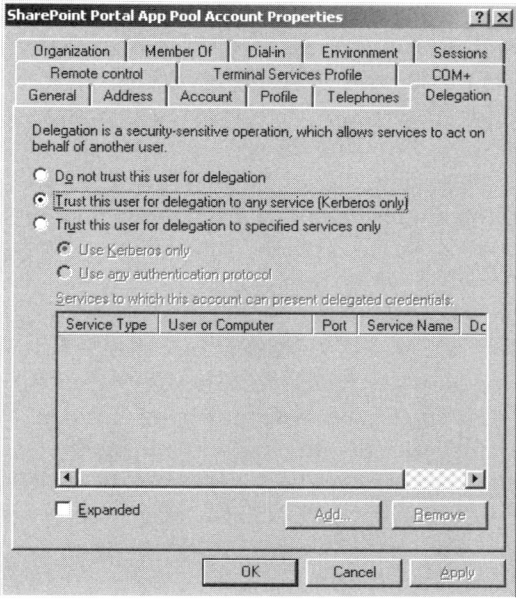

FIGURE 3.3
Delegation settings.

Based on that information, the following SetSPN commands would need to be run.

- Setspn.exe—An http/server domain\sp_farm
- Setspn.exe—An http/server.domain.local domain\sp_farm
- Setspn.exe—An http/ssp domain\sp_sspapppool
- Setspn.exe—An http/ssp.domain.local domain\sp_sspapppool
- Setspn.exe—An http/portal domain\sp_portalapppool
- Setspn.exe—An http/portal.domain.local domain\sp_portalapppool

After the SPNs are in place, you need to go into AD Users and Computers and set Trust this user for delegation to any service for the following accounts:

- Domain\sp_farm
- Domain\sp_sspapppool
- Domain\sp_portalapppool

Then find the SharePoint and SQL servers' computer accounts in AD Users and Computers and do the same step.

Next, configure your Portal Web application to run using Kerberos by going into Central Admin > Application Management > Authentication Providers. Click the proper zone and then set the IIS authentication settings to Negotiate (Kerberos). This is only necessary for the Portal Web app.

Kerberos should now be firing on all cylinders. The best way to check it is to browse to the site from a client machine. If you can get to the home page, you are in business. If you are greeted with weird authentication prompts or errors, then the first place to check is in the system log on the client PC. There should be a Kerberos error there. Seventy-five percent of the time, the issue is a typo in one of your SPNs.

A few common errors to avoid: Duplicate SPNs, nonstandard ports, and using DNS alias. If you managed to create the same SPN twice, Kerberos just fails, and you will get an error saying as much in the client's system log. If you are running your portal Web app on a nonstandard port number, then you will specify that in your SPN by http/portal:8080. If you are using the default port, this is not necessary. Also, there is a bug in several different IE browser versions that causes Kerberos to fail if you have used DNS alias or cnames. Using a host (a) record should be a requirement.

Finally, if you are setting up Kerberos to make Excel Services work, you will often need to do one additional step of configuration for your SSP. You will need to run the `stsadm` command:

```
Stsadm.exe —o —SSP <sspname> -fileaccessmethod useimpersonation
```

The repercussions of the preceding command and the entire details of making Excel Services and data connections work are the subjects of numerous books and articles and will not be discussed here. Because this command is the least mentioned yet is often required, we've included it as one last thing to check.

While it is easy to see the upside of Kerberos, once you have overcome the challenges, it is also important to note that in the SharePoint world, it still has not gone mainstream. It is estimated that fewer than 10 percent of production deployments are currently running Kerberos, so the amount of information and expertise on the subject is still very limited. But the list of companies doing this is growing and as Excel Services and SQL Reporting Services integrations become more prevalent, Kerberos will follow.

CONFIGURATION WIZARD

Configuration Wizard is a versatile tool used not only post installation, but also in ongoing maintenance of the farm. The first time you encounter the tool is post install. When running this tool, it is important to be logged in as your SharePoint

Admin account (sp_admin from earlier). This account will be given special rights to the farm and should be the only account that has been configured with the appropriate roles in SQL Server. At this point, the tool helps you either to connect your new install to an existing SharePoint farm (think configuration database) or to establish a new farm.

When creating a new farm, you will be prompted for the database server and name and for your SharePoint farm account (sp_farm). Then you will be presented with the opportunity to set the port number that the Central Admin Web application will use. This must be a unique port and should be greater than 1024. It is not possible to specify a host header. You should use a port that is easy to remember, such as 5555 or 7777, to make it easy for admins to recall later. Next, you can specify the authentication mechanism to use. NTLM is typically used here because Central Admin will not have any double-hop requirements.

When connecting to an existing farm, you will specify the database server that hosts the configuration database for the farm and then choose the appropriate database. The proper farm account will be entered, so you will only need to input the password. You must use this account, and it cannot be changed while joining to a farm. On the next screen, there will be an Advanced button, which is used only if you want to change this server to be the Central Admin site host.

After your farm is in use, Config Wizard has three primary purposes. The first is to finish the installation of SharePoint service packs and hotfixes. The second is to change what server in the farm hosts Central Admin. The third is much more severe—cleanly removing the server from the farm. Anytime you run Configuration Wizard, you should be logged in as your SharePoint Admin account. Also, keep in mind that running Configuration Wizard will stop IIS and the SharePoint services, making your Web applications unavailable while the wizard runs.

SharePoint Central Administration

After you have created your new farm, Configuration Wizard will automatically launch SharePoint Central Administration v3 (Central Admin) for you. As SharePoint does not have a GUI application for administration, this is the site you will use for day-to-day administration of SharePoint. The site is actually run as a site collection on its own Web application that you specified the first time you ran Configuration Wizard. If you were to look on your SQL server, you could find the associated content database with a name of SharePoint_Admin_GUID (referred to as the SharePoint Admin Content database in the account section). By default, all local administrators of the SharePoint server can access this site. For administration, the site is broken up into two pages of links: the Operations page and the Application Management page.

OPERATIONS

This page is full of links that are typically meant to affect the entire farm. They are broken up into multiple sections.

- **Topologies and Services.** This section contains commands for defining the servers and their associated roles in the farm. Typically, these settings are used when first building a SharePoint farm and then are left alone, other than making changes to the servers. You can use this section to do things like start-and-stop server services and to set up the flow of email through SharePoint.
- **Security Configuration.** This section is for maintaining security over SharePoint as a whole, such as setting up Antivirus, modifying service accounts, adding additional farm administrators, configuring single sign-on, and managing blocked file types. Keep in mind with blocked file types that SharePoint has 82 file types that are excluded by default, mostly executable content.
- **Logging and Reporting.** Here you will configure the logging behavior of the farm. Changing the location of the diagnostic and usage logs from C is advisable. Also, don't forget that the usage reports are disabled by default. Turning these on should be one of the first things you do in your farm. The diagnostic logging can be set to more verbose when you are troubleshooting, but for day-to-day should be left to their defaults.
- **Upgrade and Migration.** While running the upgrade process, this section is very crucial. You will see different options, depending on where you are in the upgrade cycle and which method you used. For those not doing an upgrade, you can use Convert license type to input your real license key if you initially deployed with the 180-day trial key. This is a MOSS-only section.
- **Global Configuration.** As the name implies, there are several important options here. Timer jobs are the lifeblood of SharePoint and should be monitored accordingly. Alternate access mapping is critical to configuration and is one of the top support calls to Microsoft support. There is an entire section for this command in Chapter 10, "Configuring Internet Accessible Web Sites." Solution management and managing farm features are covered in Chapter 7, "Managing Site Customization: Templates, Features, and Solution Packages."
- **Backup and Restore.** This is the out-of-the-box backup GUI tool. It has its pluses and minuses, as covered in Chapter 12, "High Availability, Backups, and Disaster Recovery."
- **Data Configuration.** Here you can change the default database server and the access account for that database server. Data retrieval service determines the allowable connection type and behavior that Web parts can use.

- **Content Deployment.** Content deployment in MOSS is used to deploy content from one site collection to another. This can be on different Web apps or even between different farms. The idea is that you can develop your entire WWW site on a dev farm and then deploy that content to your public facing farm. This is a MOSS-only section.

APPLICATION MANAGEMENT

On this page, you will find links that mostly revolve around configuring individual Web applications and their associated content. If you have MOSS, you will also find a couple other sections that didn't have a home elsewhere.

- **SharePoint Web Application Management.** These links are dedicated to the creation of new Web apps and managing settings affecting the entire Web app. You can modify the content databases, activate features, and even change things like the maximum upload size per Web app.
- **SharePoint Site Management.** In this section, you will create and manage the individual site collections. Quotas and locks can be used to set storage limits per site collection. They are the only item in SharePoint to which you can assign a quota.
- **External Service Connections.** This is where you can configure the use of a Records Center or define a document conversion service per Web app. Also, if you have any Web-based file viewers installed they would be specified here.
- **Office SharePoint Server Shared Services.** Here you are given access to configure your SSPs, including the ability to host or connect to interfarm shared services, meaning that SharePoint farm can use an SSP hosted on a different server. Also, use Check services enabled in this farm to verify the status of your farm. It does simple checks to make sure that all servers are consistent and all required services in the farm are running. Additionally, if you are using a trial key, it will tell you when that key will expire. This is a MOSS-only section.
- **Application Security.** This section allows you to configure different security behaviors in your farm, for example, controlling how Web parts are allowed to connect to each other, what permissions Web apps are permitted to use, and setting a user's access for an entire Web app. Also, from Authentication providers you can configure a Web app to use anonymous, NTLM, Kerberos, or even LDAP authentication.
- **Workflow Management.** This section is used to configure the overall rights that workflows have per Web application.

- **Search.** Managing the search service provides you with access to global config for search along with its current state. Also, there is a peek into each SSP and its current index status. Check out Chapter 8, "Configuring and Managing Enterprise Search," for everything to do with Search. This is a MOSS-only section.
- **InfoPath Forms Services.** Use this section to manage Forms services. When you start to dig into complicated forms with data connections and lookups, you will get to spend a good deal of time in these settings. This is a MOSS Enterprise or Forms server–only section.

SHARED SERVICE PROVIDERS

One of the mechanisms MOSS uses to scale is a Shared Service Provider or SSP. The quick definition of an SSP is that it is a set of centrally managed, reusable services. The idea is that there are certain services that really make sense to centrally manage and share among the various Web apps. In Figure 3.4, you can see an example of the Admin screen for the SSP to get an idea of the services available. A good example is profiles. With a SSP, you can import all of the profile information from AD once and then your various Web applications can consume the data. So if you have http://marketing and http://accounting, it doesn't make sense for each one to maintain identical profile information; instead, they should share. By connecting them both to the same SSP, they can use the following major services:

- Profiles and Audiences
- My Sites
- Search
- All of Excel Services (MOSS Enterprise Only)
- All of the Business Data Catalog or BDC (MOSS Enterprise Only)

Sometimes, the easiest way to think of Shared Services is the parent versus child relationship. The parent (your SSP) goes out and does all of the work (pulling BDC data, indexing content, hosting My Sites) and the child (your Web applications) comes to the parents to ask for $5 (request data from the BDC or view a calculated Excel sheet).

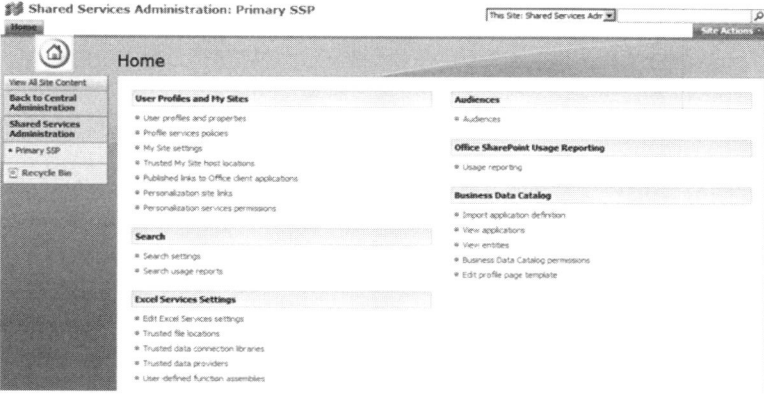

FIGURE 3.4
SSP Admin screen.

ONE OR MANY SSPS?

One of the most overwhelming things about SSPs for some people during the planning process is how many they should have. It is easy to see from the interface that you are given the opportunity to create more than one. When should you do this?

Typically, when it comes to planning SSPs, you start with one. Then you stick to that number until someone can plead his or her case and justify an additional SSP. Reasons include security isolation, management isolation, and the associated politics.

Perhaps you are considering hosting both your intranet and Internet site on the same farm. This would be a good time to argue for two unique Web apps. Think of Search in this scenario—if you are indexing all of your company's content, are you sure nothing has been exposed to anonymous users internally that should not be exposed to anonymous users externally. Very doubtful, so you could set up the Internet SSP to only index the Internet site, providing only external results when using the Search box from the external site. And you could then configure the internal SSP to index the entire enterprise, including the Internet site, and have a proper search experience from your internal site. There are lots of scenarios where security dictates your need for additional SSPs.

On more than one occasion, customers choose to have multiple SSPs for purely political reasons. The attempted justification is that there are two Web apps, one for Sales and one for Manufacturing. The VP of each division is disgusted by the thought of the other division's IT staff having any power over their Web app. So even though they both require the same SSP services, they feel the need to have only their people administrating their Web app. Politics trumps common sense every time. It may be a waste of company resources, but the VPs are happy, so everybody is happy.

ANOTHER ADVANTAGE OF SSPS

Separation of roles is another key advantage of SSPs. In some medium and large environments, it is not uncommon to have one group administering the physical server farm while another group just maintains Search. The SSP concept makes this very easy. Since the SSP administration is done from its own SharePoint site collection, you can define a user's access so they *cannot* access Central Administration but they can access the SSP. And once they get into the SSP, you can even limit them. Once inside the SSP, you can determine if they can do the following:

- Manage user profiles
- Manage audiences
- Manage permissions
- Manage usage analytics
- Manage BDC permissions (MOSS Enterprise Only)

By default, any user who is given access to the SSP can administer all of the other pieces, such as Search. Still this separation of services from the actual administration of the server can be quite useful, especially in companies where the less access a user is given, the better.

HOW TO SET SECURITY

Granting access to the various pieces of the SSP is far from intuitive so let's walk through the steps.

1. Start by logging into the SSP Admin site.
2. Now you need to add the user just like you would to any other site. Click Site Actions > Site Settings.
3. Under Users and Permissions, click Advanced permissions.
4. Click New > Add Users.
5. Enter the user's name.
6. Choose the Viewers group and press OK.

Now your user can log into the SSP and manage Search settings, the Excel Service Settings, and can view the various links list. So how do you give them more permissions? In order to do that, you need to give them some more access, so follow these steps.

1. Under User Profiles and My Sites, click Personalization services permissions.
2. Click Add Users/Groups.

3. Enter your user's name, select which permissions you would like to bestow upon them, and click Save.

What are all of these different permissions?

- **Create personal site.** This permission gives the user the capability to create and use a My Site. If you want to make that My Site link disappear, then take away this right from the users. But if you didn't give it to them, why do they have it? Go back to the Manage Permission screen. All authenticated users are given this right by default.
- **Use personal features.** This permission provides the My Links functionality and allows users to manage their Colleagues.
- **Manage user profiles.** This area allows your user to do just that. They can get in there and modify the profiles for this SSP. Give them this right and they can access these links: User profiles and properties, Profile services policies, and My Site Settings.
- **Manage audiences.** You guessed it, but now you can click that handy little Audiences link. Once you are there, you can set the schedule or define the rules for building those global audiences.
- **Manage permissions.** This permission will let that user modify Personalization services permissions (the stuff we are doing right now).
- **Manage usage analytics.** This area gives the user access to make changes to Usage reporting. Small bug here: If the user doesn't have this right, he can still open up the screen. Then if he makes a change and presses OK, he gets a 403 forbidden error.

If you have MOSS Enterprise, then there is still another set of access you can potentially grant: BDC Permissions. Here's how you do it:

1. Click Business Data Catalog permissions from the main screen of the SSP.
2. Click Add Users/Groups.
3. Enter your user, select his permissions, and click Save.

SSPs are very helpful and important to understand. They should be part of your initial planning. They can be secured at a very granular level, or they can be given broad access. Just mark this topic down as something else you need to fully think through before you start rolling out SharePoint. And when all else fails, just have one SSP.

WEB APPLICATIONS

It is important we cover a key terminology piece now. In SharePoint, we call each unique entry in IIS a Web application. Prior to this version, this has always been a very confusing issue. People have referred to the entry in IIS as a site, a Web site, a virtual site, a virtual server, and other things. This inconsistency made searching the Web or reading documentation very daunting. For SharePoint, this will always be referred to as a "Web application" or "Web app," for short.

SharePoint is a browser-based tool, so the URLs that people use to access the content require a little planning. Once you determine the proper URLs, you will then need to make sure that the corresponding DNS entries are also set up. Now it is possible that you could configure all of your sites to use the server name for access and then assign each one a unique port number. It is also possible to walk from Cincinnati to California, which doesn't mean that either is practical.

When you create each new Web app, you will need to specify the port number and the host header. These two items will need to combine to be unique compared to all other Web applications hosted on the server. This uniqueness can be achieved by not specifying a host header and setting each Web app to run on a specific port. While this may be okay for administrator Web apps, it is very confusing for users. By default, browsers assume port 80 for HTTP sites and port 443 for HTTPS sites. If at all possible, you should stick to this convention. For example, let's say you want to host two Web applications on your server: Portal and Team. You could configure Portal to be accessible via the default port and no host header (assuming you have deleted or stopped the IIS default Web site, which gives you a URL of http://server-name). Then when you create Team, port 80 with no host header is already in use. So for Team, you would have to specify a unique port number, such as 8080. Then your users would have to browse to http://servername:8080 to access the Team content. This will typically just cause lots of help desk calls and is not recommended.

A better approach is specifying a unique host header for each Web application and running all sites on the default port. Your Portal would then be located at http://portal and Team could be hosted at http://team. This would be a much more user-friendly approach. For each of these host headers, you would then need to create a DNS record. Host (A) records are preferred over aliases (cnames) and are a requirement if you plan to use Kerberos. This is due to inconsistencies in the browser's handling of DNS aliases during authentication.

Another important thing to understand about Web apps is that when you create each one, you must also specify the associated database. Each new Web app must be associated with a unique database and cannot share that database with another Web app. If you wanted two separate Web apps to share a content database and to display that same content, then what you can do is Extend an existing

Web application. This is typically done in cases where you may want to host the same content but have two different authentication methods for accessing it. So you may have http://portal using windows authentication while you have http://extranet.company.com using forms-based authentication. Then you would have two Web apps, rendering the same content but allowing access via two different mechanisms.

While each Web app must have a unique database associated with it at creation time, it still can have multiple databases. In fact, it is possible to have several content databases associated with the same Web app. This way you can spread the various site collections across different databases. The goal is that no single database should be greater than 100GB. You'll find more discussion about this in Chapter 11, "Optimizing SharePoint Performance."

SITE COLLECTIONS

After creating your first Web application, all that stands between you and your users having a SharePoint site is the creation of your first site collection at the root of the Web app. A site collection is just what the name implies—a collection of sites. You might also know the sites in this collection as subsites, Webs, or subWebs, but they are all names for the same thing. Why do we want to bring this ragtag group of sites together into one collection? For the following reasons:

- **Separation of security.** The people and groups' list is unique to each site collection. So all of the SharePoint groups that are created in any of the sites can be shared across the entire collection. Also, if you look at the All People list, it shows any user who has accessed any site in the entire site collection. This can be very important, especially in extranet environments. What if you had two sites? One that was for supplier A and one for supplier B, and they were both in the same site collection? Even though security could be set to keep user A confined to supplier A's site and user B confined to supplier B's site, they both could go to all people and see the other user listed. This can be very bad.
- **Level of ownership and administration.** When you create a site collection, you can assign a primary owner and a secondary owner. These two users are then listed with the site collection and can be notified by things like quota warnings. These two users are also placed in a group called site collection administrators. Site collection administrators have the full permissions and access to all content in the associated site collection. Additionally, there are several functions that are managed exclusively by these users. Check Figure 3.5 for those functions.

Team Site Collection
(WSS)

Publishing Site Collection
(MOSS)

Site Collection Administration

- Recycle bin
- Site collection features
- Site hierarchy
- Portal site connection

Site Collection Administration

- Search settings
- Search scopes
- Search keywords
- Recycle bin
- Site directory settings
- Site collection usage reports
- Site collection features
- Site hierarchy
- Portal site connection
- Site collection audit settings
- Audit log reports
- Site collection policies
- Site collection output cache
- Site collection cache profiles
- Site collection object cache
- Variations
- Variation labels
- Variation logs
- Translatable columns

FIGURE 3.5
Site collection administration tasks.

By default, only the owners of the site are placed in this group, but it is possible to add additional users to the group with these steps:

1. Go to the root of the site collection in the browser.
2. Click Site Actions > Site settings.
3. Under Users and Permissions, click Site collection administrator.
4. Add the users you want and click OK.

■ **Quotas.** They are the only container in SharePoint on which you can set a storage quota.

■ **Storage unit.** When you create a site collection, you create it in a specific Web app. Each Web app has one or more content databases. The site collection is automatically created in the next available database. Once created there, all content associated with that site collection (sites, uploaded documents, list items, and so on) is stored in that database. It is not possible to span a site collection across multiple databases.

SharePoint determines what the next available database is by the number of unused site collections in the database. Navigate to Central Admin > Application Management > Content Databases and take a look at the screen, as seen in Figure 3.6.

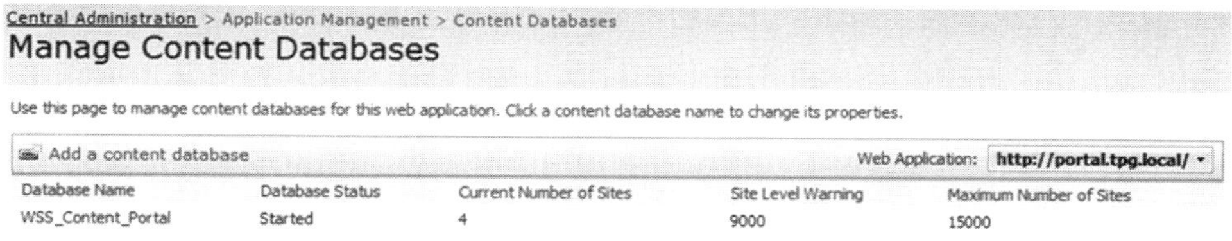

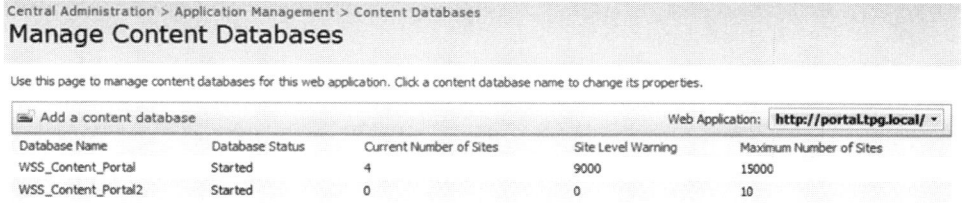

FIGURE 3.6
Manage Content Databases.

As you can see in this figure, the database WSS_Content_Portal has four site collections created (the screen says "sites" but it really means "site collections") in it and will allow 14,996 more site collections to be placed in the database.

Let's create a second database.

1. Click Add a content database from the menu bar,
2. Specify a database name of WSS_Content_Portal2,
3. Set the warning level to 0,
4. Set the maximum number of sites to 10,
5. Click OK.

The screen now looks like the one shown in Figure 3.7.

FIGURE 3.7
Manage Content Databases with two databases.

Now if you create a site collection, what database would SharePoint choose to store it in? Hope you guessed WSS_Content_Portal. Why? Because it has 14,996 free spots while WSS_Content_Portal2 only has 10 free spots.

To work around this and have the next site collection go into the new db, there are two ways to do it. You can either change the max number of sites to the WSS_Content_Portal database to four so it thinks it is full, or you can set the WSS_Content_Portal database to offline. Set the database to offline? Yes, in this interface you can click a database name and change the database status from Ready to Offline. Now, if you have a SQL background, that sounds like a really bad idea, but for SharePoint it isn't that drastic. In SharePoint, if a database is set to Offline, that only means you cannot add additional site collections to the database. It will still serve up content and allow users to add content to existing site collections, but it will not allow you to add a new site collection. Either way, you need to make it so that the Portal database will not accept new site collections, and then create your new site collection, and finally set things back to normal. If that sounds too painful, there is an even simpler way via the command line in Chapter 5, "Command Line Administration Using STSADM," to do this same process.

■ **Sharing is confined.** Site collections each have a unique set of galleries to maintain that are shared among all of the sites. These galleries include the list gallery, Web part galleries, site template galleries, and so on, and they vary by version of SharePoint.

Also, with MOSS there is a special Web part called the "Content Query Web Part" (CQWP) that can iterate through the entire site collection and return content. This Web part (and the Web parts derived from it) cannot reach outside the site collection.

As you can see, site collections set the boundaries for many things and really is the unit of scale in SharePoint. You need to plan for sites and site collections carefully and be sure to understand them before you start to build out your structure.

INSTALL MICROSOFT OFFICE SHAREPOINT SERVER 2007

For these steps, we will be using a three-server farm. Server1 will be a Windows 2008 Server, which will be assigned the Web, Query, and Excel roles. Server2 will be a Windows 2008 Server, which will be assigned the Index role. Server3 will be a Windows 2008 Server running SQL Server 2005 standard. All three servers are part of the same domain. Windows firewall has been disabled on all servers.

1. Log in to Server1 as your SharePoint Setup account. If you are following the example naming from earlier in the chapter, this should be domain\sp_admin. This account will need to be a local administrator on

both Server1 and Server2. This account will also need to be set up on Server3 with a SQL Login assigned the roles of dbcreator and securityadmin.

2. Run setup.exe from your install media or OfficeServerwithSP1.exe that you downloaded from http://www.microsoft.com/downloads/details.aspx? FamilyId=2E6E5A9C-EBF6-4F7F-8467-F4DE6BD6B831&displaylang=en. If you have preservice pack one install media, see the following section on slipstreaming.

3. Enter your Product Key and press Continue. It is possible to use a 180-day trial key at this point. At any time during the next 180 days, you may update to your purchased licensed key without doing a reinstall. For step-by-step instructions on making this update, go to http://msmvps.com/blogs/ shane/archive/2007/04/21/how-do-i-find-out-when-my-moss-trial-expires.aspx.

4. Review the Microsoft Software License Terms, click I accept the terms of this agreement, and click Continue

5. Make the right choice on this screen, because this is a very common mistake. Choose Advanced.

6. For Server Type, choose Complete.

7. Click the File Location tab and choose where you would like to install the MOSS program files and the default location of the index files. You can change this per SSP. Keep in mind that files will still be installed at c:\program files\common files\Microsoft shared\web server extensions\12, regardless of where you choose to install the MOSS files.

8. Click the Feedback tab and choose whether or not you would like to provide Microsoft with anonymous feedback.

9. Once you have double-checked all of your settings, click Install Now.

10. At the Installation Successful message, make sure the check box for Launch SharePoint Configuration Wizard is checked and click Close.

11. Configuration Wizard should open to the Welcome screen. Click Next.

12. Click Yes at the pop-up warning. This message is warning you that IIS and the SharePoint services will be stopped while Config Wizard runs. This should not be an issue since this is a fresh install.

13. From the Connect to a server farm screen, select No, I want to create a new server farm, and click Next.

14. At Specify Configuration Database Settings, specify your Database server name.

15. For database name, it is recommended that you accept the default of SharePoint_Config. The reason for the recommendation is consistency. Basically, it allows someone new to look at your environment and quickly recognize the database. It also simplifies any future troubleshooting.

16. For username, specify your chosen farm admin account. If you are following the convention from earlier in the chapter, this would be domain\sp_farm. This account requires no special permissions ahead of time. SharePoint will use the sp_admin account to elevate its permissions.

17. Enter the account password and click Next.

18. On the Configure SharePoint Central Administration Web Application, you are given the capability to specify the port number of the Central Admin. If you do not specify a port, it will choose a random number above 1024. It is recommended that you choose a number such as 5555 or 7777, something easy to remember. Do so by selecting the check box and entering your number.

19. Under Configure Security Settings, choose your authentication type. This will determine the setting that Central Admin uses. Typically, for Central Admin, you will use the default setting of NTLM. If you choose Kerberos, be certain that you have configured your SPNs properly, as outlined earlier in the chapter. After you have made your decision, click Next.

20. At this point, you can review your settings and confirm everything. If they are correct, click Next to set up your configuration.

21. After a couple of minutes, you should be brought back to a Configuration Successful screen where you will click Finish. If you have an error for any reason, you can find the diagnostic file or log file at c:\program files\common files\Microsoft shared\web server\extensions\12\logs.

INSTALLING ON ADDITIONAL SERVERS

If you have additional servers you would like in your farm, now is the time to install them. For our example, this would be Server2. You should go to each server and log in as your sp_admin account. You can then run steps 1 through 12 exactly as before. At that point, you can use these steps.

1. Select Yes, I want to connect to an existing server farm and then select Next.

2. Specify the database server name and click Retrieve Databases.

3. Choose the appropriate configuration database from the drop-down.

4. The username for your farm account (sp_farm) should appear. Enter the password and click Next

5. Verify your settings and click Next.

6. If you decided you wanted this server to host Central Admin instead of the first server you installed MOSS on, you can click the Advanced button. At that point, you can select the server to host Central Admin.
7. Click Finish at the successful screen.

Repeat these steps for all servers in the farm. Once completed, you can return to the first sever and continue on to Central Admin.

AVOIDING DCOM ERRORS

In order for SharePoint to run smoothly and not kick out DCOM errors every time a SharePoint Web app is started, you need to make a security tweak to your DCOM configuration. To do this, use the following steps:

1. Click Start > Administrative Tools > Component Services.
2. Drill down to Component Services > Computers > My Computer > DCOM Config, as shown in Figure 3.8.

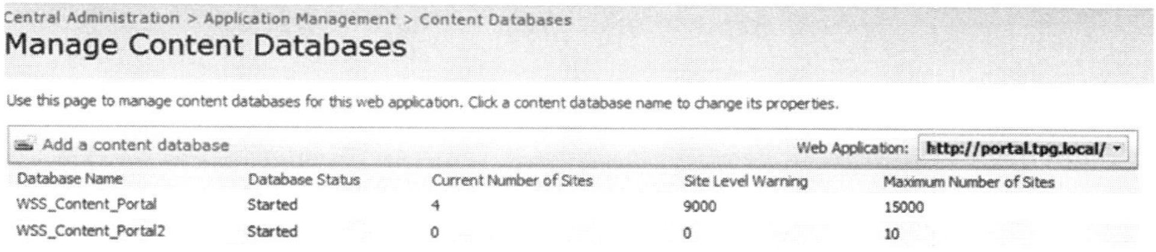

Central Administration > Application Management > Content Databases

Manage Content Databases

Use this page to manage content databases for this web application. Click a content database name to change its properties.

Add a content database			Web Application:	http://portal.tpg.local/ ▾	
Database Name	Database Status	Current Number of Sites	Site Level Warning	Maximum Number of Sites	
WSS_Content_Portal	Started	4	9000	15000	
WSS_Content_Portal2	Started	0	0	10	

FIGURE 3.8
Component Service DCOM settings.

3. Find IIS WAMREG Admin Service, right-click, and select Properties.
4. Click the Security tab.
5. For Launch and activation permissions, click Edit.
6. Click Add.
7. Click Locations and set it to your server name.
8. For name, input WSS_WPG.
9. Click OK.
10. Highlight WSS_WPG and check Allow for Local Activation.
11. Click OK twice and close the window.

By default, anytime you set an account to be an Application Pool identity in SharePoint, it will place that account in the local group on each server called WSS_WPG. And since each Application Pool account needs local activation permission, you can set the rights for the group and avoid frequent trips to Component Services. You will need to do this on each WFE in your farm.

STARTING THE SERVICES

The first step will be to configure the various services on the servers that are required by going to Central Admin. Server1 will be set up as a WFE, Query, and Excel Calculation server while Server2 will be set up to be a dedicated index box.

1. Back on Server1, Central Admin should be open. If necessary, you can launch Central Admin by going to Start > All Programs > Microsoft Office Server >SharePoint 3.0 Central Administration. If prompted, log in by using your sp_admin account.
2. Click the Operations tab
3. Under Topology and Services, click Services on server.
   You are then taken to a screen for starting services on the various servers. Notice that when you first come to the screen, you are presented with a selector, as shown in Figure 3.9.

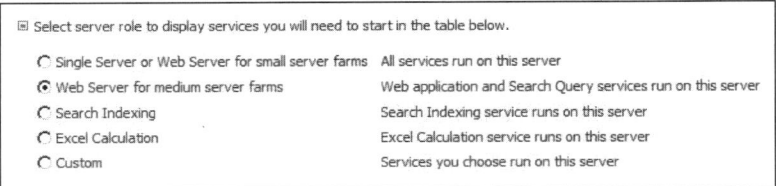

FIGURE 3.9
Select server role.

It is important to note this is just a helper. As you select the various radio buttons, the services displayed below will change. This setting does not affect the server in any way, and every time you open a new browser and return to this screen, it will be located at the default of Web Server for medium server farms. Many administrators have wasted hours wondering why their settings were not being kept—now you have just saved those wasted hours.

4. Also, you should pay attention to the Server selection, since this will show you which server in your farm you are starting services on. In the example, you should be on Server1.

5. To the right of Excel Calculation Services, click Start. After just a couple of seconds, you should be returned to this screen with the status set to "started."

6. To the right of Office SharePoint Server Search, click Start.

   In the first section, you have two check boxes. This is how you identify the server as an Index server or a Query server. For this server, select the box to the left of This is not is Figure 3.10 as shown in Figure 3.10.

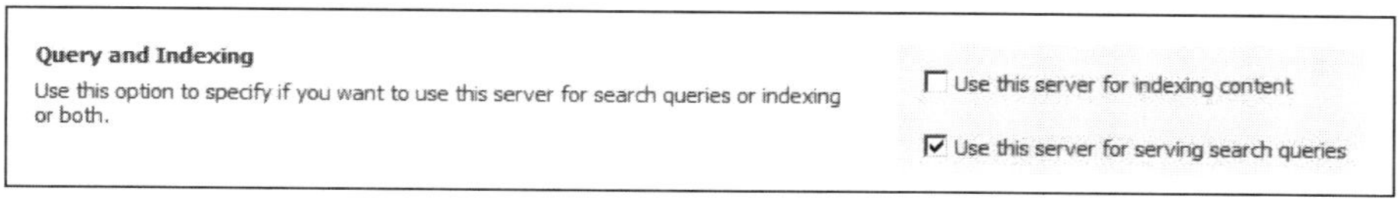

Query and Indexing

Use this option to specify if you want to use this server for search queries or indexing or both.

☐ Use this server for indexing content

☑ Use this server for serving search queries

FIGURE 3.10
Query and Indexing options

7. When you check the box, you will see additional options appear below. Fill in the email address box. This email address will be left in the logs of remote Web servers that you index, giving the administrator the opportunity to contact you if there is an issue with crawling their site.

8. For Farm Search Service Account, enter your appropriate account. If you are using the guidance from earlier in this chapter, then you would enter domain\sp_search. Keep in mind that this account will be used as the default content access for all content that you index. This account also should have read-only access to all SharePoint content. If the account has elevated privileges, it is possible that inappropriate content (such as unpublished versions) will appear in the index.

9. Enter the password.

10. Now specify the Query Server Index File Location. This is where the index will be stored on the Query server. Make sure this location has 2.8 times the size of index in free space available. Typically, putting this file on a dedicated disk is recommended.

11. In order for the index to be propagated, the location specified previously will need to be shared. It is possible (and recommended) to have SharePoint configure this share for you by putting in local administrator credentials. Your sp_admin account would work nicely for this one-time job. SharePoint does not store this account username and password.

12. Once you have your settings, click Start at the bottom of the screen.

13. Back at the Services on Server screen, find Document Conversions Load Balancer Service and click Start to the right of it.

14. After a few seconds, the status will change to started. Now click Start from the right of Document Conversions Launcher Service.

15. You are taken to a configuration screen where you need to set the Load Balancer Server to your server name and press OK.

    These two services combine to enable the Smart Client Authoring capabilities of MOSS. This feature, simply put, allows an uploaded Word Doc (docx), InfoPath form, or .xml file to be converted to a SharePoint page. For more information on this feature, please see http://blogs.msdn.com/ecm/archive/2006/06/13/629525.aspx.

16. Now that you have your first server configured, you need to switch to your second server to enable the indexing functionality. From the drop-down that says Server: ServerName, click Change Server.

17. Select your other server (Server2 in the example).

18. Now click Start to the right of Office SharePoint Server Search.

19. Check the box for Use this server for indexing content.

    Email and Account should be pre-populated, as you set this information when you started the service on the other server. Default index file location is also grayed out. This is the location you specified when you initially installed SharePoint. It's still not very important, because you will get a chance to change the index location when you create an SSP.

20. For Indexer Performance, set it to Maximum. Because this will be a dedicated Index server, it should allocate as many threads as possible.

21. For Web Front End and Crawling, accept the default of Use all front-end computers for crawling.

22. Click Start.

23. Click Start to the right of Windows SharePoint Services Search.

24. Enter your Service Account Username and Password. Be sure to use the form domain\username.

25. Enter your Content Access Account Username and Password. Be sure to use the form domain\username.

26. For most environments, the defaults for Search Database are just fine. If you need to make any adjustments, now is the time to do so; if not, keep moving down the page.

27. Indexing Schedule brings you to a decision point. In most environments, the WSS Search Service is only used to provide search capabilities for the help system built into MOSS. If this is the case, then it is best to set this service to run daily. If you plan to use the Service to provide search capabilities for some content databases, then set the schedule as needed.

28. Once everything on the page looks good, click Start.
29. The final step is to stop Windows SharePoint Services Web Application by clicking Stop. There are different scenarios (discussed in the previous chapter) where you would want your Index server to also be a WFE, but for our simple setup, this is not the case.

Configuring Outgoing Email

Outgoing email allows MOSS to send notifications out by using an anonymous SMTP relay server. Here's how to do that operation:

1. Return to the Operations page by clicking the Operations tab.
2. Under Topology and Services, click Outgoing email settings.
3. Specify the Outbound SMTP server. Keep in mind that this server must allow anonymous relay from your SharePoint servers.
4. Set the From Address and Reply-to address. They do not have to be the same. The From Address does not have to be a real account but the Reply-to should be one so that your users can get in contact with someone if needed.
5. Adjust the character set, if necessary. For most English installs, the default is correct.
6. Click OK.

Enable Usage Analysis Processing

Enabling usage analysis processing is not required, but most farm administrators like to enable the reporting. So what better time to check that off than while you are in here getting the server configured.

1. Under Logging and Reporting, click Usage analysis processing.
2. Select the check box to Enable logging.
3. Specify the location or accept the default. Each Web application will have a folder created at this location. Then for each day there will be a folder created, and the daily logs will be stored there.
   Caution here. The documentation says the server will only keep 31 days of logs, yet experience shows this not to be the case. Monitor the storage used for these logs.

4. Select the box to Enable usage analysis processing and specify a time. Because logs are only processed daily, you will never see the current day's usage stats.
5. Click OK.

CREATING YOUR FIRST SHARED SERVICES PROVIDER

Before those awful red letters !Server Farm Configuration Not Complete! will go away, you need to create your default SSP. To create the SSP, you will also need to create a Web application to host the SSP administration site collection and another Web application that will host the My Sites. Use these steps to do so:

1. From the left-hand side of the page in Central Admin, click Shared Services Administration.
2. From the menu bar, click New SSP.
3. Specify the name of your SSP.
4. From the SSP Name section of the page, click Create a new Web application. Here you are making an important deployment decision. There are two options here. You can either run the SSP on port 80 (Web default) with a host header to make it easy to access later by navigating to http://ssp/ssp/admin. Or you can just specify an uncommon port like 9999 and not use a host header. Then you would access the site by going to http://server1:9999/ssp/admin. Either one works fine, so it is just your preference. Remember if you decide to use a host header, it will need to be defined in DNS.
   In this example, let's assume that we are hosting the SSP on its own Web application at http://ssp.
5. Set the Port number to 80.
6. Specify the host header of ssp.
7. You can set a custom path for the Web application setting and configuration files or accept the default of c:\inetpub\wwwroot\wss\virtual directories\<site description>.
8. For Security configuration, the defaults should work just fine. Microsoft's internal testing has shown issues with using the SSP Web Application with Kerberos, so it is recommended that you run this Web App with NTLM.
9. The Load Balanced URL will automatically update with your previous settings.

10. Choose Create a new Application Pool. Set the username and password to be your SSP account. Be sure to use the format domain\account. If you are following the example naming from earlier in the chapter, this is sp_sspapp.

11. In our farm with only one WFE server, Restart IIS Manually is fine since there is no need to restart IIS. When you have multiple WFE servers, this Web application will be propagated automatically to those servers, but the propagation will only take effect after an IIS reset.

12. For Database Name and Authentication, the defaults will work just fine, but a change is recommended. For the database name, change it from WSS_Content to WSS_Content_SSP. This makes it easier in the future to map your databases to your Web applications. Also, once you have created a database with the name WSS_Content, the future default value will be WSS_Content_<guid>. If you are not familiar with guids, they are 32-character strings that are globally unique. These guid-named databases are very difficult to match to Web applications and generally annoy your DBAs.

13. After you have all of your settings, click OK. This will create your SSP Web application and will take you back to the create a new SSP screen. You will see lots of red warning text at the top of the page. You can just ignore it for now.

14. Scroll down to the My Site Location section and click Create a new Web application.

Once again, you have come to a place to make a choice. You can a.) choose to host My Sites on the same Web application as the SSP, b.) you can create a new Web application and host My Sites in their own environment, or c.) you can host My Sites on the same Web application as you will host your portal.

If you choose option a), you will get a warning that Microsoft recommends against this practice. For one reason, you cannot back up or restore My Sites and the SSP independently using the built-in tools. This can make recovery a pain and is generally not a good idea.

If you choose option b), this is considered the best practice according to Microsoft. Being an independent Web app gives you the most flexibility for recoverability. But this approach can cause unnecessary headaches. If you are using HTTPS, you will need a separate certificate for https://my and https://portal or a special domain wildcard certificate. If you are behind a proxy (like ISA Server), you will need two separate publishing rules. Also, if your users' browsers are not set to automatically log on to SharePoint, they will enter username/password to access http://portal. Then when they click the link to their My Site, they will be prompted again to authenticate for http://my.

If you choose option c) and host them at http://portal/mysites, this seems to be the easiest approach for your users. And if you are using a third-party backup tool, then you don't have to worry about the ability to easily recover a specific site. The downside to this method is that each My Site is going to be its own site collection and will be created in the same content database as the portal site collections. If you have only thousands of users, this could be okay. If you are going to have tens of thousands of users, you may want to avoid this method. Additionally, this method will cause you to lose some flexibility. All Web application settings like default quota template, recycle bin settings, and others will be shared between My Sites and the portal. Though, in many small shops this isn't a concern either.

For the example, we will create a unique MY Web app.

1. Set port to 80.
2. Set the host header to my.
3. Make any necessary changes to the storage path.
4. For Authentication provider, you can determine whether you require NTLM or Kerberos authentication. Remember to create the necessary SPNs if you choose Kerberos.
5. Choose Create a new Web Application Pool.
6. Enter your username/password for your App Pool. Remember to use domain\username.
7. As stated previously, determine if you need to change the IIS reset information.
8. For database name, change it to WSS_Content_My.
9. Confirm your settings and click OK. This will create your My Sites Web application and will take you back to the create a new SSP screen. You will still see lots of red warning text at the top of the page. You can just ignore it for now.
10. Under My Site Location, you can specify a relative URL, if necessary. If you created a unique Web app (as in this example), then you should just use the root /. If you choose to host My Sites under your portal Web app, then you should set the relative URL to /mysites.
11. For SSP service Credentials, enter the username and password for your SSP service account. This account gets the same permissions as the SSP Web App account and for that reason there is no reason not to use the same account as you did in step 10 in the previous set of instructions.
12. For SSP Database and Search Database, the defaults are typically acceptable.
13. For Index server, you can choose which Index server in your farm should be used for hosting this SSPs database. In most farms, this setting will be grayed out since there will only be one Index server.

14. Path for index file location finally gives you the opportunity to determine where the physical index will reside on the Index server. The default value you specified when you installed MOSS will be filled in.
15. If you would like the SSP Web services to run using SSL, check the box. Then you will manually need to deploy the SSL certificate to all Web servers in your farm. This Web application only appears in IIS and is named Office Server Web Services.
16. Once you double-check your settings click OK to create your SSP. After a minute or two, you will be taken back to Central Admin and be presented with a Success! message. Your first SSP is ready for business.

CREATING YOUR FIRST USER WEB APPLICATION

In this example, we will walk through creating another Web application, this time one dedicated to the user portal. We will also configure this Web application to use Kerberos authentication. After the Web application is up and running, we will create the root site collection using the Collaboration Portal template.

1. From Central Admin, navigate to the Application Management tab.
2. Under SharePoint Web Application Management, click Create or extend Web application.
3. Click Create a new Web application.
4. Change the port to 80.
5. Enter your host header. For this example, we have chosen portal.
6. Set the authentication provider to Negotiate (Kerberos).
7. Choose Create a new Web Application Pool.
8. Enter your username/password for your App Pool. Remember to use domain\username. Based on the guidance earlier, we will use `domain\sp_PortalAppPool`.
9. As mentioned previously, determine if you need to change the IIS reset information.
10. For the database name, change it to WSS_Content_Portal.
11. Review your settings and click OK. If you get a Kerberos warning pop-up, click OK.
    Because you have chosen Kerberos for this Web application, you need to create two very specific SPNs. The exact command would be the following:

```
Setspn.exe –A http/portal domain\sp_PortalAppPool
Setspn.exe –A http/portal.domain.local domain\sp_PortalAppPool
```

Be sure to replace `domain\` with your proper domain netbios name.

Be sure to replace `domain.local` with your proper FQDN.

Also, due to inconsistent browser handling of DNS alias (cnames), you should always use host (A records) for Kerberos host headers.

12. From the Application Created screen, click the Create Site Collection link (in blue) from the middle of the page.

13. Enter a Title and Description for your site.

14. From Select a template, choose the Publishing tab

15. From the Publishing tab, select Collaboration Portal

16. Specify a Primary Site Collection Administrator.

17. Optionally, specify a Secondary Site Collection Administrator.

Even though you can only specify two users at creation time, you can go to the site collection and add as many site collection administrators as necessary. These two named users will be notified in the case of the site being over quota and will be listed when enumerating all site collections using stsadm.exe.

18. Assign a quota, if necessary.

19. Click OK. After a minute or so, you should have a true SharePoint site ready to go.

20. When you get the Top-Level Site Successfully Created screen, click the blue link in the middle of the page to be taken to your new site collection. This is a great time to confirm Kerberos is working. So be sure to test from a client PC that you can open the site.

SLIPSTREAMING SERVICE PACK 1

If you have a pre-SP1 CD/DVD for your install, it is recommended that you slipstream service pack 1 (SP1) so that it is installed initially for you. If you are installing on Windows Server 2008, this is a requirement.

The following example is written assuming that you have extracted the MOSS installation files to c:\SharePointInstall, and you have saved the service packs in the folder c:\sp1. If you are only installing WSS, then you can skip step 6.

1. Open a Command Prompt.

2. Change directories to the location of the patches by typing the following command and pressing Enter:

```
cd "C:\sp1"
```

3. Extract WSS SP1 by typing the following command and pressing Enter:

```
Wssv3sp1-kb936988-x86-fullfile-en-us.exe
/extract:"C:\SharePointInstall\updates"
```

4. Read the EULA, check Click here to accept, and click Continue.
5. Extract MOSS SP1 by typing the following command and pressing Enter:

```
OfficeServer2007sp1-kb936984-x86-fullfile-en-us.exe
/extract:"C:\SharePointInstall\updates"
```

6. Read the EULA, check Click here to accept, and click Continue.

THE INFRASTRUCTURE UPDATE

Microsoft also has released a new set of patches and updates for both WSS and MOSS after SP1. These updates are called the infrastructure update, and you can find links to download them at http://blogs.msdn.com/sharepoint/ archive/2008/07/15/announcing-availability-of-infrastructure-updates.aspx. Multiple hotfixes have been bundled along with new enhanced Search functionality. The update does not include SP1 updates and while SP1 is not a prerequisite to installing the infrastructure update, it is highly recommended that you install SP1 prior to installing this update. It is also possible to slipstream this update for new installs following the steps previously outlined. If you are going to slipstream the update you should do it in conjunction with SP1.

4 Securing and Managing Site Content

In This Chapter

- Introduction
- Site and Content Authorization
- Web Application Authorization

INTRODUCTION

One of the key strengths of SharePoint technology is the ability to rapidly create and customize Web sites. To ensure these sites are used appropriately, user access to content must be managed according to the governance requirements of the organization. SharePoint provides the administrator with both broad scope capability in the form of Web application policies and fine grain control such as item-level permission within a Web site. Web application policies provide control over any site in the Web application. This control cannot be overridden at the site level. In the absence of Web application policies, Web sites are managed using a combination of permissions, permission levels, groups, and inheritance. Web site access can be governed at any level in the site hierarchy, which includes the site, list or library, folder and individual document, or list item. This version of SharePoint improves on the granular capability by allowing individual documents or list items to be "locked down." Inheritance is enabled by default but can be broken at any object level. Together, Web application policies and site access permissions provide both flexibility and granular control. We will begin our discussion with how Web site security is managed, and then we will discuss the details of applying Web application policies.

SITE AND CONTENT AUTHORIZATION

Maintaining control over which users can access SharePoint sites and the content they can access is critical to successful SharePoint data governance. MOSS and WSS rely on IIS (Internet Information Services) and ASP.NET to manage authentication. Once authenticated, users must be authorized in order to access sites and content. Site and content authorization are based on access rights, or permissions that can be assigned to users and groups. Permissions provide access to content and enable specific activities to be performed by a user or group. They are bundled into what SharePoint calls "permission levels." Permission levels are associated with SharePoint objects like sites. Permission levels are then assigned to users and groups, and the authorization process is complete. Sites, lists, libraries, individual list items, and documents represent securable objects, which are objects that can be "locked-down" via the appropriate permission assignment. The combination of permission levels and object inheritance govern who can access SharePoint content and what activities they can perform. We will begin the authorization process discussion with SharePoint's security architecture and components. This includes permissions, permission levels, SharePoint groups, inheritance, and the different administrator roles available for managing SharePoint sites and content.

SECURITY ARCHITECTURE AND COMPONENTS

The security architecture and components include the following items: the different types of administrator roles and their capability, the terminology used to communicate various security concepts, permission and permission levels, and SharePoint site groups. We will discuss each of the topics in detail, beginning with administrator roles in the next section.

Administration Model and Levels

MOSS provides a three-tier administrative model that is new to the SharePoint platform. This model achieves centralized management while providing the capability to differentiate roles and delegate administration to different individuals in the organization. The three different tiers are: server farm, Shared Services Provider (SSP), and site. Each tier can be managed differently, if appropriate, which enables multiple administration structures to be accommodated, depending on the company's requirements. Natively, this tiered approach contains several different administrator groups, each with different levels of authority. Tier 1 is managed by the Farm Administrators and Local Administrators. The SSP Administrator and Service Administrators manage tier 2. Tier 3 is the most pertinent tier for this chapter's discussion and is managed by the Site Collection Administrator and the Site Owner. This tiered approach separates responsibility so that things like physical server administration and the daily activities of site access and content administration can be assigned to different individuals. These different administrator groups are summarized next. A more in-depth discussion of this three-tier model can be found at: "Plan for security roles (Office SharePoint Server)" http://technet2.microsoft.com/Office/en-us/library/81b06f7d-430f-4387-8a29-122cc5928fb71033.mspx.

- **Farm Administrators.** Members of the Farm Administrators group have permissions and responsibility for all SharePoint servers in the farm, including all Central Administration functions and command-line operations. Members do not have access to individual sites or their content, but can take ownership and authorize themselves.

- **Local Administrators.** Members of the Local Administrators group on the Web server are automatically Farm Administrators. These individuals have the permission to perform all server farm administration actions plus installing new products or applications, deploying Web Parts and new features to the global assembly cache, creating new Web applications and new Internet Information Services (IIS) Web sites, and starting services. Depending on the specific organization and skill set of the local administrators, these actions may be better accomplished by a SharePoint administrator with the appropriate permissions. Members do not have access to individual sites or their content, but can take ownership and authorize themselves. The reader should revisit the recommendations of Chapter 3 with regard to which accounts should be used for each of these responsibilities and also refer to the white paper referenced previously, "Plan for security roles."

- **SSP Administrators.** These members manage which services are included in a Shared Services Provider (SSP). The SSP includes a number of services, such as the Search service and the Business Data Catalog.

- **Service Administrators.** These members configure settings for a specific service within an SSP. Individual services like Search could be delegated to a specific individual without delegating all of the SSP services responsibility.

- **Site Collection Administrators.** These members have full control permission on all Web sites within a site collection, including access to all sites.

- **Site Owners.** These members have full control permission on a specific site in the site collection.

Key Points

■ Farm and Local Administrators do not have access to SharePoint sites by default, despite their broad permission set. However, before you get too excited, keep in mind that both of them can take ownership of specific site collections, and therefore can add themselves as a site collection administrator by using the Site Collection Administrator's page in Central Administration. If this scares some folks, take heart that this process can be audited so that proper security controls can be maintained. It is also possible for these administrators to give themselves access using Web Application Policies. This topic will be discussed at the end of the chapter.

View and Modify Farm Administrators

1. Open the Central Administration Web site. Be sure you are logged in as a local administrator.
2. Click the Operations tab.
3. Click the Update Farm Administrators Group link under the Security Configuration section.
4. View the current Farm Administrators. Individual users and groups can be added by clicking the New button.

■ Members of the Site Collection Administrators group have complete authority over all sites in the collection and likewise, members of the Site Owners group have ownership and authority of their specific site. Thus, site administrators have complete authority to manage the site access and content permissions for their individual site without relying on any other administrator in the hierarchy. This includes modifying groups, creating new groups, assigning permissions, and giving the capability to manage security to other individuals. We will discuss all of these aspects in future sections.

View and Modify Site Collection Administrators

1. Open the Central Administration Web site. Be sure you are logged in as a local administrator.
2. Click the Application Management tab.
3. Click the link Site Collection Administrators found inside the SharePoint Site Management heading to reveal the Site Collection Administrators Web page, as shown in Figure 4.1.

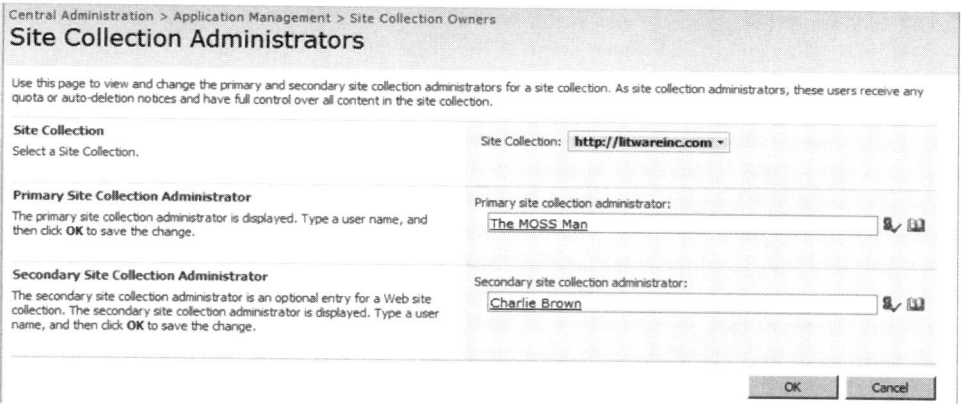

FIGURE 4.1
Viewing and modifying Site Collection Administrators.

4. Choose a Site Collection from the drop-down menu in the Site Collection section.

5. View the current Primary and Secondary Site Collection Administrators. From this page, you also have the option of updating the administrator membership, which could include adding yourself if necessary. If you're currently not one of the site collection administrators, add yourself as a primary.

6. Navigate to the specific Site Collection root site, which you chose in step 4 previously.

7. Navigate to the Site Settings Web page from the Site Settings menu. Notice that there are three links beneath the Users and Permissions heading: People and Groups, Site Collection Administrators, and Advanced Permissions. Therefore, you have the option of choosing the Site Collection Administrators' link, which would allow you to view the administrators, but we are not going to do that.

8. Click the Advanced Permissions link under Users and Permissions.

9. Click the Settings button to reveal a drop-down menu, as shown in Figure 4.2.

10. Select the Site Collection Administrators option to reveal the Web page shown in Figure 4.3. The list of administrators should match those from step 5.

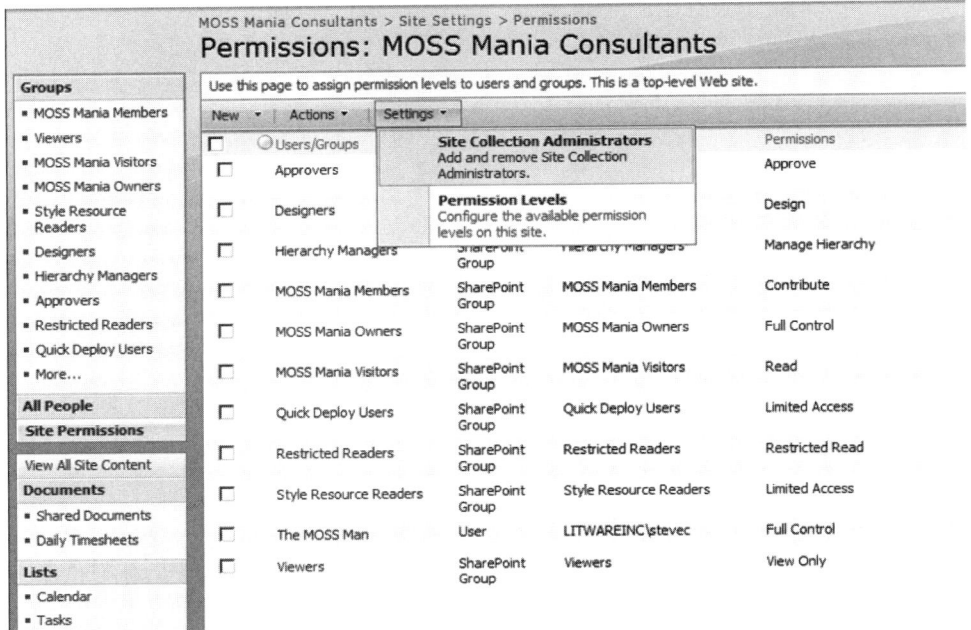

FIGURE 4.2
The option to view and modify Site Collection Administrators.

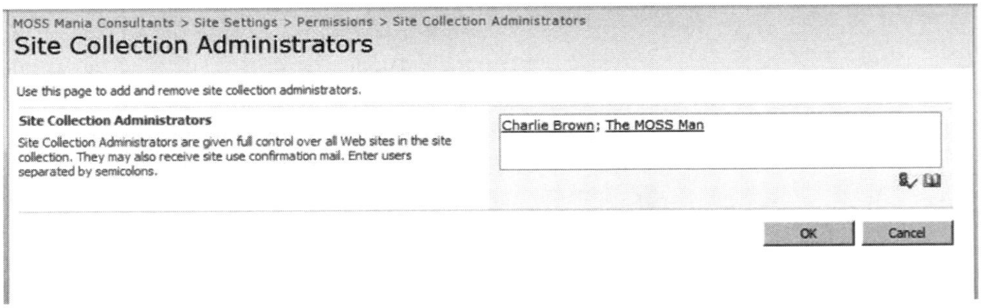

FIGURE 4.3
Viewing current Site Collection Administrators.

The three-tier model allows for separation of administrative responsibilities, which will maximize productivity and provide control where appropriate. This model gives site collection administrators and site owners the capability they need to manage their sites without requiring the intervention of the farm and local administrators. Site collection administrators and site owners will rely on permissions, permission levels, groups, and inheritance to manage their sites. The next section defines these terms to ensure clarity, and then we will delve deeper into each of the individual components. This terminology will be used throughout the chapter.

Security Terminology

There are a number of terms used routinely during the discussion of security management and particularly in this chapter. Permissions, Permission Levels, User, Groups, Securable Objects, Inheritance, and Site Groups represent a component or feature of the SharePoint authorization architecture. These terms are shown in Table 4.1 and apply to controlling access and authorization at the site collection and site levels.

TABLE 4.1 SECURITY MANAGEMENT TERMINOLOGY

Term	Description
Permissions	Individual rights that grant access to sites and content by providing the ability to perform specific actions.
Permission Levels	A defined set of permissions that grants users or groups authority to perform related activities.
User	An individual with an account in Active Directory or another user data store that can be authenticated via the mechanisms discussed previously.
Groups	A collection of users with a common role or common access needs.
Securable Objects	SharePoint entities such as sites, lists, libraries, folders, list items, and documents. Collectively, these objects comprise an object hierarchy. For example, the site is at the top of the hierarchy, then the list or library, the folder, and then the individual items like list items and documents.
Inheritance	Permissions are automatically propagated to the next object in the object hierarchy. Inheritance can be broken, if necessary, so that unique permissions can be established. For example, child site (also called subsites) inherit permissions from their parent site, document libraries inherit from their site, and so on.
Site Groups	Groups that define specific roles and permissions. By default, WSS and MOSS create a set of groups that vary depending on the type of site created and the type of functions users need to perform.

This terminology gives us the foundation for the following sections as we discuss the details of permissions, permission levels, and groups. Site access and content authorization rely on users having proper permissions. The following section defines the permissions that are available and how they can be enabled and disabled. Once enabled, they are available for all site collections and sites in a given Web application. Likewise, if disabled, they are not available for use across the Web application scope.

Permissions

A set of permissions are created and configured upon installation of MOSS. This list of available permissions can be viewed and configured from Central Administration, as shown in Figure 4.4. These permissions provide the granular control necessary for authorizing access to sites and content. Not all permissions are shown in the figure.

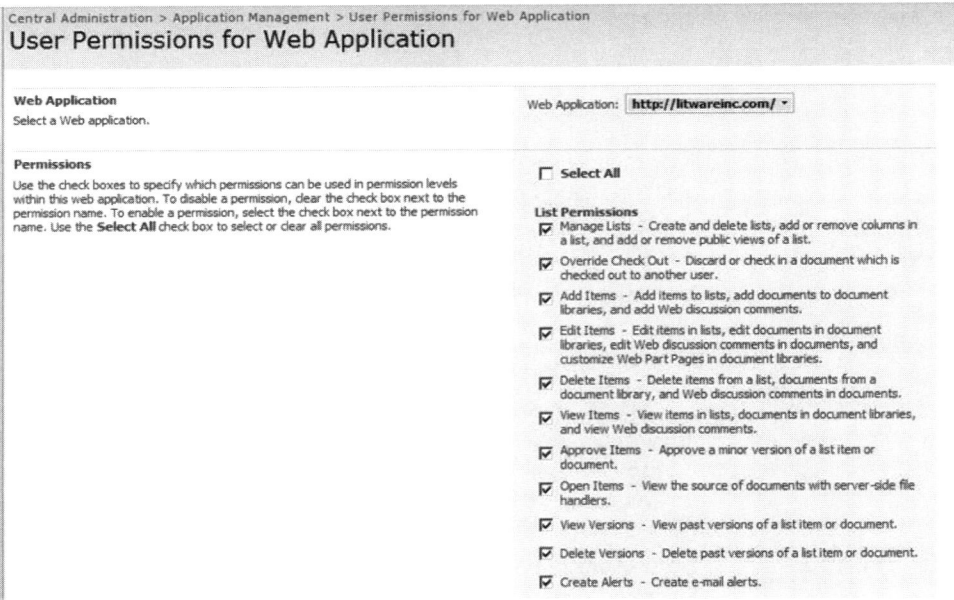

FIGURE 4.4
Web Application permissions that are currently available.

Viewing Permissions

1. Open Central Administration and click the Application Management tab.
2. From the Application Management Web page, click the User permissions for Web Application link within the Application Security section.
3. Notice that the list of permissions is categorized into three groups: List, Site, and Personal, and that all permissions are enabled.
4. Review the list of permissions and familiarize yourself with the capabilities that each provides.

These permissions collectively represent the arsenal of rights that can be used individually or grouped together to accommodate authorization requirements. The approach to SharePoint permission management will be to combine one or more permissions into groups. These groups are called permission levels. Permission levels are assigned to groups and then mapped to a specific security object, thereby providing members of the group authorization to the object. Figure 4.4 does not display the complete list of user permissions and is only meant for illustration. The complete list of permissions is shown in Table 4.2. The table also shows the mappings between individual permissions and the permission levels that SharePoint assigns by default. Permission levels will be discussed more thoroughly in the next section, but we will be referring to this table repeatedly throughout the chapter.

TABLE 4.2 PERMISSIONS AND DEFAULT USE

Permission	Description	Category	Permission Levels
Manage Lists	Create and delete lists, add or remove columns in a list, and add or remove public views of a list.	List	Design, Full Control
Override Check Out	Discard or check in a document that is checked out to another user without saving the current changes.	List	Design, Full Control
Add Items	Add items to lists, add documents to document libraries, and add Web discussion comments.	List	Contribute, Design Full Control

continued

Permission	Description	Category	Permission Levels
Edit Items	Edit items in lists, edit documents in document libraries, edit Web discussion comments in documents, and customize Web Part Pages in document libraries.	List	Contribute, Design Full Control
Delete Items	Delete items from a list, documents from a document library, and Web discussion comments in documents.	List	Contribute, Design, Full Control
View Items	View items in lists, documents in document libraries, and view Web discussion comments.	List	Read, Contribute, Design, Full Control
Approve Items	Approve minor version of list items or documents.	List	Design, Full Control
Open Items	View the source of documents with server-side file handlers.	List	Read, Contribute, Design, Full Control
View Versions	View past versions of list items or documents.	List	Read, Contribute, Design, Full Control
Delete Versions	Delete past versions of list items or documents.	List	Contribute, Design Full Control
Create Alerts	Create email alerts.	List	Read, Contribute, Design, Full Control
View Application Pages	View forms, views, and application pages, as well as enumerate lists.	List	All
Manage Permissions	Create and change permission levels on the Web site and assign permissions to users and groups.	Site	Full Control
View Usage Data	View reports on Web site usage.	Site	Full Control

continued

Permission	Description	Category	Permission Levels
Create Subsites	Create subsites, such as team sites, meeting workspace sites, and document workspaces.	Site	Full Control
Manage Web Site	Perform all administration tasks for the Web site, and manage content.	Site	Full Control
Add and Customize Pages	Add, change, or delete HTML pages or Web Part pages, and edit the Web site using a WSS-compatible editor.	Site	Design, Full Control
Apply Themes and Borders	Apply a theme or borders to the entire Web site.	Site	Design, Full Control
Apply Style Sheets	Apply a style sheet to the Web site.	Site	Design, Full Control
Create Groups	Create a group of users that can be used anywhere within the site collection.	Site	Full Control
Browse Directories	Enumerate files and folders in a Web site by using SharePoint Designer and Web DAV interfaces.	Site	Contribute, Design, Full Control
Use Self-Service Site Creation	Create a Web site using Self-Service Site Creation.	Site	Read, Contribute, Design, Full Control
View Pages	View pages in a Web site.	Site	Read, Contribute, Design, Full Control
Enumerate Permissions	Enumerate permissions on the Web site, list, folder, document, or list item.	Site	Full Control
Browse User Information	View information about users of the Web site.	Site	All

continued

Permission	Description	Category	Permission Levels
Manage Alerts	Manage alerts for all users of the Web site.	Site	All
Use Remote Interfaces	Use SOAP, Web DAV, or SharePoint Designer interfaces to access the Web site.	Site	All
Use Client Integration Features	Use features that launch client applications. Without this permission users must work on documents locally and then upload their changes.	Site	All
Open	Open a Web site, list, or folder to access items inside that container.	Site	All
Edit Personal User Information	Users can change their own user information, such as adding a picture.	Site	Contribute, Design, Full Control
Manage Personal Views	Create, change, and delete personal views of lists.	Personal	Contribute, Design, Full Control
Add/Remove Personal Web Parts	Add or remove personal Web Parts on the Web Part Page.	Personal	Contribute, Design, Full Control
Update Personal Web Parts	Update Web Parts to display personalized information.	Personal	Contribute, Design Full Control

Key Points

- Individual permissions are added together and mapped to several default permission levels. The default permission levels that contain specific permissions are shown in the table.
- Certain permissions, like Manage Permission, have dependencies on other permissions. Therefore, when Manage Permission is utilized, other permissions are also enabled by default.
- Permission levels will then be assigned to groups for a given security object.

- The Full Control permission level is the only default level to have the following permissions: Manage Permissions, View Usage Data, Create Subsites, Manage Web Site, Create Groups, Enumerate Permissions, and Manage Alerts. Site Collection Administrators and Site Owners have the Full Control permission level.
- Permissions are configurable for a specific Web Application. By enabling or disabling individual permissions, the farm or local administrator can govern those permissions, which can be used in permission levels within the specific Web Application.

Grouping permission sets into levels provides a mechanism whereby a permission level can be assigned to a group of users for a specific securable object. A different permission level can be assigned to the same group for a different object. If permissions were directly mapped to groups, then this would not be as flexible. The next section covers in more detail the default permission levels available.

Permission Levels

A permission level is a collection of permissions that can be assigned to individual users or groups. Permission levels contain one or more of the 33 permissions previously summarized in Table 4.2. WSS includes five permission levels by default, while MOSS provides an additional four; they are summarized in Table 4.3. The site collection administrator and site owner can create new permission levels and modify existing permission levels, if appropriate (except for the Limited Access and Full Control permission levels).

TABLE 4.3 DEFAULT PERMISSION LEVELS

Permission Level	WSS or MOSS	Description
Limited Access	WSS	Permission is restricted to a specific site item like a list or document without access to the entire site. Cannot be customized or deleted.
View Only	MOSS	A lot of folks get confused on the difference between View Only and Read. This permission allows the user to only view the document using a server-side viewer, like Excel Services for example; they would not be allowed to open the document using Excel, or whatever the native application.

continued

Permission Level	WSS or MOSS	Description
Restricted Read	MOSS	Read-only access to all items in a site, but does not allow the user to access previous versions or view information about other users.
Read	WSS	Read-only access to all items in the site.
Contribute	WSS	Add, remove, and edit any items in existing lists or document libraries.
Design	WSS	Create lists and document libraries, add or remove Web Parts, and change page layouts.
Approve	MOSS	Edit and approve changes to pages, list items, and documents.
Manage Hierarchy	MOSS	Create, editing, or delete individual sites, in addition to the Approve permission level privileges.
Full Control	WSS	The complete set of permissions. Cannot be customized or deleted.

Key Points

There are several points worth summarizing to ensure clarity before we move on. These are given next.

- Permission levels are managed at the site level, the top of the object hierarchy. Specifically, this would be the top-level site of the site collection.
- Permission levels and inheritance together determine the overall access rights of the user. Site collection administrators and site owners should utilize inheritance to help simplify their security management. Inheritance should be the rule and not the exception. We will discuss more about inheritance later.
- Modifying or creating new permission levels is done on the top-level site of the site collection or on any subsite that has broken inheritance and is using unique permissions. Permission management cannot be done on a subsite that is inheriting permissions. The subsite's permissions are managed when the parent site's permissions are managed. This is one of the advantages of inheritance. Keep in mind, however, that permissions that satisfy the requirements of the parent site may not be suitable for any child sites, and inheritance may need to be broken.

- All permission levels can be assigned with the exception of the Limited Access permission. The Limited Access level is assigned automatically by WSS or MOSS under certain conditions and cannot be assigned directly to users or groups. This can be a little difficult to understand, so here's an example. Consider the scenario where a user needs access to a specific document inside a library, but no other content on the site. In this situation, WSS or MOSS will grant the user the Limited Access permission level for the document library and the site. When the user accesses the site, that user will only see the document library. When the user accesses the document library, that user will only see the specific file to which he has access. If the user does not have access to the site then he will need to navigate directly to the allitems.aspx Web page in the forms folder for the library or to the name of the document directly.

- The composition of a permission level can be changed by adding or deleting individual permissions. Another option is to create an entirely new permission level from scratch or better yet, copy an existing permission level that already has what you need. Although it is easy to edit the permissions associated with one of the default permission levels shown in Table 4.3, it is better to create a new permission level with the specific permissions necessary and leave the default levels intact. Despite the fact that the Limited Access and Full Control permission levels cannot be edited, you can make permissions unavailable for the entire Web application, which essentially removes those permissions from the Limited Access and Full Control permission levels. This was discussed previously in the "Permissions" section. However, this is not a recommendation for doing such an action, only an illustration of the flexibility.

- Permission levels should be assigned to groups rather than directly to users. Group assignment is a much more efficient process versus directly managing and maintaining the permissions associated with individual user accounts. This is especially true if item-level permissions are being assigned. Team membership and roles will change, and you do not want to have to track all of those changes and continually update the permissions for uniquely secured objects. Direct user assignment should be considered the exception.

The default permission levels are created and configured upon installation and added to each site upon provisioning. Table 4.2 shows which specific permissions are associated with the WSS provisioned levels, but it does not include the same information for the MOSS-defined levels. In general, how do you determine which permissions are associated with a specific permission level? The following walkthrough is valid for the default permission levels or any custom permission level that has been created.

Viewing Permissions for a Permission Level

1. From a top-level site in any site collection, access the Site Settings Web page from the Site Actions menu.
2. Click the Advanced Permissions link under Users and Permissions.
3. Click the Settings button to reveal a drop-down list with two entries, a link to Site Collection Administrators, as seen previously, and a link to Permission Levels, as shown in Figure 4.5. If the Settings menu is not available, then you are currently at a subsite in the site collection. If so, select Manage Permissions of Parent from the Actions menu. The Settings menu is not available on the Permissions page if your site is inheriting permissions from its parent site.
4. Select Permission Levels from the drop-down menu, as shown in Figure 4.5. After selecting, a new Web page will be displayed that reveals a list of all the permission levels, both default and new levels, for the site, as shown in Figure 4.6.

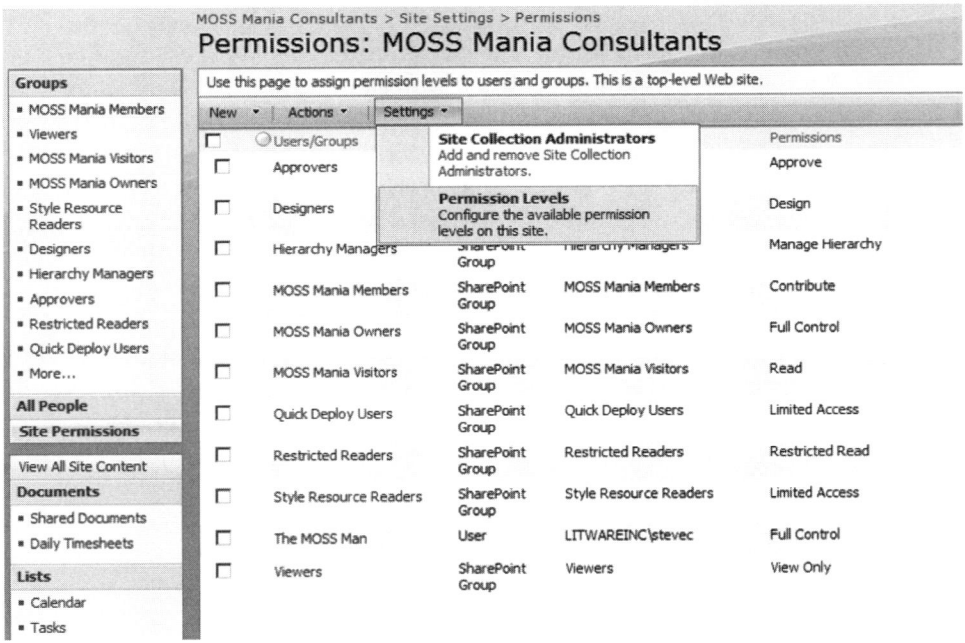

FIGURE 4.5
Site Permissions Web page and Settings options.

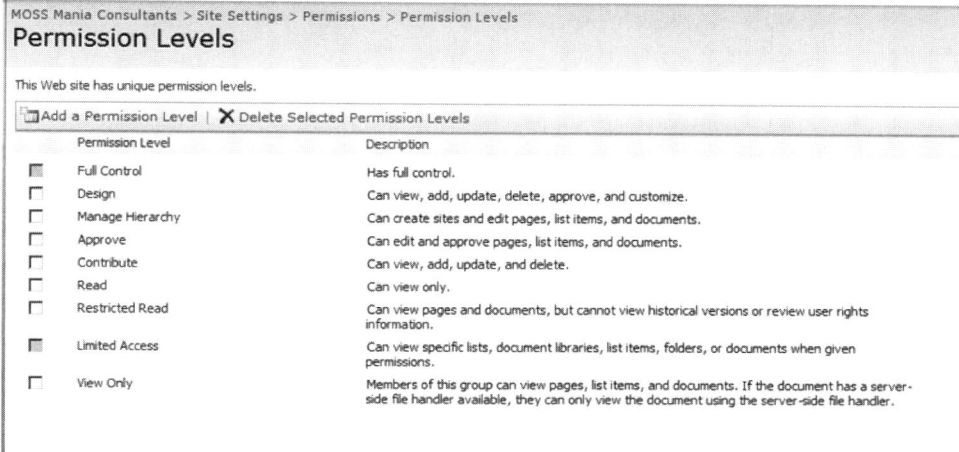

FIGURE 4.6
Web site Permission Levels.

The default permission levels simplify the site collection and site owner's security management process by providing a set of relevant permission combinations that already exist. You should plan to use the default permission levels as much as possible. However, the need will definitely arise when the default permission combinations do not meet all of the needs and new levels need to be created or existing levels need to be modified. The next section discusses this in more detail.

New Permission Levels

The default permission levels provide a good foundation for security management, but obviously they are not going to meet the needs of all situations. New permission levels can be created if none of the existing levels achieve the required security criteria. This can be accomplished by modifying existing permission levels or by creating new levels. As the site administrator, you have several different options to consider that are outlined next.

- **Copy default, modify, and save with a different name.** This is the approach you should use if the default levels are very close to what you need, and you are tempted to modify their composition directly. If so, you should copy the permissions into a new level, assign a different name to the level, and make the necessary permission modifications. This is also a good approach if you just want to rename a default level with a more descriptive name, which can also be very valuable. For example, providing a more complete description of the Approve Level would be valuable if you wanted to differentiate the scope of responsibility of different types of Approve permission levels.

■ **Create new level from scratch.** If only a few permissions are required or the desired requirements are very different from any existing level, then this may be an appropriate approach. Specifically, if you're not real familiar with the specific permissions associated with the default levels, or you don't want to take the time at the moment to become familiar, then this may be a much faster approach than reviewing existing levels for a close match.

■ **Modify existing level.** This option should be reserved for new levels that were created after the install. In other words, don't modify the default permission levels. Also, deleting a level should only be done to created levels. Modifying an existing level can have negative consequences if the scope and membership are not thoroughly reviewed.

At this point, let's familiarize ourselves with the process for each of the preceding scenarios. The following walkthrough will pick up where the previous one left off. We will begin from the Permission Levels Web page shown in Figure 4.6. From Figure 4.6, you can see that there are two buttons, one for adding a new level and one for deleting one or more existing levels.

Creating and Modifying Permission Levels

1. On the Permission Levels Web page, check the box next to the View Only permission level.
2. Click the button labeled Delete Selected Permission Levels.
3. You will receive a confirmation prompt asking you if you are sure. Click Cancel. It is that easy to delete an existing level. Be very sure when you do this and only delete new permission levels, never the default permission levels. Next, we'll illustrate the process for creating a new level by copying an existing level.
4. In the Permission Level column on the Permission Levels Web page, click the name of the permission level you want to copy, for example: Approve.
5. Scroll to the bottom of the Edit Permission Level page and then click Copy Permission Level.
6. Change the Name from Approve to List Approve and change the description to read "Can create and delete lists, add or remove columns in a list, and add or remove public views of a list. Also can edit and approve pages, list items, and documents."
7. In the List Permissions section, enable the Manage Lists permission. We could also remove permissions at this point if appropriate.
8. Once you are finished making changes, click Create. The new permission level appears on the Permission Levels page, as shown in Figure 4.7.

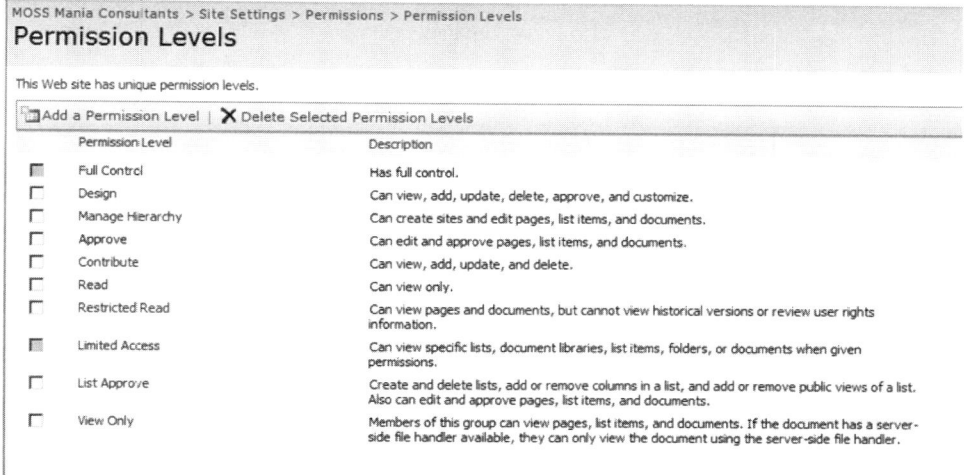

FIGURE 4.7
Permission Levels Web page showing the new List Approve permission level.

9. From the Permission Levels page, click the Add a Permission Level button.
10. For the name, enter "Permission Manager," and for the description enter "Create and change permission levels on the Web site and assign permissions to users and groups." Notice that none of the individual permissions have been assigned, and you have essentially a clean slate.
11. Under Site Permissions, enable Manage Permissions. Notice that several additional permissions were enabled once Manage Permissions was selected. These include: View Items, Open Items, View Versions, Browse Directories, View Pages, Enumerate Permissions, Browse User Information, and Open. This illustrates that certain permissions have dependencies on other permissions.
12. Click the Create button. The result is displayed in Figure 4.8.

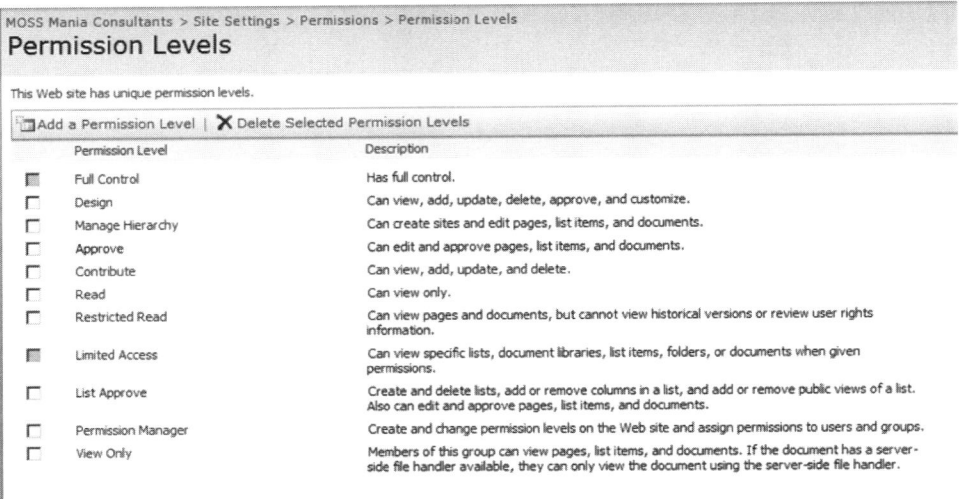

FIGURE 4.8
Permission Levels Web page showing the new Permissions Manager permission level.

13. From the Permission Levels page, click the List Approve permission level.
14. Enable Manage Alerts under the Site Permissions heading.
15. Click the Submit button to return to the Permission Levels page.

As demonstrated in the previous walkthrough, it is very easy to modify and create new permission levels. With such a simple process, it is critical that security management be implemented within the context of an overall access and authorization governance plan. The governance plan should include the company's overall security management strategy. For example, inheritance will not be broken without an approval process. Then each local site administrator has the responsibility for configuring and maintaining the company's governance requirements, as well as his or her own access management strategy for a given site. To help reduce the workload of the site administrator, WSS and MOSS automatically assign default permission levels to SharePoint Site Groups as part of the site provisioning process. SharePoint Site Groups can be viewed and modified using the Advanced Permissions link on the Site Settings page. This is discussed in the next section.

Site Groups

A site group is one of the groups on a SharePoint site that represents a collection of users. Groups are used to manage users with similar job roles or authorization requirements. Security management is accomplished by adding users to groups and assigning permission levels to the group. These groups can be a Windows security group or a SharePoint site group. Windows security groups can also be added to SharePoint groups. You should note that Active Directory Distribution Groups cannot be used. Therefore, as part of managing the security of your site, add the security group or SharePoint group to the site and assign permission levels for the respective security object. Security group membership can then be managed via Active Directory management, and SharePoint group membership is managed by the site collection administrator and site owner. By default, WSS provides three site-level groups: Visitors, Members, and Owners. MOSS provides a more extensive set of site groups that includes: Restricted Readers, Style Resource Readers, Viewers, Visitors (equivalent to the WSS Visitors user group), Members (equivalent to the WSS Members user group), Quick Deploy Users, Approvers, Designers, Hierarchy Managers, and Owners (equivalent to the WSS Owners user group). The site groups that are available upon site creation will be dependent on the site template chosen. To ensure that all of these groups are available within the site, the site will need to have the Publishing Feature enabled. These groups and their descriptions are shown in Figure 4.9.

Enabling the Publishing Site

Creating a site with the Publishing Site template will ensure that all of the groups are available. If your site has been created using a different template, you can enable the publishing capability by activating the Office SharePoint Server Publishing Infrastructure feature from the Site Collection Features Web page off the Site Settings page for the site collection.

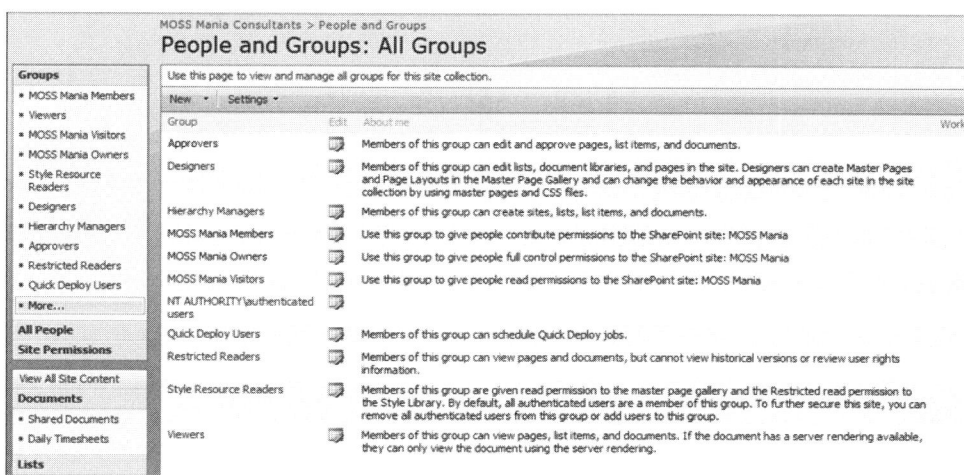

FIGURE 4.9
People and Site Groups for a site collection.

The figure illustrates the administration screen that is displayed upon navigating to Site Settings, using the People and Groups hyperlink and then clicking the Groups link at the top of the left-hand navigation. These groups are available to all sites in the site collection and therefore govern access throughout that scope as well. Several points are worth emphasizing, and they are summarized next.

Key Points

- Groups are defined at the top-level site of the site collection; they are global across the site collection. The default groups and any custom group are accessible from any site in the site collection. If you create a new group, regardless of the level in the site hierarchy, that custom group will also be available to all sites throughout the site collection. Therefore, site collection administrators have control of all defined groups in a specific site collection.
- Groups are containers for users and as such are not intrinsically associated with any specific securable object. The group must be explicitly assigned a permission level or an assignment must occur as part of the site provisioning process. Any user with the Manage Permissions permission can change the permissions for a specific securable object. From Table 4.2, only the Full Control permission level includes the Manage Permissions permission.
- Groups can be assigned different permission levels for different security objects.
- Each default SharePoint Group is assigned a permission level upon site provisioning, but the permission level for any group can be changed. As a rule, default site group permission levels should not be altered. The permission levels for the groups shown in Figure 4.9 are displayed in Figure 4.10.

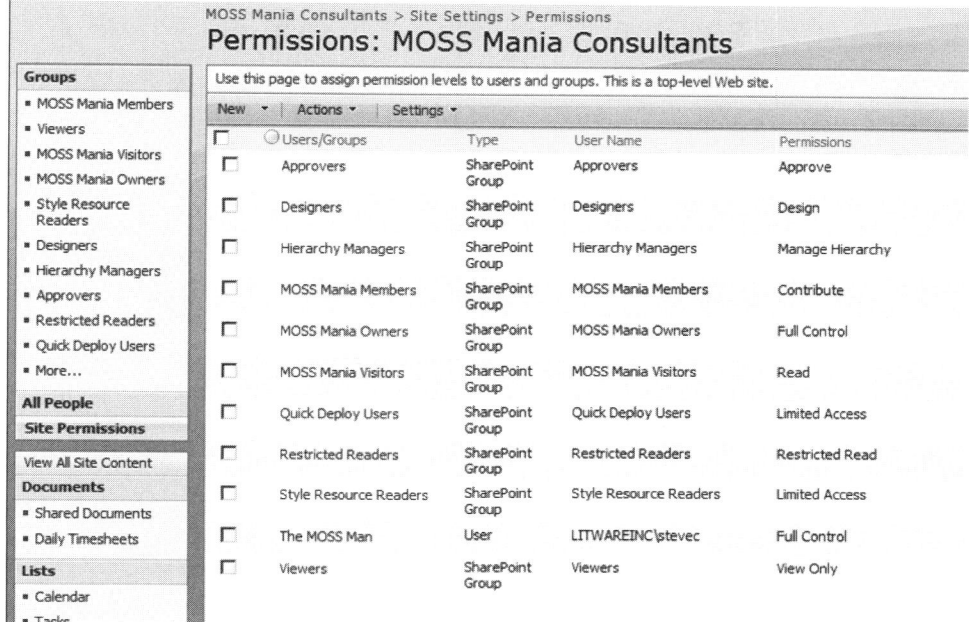

FIGURE 4.10
Permission levels assigned to groups for a site.

- New groups can be created by any user with the Create Groups permission. As shown in Table 4.2, the Create Groups permission is only included in the Full Control permission level by default.

- Use inheritance and group permissions to manage user site access and content authorization whenever possible. By default, permissions are initially controlled at the root site of the site collection, with all lists and libraries within the site inheriting the site's permissions. For example, if you authorize a user to view a site, that user is also authorized to view lists in the site and list items in each list. Use list-level, folder-level, and item-level permissions to more granularly control which users can view or interact with the site content. When a subsite is created, maintain inheritance, if possible, to ensure that permissions are propagated to the subsite. If the content access requirements dictate, an administrator can explicitly break permission inheritance at any point in the hierarchy. You can return to inheriting permissions from a parent list, the site as a whole, or a parent site at any time.

- Utilize the Authenticated Users group (the Domain Users Windows security group) if you want all domain users to have the same minimal permissions, such as being able to view content on your site. From Figure 4.10, you can see that the Authenticated Users group is available for assignment, but by default there is no assignment. You can confirm this by viewing the site permissions. Use of the Authenticated Users group also helps prevent the need for enabling anonymous access.

Groups provide the SharePoint site administrator with the capability to simplify the management process. This is directly analogous to the use of Active Directory groups and the Windows network or system's administrator. The SharePoint site administrator can use the default SharePoint site groups, create new site groups, modify existing groups, and also utilize Active Directory groups for managing security. Before we begin the process necessary for actually assigning permissions, we need to be aware of the options available for managing groups. The next walkthrough will cover these details.

Managing Groups

1. Navigate to the People and Groups: All Groups Web page, as shown in Figure 4.9.
2. Click the Settings button to display the menu shown in Figure 4.11. This menu allows you to configure which groups are displayed on the left-hand side Quick Launch menu and for configuring which WSS groups will be utilized for the site.

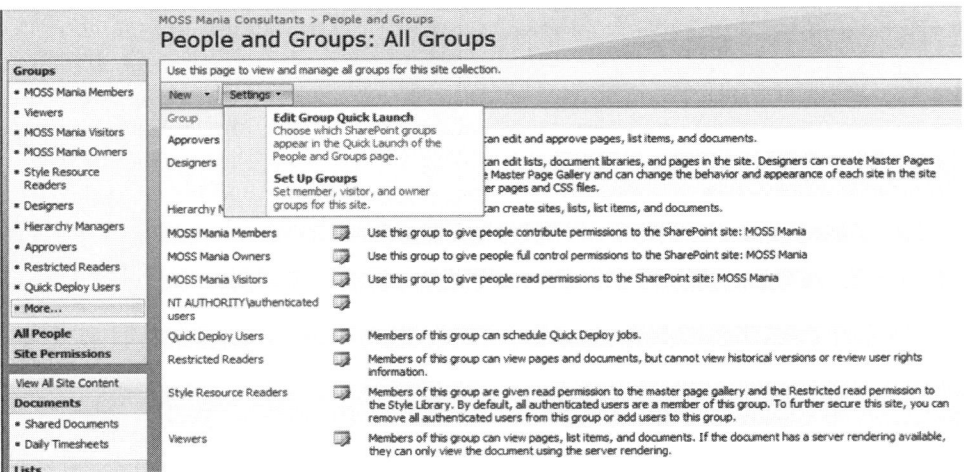

FIGURE 4.11
Settings menu options for site groups.

3. Click the Edit Group Quick Launch menu item.
4. The Edit Group Quick Launch page is displayed. Located on the right-hand side is a people-picker control. Click the little book icon in the lower-right corner above the OK and Cancel buttons. This control allows you to search for specific SharePoint groups that may be present, which is very valuable if there are a large number of groups on the People and Groups page. Overall, this feature allows you to configure which groups are displayed, which may help simplify the overall group management process.
5. Return to the People and Groups: All Groups page and select Set Up Groups from the Settings button drop-down menu; the Set Up Groups for this Site page is displayed and reproduced in Figure 4.12. (The state of the displayed page has been altered from its default condition to illustrate the various features and will differ from your view.) This management page is designed to help manage the bulk of the site users by providing a single interface that allows the administrator to select which groups will be used for visitors, members, and site owners. The administrator can utilize existing groups by clicking the down arrow revealing a list of the current groups available or create a new group by selecting the Create a new group radio button. This can be done for each of the three, independent of the others.

FIGURE 4.12
Set Up Groups for this Site Web page.

6. Click the down arrow contained inside the Visitors to this Site section and review the list of groups. Repeat the process for the other two sections.

7. Click the radio button, Create a new group inside of the Visitors to this Site section. This option allows you more granular control by creating a new group and populating it directly or adding already-existing groups. But there is one distinction here. Open the people-picker control and perform a search using a keyword that should be represented by at least one Active Directory group. If your SharePoint server is not a member of a domain, then you will not be able to search for any of the default security groups. You will need to try to utilize local accounts. For example, you could choose the keyword "DNS." There should be at least one Active Group returned. That is correct; it will return AD groups, not just SharePoint groups like we saw in step 4.

8. Click the Cancel button at the bottom of the page to return to the People and Groups: All Groups page. Next, we'll review the capabilities of managing individual groups. We will choose one group to focus on, but the walk-through discussion will pertain to any of the groups.

9. Click one of the groups displayed on the left-hand side navigation, like the Members group.

10. On the People and Groups: Members page click the Settings button and review the list of options available, as shown in Figure 4.13.

11. Select the Group Settings option at the top of the menu. The Change Group Settings page is rich in options and is shown in Figure 4.14. Review the various options on the page, taking careful notice of the default configuration of each option. In the Owner section, you can change the owner of the group. By default, it should be the site owners. You can only configure one group as the owner. Users that are entitled to view and edit the group membership can be configured in the Group Settings section. The option to allow users to request membership and an auto-accept feature can be configured in the Membership Requests section. Last, you will see that group permission levels can be modified, as well as deleting the group entirely.

12. Click the Cancel button at the bottom of the page.

13. Next, choose the View Group Permissions option from the Settings drop-down, which should open a window revealing the site collection permissions of the Members group. This is a view-only window and settings cannot be modified.

14. Click the OK button to close the window.

15. Click the Settings button and review the next two options in the list. You should recognize the Edit Group Quick Launch and Set Up Groups options as those previously reviewed in steps 3–7 of this walkthrough.

16. With the Settings menu still open, click the List Settings option. You will recognize the resulting Web page as being very similar to the List Settings page for any standard SharePoint list. The Permissions for this list option beneath the Permissions and Management heading is relevant for our discussion, but we will return to this later when we discuss configuring individual lists. For now, just realize that individual list security can be configured here as well.

17. Use the bread-crumb navigation to return one level up in the hierarchy to the Members group page.

18. Click the Actions button to reveal its menu options. Three options are revealed: E-Mail Users, Call/Message Selected Users, and Remove Users from Group. For each of these options, you need to select a user or group that is a member and then choose one of the options. You will need your SharePoint server to be email-enabled to test the email option and a SIP address for your users in the case of instant messaging. Both of these options require configuration that is beyond the scope of this chapter.

The main purpose of the walkthrough was to familiarize the administrator with the various security-related options available for configuring and managing groups. At this point in the discussion, we have defined all the parts of the story for site access and content authorization, and we are ready to begin the process for assigning permissions to users and groups.

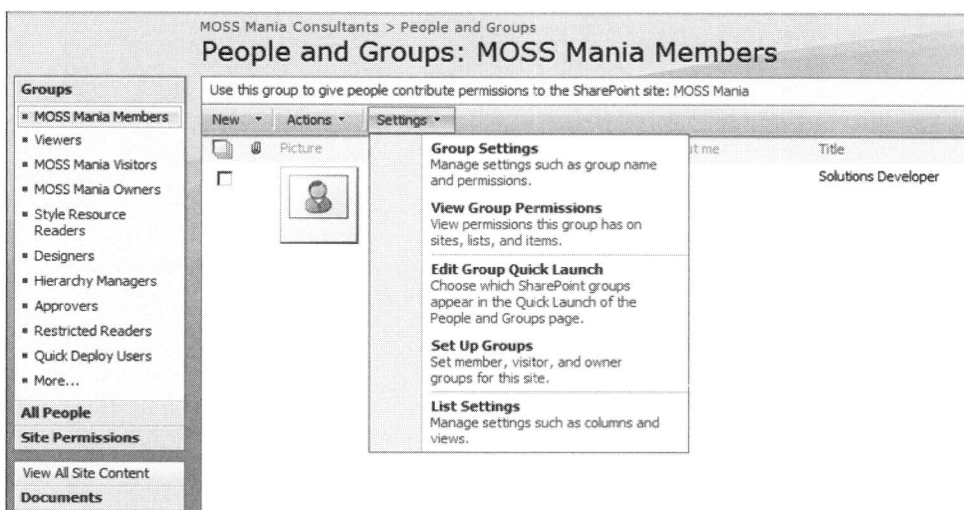

FIGURE 4.13
Settings menu options on the Members Web page.

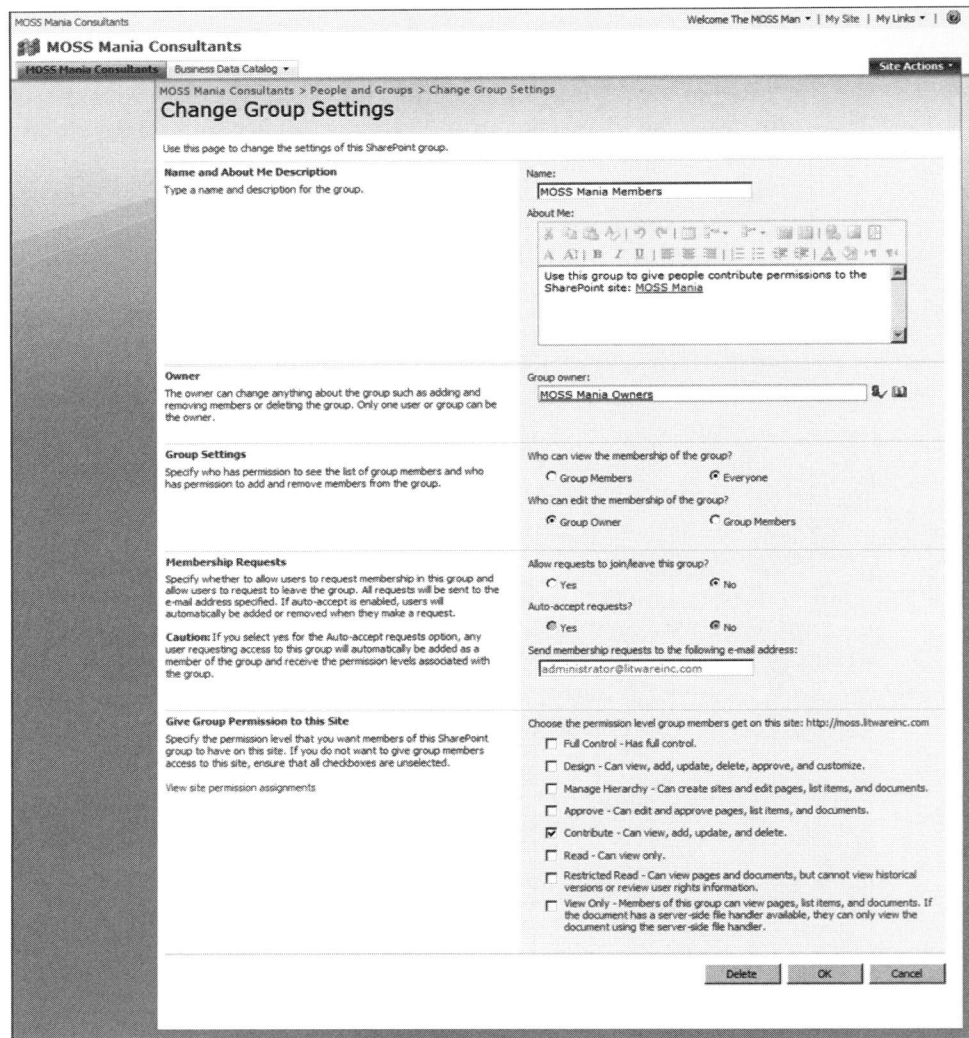

FIGURE 4.14
Change Group Settings page in the Web site.

PERMISSION MANAGEMENT

The discussion up to now has focused on the different security features of the architecture that represents the "under the hood" details of how security management is accomplished for SharePoint sites and their content. These include: Permissions, Permission Levels, and Groups. Permissions define the activities that users are allowed to perform. Permissions are grouped together to form Permission

Levels. Permission Levels are better suited to be mapped to user roles, since users perform activities based on their role in the organization. The other half of the authorization process is to add users to groups. Similar to the recommendation for managing Active Directory users in a Windows environment, SharePoint site administrators are encouraged to add users to groups. These groups can be one of three types: SharePoint site groups, custom SharePoint groups, and AD security groups. This completes the authorization process for a given site or security object when permission levels are assigned to groups. Let us consider the types of groups we should be using, SharePoint groups or Active Directory groups, or both.

SharePoint Groups Versus Active Directory Groups

You can use AD security groups to control permissions for your site by directly adding the security group to the SharePoint site and assigning the appropriate permission levels. This eliminates the need to manage the individual users in the SharePoint environment. These groups are already being managed by the network administrators responsible for the directory structure. However, AD groups are usually aligned around the organization's enterprise access requirements. These requirements may not match those needed for SharePoint sites. Also, SharePoint site administrators will generally not have the necessary privileges to manage the Active Directory structure, and likewise the network administrators that manage AD will not have SharePoint site administration rights. In the absence of an overall governance plan, the SharePoint site administrator will need to decide whether Windows security groups should be used and if so, which groups. Let's review some of the details.

■ **Should Windows security groups be used?** There are clearly advantages to using them, but there are potential challenges as well. The groups already exist, and they are being managed. Since AD has been used routinely for much longer, the organization already has governance in place and a process for creating and maintaining AD security groups. Also, the organization may have a set of tools, which simplifies the administration process. One of the strongest arguments from a security perspective is that the AD administrators are, with few exceptions, technical professionals. SharePoint site administrators could be business users and in practice they tend to be in a lot of cases. Therefore, asking a nontechnical individual to manage security may not be the best solution. However, AD security groups are tied to either an organizational hierarchy or an organizational function with permissions associated with that function. This permission may not align with SharePoint access requirements. For example, the SharePoint site administrator may want to add someone to the group who doesn't functionally belong in that AD group, like adding a software developer to the Marketing AD security group. The developer shouldn't be in that AD security group because of the other Windows functions that group can perform. Therefore, you would add that person to a SharePoint group without having to make special concessions in the AD group. The scope of the groups is one last point to consider. AD security groups deliver capability across the enterprise. The SharePoint group's scope is the site collection, by default. As you can see, good arguments can be made for either using or not using AD security groups.

- **Which Windows security groups should be used?** Any group that meets the following criteria is a candidate: a group whose membership is small enough so that a common SharePoint role can be defined, and is resistant to frequent changes so that group membership doesn't have to be reviewed by the SharePoint site administrator. If you are going to use Windows security groups, then you need to ensure that a mechanism is in place for informing the SharePoint administrator when AD group membership changes. This will help ensure that access is not given to the wrong individual. One could also consider creating "SharePoint" security groups in AD. What this means is this: deciding the type of SharePoint membership required and creating an AD security group with those members. This would transfer the responsibility of maintaining the group but would remove control from the SharePoint site administrator. In practice, most organizations reject this option.

- **Should the Authenticated Users group be used?** Using this group may be useful in rare situations to ensure that a minimal permission set is available for all users within your domain. Doing this would alleviate managing infrequent users, for example. However, this option is used very infrequently. Obviously, this approach requires that Windows Integrated Security is being used to authenticate users.

- **Should anonymous users be allowed access?** This is a more pertinent question for Internet-facing sites than intranets. Anonymous access must be granted at the Web application level. Once enabled at the Web application level, individual site administrators must decide whether they will grant access. They could refuse access and therefore no action would be required, or they could grant access at the site level or only to lists and libraries. One potential issue is that anonymous access utilizes the IUSR_ComputerName account, which is created and maintained by Microsoft Internet Information Services (IIS) Web server, not the SharePoint site administrator. You should consider this option very carefully before utilizing it.

So what is the right answer? Unfortunately, there isn't one answer that fits all situations. Each organization manages its AD and SharePoint environments differently. The general recommendation is to use both AD groups and SharePoint groups because each has its own advantages as we've discussed. This maximizes the flexibility while minimizing administration. If the site administrator technically understands the security model and ramifications, he or she should use SharePoint groups and add AD security groups to SharePoint groups.

Inheritance

The combination of Permission Levels and inheritance will govern the site access and content authorization for a given user. Inheritance is the easiest way to manage a group of Web sites, and a site collection is a group of Web sites. Inheritance alleviates the need to track and update individual permission levels associated with uniquely secured objects. Now you probably believe that item-level security is a very powerful feature, and it is. Being able to assign an individual document a more limited permission level definitely provides much greater granular control. Unfortunately, you should expect that team memberships will change, as well as individual responsibilities of team members. Therefore, the rule is to utilize groups and inheritance as much as possible.

Key Points

- Permission management is easiest when there is a clear set of permissions and an inheritance hierarchy. Management is more difficult when some lists within a site have item-level permissions applied. This is further complicated when some sites have subsites with unique permissions and other subsites with inherited permissions. As a design target, arrange sites and subsites and lists and libraries so that a common set of permissions meets the access requirements. Content that requires more limited access should be separated into its own subsites, lists, or libraries. Always govern at the highest level in the object hierarchy possible.
- Permissions and permission levels within a site collection are inherited from the top-level site to all subsites by default. This is a clear inheritance hierarchy. When a site is provisioned, the creator has the option of maintaining inheritance or breaking inheritance and establishing unique permissions.
- Inheritance provides a shared set of permissions. If a subsite inherits permissions from its parent, both sites share the set of permissions. This means that the site owners of subsites that inherit permissions from the parent site can edit the permissions of the parent site. If you want to change permissions for the subsite alone, you must stop inheriting permissions and then make the change.

- Creating unique permissions for a subsite copies the groups, users, and permission levels from the parent site to the subsite, and then breaks the inheritance. If you return to inheritance at a later time, you lose any users, groups, or permission levels that you uniquely defined in the subsite.
- Permission levels can also be unique. By default, they are inherited via the object hierarchy. This means that the Read permission level is the same, no matter what object it is applied to.

Inheritance is a very powerful ally, but it may not achieve the desired results all the time. Therefore, it is important to define a structure that establishes a balance between ease of administration, performance, and the need to control specific permissions for individual items. As you increase the use of item-level permissions, whether this is a list, library, folder, or individual document, you will be spending more time managing the permissions, and users may experience slower performance when they try to access the site's content. Let's take a look at what's involved in breaking inheritance at the site and lower object levels.

Breaking Inheritance

1. From the Site Settings Web page of a subsite, click the Advanced Permissions link. If your setup doesn't include a subsite, then navigate to the root of a site collection and create a new subsite.
2. Click the Actions button to reveal the menu options shown in Figure 4.15. Notice that you are able to manage the permissions of the parent site by selecting the first item in the menu. Essentially, this is telling you that if you want to manage the permissions for your site, then you need to manage them at the parent site level, since the subsite is inheriting permissions from the parent site.

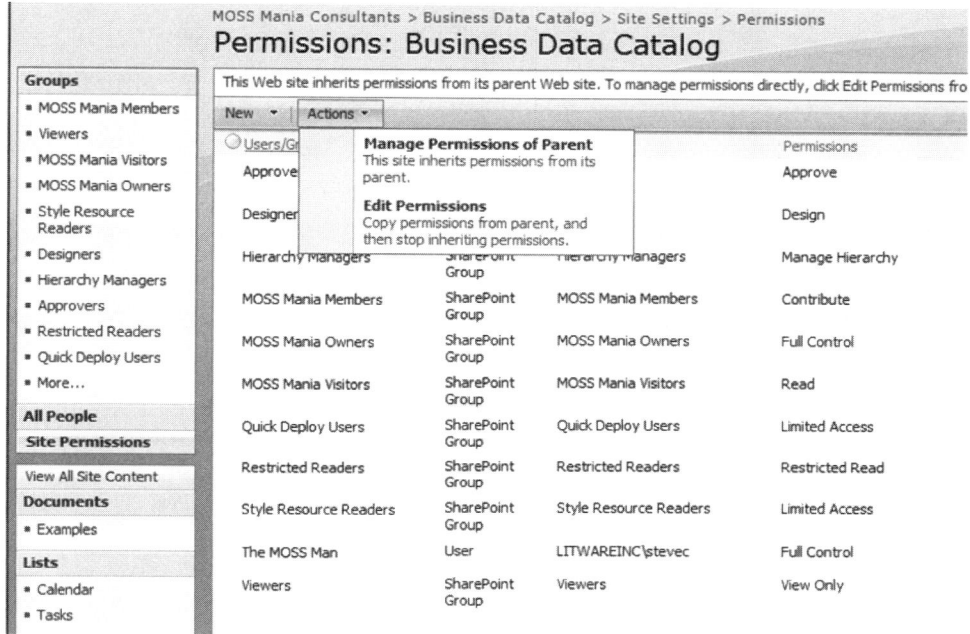

FIGURE 4.15
Site Permissions Web page and the Actions menu options.

3. Make a mental note or write down the bread-crumb trail for your current location. Click the Manager Permission of Parent from the drop-down menu.

4. As you can see from the bread-crumb trail, you just jumped up the hierarchy to the parent site. We have already discussed how to manage permissions and permission levels for groups so we won't duplicate it here.

5. Return to the subsite and choose the Edit Permissions option from the Actions drop-down menu. You should be prompted, telling you that you are about to create unique permissions for this Web site. Remember, only do this when absolutely necessary.

6. Click the OK button to break inheritance.

7. You are returned to the same Permissions page and nothing appears to have changed. However, if you look at the sentence of text above the button bar you will notice that this site now has unique permissions. Click the Settings button to reveal a new menu selection. The only option now is a choice called Permission Levels, as shown in Figure 4.16. You may also see a second option called Access Requests if you created your site using a collaboration portal template instead of a publishing site template.

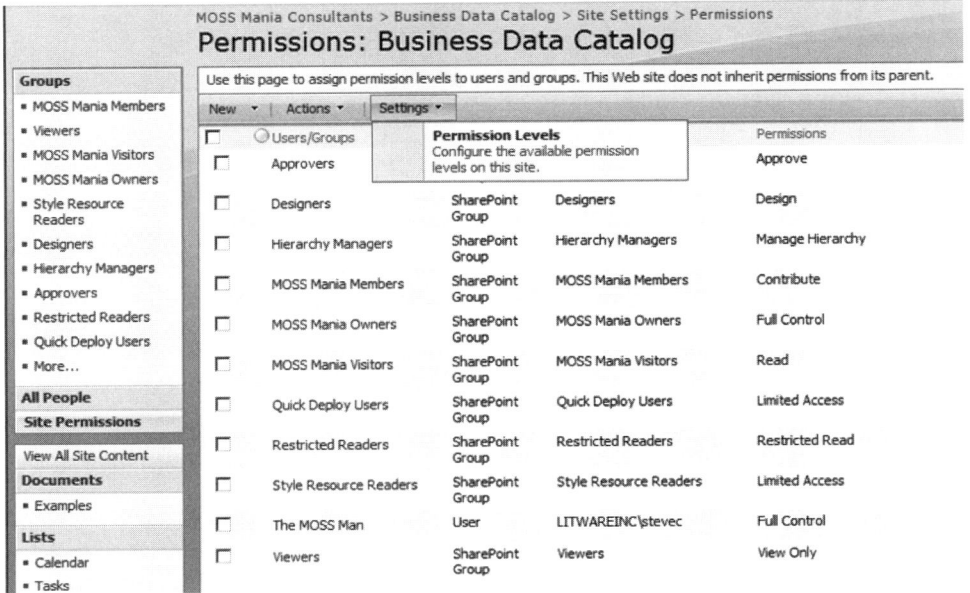

FIGURE 4.16
Site Permissions Web page and the Settings menu options.

8. Click the Permission Levels option. Notice that resulting page has a caption that says "This Web site inherits permission levels from the parent Web site." Even though we broke site group inheritance, we are still inheriting permission levels.

9. Click the button labeled Edit Permission Levels.

10. You will be prompted that "You are about to create custom groups and custom permissions for this site. Changes to the parent groups and permissions will no longer affect this site." Click the OK button to see the result shown in Figure 4.17. This page should look very similar to the page created in Figure 4.6, except there is one difference. Figure 4.17 contains an additional button labeled Inherit Permission Levels from Parent Web Site, which allows you to re-enable inheritance.

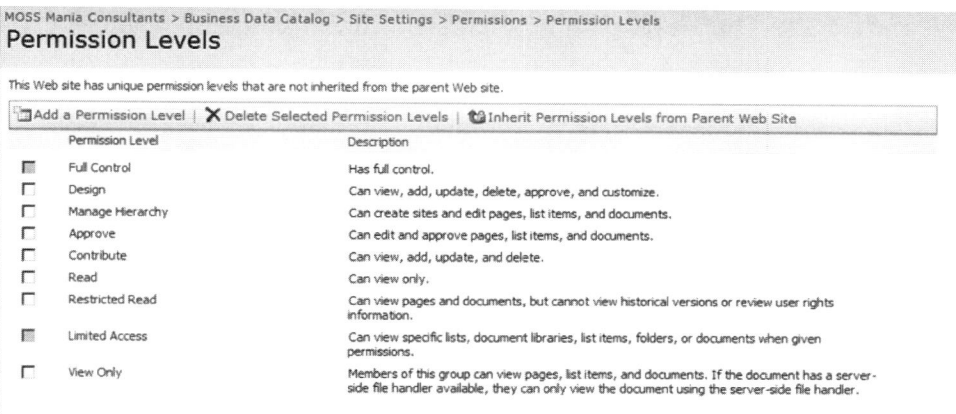

FIGURE 4.17
Permission Levels for a Web site that has unique permissions.

11. Return to the Permissions page by clicking the bread-crumb trail.
12. Click the Actions button to reveal the different menu options. The option of interest is called Inherit Permissions.
13. Click the Inherit Permissions option. You are prompted with a message that says "Changing to inherited permissions may prevent you or other users from being able to access this Web site." As mentioned previously in the Key Point section, reverting back to inheritance will cause you to lose any custom group information and that is the basis for the prompt.
14. Click the OK button. This should return the security configuration to its original state.
15. Navigate to the home page of the top-level site in the site collection.
16. Click the Shared Documents link on the left-hand side Quick Launch. If a document library named Shared Documents is not present, click any other document library of your choice.
17. Click the Document Library Settings option in the Settings drop-down menu.
18. From the Customize Shared Documents page, click the Permissions for This Document Library link under the Permissions and Management heading.
19. On the Permissions page, click the Actions button. Do the menu options look familiar? They are exactly the same as we saw when we attempted to edit subsite permissions before we broke inheritance. Therefore, the process is the same for breaking inheritance at any point in the object hierarchy.
20. The reader should confirm that the process for breaking inheritance on lists is accomplished in exactly the same way.

21. The process is a little different for breaking inheritance for folders, list items, or documents. When you mouse-over the item, the Edit Control Block menu is revealed and by clicking the down arrow you will see the Manage Permissions option. From that point, everything else is the same. The reader should confirm the details on his own.

The walkthrough demonstrated how easy it is to remove inheritance and the potential ramifications that may occur if this is done. Obviously, the default groups and permission levels will likely not meet all of your security management needs, and therefore, a time will arise when the site administrator will need to break inheritance. Make sure that you are designing your site structures with this in mind and that breaking inheritance is consistent with your overall governance plans.

Permission Assignment

Security management is accomplished by adding users and AD groups to SharePoint groups, assigning permission levels to SharePoint groups, and utilizing inheritance to propagate permissions to all security objects in the site collection. We have discussed in detail each of these steps, except the mechanics of adding users or AD groups to SharePoint groups. This is the next and final step in the process. Keep in mind, however, that security management is not a static process; it is constantly changing because team membership changes and roles change. Prior to the walkthrough that illustrates the steps for adding users to SharePoint groups, we should briefly review the process for accomplishing security management. Keep in mind that there isn't one correct process that is going to meet everyone's needs all the time, but the following guidance should provide a baseline from which to begin.

Overall Permission Management Guidance

1. Follow the principle of least privilege. Users should have only the minimum permission levels they need to accomplish their role.
2. Utilize and maintain inheritance where possible by establishing permissions at the site collection level for the easiest administration experience.
3. Utilize the default SharePoint groups where possible, Members, Visitors, and Owners.
4. Add most users to the Visitors or Members groups. This can be simplified by adding AD security groups to these groups. Assign users or AD groups to other SharePoint groups and create new SharePoint groups when necessary.
5. Break inheritance only as the exception. When it's necessary, make sure to restructure your sites to establish unique permissions at the highest level in the object hierarchy.

6. Minimize the number of users assigned to the Owners group. Obviously, the more users with site administrator privileges, the more difficult it is to ensure consistency and proper management.

Assigning Permissions to Users and Groups

1. Navigate to the People and Groups: All Groups page by clicking the People and Groups link from Site Settings. The page should display the members and options for configuring the Members group by default.
2. Click the down arrow next to the New button and notice two options: Add Users and New Group. We have already discussed how to create new groups so we won't duplicate the discussion here.
3. Click the Add Users item. The Add Users Web page provides the capability to add users or groups to the Members group and assign permissions to those users.
4. Click the open book icon to reveal the People Picker dialog box. This dialog allows you to search for users, AD security groups, and SharePoint groups and then add them to the Members group.
5. From the Give Permission section, you'll notice that you are adding the users that you entered to the Members group, but by clicking the drop-down arrow you can choose any other group available. Notice that the default is to assign the users to a group. If you are uncertain of the permissions associated with a specific group, you can click the hyperlink beneath the list box.
6. Once you're finished reviewing the options, click the Cancel button.
7. Return to the Members page and click the Actions button. You can see that the option to Remove Users from Group is available. This is one approach for removing users.
8. Click the Site Permissions link located in the left-hand Quick Launch navigation.
9. Click the drop-down arrow next to the New button and confirm that you have the same two options seen previously in step 2. Repeat steps 8 and 9 for the Groups link at the top of the Quick Launch section.
10. From the Permissions page, click the Actions button and confirm that Remove User Permissions and Edit User Permissions are options. This is a different way to accomplish modifying current users than using step 7, but the result is the same. You are now familiar with the different approaches to adding users and groups to SharePoint groups and modifying group membership.

This walkthrough completes the process for managing users and groups. As we saw, there are several different ways to complete activities, each from different pages in the site. Site and content access management is not a difficult process, but an understanding of each of the security components is critical to successful administration. Some level of technical understanding is a requirement. One of the challenges that most administrators run into, technical or not, is that the SharePoint administration pages do not provide a way to view all of the permissions specific to lists, libraries, folders, items, or documents within a site. This makes it very difficult to quickly ascertain who has permissions on which securable objects, what permissions a specific user has across the farm, and also difficult to reset any item-level permissions. The administrator may want to invest in a commercially available product that helps with user and object security discovery.

Security Management

DeliverPoint: Permissions is a tool that provides a large number of security management features including object and user account permission discovery.

Up to now, we have been discussing how site and content access to information is governed by permissions assigned to users and groups and inheritance. This access is governed at the site collection level, and propagates throughout the collection to all subsites as long as inheritance is maintained. There is another option for governing site access, and it's called Web Application Authorization through the use of Web Application Policies. This is discussed in the next section.

WEB APPLICATION AUTHORIZATION

MOSS introduces a new option for managing site access, and it is called Web Application Policies. These policies cover all site collections within the Web application where they are configured, and they will override any settings at the site collection or site level for that user. Web Application Policies allow administrators to grant or deny access to accounts and security groups for all sites in the Web application. This greatly simplifies administration and eliminates the need to create site access permission manually for all sites. Why would you want to do this? Well, a good example that affects most companies involves help desk personnel. These people may need administrative access to SharePoint sites during the process of responding to support calls. A simple way to accomplish this access is to create a Web application policy for help desk staff accounts and grant the appropriate permissions. Policies can be viewed and configured using the following steps.

POLICY MANAGEMENT

1. Navigate to the Application Management Web page.
2. Click Policy for Web Application on the Application Management page in the Application Security section. The Policy for Web Application Web page is shown in Figure 4.18.

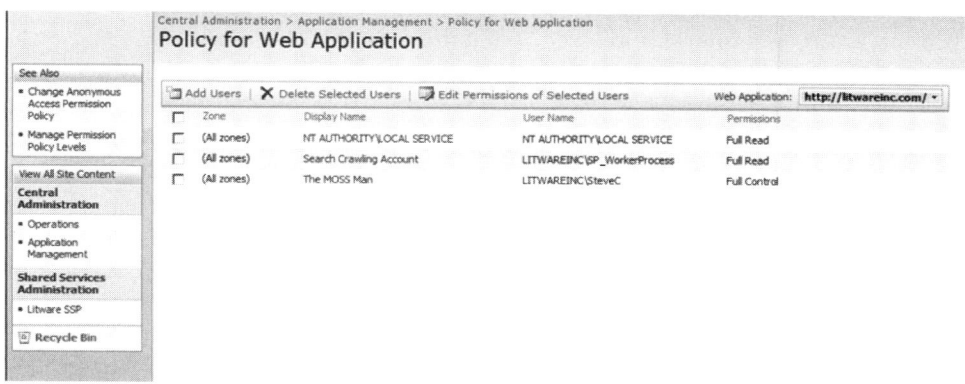

FIGURE 4.18
Policy for Web Application Web page.

3. Figure 4.18 shows three policies that have already been created. Web application policies give the administrator the capability to assign permissions to users or accounts that are critical to some necessary process. This circumvents the need for the site collection administrators and site owners to be involved. For example, one of these scenarios includes the SharePoint indexing or crawling process. You will notice that one of the policies shown in Figure 4.18 is for the account used by the indexing process: Search Crawling Account. From the Policy for Web Application page, the administrator can add new users and define the corresponding policy, edit permissions for existing policies, and delete policies. From the left-hand side navigation, you'll also notice that you can enable anonymous access and manage permission policy levels.

Search Crawling Account Policy

MOSS provides excellent capabilities for searching content. One of the requirements for searching content is the ability to index or crawl the content. Content is crawled using an account defined during SharePoint installation, but it can be changed at any time. The crawler account must go through the same authorization mechanism as any other account, and therefore it can only index content that it has been authorized to access. By configuring a Web application policy for the crawler account, it will be able to access and index all existing and future content without the requirement of the site administrator granting it explicit access. The search service uses a "Full Read" policy on the Web applications to give its crawler permission to read all content on that Web application.

4. On the Policy for Web Application page, click Add Users. Notice that you can select which Web application and which zones where the policy will apply. Because policies are tied to both the Web application and their zones, this ensures that a policy applied to one zone doesn't affect other zones.
5. Accept the default settings and click the Next button. This will take you to the Add Users Web page, as shown in Figure 4.19.

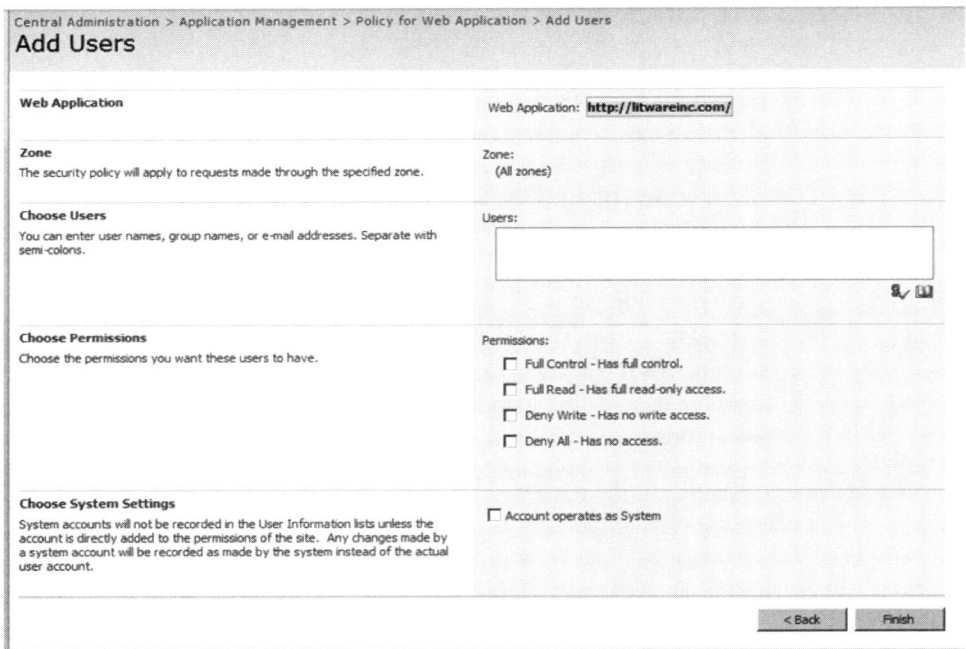

FIGURE 4.19
Web page for adding users and configuring a policy.

6. Review the Add Users Web page in Figure 4.19 and the options that are available. The Choose Permissions section lists the permissions that you want the policy to govern and apply to the users. You will notice that the permissions list includes two new permissions not available at the site collection and site levels; these include: Deny Write and Deny All. If either or both of these permissions are enabled for a user, the deny settings will govern their actions for all of the site collections and sites in the Web application, regardless of the specific site collection and site settings. For example, consider the scenario where only employees are allowed access to content in a given Web application, but contractors are allowed access in a different Web application or zone. You could create a Web application policy to deny the Contractor security group or SharePoint group that includes all contractor personnel.

7. The last option on the page allows the specified user account to behave as a system account by selecting the Account operates as System check box. Any changes made by this user account are logged as being made by the system account instead of the actual user account. After you're done reviewing the options or if you have created an actual policy, then you can click the Finish button. Otherwise, return to the Policy for Web Application page.

8. The administrator can also edit permissions and delete users by selecting the appropriate check boxes for the user policies that you want to edit and clicking the respective button.

9. One other feature to note is the ability to add new policy levels. Click the Manager Permission Policy Levels link on the left-hand side. The reader should confirm that creating new permission policy levels is very similar to creating new permission levels discussed earlier in the chapter. Once new policy levels are created, they will be available as options in the Choose Permissions section of the Add Users Web page.

The process of creating Web application policies is very simple by using the browser interface, and it provides the administrator with the flexibility of applying "blanket" permissions across all sites in the Web application. This broadens the scope of governance to the Web application level with granular control of access policies and the ability to override any access permission configured at the site level.

Security management is one of the key ongoing responsibilities of the SharePoint administrator. SharePoint provides both site-level management and Web application–level management capability, which helps ensure that the diverse access requirements of an organization can be satisfied. In the absence of Web application policies, Web sites are managed using a combination of permissions, permission levels, groups, and inheritance. Inheritance is enabled by default to help minimize the administration workload, but inheritance can be broken at any object level in the site to achieve the proper access requirements. Web application policies provide an additional degree of granular control and give the administrator the ability to provide a set of permissions that span all sites in the Web application. Also, Web application policy permissions override any permission set at the site collection or site level. Together, Web application policies and site access permissions provide both flexibility and granular control.

5 Command Line Administration with STSADM

In This Chapter

- Introduction
- An Overview of STSADM
- Common Operations
- Advanced Management
- Things You Can Only Do in STSADM

INTRODUCTION

The administrative picture in SharePoint is pretty good. Those of us grizzled old veterans who used the 2003 or even 2001 versions of SharePoint can really appreciate the new functionality and layout of the Central Administration Web site. It's almost enjoyable going in Central Admin and tweaking something. The site collection administrative experience has also changed for the better in SharePoint 2007. Adding users and content is easier than ever now. Microsoft also added some muscle to the command line administration experience. The UI is great, but when you have to perform the same actions more than once, you'll begin to appreciate the real power of the command line and scripting with STSADM. In this chapter, we are going to look at the magic that you can perform with STSADM during your daily administration of SharePoint. We'll cover basic functionality as well as advanced features that it brings to the table. While the new administrative UI is very good, by the end of this chapter, you may never need to use it again.

An Overview of **STSADM**

STSADM.exe is a command line utility that has been included with every version of SharePoint since the 2003 days. It even appeared in SharePoint 2001 but under the name OWSADM.exe. Like the name suggests, STSADM is an administrative tool for SharePoint. But before you can harness the power of STSADM, you must agree to a few restrictions. First, it only runs from the command line. Second, you must run it on a member of the SharePoint farm that you want to affect. STSADM uses the SharePoint Object Model to do its work, so it will not work from a client, but only on a SharePoint server itself. Finally, you must be a local administrator on the machine where you execute it. If none of those restrictions slow you down, then let's dig in and take STSADM for a spin.

Before you can use STSADM, you have to find it. It lives in a place we SharePoint aficionados call the "12 Hive." We are a creative bunch. The 12 Hive is where all of SharePoint's files live, so STSADM is right at home. Unless you point it somewhere else during install, the 12 Hive is located at C:\Program Files\Common Files\Microsoft Shared\Web Server Extensions\12. The "12" part relates to the current version of SharePoint that was moved to 12.x to match the Office version number. The SharePoint 2003 version was 6.x to match the version of Windows. STSADM lives in the Bin directory of the 12 Hive, which is not a very handy location at all. One of the first things you should do when installing SharePoint on a new box is to add that folder to the Path system variable. That way you can enjoy STSADM wherever you are in the file system. Make sure to add it through Control Panel > System. If you add it from the Command Prompt, the setting will not persist outside of that session. If you cannot change your Path variable for whatever reason, then create a shortcut to CMD on your desktop and set the working directory to the Bin directory in the 12 Hive. Microsoft has even been kind enough to include an icon with STSADM for you to use, as shown in Figure 5.1.

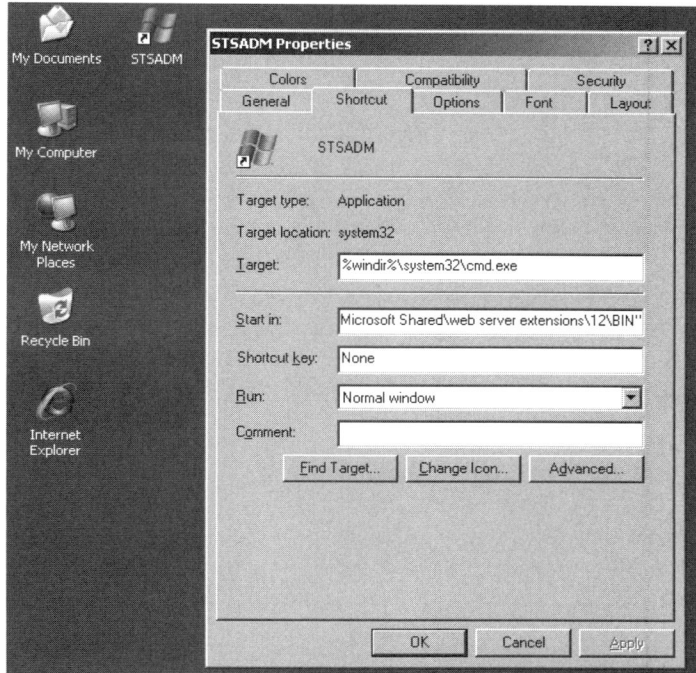

FIGURE 5.1
STSADM shortcut properties.

Now that you have made STSADM accessible, let's get some of the basics under our belt. Once you start using STSADM, you will notice that it is not interactive at all. If you do not give it all the information it needs to complete its task, it will simply fail. It will not prompt you for more information. While you might not appreciate STSADM's tough love, the fact that it is not being interactive makes it a great candidate for scripting. For example, you know your scripts will never hang because of STSADM waiting for input from you. When you issue STSADM commands, they will consist of an operation name and optional parameters. If you want STSADM to execute the operation, then precede it with –o. If instead you would like help with an operation, use the –help parameter instead.

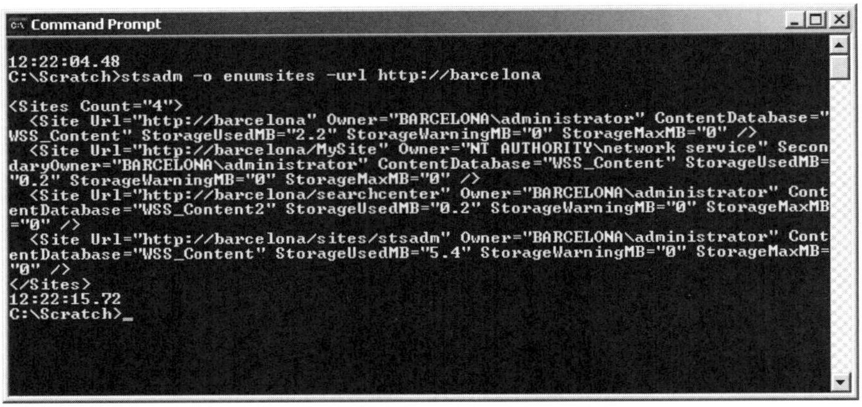

FIGURE 5.2
Output from `enumsites` operation.

Figure 5.2 demonstrates the `enumsites` operation. It does not require any parameters, so none were passed. How do you know if it requires any parameters? Run it with `-help`, as shown in Figure 5.3 to see the usage.

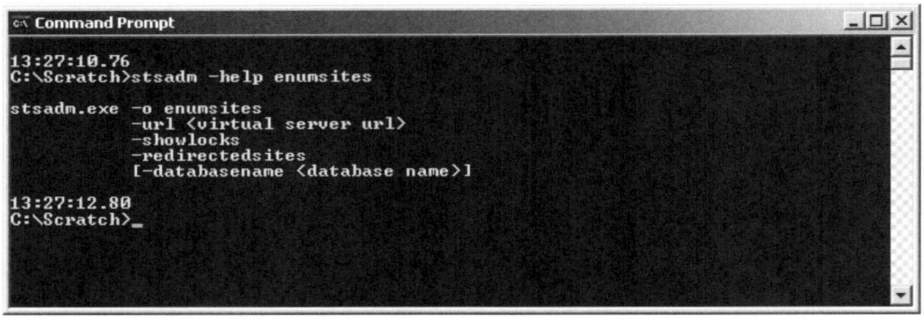

FIGURE 5.3
`Enumsites` usage.

Each and every STSADM operation has a `-help` option. It is required by the STSADM framework. Now, whether the output of `-help` is actually helpful is another issue entirely. There are some operations where the `-help` output references a completely different operation. That will be covered later in this chapter. Consider it something to look forward to.

Microsoft Office SharePoint Server (MOSS) has 184 operations in STSADM. Subsequent patches add even more. To see all the operations that are available, run STSADM with no parameters. Since you did not give it enough information to complete any tasks, it gives you a list of all the operations it has. How can you keep track of all these operations? How are you supposed to be able to find one when you are looking for something? There is no way out of the box to help you manage it. The best option you have is to make sure your scrollback is large enough for all the output so you can scroll through it. You can use the Find command to filter the output of STSADM to pare down the list of operations to a more manageable list. For instance, if you want to see only the list operations that relate to sites, you would use a command like the one in Figure 5.4.

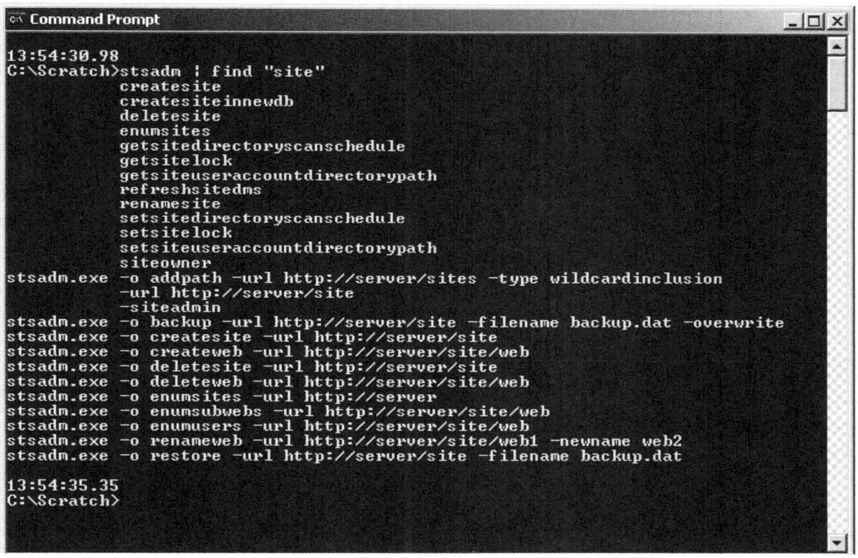

FIGURE 5.4
Filtering STSADM output for operations dealing with sites.

Now you have a secret weapon for taming STSADM, which is FIND. Whenever you are faced with a task, and you wonder if STSADM has an operation that can help, use FIND to try to find out. If you are going to be doing something with sites, use the command in Figure 5.4. If you are going to be manipulating users somehow, try the command in Figure 5.5 instead.

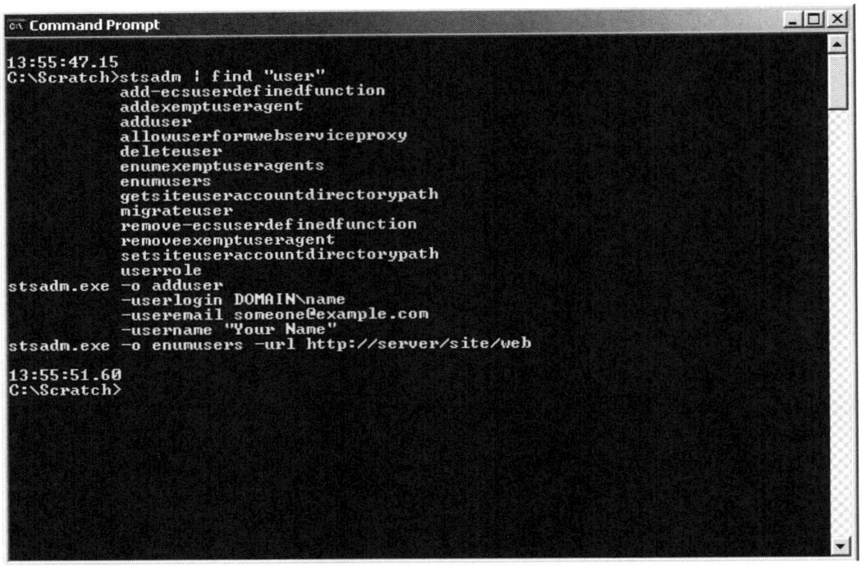

FIGURE 5.5
Filtering STSADM output for operations dealing with users.

As a general rule, search for the singular form of the noun, so "site" as opposed to "sites." This catches both `createsite` and `enumsites`.

Time on Your Side

You may notice that the Command Prompt in my screenshots displays the time above the path. I started using this as a rough method to keep track of how long my scripts took to complete. You can customize your own prompt however you would like. To see what your options are, type `prompt /?` in your Command Prompt window. This gives you a list of all the special codes you can use. To set your prompt like mine, enter the following command:

`Prompt $T$_$P$G`

That sets the prompt to the Time, a Carriage Return, the Path, and a Greater-than sign. You will notice if you do this that you have to enter your prompt settings each time you open a new Command Prompt, because they do not continue across sessions. To make the change permanent, create an environment variable called "prompt" and set its value to the string you passed the `prompt` command. In order for this to continue system-wide, you will have to create the variable in Control Panel > System > Advanced > Environment Variables.

> **A Pictures Is Worth a Thousand Words**
>
> The SharePoint Product team has also pitched in to help you keep track of all the wonderful things STSADM can do. They recently released STSADM posters that map out all the built-in operations. Download your own copy here at http://blogs.msdn.com/sharepoint/archive/2008/05/12/posters-for-sharepoint-stsadm-command-line-parameters-now-available.aspx. We expect this poster to be a big hit on teenage bedrooms all over the world.

COMMON OPERATIONS

Now that you have a basic understanding of how to use STSADM, let's spend some time going over operations that you may use in your day-to-day lives as a SharePoint administrator. Granted, some of the scripting might seem like overkill for your environment. Perhaps you only have 10 or 20 site collections in your organization and you do not create new ones frequently. While most of these techniques will probably benefit those with larger organizations, most smaller farms can also benefit from them. First, these techniques allow for some sort of standardization. You can be sure that every person on your team will perform a specific task in the exact way that everyone else does. Second, following the same practices will make business continuity or disaster planning much easier. If you have scripts to create your sites, or create Alternate Access Mappings, or install Solutions, then recovering from a disaster will be a much less stressful experience, and the scripts will give you the benefit of instant documentation. Finally, you should have a test environment. Having scripts that create or restore your sites makes creating that test environment much easier.

WORKING WITH SITES

Since we were talking about sites last, let's start there. In STSADM operations any time you see "site," the operation is dealing with Site Collections. STSADM uses web to refer to subsites. From Figure 5.4, you can see that you have the following operations available that manipulate sites:

```
createsite
createsiteinnewdb
deletesite
enumsites
getsitedirectoryscanschedule
getsitelock
getsiteuseraccountdirectorypath
```

```
refreshsitedms
renamesite
setsitedirectoryscanschedule
setsitelock
setsiteuseraccountdirectorypath
siteowner
```

We will not cover each and every one of these, but there are a few that definitely deserve some attention. We will start at the top with createsite. Createsite is how you create site collections with STSADM. Pretty simple, huh? Using the –help parameter, you can see that createsite has the following options shown in Figure 5.6.

FIGURE 5.6
Createsite usage.

The -help shows that createsite only has two mandatory parameters. This is one of those cases where –help is not quite as helpful as you would like it to be. In most cases, there are actually three mandatory parameters. STSADM starts with asking for a URL. it wants the location to create the new site collection. Next, it asks for the owner's email address. If you were to believe help, you could create a site with just that information alone. Go ahead, try it, but you will be disappointed. Unless you are running SharePoint in Active Directory Account Creation Mode, you also need to specify the ownerlogin. Let's go ahead and create a site collection with STSADM and see how it goes.

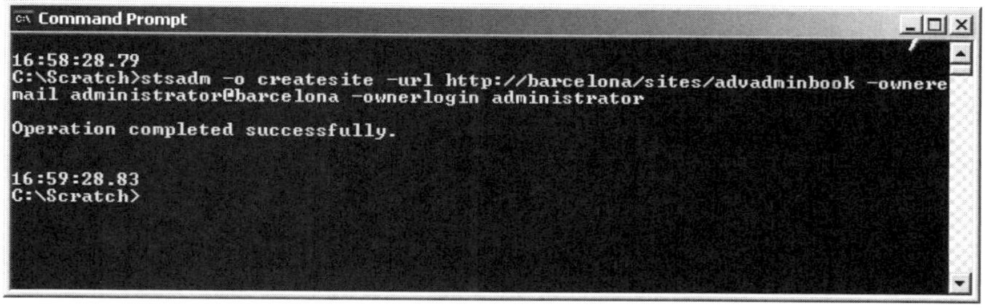

FIGURE 5.7
Creating a site with the `createsite` operation.

The command `stsadm -o createsite -url http://barcelona/sites/advadminbook` `-owneremail administrator@barcelona -ownerlogin administrator` in Figure 5.7 created a site collection at /sites/advadminbook and assigned the local administrator as the owner. You will notice that we did not specify a site template for this new site. This is one advantage of creating sites with STSADM over the UI. In the UI, there is no way to create a site with no template. You can create one with a blank template, but that's not the same thing. If you want to give your users the power to set their own templates, there is no way to do that for site collections in the UI. You have to select a template. If you create the site collection with STSADM, you can leave the template name blank, and the owner will get the template picker page when he hits the site for the first time. This is a great compromise; it allows IT to keep control of site collection creation while giving users all the flexibility they want: IT and users working together. If STSADM touches just one life, it was all worth it.

The minimalist approach is not the only one we can take when creating sites with STSADM. Another advantage of creating sites with STSADM is that you can specify all the details about the site so they are all created exactly the same way. For example, you can verify a specific site template is used or that a quota is always applied. Figure 5.8 demonstrates a more aggressive site creation command.

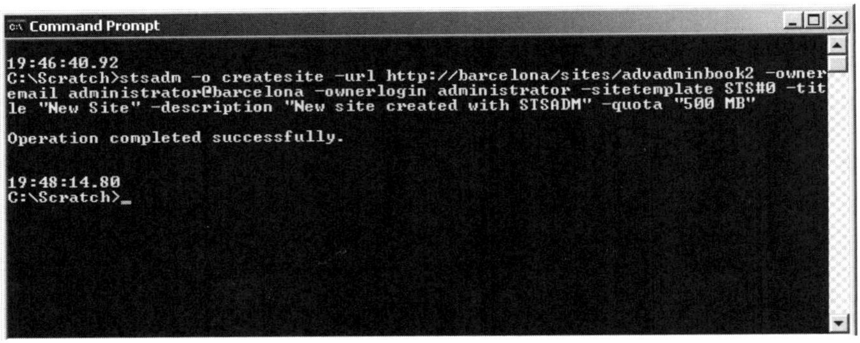

FIGURE 5.8
Creating a site collection and assigning a quota.

What's in a Name?

For the template name in Figure 5.8, STS#0, we created a team site. Where is this documented? Well, unfortunately, Microsoft did not make it very easy to discover the names of the built-in site templates. There is an STSADM operation for enumerating templates, enumtemplates, but it only lists the templates that have been added by administrators. It does not show the built-in templates. Microsoft does not make it easy either to get the names of the built-in templates, so we have listed some of the most common built-in site templates and their names in the following list. Depending on whether you have WSS or MOSS installed, the built-in templates will be different. The templates will work with both.

```
STS#0 = Team Site
STS#1 = Blank Site
STS#2 = Document Workspace
MPS#0 = Basic Meeting Workspace
MPS#1 = Blank Meeting Workspace
MPS#2 = Decision Meeting Workspace
MPS#3 = Social Meeting Workspace
MPS#4 = Multipage Meeting Workspace
WIKI#0 = Wiki Site
BLOG#0 = Blog
```

The command in Figure 5.8 is `stsadm -o createsite -url http://barcelona/sites/advadminbook2 -owneremail administrator@barcelona -ownerlogin administrator -sitetemplate STS#0 -title "New Site" -description "New site created with STSADM" -quota "500 MB"`. This command builds on the previously used command by adding a template, title, description, and quota. Using scripted commands ensures that the site is created exactly the way you intend—each time you run that command, just change the name of the URL and the owner, if need be. To make it smoother, put that command in a script and pass parameters to it. Create a text file and call it `createsite.cmd`. Then paste the following line into it:

```
stsadm -o createsite -url %1 -owneremail admin@barcelona -ownerlogin
barcelona\administrator -sitetemplate STS#0 -title "Created with
STSADM" —quota "500 MB"
```

To use it, type the command in Figure 5.9 at the Command Prompt.

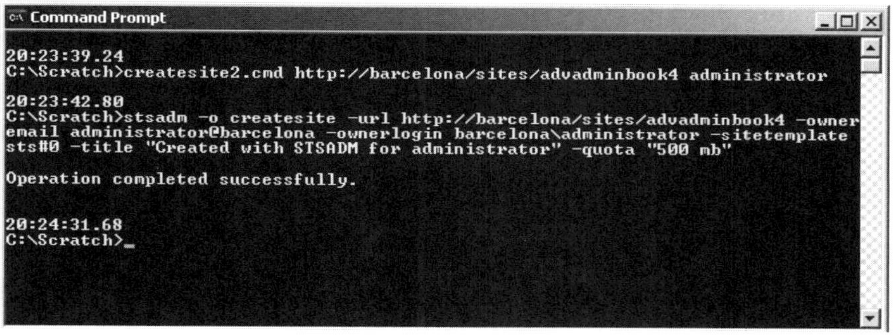

FIGURE 5.9
Using a script to create a site collection.

This command will create a team site at the location in the parameter you pass it and give it the quota named 500 MB. If you wanted to get fancy and pass the owner's name as well, change the script file to this:

```
stsadm -o createsite -url %1 -owneremail %2@barcelona -ownerlogin
barcelona\%2 -sitetemplate sts#0 -title "Created with STSADM for %2" -
quota "500 mb"
```

This script takes two parameters, as shown in Figure 5.10.

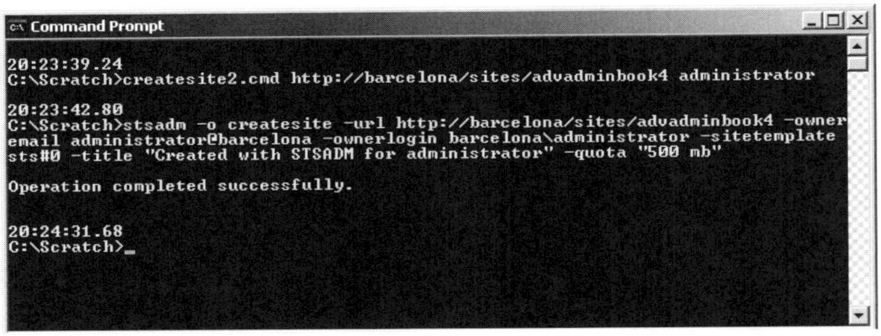

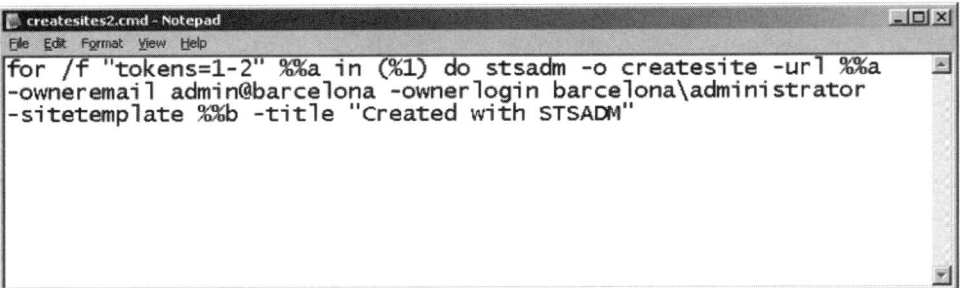

FIGURE 5.10
Passing the administrator's name to the site creation script.

As you have probably figured out, %1 is expanded to the first parameter you pass the script, %2 the second parameter, and so on. You can add any additional parameters you would like, if they meet your needs better.

Earlier, it was mentioned that you could pass a file to an STSADM script instead of individual values. To do that, we will incorporate the FOR command. Again, you can hardcode as many or as few of the parameters as makes sense for your situation. Figure 5.11 shows the script file.

```
for /f "tokens=1-2" %%a in (%1) do stsadm -o createsite -url %%a
-owneremail admin@barcelona -ownerlogin barcelona\administrator
-sitetemplate %%b -title "Created with STSADM"
```

FIGURE 5.11
Site collection creation script that accepts file input.

Figure 5.12 shows the text file you would pass to the script.

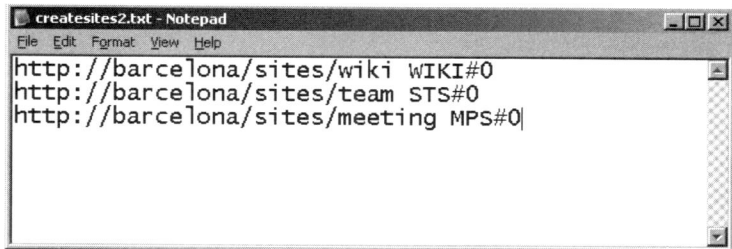

FIGURE 5.12
List of site collections to pass to the script.

In this example, we are passing the URL and the template for each site that is being created.

The FOR command could use some explanation. Like FIND, FOR is included in Windows, so there is nothing extra to install. FOR has several modes it can work in, but we only care about the file mode. The /f parameter tells FOR to use that mode. The tokens parameter tells FOR which parts of the line in the file to use. The script in the example has the tokens set to 1-2, which tells FOR to use the first two tokens in the line. If you want to use more than one value, make the token's line reflect the number of values you want to use. The %%a part tells FOR which variable to start assigning values to. In the example script, we are taking two values (tokens 1-2) and starting the assignments at %%a. The first token will be assigned to %%a and the second to %%b. If you use more than two values, they will continue at %%c and so on. The next part in (%1) tells FOR from where to get its list of lines. In this case, we are passing the script a filename, which resolves in the spot of %1. The last part of the FOR statement is the DO statement. Everything following that is what FOR executes for each loop. This means the FOR loop walks through the file you pass it, takes the first value of each line and uses it as the URL, and takes the second value and uses it for the template. FOR uses whitespace to determine where one value ends and the next one begins, so it will not work in this form with a URL with a space in it.

All of these scripting techniques work as well for other operations, like deletesite. The help for deletesite is pretty basic:

```
stsadm.exe -o deletesite
          -url <url>
          -deleteadaccounts <true/false>
```

All `deletesite` needs is a URL. If you are running in Active Directory Account Creation Mode, optionally you can have `deletesite` delete the AD accounts that were created for that site collection. When you execute `deletesite`, it removes all content of the site collection—every document, every list, every library, every subweb, everything. As mentioned earlier, STSADM is not interactive, so there will not be any "Are you sure?" prompts; the site collection will just be deleted. Like `createsite`, `deletesite` can be scripted. The scripts look nearly identical. If you wanted to delete a group of site collections at one time, you could use a script like the one in Figure 5.13.

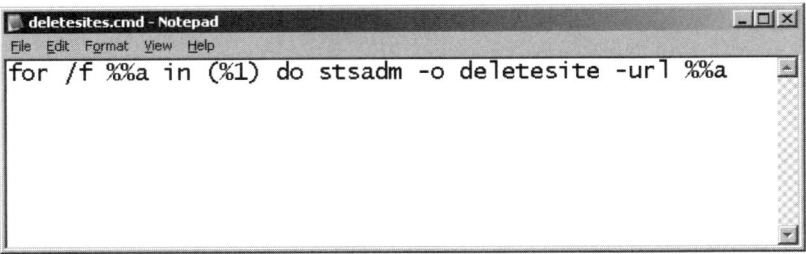

FIGURE 5.13
Script to delete site collections.

You can use the same text file format as Figure 5.12. Of course, it will take the first value, which is the URL. The FOR loop will walk through the text file and delete all the URLs. Scripting site deletions and site creation are handy for creating and working in test environments. It gives you the ability to create a large number of sites, test processes, and then delete the sites.

In many instances, STSADM offers more functionality than the UI. Site creation is one example of this. With STSADM not only can you create new site collections, but you can also have the new site collection created in its own content database. The operation `createsiteinnewdb` does just that. Here is the usage:

```
stsadm.exe -o createsiteinnewdb
          -url <url>
          -owneremail <someone@example.com>
          [-ownerlogin <DOMAIN\name>]
          [-ownername <display name>]
          [-secondaryemail <someone@example.com>]
          [-secondarylogin <DOMAIN\name>]
          [-secondaryname <display name>]
          [-lcid <language>]
          [-sitetemplate <site template>]
```

```
[-title <site title>]
[-description <site description>]
[-hostheaderwebapplicationurl <web application url>]
[-quota <quota template>]
[-databaseuser <database username>]
[-databasepassword <database password>]
[-databaseserver <database server name>]
[-databasename <database name>]
```

You can see it has many of the same parameters as `createsite`. The last four parameters deal with the database creation, and they are optional. If you do not pass any parameters, STSADM will create the content database on the default content database server defined in Central Admin. It will use Windows Authentication, and it will name the database `WSS_Content_` followed by a long, ugly GUID. A best practice would be to supply a database name at a minimum. Give it a name you will recognize when you are looking at it in SQL Server and Central Administration. You will also need to go into Central Admin to define a Search server for your new content database, or your search results will be inconsistent. Finally, unless you set the database to `offline` or `stopped`, then newly created site collections may be created in it as well.

That Doesn't Mean What You Think It Means

Take my databases offline? Stop them? Are you mad? The toughest hurdle in Share-Point is the terminology. This is another fine example of that. Content databases can have two states, as far as SharePoint is concerned. What those two states are called varies from screen to screen. In Central Admin > Application Management > Content Databases (`/_admin/CNTDBADM.aspx`), you will see the database status is either `Started` or `Stopped`. Seems clear enough. But, if you click a database name to change any of its settings (`/_admin/oldcntdb.aspx`), those statuses magically change to `Ready` and `Offline`. Confusing? We thought so. What that status means is even more confusing. `Started` (or `Ready`) means that when new site collections are created, this database is available for them to be housed in. It does not mean they will go in there, but it means it is possible, based on how many site collections the database has already, and how many before it hits its maximum value. `Stopped` (or `Offline`) are not as scary as they sound. They do not mean the database is offline, or that the content in that database is unavailable. The sites in that database render just fine, and there is no way to tell from the end user experience that the database is in the `Stopped` (or `Offline`) state. It just means that new site collections cannot be placed in this content database. The bad news is that this is horribly confusing. The good news is that now that you understand it, you can impress your coworkers with how smart you are. Make sure and mention this book.

Now that you have gone hog wild and created all those sites, how do you and your users keep track of them? Of course we would not be asking this if STSADM did not have a way to address this problem. As we saw earlier, the operation `enumsites` can do this. `Enumsites` enumerates all the site collections in the given Web application. If you are using MOSS, you have a couple of site management options with functionality like the Site Directory and My SharePoint Sites in the My Sites. WSS does not have those, so how can you leverage `STSADM –o enumsites` for your users? It can be done with a Data View Web Part (DVWP). DVWPs are created with SharePoint Designer (SPD), and their sole purpose in life is consuming and displaying XML. Fortunately for us, the output of `enumsites` is XML. It is a perfect combination!

Let's go over the steps of how to amaze your users with a customized list of all the sites in your farm. First, you will need to make sure you have SPD installed somewhere. That is how you will create and customize the DVWP. Then you need to decide where you are going to store and display the output of `enumsites`. A good place is near the root of your site, maybe as part of a Help or FAQ section. It makes a great answer to the FAQ "How do I find a site if I forgot to bookmark it?" After you have determined that location, find a document library to save the output from `enumsites`. We usually recommend that it be in the same site, so that it is easy to keep track of. Now let's capture the output of `enumsites` and get that DVWP built. You can do this by piping the output to a file like this:

```
Stsadm –o enumsites –url http://localhost > sites.xml
```

Of course, you will use the address of your Web application instead of `http://localhost`. Now, upload `sites.xml` to the document library. After you have done that, open up SPD and navigate to the page where you will display the DVWP. Select the Web part zone where you will display the DVWP and click Data View in the menu bar, followed by Insert Data View. The Data Source Library will show up on the right. Expand the XML Files section and click Add an XML file. Browse to the `sites.xml` file you just uploaded. After it has been added to the library, click it and click Show Data from the drop-down list. You will be taken to the Data Source Library pane. You can see all the fields that exist in that XML file, which match the fields that `enumsites` outputs. To get this onto your page, click the Site heading where the list of sites starts and drag it over to the Web part zone of your choosing. Poof! Now you have a list of all your Site Collections in one place where your users can see them. The DVWP is wildly customizable, and we will not go over all the things you can do here. We will show one customization that will help your users though, to get you started.

Go to the first row of the sites and highlight the whole URL. Now right-click and select Hyperlink. On the bottom next to the Address: box, click the Formula button. The default value is URL. Click OK. When you return back to the Insert

Hyperlink dialog box, the Address: box should contain {@Url}. Click OK. Save the changes to your page and view it in Internet Explorer. Now the URLs are clickable as hyperlinks. Once your users see the site they want, they can just click it and be taken there.

There are other ways to customize the DVWP. You may want to look at how to remove columns you do not want displayed, like ContentDatabase. You can also filter the rows shown. Since there is no security trimming with this, you may have sites you do not want to show up. You could also do this if you wanted a DVWP of only sites that matched a pattern, like MySites, for instance.

There are a couple of other site-related operations that we want to mention. Two complimentary operations are `setsitelock` and `getsitelock`. Like the names suggest, these two operations set the lock status of a site collection and retrieve it. In most cases, you do not need to change this status. However, there is one situation where it is very important—when doing site collection backups. That will be covered in more detail in a later section.

Finally, there is an operation called `renamesite`. Before you get too excited, this does not do what you might think it does. It does not rename site collections in most instances. It only works if your site collection was created in host header mode, which is by far the minority of installations. We only bring it up in case you stumble onto it and think the guys that wrote this book did not know what they were talking about and there was a way to rename sites. Sorry Virginia, there is not.

Working with Webs

Let's move on to the next logical step, which is Webs. If you execute `stsadm | find "web"`, you will see the operations that deal with Webs are very similar to the ones that deal with sites. You have the old standbys, `createweb` and `deleteweb`, which function like you would expect they would. `Createweb` does not require any owner information, since Webs do not have owners. It does have a switch that keeps it from inheriting the parent permissions, `-unique`. As with `createsite`, if you do not specify a template the first time users with permission hit the Web, they will be prompted to select one. `Deleteweb` works like you would expect, but it does not recurse. It will not delete a Web that has subwebs itself. You will need to delete them first. To complement `enumsites`, there is an `enumwebs` operation. It works the same way, with one caveat. It also does not recurse. It will only show you the subwebs of the URL you provide, but it will not show you any subwebs those subwebs have. Put another way, it will show you the children of the URL you provide, but not the grandchildren. There is one bright shining star in the Web suite of operations: `renameweb`. Unlike the disappointing `renamesite`, `renameweb` actually does rename the Web the way you want it.

Like sites, you can use STSADM to script the creation or deletion of Webs. The good news is that the scripts are nearly identical, as all the corresponding parameters are named the same. To script the creation of Webs, create a batch file that contains this line:

```
stsadm -o createweb -url %1 -title "Created with STSADM"
```

Then pass the script a URL. You could also use the script with the FOR loop to bulk create Webs for test environments. The same goes with deleteweb. If you wanted to delete bulk Webs, you could use the same approach. Just remember that you will need to delete subwebs before deleting their parent Webs.

Working with Users

Sites and Webs are not the only SharePoint objects you can manipulate with STSADM. You can also work with users from STSADM. Like sites and users, you have your basic add and delete operations, adduser and deleteuser. Adduser has the following usage:

```
stsadm.exe -o adduser
           -url <url>
           -userlogin <DOMAIN\user>
           -useremail <someone@example.com>
           -role <role name> / -group <group name>
           -username <display name>
           [-siteadmin]
```

You need to provide the URL, the user login, the user's email address and display name, and the role or group you are adding them to. While it would seem that SharePoint would be able to get the display name and email address from Active Directory, it is important to remember that SharePoint supports any ASP.net authentication provider, so getting that information from another back-end authentication source may not be possible. It also gives you the option of specifying an email address that is not the user's default if you are trying to match an IM address so that you get presence information. Getting the role and group information correct can be a little tricky. Fortunately, STSADM has two operations, enumgroups and enumroles, which list the roles or groups to which you can assign a user. Make sure to surround any group, role, or display names in double quotes if they have spaces in them.

Deleteuser and enumusers do not seem to behave exactly like you would expect. Deleteuser does remove the user from the site provided. However, the UI does not seem to be updated immediately, so by looking at People and Groups in the UI, it may appear it did not work, but the user will no longer be able to access the site, and the UI will catch up eventually. Enumusers is very confusing. It does not show you all the users that have access to the site collection, like you might believe. That list is on the People and Groups page at /_layouts/People.aspx. Instead, the Enumusers operation lists the individual users that have been given user permissions. This page is found in the UI at /_layouts/user.aspx. The functionality is not quite as useful as it could be, unfortunately.

Migrateuser is a somewhat new operation. Most of the operations we have looked at so far existed in SharePoint 2003 also. Migrateuser was added with a service pack to SharePoint 2003 and stayed for SharePoint 2007. It migrates user permissions from one user to another, and when needed, it is extremely handy. The most obvious need for migrateuser is when you are combining two domains or splitting them. With migrateuser, you can be assured that NEWCOMPANY\jsmith gets the same permissions that OLDCOMPANY\jsmith had when the OLDCOMPANY domain is retired. The usage for migrateuser is pretty straightforward:

```
stsadm.exe -o migrateuser
          -oldlogin <DOMAIN\name>
          -newlogin <DOMAIN\name>
          [-ignoresidhistory]
```

Simply put, use the old login in for the –oldlogin value and the new login in for –newlogin. When you run the command, the account specified as –newlogin must exist. It is okay if –oldlogin does not. If both –oldlogin and –newlogin have permissions to an object, the permissions that –newlogin has are removed and replaced with the permissions –oldlogin had. The permissions are not merged, and –newlogin is not given the greater of the two. If the permissions looked like this before the command is executed:

```
OLDCOMPANY\jsmith —Visitors
NEWCOMPANY\jsmith —Owners
```

and the command executed is this:

```
Stsadm —o migrateuser —oldlogin OLDCOMPANY\jsmith —newlogin
NEWCOMPANY\jsmith
```

then the permissions NEWCOMPANY\jsmith had will be deleted and replaced with the ones OLDCOMPANY\jsmith had, and this would be the result:

```
NEWCOMPANY\jsmith —Visitors
```

Keep this in mind. The lesson here is not to assign permissions to the new accounts if you can avoid it. This opens you to one particularly nasty problem. If `OLDCOMPANY\jsmith` is the only owner of a site collection, then the administration of that site collection will be broken if you run `migrateuser`. As the process goes through, it evaluates the permissions that –oldlogin has, removes –oldlogin, and then assigns those same permissions to –newlogin. The problem with site collection ownership is that the site collection must have an owner to be manageable. Once `migrateuser` gets to the step where it removes –oldlogin, the site collection cannot be administrated anymore, which means that –newlogin cannot be made the owner in place of –oldlogin. You get a site collection with no owner and no way to assign one. Some places require all site collections to have a secondary site collection owner. If you are going to be using `migrateuser`, that is a good idea.

Groups and Roles

STSADM includes a handful of operations that deal with groups and roles. For the most part, they function as expected with a couple of small exceptions. Here is a list of the relevant operations:

- `userrole`
- `enumroles`
- `creategroup`
- `deletegroup`
- `enumgroups`

The bottom four operations behave the way their –help information says they will, so they are pretty easy to use. `Userrole` is different, though. Here is the –help entry for it:

```
stsadm.exe -o userrole
          -url <url>
          -userlogin <DOMAIN\name>
          -role <role name>
          [-add]
          [-delete]
```

That information would lead you to believe that you used this to assign a particular user to a role. That would be incorrect, sort of. This command does not add users to sites; it assigns permission levels (refer to "role" in the –help) to users or groups. Because of that, the user or group must already exist on the Site Permissions page (/_layouts/user.aspx) before you can use the `userrole` operation to assign a permission level to it. You can verify the user exists with the `enumusers` operation. If the user exists, you can use the `follow` command to assign the Design permission level to the user administrator:

```
stsadm -o userrole -url http://barcelona/sites/stsadm -role Design -
userlogin barcelona\administrator
```

The –`help` does not call it out, but you can also use this to assign a permission level to a group, like the following:

```
stsadm -o userrole -url http://barcelona/sites/stsadm -role Design -
userlogin "STSADM site Visitors"
```

BACKUP AND DISASTER RECOVERY WITH STSADM

Now that you have a handle on how to use STSADM and can see what it can do, it is time to look at some of the more advanced functionality it has to offer. We will start with Backup and Disaster Recovery. When discussing this topic, it is usually in relation to one of three situations: content recovery, disaster recovery, and high availability. Content recovery is defined as protecting individual documents, list items, and things considered content. Disaster recovery usually involves recovering entire environments from hardware failure or data center loss. High availability is keeping content available during a disaster. STSADM does not really help with the last one—high availability. This section will mainly be dealing with content recovery and disaster recovery.

Web Level

We will start by covering what STSADM can do at the Web level. In SharePoint 2003, STSADM did not deal with Webs when it came to backing up or restoring. You had to use a separate tool, SMIGRATE.exe. SMIGRATE had a lot of limitations and for large amounts of content, it was completely unusable. Fortunately, the picture is much better in SharePoint 2007. Microsoft cleaned up the Web functionality of SMIGRATE and included it with STSADM. It has two new operations, `export` and `import`, that deal with Webs. You may be asking yourself, why not just use the old standbys of `backup` and `restore`? Good question, and we are not entirely sure what the answer is. In the background, `import` and `export` use the same APIs (sometimes referred to as "Prime") as Content Deployment, so that might be why they are named differently. Maybe it is just to keep us on our toes. We can say that using the content deployment API gives `import` and `export` a lot of functionality. Let's look at the –`help` entries for them:

```
stsadm.exe -o export
            -url <URL to be exported>
            -filename <export file name>
                [-overwrite]
            [-includeusersecurity]
            [-haltonwarning]
            [-haltonfatalerror]
            [-nologfile]
            [-versions <1-4>
                1 - Last major version for files and list items (default)
                2 - The current version, either the last major or the last minor
                3 - Last major and last minor version for files and list items
                4 - All versions for files and list items]
            [-cabsize <integer from 1-1024 megabytes> (default: 25)]
            [-nofilecompression]
            [-quiet]

stsadm.exe -o import
            -url <URL to import to>
            -filename <import file name>
            [-includeusersecurity]
            [-haltonwarning]
            [-haltonfatalerror]
            [-nologfile]
            [-updateversions <1-3>
                1 - Add new versions to the current file (default)
                2 - Overwrite the file and all its versions (delete then insert)
                3 - Ignore the file if it exists on the destination]
            [-nofilecompression]
            [-quiet]
```

As you can see, there are quite a few options for just backing up your content. Let's start by looking at export. You need to provide a URL so that STSADM knows what to export. That URL can be to a subweb or to the rootweb of a site collection—either works fine. You cannot go any deeper than a subweb, though. You cannot give the URL to a document library, for instance. Next, you need to provide a filename. If you do not specify an extension for the file, STSADM will add the extension CMP for Content Management Package. The –cabsize option alludes to this, but the files created are simply CAB files. If you add .CAB to the name of one, you can open it up in Explorer and look around. If you do, you will notice many .DAT files and a few .XML files. The .DAT files are the actual content that was backed up. This includes documents, list items, master pages, ASPX pages, and so on. The XML files describe what those files are, as well as other settings. Starting from the top, `ExportSettings.xml` has the settings that were used when the export was performed. The next file, `Manifest.XML` is the big daddy. Using `Manifest.xml`, you could crack one of these .CAB files open and pull out individual documents if you wanted. Each .DAT file is mapped to an object in `Manifest.xml`. If you are ever bored and want to see how SharePoint stores and handles information, this is a great place to start looking. The other file we want to mention is the `UserGroup.xml` file. All the group information is mapped out in this file, including the group names, the users who are members, and settings for the group. We will cover this more in the farm-level backups, but in a few cases we will recommend backing up things that you will never restore. That may seem like a bad idea, but it makes for great reference information. This is an example of that. This document will lay out how your groups are structured and what their settings are.

The —includeusersecurity, -overwrite, and -nologfile options work the way you would expect them to. `-Includeusersecurity` maintains the user information for objects that are exported. —nologfile prevents the `export.log` file from being created. The —versions switch gives you control of how many versions of each item are exported. The default is to export only the last major version. Passing 4 to —versions gives you all versions. —Cabsize lets you choose the size of the output files. By default, `export` breaks the files up into 25MB chunks. This is another reference to its content deployment background. If you were moving these files across a WAN, you might want to tune them to your available bandwidth. If you would like, you can have the files go up to 1GB in size. The —nofilecompression option gives you an uncompressed version of the backup files. Instead of writing the export to a .CAB file, a folder is created with the name you specify, and the files are written there instead. Finally, the —quiet tells STSADM not to echo everything out to the console that it is doing.

After you have some content exported out, you use `stsadm —o import` to bring it back in. The parameters for `import` are nearly identical to `export`. Supply the destination URL and the name of the file to import, and that is all you need. You will need to create the destination for the `import` first if it does not already exist. This is a good situation to use `stsadm —o createweb` with no template. The `import` will take care of all of that for you. Also, if you use a template, `import` will combine the contents of the lists and libraries that are the same, unless you tell it not to do so.

We've mentioned a couple of times that working with STSADM makes creating test environments much easier. This is another example of that. When you export out a subweb, it can be imported anywhere. That includes its original location, another Web in the same farm, or a completely different farm entirely. This is one way to populate your test environment with content, if you want to. Just make sure both of your farms are at the same patch level.

Another use for `import` and `export` is promoting a subweb to be its own site collection. On more than one occasion as SharePoint administrators, we thought we had our taxonomy planned out correctly, just to have a subweb somewhere need to be broken out as a site collection. Normally, this is done for quota reasons or management purposes. In SharePoint 2003, your options were limited, if not completely nonexistent. You could do some of it with STSADM and SMIGRATE, but most of the time it left you wanting more. With the introduction of `import` and `export`, the dream of breaking a Web out is now a reality. It is pretty easy, too. Use `export` to make a backup of the subweb you want to break out on its own. Make sure to use the `–includeusersecurity` and `–versions 4` options to get everything. Then use STSADM `–o createsite` to create a brand-new site collection. Do not assign it a template or browse to it. Then use STSADM `–o import` to import your subweb to the root of the site collection you have just created. The last step, after you have verified that everything looks good in your shiny new site collection, is to delete the Web on the original site collection.

As with other STSADM operations, `export` can be easily scripted for periodic exports of specific content.

Site Collection Level

Much like the Web level, STSADM has two options for disaster recovery at the site collection level: `backup` and `restore`. Unlike `export` and `import`, `backup` and `restore` do not use the content deployment API, which may explain why their names are different. Let's start by looking at the `backup` operation. Here is the `–help` listing:

```
For site collection backup:
    stsadm.exe -o backup
      -url <url>
      -filename <filename>
      [-overwrite]
```

Those of you following along might notice we've left something out. Both `backup` and `restore` can operate in two modes, site collection and catastrophic, which we call farm level. It is less scary that way. When you execute `–help`, you get the usage for both. In this part of the chapter, we are only dealing with site collection–level options, so we have only included the site collection–level usage. We will cover the farm-level backups in the next section.

From the usage, you can see that `backup` is pretty simple. You supply it with a URL and a filename, and it gives you a nice backup of that site collection in return. Pretty easy. As a best practice, you can make filenames in the form of `managed path--sitename.stsadm`. A site located at `http://barcelona/sites/book`

would be backed up to `sites--book.stsadm`. We do this for two reasons. It is possible for sites in different managed paths to have the same name. Including the path in the filename removes doubt as to which is the correct one. We also use the extension `stsadm` to differentiate these backups from other backups, such as export backups or SQL-level backups.

The `backup` operation backs up all aspects of your site collection that are stored in the content database. This includes every Web, all content, all user information, the template galleries, and all site collection settings. It does not include anything that you have changed either on the Web front-end file system or things that are stored in the config database. This means that custom themes, custom images, installed Features, Solutions, or Web parts are not included in this backup. Your backups will not function completely if the environment you restore it to does not include everything it needs.

When STSADM is backing up your site collection, it uses the Temp directory on your Web front-end as it is creating its output file. Make sure that the drive your Temp directory is on has at least as much free space as the size of the site collection you are backing up. If not, your operation will fail. This is true for restores as well.

`Backup` works very well for backing up discrete site collections for small to mid-sized environments, but it does not scale very well. It is not a fast operation, so as your content grows, the amount of time it takes to back up your content will soon grow larger than your backup window. You can mitigate that somewhat by running multiple `backup` operations on multiple machines in your farm. Also, as your content databases grow, it is possible for STSADM to lock your content database while it is backing up a site collection that is in it. For this to happen, your content database has to be large and have a large number of rows in specific tables, but it is not a risk you want to take. If your content database is locked, the site collections that are in that database will be completely unavailable to your user population until the lock is released. Your users would not be very understanding about that. Not quite pitchforks and torches at your office door, but it might be close.

When you are backing up a site collection with STSADM, it is a best practice to lock the site collection as `no access` before you do it. This can be done with `STSADM –o setsitelock –lock noaccess`. If you do not do this, you run the risk of your backups not restoring. There are a few reasons for this. The first is if the backup is in an inconsistent state when it is being backed up. This can come from large amounts of content being added to the site when the backup is running. You would think that setting the site lock to `read-only` would solve that. You are correct, it will. But that is not the only problem that can keep your backups from restoring. If your site is large, and a user tried to access it while it is restoring, the restore may fail as well. When a user is able to successfully access a site, a record is created in the `UserInfo` table of the content database. If that record is written before the STSADM restore process gets to the table, it will fail. Setting the site collection to `no access` before backing it up is the safest way to go. Unfortunately, there is no way to know if your backup will restore until you need it, which is often too late. Of course, you will need to run `stsadm –o setsitelock –lock none` after you restore the site so that users can get in. You will also need to run it after the backup job if you lock it to `noaccess` beforehand.

As we have mentioned before, a lot of STSADM operations can be used to shuffle content between locations, and this is another one of them. Backups made with `backup` can be restored to the location they came from, another location in the same farm, or a completely different farm. Like `export`, if you restore to a different farm, it must be at exactly the same patch level as the source farm. If you are restoring a backup to another location in the same farm, the site collection must end up in a different content database than the original. The backup file maintains several GUIDs that are used by SharePoint to keep track of sites, Webs, lists, and libraries. If the second instance of the site tries to go into the second content database as the original version, the GUIDs will collide and will no longer be unique. The fix for this is to create another content database. SharePoint is smart enough to look for another one if it cannot restore into the first one it attempts.

We have touched on a few parts of site collection `restores` in the previous paragraphs. Let's give it a little closer look. Here is the usage for `restore` at the site collection level:

```
stsadm.exe -o restore
    -url <url>
    -filename <filename>
    [-hostheaderwebapplicationurl <web application url>]
    [-overwrite]
```

Again, like backup, the options are very simple. You need to provide a URL and a filename. Optionally, you can restore to a host header Web app or overwrite an existing site collection. There is not a lot to say about `restore` that has not already been covered. It works like you would expect. One thing of note is that you should not use Ctrl-C to interrupt a `restore` if you realize something is incorrect about it, like it is going to the wrong path or it is the wrong filename. Stopping a `restore` will likely result in orphaned objects in your content database. You can use the STSADM operation `databaserepair` to fix them, but it is trouble you should avoid if you can. There is also no way to determine which content database a restored site collection will go in from the `restore` command itself. You will need to adjust the status of your content databases to make this happen.

Farm Level

Working our way up from Webs to sites, we have finally reached the top of the disaster recovery mountain, farm level. The same two operations, backup and restore, do double duty and also work at the farm level. Here is their farm-level usage:

```
For catastrophic backup:
    stsadm.exe -o backup
        -directory <UNC path>
        -backupmethod <full | differential>
         [-item <created path from tree>]
        [-percentage <integer between 1 and 100>]
        [-backupthreads <integer between 1 and 10>]
        [-showtree]
        [-quiet]

For catastrophic restore:
stsadm.exe -o restore
    -directory <UNC path>
    -restoremethod <overwrite | new>
    [-backupid <Id from backuphistory, see stsadm -help backuphistory>]
    [-item <created path from tree>]
    [-percentage <integer between 1 and 100>]
    [-showtree]
    [-suppressprompt]
    [-username <username>]
    [-password <password>]
    [-newdatabaseserver <new database server name>]
    [-quiet]
```

The usage for farm-level backups is quite different than Web or site collection. First, you will notice that you are not asked for a URL. Since this is a farm level, a URL would be useless. Second, instead of providing a filename, you need to provide a directory name. You can probably tell that this backup will be big—it is not messing around. Notice the help asks for a UNC path, not a local path. This is important. The farm-level backup process happens in several locations, and depending on your topology, not necessarily all on the same server. If you provide a path like D:\Backups, that works great on the server you are on, but makes it very difficult for a remote server to get access. Make sure that you use a UNC-like \\server\backups instead. With the backup happening in different locations, it may also be running as different users. Make sure that the account where you are running STSADM, the App Pool account where Central Admin is running, and the service account SQL is running have read-and-write access to that location. They each take part in the backup and restore process.

You do have the option of doing a full or differential backup of your farm. In order to run a differential, you must have at least one successful full backup in your directory. Instead of specifying a URL for farm-level backups, you specify an item in the farm path to back up. Run `stsadm –o backup –showtree` to see the list of items you can back up. Here is an example of the output of `showtree`:

```
C:\Scratch>stsadm -o backup -showtree

    Farm\
        [SharePoint_Config_5deead6d-5d40-4ec7-ab2e-ac3e66e4fe80]\
        Windows SharePoint Services Web Application\
            SharePoint - 80\
                WSS_Content\
                WSS_Content2\
                WSS_Content_Move\
                WSS_Content3\
                WSS_Content_d1922aff200b48c2a0868a55068c8665\
            SharePoint - extranet80\
                WSS_Content_Extranet\
        [WSS_Administration]\
            [Web Application]\
                SharePoint_AdminContent_33b9c499-f1ed-4a56-8a1d-b940908abf68\
        SharedServices1\
            [SharePoint - 15843]\
                SharedServicesContent_95827fde-2007-425f-99e5-13333938c5db\
            [SharedServices1_DB_abb922fd-29a6-48ea-a4a4-b8e421feb4c6]\
            [UserProfileApplication]\
            [SessionStateSharedApplication]\
            [Shared Search Index]\
            [SharedServices1_Search_DB_0e7a682d-2bdc-4073-baf0-3800377e1e2b]
\
            Global Search Settings\
            Windows SharePoint Services Search\
              [Search instance]\
                  [WSS_Search_BARCELONA]\

        [ ] - item cannot be selected.
        *  - not selected to be backed up.
```

To start the backup or restore process, run the command again omitting the `–showtree` option.

The items in brackets, like the config database, cannot be backed up on their own. They must be done as part of a parent item. The tree shows that you can back the entire farm up by specifying "Farm" as the item, or you can do individual Web applications or databases. This tree may look familiar to you. It is the same tree of options you get if you do a backup in Central Admin, as shown in Figure 5.14.

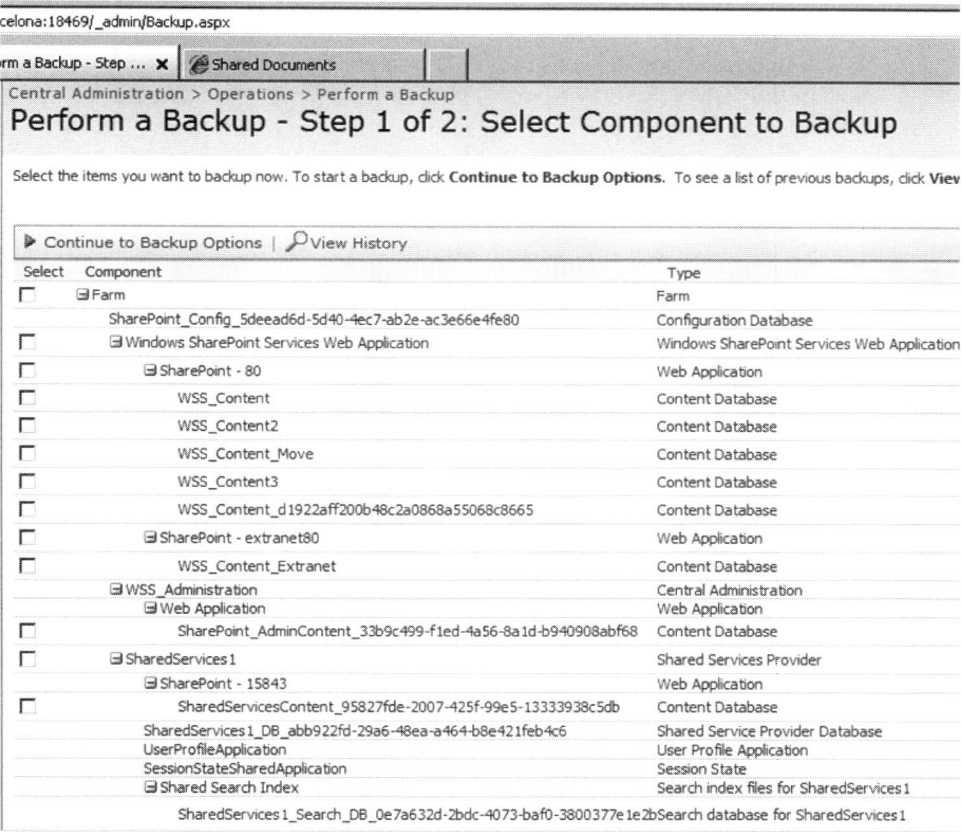

FIGURE 5.14
Doing backups in Central Administration.

The backups you do from STSADM are the same backups that are done in Central Admin, which gives you tremendous flexibility. You can do backups in either STSADM or Central Admin and restore with either as well. Just make sure that you point both STSADM and Central Admin at the same UNC location when doing backups and restores, and they will be able to see each other's work. This means that you can create a script and schedule backups with STSADM, something you cannot do in Central Admin.

Once you have decided which item you are going to back up, you can configure how often STSADM updates you with its progress as it backs up items. It will update you at whatever percentage interval you specify with `–percentage`. This is the per-item progress, not the overall progress. If you pass it `–percentage 12`, you will get updates at 12 percent intervals for each item, like this:

```
Progress: [WSS_Search_BARCELONA] 12 percent complete.
Progress: [WSS_Search_BARCELONA] 24 percent complete.
Progress: [WSS_Search_BARCELONA] 36 percent complete.
Progress: [WSS_Search_BARCELONA] 48 percent complete.
```

The `–backupthreads` parameter allows you to specify how many threads the backup process can use. This can be very handy on boxes with multiple processors.

That covers backups. `Restore` starts with the same parameter as `backup`, `directory`. Since the entirety of the backup lives in that directory, you can have multiple directories if you want. Just make sure that you pass `restore` the directory that contains the correct backup set. The `–restoremethod` parameter specifies whether you will be overwriting existing content or restoring it to a new location. Like the other backup methods we have discussed, these backups are portable. They can be restored to another environment. If you do, use the `–newdatabaseserver` option and provide the new server name. STSADM will correct any references to the old SQL server name.

When you do restores, you do not have to restore all that was backed up. You can specify discrete parts of a backup to restore. You use `–backupid` and `–item` to determine what content you are restoring. To drill down to the item you want, start with `stsadm –o backuphistory –directory` and point it at the directory where your backups are. This will list when the backups have been run, along with their BackupId. Use that BackupID with `stsadm –o restore -directory –showtree –backupid`. The end of that output will show you the items you can restore. Items preceded by an `*` or surrounded by brackets cannot be restored. Choose the item you want to restore and add it as `–item`. You will need to provide the entire path, like this:

```
stsadm -o restore -directory \\server\Backup -backupid 2d9dbbc2-0b88-
43cf-b407-70c21ef34981 -item "Farm\Windows SharePoint Services Web
Application\SharePoint - 80\WSS_Content" -restoremethod overwrite
```

This path will restore a single content database from that backup job to its previous location, overwriting the database that is there.

There are other ways to recover data, and we will cover them in more detail in Chapter 12, "High Availability, Backups, and Disaster Recovery."

ADVANCED MANAGEMENT

Now let's move on to some more advanced operations of using STSADM. We will look at the management of several SharePoint objects, as well as cover some things you can only do with STSADM

SOLUTION MANAGEMENT

STSADM has several operations that allow you to work with the SharePoint Solution Store, and they include the following:

```
addsolution
deletesolution
deploysolution
displaysolution
enumsolutions
removesolutiondeploymentlock
retractsolution
syncsolution
upgradesolution
```

> **How Much Is That Solution in the Window?**
>
> We'll mention the Solution Store a few times in this section. What is the Solution Store, exactly? It is a virtual location that is a combination of the contents of two tables in the Configuration database. We will cover it in more detail in Chapter 13 when we cover how SharePoint uses SQL Server.

Wise Words from Todd

This time is as good as any to talk to you about Solutions and Features, and how very important they are to you, the administrator. If at all possible, anything you add to your SharePoint environment should be packaged as a Solution and a Feature, if fitting. If you are like me, an old-school SharePoint administrator, you remember the good old days of SharePoint 2003 where there were no Solutions or Features. If you needed to add some files to your SharePoint server, you just did it. And if you had Web Parts to add, you went to each Web front-end (uphill, I might add), and you added them, and you liked it! Now SharePoint 2007 has these newfangled Solutions. By packaging your changes and functionality as a Solution, you give yourself much easier management. You don't need to remember every location where a file was installed, or what changes it made to your web.config. You can just use STSADM to delete it. You also don't need to worry about keeping your SharePoint servers in sync, because that is done automatically for you when you use Solutions and Features. A Timer Job will automatically push out Solutions to new machines that are added to the farm.

If you are having a developer create some SharePoint functionality for you, make sure they provide it for you as a Solution. You'll thank me in the long run.

As you can imagine, the whole process starts with addsolution. This operation adds a Solution to the Solution Store. Using STSADM is the only way to add a Solution without writing custom code. It cannot be done in Central Admin. Adding the Solution is very simple, because you only need to provide the name of the Solution file, which commonly has the extension WSP. The Solution Store is scoped at the farm level, so there is no need to provide a URL. After you have added the Solution to the Solution Store, use the deploysolution operation to deploy it to your farm. Deploysolution has a few more parameters:

```
stsadm.exe -o deploysolution
          -name <Solution name>
          [-url <virtual server url>]
          [-allcontenturls]
          [-time <time to deploy at>]
          [-immediate]
          [-local]
          [-allowgacdeployment]
          [-allowcaspolicies]
          [-lcid <language>]
          [-force]
```

You can see there are a lot of options when deploying Solutions. Once the Solution is in the Solution Store, you can publish it to select Web applications, called virtual servers in the –help, or to all URLs with –allcontenturls. If you would like to schedule the deployment of the Solution, you can use the –time parameter or use –immediate to have it deployed immediately. You can use –local if you only want the Solution deployed to the server you are running the command on. If you choose that option, the Solution will not be marked as "deployed" in the config database. If your Solution requires GAC deployment or a CAS policy, you can provide the appropriate parameter. Jobs that are submitted as –immediate are run by a timer job, and by default that job runs every five minutes. If you would like it to run sooner, then execute stsadm –o execadmsvcjobs. That will force the job to run even more immediately.

After your Solution is deployed, you can see all the Solutions in the Solution Store by using the enumsolutions operations. Alternately, if you want information only on a specific Solution, use displaysolution instead. It gives the same information as enumsolutions, but only on a single Solution. Once a Solution has been added, you can upgrade to a newer version with the upgradesolution operation. This works on Solutions whether they have been deployed or not. If the Solution has been deployed, you can use –immediate and –time to control when the Solution is upgraded. This allows you to have the Solution upgraded during a maintenance window. This is important because as the Solution is being upgraded, it may not be available until the upgrade is complete.

You can use syncsolution to have a Solution redeployed if they get out of sync. This may happen if you use the –local parameter with deploysolution. Syncsolution will remove the Solution files from the cache and WFE file system and redeploy them from the Solution Store. To round out your management tasks, there is an operation retractionsolution that retracts Solutions. It removes any files from the SharePoint servers that the Solution added, but does not remove them from the Solution Store. To remove the Solution completely, use deletesolution. Unless you use the –override parameter, you will have to retract the Solution before you can delete it. Deletesolution removes the Solution from the Solution Store.

FEATURE MANAGEMENT

On the heels of Solution management is Feature management. The installfeature operation installs the Feature specified by the filename parameter or the folder in the name parameter. If you do not know the filename or folder, you can use the scanforfeatures operation to scan the Features directory for new Features and install them automatically. You can use –displayonly to simply list the Features without installing them. After Features are installed, you can use activatefeature to activate them if they were not already activated when they were installed. The –url is not needed if the Feature is scoped at the farm level. You can deactivate the Feature with the `deactivatefeature`. The Feature is not uninstalled, so it can easily be reactivated without reinstallation. Finally, you can uninstall the Feature completely with `uninstallfeature`.

Does This Template Make Me Look Fat?

When you save out a site template with content, it can get large. Too large, in fact. So large that STSADM refuses to upload it to the template repository. There is a template size limit of 10MB. Any larger than that, and you cannot upload it. Fortunately, STSADM taketh away, but STSADM giveth as well. You can use the STSADM operation `setproperty` to increase the maximum template size. Here is the command you would run:

```
stsadm -o setproperty -propertyname max-template-document-size -
propertyvalue 25000000
```

That sets the maximum template size to 25MB. That particular `propertyname` is tricky because it is not listed by the `-help` for either `setproperty` or `getproperty`. You have to know it exists to use it. Luckily, you bought this book.

TEMPLATE MANAGEMENT

You can also manage site templates with STSADM. The `addtemplate` operation takes a site template in an STP file and adds it to the farm site template repository. This is the only place to add a template and make it available to your entire farm. If you do it through the Site Settings UI, it is only available in that site collection. When you add the template, the text you provide with the `-title` parameter is the name that will appear in the site template picker. You can remove a template from the repository with the `deletetemplate` operation. It is not explicitly spelled out anywhere, but you cannot use `addtemplate` to add list templates to a central repository. `Addtemplate` only works for site templates. `Enumtemplates` enumerates all the custom site templates that have been added with `addtemplate`. It will not enumerate the built-in templates. If you run `enumtemplates` and nothing shows up, don't panic, because all the built-in templates are still available.

CONTENT DATABASE MANAGEMENT

Content databases are another object that can be manipulated easily with STSADM. Out of the box, you have three operations to work with them: `addcontentdb`, `deletecontentdb`, and `enumcontentdb`. `Addcontentdb` will add an existing content db to the Web application that is given as the –`url` parameter. This is the same as attaching a content database in Central Admin. Besides adding an existing database, it will also create a new database if the `databasename` you provide does not already exist in SQL. If you do not provide any parameters besides the `databasename`, STSADM uses the defaults. It uses the default content database server, uses Windows Authentication, sets the `-sitewarning` at `9000` and the –`sitemax` at `15000`. The –`enumcontentdbs` operation lists all the content databases for the URL you provide. It gives you their name, as well as the SQL instance they are in. To detach a database, use the `deletecontentdb` operation. This operation does not actually delete the database in SQL, it merely detaches it from SharePoint. You will have to remove the database from SQL manually.

If you plan on moving a database from one MOSS installation to another, you must run `stsadm –o preparetomove` before you run `stsadm –o deletecontentdb`. If you do not, the profile pieces inside the database will not be set correctly when you add the database to the new farm, and you will have all kinds of weird problems. Also, if you restore a content database in SQL and overwrite an existing one, you must detach and then reattach (`deletecontentdb` then `addcontentdb`) the database in SharePoint. When SharePoint adds a content database, it interrogates it for things like the site collections it contains. If you replace the database in SQL without SharePoint being able to do an inventory of it, your configuration and content databases will get out of step. Sites may not render, and data could be lost.

SP1 for SharePoint introduced a new operation that deals with content databases, `mergecontentdbs`. This little gem allows you to move site collections between content databases in a single command. Before SP1, moving a site collection to a different content database was roughly these steps:

1. Lock site collection for no access.
2. Back up site collection.
3. Delete site collection.
4. Set all of your databases to offline, except the one you want the site collection to go into.
5. Restore site collection.
6. Unlock site collection.

It wasn't a fun process at all, and it had a lot of risk. There was always the risk that your site collection would not restore after you had deleted it. Putting your databases offline also carried the risk that someone else might create a site collection, and it would go into your content database. Fortunately, the `mergecontentdbs` operation takes all of the risk out of this procedure. Let's take a look at the –`help`:

```
stsadm.exe -o mergecontentdbs
          -url <url>
          -sourcedatabasename <source database name>
          -destinationdatabasename <destination datbabase name>
          [-operation <1-3>
                1 - Analyze (default)
                2 - Full Database Merge
                3 - Read from file]
          [-filename <file generated from stsadm -o enumsites>]
```

See also:

```
stsadm -o enumcontentdbs -url <url>
stsadm -o enumsites -url <url> -databasename <database>
```

While it is easy to use, the –help is a bit misleading. The –url parameter is not the URL of the site collection you want to move; rather, it is the URL of the Web application that the site collection and content database are in. It is helpful that the -help refers you to the enumsites and enumcontentdbs operations to get the list of sites and databases. That is a nice touch. Let's walk through using mergecontentdbs. Let's start by looking at the list of sites that we have:

```
C:\Scratch>stsadm -o enumsites -url http://barcelona

<Sites Count="4">
  <Site Url="http://barcelona" Owner="BARCELONA\administrator"
ContentDatabase="WSS_Content" StorageUsedMB="2.2" StorageWarningMB="0"
StorageMaxMB="0" />
  <Site Url="http://barcelona/MySite" Owner="NT AUTHORITY\network
service" SecondaryOwner="BARCELONA\administrator"
ContentDatabase="WSS_Content" StorageUsedMB="0.2" StorageWarningMB="0"
StorageMaxMB="0" />
  <Site Url="http://barcelona/sites/advadminbook5"
Owner="BARCELONA\administrator"
ContentDatabase="WSS_Content_d1922aff200b48c2a0868a55068c8665"
StorageUsedMB="0.5" StorageWarningMB="480" StorageMaxMB="500" />
  <Site Url="http://barcelona/sites/stsadm"
Owner="BARCELONA\administrator" ContentDatabase="WSS_Content"
StorageUsedMB="32.8" StorageWarningMB="0" StorageMaxMB="0" />
</Sites>
```

From that output, we can see that we have one content database with a very ugly name, WSS_Content_d1922aff200b48c2a0868a55068c8665. Let's move the site collection in that database into a database with a more respectable name, like WSS_Content. The first step is to run an analyse operation like this:

```
C:\Scratch>stsadm -o mergecontentdbs -url http://barcelona -operation 1
-sourcedatabasename WSS_Content_d1922aff200b48c2a0868a55068c8665 -
destinationdatabasename WSS_Content

WSS_Content_d1922aff200b48c2a0868a55068c8665:
  Disk Size: 18 MB.
  Sites: 1.
  Maximum Sites: 15000.
  Maximum number of sites that can be added : 14999.
WSS_Content:
 Disk Size: 88 MB.
 Sites: 3.
 Maximum Sites: 15000.
 Maximum number of sites that can be added : 14997.

Suggested steps:
  Retrieve all the site collections from the source:
    stsadm -o enumsites -url http://barcelona/ -databasename
WSS_Content_d1922aff200b48c2a0868a55068c8665 > mysites.xml
  Removes unneeded site collections:
    notepad mysites.xml
  Merge databases:
    stsadm -o mergecontentdbs -url http://barcelona/ -
sourcedatabasename WSS_Content_d1922aff200b48c2a0868a55068c8665 -
destinationdatabasename WSS_Content -operation 3 -filename mysites.xml
```

The analyze option is quite helpful. It gives us the exact commands we need to run. Since the database we want to empty only has one site collection in it, we can also do a Full Database Merge instead of doing the Read from file method outlined earlier. To do that, we use the same command we used before, but change the operation number from 1 (Analyze) to 2 (Full Database Merge):

```
C:\Scratch>stsadm -o mergecontentdbs -url http://barcelona -operation 2
-sourcedatabasename WSS_Content_d1922aff200b48c2a0868a55068c8665 -
destinationdatabasename WSS_Content

Moving sites...
Operation completed successfully.

IIS must be restarted before this change will take effect. To restart
IIS, open a command prompt window and type iisreset.
```

That is all there is to it. Now an `enumsite` shows that the site collection `http://barcelona/sites/advadminbook5` is now in the `WSS_Content` content database.

```
C:\Scratch>stsadm -o enumsites -url http://barcelona

<Sites Count="4">
 <Site Url="http://barcelona" Owner="BARCELONA\administrator"
ContentDatabase="WSS_Content" StorageUsedMB="2.2" StorageWarningMB="0"
StorageMaxMB="0" />
 <Site Url="http://barcelona/MySite" Owner="NT AUTHORITY\network
service" SecondaryOwner="BARCELONA\administrator"
ContentDatabase="WSS_Content" StorageUsedMB="0.2" StorageWarningMB="0"
StorageMaxMB="0" />
 <Site Url="http://barcelona/sites/advadminbook5"
Owner="BARCELONA\administrator" ContentDatabase="WSS_Content"
StorageUsedMB="0.5" StorageWarningMB="480" Stor
ageMaxMB="500" />
 <Site Url="http://barcelona/sites/stsadm"
Owner="BARCELONA\administrator" ContentDatabase="WSS_Content"
StorageUsedMB="32.8" StorageWarningMB="0" StorageMaxMB
="0" />
</Sites>
```

We can delete the `WSS_Content_d1922aff200b48c2a0868a55068c8665` database and not lose any content.

While the name is `mergecontentdbs`, this operation can be just as easily used to split content databases. To do that, use the third operation type, `Read from File`, and edit the `mysites.xml` file like the `Analyze` operation suggests. When you do this, you will have some white space in the databases that you move site collections out of. They will not automatically shrink.

MANAGED PATHS AND ZONES

Managed paths and zones can also be manipulated with STSADM. The support for managed paths is pretty slim. You can add or delete managed paths with `addpath` and `deletepath`. Curiously, there is no `enumpaths` to get a list of existing managed paths. We think using scripts to create managed paths is a great idea. Having scripts to do this takes you a long way toward disaster recovery or building a test environment. Not only does it make the work easier, but it is also documentation of your settings. Bosses love that kind of stuff.

You can also script the creation of zones and alternate access mappings. These really benefit from being scripted because they are not restored if you do a catastrophic recovery. Having scripts that create them for you in the case of a disaster will ensure that you have the same settings. Fortunately, there are enumeration operations for both zones and alternate access mappings. We recommend that you pipe the output of both to files and include them in your nightly backups. Here are the Zone and AAM operations:

```
Zones:
addzoneurl
deletezoneurl
enumzoneurls
geturlzone

Alternate Access Mappings:
addalternatedomain
deletealternatedomain
enumalternatedomains
```

The key to remembering the AAM operations is to think of them as DNS domains. To keep a copy of the settings, use the following two commands:

```
stsadm -o enumzoneurls > zones.xml
stsadm -o enumalternatedomains > aams.xml
```

While the `-help` for both of those operations asks for a `-url` parameter, it is optional. Piping the output to a text file gives you a reference should you need to rebuild your environment. We will cover more about disaster recovery in Chapter 12. You can use the `geturlzone` operation to get all of the zone URLs for a given URL.

WEB APPLICATION MANAGEMENT

The last management piece we want to talk about is Web application policies. They can be altered with STSADM as well. There are several operations that apply, including the following:

```
addpermissionpolicy
changepermissionpolicy
deletepermissionpolicy
managepermissionpolicylevel
```

Let's start at the bottom with managepermissionpolicylevel. This operation lets you define policies that can be applied to users or groups. This can also be done in Central Admin > Application Management > Policy for Web Applications; then click Manage Permission Policy Levels on the left nav. Here is the usage:

```
stsadm.exe -o managepermissionpolicylevel
            -url <url>
            -name <permission policy level name>
            [{ -add | -delete }]
            [-description <description>]
            [-siteadmin <true | false>]
            [-siteauditor <true | false>]
            [-grantpermissions <comma-separated list of permissions>]
            [-denypermissions <comma-separated list of permissions>]
```

Use –add or –delete to create or delete the policy. Use the –grantpermissions or –denypermissions to define the policy. Unfortunately, you cannot use the same permission names that you see in the UI because they have spaces in them. Surrounding them in double quotes does not seem to work either. Table 5.1 is mapping the permissions in the UI to the value you have to enter on the command line. The permission names are case sensitive. You will get an error if you do not enter them exactly as they are shown here.

TABLE 5.1 BASE PERMISSIONS MAPPING BETWEEN STSADM AND CENTRAL ADMINISTRATION

STSADM Permission	Central Admin Permission
ManageLists	Manage Lists
CancelCheckout	Override Check Out
AddListItems	Add Items
EditListItems	Edit Items
DeleteListItems	Delete Items
ViewListItems	View Items
ApproveItems	Approve Items
OpenItems	Open Items
ViewVersions	View Versions
DeleteVersions	Delete Versions
CreateAlerts	Create Alerts
ViewFormPages	View Application Pages
ManagePermissions	Manage Permissions
ViewUsageData	View Usage Data
ManageSubwebs	Create Subsites
ManageWeb	Manage Web Site
AddAndCustomizePages	Add and Customize Pages
ApplyThemeAndBorder	Apply Themes and Borders
ApplyStyleSheets	Apply Style Sheets
CreateGroups	Create Groups
BrowseDirectories	Browse Directories
CreateSSCSite	Use Self-Service Site Creation
ViewPages	View Pages
EnumeratePermissions	Enumerate Permissions
BrowseUserInfo	Browse User Information

continued

STSADM Permission	Central Admin Permission
ManageAlerts	Manage Alerts
UseRemoteAPIs	Use Remote Interfaces
UseClientIntegration	Use Client Integration Features
Open	Open
EditMyUserInfo	Edit Personal User Information
ManagePersonalViews	Manage Personal Views
AddDelPrivateWebParts	Add/Remove Personal Web Parts
UpdatePersonalWebParts	Update Personal Web Parts

Separate multiple permissions with a comma and no spaces. Here is an example:

```
stsadm -o managepermissionpolicylevel -url http://barcelona -name "Book
Example" -add -description "Example from book" -grantpermissions
UpdatePersonalWebParts,ManageLists
```

You can verify the creation of the policy in Central Administration. Once the policy is created, you can use `changepermissionpolicy` to alter the permissions or use `deletepermissionpolicy` to remove it completely. You can also use `addpermissionpolicy` to assign your policy or any of the included ones to a user or group.

THINGS YOU CAN ONLY DO IN STSADM

The final part of this chapter will cover functionality that is not in the Web UI. This functionality is only available with STSADM.

WORKING WITH PROPERTIES

We will start with two of STSADM's more powerful operations: `getproperty` and `setproperty`. These two operations allow you to set or get internal SharePoint properties, many that are not exposed anywhere in the UI. The list of exposed properties is provided in the `-help` operation for either command. Here is the list:

```
stsadm.exe -o setproperty
          -propertyname <property name>
          -propertyvalue <property value>
          [-url <url>]

SharePoint cluster properties:
        avallowdownload
        avcleaningenabled
        avdownloadscanenabled
        avnumberofthreads
        avtimeout
        avuploadscanenabled
        command-line-upgrade-running
        database-command-timeout
        database-connection-timeout
        data-retrieval-services-enabled
        data-retrieval-services-oledb-providers
        data-retrieval-services-response-size
        data-retrieval-services-timeout
        data-retrieval-services-update
        data-source-controls-enabled
        dead-site-auto-delete
        dead-site-notify-after
        dead-site-num-notifications
        defaultcontentdb-password
        defaultcontentdb-server
        defaultcontentdb-user
        delete-web-send-email
        irmaddinsenabled
        irmrmscertserver
        irmrmsenabled
        irmrmsusead
        job-ceip-datacollection
        job-config-refresh
        job-database-statistics
        job-dead-site-delete
        job-usage-analysis
        job-watson-trigger
        large-file-chunk-size
        token-timeout
        workflow-cpu-throttle
        workflow-eventdelivery-batchsize
        workflow-eventdelivery-throttle
        workflow-eventdelivery-timeout
```

```
            workflow-timerjob-cpu-throttle
            workitem-eventdelivery-batchsize
            workitem-eventdelivery-throttle

SharePoint virtual server properties:
            alerts-enabled
            alerts-limited
            alerts-maximum
            change-log-expiration-enabled
            change-log-retention-period
            data-retrieval-services-enabled
            data-retrieval-services-inherit
            data-retrieval-services-oledb-providers
            data-retrieval-services-response-size
            data-retrieval-services-timeout
            data-retrieval-services-update
            data-source-controls-enabled
            days-to-show-new-icon
            dead-site-auto-delete
            dead-site-notify-after
            dead-site-num-notifications
            defaultquotatemplate
            defaulttimezone
            delete-web-send-email
            job-change-log-expiration
            job-dead-site-delete
            job-diskquota-warning
            job-immediate-alerts
            job-recycle-bin-cleanup
            job-usage-analysis
            job-workflow
            job-workflow-autoclean
            job-workflow-failover
            max-file-post-size
            peoplepicker-activedirectorysearchtimeout
            peoplepicker-distributionlistsearchdomains
            peoplepicker-nowindowsaccountsfornonwindowsauthenticationmode
            peoplepicker-onlysearchwithinsitecollection
            peoplepicker-searchadcustomfilter
            peoplepicker-searchadcustomquery
            peoplepicker-searchadforests
            peoplepicker-serviceaccountdirectorypaths
            presenceenabled
            recycle-bin-cleanup-enabled
```

```
recycle-bin-enabled
recycle-bin-retention-period
richtexteditorshortcutenabled
second-stage-recycle-bin-quota
send-ad-email
```

The properties have two scopes: farm and Web application. We could spend pages and pages explaining each operation, but we will only cover a few that you are likely to use.

1. `Days-to-show-new-icon`: This value determines how long the "!new" tag is displayed next to items in lists and libraries. Set the value to the number of days you would like the tag to stay on new items. Set it to 0 to disable the tag completely

2. `Job-immediate-alerts`: When alerts are set to "immediate" they are checked on an interval. By default that interval is every five minutes. To make that interval longer or shorter, set this value in minutes to the time you would like.

3. `Recycle-bin-enabled`: This sets whether the recycle bin is enabled. When scripting installs, this can be set to verify that the recycle bin is enabled.

4. `Recycle-bin-retention-period`: This sets the duration in days that items stay in the first-stage recycle bin. The default is 30 days. If you have the drive space, consider making this value longer. It is good insurance against needing to restore databases to get documents back. This value can be set in each site collection's settings, but if you have many site collections, it is easier to do it from the command prompt.

5. `Second-stage-recycle-bin-quota`: This is the complement to #4. This sets the percentage of the site collection quota that the second stage can consume. The default is 50 percent. Again, consider increasing this if you have the drive space.

6. There is a hidden property `max-template-document-size` that sets the maximum size of a site template. By default, you cannot upload a site template larger than 10MB, which is very restrictive if you are saving content with your templates. The value you pass is in bytes, so if you want to set the limit to 20MB you would use the value 20000000. This is covered in a sidebar earlier in the chapter, but it is important enough to repeat. It also does not show up when `setproperty` or `getproperty` list properties. You need to know it is there.

When using `setproperty` and `getproperty`, you can abbreviate the parameter –propertyname as –pn and –propertyvalue as –pv.

OTHER STSADM-ONLY OPERATIONS

If a backup or restore operation fails, you can end up with orphaned items in your databases. If you find yourself with orphans, you can remove them with the data-baserepair operation. The usage is pretty simple:

```
stsadm.exe -o databaserepair
        -url <url>
        -databasename <database name>
        [-deletecorruption]
```

The –url is the URL of a Web application, not of a site collection, and –data-basename is the name of the content database you would like to scan. First, run it without the –deletecorruption parameter to get a list of any orphans that may exist. If you find orphans, add the –deletecorruption parameter to remove them. Run it several times, as each set of orphans that is removed may orphan other objects.

Earlier in the chapter, we mentioned that the –help entry for one operation referenced a completely different operation. That operation is forcedeletelist. Here is the usage:

```
stsadm.exe -o forcedeleteweb
        -url <url>
```

Notice the reference to forcedeleteweb, an operation that does not exist. The operation, when you use the correct one, is pretty easy to use—simply supply the URL of the list that will not delete from the UI.

If you are doing a gradual upgrade, you can do upgrades either from Central Admin or with stsadm –o upgrade. There is nothing exciting about that. However, you can get yourself into a spot where you can only do upgrades with STSADM. If you install a language pack after you have started your upgrade, Central Admin may refuse to do the upgrades for you. You can use STSADM to perform them, though. Is there anything STSADM can't do?

If you have alerts that have incorrect URLs because addresses have changed, until you bought this book, your only option was to have your users re-create them all. Again, not something that makes you popular with your user base. Microsoft recently released a tool called the SharePoint Administration Toolkit at http://www.microsoft.com/downloads/details.aspx?FamilyID=263CD480-F6EB-4FA3-9F2E-2D47618505F2&displaylang=en. This toolkit includes a plug-in for Central Admin and an extension for STSADM, updatealert. This new operation will remap all the URLs in your alerts to the new URL. The usage is pretty straightforward.

```
C:\>stsadm -help updatealert

stsadm -o updatealert
        stsadm.exe -o updateAlert -url <siteUrl> -oldUrl <siteUrl> [-
nologfile] [-quiet]
```

Simply supply the old and new URLs and STSADM does the rest.

EXTENDING STSADM

While this is a book for administrators, we would be remiss if we did not mention STSADM's expandability, which was alluded to in the previous section. STSADM supports extensions, so you can add your operations to it to expand its functionality. The extensions themselves consist of two files: an XML file that contains a list the operations added and the assembly that contains the actual code. This XML file is in the form of `stsadmcommands.function.xml` and exists in the C:\Program Files\Common Files\Microsoft Shared\web server extensions\12\CONFIG directory. The second file is the DLL that contains the code. That file goes into the Global Assembly Cache (GAC). While it is easy enough to copy the files manually, a best practice is to package them as a Solution for easy installation and removal. This book will not cover creating an STSADM extension here, but we will point you toward some great references. MSDN has an explanation of how to extend STSADM here at http://msdn.microsoft.com/en-us/library/bb417382.aspx. That article includes code for both the XML and DLL components. To see what STSADM can really do, check out fellow MVP Gary Lapointe's blog at http://stsadm.blogspot.com. He has written over 100 STSADM extensions that he has made available for download. If that were not enough, he has also created a Codeplex project with just the extension framework. You just need to provide the C# code, and Gary does the rest. His project will also automatically create a Solution for your extension and deploy it for you. Is this guy a saint or what? If you are interested in expanding STSADM's functionality, his Web site is the place to start.

The UI in SharePoint 2007 is phenomenal, both the end user and administrative interfaces. However, in large environments, administrators need the power of command-line scripting to get their jobs done efficiently. STSADM provides that interface. STSADM allows you to perform actions you would normally need to do in Central Administration. It also allows you to do things you cannot otherwise do without custom code. STSADM can also be extended with custom code to perform any operations it does not support out of the box. STSADM is a great tool to add to any SharePoint administrator's toolbox.

6 SharePoint Navigation and Governance

In This Chapter

- Introduction
- Navigation
- IT Governance

INTRODUCTION

This chapter explains two interrelated yet distinct topics: navigation and IT governance. Both are crucial to a successful deployment and should not be taken lightly.

With navigation we will take an in-depth look at all of the flexibility built into the product. Navigation out of the box is very low maintenance, but to really have fun with it takes some understanding. As administrators we will skip the discussions on information architecture and how the arrangement of navigation was determined, and instead we'll concentrate on all of the settings at our disposal to build what has been designed.

Then we'll take a look at IT governance, where we will try to manage SharePoint infrastructure. This section will concentrate on making sure you are thinking through the right questions and know what you need to be managing. Too often we see projects where lots of thought goes into building things but very little time and energy go into controlling the growth that will follow. SharePoint will snowball in your environment, and if you aren't ready to maintain that growth, you will be in trouble.

The goal of this chapter is twofold—make sure when the project planners come to you for help in making navigation submit to their wills that you are equipped with all of the knowledge necessary. And we also want to make sure that this great infrastructure you have designed can sustain the test of time. You have built it, they are coming, now what are you going to do? Read on.

NAVIGATION

Navigation is one of the keys to discovering content in any Web site. While being an administrator may preclude you from deciding what links to expose and the placement of those links, you will be the first one asked "How do we set this up?" In this section, the goal is to gain a thorough understanding of the different options available for configuring navigation and to give you some guidance on using that power.

Both WSS and MOSS expose a great deal of flexibility for navigation out of the box with just some slight variances. Of course, as with all features, the truly cool stuff is saved for MOSS. Still, across the board, both do security trimming, auto-maintained bread crumbs, flexible administration of the navigation links, and other little things. With MOSS, you add audience targeting of navigation and even more flexibility. Let's first take a good look at functionality common to both products.

In Figure 6.1, you can see a screenshot of a MOSS site where you have navigated to the Invoice Folder folder within the Shared Documents document library on the Marketing subsite of the Company Portal. As you can see from the figure, there are several navigation elements on the page.

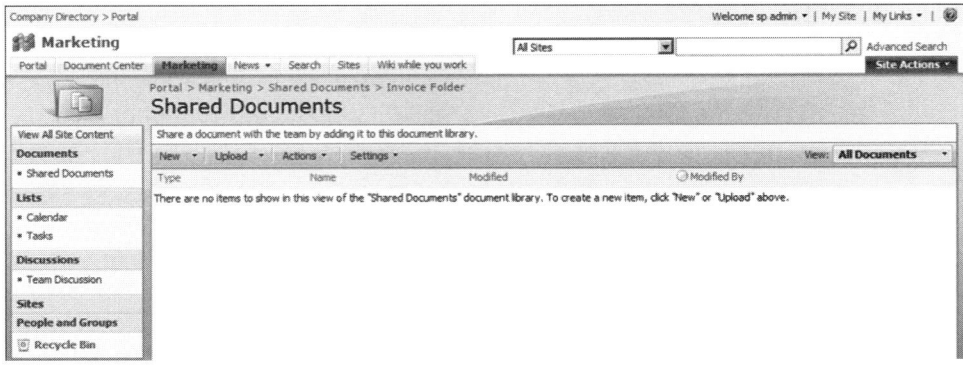

FIGURE 6.1
A typical SharePoint page with all of its navigational elements.

GLOBAL BREAD CRUMBS

Across the top, you have the global bread crumb. SharePoint will automatically maintain this bread crumb so there is no administrative interface for it. The bread crumb will start at the root of the site collection and will add an item each time you break navigation inheritance. So if you create a subsite for Projects and choose to use unique navigation, there would be an entry added to the bread crumb anytime you are on the Project's site or below. If you created a subsite for Project 1 beneath Projects and chose to have unique navigation again, then you would have a bread crumb as Portal > Projects > Project 1 while you were on the Project 1 subsite. If you navigated back to the Project's subsite, then you would only see the bread crumb as Portal > Projects. Each time you choose to use unique navigation, the bread crumb will update. Bread crumbs only span a site collection and are not affected by changes to other site collections.

As a site collection administrator, there is an option to control the root or first item of the bread crumb. Through the option Portal Site Connection, you can add an item to the bread crumb pointing to any URL you would like. Often, this is used to provide a link from a site collection in the site's path to the site collection at the root of the Web application. So you might have a site collection at http://portal.company.com/sites/marketing where you add a Portal site connection to http://portal.company.com. This will help "link up" the user experience between different site collections. To accomplish this, use the following steps:

1. Navigate to your site collection and make sure that you are logged in as a site collection administrator.
2. Click Site Actions > Site Settings.
3. Under Site Collection Administration, click Portal site connection.
4. Click the radio button for Connect to portal site and then input the URL you would like to send the user to.
5. Enter the Portal Name for the link.
6. Click OK.

Updating the Bread Crumb for All My Sites

One common challenge you may encounter is that by default since all My Sites are separate site collections, they are not linked back to the main SharePoint site. For users, this can be very confusing because one minute they are in a SharePoint site and then they click the link to My Site and even though they are still in "SharePoint," there is no way to get back to where they were.

Out of the box, there is no way to send them back to exactly where they were before (unless you hit the Back button), but you can use the Portal site connection to send them back to a specified place every time, like the root of your corporate portal. The challenge of this technique is that there is no obvious way to do this, short of explaining to each user how to configure it for himself.

Fortunately, for all My Sites that have not been created yet, you can set a default. You do this by setting the Portal site connection for the My Site Host, and then any My Site that is created will take that setting. Changes to the Portal site connection of the My Site Host will not affect any existing My Sites.

The real tricky part of all of this is finding the location to make the change. Say, for example, you specified in your SSP that the My Site Host is at http://my.company.com and My Sites are created at http://my.company.com/personal. Then you would need to manually enter the URL of http://my.company.com/_layouts/settings.aspx into your browser to get to the Site Settings page. From there, you could follow the directions for adding a Portal site connection URL. Since only future My Sites will be created with the link, you should consider making this change early in your deployment.

GLOBAL NAVIGATION

The next major navigational element you encounter is global navigation. These are the tabs across the top of the page (in Figure 6.1, they are the tabs of Portal, Document Center, Marketing, News, Search, Sites, and Wiki while you work). Global navigation also will be referred to as the "Top link bar" and "horizontal navigation." This navigation element is often used to present the primary navigation options and should be kept as consistent as possible from site to site. This consistency will prevent your users from feeling confused. For example, often if they click a link and are taken to a new navigation element, they assume they have gone somewhere else. By default, this navigation is configured at the root of the site collection and all subsites will inherit from the parent. As noted previously, anytime you break this inheritance, the global bread crumb will be updated. Global navigation can also make use of flyouts (sometimes called "cascading menus") where you see additional items when you hover over a tab in navigation. The behavior and capabilities of flyouts are defined in the master page for the site.

When planning your global navigation, it is important to keep good usability in mind. Most SharePoint deployments that are done "ad hoc" run into the problem of too much navigation. As a general rule of thumb, you want to have no more than seven to nine tabs in global navigation; any more than that, and there might as well be none. If the user is overwhelmed with too much information, he will ignore all of the tabs. What is the point of having navigation if users don't use it? Additionally, you should attempt to be very mindful of consistent navigation as much as possible. When it comes to navigation, users need consistency to feel comfortable—change is bad.

Global navigation has complete flexibility where you can allow SharePoint to be self-maintaining and automatically display subsites in navigation and where you can add your own tabs manually. Of course, you can also reorder the tabs and even remove the ones you don't want. These options are all slightly different, depending on whether you are using WSS or MOSS, so they will be covered independently later in the chapter.

Quick Launch

If you look down the left-hand side of the page, you will see the Quick Launch bar. This navigational element is also referred to as "left-hand nav" or "current nav." Typically, this navigation tool is used to present the user with links and items related to the current site. So after your users have used your global navigation to find the appropriate subsite, they would then be able to discover content on the subsite through the Quick Launch bar.

The Quick Launch bar is almost identical to global nav in its customization options. With WSS you will only be able to show items automatically from the current site, while MOSS will add the ability to show the parent's Quick Launch bar or content from the sibling's sites. Once again, since WSS and MOSS are different in how you maintain the Quick Launch, they will be covered separately later.

Right below the Quick Launch bar, you have the option of enabling a Tree view control, as pictured in Figure 6.2. While this sounds like a useful feature on the surface, most administrators quickly lose interest. The reason is that the tree view is simply on or off; there are no options for controlling what items it displays or what items are expanded. Also, typically in anything more than a simple site, you will have scroll bars for the tree view, which is not exactly ideal.

FIGURE 6.2
A SharePoint page with the Tree
view control enabled on the
Quick Launch bar.

To try out the tree view for yourself, use the following steps:

1. Navigate to your site collection and make sure you are logged in as a site collection administrator.
2. Click Site Actions > Site Settings.
3. Under Look and Feel, click Tree view.
4. Select the box for Enable Tree View and click OK.

Notice that you can also use this screen for completely disabling the Quick Launch if you would like. The problem with disabling the Quick Launch is the space on the page for the Quick Launch bar is still there, but it is just blank. If you do not want to have a Quick Launch on your site, a better option would be to customize your master page and remove the placeholder.

Current Bread Crumb

These links are not always readily apparent to the user, but once they do discover them and get in the habit of using them, moving around in SharePoint becomes very efficient. In Figure 6.1, you can see the bread crumb right below global nav. The link is Portal > Marketing > Shared Documents > Invoice Folder. This tells the user exactly where he is within the site collection and gives him a quick way to move back up the tree anywhere. This bread crumb is completely self-maintaining with no administration options at all, you can look at modifying the masterpage if you need to change the behavior.

Security Trimming

Nothing upsets users more than when they are navigating through a site, they click a link, and all of a sudden they are prompted for credentials. Then they type in their username and password three times to no avail. Finally, they will call the help desk very annoyed. Luckily, SharePoint takes care of this for you when displaying automatic SharePoint content. Exactly what does this mean? Things like the links to My Sites or the Site Actions button are automatically only displayed for users with access, and the same goes for SharePoint sites, pages, and libraries that appear in navigation automatically. When it comes to navigation, though, items that are manually added through headings and links are not security trimmed. So that link you gave a user to another site collection will not be trimmed, but all of those subsites will be.

There is one consideration when it comes to security trimming, which is the performance cost. When a page is rendered, it requires CPU cycles to confirm the user can or cannot access all items that aren't using inherited security. So if you have 40 items on the page and they all have unique security, then SharePoint will have to check each of those items before it renders the page. This can add a tremendous burden to your server. Some of this load can be eliminated through the use of caching, as discussed in the performance chapter. The best piece of advice to offer is to try to be mindful of high-traffic pages and what you display. Take, for example, the home page of a portal. You wouldn't want to have lots of security trimming happening on this page, whereas at a department site with low traffic, this might be permissible.

WSS Navigation

There is more than meets the eye when it comes to WSS navigation. Typically, users create team sites and then assume the navigation they are presented with is all they get. The default settings of subsites automatically populating in global navigation and the list and libraries showing up on the Quick Launch are more than adequate for most sites. But in reality, there is a great deal of flexibility to be had by digging a little deeper.

This Section Is Not for WSS Administrators Only

Even if you do have MOSS, you will not necessarily have all of the navigation options available to you. Anytime you are in a site collection that does not have the publishing infrastructure feature activated, you will not get the "fancy" navigation options discussed in the MOSS section, but instead will see these same WSS-only features. So learning this section is important for all readers.

Maintaining Navigation as You Go

When you first create your site collection, there is only one tab and that is for the root site of the site collection. When you create your first subsite, you are presented with options that will give you some choices about updating navigation, as shown in Figure 6.3. This allows many administrators to just make simple choices and have WSS deal with keeping navigation correct.

Navigation
Specify whether links to this site appear in the Quick Launch and the top link bar of the parent site.

Display this site on the Quick Launch of the parent site?
⦿ Yes   ○ No

Display this site on the top link bar of the parent site?
⦿ Yes   ○ No

Navigation Inheritance
Specify whether this site shares the same top link bar as the parent. This setting may also determine the starting element of the breadcrumb.

Use the top link bar from the parent site?
⦿ Yes   ○ No

FIGURE 6.3
Navigation choices made while creating a new subsite.

The first choice you have when creating the subsite is whether you would like the Quick Launch bar to automatically have a link added in the sites section for this site or not. Then you can make the same choice for having this site added to the Top link bar—both are Yes by default.

In the next section, you are choosing whether you would like the subsite you are creating to use the parent's navigation (default), or if you would like to break navigation and have the subsite use its own. If you choose unique navigation, then the global bread crumb will automatically add an entry for the subsite.

These choices are not permanent, though. Once you make these decisions and the site is created, you can modify all of these settings by using the Top link bar and Quick Launch options from the Site Settings page.

You are also presented with navigation options when you create a new list or library. As shown in Figure 6.4, when creating a list, you can choose to have it included on the Quick Launch or not. The default is Yes, and if you accept the default, the list will be put into the appropriate section of the Quick Launch bar.

FIGURE 6.4
Navigation choice when creating a new list or library.

If, after the fact, you change your mind about having a list or library displayed in navigation, then you can use the Quick Launch menu to modify the display of the item, or you can go straight to the list. To modify the display of a list or library from the list, follow the steps below:

1. Navigate to the list.
2. Hover over Settings and click List Settings.
3. Under General Settings, click Title, description, and navigation.
4. Now you can change the Navigation setting and click Save.

Top Link Bar

Top link bar, which we recall from earlier, is just another name for global navigation. Starting at the root of your site collection, anytime you create a subsite from the root, it will automatically be displayed in the navigation bar across the top of the page.

By navigating to the Site Settings page, you will find the Look and Feel section. In this section is the option of the Top link bar. Click the link, and you will be able to view the settings. From this screen, you have the ability to create a new link, change the order of the links, or modify one of the existing links. If you would like to delete one of the links, click the Edit icon to the left of the link and on the Edit screen is a Delete button.

From the Edit screen, you will notice you do not have the ability to edit the URL for the automatically added links, but you will have the ability to edit any new link you may have created.

If you are on a subsite that is displaying the parent site's navigation, you will still have the option of clicking Top link bar from Site Settings. When you do, you will only see one button, Stop Inheriting Links. If you click this button, your subsite will now display unique navigation and the global bread crumb will be updated. After manually updating the navigation, if you decide you would like to once again inherit, you can choose the button for Use Links from Parent. If you choose this option, any new links you have created will be permanently deleted.

Quick Launch

The Quick Launch bar, also known as "current navigation" and "left-hand navigation," is the first column that runs down the left-hand side of the page right below global nav. This navigation bar is used to present the user with links that relate to the current site.

While Quick Launch can be self-maintaining, as discussed earlier in the chapter, there is always the flexibility to adjust it by adding or deleting items and reordering them, much the same way you can with the Top link bar. To take a look at these various options available to you, navigate to Site Settings, and under the Look and Feel section, click Quick Launch.

The New Link and Change Order buttons behave exactly the same as with the Top link bar, but there is a new button added, New Heading. Headings are used in the Quick Launch to group navigational elements. Headings behave exactly as links do, but they are just bolded with links appearing as bulleted items beneath them.

Meeting Workspaces

While team sites, blogs, and wikis share the same navigational behaviors, there are a couple of unique things about how the various meeting workspace templates handle navigation. The key difference is that meeting workspaces do not use the Quick Launch bar or tree view, even though you will see the options in Site Settings > Tree view to enable the functionality. Also, these templates use a "pages" concept for navigation that should not be confused with the pages functionality offered in MOSS.

In the workspaces from the Site Actions button, you can choose Add Pages. You can then enter a page name and click Add. This will now add a level of tabs slightly beneath the global navigation to display a link to the page. The page itself is just a simple Web part page.

From the Site Actions menu, you can also choose Manage Pages to take you to the screen for modifying the order of the pages. From the Pages toolbar that appears on the right side of the page when you choose Add Pages or Manage Pages, there are also two other options that are slightly hidden. If you look at Figure 6.5, you will see that by clicking the drop-down to the right of Order, you have the extra options of deleting Pages or Settings, which allows you to rename a page.

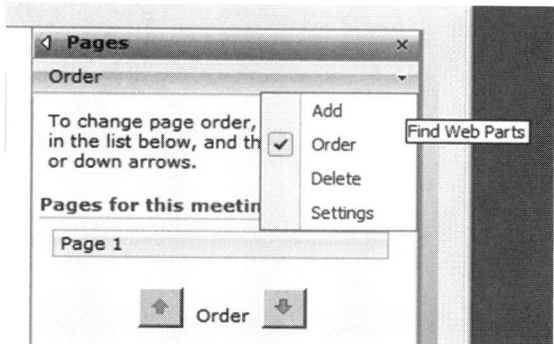

FIGURE 6.5
Options for working with pages in a Meeting Workspace.

MOSS NAVIGATION

With MOSS you can take all of the features you just discovered and go one step further with the addition of the publishing infrastructure Feature. Now instead of Top link bar and Quick Launch menu options, you will get just a single menu called Navigation. From this menu, you can control the setting for navigation elements with some additional flexibility, such as the display of pages and the ability to have Quick Launch inherit from the parent site or show its sibling sites. Also, you get some options around targeting navigation elements to specific groups. Even if you have MOSS, you should still read the entire WSS section of the chapter, because most of those behaviors are identical even with the addition of MOSS.

The ability to use the Navigation option from Site Settings comes from the activation of the Feature Office SharePoint Server Publishing Infrastructure, which is scoped at the site collection level. By default, if you choose the Collaboration Portal or the Publishing Portal template when creating your site collection, this feature will be activated. If you create a site collection using any other template, you will get the same features as discussed for WSS, even if you have MOSS. This is a common point of confusion for administrators.

From the root of your Collaboration Portal, click Site Actions > Site Settings > and choose Modify Navigation. You will be taken to a screen similar to Figure 6.6.

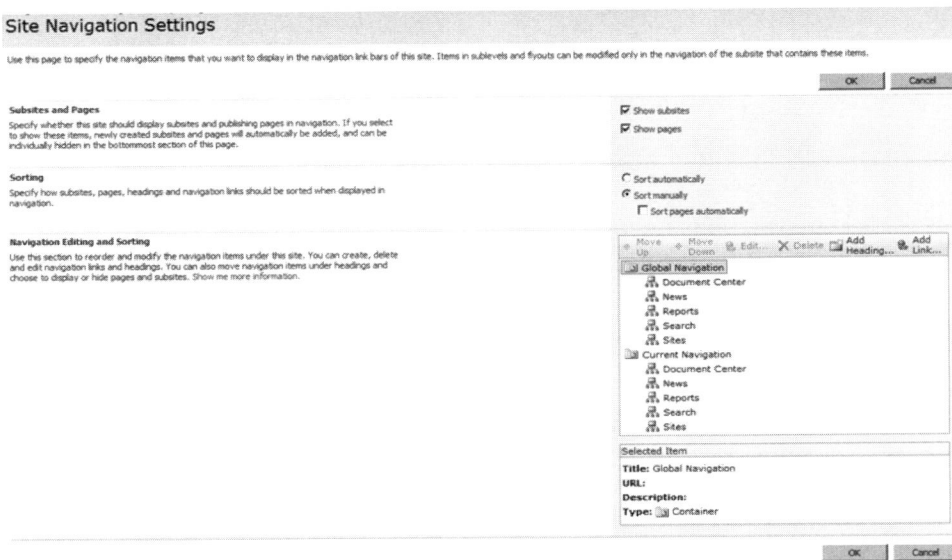

FIGURE 6.6
Site Navigation Settings available when the Office SharePoint Server Publishing Infrastructure Feature is activated.

In the first section, you have the ability to control whether or not subsites and pages are automatically added to navigation. By default, both options are checked. It is important to remember that only published pages will show up in navigation, and users will only see pages or subsites that they have been granted access to, thanks to security trimming.

In the Sorting section, you can control if navigation is arranged automatically or manually (the default). If you choose automatically, a new control will appear on the page allowing you to choose if sorting is by Title, Created Date, or Last Modified Date, and then if the items are sorted in ascending or descending order. In most environments, manual sorting of navigation seems to work best.

The final section allows for the complete control of navigation, much like Top link bar and Quick Launch, but with greater features. Move Up and Move Down work as advertised, as long as you have Sorting configured to manual. The Edit button will be disabled for automatic items in navigation and can only be used for links or headings you have created. The fourth button will vary between Hide and Delete, depending on which item in the list you have chosen. Automatically added items can only be hidden while manual additions cannot be hidden, only deleted. If you have hidden the item, the button will turn to Show. If you delete the item, it is just gone, so you will have to re-create it if you want it back.

Use Add Heading to create headings in Navigation. Headings in MOSS have a couple of unique attributes compared to their WSS counterparts. Headings when added to Global Navigation allow you to place links below them; this will create fly-out or cascading menus. So when you hover over the heading, you will see the links beneath. Also, when creating a heading, you can specify a title without giving it a URL. This way you could create a heading called Departments with no link in global navigation and then add links below it for Accounting and Human Resources. Now when a user hovers over Departments, he will see links to Accounting and Human Resources but will not be able to actually click Departments. This is improved over WSS where if you created the same type of behavior, Departments would have to be linked to something. Look at Figure 6.7 to see the screen for adding a heading. The screen for adding a link is identical.

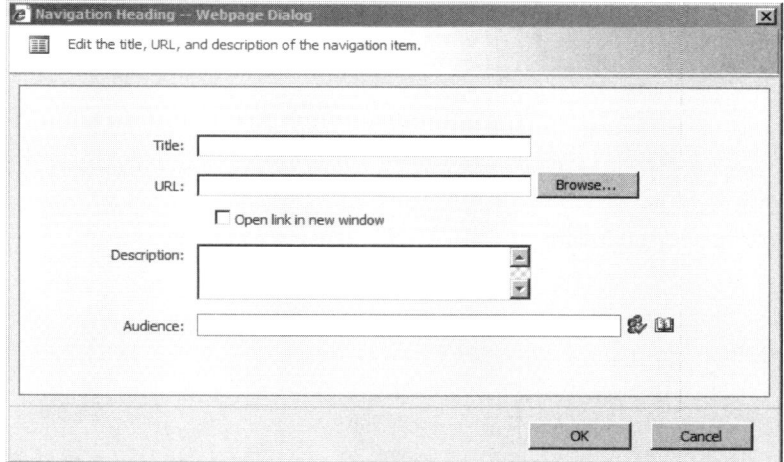

FIGURE 6.7
Screen for adding a new navigation heading.

The next option is the ability to Open link in a new window. Typically, if creating navigational elements pointing to content within the portal, you wouldn't want to open a new window, but if you had links to other Web sites, then opening a new browser is ideal. This way your users don't lose their place in SharePoint if you need to send them elsewhere.

Anything you enter in the Description box will show up as a tool tip, which appears when the mouse pointer is hovering over the navigation link.

You can use the Audience field to target this heading/link to a specific SharePoint Audience, a distribution list, a security group, or a SharePoint site group. This allows the designers and information architects some very powerful control of navigation. Targeting links only to users who need to see them is a great way to reduce the number of items appearing in navigation while still keeping everyone happy. Remember, though, that targeting is not security. It is only controlling what information is presented to a user. Look at Chapter 9, "Personalization and People Search," for detailed information on audiences and targeting of content.

Something else that is important to pay close attention to when updating navigation is to make sure you click OK at the bottom or top of the page when you are done; if you do not do this, then your changes will not be saved. More than one administrator has made all of his changes to navigation and then clicked another link only to realize his changes have been lost. Even though you see your changes in the window, they are not committed until you click OK at the bottom or top of the page.

If you are on a subsite within the site collection, you will get a couple of additional options on the Navigation page, as shown in Figure 6.8.

FIGURE 6.8
Options for controlling navigation inheritance on subsites.

For Global Navigation, it is a simple decision whether you want to inherit navigation from the parent site or not. Like WSS, when you created the subsite, you were given the choice of inheritance, and if you chose not to, then the global bread crumb would automatically be updated.

The Current Navigation (another name for Quick Launch) setting is not chosen when you create the subsite; instead, it is based on the template you chose for the subsite.

The publishing site templates will default to Display the current site, the navigation items below the current site, and the current site's siblings. This setting will show any navigational items added to the Quick Launch bar for this site and will also show all of the other sites that have the same parent site. This allows you to create a feel where all of the subsites have the same navigation links but with the addition of content from the subsite. Consistency is the cornerstone of any good navigation, so in a structured portal, this setting is ideal.

All of the other templates will use the setting of Display only the navigation items below the current site. This is the same as the normal behavior of a WSS template where you only see navigational items from the current site. The same options for updating navigation when creating list and libraries that are available in WSS are available. Of course, you could also choose the option to display the current navigation from the parent site.

Why Are There Flyouts Under News?

You just created a brand-new collaboration portal and when you go to the portal, News has flyouts. You then go into Modify Navigation to get rid of them. First, you look in the navigation section looking for the items of Sample News Article and News Archive to be links under the News site so you can just hide them, but they are not there. Interesting. Well, you know they are pages so you try deselecting Show pages and click OK. No luck. How do you get rid of those flyouts then?

Flyouts for subsites are controlled at the subsite level, even if the subsite is inheriting global nav from the parent site. So in this case, to get rid of the flyouts you would need to go to the News Site, Modify Navigation, deselect Show pages, and click OK. Now the flyouts are gone below News.

IT GOVERNANCE

You may have heard of governance before as it relates to information architecture. The idea is that it allows a company to put into place controls for managing change and growth of the information within the portal going forward. This keeps the portal from going stale, or worse, spiraling out of control because no effort is made to keep the information in line with the original intentions and structure. This type of governance and oversight is usually handled from the business side of the company and typically does not interest you, the SharePoint administrator.

While controlling how the information evolves is not your priority, you should be looking to your own governance strategies—not around the organization of the information, but instead how the infrastructure is going to be maintained going forward. This doesn't just mean the additions of hotfixes or service packs but also change. What will your policy be on adding custom code? What will you do if they add 500GB of data to a site collection? What are the service level agreements (SLAs) for SharePoint's availability? What happens if one of the departments brings its own SharePoint Farm online? How will you even know if they do? These are just some of the important questions you need to be asking and planning for.

The responsibility is placed on you. No one will ask these questions typically until it is too late. Your goal should be the creation of detailed documents and procedures that will outline all of the decisions you have made and the assumptions that went into each. Then, as necessary, you should document the action items to be taken for each event. If the datacenter is flooded by interns playing volleyball in the computer room and hitting the sprinkler, what do you do?

CONTROLLING DOWNTIME

Does your farm need to have high availability? Or do you just need to make your best effort? As discussed in Chapter 2, "Architecture and Capacity Planning," if you need true high availability, you will need to use redundant hardware both on the front end (your Web servers) and on the back end (SQL Server) to achieve this and at a minimum, you will need to start with a medium server farm. But don't stop there. If you have multiple front ends, and you have some type of network load balancer, is it redundant? What about your network? Can one switch failure bring your whole farm down? These types of questions don't seem as if they are the function of a SharePoint administrator since they pertain to networking and infrastructure components outside the farm. In reality, those are pieces your SharePoint farm needs to operate, so their uptime is your problem.

In the backup and recovery chapter, you should review the various high availability options that you have. Do you need to have a disaster recovery site? Or are offsite backups good enough? These questions need to be addressed in your plan, and the answer is different for each company. Also, don't forget that along with backups, you should really test your Restore process periodically. In the field, it is very common to find companies who think they have backups and they turn out to be unusable—either the backups are corrupt, or they were not backing up all of the necessary data. Test your capability to recover from your backups before it is too late. This does two great things for you. One is that it confirms the data in your backups is usable and everything you need is there. Second, you now have confirmed that you actually know how to recover from a backup—sometimes it's easier said than done.

With SharePoint, anytime that you install an update or service pack, your entire farm will be offline; there is no way around this. So you need to make sure you plan for maintenance windows for the deployment of these updates. Some administrators assume since they are using a multiserver farm that they can just update one server at a time without affecting the other server. The problem lies in the data. When you run Configuration Wizard to update the databases, all of the data will be unavailable. The amount of time this process takes is directly dependent on the amount of data you have. If you cannot afford to have your site offline for this upgrade (such as a public-facing Web site), you could consider having a second farm that was read-only and redirect traffic there while your primary farm is offline for the upgrade. Cory Burns of Microsoft IT has a detailed blog posting on this at http://blogs.technet.com/corybu/archive/2007/08/02/high-performance-upgrades-for-moss-2007-wss-3-0-database-migration-methods.aspx. His discussion is in the context of doing an upgrade, but in reality that is what you are doing anytime you install an update or service pack to SharePoint—you are upgrading the database to the latest version.

Managing Growth

Your SharePoint environment is going to grow, by leaps and bounds, no matter what. Customers who start with 2GB of data with plans for storing up to 20GB find themselves dealing with 200GB of content six months later. How will you handle this plethora of data? First thing to look at are your SQL server(s). As users add data, it is going straight into the content db. Do you have enough drive space? But your storage woes don't stop there. Now your index is going to grow, which is stored on the file system of the Index server and is being propagated to your Query servers. Can they handle such radical growth? It is hard to anticipate such growth, but at a minimum you can plan to monitor it so you'll get a heads-up at 50GB instead of 200GB when the server comes to a grinding halt from running out of drive space.

Quotas

One of the tools to use for keeping the growth in check is the use of site collection quotas, which can be maintained from Central Admin. This allows you to keep a lid on those rogue site collections. While these may not be well suited for your primary site collections that should grow as necessary, they are outstanding for ad hoc and collaboration site collections. If you have a Web app for http://projects where you create new site collections for each project and you limit each project to 2GB quotas, then you know that if you limit the content database to only store 50 site collections, you should never exceed your goal of limiting content databases to 100GB. Technically, you could still exceed your database size because the second-stage recycle bin does not count against the site collection quota and by default it can be up to 50 percent of the size of the site collection. Generally, it's not something to be alarmed about but important to keep in mind. The addition of content databases and quotas are covered in Chapter 3, "Installation and Configuration," in the "Site Collections" section.

Content Databases

What would you do if you found yourself needing to create more site collections in the projects Web app? You would add another content database, of course, and limit its growth to 50 site collections. Now that you have a new database created, will your current backup tool automatically back it up? Or do you have to go adjust the backup program or the SQL Maintenance job to recognize the new database? What is your plan for communicating the creation of the database to the person who is responsible for backups?

Blocked File Types

When looking for other clever ways to minimize unnecessary storage, take a second look at blocked file types. SharePoint focuses on blocking executable code from being stored in the database. To control growth, you may want to look at file types that lack true business purpose. This could be MP3s, AVIs, or other multimedia file types. You can control the file type list per Web application also, so this gives you the flexibility to do things such as stopping mp3s from being stored within the My Site Web application while still permitting them in the portal where marketing is using them to promote the new product line.

SharePoint Versus File Shares

It turns out there is more than one person running around telling people that the file share is dead, that SharePoint has killed it, and you should shut all of them down and migrate it all to your document libraries. This is just plain incorrect. If your project plan calls for you to copy all of the data off your file share and dump it into SharePoint, you need a new project plan.

While a document library with its alerts and metadata columns and filtered views has a tremendous advantage over the file folder, that doesn't mean it is always better. Remember those fancy features come at a price. While there are no official calculations to quote, you have to figure that storage in SharePoint is several times more expensive than storage on a file share. This is because the file and its metadata are kept in the SQL database for SharePoint, which costs much more than a simple NTFS file share. So storing unused archives or things like log files just doesn't make sense in SharePoint.

Another reason not to just dump is that typically file shares are pure chaos of mismatched folders and duplicate data, and this is probably why your company is pursuing SharePoint. If you drag and drop that into SharePoint, what have you gained? Nothing. You should have a plan for data cleanup and structuring as you transition from the file share.

There are lots of articles on the Internet weighing the pros and cons. We recommend starting with a series by Joel Oleson, which can be found here http://blogs.msdn.com/joelo/archive/2007/04/12/roi-from-file-shares-to-sharepoint.aspx. Passing these links on to the project managers for the SharePoint project can save you lots of unnecessary storage headaches later.

USAGE

Both WSS and MOSS come with some basic usage reporting capabilities. As outlined in Chapter 3, from Central Admin you enable the logging and processing necessary to do reporting. These reports can be broken down by day or month and report on Page access, User activity, OS or browser used, and the referring URL. To look at these reports, go to any site, navigate to Site Settings, and under Site Administration, choose Site usage report. This same data can be accessed using SharePoint Designer, giving you a little more flexibility to work with the data. Additionally, if you are a site collection administrator, you can run the Usage summary from the Site Collection Administration section. This report will show you storage, number of users, and activity for the entire site collection.

There is also a third usage report for storage used that is only available when you enable a site collection quota. Look at Figure 6.9 for a sample.

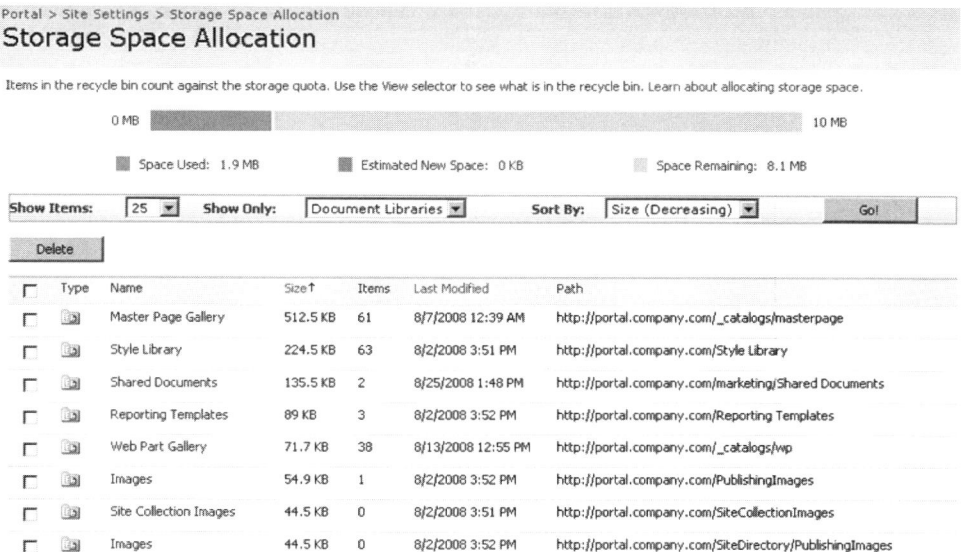

FIGURE 6.9
Site collection Storage Space Allocation report.

This is a very powerful report that gives you the chance to look at storage allocation throughout your site collection, which makes finding those large lists a breeze. You can view the report filtered by document libraries, documents, lists, and the recycle bin. This report is accessed by logging in as a site collection administrator, navigating to Site Settings, and clicking Storage space allocation under Site Collection Administration. When you go looking for this report, you may find that you don't have it as an option on your menu. The reason for this is the site collection has to have a quota enabled for this report to be available. Since all of your site collections may not have quotas enabled, you may find it necessary to set up a temporary quota for the site collection to access this report. To set up a quota for the site collection http://portal.company.com, follow the steps:

1. Open Central Admin.
2. Click the Application Management tab.
3. Under SharePoint Site Management, click Site collection quotas and locks.
4. Click the Site Collection and choose Change site collection.
5. Click the appropriate site collection and click OK.
6. Select the box for Limit site storage to a maximum of and specify a value that is greater than the current usage. You can see the current storage used right above the OK button.
7. Click OK. Now you will have the option to view Storage space allocation.

More information on quotas is available in the next section.

If you have purchased MOSS, you gain some additional reporting capabilities. These updated reports come from the SSP and must be first enabled in order to use them. To enable the reports, use the following steps:

1. Open your SSP Administration site.
2. In the Office SharePoint Usage Reporting section, click Usage reporting.
3. Select the box for Enable advanced usage analysis reporting and click OK. You will need to make sure you have already enabled basic usage reporting from Central Admin.
4. The option for Enable search query logging is checked by default.

Also, you will need to confirm that either the site Feature of Office SharePoint Server Enterprise Site features or Office SharePoint Server Standard Site features is activated. By default, this Feature is only not activated in Publishing portals.

After the features have been enabled, the link under Site Administration will take you to a different page; look at Figure 6.10 for an example report.

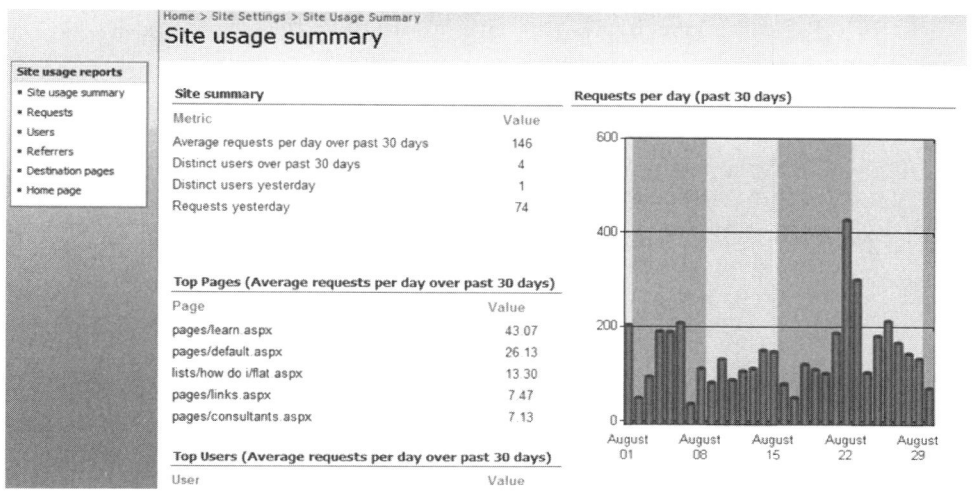

FIGURE 6.10
An example Site usage summary report from a SharePoint site that is
associated with an SSP that has advanced usage analysis processing enabled.

You can see these reports include graphs and are taking the same basic infor-
mation and breaking it down for you a little better. You can use the links in the
Quick Launch to see the various reports that have been generated. The report for
Site collection usage summary is also updated with the same interface.

Enabling SSP usage reporting also added the capabilities to do very rich, detailed search reporting. You can view both usage reports to look at volume and results reports to see potential areas of improvement. Search reports are covered
along with Search in Chapter 8, "Configuring and Managing Enterprise Search."

Quotas

In the previous section, you looked at how to assign an individual quota to a site
collection. Quotas can only be set at the site collection and are used to help control
the amount of storage consumed. When a site reaches its quota, users will receive a
message they have exceeded their quota and that they should contact their administrator. By default, only personal sites will receive a quota, which is 100MB. All
other site collections, by default, will have no quota. This quota is applied by using
a quota template, which is configured from Central Admin.

1. Open Central Admin.
2. Go to the Application Management tab.
3. Under SharePoint Site Management, click Quota templates.

From this screen, you will have the ability to modify a template or create a new one. Once you have created one of these templates, you can apply it to an existing site collection or when creating the site collection, you can use the template. It is important to note that the templates do not work exactly as you might expect. For example, create a quota template for 500MB called Team Quota. Then create a site collection at http://portal.company.com/sites/team and apply the Team Quota template. Now you have a site collection that is allowed a maximum amount of storage of 500MB. Now update the template to be 800MB. Does this affect the site collection you created at /sites/team? No. Site collections take the templates settings at creation time but are not tied to the template. If you were to go into the Manage site collection quotas and locks screen, it would like look the site now had an 800MB limit, but if you tried to upload data past the 500MB capacity, you would be stopped. Also, if you were to run stsadm.exe –enumsites, you would see the quota is still 500MB. If you would like the site collection to use the new template settings, you will need to reapply the quota template from within Central Admin. Simply open the Manage quotas and locks page, select the site collection, and click OK. Let's just call this a feature.

The last piece of functionality you may notice for quotas and locks is the ability to lock down a site collection. You can set it to no additions, read only, or no access. This gives you some flexibility when trying to decommission site collections or transition users from one to the other.

MANAGING THIRD-PARTY CODE

No matter how much administrators fight it, sooner or later you will be forced to deploy third-party or custom code. This is always a very sad day. Luckily, thanks to Features and Solution Packages (WSPs), you can make these changes to your farm in a very controlled manner. In Chapter 7, "Managing Site Customization: Templates, Features, and Solution Packages, you will find everything you need to know about maintaining and deploying these changes. From a governance perspective, this is the most important chapter in the entire book—you must insist on WSPs for all code additions. Also, make sure that you are backing up those WSPs as part of your backup strategy; they will be required to recover your farm.

CONTROL SITE PROLIFERATION

Another tough fact for everyone from the site designers to the administrator, the process of creating new sites needs to be addressed at the beginning of your Share-Point project. One of the challenges is that SharePoint provides either the ability to create a site or not—there is no gray area. In most deployments, the plan calls for a method where sites are requested and some form of a workflow takes place with an approval step before the site is created. This is great, but at the same time, the process needs to be very easy for both the requestor and the approver of the new site. Out of the box, SharePoint just does not provide this, so you are left looking for third-party solutions or having your developers create one for you. There are several very good third-party solutions to this problem, and unfortunately that is where you will need to look if the process needs to be automated.

Many shops end up choosing the manual process where users put in a request to the Help desk for site creation, or they completely empower the user community to create their own sites and then deal with the sprawl—well, actually, they just have site proliferation and hope it doesn't get out of control. If you do have to empower the users, make sure they are only creating sites within site collections that have quotas so you can have some level of control.

The one point of caution with trying to control site creation is not to make it too difficult for the users. If you make creating a subsite very difficult for users of the HR site collection, but they can easily create a subsite on their personal site, they are more likely to follow the path of least resistance. Now your information architecture is compromised and worse yet, they may be storing confidential information on their public personal site instead of in the locked-down HR site collection. That is a scary reality that you should look for ways to avoid.

SECURITY AND SITE AUDITING FOR SHAREPOINT

Auditing is another very important topic where SharePoint will leave you wanting more. Initially, there is no way to quickly view permissions of your farm from top to bottom or to even quickly find a listing of all of the sites and their subsites. This is another spot where third-party code becomes very important. You can look to vendors and purchase full-featured tools that will become your best friend when it comes to management. These tools will not only help you audit what you have in place, but will also give you options for mass creation of data or help you do things like copy permissions, deploy customizations in bulk, or discover rogue SharePoint servers. If you are trying to keep tabs on a large SharePoint environment, this is a must. If you don't want all of those fancy features or don't have the budget for it, you can also look to a free tool at http://www.codeplex.com/sushi. This tool will do several of these items in a much simple form, but the price is great.

When it comes to security, this is the balancing act. Some deployments lock down everything and only a couple of people within IT can make any changes, including creating new sites or modifying permissions. While this is great for keeping SharePoint 100 percent in control, it is awful for empowering the users. One of the best features of SharePoint is the fact that basic site management can be delegated down to the user community, removing these tasks from over-burdened IT departments. There is no value added in a $60,000-a-year IT administrator updating permissions on a list that a $6-an-hour intern can do just as well.

While locking everything down isn't going to work very well, neither is setting everyone to full control and then hoping they will not destroy all that you have built, because they will. Instead, you need to find that happy medium. Sometimes that means setting physical controls through approval processes or change request forms, and sometimes it is as simple as having a clear policy on how sites should be used and where what content lives where. Communicating this information clearly to the empowered users then puts the burden for keeping their data organized on them. This type of policy is very powerful in the hands of a well-backed governance committee that will be responsible for policing the changes.

COMMUNICATION

As you work through this section of the book and you start establishing your SLA for uptime and lengths of how long you will maintain copies of backups, you need to document this information and then communicate it to the community. There is very little value to the business if IT is keeping backups of SharePoint data for two years and no one in the business knows they can request data from that long ago. You must clearly communicate your IT governance policies for them to be effective. This also includes defining your maintenance window and then doing your best to stick to it. Users are much more likely to trust and adopt SharePoint if they understand the tremendous efforts IT is going to in order to keep the environment accessible. Or maybe it is the opposite and the decision has been made not to have SharePoint available at the disaster recovery site. This needs to be communicated to the business as well. You can imagine their surprise when all of their documentation for business continuity is stored in a team site and that team site isn't available during a failover.

MORE GOVERNANCE RESOURCES

For governance we tried to touch on some of the high-level things that will get you thinking about governance from the IT perspective, but we did not even attempt to try and discuss portal governance, which is usually led by the business side of the house. There are a couple of resources you should check out if you are part of either governance committee: http://www.codeplex.com/governance has several free tools that have come out of the Microsoft internal deployment. Tools such as the Site Undelete tool are must-haves for all deployments. Also, the official starting point for SharePoint governance is available on TechNet at http://technet.microsoft.com/en-us/office/sharepointserver/bb507202.aspx. From there, the sky is the limit; you can look into dedicated governance books or even training classes (such as this one http://www.tedpattison.net/courses/spg301.aspx) as this hot topic continues to evolve. Whatever you do, no matter how deep you want to go, you need to at least think about governance and how much of it makes sense for your environment.

7 Managing Site Customization: Templates, Features, and Solution Packages

In This Chapter

- Introduction
- Site Creation and Customization
- Custom Site Templates
- Site Definition
- Custom Site Templates Versus Site Definitions
- Features
- Solution Packages

INTRODUCTION

One of the key strengths of SharePoint technology is its ability to create Web sites rapidly. Web sites are created according to the specifications defined inside a template. This is very similar to the process of creating a new Microsoft Word document, something with which most readers should be familiar. SharePoint Web sites are created from two different types of templates, which are called "site definitions" and "custom site templates." Site definitions are available out of the box for creating several different types of Web sites. These templates provide the specifications for creating the Web site and for customizing the Web site; a process referred to as "site provisioning." Site customization includes such things as establishing which Web parts, lists, document libraries, and so on will be immediately available for use.

The site owner and users of the site can further customize the site. Once the site has been customized, the site and its content can be saved and reused to provision other Web sites, just like the site definition was used initially.

Custom site templates are templates that have been created from an existing Web site that has already been provisioned and further customized. The custom site template is now available to be used to create new Web sites. The architecture for creating and customizing Web sites has been improved from the previous version of SharePoint with the addition of the Feature framework. Features modularize functionality and allow specific customizations to be enabled and disabled very easily. In addition to Features, the deployment and installation of customer artifacts, such as custom Web parts and custom Web pages, has been improved with the introduction of Solution Packages. Templates, Features, and Solution Packages all play a role in the customization of SharePoint Web sites. The purpose of this chapter is to familiarize the SharePoint administrator with each of these different technology components so that they understand their capability and can manage the SharePoint environment effectively.

SITE CREATION AND CUSTOMIZATION

Windows SharePoint Services v3.0 is a Web site provisioning engine. It is designed as a platform to create and support different types of sites. SharePoint sites are different in many ways from the standard Web sites with which most people are familiar. With these sites, each Web site is made up of a number of Web pages that physically exist in some type of folder hierarchy. SharePoint sites are created using a predefined recipe or template. Once created, the site is defined by the information in a row inside the Docs table in the content database. This information is used to generate Web pages dynamically upon request. The provisioning process (site creation + customization) can create sites with different characteristics by utilizing different templates.

The template architecture consists of site definitions and custom site templates. Site definitions consist of multiple XML files located in the file system of a front-end Web server. Custom templates are created through the user interface after a site has been customized. Before a SharePoint site can be customized, the site must already exist. So we will begin our discussion with how a new site is created.

A new site can be created by using the Web browser interface. (A new site can also be created using the object model, but our focus here is not development.) This process includes selecting a preconfigured definition, which will determine the starting conditions for the new Web site; these conditions include things like the type of lists that will be present, the document libraries, Web parts, workflows, files, and so on, and settings for the new SharePoint site. There are two different types of definitions that can be chosen: a site definition and a custom site template.

A site definition is essentially a blueprint for the new site and includes multiple XML files and .NET Web pages. This information is stored on the front-end Web servers in the Template folder located in the "12 hive" (c:\Program Files\Common Files\Microsoft Shared\web server extensions\12\TEMPLATE). These blueprints are reused over and over again to provision new SharePoint sites. Once a new site is created from a specific site definition, the new site will utilize a set of pages commonly referred to as *ghosted* or *uncustomized* pages.

CUSTOMIZED AND UNCUSTOMIZED PAGES

Uncustomized pages are shared by multiple Web sites. For example, each Web site does not have its own unique copy of the default home page default.aspx. This and other files like this exist once and only once on each of the front-end Web servers. Sites that utilize these pages include a reference to the specific ghosted file inside of SharePoint's content database. Therefore, each site appears to have its own copy, but in reality the pages are actually shared across all sites that use the same definition. The ghosting process saves space, and it improves performance. Space is dramatically reduced by having sites share physical pages, which also helps in SharePoint's scalability. Performance is dramatically improved because the number of files that have to be cached is less, which reduces the overall load freeing up memory for other purposes, and files needing to be cached are retrieved from the local file system, eliminating the need to make a database request, which reduces overhead. Unfortunately, the benefit of having multiple sites use the same pages gets in the way of customization.

Site customization performed using the Web browser does not alter the ghosting mechanism, but customization using SharePoint Designer 2007 produces unghosting or a customized page. As part of the page editing process, a copy of the original page is made and the customized copy is said to be unghosted and is stored inside the content database. Clearly, the benefit is the ability to customize a site without negatively impacting other sites but at a cost of potentially reducing performance. Also, any changes to the original ghosted page will not propagate to the customized site. Obviously, customization without unghosting sounds the "best." Custom site templates provide an alternate mechanism for reusing sites.

Custom site templates and site definitions both provide the capability to create SharePoint sites and reuse configuration information. The difficulty with working with and customizing sites using site definitions has been reduced with the introduction of Features in WSS v3.0. Features simplify site definitions by modularizing their composition into smaller chunks of functionality, which reduces the complexity involved in making site customizations, deploying upgrades, and activating or deactivating functionality. In the following sections, we will discuss custom site templates, site definitions, and Features in a lot more depth so that the SharePoint administrator has a good understanding of how to utilize and manage this capability.

CUSTOM SITE TEMPLATES

Custom site templates are based on existing sites. Therefore, before you can create a custom site template, you must have already created a site, and this site must have been provisioned using a site definition. A custom site template represents site customization that is above and beyond the provisioning specified in the site definition. Custom site templates are created after an existing site has been modified to an extent that is acceptable to the site owner, team, or workgroup. These templates are stored in SharePoint's content database inside SQL Server. The custom template represents another approach to reusing sites, but in this case, sites that you have already customized.

Custom site templates represent an easy way to save your entire site into a single file for either archiving purposes or site reuse. This file includes all pages, lists, libraries, and contents. Custom site templates are created using the user interface of the Web browser or SharePoint Designer 2007. SharePoint users are generally more familiar with site templates than site definitions because the former are readily visible from the Web browser, while site definitions require access to the file system to be viewed. Site templates have two key strengths: they are easy to create, and they are easy to reuse.

TEMPLATE COMPOSITION

A custom site template represents any changes or customization applied to a SharePoint site after it has been provisioned. The template content adds to, but does not repeat, the structural and content information from the original site definition. The process of customization occurs when a user with at least Design privileges changes a Web site using the Web browser user interface or SharePoint Designer 2007. Essentially, the custom template represents the difference between the state of the original Web site before customization, and the state of the Web site at the time that the custom template is generated. For example, site templates track changes to navigation, Web parts, lists, and libraries, and optionally, changes to the content of a site. Site templates include data for the entire site and can optionally include the content of the site as well.

SITE DEFINITION DEPENDENCY

Custom templates remain dependent on the original site definition used to create the original site. The custom site template maintains a unique identifier in relation to the original site definition from which the source site of the site template is derived. This means that a site template will not function unless the original site definition is present on the front-end Web server or servers. Therefore, if the original site definition is not present when attempting to use the custom template to provision a site, the process will not work. Also, if the definition is present but has been changed, it is likely that existing sites based on that definition will break. Hence, never modify an existing site definition after any sites have been provisioned.

SAVING A TEMPLATE

A custom site template is created by selecting Save site as template option from the Site Settings page, as highlighted in Figure 7.1. The process generally includes creating a SharePoint site using one of the out-of-the-box site definitions or another custom template, modifying the provisioned site to meet the needs of the specific organization, and then creating the custom template. Once saved, site templates are stored in the Site Template Gallery of the top-level site in a site collection and are available for subsite creation on all Web sites in the site collection.

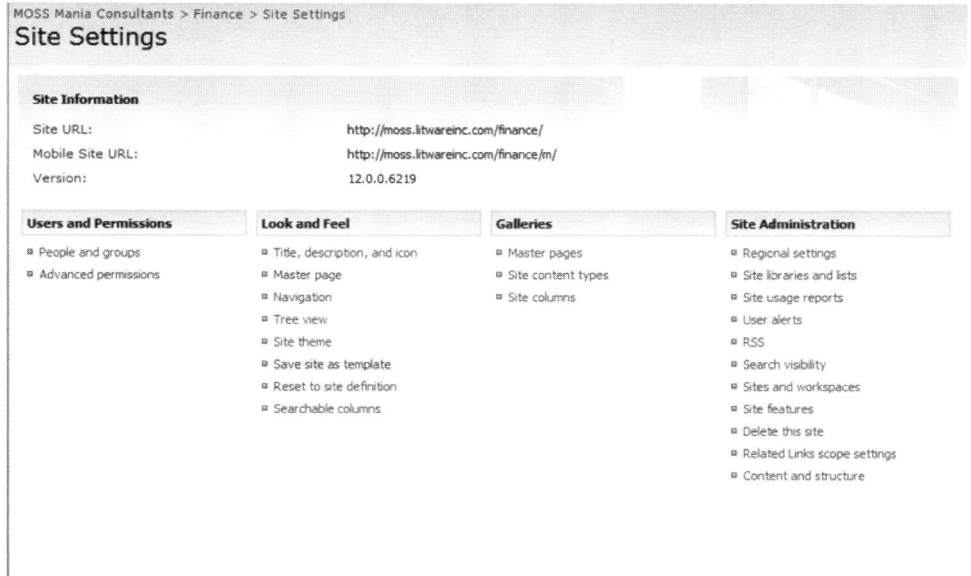

FIGURE 7.1
The Site Settings page showing the Save site as template option.

NOTE

Save Site Link Not Present

The Save site as a template link will not be available on the Site Settings page if the site is a Publishing site; a Publishing site is a site where the Office SharePoint Server Publishing Feature is activated.

Custom site templates are saved as a file with a .stp extension, as can be seen in Figure 7.2, which shows the Save Site as Template Web page. From the figure, you'll note that the template can also include content by enabling the check box at the bottom of the page. By default, there is a 10MB limit to the size of the site template.

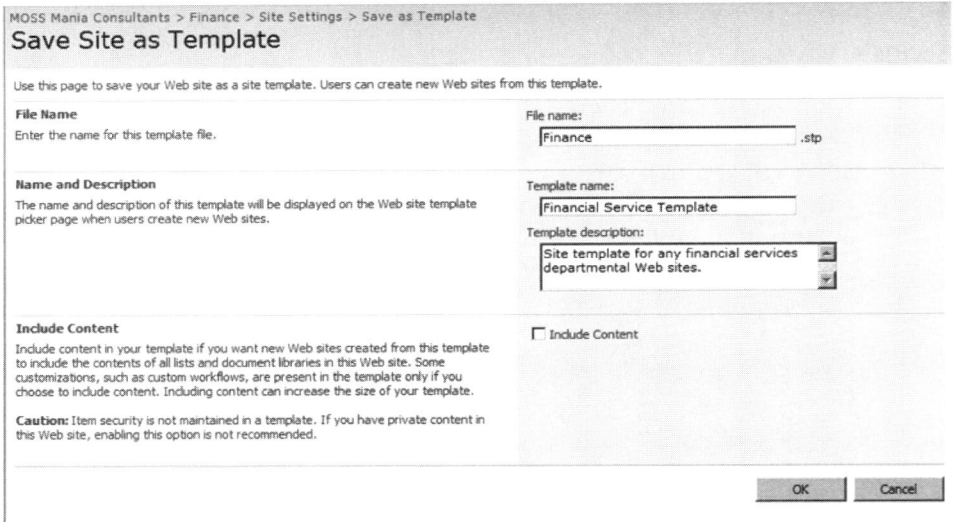

FIGURE 7.2
The Web page for saving a site as a template.

NOTE

Site Template Size

The following STSADM command can be used to increase the size of the site template that can be saved:

```
STSADM —o setproperty —pn max-template-document-size —pv template_size
```

The —pv value template_size *is in bytes with a maximum value of 500MB or 524,288,000 bytes. Execute the command replacing* template_size *with the desired size of the site template. The command changes the maximum size of both site and list templates.*

The figure shows that a template called Financial Services Template is being created. Once created, the template is automatically stored in the Site Template Gallery at the root of the site collection, as shown in Figure 7.3. The custom template file is physically stored inside the SharePoint content database. During the site creation process, the new template will be available as one of the choices, as illustrated in Figure 7.4. The template can be saved to another location by clicking the hyperlink and choosing a location on the SharePoint server.

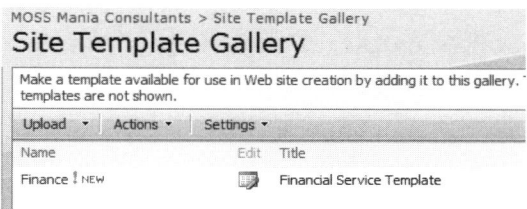

FIGURE 7.3
Site Template Gallery.

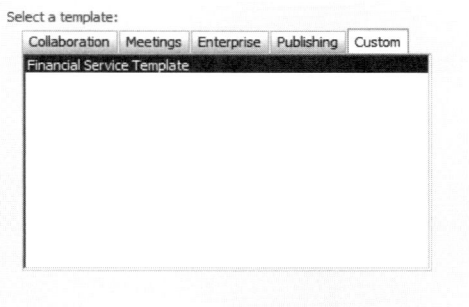

FIGURE 7.4
Site template gallery.

The template file is actually a .cab file. To view the contents of the template file, save it to an alternate location and rename the .stp extension to .cab. Once renamed, the contents can be viewed using Windows Explorer. This file includes a manifest.xml file. View the contents of this XML file and notice the specific schema called "Collaborative Application Markup Language (CAML)." CAML is the XML-based language that is used to build and customize SharePoint Web sites. Specifically, CAML is used to render Web pages by defining the type of data that is contained within a field and to construct HTML that is displayed in the browser.

GLOBAL USE OF THE TEMPLATE

Site templates can be downloaded and uploaded to other site collection galleries. They can also be added to the Central Site Template Gallery, where they become available for top-level site creation in addition to subsite creation. To add the template to the central gallery and make it globally available, you need to perform the following steps. Once added to the central gallery, the template will be available from the Create Site Collection Web page, as shown in Figure 7.5.

1. Download the site template from the site collection gallery and save the .stp file in a convenient location where you can access it from step 2.
2. Run the STSADM Command Line tool with the following syntax, making sure to prefix the template file name with the full location.
   stsadm.exe -o addtemplate -filename *Site*_Template_File_Name -title *Site_Template_Title* [-description *Site_Template_Description*]
3. Reset Internet Information Services (IIS) by typing **IISRESET** at the Command Prompt.

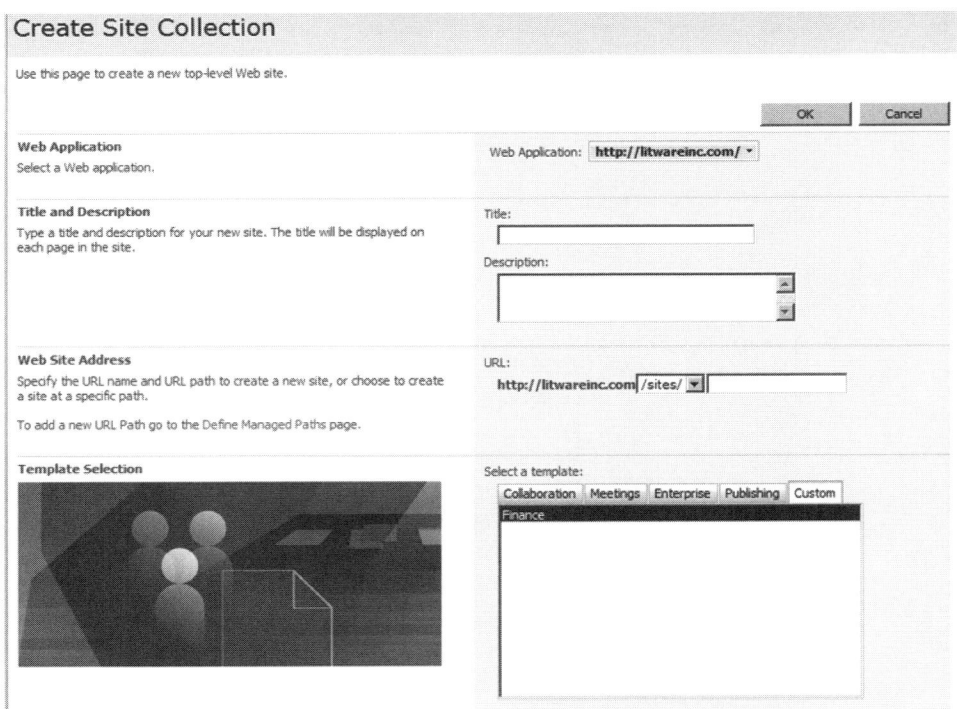

FIGURE 7.5
Create Site Collection Web page.

Custom List Templates

Just like a customized site can be reused by creating a site template, lists can also be reused by creating a list template. The list author would create the custom list with the necessary columns and data types and then save the list as a list template. This template can then be used to provision a new list. The focus of this chapter is on site customization and reuse, so it is left up to the reader to investigate the process for creating and reusing list templates.

The custom site template can be created easily by utilizing the Web browser or SharePoint Designer 2007 user interface and reused via the same browser interface. Site definitions represent a more complex approach to site customization. They represent the foundation with which sites are created. The following section describes the details of the site definition and how they can be customized. The intent is not for administrators to create new site definitions, but to provide an understanding of how they are created and how to communicate with those whom may be creating new definitions.

SITE DEFINITION

A site definition is a very powerful and reusable template for creating fully customized Web sites; they are the blueprint for a unique SharePoint site. Each definition includes a group of files that reside on the front-end Web servers. Site definitions represent one of the ways WSS optimizes performance using a set of ghosted or uncustomized files to create every site based on that definition, as we discussed previously. A single change to these files will propagate to all sites created from this definition. Contrast that to sites created from a custom template, which would have to updated individually. The site collection or site creation process requires you to select a template; this template represents the site definition for that specific site unless custom site templates have been created, as shown previously. The following discussion provides an overview of the components of a site definition and how they are used to define Web site composition. It is not meant to serve as a tutorial for creating new site definitions.

DEFINITION FOLDER HIERARCHY

Several site definitions are natively installed by WSS, which include STS for team sites, MPS for meeting workspaces, CENTRALADMIN for central administration sites, WIKI, and BLOG. MOSS installs several others like SPSMSITE for My Sites and PUBLISHING for a publishing site. Each of these definitions is represented by a folder hierarchy, which must contain an XML folder and a default.aspx Web page. Each definition also contains an ONET.XML file inside of the XML folder. Some of the definitions like BLOG and MPS, for example, are more complex and include additional items like a Lists folder and additional Web pages. This hierarchy is shown in Figure 7.6.

Site definitions can be seen by viewing the subfolders inside of the \Templates\ SiteTemplates folder in the 12 hive, as shown in Figure 7.6. As you can see, each site definition has its own subdirectory, and each folder is named for the type of definition it represents. The folders may also contain one or more files including .xml, .aspx, .ascx, and .master page files, as well as document template files (.dot, .htm, and so on), and content files (.gif, .doc, and so on). If the reader is following along with an open instance of MOSS, he should open the SiteTemplates folder and browse the different folders and view their respective compositions.

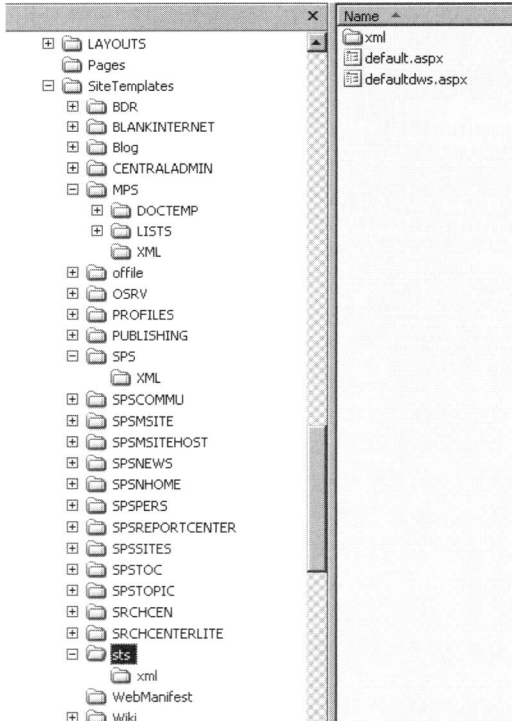

FIGURE 7.6
SiteTemplates hierarchy containing subfolders
for each of the site definitions.

Defining Terminology

The reader will note that the common terminology, including that used by this book and that of the Sharepoint SDKs, refers to Site Templates as .stp files that are generated when you save a site as a template, and to file-based site templates as Site Definitions, despite the fact that the name of the directory that houses the site definitions is named SiteTemplates.

DEFINITION DESCRIPTION AND REGISTRATION

Site definition configuration information is defined in another XML file called WEBTEMP.XML, which is available in C:\Program Files\Common Files\Microsoft Shared\web server extensions\12\TEMPLATE\1033\XML folder. The reader will also notice that there are other WEBTEMP files that match the format WEBTEMP<NAME OF SITE DEFINITION>.XML. The purpose of the WEBTEMP file is to register and describe the site definition; this file contains the name of the site definition, as displayed in the Create Site page in a site or the Create Site Collection page in Central Administration. If you open the WEBTEMP file, you'll notice that the XML is composed of a series of Template tags. A portion of the contents of the WEBTEMP file is shown in the following text.

Each Template node contains one or more configuration nodes, and these describe the site definition. The value for the Name attribute of the Template node must match the name of a subfolder inside of the SiteTemplates directory. SharePoint now knows to look for the ONET.XML file inside the XML folder for the actual site definition information. The Template ID must be unique across the SharePoint farm. A Configuration element is used to identify an existing site definition configuration within a site definition. The reader who is familiar with creating sites will notice that the Configuration node attributes ImageUrl, Description, and DisplayCategory information are defining what is displayed to the user on the site creation Web page. A site definition can also include more than one site definition configuration. For example, the STS definition includes configurations for Team Site, Blank Site, and Document Workspace, as illustrated by the XML fragment below.

```
<Template Name="STS" ID="1">
<Configuration ID="0" Title="Team Site" Hidden="FALSE"
    ImageUrl="/_layouts/images/stsprev.png" Description="A site for teams
    to quickly organize, author, and share information. It provides a
    document library, and lists for managing announcements, calendar
    items, tasks, and discussions." DisplayCategory="Collaboration" />
<Configuration ID="1" Title="Blank Site" Hidden="FALSE"
```

```
    ImageUrl="/_layouts/images/blankprev.png" Description="A blank site
    for you to customize based on your requirements."
    DisplayCategory="Collaboration"
    AllowGlobalFeatureAssociations="False"/>
<Configuration ID="2" Title="Document Workspace" Hidden="FALSE"
    ImageUrl="/_layouts/images/dwsprev.png" Description="A site for
    colleagues to work together on a document. It provides a document
    library for storing the primary document and supporting files, a
    tasks list for assigning to-do items, and a links list for
resources
    related to the document." DisplayCategory="Collaboration" />
</Template>
```

Feature Association

The reader will also notice that the Blank Site Template definition includes the Configuration attribute AllowGlobalFeatureAssociations="False". *The value of false prevents features that have the* templatename='global' *from being associated with this site upon provisioning. The* templatename='global' *property is defined inside of the feature.xml file and signifies that the corresponding feature will be stapled to all site templates. We will cover Features and Feature Stapling in the next section.*

The configuration declaration information can have other attributes providing additional site provisioning control, as can be seen from the SPSPORTAL site definition Template node from the WEBTEMPSPS.XML file, as shown in the following XML fragment. This is configuration information for a Collaboration Portal site. It specifies that the Collaboration Portal site definition can only be used to create top-level sites in the site collection because of the attribute RootWebOnly="TRUE". You could also specify that the site only exist as a subsite within a site collection using SubWebOnly="TRUE". This provides a level control on how the site definition can be used, and provides a mechanism to control how certain features are enabled. The VisibilityFeatureDependency controls the visibility of the configuration information based on the activation of a feature, specifically in this case, BaseSiteStapling feature whose ID value is 97A2485F-EF4B-401f-9167-FA4FE177C6F6. This essentially says that the Collaboration Portal site definition contains features that depend on the BaseSiteStapling feature and if BaseSiteStapling has not been activated, you will not be able to select this definition in the site provisioning process.

```
<Template Name="SPSPORTAL" ID="47">
<Configuration ID="0" Title="Collaboration Portal"
Type="0"Hidden="FALSE"
    ImageUrl="/_layouts/1033/images/template_corp_intranet.png"
    Description="A starter site hierarchy for an intranet divisional
    portal. It includes a home page, a News site, a Site Directory, a
    Document Center, and a Search Center with Tabs. Typically, this site
    has nearly as many contributors as readers and is used to host team
    sites." ProvisionAssembly="Microsoft.SharePoint.Publishing,
    Version=12.0.0.0, Culture=neutral, PublicKeyToken=71e9bce111e9429c"
    ProvisionClass="Microsoft.SharePoint.Publishing.
    PortalProvisioningProvider"
    ProvisionData="SiteTemplates\\WebManifest\\PortalWebManifest.xml"
    RootWebOnly="TRUE" DisplayCategory="Publishing"
    VisibilityFeatureDependency="97A2485F-EF4B-401f-9167-FA4FE177C6F6"
/>
</Template>
```

The Collaboration Portal site definition creates multiple sites as part of its overall provisioning process using the attributes ProvisionClass, ProvisionAssembly, and ProvisionData. The ProvisionClass attribute specifies the name of a class that actually does the additional work of provisioning other sites. This code resides in the .NET assembly specified by the ProvisionAssembly attribute. The class is passed the value of the ProvisionData attribute, which is generally a path to an XML file, in this case PortalWebManifest.xml. This file contains instructions on the sites to create as part of the Portal Definition. From a portion of the content of the PortalWebManifest.xml file which is shown below, the name attribute of the Web element indicates that four sites are created: News, Site Directory, Search Center, and Document center.

```
<webs>
 <web name="News" siteDefinition="SPSNHOME"
   displayName="$Resources:spscore,PortalManifest_News_DisplayName;"
   description="$Resources:spscore,PortalManifest_News_Description;" />
 <web name="SiteDirectory" siteDefinition="SPSSITES"
   displayName="$Resources:spscore,PortalManifest_SiteDirectory_DisplayName;"
   description="$Resources:spscore,PortalManifest_SiteDirectory_Description;"/>
 <web name="SearchCenter" siteDefinition="SRCHCEN"
   displayName="$Resources:spscore,PortalManifest_SearchCenter_DisplayName;"
   description="$Resources:spscore,PortalManifest_SearchCenter_Description;" />
 <web name="Docs" siteDefinition="BDR"
   displayName="$Resources:spscore,PortalManifest_DocumentCenter_DisplayName;"
   description="$Resources:spscore,PortalManifest_DocumentCenter_Description;"/>
</webs>
```

DEFINITION CONFIGURATION

The XML folder contains the ONET.XML (Office .NET) file. This file contains the CAML that represents the actual site definition information, including, for example, navigational areas, Web parts, list templates, document templates, configurations, modules, and components. The file is broken into several different sections. The reader is encouraged to open up the ONET.XML file and browse through it to become familiar with its contents. If we open the file for Team Site definition, you'll notice the NavBars element, which contains definitions for the top navigation and side navigation displayed on the home page. The ListTemplates section specifies the list definitions for the site definition; this section is not used since the introduction of Features in WSS v3.0. The new approach is to use list definition Features and element .xml files to define its list templates. The DocumentTemplates section defines the document templates used in document libraries. Since the STS site definition, as partially shown previously in the Description and Registration section, is used to provision three different sites, there are three different Configuration elements in the Configurations section, which specify the lists and modules that are created upon provisioning. Note the presence of list definition Features and the specification of Features inside WebFeatures and SiteFeatures elements. In the previous version of SharePoint, site definitions were much more complex. The CAML for each of the desired functionalities was hard coded into the definition, making modification and post-site creation customization much more difficult. For the reader interested in a more in-depth description of the ONET.XML file, the following link provides a good discussion http://msdn2.microsoft.com/en-us/library/ms474369.aspx.

The site definition includes a very granular approach to defining what gets included in the provisioning of a new SharePoint Web site. An individual desiring to understand the details of the site definition is also required to understand CAML. Although we did not cover every aspect thoroughly, it is clear that a more in-depth understanding is necessary to fully leverage site definitions, and therefore creating site definitions is a more complex process than creating custom site templates.

Custom site templates and site definitions both provide the capability to create SharePoint sites and reuse configuration information. The difficulty with working with and customizing sites using site definitions has been reduced with the introduction of Features in WSS v3.0. Features simplify site definitions by modularizing their composition into smaller chunks of functionality, which reduces the complexity involved in making site customizations, deploying upgrades, and activating or deactivating functionality. We saw that several sections of the site definition included reference to Features, thus making the definition much more modular.

One can also envision how easy it would be to modify the site definition by adding new Features or replacing existing Features. Thus, Features provide a very convenient approach for creating and modifying site definitions. Features will be discussed in depth in an upcoming section, but first we will discuss the advantages and disadvantages for using custom site templates and creating new site definitions.

CUSTOM SITE TEMPLATES VERSUS CUSTOM SITE DEFINITIONS

The previous sections have outlined the details of custom site templates and an overview of site definitions, including how they are used to provision Web sites. We have purposely not included a discussion for creating custom site definitions because it is beyond the scope of this chapter, and it is our recommendation not to encourage the creation of custom site definitions as a general practice. However, for interested readers, they are directed to the following excellent article, "Creating a Custom Site Definition in WSS V3 / MOSS" at this location: http://www.sharepointblogs.com/ tbaginski/archive/2007/08/16/creating-a-custom-site-definition-in-wss-v3-moss.aspx. Therefore, to understand where these two approaches should be used, let's review each of their advantages and disadvantages, as shown in Table 7.1.

Clearly, both site provisioning approaches have their strengths and weaknesses. As a general rule, we do not recommend creating new site definitions (with one exception discussed in the note below), but instead strongly encourage the use of site definition modification called "Feature Stapling." We discuss Features and Feature Stapling in the next section with the intent of providing the administrator with an understanding to help in managing a SharePoint environment. Features provide a mechanism for customizing new and already-existing sites.

Creating Custom Site Definitions

The authors do recommend creating custom site definitions for one scenario: creating a template for a publishing site. Since creating a custom site template is not an option, the requirements for provisioning and reusing a publishing site may dictate the need. For those interested in this approach, they are referred to Chapter 5 in the book by Andrew Connell, SharePoint 2007 Web Content Management Development.

TABLE 7.1 ADVANTAGES AND DISADVANTAGES FOR CUSTOM SITE
TEMPLATES VERSUS SITE DEFINITIONS

	Key Advantages	**Key Disadvantages**
Custom Site Template	Easy to create using the Web browser interface and to reuse to create new sites. Existing custom site templates can be modified without affecting existing sites created from that original template. Server administrator is not needed for creation or deployment.	Stored in the content database and therefore may negatively impact performance. Since they are a customization of the original site definition, they maintain a dependency on the site definition used to create the original site that was saved. Cannot be used for Publishing sites, sites with the Publishing Feature enabled. Site templates are a customization approach useful for one-off scenarios and not a development approach useful across the enterprise.
Custom Site Definition	Performance is typically better since the information is stored in the file system and can be successfully cached. A greater and more granular level of customization is possible compared to site templates created through the Web browser. Useful for implementing site provisioning requirements across a large number of sites.	More complicated to create, debug, and deploy. Server administrators are always required for deployment since access to the local server file system is required. Site definitions should not be edited once sites have been created because of the risk of breaking existing sites. You could only add to a custom site definition once deployed.

FEATURES

Windows SharePoint Services 3.0 introduces a new capability to the SharePoint tool arsenal, and it's called "Features." In general terms, Features provide a number of advantages:

- Customizing site provisioning configuration by modularizing site definition information
- Changing or adding new functionality to existing SharePoint sites
- Selectively enabling and disabling customizations
- Reusing code

Features are a part of provisioning a Web site with a specific set of functionality, and they also provide the capability to "light up" or activate or deactivate other capabilities after the site has already been created, further customizing the already-existing site. The ability to toggle functionality on and off is a tremendous advantage to modifying existing Web sites. Our discussion will focus on providing the SharePoint administrator with an understanding of Features technology and how to effectively manage Features. Resources are provided for those who may want to know how to create new Features.

FEATURE FOLDER HIERARCHY

Just as we saw with site definitions, Features are represented by a folder hierarchy. WSS and MOSS install Features inside of the 12 hive in the following subdirectory: \TEMPLATE\FEATURES. Do you continue to see the importance of the 12 hive? The FEATURES folder contains named subfolders for each Feature that has been deployed to the server and any custom Feature that has been created. The reader should take a minute to review all of the Features present on a MOSS install. Some of the installed Features can be viewed using the browser interface by navigating to Site Settings Web page and choosing either the Site Features or Site Collection Features link. This will not display all of the installed Features, since some of the Features are hidden.

FEATURE DESCRIPTION AND FEATURE.XML

Each Feature directory must include a manifest file called the Feature.xml file and generally include supporting information, which is represented by a set of subfolders and files that contain CAML. The Feature.xml file defines the high-level attributes of the Feature, and is used in the deployment of the Feature. For example, the SlideLibrary Feature directory contains three subfolders: ListTemplates, Resources, and SldLib. The following XML shows the contents of the SlideLibrary Feature.xml file. The Feature element defines a set of child elements and attributes that collectively specify the location of assemblies, files, dependencies, or properties that support the Feature. For a detailed discussion of the contents of the Feature.xml file and the Feature schema, consult the WSS Software Development Kit.

```
<Feature xmlns="http://schemas.microsoft.com/sharepoint/"
  Id="0BE49FE9-9BC9-409d-ABF9-702753BD878D
  Title="$Resources:SldlibDisplayName"
  Description="$Resources:SldlibDescription"
  Version="1.0.0.0"
  Scope="Web"
  Hidden="TRUE"
  DefaultResourceFile="_Res">
    <ElementManifests>
       <ElementManifest Location="ListTemplates\SlideLibrary.xml" />
       <ElementManifest Location="ListTemplates\EventReceiver.xml" />
    </ElementManifests>
</Feature>
```

Every Feature must have a unique ID, which is represented by a GUID. For new Features, this GUID is created using Visual Studio or another equivalent tool. Also note that Features can be hidden so that they can't be viewed from the Site Settings page using the browser by defining the Hidden attribute as True. Hidden Features must be activated and deactivated from the command line using the STSADM tool, using the SharePoint object model, or by deploying the Feature as part of a site definition.

Features have a scope that defines how broadly their functionality will be available within the SharePoint farm. There are four different values for the Scope attribute, and they are listed in Table 7.2. Once the Feature is installed and activated, it will provide functionality across the specified scope. Features with Farm scope are activated by default when they are installed.

TABLE 7.2 FEATURE SCOPE

Value of Scope Attribute	Description
Web	Applies to a specific Web site in a site collection.
Site	Applies to all sites in a site collection.
WebApplication	Applies to the specific Web application, any extended Web application, and all site collections in the Web application, which includes all sites in the site collection.
Farm	Applies to the whole SharePoint farm.

Other types of supporting files called "Element" files may be referenced from the Feature.xml file, and these files are called "Element Manifests." These files contain CAML and define the specific functionality of the Feature. A detailed discussion of the contents and schema of the Element files can be found in the WSS SDK. The SlideLibrary Feature.xml file references two files that are part of the ListTemplates folder: SlideLibrary.xml and EventReceiver.xml. The contents of the SlideLibrary.xml file are shown below, and they are used to specify a ListTemplate element, which defines a list definition or template that will be provisioned as part of the Feature. The Elements portion of the EventReceiver.xml file contains three different Receiver elements contained inside of the Receivers element, of which only one is shown for illustration. The Receiver element is used to register the .NET assembly and class for an event handler, which is deployed as part of the Feature.

```
<Elements xmlns="http://schemas.microsoft.com/sharepoint/">
    <ListTemplate
                Name="sldlib"
                Type="2100"
                BaseType="1"
                OnQuickLaunch="TRUE"
                SecurityBits="11"
                DisplayName="$Resources:SldlibDisplayName"
                NewPage="slnew.aspx"
                EditPage="sledit.aspx"
                Description="$Resources:SldlibDescription"
                Image="/_layouts/images/itsl.gif"
                DocumentTemplate="100" />
        </Elements>
```

```
<Elements xmlns="http://schemas.microsoft.com/sharepoint/">
    <Receivers ListTemplateId="2100" ListTemplateOwner="">
        <Receiver>
                <Name>Slide Library Item Adding event handler</Name>
                <Type>ItemAdding</Type>
                <SequenceNumber>1000</SequenceNumber>
                <Assembly>Microsoft.Office.SlideLibrary,
                    Version=12.0.0.0,
                    Culture=neutral,
                    PublicKeyToken=71e9bce111e9429c</Assembly>

    <Class>Microsoft.Office.SlideLibrary.SldLibEventHandlers
    </Class>
        <Data />
        </Receiver>
…
…
    </Receivers>
</Elements>
```

FEATURE DEPENDENCY

Features can be dependent on other Features being installed and activated. A Feature activation dependency specifies a relationship between a Feature and another Feature that is required for the dependent Feature to work properly, ensuring that other Features are activated before activating the dependent Feature. This dependency is specified by adding the ActivationDependencies element to the Feature element node in the Feature.xml file and including an ActivationDependency node for each specific dependency. This is illustrated in the XML fragment below from the Feature.xml file of the PublishingSite Feature. As can be seen, this Feature has four dependencies. When the PublishingSite Feature is activated, it ensures that these other Features have also activated; if not, then they will be activated. Features will not be deactivated as long as other Features that maintain a dependency remain active. For a Feature to be automatically activated as part of a dependency, its Hidden attribute must be defined as TRUE.

```
<Feature
    Id="F6924D36-2FA8-4f0b-B16D-06B7250180FA"
    Title="$Resources:osrvcore,PublishingUberSiteFeatureTitle;"

Description="$Resources:osrvcore,PublishingUberSiteFeatureDescription;"
    Version="12.0.0.0" Scope="Site"
```

```
                    xmlns="http://schemas.microsoft.com/sharepoint/">
        <ActivationDependencies>
            <ActivationDependency FeatureId="A392DA98-270B-4e85-9769-
                    04C0FDE267AA" />
            <ActivationDependency FeatureId="AEBC918D-B20F-4a11-A1DB-
                    9ED84D79C87E" />
            <ActivationDependency FeatureId="89E0306D-453B-4ec5-8D68-
                    42067CDBF98E" />
            <ActivationDependency FeatureId="D3F51BE2-38A8-4e44-BA84-
                    940D35BE1566" />
            </ActivationDependencies>
        </Feature>
```

FEATURE DEPLOYMENT

Features are deployed by first installing the Feature and then activating the Feature. Deployment requires individuals with administrative privilege since access to the SharePoint server console is required. Features are installed using either the STSADM Command Line tool or a solution package, which is covered in the last section of the chapter. Farm administrators are required for Farm and Web Application scopes and Site Collection administrators for Site and Web scope. You can also use the SharePoint API, but this is generally not something that will be used by administrators directly, or the code accessing the API will be part of the solution package that is being installed by the administrator. Once installed, activation and deactivation can be performed using the Command Line tool or the browser interface. As stated previously, the Web browser interface can only be used to activate and deactivate Features that are not hidden. Table 7.3 summarizes the different approaches for managing Feature deployment and removal.

TABLE 7.3 FEATURE MANAGEMENT OPTIONS

	STSADM	Object Model	Browser UI	Site Definition
Installation	Yes	Yes		
Uninstall	Yes	Yes		
Activate	Yes	Yes	Yes	Yes
Deactivate	Yes	Yes	Yes	

The following STSADM commands are included for reference and used to install, uninstall, activate, and deactivate a Feature using the Command-Line tool. Some of the STSADM commands were also covered in Chapter 5. By default, Features are set to be deactivated upon installation, except for those Features that are deployed as part of a site definition upon which activation may occur as part of provisioning. For STSADM help, use the following command `stsadm –help <commandname>`. Make sure to issue an IISRESET after installing or reinstalling a Feature. Features should be deactivated before they are uninstalled unless their scope is Farm or WebApplication. The Feature's folder in the 12 hive is not removed by the STSADM uninstallfeature command.

Install Feature or Reinstall Feature

```
stsadm -o installfeature –name <feature_name>
stsadm -o installfeature –name <feature_name> -force
```

Uninstall Feature

```
stsadm –o uninstallfeature –name <feature_name>
```

Activate Feature

```
stsadm -o activatefeature –name <feature_name> -url <target_site>
```

Deactivate Feature

```
stsadm -o deactivatefeature –name <feature_name> -url <target_site>
```

CREATING A NEW FEATURE

A new Feature is created by adding a subfolder to the Features directory. After creating the Feature folder, the Feature is installed and activated using the STSADM Command Line tool or through the SharePoint object model. A Feature can also be activated through the browser interface, as long as it is not a hidden Feature. Installing a Feature makes its definition and elements known throughout a server farm, and activating the Feature makes the feature available at a particular scope. The following white paper discusses the creation and deployment of a new Feature: "Creating a Custom Feature in Office SharePoint Server 2007," at http://msdn.microsoft.com/en-us/library/cc263911.aspx.Feature Stapling.

Feature Stapling provides the capability to add new functionality to existing site definitions. As we discussed in the section on Site Definitions in Table 7.1, you should not modify the site definition after it has been used to create sites. Therefore, the option of Feature Stapling provides this modification capability. Once a Feature has been associated or stapled to an existing site definition, any future site provisioning will automatically activate the stapled Feature. This is accomplished using the FeatureSiteTemplateAssociation element. Feature Stapling won't affect any sites that have already been created from the original site definition, only subsequent sites. A stapled Feature can be removed by deactivating the Feature. For a real example, open the publishingstapling.xml file that is part of the PublishingStapling Feature and notice the CAML being utilized.

Features represent a very powerful tool for customizing SharePoint sites. This includes simplifying the site definition so that it is more modular and less complex and providing an approach to selectively adding or removing functionality through activation and deactivation. There is another approach to deploying Features that is discussed in the final section of the chapter: "Solution Packages." Solutions, for short, can be utilized to deploy other customization content as well, such as Web parts. The next section provides the administrator with the knowledge for deploying and managing solution packages.

SOLUTION PACKAGES

WSS v3.0 includes new capability for deploying custom content such as Features, Web parts, site definitions, .NET assemblies, and so on, and it is called "Solution Packages." This deployment mechanism is essentially a CAB file with a .wsp filename extension (WSS solution package) that contains all the files that must be deployed on the front-end Web server and an XML-based manifest file that defines what SharePoint should do with the package components. Solution packages are designed to simplify the deployment mechanism after developers have created custom solutions.

KEY POINTS

- The solution framework achieves a number of advantages for both the administrator and the developer and these include:
  One deployment mechanism. Solution packages are the mechanism for making changes to site functionality. Deploy new solutions and upgrade existing solutions across the farm.
  Single file installation. Solutions are deployed as a single entity across all Web front-end servers in the farm. Synchronize a front-end Web server so that its state is consistent with the state of other servers in the farm.

File type inclusion flexibility. Solution packages can include .NET assemblies, Web parts and their associated definitions, code access security policies, and essentially any type of file included in the 12 hive. Assemblies can be deployed to the Global Assembly Cache (GAC) or to the \bin folder of the extended Web application.

■ Solutions include an instruction file called a "solution manifest" that tells SharePoint what to do with all the files in the package. This file is named manifest.xml, and it contains the CAML that defines the parts of a solution, including its files, assemblies, code access security, Web Parts, Features, site definitions, and other resources.

■ Developers can create the manifest.xml file based on the specific site customizations required and then create the solution package. The solution schema that governs the type and syntax of the CAML included in the manifest.xml file is covered in the WSS SDK. Once the manifest.xml file is created, it is compiled into a CAB file with all the other required files. This can be accomplished using the MAKECAB Command-Line utility. This tool requires a Diamond Directive File (.ddf file) that tells the MAKECAB tool which files to compress and include in the CAB file. Executing the MAKECAB tool using the .ddf file will generate the .wsp file ready for deployment.

Creating Solution Packages

The process for creating a solution package is covered here, "Creating a Solution Package in Windows SharePoint Services 3.0," http://msdn.microsoft.com/en-us/library/bb466225.aspx.

■ Solution deployment refers to the process of distributing, unpacking, and installing solution files to the front-end Web servers. The first step in deployment is adding the solution package to the solution store, a centralized location for solutions installed on the SharePoint farm. The second step is uniform deployment to all the front-end Web servers, which includes synchronizing the state of all Web servers so that each contains all deployed solutions. Administrators can deploy the solution to a single Web application or all Web applications across the farm. The STSADM command for adding a solution to the solution store is shown below. Once added to the store, the solution is viewable and managed from the Solution Management Web page in central administration. This page is accessible from the Operations tab under the Global Configuration section via the Solution Management link. Deployment can be scheduled for immediate or future deployment.

```
stsadm –o addsolution –filename <filename.wsp>
```

Central Administration Capability

The central administration Web site cannot add solutions to the store; it can only be used to remove solutions from the store.

■ Solutions can be upgraded once they have been deployed using the `upgrade-solution` command. This adds the solution to the store just as the `addsolution` command did, and it overwrites the existing solution after making a backup for rollback purposes. The solution will then be automatically re-deployed if the original solution was deployed. Administrators can also retract the solution using central administration or the STSADM retractsolution command.

The `addsolution`, `upgradesolution`, and `retractsolution` commands have been covered in Chapter 5, and the reader can review that discussion for more information. The solution framework represents a major improvement for deploying custom SharePoint solutions. Developers create a solution package containing all of the code and files required to implement their custom solution and administrators deploy the solution.

8 Configuring and Managing Enterprise Search

In This Chapter

- Introduction
- Shared Service Provider Architecture
- Search Administration and Management

INTRODUCTION

Deploying and configuring the MOSS Enterprise search solution requires that you be familiar with a number of the key components in the SharePoint farm. A MOSS farm consists of three server roles: Web server role, Application server role, and Database server role. As discussed in the earlier chapters, these server roles can physically reside on a single server or be split across a number of servers in a multi-server farm. Additionally, two other roles specific for delivering search functionality are the Index role and the Query role. These latter two roles are collectively referred to as the "search services." These roles can physically reside on the same physical server in a single-server deployment, or they can be split across Web and Application servers. The MOSS search engine actually consists of two different major components, the index engine and the query engine. These coincide with the Index and Query roles mentioned earlier. There are also a number of different options and features that require proper configuration in order to maximize the benefits of the search capability. This chapter will focus on "getting search up and running," as well as discuss the various features and configuration options available for implementing MOSS search, including the new features provided by the Infrastructure Update. As introduced and discussed in Chapter 3, "Installation and Configuration," the Shared Services Provider (SSP) is critical to managing MOSS services, which includes some of the search services.

Infrastructure Update

For those not familiar with the MOSS infrastructure update, please see "Availability of Infrastructure Updates" at http://blogs.msdn.com/sharepoint/archive/ 2008/07/15/announcing-availability-of-infrastructure-updates.aspx. This update provides a set of new search features. The following hotfix should also be reviewed: http://support.microsoft.com/kb/956248.

SHARED SERVICE PROVIDER ARCHITECTURE

MOSS relies very heavily on the SSP to deliver a set of core services across the farm. These services include such things as user profiles and My Sites, Forms services, Excel services, search, and the Business Data Catalog. These services are centrally managed by administrators that create and configure SSPs so that they are available across many different MOSS portal sites and WSS Web sites in the farm. An administrator assigns each Web application in the farm to an SSP, and each Web application can only be associated with one SSP. Multiple SSPs can be created, but, in general, a single farm will usually only have one SSP. From a search perspective, the SSP manages the Index server role, and it provides indexing services and index management capabilities. An SSP can only be assigned to use one Index server and a single index. Therefore, unlike the previous version of SharePoint, multiple index files cannot be utilized. The Index server will index or "crawl" your content and make it available to users.

Maximum Number of SSPs

A maximum of 20 SSPs can be created per farm, although the recommended maximum is three SSPs per farm. Search scenarios that include multiple Index servers are very infrequent, but this topic is addressed later in the chapter.

INDEX SERVER ROLE

The Index server or server role provides the indexing services for the farm. Specifically, this includes crawling and indexing content, managing when indexing occurs, which is referred to as crawl schedules, and specifying how content should be indexed by defining crawl rules.

Single Role per SSP

The Index server role is managed by a single SSP, and a single SSP can only manage one single index. The role can reside on the Web front-end server in a multi-server farm or reside with the Application server. So the indexing requirements for a single index role or SSP cannot be spread across multiple physical servers.

Content Source

Content sources represent the storage systems that contain information that is going to be crawled and indexed. This storage system is characterized by type, location, and starting address. An SSP can define up to 500 content sources. MOSS indexes content from the following content sources:

- SharePoint sites and data
- Non-SharePoint Web sites
- File shares
- Exchange Public Folders
- Line of business data from relational databases, Web services, and custom third-party storage systems using the Business Data Catalog
- Lotus Notes documents

NOTE

Indexing Lotus Notes Content

Unlike all other types of content sources, the Lotus Notes content source option does not appear in the Central Administration user interface until you have installed and configured the appropriate prerequisite software. For information about enabling this protocol handler, see "Configure Office SharePoint Server Search to crawl Lotus Notes (Office SharePoint Server 2007)," at http://technet.microsoft.com/en-us/library/cc262927.aspx.

Indexing Process

Crawling and indexing content is part of the indexing process that includes accessing and parsing content and its properties, and leads to building a content index for resolving search queries. Each SSP that is configured for search will have its own content index. The SSP content index includes an index file physically stored on the Windows file system and a property store in a SQL Server database. The index file is composed of a list of keywords obtained during the index process and a list of references to all documents in which the keyword appears, including all the positions in the document the keyword appears. Properties or metadata that are indexed during the crawl process are stored in the property store, including access control information for each item. Structurally, the property store consists of a table of properties and their values. Each row in the table corresponds to a separate document in the full-text index. The crawler account accesses individual files or pieces of content, and the keywords and metadata for the crawled content are stored in the content index. Search queries are processed by utilizing a mapping between the keywords, the metadata, and the URL of the source from which the content was crawled. During the indexing process, the indexing account accesses the stored information inside the content source through a component called a "protocol handler (PH)." A PH is required for each content source that is to be crawled. MOSS includes a number of PHs, but it also provides an extensible architecture so other PHs can be added. The PH is essentially responsible for 1) connecting to a source system utilizing the necessary protocol (such as HTTP:// or FILE://), 2) traversing the source system (the FILE:// protocol handler traverses folders, subfolders, and files, whereas the HTTP:// protocol handler follows hyperlinks), 3) identifying different types of content, such as files or Web pages, and 4) invoking an iFilter to read each type of content.

An iFilter for each type of content, such as Word files or PDF files, must be installed before indexing of that content will be enabled. An iFilter is a software component that plugs into the architecture and is responsible for opening and reading the content from the file. It also retrieves metadata that may be included in the file, such as Microsoft Office document property sheet values. Without an appropriate iFilter, file contents cannot be indexed.

As the crawl process proceeds, the PH retrieves content through the iFilter and returns two different types of data to the indexing engine: one for metadata and permissions, which is saved in the property store, and another for content that is saved to the index file. Permissions are stored in the search database and are used at query time to filter the search results so that users see only content appropriate to their permission levels.

Before content that is returned by the PH is added to the content index, word breakers are used to break the content stream into words. Noise words, such as "the" or "it," are removed since they are so common that there is limited value in indexing them. The noise word list can be customized using the noise word files.

Content is indexed on a frequency defined by the Crawl Schedule, which is one of the configuration options in the SSP. The frequency of indexing affects the relevancy of your search results and load on the SharePoint servers. When your content changes, it will only be retrievable after it has been indexed. Frequent indexing increases the load on the server farm and will affect the architecture necessary for meeting search requirements. An Incremental index only indexes content that has changed since the previous index process, while a Full index crawls all content.

Crawl Rules define a set of instructions for how content should be indexed. For example, an administrator could specify that content within a particular path be excluded from indexing.

32-Bit Versus 64-Bit

MOSS can be purchased in either 32-bit or 64-bit versions; the latter is recommended for performance and scalability reasons. If you install the 64-bit version of MOSS on your Index server, then you must ensure that you use the 64-bit version of the protocol handler as well as the 64-bit version of any iFilter.

Content Index

Crawled content is stored in the content index and the search database in SQL Server. The content index represents a full-text catalog that is physically stored on the file system. Only one logical full-text catalog file is required on the Index server, even though indexed content may come from many different sources. Indexed properties are also stored in the full-text catalog in a tokenized format just like the indexed content.

The full-text catalog file on an Index server can be viewed as a single logical file, even though it is actually managed as a series of files, which includes a main master index file and a series of shadow index files. This approach enables small shadow files to be created and updated while indexing is occurring, which is a much more efficient process than having to update the larger master index file when new content is indexed. When the combined size of the shadow indexes reaches about 10 percent of the size of the master index file, they are all merged into the master, and then new shadow index files will be created.

Index Propagation

The index file is propagated to the query servers in the farm and is used to respond to actual search queries requested by users. Index propagation to the Query server only occurs if the Query server role and Index server role reside on different physical servers. If a single server is configured to perform both the Query Server role and the Index server role, index propagation does not happen.

The index is propagated continuously to the Query server while crawls are occurring and the full-text catalog file is being updated on the Index server. This is in contrast to the previous versions of SharePoint technologies where index propagation did not begin until the crawl was fully complete. Continuous propagation minimizes latency by ensuring that the Query servers always have a relatively fresh copy of the index from which to serve user queries. Continuous propagation occurs automatically and does not require any administrator configuration or management.

Adding an Index Server

Adding an Index server to the farm is done through the Central Administration Web site and is discussed in the following steps. This process is not a difficult one, but a lot of planning is required to ensure the best configuration possible as the discussion will highlight.

1. From Central Administration select the Operations tab and then click the Services on server link to reveal the Services on Server Web page, as shown in Figure 8.1.

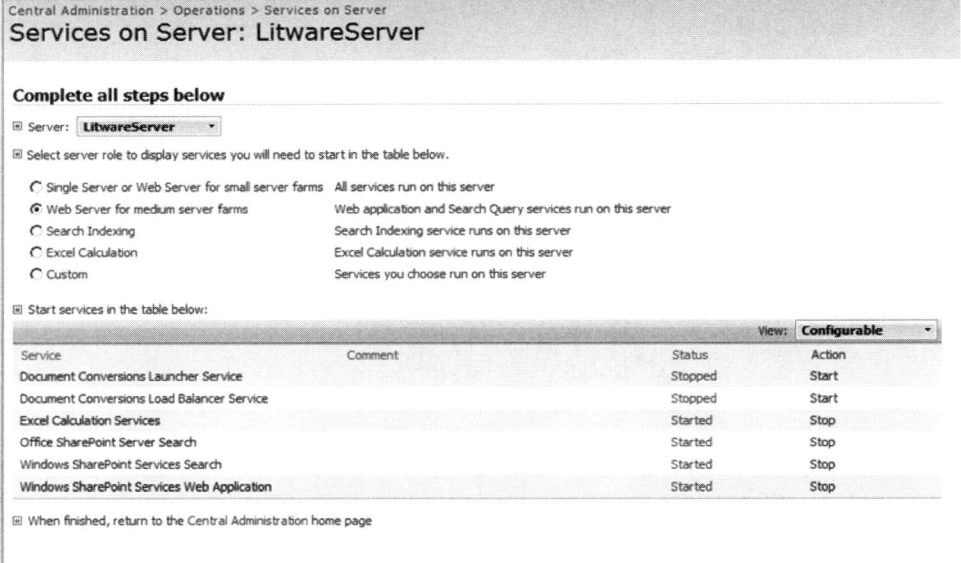

FIGURE 8.1
Services on Server Web page in Central Administration.

2. Choose the name of the server you want to become the Index server by selecting the inverted triangle in the upper-left corner and selecting the Change Server option. Select your server from the list of servers. After you've chosen your server, you will be returned to the Services on Server page.

3. Start the Office SharePoint Server Search service by clicking the Start link to the right of the Office SharePoint Server Search link, which will take you to the Configure Office SharePoint Server Search Service Settings on server Web page, as shown in Figure 8.2.

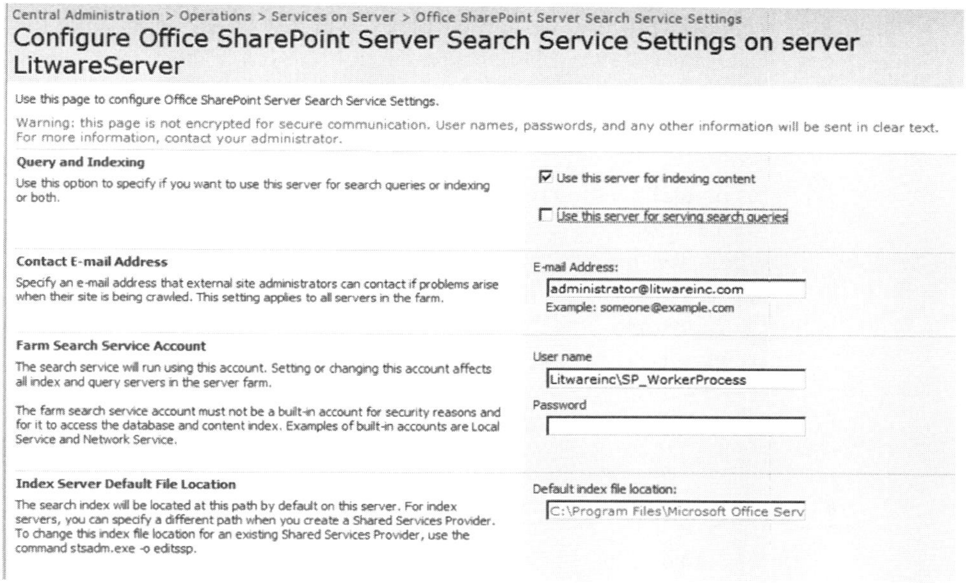

FIGURE 8.2
Configure Office SharePoint Server Search Service Settings on server Web page.

4. Select Use this server for indexing content. The contact email address and the Farm Search Service Account should already be populated. If not, then add this information. The Index Server Default File Location option is likely set to the C: drive and not available for change (it should be grayed out). The index file location can be configured as part of creating an SSP.

5. Make sure that the Indexer Performance setting is set to Partly reduced, which is the default setting. A lower value reduces the speed at which items are indexed, while increasing the value will affect performance of servers in the farm. For example, increasing indexing speed places increased demand on the Index server, the writing of metadata to the search database becomes more frequent, and the requests to Web front-end servers also increase. For a more in-depth discussion on setting the Indexer Performance level, the reader should see http://technet.microsoft.com/en-us/library/cc788930.aspx.

6. Choosing the proper setting for the Web Front End and Crawling option is dependent on the number of servers in your server farm and the amount of content being indexed. MOSS supports two options: Use all Web front-end computers for crawling and Use a dedicated Web front-end for crawling. As we've discussed, the indexing process produces a lot of network traffic between the Index server, the Front-end Web server, and the Database server. When crawling content, the Index server sends requests to the Front-end Web server that retrieves the content and sends it back to the Index server. When your server farm is configured to Use all Front-end Web servers for crawling, the Index server sends requests to each Front-end Web server in the farm. This produces quite a bit of traffic since these requests include the start address from which to start crawling, the file types to include, and how many levels deep from the starting address to crawl. For best performance, the recommendation is to configure the Index server as the dedicated Front-end Web server for crawling if your Index server has the memory capacity for both roles. By using the same server as both the Index server and dedicated Front-end Web server, you im-prove crawl performance and reduce network traffic by eliminating the need for the Index server to send requests to a different server when crawling con-tent. If this is not possible, you can use a different server in your server farm. In general, the recommendation is to use a dedicated Front-end Web server for crawling in a three-server farm or greater, especially if you are crawling a server farm that contains more than 500 gigabytes (GB) of content. In this case, your dedicated Web Front-end would not be a part of a load-balanced cluster. There are two ways to configure a dedicated Front-end Web server for crawling: 1) use the Configure Office SharePoint Server Search Service Settings on server page in the Central Administration Web site, or 2) update the server's Hosts file directly. The reader is encouraged to review the fol-lowing white paper before choosing the best approach for configuring a ded-icated Front-end Web server for crawling, http://technet.microsoft.com/ en-us/library/ cc179342.aspx.

7. Once you've chosen the setting for the Web Front-end and Crawling option, click the OK button at the bottom of the page, which will return you to the Configure Office SharePoint Server Search Service Settings Web page.

8. The last step is starting the WSS search service. In a MOSS farm, the WSS search service is responsible for indexing the help system and providing search capability within the help windows. It is customary to enable the WSS search service on the same server that holds the index role, since its pri-mary function is indexing. To start the WSS search service, click the Start link beneath the Action column, which should take you to the Configure Windows SharePoint Services Search Service Settings on server Web page,

as shown in Figure 8.3. For the Service Account option, you can utilize the same account that was used for the Office SharePoint Server Search service. The account specified will be added to the local security group WSS_WPG and granted the Log on as a service local security policy.

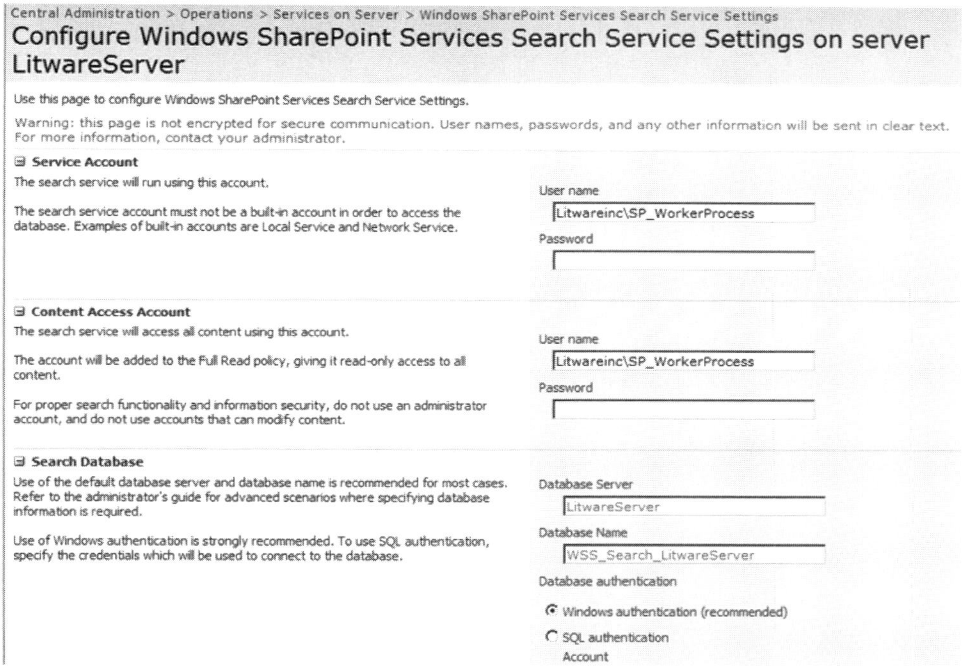

Central Administration > Operations > Services on Server > Windows SharePoint Services Search Service Settings

Configure Windows SharePoint Services Search Service Settings on server LitwareServer

Use this page to configure Windows SharePoint Services Search Service Settings.

Warning: this page is not encrypted for secure communication. User names, passwords, and any other information will be sent in clear text. For more information, contact your administrator.

Service Account
The search service will run using this account.

The search service account must not be a built-in account in order to access the database. Examples of built-in accounts are Local Service and Network Service.

User name
Litwareinc\SP_WorkerProcess
Password

Content Access Account
The search service will access all content using this account.

The account will be added to the Full Read policy, giving it read-only access to all content.

For proper search functionality and information security, do not use an administrator account, and do not use accounts that can modify content.

User name
Litwareinc\SP_WorkerProcess
Password

Search Database
Use of the default database server and database name is recommended for most cases. Refer to the administrator's guide for advanced scenarios where specifying database information is required.

Use of Windows authentication is strongly recommended. To use SQL authentication, specify the credentials which will be used to connect to the database.

Database Server
LitwareServer

Database Name
WSS_Search_LitwareServer

Database authentication

◉ Windows authentication (recommended)

○ SQL authentication
Account

FIGURE 8.3
Configure Windows SharePoint Services Search Service Settings on server Web page.

9. The Content Access Account is used by the protocol handler to read the content that is indexed. As in step 8, you can reuse the same account as the MOSS search service. This account will be given read access to the content.

10. The default settings should suffice for the Search Database option, including the use of Windows authentication.

11. The Indexing Schedule option should be set to Daily during a low usage time. Since the help system's content isn't going to be changing, there is no need to index more frequently. Although you may be tempted to start the service, create the index, and then stop the service, this is not recommended since the index will be deleted, and the help system's search capability will not be available.

12. Click the OK button to complete the setup. This completes the setup for a new Index server.

The Index server is responsible for indexing content so that the content can be searched or queried by SharePoint users. Search requests or queries are executed by retrieving the search request from the Query server. The Query server is managed at the farm level, unlike the Index server, which is managed by the SSP. The Query server role is described in the next section.

Crawled Properties and Managed Properties

Information that is indexed by SharePoint usually contains two different types of content: the content that comprises the bulk of the document or Web page and properties that are also part of the document. Both types of content will be indexed, and the latter are referred to as "Crawled Properties." Each different type of content exposes a different number and type of properties. For example, file shares expose properties such as Modified Date, whereas SharePoint lists and libraries can present many different properties of varying data types. Also, some file types, like text files, do not contain property sheets, whereas Office documents present extensible property sheets. When content gets crawled, properties (or "metadata" as it is sometimes referred to) is collected and stored by the crawler in the property store, which is one of the databases under the control of the SSP. During the search request process, content that includes crawled property values that match the query terms will be returned as part of the results. Site owners can have some control over what properties are indexed by configuring the Search settings for fields Web page, which is accessible from the Searchable columns link on the Site Settings page. This provides a way to protect potentially sensitive information, such as employee salaries or patient details, from being exposed during searches.

Crawled properties can be mapped to Managed Properties. Managed properties represent a set of properties that is mapped to one or more crawled properties and provide several advantages during the search process. For example, you could map a managed property called "Product" to three different content sources, one that specifies a Products indexed property and two others that specify Prod and ProductInfo. The benefits of this approach are twofold: 1) managed properties can be used as property filters during searches so that items from multiple sources will be returned where the crawled property that maps to the Managed Property contains the value in the filter, and 2) scopes can be created based on property filters. Creating managed properties will be discussed later in the chapter.

QUERY SERVER ROLE

The Query Server or Query role is responsible for performing and managing search queries. User search requests or queries, as they are called, are processed using the file index from the crawl process and the search database. When a user makes a search request from a portal or SharePoint Web site, the Web server contacts the Query server to process the request using information contained in the index file (the Web server may also be the Query server if it's hosting the Query role). The Web server also contacts the database server to retrieve property values and access control lists (ACLs). The Query server processes the request, filtering the search results based on the ACLs for the individual user making the request (a process known as "security trimming"), and the results are returned to the Web front-end to be displayed to the user. An exception to this process occurs when a user is making a property search. In this case, the Web Front-end can satisfy the query using the search database without using the full-text catalog so the Query server does not need to be contacted.

Multiple Query Servers

Multiple Query servers can be added to a multi-server farm, up to a recommended maximum of eight servers (theoretical limit of 32), which provides the ability to spread the query load and improve performance (scale out). This is only possible if the server hosting the Query role does not also host the index role, as was mentioned in the previous section.

Index Management

Index files are propagated from the Index server to all Query servers in the farm. File propagation occurs continuously while the Index server is indexing content and building the index file, providing a more efficient mechanism. As with Index servers, the full-text catalog is actually managed by the Query servers as a main master index file and a series of shadow index files. When the combined size of the shadow indexes reaches about 10 percent of the size of the master index file, they are all merged into the master, and then new shadow index files will be created. The Query server has the ability to manage the collective set of files, including the master index file and multiple shadow indexes so that queries can be still be satisfied based on the entire index set.

Adding a Query Server

Adding a Query server is very similar to the steps taken to add an Index server. The following steps will add a Query server to the MOSS farm.

1. From Central Administration, select the Operations tab and then click the Services on server link to reveal the Services on Server Web page, as previously shown in Figure 8.1.
2. Choose the name of the server you want to become the Query server by selecting the inverted triangle in the upper-left corner and selecting the Change Server option. Select your server from the list of servers. After you've chosen your server, you will be returned to Services on Server page.

3. Start the Office SharePoint Server Search service by clicking the Start link to the right of the Office SharePoint Server Search link, which will take you to the Configure Office SharePoint Server Search Service Settings on server Web page, as previously shown in Figure 8.2.

4. On the Configure Office SharePoint Server Search Service Settings on server Web page, in the Query and Indexing section, select the option for serving search queries.

5. In the Contact E-mail Address section, specify someone whom site owners can contact if problems occur when sites are being crawled. This is also the email address that will occur in the logs as SharePoint crawls remote content.

6. In the Farm Search Service Account section, provide a name and password for a domain account using the format domain_name\user_name. This account will be granted read access to content and be the default access account. It is critical that this account not have any elevated privileges, or content that should not be indexed, may be indexed.

7. The Query Server Default File Location section contains the file system address that will be used to store the index files when they are propagated from the Index server. The default location is c:\Program Files\Microsoft Office Servers\12.0\Data\Office Server\Applications. Because of the potential size of this file, the recommendation is not to store this on the C: drive. To change the location, specify the new path in the text box provided.

8. The final step is to specify an account with administrative privileges. This is a one-time requirement since SharePoint needs to create a file share that maps to the location of the index file created in step 7. The Farm Search Service Account and the WSS_Admin_WPG local security group are given full control of the share.

9. Click the Start button at the bottom of the page to complete the process.

As we've seen, part of the search information is stored inside of the search database in SQL Server. The next section discusses the Database server role and how it pertains to search capability.

DATABASE SERVER ROLE

Search indexing and query processing relies heavily on the search database, which resides inside SQL Server. The search database stores configuration information such as content source definitions, crawl schedules, crawl rules, and search scopes. Besides configuration data, the Database server also stores data that is retrieved during the crawl process, such as managed property information and access control lists. Managed properties are stored in the Property Store table in the search database. Access control lists are also stored in the search database, so that they can be retrieved at query time to enable security trimming by Web servers.

WEB SERVER ROLE

This role accepts the search request and then responds by returning the results to the users or applications making the request. The end-to-end search request process is described next. In a multi-server farm, this role could be fulfilled by more than one Front-end Web server.

End-to-End Search Request Process

The first step in the process requires aggregating the search request information. This includes collecting information about the terms or keywords specified in the request and obtaining contextual information, such as the identity of the process issuing the request and the location the request is originating. The Query engine is responsible for processing queries from the Search Center (which we will discuss later) and any query using the application programming interface (API). Once the request information has been collected, the query is passed to a wordbreaker, and a stemmer. Word breaking isolates ("breaks down") the important words out of the query, while stemming adds word variations such as running, runs, and so on for the query "run" (stemming is not enabled by default). Once these steps are complete, which improve the relevance and effectiveness of the results, the refined query is passed to the content index and the results are security-trimmed. Once trimmed, the results are rendered within search Web parts or returned to the calling application. Security trimming ensures that 1) users are not prompted for authentication only to be denied access when they click a result for which they do not have permission, and 2) users are not made aware of even the existence of potentially sensitive information during the search process. Therefore, users only see results for which they have permissions.

   This portion of the chapter has covered the architecture and key components of an enterprise search solution and briefly discussed how to add an Index server and Query server, two key server roles, to the SharePoint farm. The next section discusses in more detail the overall administration and management of the MOSS search solution.

SEARCH ADMINISTRATION AND MANAGEMENT

Search is managed at several different locations by the SharePoint administrator, and each of these locations or levels impacts the search deployment in various ways. The different levels of administration include Server, farm, SSP, and Site Collection. The previous section discussed server-level changes when the Index and Query servers were added to the farm. The Central Administration Web site and the SSP Web site provide additional configuration options that impact various levels in the search solution. These are discussed next.

FARM-LEVEL ADMINISTRATION

The Manage Search Service Web page is accessed from the Search section on the Application tab in the Central Administration Web site and is shown in Figure 8.4. There are three different sections on this page, which include Farm-Level Search Settings, Query and Index Servers, and Shared Service Providers with Search Enabled. The latter two sections are informational only, but the first provides the ability to configure several different search options, which include Farm-level search settings and Crawler impact rules.

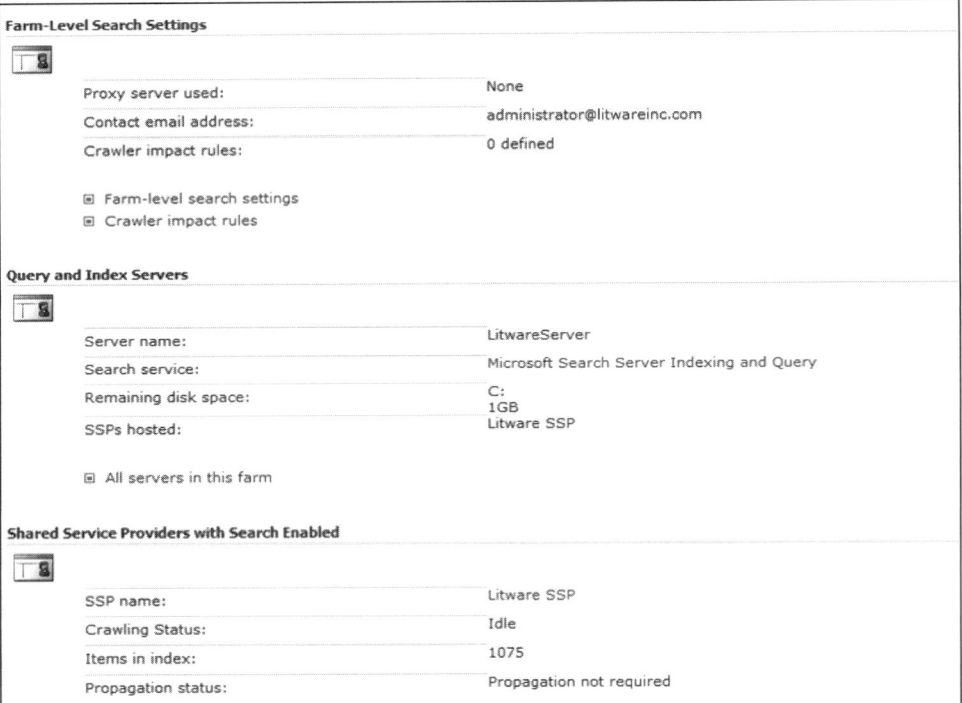

FIGURE 8.4
Manage Search Service Web page.

Farm-Level Search Settings

The Manage Farm-Level Search Settings Web page, as shown in Figure 8.5, has options for configuring contact email address, proxy server settings, timeout settings, and SSL (Secure Socket Layer) certification warnings. Some of these options are similar to those we have already been exposed to, while others have not yet been discussed.

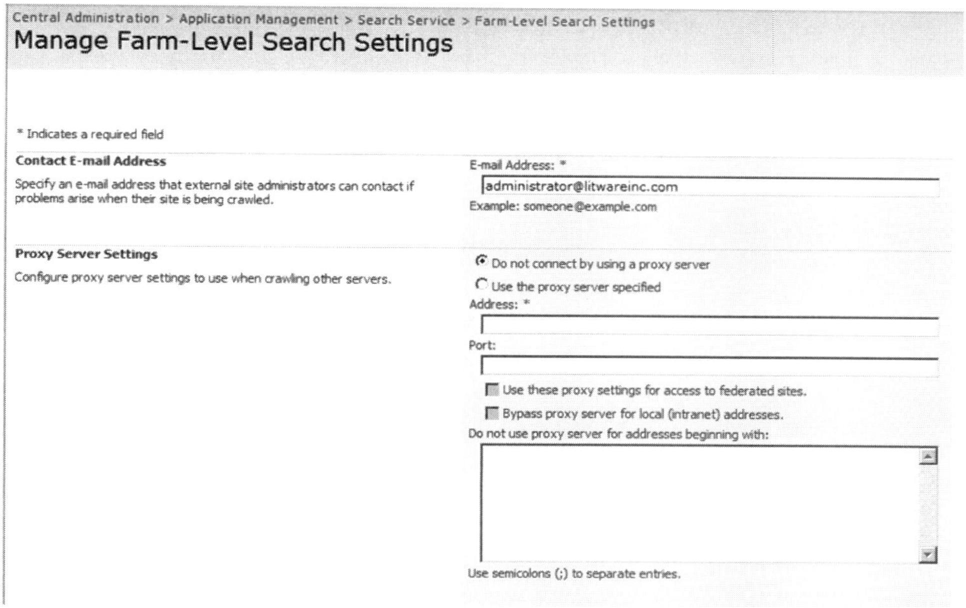

FIGURE 8.5
Manage Farm-Level Search Settings Web page.

Configure Settings

The Contact E-mail Address option is the same option we specified earlier when we configured the Office SharePoint Server Search Service Setting on server Web page. Recall this is the email address or distribution list that external site administrators can contact if problems arise when their site is being crawled. It could be modified at this location as well, if necessary.

The option to configure a proxy server to access and crawl a content source is available under Proxy Server Settings. The default value of Do not connect by using a proxy server is generally the option of choice. The Address can be either the NetBIOS name or the IP address of the proxy server, while the listening port value is specified for the Port option. The access to federated sites option is new with the infrastructure update to MOSS, and, if checked, specifies that the server should be used for querying federated search sources. There are actually two different ways to specify proxy settings. The first is the approach we just mentioned, and it will apply to all federated locations. This is the recommended approach if you only have one proxy server for querying federated sources. The second approach utilizes the web.config file of the SharePoint site hosting the federated location, allowing you to specify different proxy settings for different federated locations. These settings are the default proxy server settings used by MOSS unless the proxy server was configured using the first approach, and then those options will take precedence.

It is also possible to use the proxy server for querying some content sources but not for others. If this is desirable, then check the box Bypass proxy server for local (intranet) addresses and enter the addresses, which should be accessed directly without using the proxy server.

Anytime a content source is accessed, there is an opportunity for connection problems, and the timeout settings specify how long the index process should wait. The default value is 60 seconds. One might think that it would help to increase its value, but keep in mind that having the index process wait longer will increase the overall indexing time. If you notice that there are timeout errors in the crawl logs, then this is the time to increase this value.

The indexing process may produce certificate errors when attempting to access secure content via HTTPS. Select the Ignore SSL certificate name warnings check box if you want to trust that sites are legitimate, even if their certificate names are not exact matches.

Crawler Impact Rules

As the name implies, these rules affect the impact that the crawler has on a remote content source, and as a general rule should be implemented when crawling external servers. SharePoint indexing could put a heavy load on a remote server, which could affect the performance and responsiveness of that server, which could lead to access being disabled. Crawler impact rules enable administrators with the capability to manage this load. Each rule can specify a single URL or a block of URLs using wildcard characters in the URL path. After the URLs are defined, you can then specify how many simultaneous requests for pages will be made to the specified URL, or you can choose to request only one document at a time and wait a number of seconds that you choose between requests. Initially, your installation will not have any crawler impact rules defined so you will need to create them. The following section discusses creating new rules. Keep in mind that you must have farm administrator permissions to complete the following steps.

Creating a New Rule

1. On the Manage Search Service page in the Farm-Level Search Settings section, click Crawler impact rules.
2. On the Crawler Impact Rules page, click Add Rule, which will display the Add Crawler Impact Rule Web page, as shown in Figure 8.6.

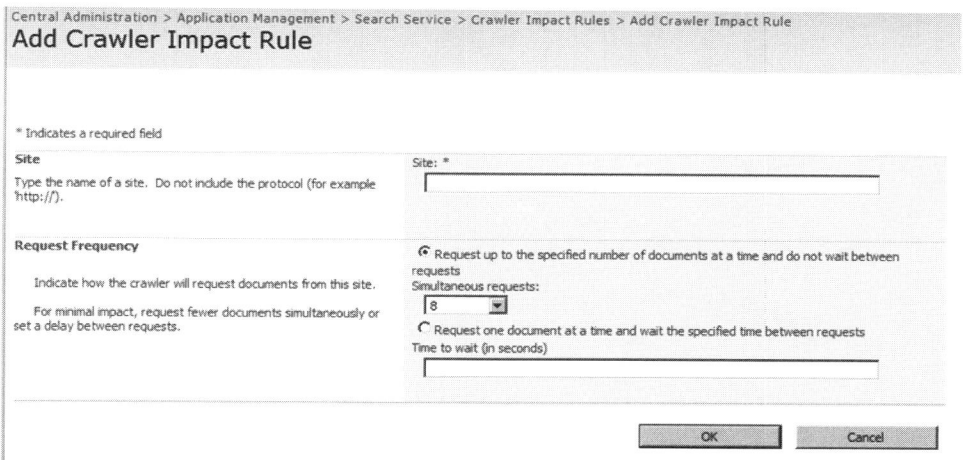

FIGURE 8.6
Add Crawler Impact Rule Web page.

3. In the Site section in the Site box, type the site name that will be associated with this crawler impact rule. Do not include the protocol when typing the URL; for example, do not include http:// for a Web site or file:// for a file share. You could type *.com to have the rule apply to all .com sites. The different wildcard characters that can be used in the site name are in Table 8.1.

TABLE 8.1 WILDCARD CHARACTERS FOR CRAWL RULES

Site Name with Wildcard Character	Outcome
*	Applies the rule to all sites.
*.com	Applies the rule to all Web sites with a .com domain.
?	Applies the rule to sites with a single character difference in the name. For example *.demo?.com would apply to all sites in the domains *.demo1.com and *.demo5.com.

4. You have two different choices for the Request Frequency: Simultaneous requests or Time to wait. If you choose the former, then select Request up to the specified number of documents at a time and do not wait between requests,

and then use the Simultaneous requests list to define how many documents should be requested. The value can be: 1, 2, 4, 8, 16, 32, or 64. The alternative choice is to select Request one document at a time and wait the specified time between requests. The delay (in seconds) between requests must be in the range of 1 to 1,000. When this option is selected, the Office SharePoint Server Search service makes one request per site at one time, and then it waits for the specified amount of time before making the next request.

5. Click OK to complete the rule. The completed rule is shown in Figure 8.7. You should notice from the figure that rules have an Order associated with them. Since this is the first and only rule, the order is of little significance. When more than one rule is present, site name expressions are evaluated in order, and this is the purpose for providing the ability to re-order rules using the Order drop-down menu. Since expressions are evaluated in order, you should generally order the crawler impact rules from most-specific to most-general because the first matching rule is applied. For example, * must always be the last rule in the list, or any rules listed later will not be applied.

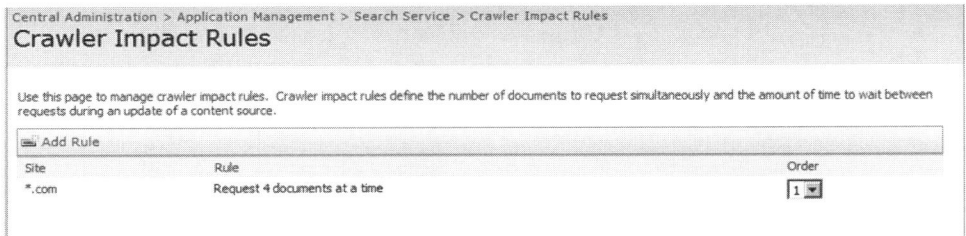

FIGURE 8.7
Completed impact rule shown on the Crawler Impact Rules Web page.

Crawler Impact Rules

Crawler Impact Rules take precedence over Indexer Performance Settings discussed earlier. Any new rule created while a crawl is in progress becomes effective as soon as it is saved and will apply to any content that has not already been crawled.

Crawler impact rules should be set based on the performance and capacity of your servers. This knowledge is known or could be determined for internal Web sites. For external sites, this knowledge will generally not be known, which makes setting the crawl rules more difficult. Therefore, rules should be applied for all external sites using the mindset of crawling too little rather than too much. This way you can minimize the risk that you will lose access to the external site or have your bandwidth limited.

Initially, set the rules to minimize impact while still crawling enough content and crawling frequently enough to ensure the most up-to-date index as possible. These settings can then be adjusted after you have more experience.

SSP-Level Administration

A Shared Services Provider (SSP) provides a common set of centralized services to the Web applications and their Web sites across the MOSS farm—specifically, the SSP provides personalization services, Excel services, the Business Data Catalog, and search services. The search services provide a single index of all content across all sites and other content sources. When the MOSS farm was installed, the default SSP is created as one of the first tasks once the software is installed. The search services provided by the SSP will apply to all Web applications that are associated with the SSP. Each Web application is associated with one and only one SSP. Therefore, the SSP search services propagate to all site collections and sites, and they cannot be disabled at the site collection or site level. For the following discussion, it is assumed that an SSP has already been created as part of the installation process as discussed in Chapter 3, and we will proceed with configuring the SSP so that the search services can be fully utilized. The discussion will focus on only configuring the search-related options.

Configuring and Utilizing the SSP for Search

The Shared Services Administration Web site contains a section called "Search," which contains three different options: Search Administration, Search Settings, and Search Usage Reports. These three different sections contain quite a few different options that pertain to search configuration, and it can appear somewhat daunting at first so we will begin with a goal. Let's begin with the basic steps for configuring Search so "we can get it up and running." The basic configuration can be broken down into five administrative steps, which include the following:

1. Start the MOSS search service. This was previously demonstrated when we discussed adding an Index and Query server.
2. Create an SSP. This was done as part of the initial installation covered in Chapter 3.
3. Configure the Content Sources. Content sources represent the data stores that contain the data that will be indexed. In a previous section, we briefly discussed the different sources, such as file servers, Web sites, SharePoint Sites, and so on.
4. Configure Indexing and Scheduling. This will allow you to initiate your first crawl so you can perform your first search requests.

5. Build a Search Center. The Search Center is used as a centralized location for executing search requests and viewing the results.

We will begin with step 3, and this process begins with configuring the content sources defined in the SSP.

Configuring the Content Source

Content sources represent content that should be crawled by the search service, along with crawl information. Specifically, they contain a collection of start addresses, and they also specify settings that define the crawl behavior and the schedule on which the content will be crawled. One valuable change from previous versions of SharePoint technology is that multiple start addresses for a single content source are now allowed, which reduces the number of sources that are required and simplifies the management process. MOSS provides several different types of content sources by default. These include content sources for SharePoint information, non-SharePoint Web sites, file shares, Exchange public folders, and line-of-business data using the Business Data Catalog (BDC). Other types of content can be indexed by creating a custom content source using a custom protocol handler or using the BDC if the content sources exposes its content via a Web service or .NET provider. A Lotus Notes content source is also available, but it is not configured by default.

Content sources are configured by selecting the Search Settings link beneath the Search heading on the Shared Services Administration Web page. This should take you to the Configure Search Settings Web page, as shown in Figure 8.8.

This page has several different options, but we are going to focus on the content sources and crawl schedule options. Navigate to the Manage Content Sources Web page, as illustrated in Figure 8.9, by clicking the link labeled Content sources and crawl schedules. By default, one content source is configured, the Local Office Share-Point Server Sites content source, and this source is called the "default content source." Shared services administrators can use this content source to crawl and index all content in all Web applications associated with the SSP. Therefore, this source includes all content that is stored in all the corresponding site collections and sites, as well as user profiles. (We will discuss user profiles and their configuration in Chapter 9, "Personalization and People Search.")

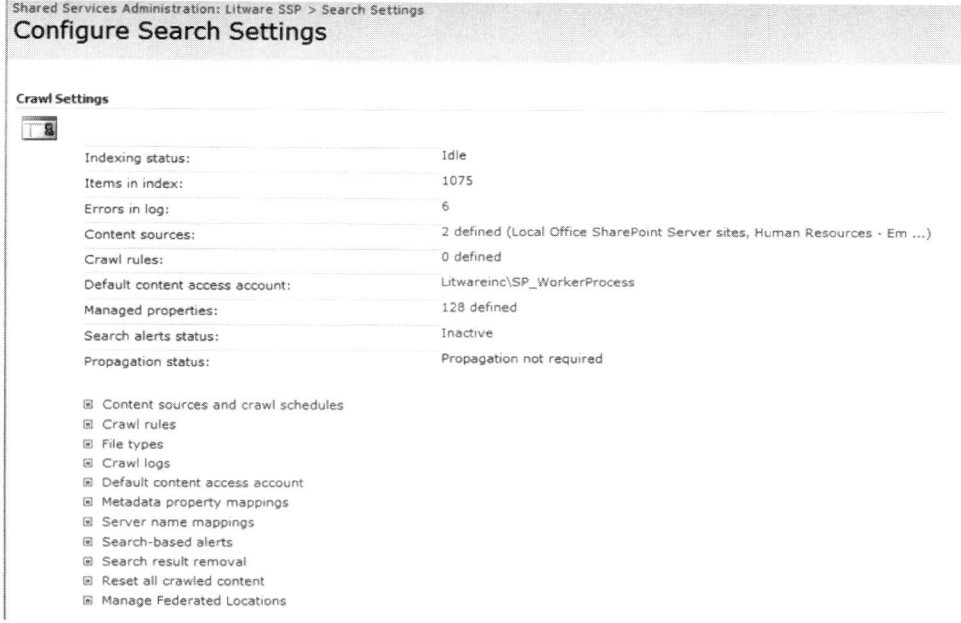

FIGURE 8.8
Configure Search Settings Web page.

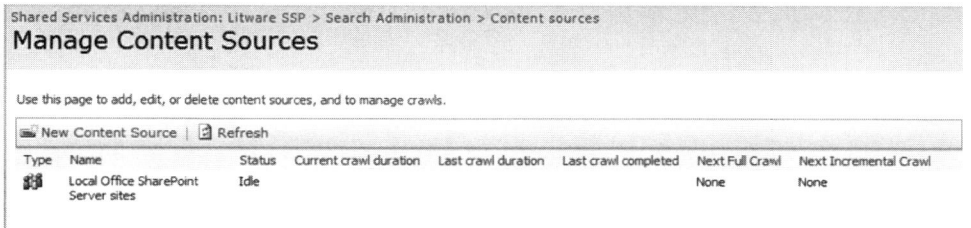

FIGURE 8.9
Manage Content Sources Web page.

We can view the details of the default content source or edit the source by hovering over the name and clicking the drop-down arrow that will reveal a list of menu options, as shown in Figure 8.10. By choosing the Edit option, the Edit Content Source Web page is revealed and displayed in Figures 8.11a and b.

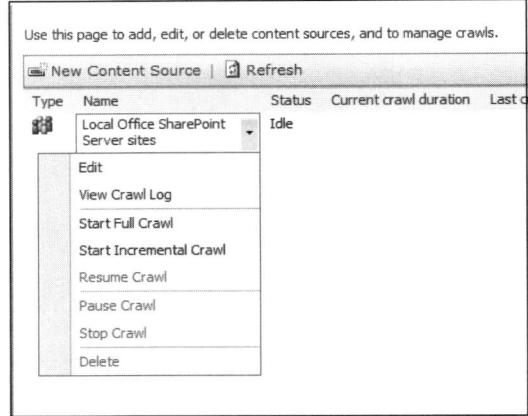

FIGURE 8.10
Options menu that defines what actions can be
taken against the content source.

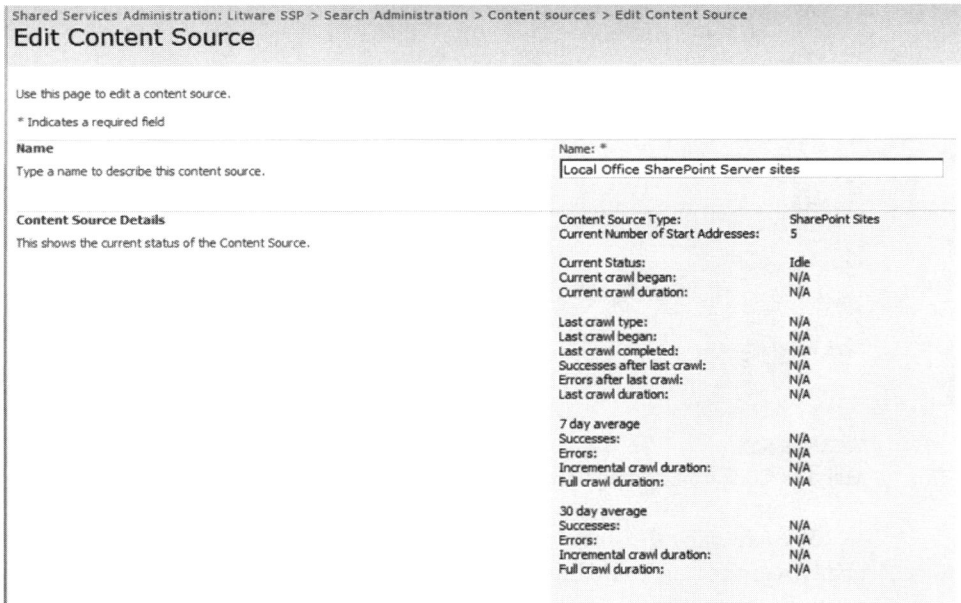

FIGURE 8.11a
Content Source name and details section.

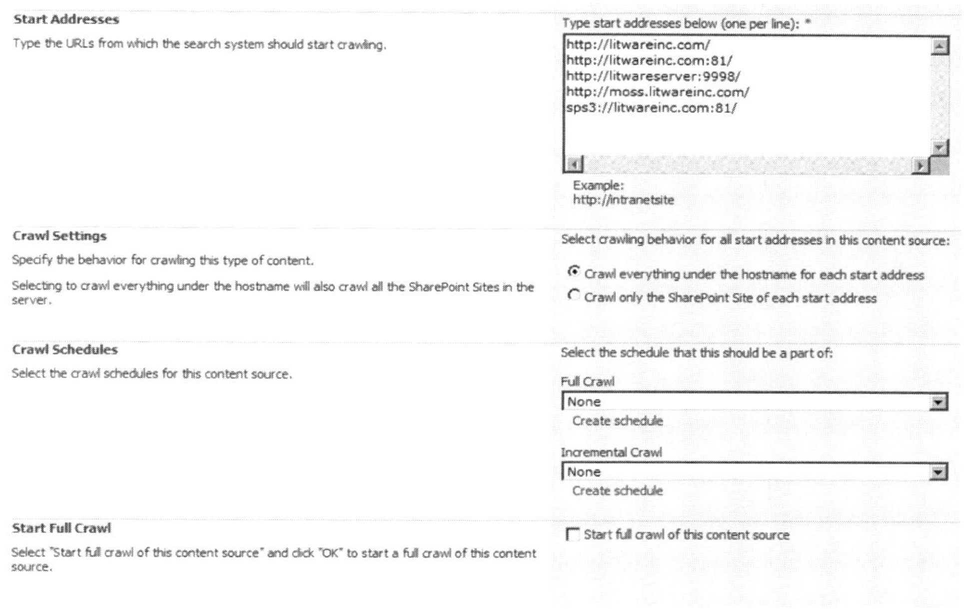

FIGURE 8.11b
Additional settings for the content source.

As can be seen in Figure 8.11a, there are a lot of details about the content source and the last crawl process in the section titled "Content Source Details." Take a minute and review all of the information presented. Figure 8.11b displays the remainder of the page and contains information for the start addresses, crawl settings, and crawl schedule, along with the ability to initiate a full crawl. You should note that several start addresses have already been added to the list. By default, MOSS adds the start address (in this case a URL) of each top-level site in the Web application that is associated with this SSP. This content source is dynamically updated as you create new sites and site collections. The Crawl Settings section allows you to specify whether to crawl all sites in the site collection contained in the Web application or only the top-level site in the site collection. Generally, you would accept the default value of Crawl everything under the hostname for each start address. The last configuration option allows you to define the schedule for crawling content. Content can be indexed by configuring a full crawl, an incremental crawl, or both. Before we configure the crawl schedule and the indexing process, let's take a brief side road to discuss creating and utilizing non-SharePoint content sources. Then we will return to the indexing process.

Other Content Sources

The default content source is ready and available without any configuration and provides the mechanism for indexing SharePoint content. SharePoint extends this capability by providing content sources for information that is stored outside of SharePoint, so this external content can be monitored and retrieved as part of the enterprise search process. Let's take a look at the available content sources that can be configured using the default installation as the context. Access the Manage Content Sources Web page by clicking the Content Sources link in the left-hand side navigation. Then click the New Content Source button to reveal the page shown in Figure 8.12.

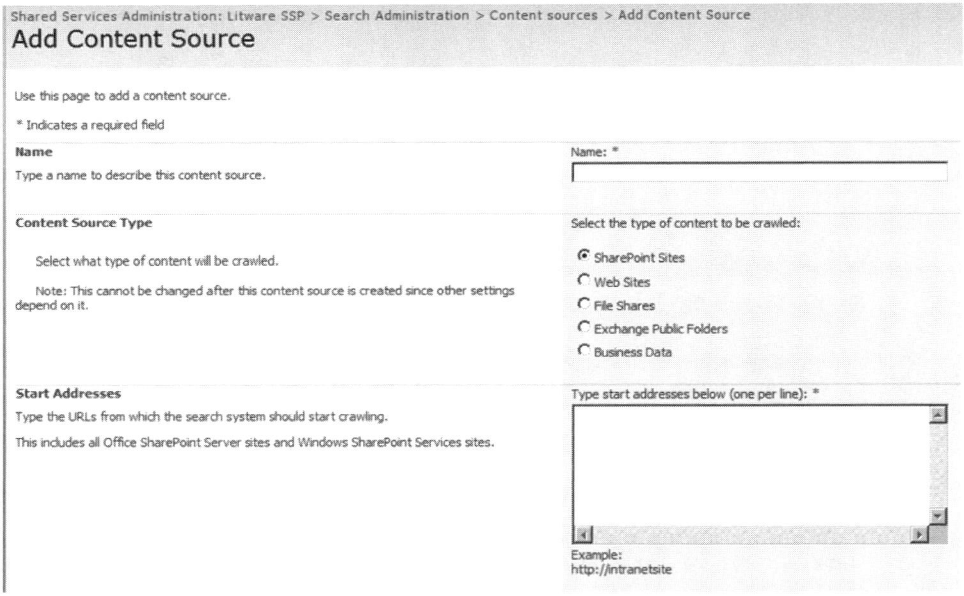

FIGURE 8.12
Add Content Source Web page.

You'll notice a lot of similarity between Figure 8.12 and Figure 8.11b, with the exception of the Content Source Type selection. The SharePoint site's content source we have discussed previously since that is the type for the default content source.

Selecting the Web site's content source exposes new Crawl Settings options so that you can crawl external, non-SharePoint Web sites. If the external site requires a custom login, this can be accomplished using crawl rules. As can be seen from Figure 8.12, we can specify that crawling remain within the server of each start address and not index any linked content on a different physical server. We can also specify that only the first page of each start address be indexed. The Custom option allows you to specify page depth and server hops. Limit Page Depth determines how many linked pages deep the crawler will go to index processed content. Limit Server Hops controls how many hops to other Web sites should be included in the indexing process. Clearly, Unlimited may not be the best choice for either of the options, so choose the proper level based on the best information at hand, keeping in mind that it can be revised once you have more experience indexing the external sites.

File shares can be indexed using the default choice: The folder and all subfolders of each start address or only the starting address folder. Crawl rules will also provide additional granular capability by allowing certain paths to be excluded (more on this later). Indexing Exchange public folders has similar options to indexing file shares, with the same logic being applicable to both.

The Business Data Catalog (BDC) is the last Content Source option. This option may not be available in your specific installation unless you have purchased the Enterprise Client Access License. The BDC can access any external data source that exposes its data through a .NET provider mechanism or a Web service. The use of the BDC content source requires that you have already created and installed the appropriate application definition files (ADF), which are used by the BDC to access external data sources. A discussion of the BDC and its proper use is beyond the scope of this chapter, but the interested reader should see the book titled *Inside the Index and Search Engines* by Patrick Tisseghem and Lars Fastrup, for an excellent coverage of this topic. If BDC applications have been added to your server, you will see them listed beneath the Crawl selected applications option. This completes the discussion on all of the preconfigured content sources available by default. One other option not listed by default is the content source for indexing Lotus Notes content. The following resource provides the necessary information for configuring MOSS search to index these type of content sources: http://technet.microsoft.com/en-us/library/cc179399.aspx. Now that we have a good understanding of content sources, let's return to the configuration of the indexing process.

Configure Indexing

The indexing process is initiated by either manually starting the process or creating a schedule that determines when content will be crawled. The next section covers crawl schedules and their creation.

Crawl Schedules

SSP administrators need to decide how often content is crawled. As we saw from earlier figures, we can configure a different crawl schedule for each content source, giving us maximum flexibility. The larger the volume of content, as well as the type of content that is being crawled, the more likely it is that you will need different schedules. Some reasons for crawling content on different schedules include: 1) content that is updated more frequently, 2) content that is hosted on slower servers separately from content crawled on faster host servers, and 3) content crawling that is scheduled to accommodate downtimes and periods of peak usage. Even though all the necessary information for establishing the best crawl schedule is seldom known, it is always a good idea to consider as many factors as possible.

Full and Incremental Crawl Schedules

Crawl schedules can be configured independently for each content source. Each content source can be configured for a time to do a full crawl and a separate time to do an incremental crawl. A full crawl must be run for a particular content source before you can run an incremental crawl. If you choose an incremental crawl for content that has not yet been crawled, the system performs a full crawl.

During a full crawl, all content in a given content source will be crawled, even if the content already exists in the index. A full crawl must be initiated for each content source individually. Note that using the Start all crawls link on the Manage Content Sources page results in all content sources being crawled using an incremental crawl, unless the system detects that a full crawl is required. An incremental crawl will index content that does not already exist in the index—content that does exist in the index but has been updated since the last crawl. An incremental crawl also removes content from the index that no longer exists on the server. As mentioned previously, you can start an incremental crawl for a specific content source or for all content sources at once. Incremental crawls are much less resource intensive because they are indexing only those items that have changed. Whether an item has changed is determined by the change log. An incremental crawl will write its changes directly to the current index instead of creating a new index.

NOTE

Change Log

The Change Log is a SQL table that resides in each content database. Changes to items, files, folders, list metadata, site metadata, and permissions represent a transaction that is written to the log. The specific changes being monitored are the following: add, update, delete, rename, and move.

There are several reasons one should initiate a full crawl, and they are as follows:

■ When new ASPX pages are added or current pages are modified within a site. This is especially important for sites using Web content management since the crawler cannot discover when Web pages on a given site have changed. Therefore, a full crawl is recommended on a weekly basis at a minimum.

- Software updates to the server, such as hotfixes or service packs.
- A new crawl rule has been added or an existing one has been modified.
- A new managed property has been added.
- The content access account has been changed.
- The list of included file types has been modified.

A full crawl is performed automatically when:

- A previous crawl was stopped before completing.
- A content database was restored from backup.
- A content database has been detached and reattached.
- A full crawl of the content source has never been done.
- To repair a corrupted index that has been detected.

Configuring the Crawl Schedule

Crawl schedules should be based on the availability, performance, and bandwidth considerations of the servers running the search service and the servers hosting the crawled content. A few points to consider as you establish your schedules are the following:

1. Schedule incremental crawls during off hours and stagger crawl schedules so that the indexing load is distributed over time.
2. Create content sources that contain start addresses that have similar availability and overall resource usage.
3. Schedule full crawls when necessary, based on the guidance provided in the previous section. Full crawls should be performed less frequently than incremental crawls. To minimize the number of full crawls, implement necessary administration changes that will require a full crawl immediately prior to the next scheduled full crawl.

To start the process of creating a crawl schedule, click Create schedule below Full Crawl in the Crawl schedules section on the Edit Content Source Web page. You will be prompted with a dialog window, as shown in Figure 8.13.

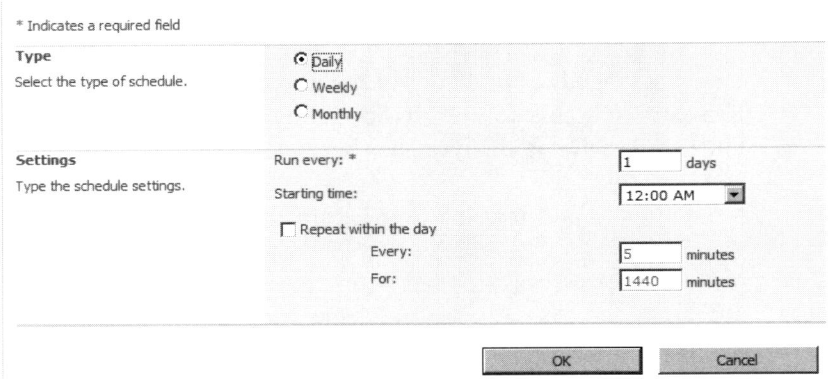

FIGURE 8.13
Web page dialog box for configuring a full crawl.

As you choose different options in the Type section, you will notice that the options in the Settings section also change. Let's configure the full crawl to run weekly, so set the Type to Weekly and choose Friday at 12:00 a.m. as the start time. Whatever Start time you choose, try to ensure that your backup schedule and your full crawl schedule do not overlap since they are both resource intensive. Click the OK button to finish the schedule. An incremental crawl schedule is created in a similar fashion. You will want to schedule incremental crawls more frequently, at least once a day, but likely more than once a day if your content is changing daily, which it will under typical use. Once complete, click the OK button, and you are ready to initiate a full crawl. This can be done by selecting the check box in the Start full crawl section at the bottom of the page or from the drop-down menu shown in Figure 8.10.

On the left-hand side of the Manage Content Sources Web page, you will notice a number of options that all pertain to managing and configuring search in the SSP. These include the headings labeled Administration, Crawling, Queries and Results, and Usage Reports. One of the options is the crawl log, which is discussed next.

Viewing the Crawl Log

The crawl log provides a summary of the crawl process, including whether the crawl was successful, whether content was excluded because of a crawl rule, or whether an error caused indexing to fail. This information is very valuable for troubleshooting. The log also contains information such as the time of the last successful crawl, the content source since there can be more than one, the content access account used, and whether any crawl rules (discussed in the next section) were applied. Filters can be applied to the log's data to simplify the viewing, displaying only the data you would like to see, since the log will generally be pretty long. The crawl log can be viewed by clicking the Crawl log hyperlink beneath the Crawling heading on the Manage Content Sources Web page. The log displays the information by host name on the Crawl Log Web page, as shown in Figure 8.14. Specific crawl log entries can be seen by clicking one of the hostname links, which takes you to the URL summary page for the specific host name. This page is shown in Figure 8.15. In the displayed example, you can see that the crawl was successful. One of the key strengths of the log page is the filtering capability user interface that is visible at the top of the page.

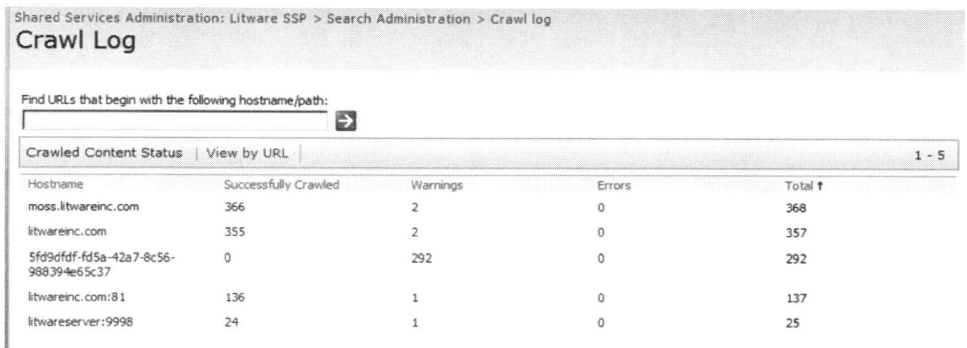

FIGURE 8.14
Crawl Log Web page.

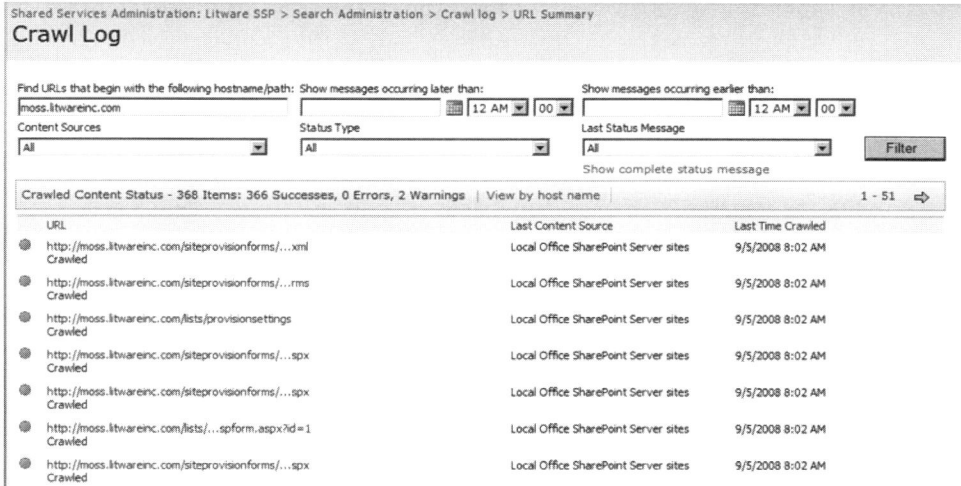

FIGURE 8.15
URL summary page in the Crawl Log.

While you are viewing the crawl log, another page worth viewing is the Search Administration page. Access to this page is also provided by the link on the left-hand side of the page labeled "Search Administration." This is the same link we saw previously on the SSP home page. This page provides a more complete summary of the overall search process and the status of many of the search-related parameters. It is left up to the reader to view this page and become familiar with the type of information provided. Since the earlier discussion has mentioned the topic of crawl rules, let us take a moment to discuss this capability. Crawl rules are an integral part of the indexing process.

Crawl Rules

Crawl rules provide a finer degree of control when crawling a specific path within a content source. This control includes excluding content from being crawled, including content that, for whatever the reason, would otherwise be excluded from the crawl, and specifying authentication credentials for Web sites that require the crawler to log in or use credentials that may be different for the credentials of the default crawler account. For example, say a content source has a URL path such as http://www.mossdemos.com/, and you want to prevent content from the "secure" subdirectory http://www.mossdemo.com/secure/ from being crawled. You could establish a crawl rule for the URL and exclude content from that subdirectory.

Click the Crawl Rules link on the left-hand side navigation to manage crawl rules and create new rules. The options for creating new rules can be seen by clicking the New Crawl Rule button, which will display the Add Crawl Rule Web page shown in Figure 8.16.

To start the process, add the path that will be subject to the new rule. You can use wild-card characters as appropriate, as illustrated by the examples beneath the Path text box. The path syntax for a file share or Web site would be represented as file://server/share or http://url, respectively. By default, the Exclude all items in this path option is selected so if exclusion is what you desire, then you only need to consider if complex URLs should be included as part of the exclusion; they are excluded by default. A complex URL contains query strings in the URL (the URL is encoded with a question mark, ?, as one of the parameters). You should note that the additional options are grayed out, including the options in the Specify Authentication section. These can be enabled for configuration by selecting the Include all items in the path radio button option.

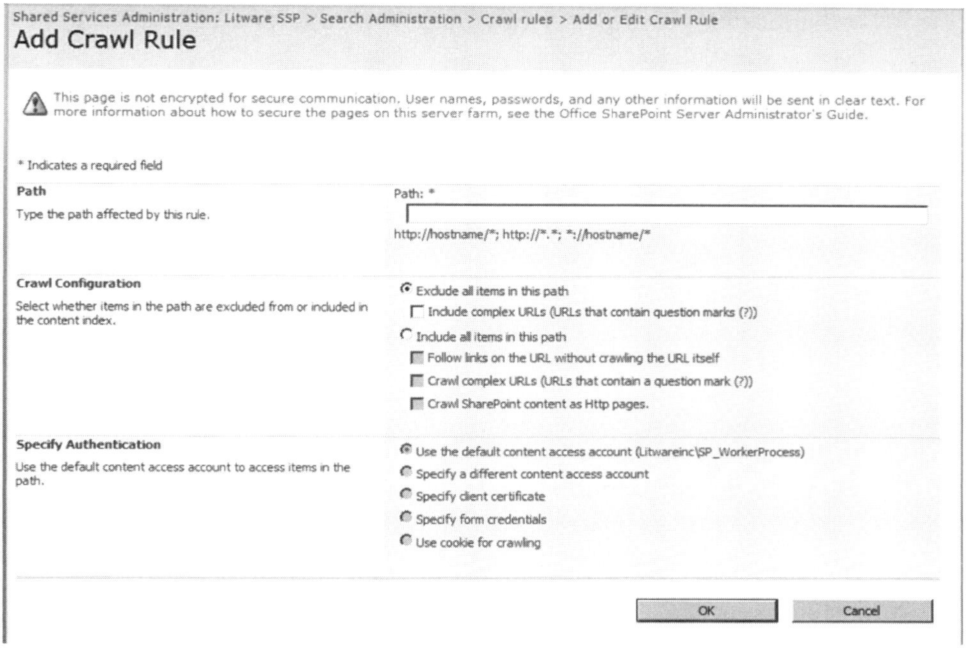

FIGURE 8.16
Add Crawl Rule Web page.

If you have a scenario where you have a home page or landing page that serves to orient users with navigation options, but the content on the page is redundant and exposed on other pages, you could enable the Follow links on the URL without crawling the URL itself check box. For content that requires parameters to be passed in the URL, you would select the Crawl complex URLs (URLs that contain a question mark (?)) option. SharePoint content is normally crawled using a special protocol, but it can be crawled as HTTP pages by selecting the Crawl SharePoint content as Http pages option. Practically, this option is seldom used because SharePoint permissions are not maintained when content is crawled by using the HTTP protocol.

Frequently, you will have the requirement of indexing a content source that requires logging into the Web site as a prerequisite, for example, using a custom authentication mechanism. By enabling the Include all items in the path radio button, you have the capability to define a custom authentication setting, and this is one of the key reasons for choosing such an option. Once enabled, the Use the default content access account is the default setting for custom authentication.

Choosing a different radio button option provides you with new fields. For example, selecting the Specify a different content access account option will enable options for entering the account username and password that will be used for authentication. Also notice that Basic authentication is not available by default because credentials are transmitted as clear text. As with any Web site considering Basic authentication, this should only be used in combination with Secure Socket Layer (SSL) encryption. To utilize a client certificate, you can select the radio button Specify client certificate, which will then allow you to choose one of the registered certificates from your Index server.

Crawl rules can also log into Web sites that utilize Forms Based Authentication or FBA. The Specify form credentials option allows you to specify the URL of the login page for the site. Once you enter the URL, click Enter Credentials, and this will display a proxy window to enter your credentials. If a more complex form submission process is required beyond the standard single login form-submit process approach, this configuration will not work. Also, since a single account is being used to log into the content source, this content will be available for all users and SharePoint will not do any form of security trimming. For those interested in using a custom security trimming mechanism, they should review the following white paper, "Custom Security Trimming for Enterprise Search Results Overview," at http://msdn.microsoft.com/en-us/library/aa981236.aspx.

The crawler can also use a cookie for authentication by selecting the Use cookie for crawling option. By specifying the full location for the cookie in the Obtain cookie from a URL box, a cookie can be retrieved by clicking the Get Cookie button. You can also browse to a specific cookie using the Specify cookie for crawling option. With the cookie option, you can also specify an error page when the cookie expires. As mentioned with FBA authentication, the content will not be security-trimmed and available to all users. This completes the discussion for reviewing the options available when creating a new crawl rule.

File Types

Content is indexed only if the specific file name extension representing the content is included in the file-type inclusions list and an iFilter is installed on the Index server that supports those file types. By default, MOSS is configured to index 38 different file extensions. All other file extensions will be ignored during the indexing process. For the complete list of the installed file types, click the File types link on the left-hand side of the screen. A new file type is entered by clicking the New File Type button in the menu bar and entering the file extension without the period. Once a new file type is registered, you should add the appropriate icon image so that this image is displayed as part of the search results for easy recognition. Otherwise, the familiar Windows icon will be displayed by default. Microsoft has released an article that covers the proper procedure for updating the images at http://support.microsoft.com/kb/832809. In addition to adding a new file type, a file extension can also be removed from the list by hovering over the extension and clicking the drop-down menu and selecting Delete.

An iFilter must also be installed in addition to the file extension being registered. Recall earlier in the chapter when we defined the purpose of the iFilter. It is a software component that is called by the protocol handler during the indexing process to actually open the file and read the content. The procedure for installing an iFilter may vary with the specific file extension, so you should consult the manufacturer for instructions.

One last check is to ensure that the specific file type of interest has not been configured as a member of the blocked file type list. This list is accessible from the Operations tab in Central Administration. By default, 90 different file types are blocked.

As part of planning which content sources you should index, you need to decide what file types need to be crawled to ensure that the proper content is represented in the search process. As you view the left-side navigation pane on the Configure Search Settings Web page, you will notice one other option under the Crawling heading, which is labeled Reset all crawled content. We will discuss this option, which will complete the indexing discussion.

Reset All Crawled Content

The current content index and the property store can be deleted from the Reset Crawled Content Web page. Therefore, search results will not be available until after a crawl has been completed. As you can see, the implications of this reset operation are pretty significant and should not be done without careful consideration. From the Web page, you will notice that the default recommendation is to deactivate search alerts during the reset so users will not receive unnecessary emails during the indexing process. Alerts can be re-enabled after the index has been rebuilt. Make sure to initiate full crawls across all content sources. If the reader is unfamiliar with search alerts, they are discussed in the next section.

Search Alerts

Search alerts are a part of SharePoint's subscription capability. Alerts provide a mechanism for notifying a user that the results from a previous search query have changed. This notification will occur once a user creates an alert through the search user interface. Alerts can be enabled and disabled through the SSP Web site by an administrator with SSP administrator permission. From the Search Administration Web page, alert status can be viewed and enabled/disabled using the Search Alerts Status option beneath the Search Status heading, as illustrated in Figure 8.17. Alert status can also be viewed and changed by clicking the Search-based alerts option on the Configure Search-based Alerts Web page, as shown in Figure 8.18.

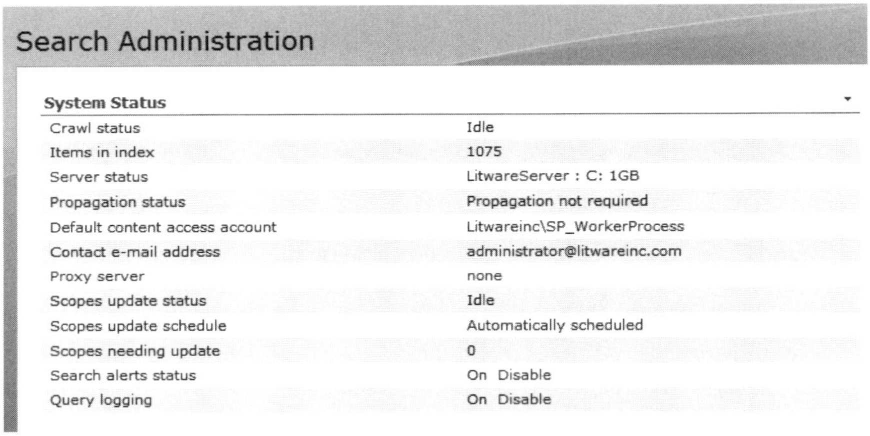

FIGURE 8.17
System Status on the Search Administration Web page.

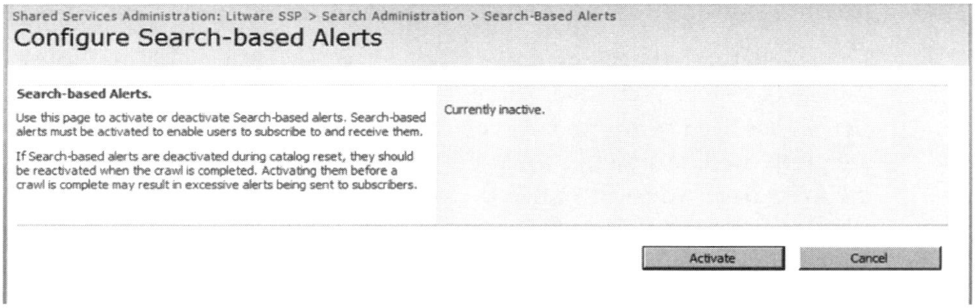

FIGURE 8.18
Configure Search-based Alerts Web page.

The process for "getting MOSS search up and running" is almost complete, at least as a first pass that will likely require some refinement. We have discussed the options for indexing and configuring the index process. At this point, we have completed a full crawl across all of our content sources and made any necessary crawl rule configurations for optimizing the index process. Therefore, content is available for search and that is the focus of the following sections. The next section covers step 5, the final step in "getting search up and running." This step in the process includes creating the search center that will represent the user interface for executing queries and displaying the results. We will also cover other SSP administrative topics that include authoritative pages, federated locations, managed properties, search scopes, and server name mappings. These latter topics impact the query and result process.

Creating and Customizing the Search Experience

The user's search experience can be optimized and customized by creating a search center, which is the centralized location and user interface for executing search requests and viewing the results. The search center is a new type of site that is automatically created by default within the site collection when you provision a Collaboration Portal using the corresponding template. Its purpose is to provide users with a customized search experience and to replace the familiar search box that is available at the top of the Web pages in the portal.

The search center can be created using one of two different templates: the Search Center Lite and the Search Center with Tabs. The Search Center Lite is typically added to site collections where the publishing features are not activated, such as site collections with only team sites. The Search Center with Tabs offers more customization options using a tab-based user interface, but it requires the publishing features to be enabled (a Collaboration Portal has the publishing features enabled as part of the provisioning process). Both of these search centers are ready to use once they are created, but some additional configuration may be necessary to provide the customized search experience desired by the organization. Our discussion will focus on the search center with tabs. The result of creating the search center from the template or provisioning a Collaboration Portal is shown in Figure 8.19.

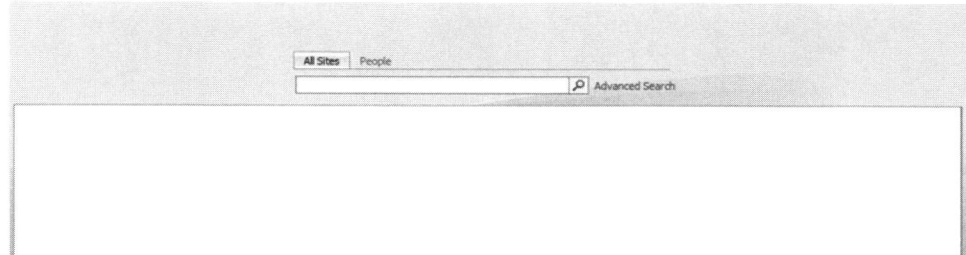

FIGURE 8.19
Search Center with Tabs created from the corresponding template.

Enable Publishing Feature

If the Search Center with Tabs template is not available, then likely the publishing feature has not been enabled. To enable, navigate to the Site Features page for the site collection and activate the Office SharePoint Server Publishing feature. Once activated, proceed with creating a search center using the Search Center with Tabs template.

This search center is ready to use to accept user queries as is, but it may need some additional customization. The People tab refers to the people search capability built into MOSS and will be discussed in depth in Chapter 9. Readers interested in customization of the user interface are directed to review "Creating a Custom Search Page and Tabs in the Search Center of SharePoint Server" at http://msdn.microsoft.com/en-us/library/bb428855.aspx. The article covers the process for adding custom search pages and tabs, along with how to alter the display of the search results using custom XSLT.

The user experience can be simplified using the Advanced Search Web page. This is revealed by clicking the Advanced Search link to the right of the query text box, as shown in Figure 8.20. This page helps the user build a search query, which simplifies the query process. There are several additional MOSS search features that enhance the end user experience, and require the administrator to configure for proper use. These include the following:

- Managed Properties
- Search Scopes
- Authoritative Pages
- Server Name Mappings
- Federated Locations

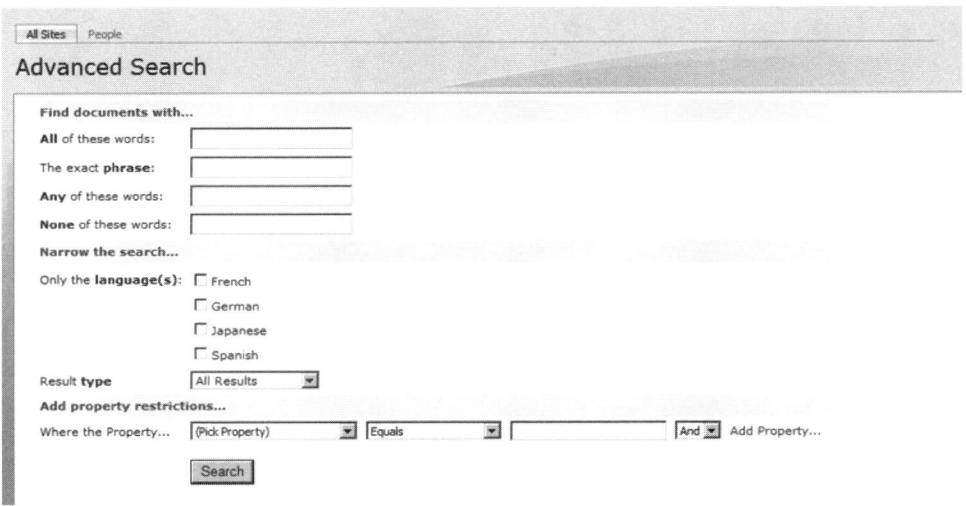

FIGURE 8.20
Advanced Search Web page.

The use of managed properties simplify the user search experience by providing options to choose from, as shown at the bottom of Figure 8.20. The next section covers managed properties in detail.

Managed Properties

As part of the indexing process, content properties, also known as "metadata," is collected and stored by the crawler in the Property Store, one of the databases in SQL Server and controlled by the SSP. Metadata originates by content creators assigning property values to their content, including such things as document titles, file names, and author. Any SharePoint library or list can be customized to include custom metadata, and metadata can also be associated with content types. This metadata is indexed and referred to as a "crawled property," and it can be used as part of the search process. Crawled properties can be mapped to managed properties to further enhance the search experience. This allows users to specify the managed property in their search query using the Property Picker on the Advanced Search Web page, as shown at the bottom of Figure 8.20.

How do you add managed properties to the Property Picker drop-down list? From the SSP Web site, administrators can map one or more of these crawled properties to a managed property, which will then show up as one of the entries on the list of the Property Picker.

Why would you want to map more than one crawled property to a single managed property? For example, an organization might have three metadata definitions for a property identifying the content author: Author, Writer, and Originator. You can map each of these crawled properties to the Author managed property so that when a user queries by Author, appropriate results from the three metadata types are included.

Viewing and Configuring Managed Properties

Managed properties are viewed and created by navigating to the Search Administration Web page and clicking the Metadata Properties link on the left-hand side column. The Metadata Property Mappings Web page is partially shown in Figure 8.21. You can view a listing of the crawled properties by clicking the Crawled Properties button at the top of the page. This list contains every property that the indexer has discovered as part of the crawl process. Crawled properties can be categorized by administrators by editing and deleting the folders present. An individual property can be viewed by selecting one of the folders, such as SharePoint, and then clicking the property ows_FullName(Text). This reveals the Edit Crawled Property page, which indicates the name and information of the property, a list of the indexed content containing this property, any mappings to managed properties, and whether or not this property is included in the search index. To locate a specific crawled property, use the search box above the menu bar on the Metadata Property Mappings Web page.

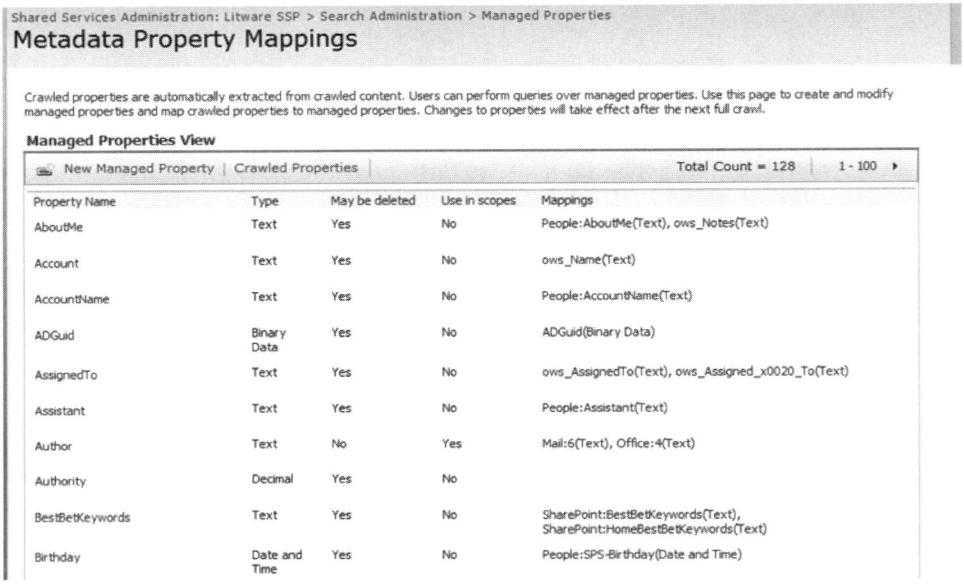

FIGURE 8.21
Metadata Property Mappings Web page.

A listing of the managed properties can be seen by clicking the Managed Properties button to return to the Managed Properties View. To create a new property, click the New Managed Property button, which will take you to the New Managed Property Web page, as shown in Figure 8.22.

Property name is a required field and must be unique. You should always add a description because this will simplify management of multiple properties, some of which may be very similar. Choose the property type carefully and use the option which best fits the type of property you're creating since this will determine your options for searching the data using the Advanced Search Web page.

The Mappings to Crawled Properties section gives a list of crawled properties mapped to this managed property. When creating a new property, you have two options: Include values from all crawled properties mapped or Include values from a single crawled property based on the order specified. Content that contains more than one mapped property will be impacted by this setting. The managed property will either be assigned multiple values based on all the mapped properties or assigned a single value based on the order specified.

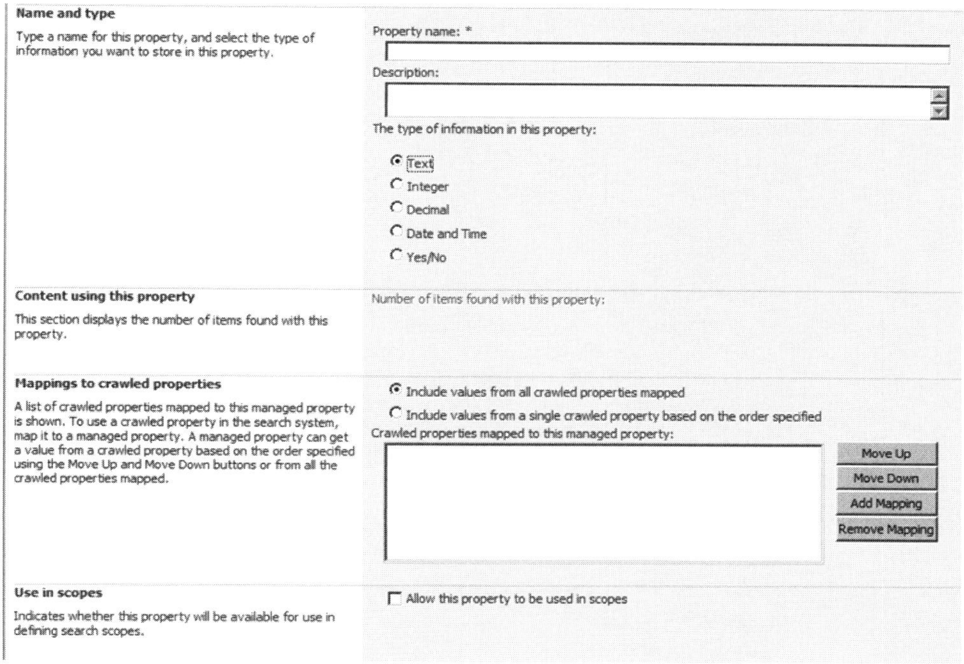

FIGURE 8.22
New Managed Property Web page.

Managed properties can also be used in search scopes by enabling the check box Allow this property to be used in scopes. Scopes are covered in the next section.

Search Scopes

Content sources have the information that is indexed and made available through the search process. Search scopes define a subset of the content and allow queries to be focused on a smaller set of data, which improves performance and helps improve relevance as long as the scopes have been created properly. By default, a user performs a search using the All Sites scope, which will include security-trimmed results from all of the content sources. By default, the Scope Picker drop-down list is not shown in the search center but can be enabled to display, as shown in Figure 8.23 by configuring the Web part properties on the page. It can also be enabled for the Advanced Search page using the same process. If the administrator knows that users will be querying a specific content source, for example, the file shares content source, he can create a custom scope that represents this content and only results from this source will be returned in the result set. This custom scope can be made available inside the Scope Picker for the user to choose for his specific query. Another approach would be to create a custom search center that defines a custom scope as the default, which would simplify the process for the user. The search services administrator or SSP administrator defines the default scopes, or "shared scopes" as they are called, that can be used by the entire site collection. Site collection administrators can add and modify scopes, add scope display groups, and choose and arrange scopes within them. As a result, site owners can apply the groups to modify instances of the scope list on their pages. Additionally, site collection administrators can define local search scopes, which can only be used within that specific site collection.

FIGURE 8.23
Search Scopes drop-down list enabled for the search center.

Creating and Using Search Scopes

Administrators define scopes that they expect their users to need based on particular locations and content during the planning portion of the MOSS deployment. Scopes are created using rules that define what is included and not included in the scope. When defining a scope, you can combine location rules with property rules to limit searches as desired. For example, a scope can direct a query to specific sites or to documents marked with particular property values.

The current scopes can be viewed by navigating to the Search Administration page and clicking the Scopes link on the left-hand side. From this screen, you can see both the shared scopes and a listing of each site collection, including any local scopes that may have been created, as shown in Figure 8.24.

A new scope can be created by clicking the New Scope button on the menu bar to reveal the Create Scope Web page shown in Figure 8.25. Add an appropriate title and description for the new scope. We can have the search results sent to the default results page or to another page. This gives us the flexibility to control the output based on the scope being used. For now, you can accept the default page. Once you're finished, click the OK button, which will return you to the View Scopes Web page. Click the Add rules link that is next to the scope you just created to display the Add Scope Rule Web page shown in Figure 8.26. By selecting different rule types, you will notice that the remaining sections on the page change, providing different options for each different rule type. Select the radio button for Web Address to see the first set of options.

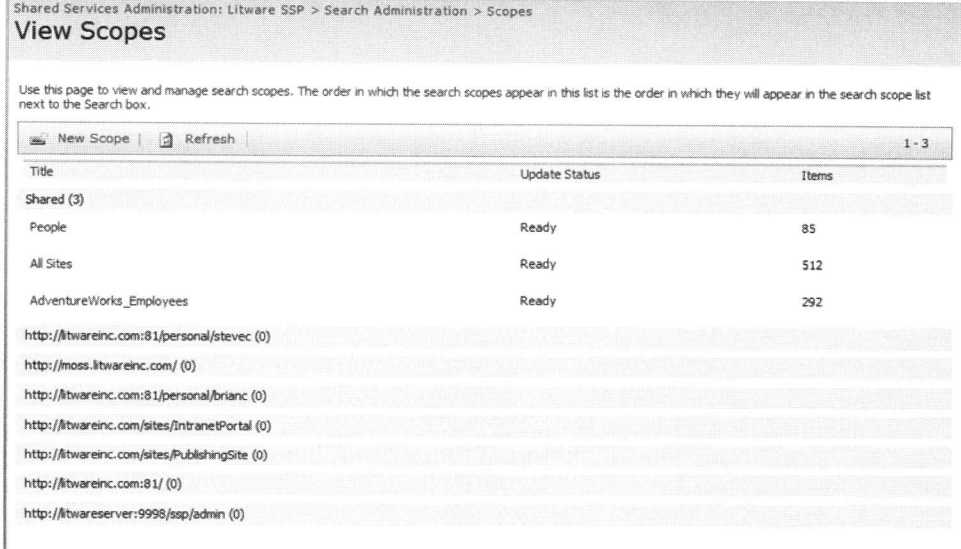

FIGURE 8.24
View Scopes Web page.

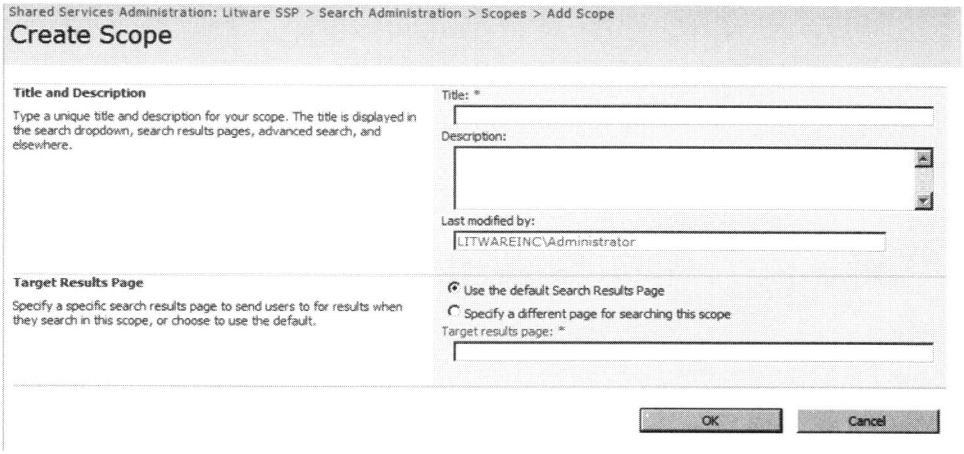

FIGURE 8.25
Create Scope Web page.

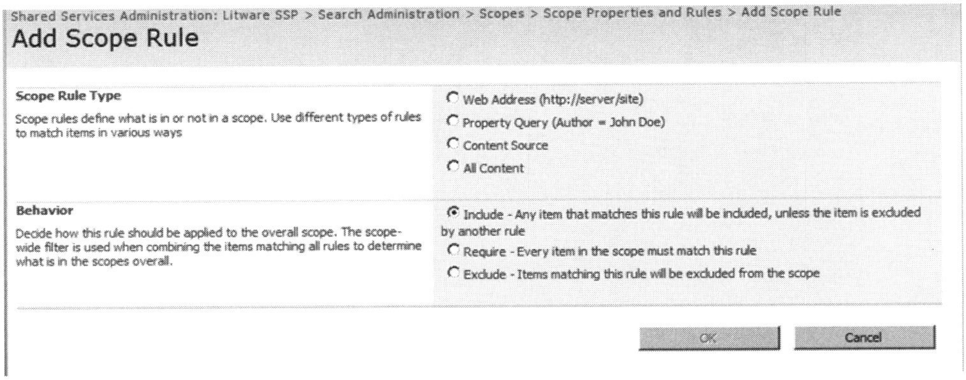

FIGURE 8.26
Add Scope Rule Web page.

Web Address scope rules include content in Web sites, file shares, exchange public folders, or any other content in the search index that has a URL. Folder rules include all items in the folder path, and domain or hostname rules include all items within the specified domain or hostname.

The Property Query rule type allows you to specify inclusion of managed properties based on the property equaling some value. The property restriction specifies the value that is to be compared. All items matching the property query will be added to the scope. Navigate to the managed properties list and select Allow this property to be used in scopes for the specific managed property to make it available for use in scope rules. This provides you the flexibility to create content-specific scopes.

The Content Source type is used to create a rule that returns all items from a specific content source. For example, a search can be created that only covers the content in file shares, Exchange Public Folders, and so on.

The All Content rule type returns everything in the index. The default All Sites scope uses this rule type along with an exclusion of the content associated with people. This can be verified by returning to the View Scopes page and selecting the Edit Properties and Rules option from the All Sites drop-down menu. This will take you to the Scope Properties and Rules page, which will show the rules for this specific scope. Rules may also have a behavior that specifies how this rule should be applied to the overall scope. The behaviors are Include, Require, and Exclude.

The behavior determines how a specific rule combines with other rules to define the overall scope. Include behavior specifies that any content that meets this particular rule will be included in the scope. If two rules are configured, A and B, then if the content satisfies rule A or the content satisfies rule B, it is included as part of the scope. Required specifies that for any content to be included, it must satisfy all rules, which means the content must satisfy rule A *and* it must satisfy rule B. Exclude means that any documents that match the rule will be excluded from the index. Content will be excluded if it satisfies rule A and not rule B.

Scopes are compiled automatically every 15 minutes by default. The automatic compilation can be disabled, and scopes can be compiled on demand from the Configure Search Settings page. Beneath the Scopes section of the settings page, you can configure the Update Schedule option to either Automatically scheduled or On demand updates only. Scopes can be compiled manually by selecting the Start update now option. A new scope does not appear in a search box scope list until after its first compilation.

New scopes can also be created by copying an existing scope. This is accomplished from the drop-down menu for a specific scope on the View Scopes Web page. You should notice that the drop-down menu has three options: Edit Properties and Rules, Make Copy as Shared, and Delete. Once you make a copy, you can edit the scope and change its name. This process simplifies creating shared scopes and creating a shared scope from a local site collection scope. Once shared scopes are created, they can be used within the site collection. The site collection administrator also has the ability to create display groups, which provide additional capability for customizing the search experience.

A site collection administrator can utilize shared scopes or create scopes local to the site collection. Scopes are displayed by creating a display group, which allows a scope to be included or excluded as well as the order they are shown. This is accomplished from the Search Scopes page, which is accessible from the Site Settings page of the top-level site in the site collection. This link takes you to the View Scopes Web page, as shown in Figure 8.27. From this page, an administrator can create a local scope using the New Scope button and create a new display group using the corresponding button. The display group allows the site collection administrator to specify which scopes are included and their specific order of display. Once created, a site owner can change the scopes available from the scope list beside a search box, and can use display groups to modify the scope list in instances of the Search Box Web part using its property settings.

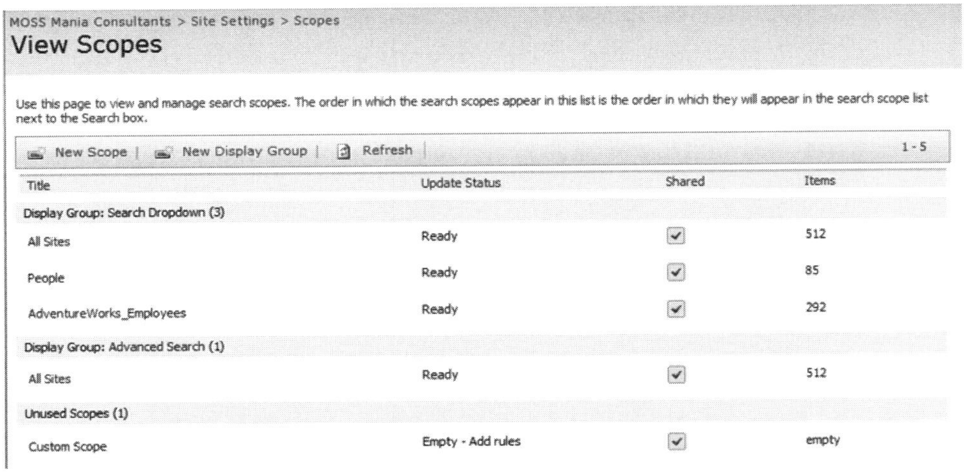

FIGURE 8.27
View Scopes Web page.

Authoritative Pages

Authoritative pages are sites that contain the most relevant content or link to the most relevant information. You can specify authoritative pages from the most valuable, to the second most valuable, and to a third level using the Specify Authoritative Pages Web page. The search engine uses this list to calculate what is referred to as the rank of every page in the index. Item ranking affects the order that search results appear in the search results list. Relevance rankings for items are determined in part by the distance (in clicks) that items are from URLs that are listed as authoritative, second-level authoritative, or third-level authoritative. The latter two types of URLs receive a penalty click of one and two, respectively. That is, being close to a third-level authoritative URL is good, but it is one click worse than being close to a second-level authoritative URL. The same is true for a second-level authoritative URL and a most authoritative URL. Clearly, click distance is used when calculating overall content relevance. Authoritative pages are administrator-maintained and can be adjusted to influence this weighting process. You can also mark URLs as non-authoritative so that they appear lower in the search results list. A discussion of the topic of search relevance is beyond the scope of this chapter, but interested readers are directed to the white paper "Evaluating and Customizing Search Relevance in SharePoint Server 2007" at http://msdn2.microsoft.com/en-us/library/bb499682.aspx.

Server Name Mappings

Server name mappings change how search-result URLs are displayed. Server name mappings are typically needed when the URLs used by the crawler to access content are different than the URLs that users use to navigate to the same files. For example, local file shares content was indexed, but it needs to be accessible by users from the Internet. Server name mappings are configured from the Server Name Mappings page using a link on the Search Administration page. Alternate Access Mappings (AAM) may also be used in this scenario, and for all practical purposes may be the better approach, since they would have to already have been configured for proper access to the site from both the intranet and Internet. AAM should be used when a different server name or port is used for accessing the entire portal site. Use server name mappings to specify a protocol or server for an address that appears in search results that is different from the address from which that content was crawled. The interested reader is directed toward the following discussion for more information: http://blogs.msdn.com/sharepoint/archive/2007/03/06/what-every-sharepoint-administrator-needs-to-know-about-alternate-access-mappings-part-1.aspx.

Federated Locations

As we have discussed, MOSS search queries are processed using the content index. MOSS also has the ability to display search results for content that is not indexed by MOSS. The latter refers to federated search. With federation, the query can be performed over the local content index, or it can be forwarded to an external content repository where it is processed by that repository's search engine. The external search engine returns the results to MOSS, which formats and renders the results within the same search results page as the MOSS search results. Thus, users can simultaneously query more than one search engine. The external search engine must support the OpenSearch standard to be considered a source for federation. A MOSS federated location defines the connection to the external content repository, and is configured from the Managed Federated Locations Web page in the SSP Web site. The interested reader is directed to the white paper "Federated Search Overview" at http://msdn.microsoft.com/en-us/library/bb931080.aspx and to the book *Inside the Index and Search Engines* by Patrick Tisseghem.

This completes our discussion for getting "MOSS search up and running." MOSS provides a very comprehensive and feature-rich search system, and it is impossible to cover the search capability in one chapter. Whole books have been devoted to MOSS search, so our purpose was to provide the administrator with just enough information to begin using this great capability and optimizing the search experience.

9 Personalization and People Search

In This Chapter

- Introduction
- User Profiles
- People Search
- My Sites

INTRODUCTION

Microsoft Office SharePoint Server 2007 (MOSS) provides several different features to help ensure that content is relevant for each user when he accesses a SharePoint site. The key features include: user profiles, My Sites, and Audiences. MOSS search also has the capability to index user profiles and search people information. Therefore, People Search is also tightly integrated with MOSS's social networking capability; this will be discussed in the second half of the chapter. This chapter will cover user profiles and My Sites since they are the key components of the personalization architecture.

My Sites represents a personal Web site, or "personal desktop" if you will, for a user and a location where that person can store content that is relevant to him. This central location also contains personal information about the user that may be relevant for other business users. Each My Site is a site collection with the individual user as the site owner. This gives users the autonomy to build a site hierarchy appropriate for their information, if necessary. A critical component to establishing and utilizing My Sites is creating and populating user profiles.

Personalization configuration, including user profiles and My Sites, is done using the Shared Services Provider (SSP) Web site, as we have seen previously with search services in Chapter 8, "Configuring and Managing Enterprise Search." The SSP provides a centralized location for administrators to manage these settings. The Personalization discussion will begin with the details for configuring and utilizing user profiles.

USER PROFILES

User profile information is critical to all of SharePoint's social networking features. Most organizations store people information (for example, Name, Job Title, Department, Phone, Email, and so on) in their Active Directory database, another directory services database such as a Lightweight Directory Access Protocol (LDAP) database, or a database such as SQL Server. Additionally, other pertinent information (such as Hire Date, Employee ID) may be stored in line-of-business (LOB) applications or an HR database. Therefore, a complete and consistent representation of the people in the organization will require data to be aggregated from several different and diverse data sources. Before we discuss how to populate and configure the user profiles, let's review some of the key aspects and features that make this information so valuable.

- Profile information can be imported directly from Active Directory directory service or entered manually. It can also be imported from LOB systems using the Business Data Catalog (BDC) feature. Each profile contains several properties that can be customized according to the needs of the organization. These properties can be mapped to attributes inside of Active Directory, other directory services, or other data stores. User profile data is stored in a database inside of SQL Server.
- It is used to generate a My Site or personal site for individual users that they can personalize. A user's My Site can be configured to display relationship information that is contained in the profile properties using SharePoint's out-of-the-box Web parts. A user can view and change his own user profile from his corresponding My Site. Only profile properties that are marked as editable can be changed. A My Site has both a public view and a private view.
- The profile can be viewed using either the private view or the public view. The public view is visible to all other site users. You can edit your profile from either

view, but the actual profile details are only displayed on the public view by default. The private view contains private information that is viewable only by the owner.

- User profile information can be searched once information has been entered or imported by performing an index of the content and thus provide better search results. We will discuss this further when we get to the people search portion of the chapter.
- Profile content is used to personalize content for users by targeting content via the audience feature.
- Site users with the Manage Profiles right can manage user profiles.

Therefore, user profiles can be used in several different ways, such as to identify connections and relationships among users, establish common managers and colleagues, and locate subject matter expertise and identify Web site membership. Relationship information can be used to help facilitate more efficient collaboration with colleagues and across teams. Populating the profile database is a prerequisite to using the profile information and generally this is done by importing the necessary data. A complete profile import requires that import connections be configured, profile properties be defined and mapped to directory services properties, and that profile services policies be established to govern the visibility of the information. The following section describes the details for managing and configuring user profiles, including the import configuration process.

PROFILE MANAGEMENT AND CONFIGURATION

User profile management should be a part of the planning process for deploying and configuring MOSS. Profile management includes the following:

1. **Import Connections.** Configure the connections that will be used to access the data stored in the Active Directory database, an LDAP directory, or a LOB application.
2. **Property Definition and Configuration.** Establish the properties that collectively will represent the users' profiles and define their visibility or policy.
3. **Property Mapping.** Configure the mapping between the profile properties and properties native to the directory service or LOB application.
4. **Profile Indexing.** Perform an index of the content so that profile information will be available through the search process and ongoing indexing as the content gets updated.

We will continue our discussion of profile management with the details associated with configuring import connections, followed by an example import to illustrate the process. Then we will move on to define and map the profile properties.

Import Connections

Profile Services is the shared service for people and personalization features within MOSS. Therefore, all configurations are done through the SSP previously created and defined as part of the MOSS setup. Profile Services connections establish the way information contained within the external data source is to be imported into user profiles inside of MOSS. Properties are imported into user profiles by connecting to the relevant service or database and mapping the unique identifier for each property in the shared service to the unique identifier of the corresponding property in the external data source or business application.

Key Points

There are several different aspects of the import process and services connections that need to be highlighted. They are summarized next.

- The import process is managed by a profile services administrator. This individual may also be the SSP administrator or the responsibility can be delegated to a completely different individual since the profile services administrator has additional permissions that are not available to SSP administrators. Performing an import requires the administrator to have the Manage user profiles permission.
- Importing from Active Directory in the current domain does not require any custom configuration of the import connections. Custom connections must be created to import from an LDAP database, the Business Data Catalog, or resources on multiple servers or across multiple forests. The Active Directory or LDAP connection represents a primary connection.
- Manual editing of profile data that is mapped to attributes in a primary connection is not recommended since the next import will overwrite the manual modifications.
- The MOSS profile database information is kept relevant and in synchronization with the data stores using regularly scheduled imports. As part of ongoing profile management, new connections can be created, out-of-date ones can be removed, and property mappings can be modified to support enterprise data requirements that change over time. After you add or remove connections, or change the settings for an existing connection, you must perform a full import since user profile information is not updated automatically.
- Data imports synchronize content contained in the user database with properties in the profile database in MOSS. This is a one-way process. MOSS cannot write to or export profile data from the profile database and update content inside of the source databases.
- The BDC can be used to import content from LOB systems. This import connection is considered a secondary connection and does not overwrite existing

imported data. BDC imported properties augment existing user profiles and cannot be used to create or import new user profiles.

Import connections enable MOSS user profiles to be populated with information from across directory services and business applications. User information is synchronized across all site collections in the SharePoint farm that use the same SSP. The next section walks through the process of configuring import connections.

Performing a Profile Import

The following steps illustrate the process to import data from Active Directory in the current domain. Importing Active Directory data from the current domain does not require the addition of a separate connection or any configuration. Keep in mind that data is retrieved from all connections when an import is launched. Full imports include all data in user profiles, while incremental imports include only the user profiles added since the last import.

1. Access the SSP Web site from the Central Administration Web site using a farm administrator account or equivalent with appropriate permission. An example SSP Web site is shown in Figure 9.1. Our focus will be the User Profiles and My Sites section and specifically the User profiles and properties link.

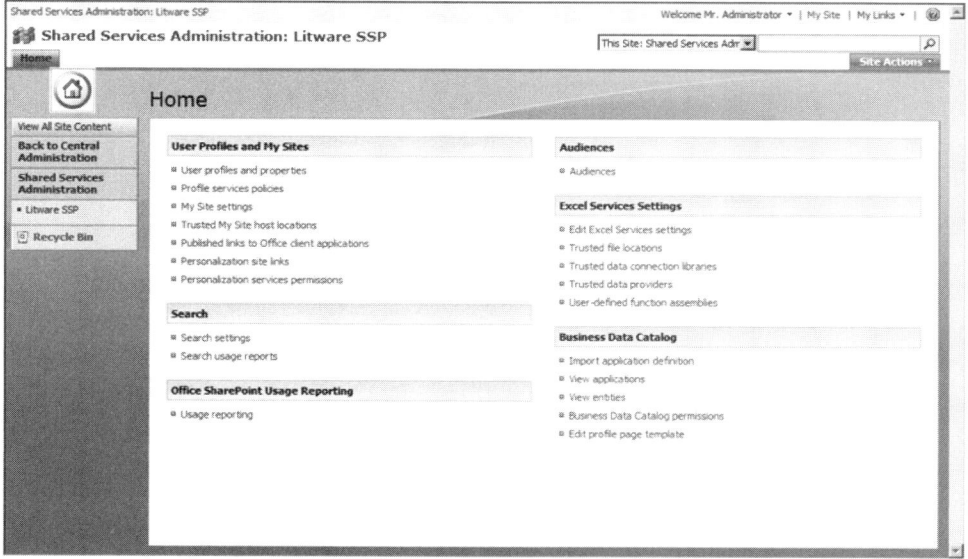

FIGURE 9.1
An example SSP Web site.

2. View the User Profiles and Properties Web page, as shown in Figure 9.2. Notice that there are two sections: Profile and Import Settings and User Profile Properties. Review the different options in each of the two sections on the User Profiles and Properties Web page. We will be discussing each of the options at some point during the chapter. During this walkthrough, we will focus on the Profile and Import Settings section in the following steps.

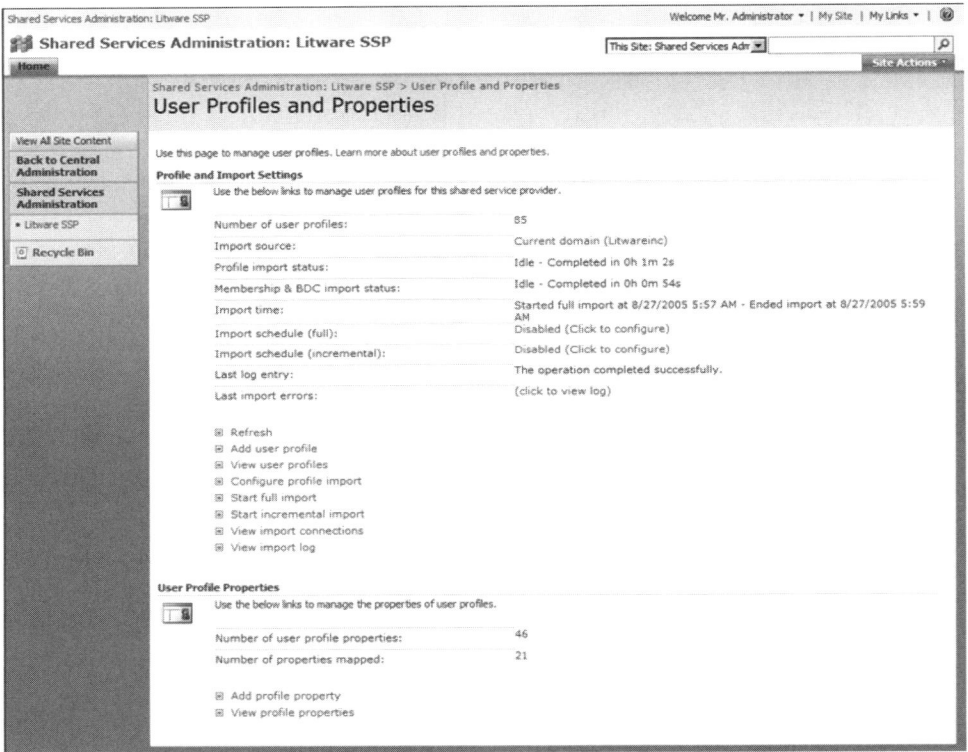

FIGURE 9.2
User Profiles and Properties Web page.

3. The data source for the import is configured by clicking the Configure profile import link. The account used to access the data source and the import schedule can also be configured from this page. Within the Source section, the current domain should already be selected, but you have the option of selecting the source for the import. Since we will be importing from Active Directory in the current domain, no change needs to be made. No other changes are required on this page.

Security Best Practices

Security best practices suggest that you should specify an actual account rather than relying on the default content access account. An import schedule is not required but in practical terms is necessary since it will help ensure that periodic updates are performed and data synchronicity is maintained. An import should be performed at a frequency that data source content changes.

4. Click the OK button at the bottom of the page once your configuration is complete. If you are importing data for the first time, then you will need to perform a full import. A full import can be initiated by clicking the Start full import link. Once the import has begun, refresh the page until the Profile Import Status returns to Idle. View the import log once the import process has completed to review any errors and familiarize yourself with the log format and content.

5. The details of the import connection can be viewed by clicking View Import Connections from the User Profiles and Properties page. This connection was created to access the Active Directory database when the import was initiated. Open the existing connection by placing the cursor over the connection name and clicking Edit from the drop-down menu.

6. The Edit Connection page demonstrates all the configuration information necessary for establishing and maintaining a connection to the data source. The reader should review each of the options and note the existing LDAP user filter string. The default string that is displayed, (&(object Category=Person)(objectClass=User)), will import all user accounts, even disabled accounts. If you only want to import active user accounts, then the string should be changed to:(&(objectCategory=person)(object Class=user)(!(userAccountControl:1.2.840.113556.1.4.803:=2))). The following knowledge-base article discusses making this change: http://support.microsoft.com/ default.aspx?scid=kb;en-us;827754.

A more detailed discussion for creating a connection to Active Directory can be found here: "Add connections to Active Directory" at http://technet.microsoft.com/en-us/library/cc262776(TechNet.10).aspx. The details for creating an LDAP connection are here: "Add connections to LDAP" at http://technet.microsoft.com/en-us/library/cc263081.aspx. A BDC connection can be configured using "Add connections to the Business Data Catalog" at http://technet.microsoft.com/en-us/library/cc263388(TechNet.10).aspx. For creating and managing connections to directory services across Active Directory forests, the reader can refer to "Manage connections across domains in multiple forests" at http://technet.microsoft.com/en-us/library/cc262116.aspx.

7. Perform a full import once again as done previously and review the import log once completed.

The reader should now be familiar with the process for configuring and performing a profile import. One of the key aspects in populating the profile database is defining the specific properties in the profile and the corresponding property mappings that govern how data is imported and associated with these properties. In practice, we would define properties and their mappings before we completed an import. The following section discusses profile properties and how to configure mappings and policies.

Profile Properties and Mappings

User profiles will require both planning and ongoing management to ensure that the information is up-to-date and as useful as possible. Specifically, this will include property definition, mapping, policy definition, and customization. Let's review some of the key points and details regarding how properties and mappings are configured.

■ User profiles represent two things: a list of users and a set of properties that may or may not contain values for each user. However, user profiles are not user accounts and therefore, not used for authentication. The list of profile properties will need to be configured and managed on an ongoing basis. The user profiles in the profile database can be viewed by clicking the View user profiles link on the User Profiles and Properties page in the SSP Web site. A portion of a populated profile is shown in Figure 9.3. From the User Profiles Web page, you can search for specific users by account name, preferred name, or email alias. You can also add new profiles or delete existing user profiles. To edit an existing user profile, place the cursor over the user account in the list and a drop-down menu will be displayed with three options: Edit, Delete, and Manage personal site. Click the Edit option, and you will be taken to the Edit User Profile page. Keep in mind that any manual modifications may be overwritten as part of the next import and these modifications only affect this user account.

■ User profiles can be added for users not listed in the current connections to directory services. New user profiles can be manually added to the profile database from the Edit User Profile page or by clicking the Add user profile from the User Profiles and Properties page. Any profiles created using this approach will not be affected by subsequent imports from primary connections and will need to be managed manually.

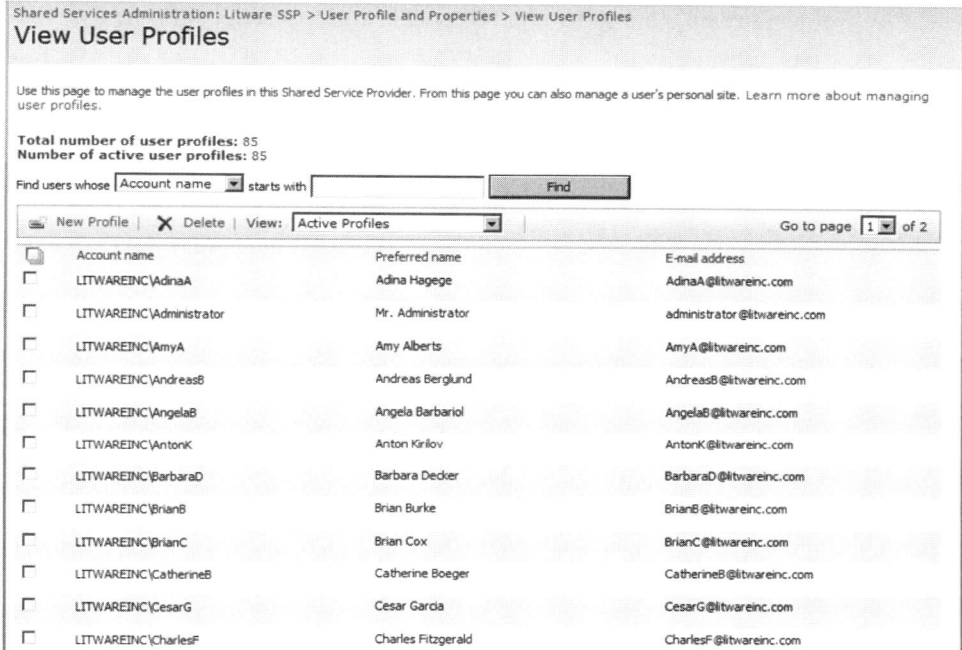

FIGURE 9.3
User Profiles Web page used for profile management.

■ All user profiles contain the same list of properties with different values for each user. From the Edit User Profile Web page, the values for each of the profile properties can be changed, as shown in Figure 9.4. The profile page shows the property name, the current value which can be modified, and the visibility of the property or policy defining who is allowed to view this property. Only the property value can be modified, not the property name or policy. You will also notice that this page shows which properties are mapped for import and which are required.

■ Administrators can modify existing properties, as well as add or delete properties in the profile list and set personalization policies for each property. Any change to the properties list or an associated policy will be reflected in every user profile. Properties can be modified by clicking the View profile properties link under the User Profile Properties section of the User Profiles and Properties Web page. As shown in Figure 9.5, each property, the display order, property type, mapping, whether it's a multivalue property, and its alias are listed. The Property Name represents the property's display name, the name that is displayed when the property appears in the public profile and any Web sites. The actual property name displayed in the user profile itself is the property that is used by Web parts, custom applications, and other programming-related tasks. This property is often different from the display name. The actual property name is visible by editing an individual property. The Mapped Attribute is the attribute in a profile import from a directory service to which each profile property is mapped. Properties can contain more than one value, as shown by the Multivalue column. The check mark in the Alias column indicates that the property is related to the user's name and account. From the View Profile Properties Web page, administrators can add, edit, organize, delete, or map user profile properties. These are all key functions in managing user profile data. Each property can be edited by using the drop-down menu, as shown in Figure 9.5. Profile properties can be mapped to Active Directory, LDAP-compliant directory services, as well as Application Entity Fields exposed by the Business Data Catalog.

Shared Services Administration: Litware SSP > User Profile and Properties > View User Profiles > Edit User Profile

Edit User Profile

Use this page to edit this user profile by changing values for the following properties. Properties that are mapped to the external data source will be overwritten the next time user profiles are imported.

💾 Save and Close | Cancel and Go Back

* Indicates a required field
Indicates a field mapped for profile import

		Show To
Account name:	LITWAREINC\AdinaA	Everyone
First name:	Adina	Everyone
Last name:	Hagege	Everyone
Name: *	Adina Hagege	Everyone
Work phone: *	(425) 555-0172	Everyone
Office: *	N1043	Everyone
Department: *	Operations	Everyone
Title: *	Fullfillment	Everyone
Manager:	Don Funk	Everyone

FIGURE 9.4
A portion of the Edit User Profile Web page for a specific user account.

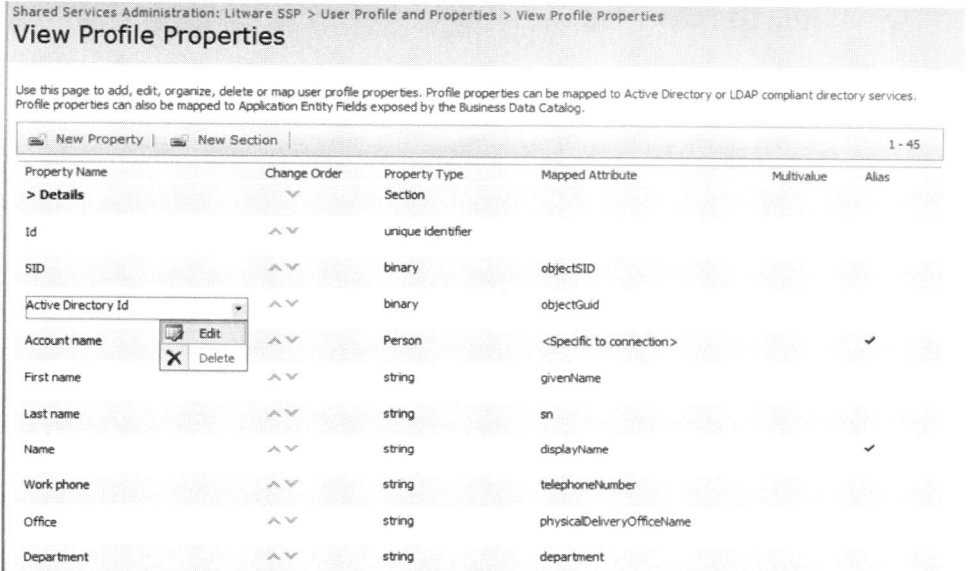

FIGURE 9.5
User profile properties and mappings.

■   New properties can be created in two ways: by clicking the New Property button on the View Profile Properties Web page and by clicking Add profile property in the User Profile Properties section. The process for creating a new property would be as follows. From the Add User Profile Property Web page, a portion of which is shown in Figure 9.6, you would type a name for the property in the Name box and a Display Name in the Property Settings section. Properties also support multiple languages, as you can see by clicking the Edit Languages button. Choose the data type for the property from the Type menu (for example, string, float, or date). In the Length box, type a value for the maximum length of the property. (This option will not appear if it is not applicable for the property type.) Enable multiple values if appropriate by selecting the Allow multiple values check box. If you select this option, indicate how values are separated by clicking either Comma: A,B,C... or Semicolon: A;B;C;... on the Multivalue Separator menu. Properties can be assigned a choice list by selecting the Allow choice list check box. Enabling this option creates a new section called "Choice List Settings." Options for the choice list can be defined by selecting Defined Choice List. Users can be enabled to add their own choices by selecting the Allow users to add to choice list check box. A comma-delimited list can be imported.

Alternative Display Names

Alternative display names can be provided for each language by clicking the Edit Languages button, clicking Add Language, selecting a language from the menu, and then typing the display name in the new language. The name that is displayed depends on the operating system language being used by the user viewing the property. You cannot change a property to a multi-valued property if it was initially created as a single-value property. A property that was initially created without a choice list cannot be subsequently changed to have a choice list. Therefore, if you think that you may want a choice list in the future, you should select the Allow choice list check box at creation.

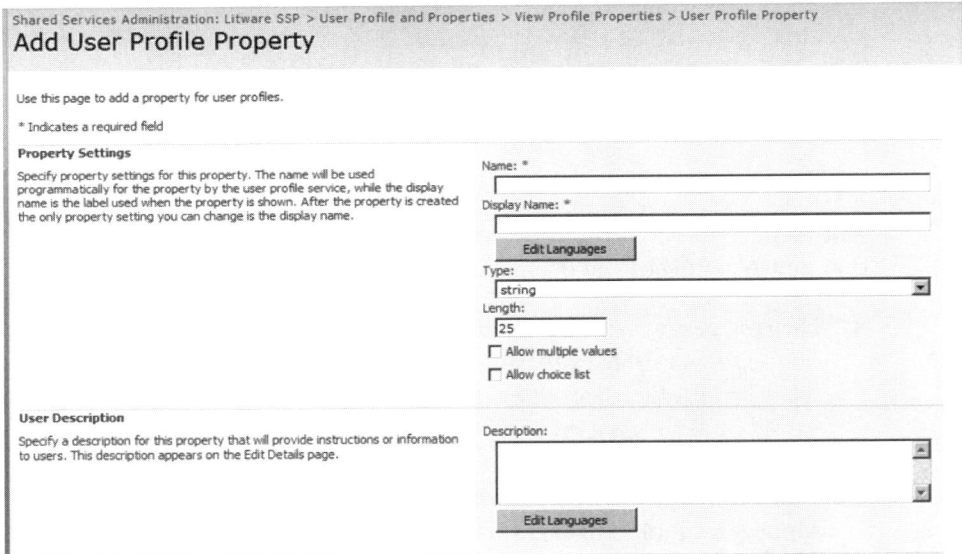

FIGURE 9.6
A portion of the Add User Profile Properties Web page.

- Property visibility is controlled by the privacy policy. The configuration of the Policy Settings section of the Add User Profile Property Web page defines the property policy. In the drop-down list box inside the Policy Settings section, you will need to choose whether a privacy policy is Required, Optional, or Disabled. The property may contain information if its policy setting is Optional and must contain information if the policy setting is Required. Select Disabled to prevent anyone but the SSP administrator from viewing the property or feature. On the Default Privacy Setting menu, click one of the following: Only Me, My Manager, My Workgroup, My Colleagues, Everyone. The description of each of these settings is given in Table 9.1. My Workgroup limits visibility to the user and all users who report to the same manager. Choose Everyone to share the information with all users who have the Use personal features permission. Select the User can override check box to allow users to change the default privacy setting. In general, this should not be chosen without careful consideration. Properties can be replicated to every site collection in the SharePoint farm by selecting the Replicable check box. The Replicable check box may be grayed-out and not available for selecting. The privacy policy must be set to Everyone, and the User can override check box must not be selected to enable the replicate option. Replication occurs during profile imports. Determine if users will be allowed to edit property values by selecting the appropriate check box in the Edit Settings section, as well as where the property will be displayed on the user's My Site in the Display Settings section. The Show in the profile properties section of the user's profile page option will be grayed-out if Only Me is chosen for the privacy.

TABLE 9.1 PRIVACY SETTINGS

Setting	Description
Only Me	The owner of the My Site.
My Manager	The manager property is dynamically assigned, according to the Manager property in Active Directory, once imports have been configured.
My Colleagues	Other user profiles that share common attributes (such as members of the same site) with a My Site owner can be added to the individual's My Site. This can be accomplished as part of the people search process or suggested by SharePoint.
My Workgroup	One of the preconfigured groups in the My Site. Colleagues can be added to this group as colleagues are added to a My Site.
Everyone	All users with at least Read access to My Sites.

NOTE

Property Visibility

To display the property in the profile properties section of the user's profile page, select Show in the profile properties section of the user's profile page. Show on the Edit Details page displays the property on the Edit Details page available from the personal page of My Site. Show changes in the Colleague Tracker Web Part displays changes to the property in the Colleagues section of My Site and all other instances of the Colleague Tracker Web Part.

■ Property indexing can be enabled from the Add User Profile Property Web page in the Search Settings section by selecting the Indexed check box, which also ensures that it is part of the people search scope schema. Select the Alias check box to treat the property as a user name or account name. An alias property will be used when searching for items authored by a user, targeting items to a user, or displaying items in the Documents Web Part of the user's personal site. This option will not be available if Only Me is the privacy setting.

■ Property mapping defines what attribute values are imported and assigned to a profile property during a profile import. The Property Import Mapping section is the last section on the Add User Profile Property Web page and is shown in Figure 9.7. The Source Data Connection menu will display current connections. This menu includes the Master Connection for all directory services connections and each of the connections to entities in the BDC. Choose the appropriate data connection for the property mapping. In the Data source field to map box, select the property in the data source that is to be mapped to the specific profile property. All properties from SSPs in trusted domains appear in this list. To map to a property in the master connection, select Data source field to map and then click a property in the menu, or select Enter field to map and type the name of the data source field. Property values are mapped when the next import occurs.

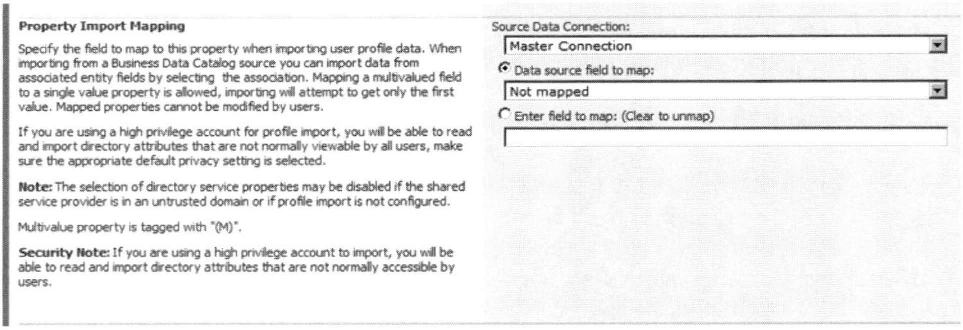

Property Import Mapping

Specify the field to map to this property when importing user profile data. When importing from a Business Data Catalog source you can import data from associated entity fields by selecting the association. Mapping a multivalued field to a single value property is allowed, importing will attempt to get only the first value. Mapped properties cannot be modified by users.

If you are using a high privilege account for profile import, you will be able to read and import directory attributes that are not normally viewable by all users, make sure the appropriate default privacy setting is selected.

Note: The selection of directory service properties may be disabled if the shared service provider is in an untrusted domain or if profile import is not configured.

Multivalue property is tagged with "(M)".

Security Note: If you are using a high privilege account to import, you will be able to read and import directory attributes that are not normally accessible by users.

Source Data Connection:

Master Connection

Data source field to map:

Not mapped

Enter field to map: (Clear to unmap)

FIGURE 9.7
Property Import Mapping section on the Add User Profile Property Web page.

■ Users are added to the profile and individual properties within each profile are populated with values based on mappings created between the data directory or BDC and the profile property during each and every import. Property values will be overwritten every time profiles are imported from the master connection; BDC imports are supplemental only. Additional properties, or custom properties, can be added to the user profile and can be configured not to be affected by master data source imports. Custom properties can also be mapped.

■ All user profiles can be indexed and be available by searching and through personalization features. The profile database must be indexed after each and every import to ensure that the search results are as up-to-date and relevant as possible. User profiles can be deleted so information about a user cannot be used in personalization features, even though an individual user is a member of a group imported from directory services.

■ User profiles can be deleted and then subsequently re-added manually or re-imported from the source directory. Unfortunately, once the profile is deleted, the corresponding My Site will not be accessible.

This completes the overview of property definition and mapping. The last step in profile management is profile indexing. Indexing of the profile database content allows the information to be searched and made available to personalization Web parts. Do you recall the search discussion in Chapter 8 and the People tab in the Search Center with Tabs? This is the location that is used to perform people queries and seeing the results once the user profile information has been indexed.

At this point, you should create an incremental import schedule. The frequency will be dependent on how often the data is changing. An incremental import will perform a full import the first time it is initiated. A full import does not have to be scheduled and can be reserved for "clearing the slate" and starting over. Chapter 7, "Managing Site Customization: Templates, Features, and Solution Packages," discusses the details for creating both full and incremental imports. The reader is encouraged to review that discussion. The next section covers people search.

MOSS imports data from a master connection by default, which is typically an Active Directory or LDAP data source. This import creates new user profiles, updates existing profiles, and populates all profile properties mapped to data source attributes. Imports from a BDC connection are supplemental, and they populate properties in profiles that already exist but that are not populated by the values retrieved from the master data connection. The reader interested in utilizing the BDC in general and specifically supplemental profile imports using the BDC is referred to the excellent book titled *Inside the Index and Search Engines* by Patrick Tisseghem.

PEOPLE SEARCH

Once user profiles have been created and a full crawl has been completed, then profile information is available through the search process. MOSS search includes people search capability, as we have briefly seen in Chapter 8. People search is available with or without My Sites. This is an important point since many organizations will not deploy My Sites initially.

Many times we need to identify a technical resource or subject matter expert associated with a given technology, rather than technical information about a given subject. MOSS has the ability to search for people with certain knowledge and expertise. People search functionality supplements the capability for finding content and allows users to find and leverage the knowledge held by other individuals throughout the organization. People search capability is available through the MOSS search center. We will begin the people search discussion with a discussion of the search center. Search center information was briefly discussed in Chapter 8, but the focus there was on "getting search up and running" and was not on the topic of people search or any specifics of the search center. Therefore, some of the information may be repeated, but if so it is minimal, and the author has deemed it necessary for the discussion. The purpose of the discussion is to provide the administrator with the necessary information to get "people search up and running."

Search Capability

Windows SharePoint Services v3.0 and the different versions of Search Server 2008 do not provide the people search capability.

Search Center

MOSS comes with two different search site templates: Search Center and Search Center with Tabs. The following discussion will focus on the latter. Search Center plays a central role in the user experience with MOSS search by providing a more functionally rich and pleasing interface to the small search box that populates all sites. The tabbed site can only be created from the corresponding site template and included as part of a site collection that has the publishing features activated. Also, a tabbed site is automatically created as part of the Collaboration Portal site template. Figure 9.8 displays a tabbed site that was provisioned from the Search Center with Tabs site template. We will begin by discussing the People Search Web page and the tabbed user interface.

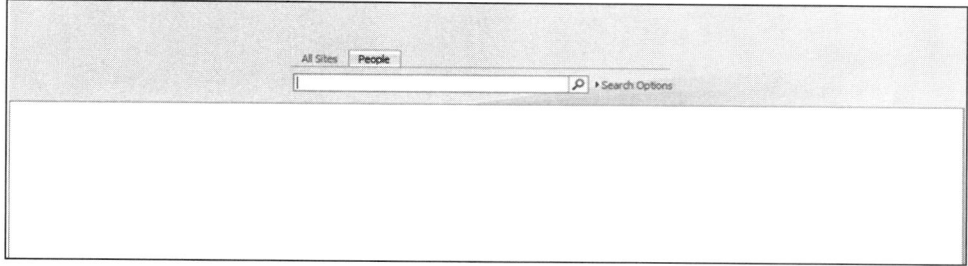

FIGURE 9.8
The Search Center with Tabs Web site.

People Search Page and Tab

The site in Figure 9.8 displays two tabs by default: All Sites and People. Each tab includes a query box centered on the page, with an area beneath for displaying search results. The tabbed structure is extensible; existing tabs can be modified and new tabs can be creating by editing the page. The All Sites tab is selected by default when a user browses to the site. It is associated with the default.aspx page, which is the default or home page for the site. The query search box in the center of the page is configured to work with the All Sites search scope by default. The people.aspx search page is associated with the People tab. The people search page contains Web parts and options that are specific to people search functionality.

The people.aspx Web page contains a similar type of search box Web part to the one on the default.aspx page; both allow the user to enter and execute keyword queries. The search box Web part on the People tab page can be revealed by entering edit mode on the page, which will reveal the People Search Box Web part, as shown in Figure 9.9. You can see from the figure that existing tabs can be edited and new tabs created, as well as modify the properties of the People Search Box Web part. By clicking the Search Options link directly to the right of the search box, the Search Options pane is revealed, as shown in Figure 9.10.

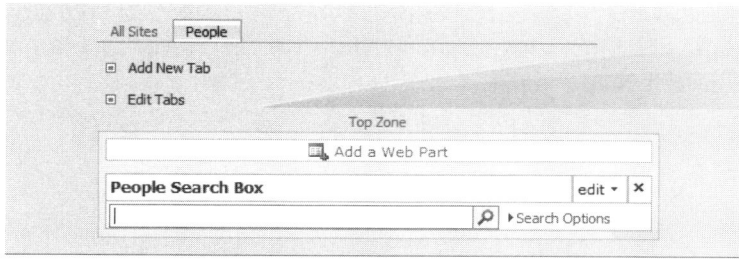

FIGURE 9.9
The Search Web page in edit mode.

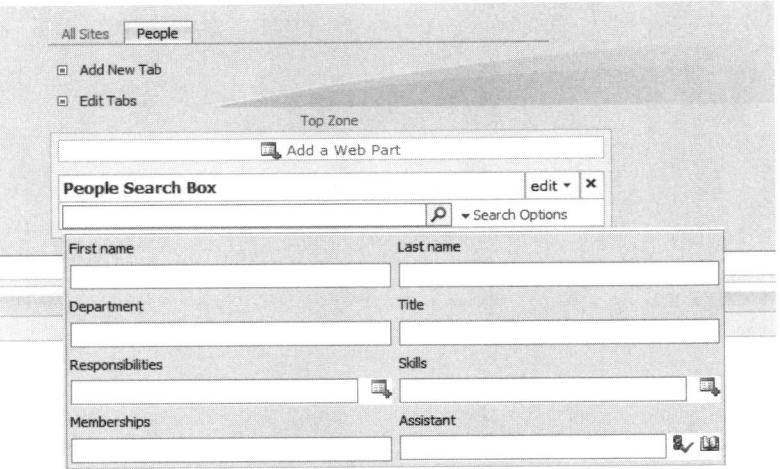

FIGURE 9.10
The People Search Options pane.

The reader may notice that some of property titles in the Search Options pane are the names of properties contained inside of the user profile. These properties can be used to search for people with property values equal to those entered into the query. Therefore, this pane simplifies the user experience by helping them formulate people queries, just like the Advanced Search page helps in searching for specific values of managed properties like we saw in Chapter 8. Therefore, people in the organization whose profile attribute values equal values entered into the search pane will be returned as part of the search results. This emphasizes the power of information contained in the user profile and the flexibility available for populating the profile, as we discussed in the first part of the chapter. Properties in the option pane can be configured to assist the user in determining the words to enter into the query. For example, notice the Assistant property and the two icons directly to the right of the text box. By clicking the open book icon, a dialog box allowing the user to perform a lookup is revealed and shown in Figure 9.11. You could enter a name, such as John, and perform a lookup and then choose a value returned from the directory service lookup. You can also use the check names icon to check that a specific name exists in the directory.

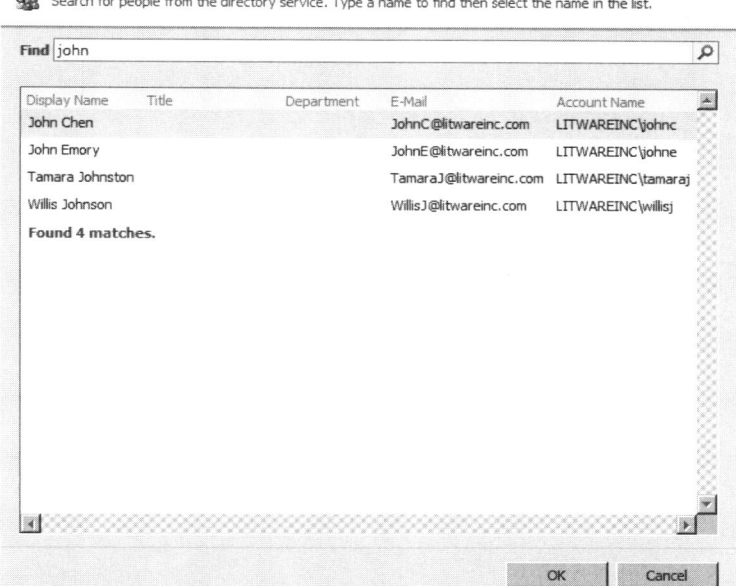

FIGURE 9.11
The directory Search dialog box.

A new tab can be created by clicking the Add new tab link on the search page in edit mode. This reveals the Tabs in Search Pages Web page shown in Figure 9.12. You will notice from the figure that you must associate a specific search results page with the new tab. If you don't, you will not be allowed to create a new tab. For example, you could create a tab called "Customer" and have the results mapped to a different page that only displays customer results. Once you are finished and click the OK button, you will be redirected to the Tabs in Search Pages list. This list has all the expected features of any SharePoint list. You will also need to create a tab on the search results page with the corresponding name. This can be accomplished from the Tabs in Search Results list. Both of these lists are available from the All Site Content page. The reader who is interested in the specific steps for creating a custom search page and tab is directed to the white paper "Creating a Custom Search Page and Tabs in the Search Center of SharePoint Server" at http://msdn.microsoft.com/en-us/library/bb428855.aspx.

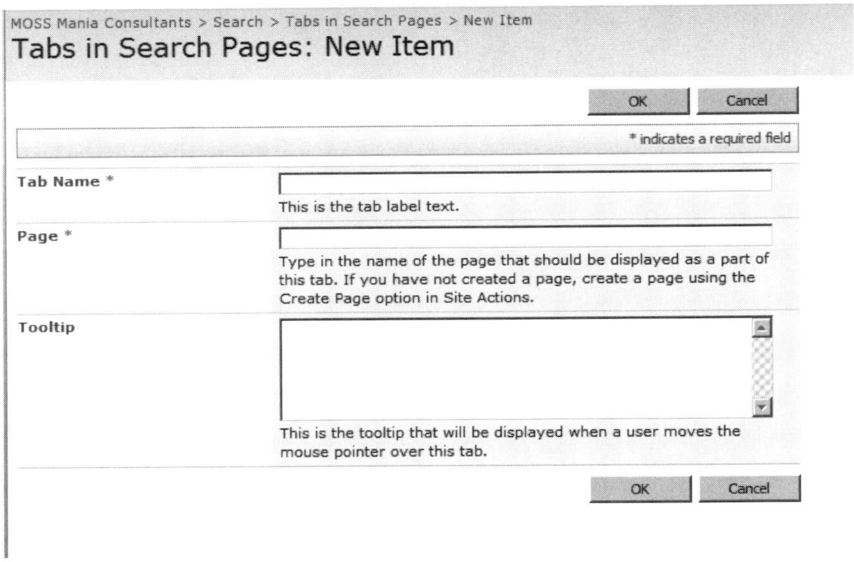

MOSS Mania Consultants > Search > Tabs in Search Pages > New Item
Tabs in Search Pages: New Item

OK   Cancel

* indicates a required field

Tab Name *

This is the tab label text.

Page *

Type in the name of the page that should be displayed as a part of this tab. If you have not created a page, create a page using the Create Page option in Site Actions.

Tooltip

This is the tooltip that will be displayed when a user moves the mouse pointer over this tab.

OK   Cancel

FIGURE 9.12
Tabs in Search Pages Web page.

People Search Results Page

When you perform a people search, for all users named John, the search results are displayed on the peopleresults.aspx Web page shown in Figure 9.13. Two results are shown for this query, and they are sorted by Social Distance, which is the default. Social Distance is based on colleague relationships; it represents a relationship between the person issuing the query and his or her colleagues. For example, a user will see search results containing people at a similar level in the organizational hierarchy displayed higher in the list because of their higher relevance. The results will be displayed as groups—the first group will be your colleagues, the next group will be colleagues of your colleagues, and then everyone else will be grouped last. Within each group, the ordering of the results is based on relevance. People search uses the same relevance algorithm as MOSS search discussed in Chapter 8. Conceptually, a user's profile is treated as a document with their name as the title. Simplistically, the more search query terms that appear in the person's profile, the more relevant the result will be.

Figure 9.13 illustrates that each result contains a picture, their name, and additional information from their user profile. From the search results, you can also tell if the individual is available. This is done by viewing the user's presence information, which is shown by noting the color of the circle directly to the left of the individual's name.

FIGURE 9.13
The people search results Web page.

Presence information is a result of integration of MOSS with Microsoft Communication Server or equivalent and provides a status of the individual, such as they are currently online and available, or they are busy and not available. If they are available, you could initiate an instant messaging session or call them directly.

Search results can be further refined by user profile properties, such as job title and department, as can be seen from the links on the left-hand side of the results page. Also, the results can be viewed based on search term relevance by clicking the View by Relevance link. People search relevance is based on profile properties. The more search query terms that are present in the person's profile, the more relevant that person will be in the results.

You can find out more information about the individual by clicking his or her name, which is actually a hyperlink that will take you to that person's corresponding personal site, as shown in Figure 9.14. What if a user hasn't created a My Site? A portion of the My Site (the My Profile page) is generated automatically as part of the user profile creation process. During the profile import, a profile page is created for that specific user. So even though the My Site has not been explicitly created by the user, the user's profile page will exist.

My Site Details

A My Site is represented by a My Home page (default.aspx) and a My Profile page (person.aspx). The My Profile page is provided for every user in the portal, regardless of whether they have a My Site, or even if My Sites are disabled for the organization. Yes, even if the My Site functionality is disabled for the user or the organization, the user will still have a profile page. See the My Site Creation section for more details.

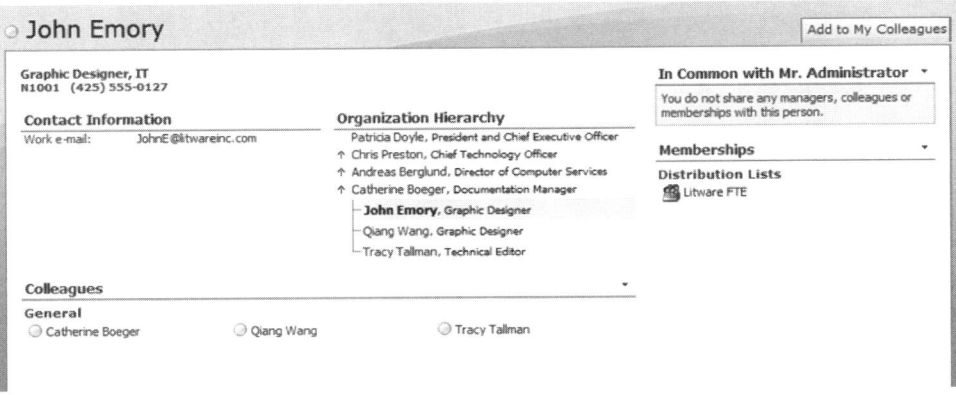

FIGURE 9.14
Example My Site for an individual in the organization.

Each result also has an Add to My Colleagues link, which represents one of the social networking features of MOSS. The profile database maintains a list of your colleagues that is populated during a profile import. Initially, this list is populated with a set of "immediate colleagues" that are computed from your profile properties: manager, peers, and direct reports. You can also add and remove colleagues from your My Site or your My Profile page. By clicking the Add to My Colleagues link, the Add Colleagues Web page is displayed, as shown in Figure 9.15. This page allows you to set the privacy policy for who can view this colleague and gives you the ability to assign the colleague to an existing or custom group to improve organization of your colleagues. Once you complete this page, that user will be added to the Colleagues Tracker Web part and you will be returned to the search results page. You will notice that the results page has changed, as seen in Figure 9.16.

After adding John Emory as a colleague, the search results are displayed with John Emory grouped within My Colleagues and ranked higher than John Chen, who is contained in the Everyone Else group.

The search results also provide the user with the option of creating a search alert using the Alert Me link. Search alerts were discussed in Chapter 8, but essentially allow the user to be notified when any of the search results change for a specific query they have previously executed. MOSS search also supports RSS feeds, as can be seen from the previous figures.

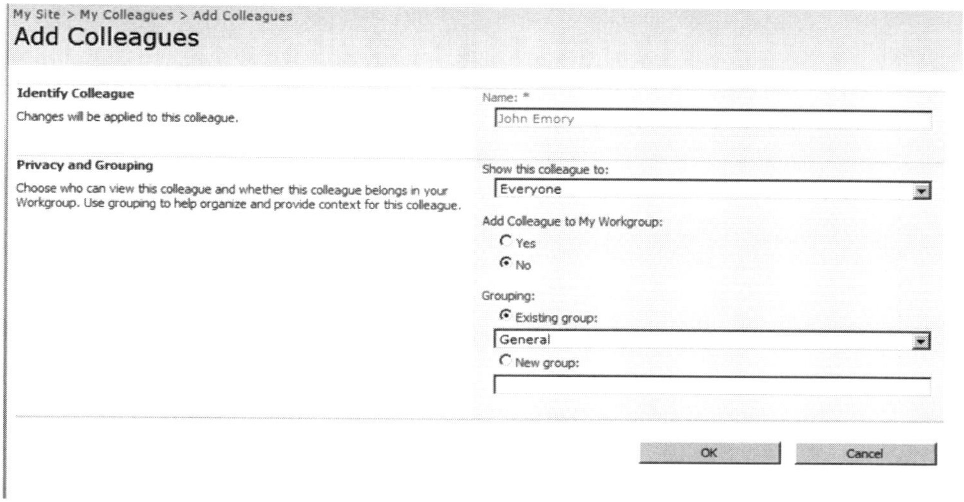

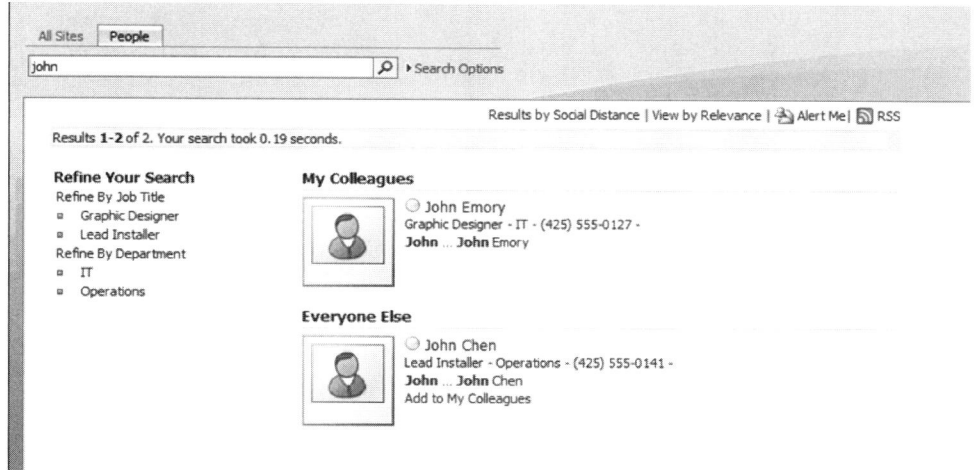

FIGURE 9.15
Add Colleagues Web page.

FIGURE 9.16
Revised people search results page after adding a colleague.

You can see that user profile information can be returned as part of the people search results. Keep in mind that the privacy controls specified in Table 9.1 govern what will be visible and to whom. For example, if a specific user has configured the Skills property to only be visible to him (Only Me), any information from this attribute will not be returned as part of the search results. However, one exception may occur. Let's consider that the property's visibility was changed from Everyone to Only Me. The Only Me policy will not take effect until an incremental crawl is performed, and therefore members of the Everyone group will continue to see the Skill property values.

My Sites

A SharePoint My Site represents a user's personal desktop. My Sites require MOSS and is not available on WSS-only installations. This desktop has both a public view and a private or personal view. From this desktop, users can view and centrally manage all of their documents, tasks, links, calendar, colleagues, and other personal information. It also provides a way for other users to view your information and learn about you and your areas of expertise, current projects, and colleague relationships.

My Sites are a SharePoint Web site so they have the features you would expect from sites such as Web parts, lists, and libraries. Actually, My Sites are site collections so things like quotas can be established. My Sites also allow user profile property information to be shared and as we have seen, the visibility of these property values is governed by policies. Information can also be targeted to you by content providers based on your profile.

My Sites can display lists of memberships, such as distribution lists, a listing of your colleagues, and an organization hierarchy diagram to show your position within your immediate team. When other people visit your My Site, they can quickly see what they have in common with you—colleagues whom you both know, memberships that you share, and the first manager whom you both share.

A user's default view of his My Site includes two tabs: My Home and My Profile. My Home is the user's private page and only viewable by the My Site owner. The My Profile page contains the user's information that will be made available to others based on the privacy controls specified by the owner and summarized in Table 9.1. These privacy controls govern what information is displayed on the user's public My Site page. Therefore, the public My Site page displays information based on the specific user that is viewing the page and the policy settings.

MY SITE CREATION

My Sites are activated at the Web application level, since a Web application is associated with a single SSP and My Sites are one of the offered services. Therefore, if any of the sites in the Web application will benefit from My Site capabilities, My Sites should be enabled and utilized. However, My Sites can represent a large storage requirement since each site is actually a site collection and personal sites can dramatically grow in size if utilized extensively by a large number of users. A My Site is composed of a public Web page called "My Profile" and a private page called "My Home." These two different pages are actually stored in two different site collections. This can be confirmed by looking at the two different URLs for these two pages. The My Profile page is automatically created and is rendered from the http://mysite/person.aspx Web page. The person.aspx page has code that displays a "My Home" tab linking to the user's My Site at http://mysite/personal/userid/default.aspx if it exists. The term mysite in the two previous sentences represents the URL of the Web application that is hosting your My Site and userid is your user ID. The My Home tab makes it appear that My Home and My Profile are part of the same site, while in actuality they are in separate site collections.

Therefore, as an administrator and planning for My Sites, Web applications that have a large number of users, a high volume of content, and relatively little need for personalization or collaboration might not benefit from My Sites. By default, users that are members of the NT Authority\Authenticated Users group have permission to create a My Site. As soon as My Sites are activated, any user profiles are replaced by the public profiles (My Profile pages) that are part of My Site. As each additional user profile is created, a subsequent My Profile page is also created. This My Profile page (person.aspx) holds profile information associated with the import and does not contain the collaboration features of a standard My Site. A My Site link is added to the top menu bar for all sites in the site collection, along with the My Links menu. An individual user's My Site (My Home + My Profile) is created the first time the user logs into a SharePoint site and clicks the My Site link in the top menu bar. The user is added to the Site Collection Administrators group, and he has full control over his My Site. At this point, the user's My Site will appear on the Site Collection List Web page in Central Administration. If a My Site has not been explicitly created and only the My Profile page exists, then the Site Collection List will not contain an entry for the My Site. The My Profile page will exist even if My Site creation is disabled. My Site creation can be disabled using the following process.

Disabling My Site Creation

Navigate to the Manage Permissions: Shared Service Rights Web page by clicking the Personalization services permissions link on the SSP home page. This will reveal the page that is shown in Figure 9.17. From this figure, you'll notice the Authenticated

Users group. Deleting this group will remove the ability of users to create My Sites. If you choose not to enable My Sites initially, the authors recommend enabling My Sites for a small and select group of users so that the functionality can be assessed for its applicability for the organization. This could be accomplished by adding a group to this list and providing them with the necessary permissions for site creation. The default permissions of the Authenticated Users group can be seen by clicking the group name, which is actually a hyperlink to the Modify Permissions: Shared Service Rights Web page shown in Figure 9.18. You will notice from the figure that the Create personal site and Use personal features permissions are enabled. Disabling the Create personal site permission will remove the My Site link from the top menu bar of all pages, and it will also remove the My Home tab from any My Site that already exists. No new My Sites will be allowed to be created once the permission is disabled. However, any existing My Site can still be accessed by entering the URL of the My Site directly into the browser, http://mysite/personal/userid/default.aspx. To prevent browsing to existing My Sites, disable the Use personal features permission. In both of these cases, the My Profile tab is still visible and the profile page is still accessible by entering http://mysite/person.aspx directly into the browser. You can also access the My Profile page using the user link provided via People search results in the search center.

Office SharePoint Server Standard Web Application Feature

My Sites are activated by default as part of the Office SharePoint Server Standard Web application feature. This feature can be deactivated at either the Web application or at the site collection or site level. Unfortunately, you will also lose the search functionality by deactivating this feature, so this is not recommended.

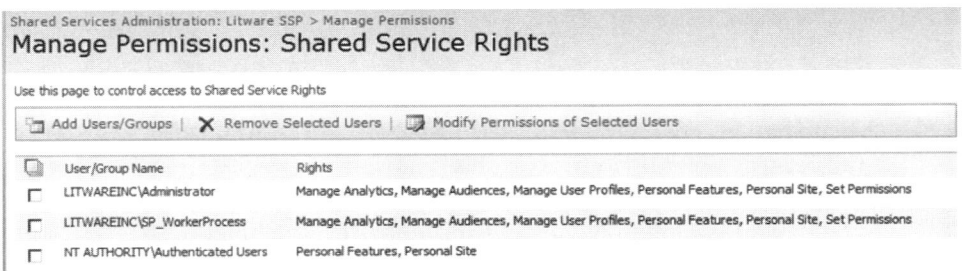

FIGURE 9.17
Manage Permissions: Shared Service Rights Web page.

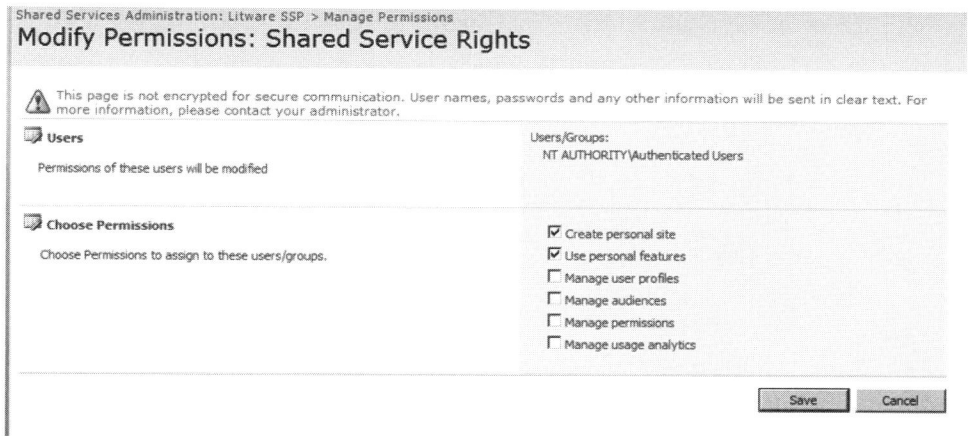

FIGURE 9.18
Modify Permissions: Shared Service Rights Web page.

USING MY SITES

My Sites and people search represent the key components of SharePoint's social networking capability. Users can add custom Web parts, such as the Colleague Tracker Web part, which will display and highlight any change to a user's colleague's profile or memberships. Users can locate other users based on similar interests and suggest colleagues that users may be interested in getting connected. The My Profiles page allows the site owner to selectively expose information based on the configuration of privacy controls, as we have already discussed.

The first time the user creates his or her My Site, he or she is prompted with the Configure My Site for Microsoft Office dialog box shown in Figure 9.19. This may seem like a strange question to be asking the user, but keep in mind that the user could have more than one My Site. This can occur because My Sites are configured within the SSP and associated with a Web application. An organization could have multiple SSPs and more than one Web application for creating My Sites. In the case of multiple SSPs, only one should be enabled for My Site creation and all others disabled, as we discussed in the previous section. The user can choose not to accept at this time, and he will still have the option later by clicking the Set As Default My Site tab on the My Home page. Once the default is established, the My Site location is saved to a registry key on the user's client machine and the location is also written to the Active Directory. The benefit of this is that the user's My Site location will be included as part of Save dialog boxes and links published to Office desktop applications. The specific user automatically becomes the owner and administrator of the My Site, which you'll recall is a site collection. This enables the user to manage the access permissions for those in the organization. The default appearance of the My Site immediately after creation is shown in Figure 9.20.

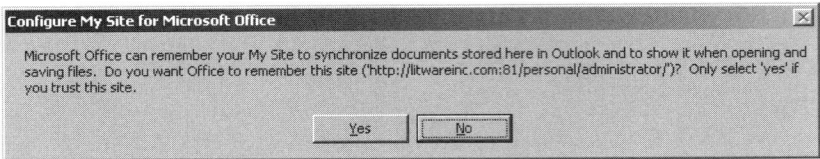

FIGURE 9.19
Configure My Site for Microsoft Office dialog box.

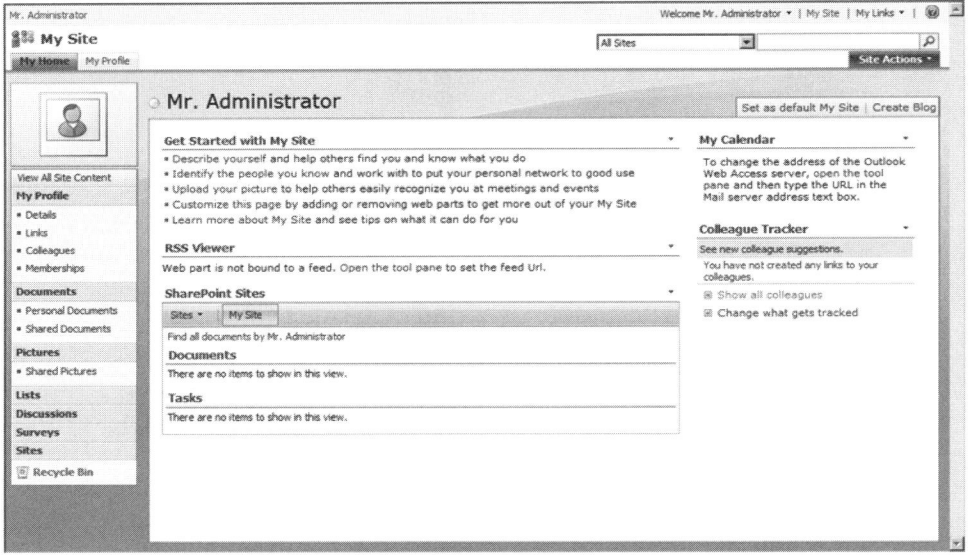

FIGURE 9.20
Default My Site upon first creation by user.

You'll notice that a new My Site has a similar appearance to a new team site. The two different tabs that we have been discussing, My Home and My Profile, are visible on the left-hand side horizontal navigation. The default view is the private view of the My Home home page. Set As Default My Site tab is also visible on the right-hand side and provides the ability to establish this My Site as the default, as we have previously discussed. A tab for creating a new blog site is also present. If you click the Create Blog link, it will take you to your blog site with an initial post entitled "Welcome to your Blog." Once you return to your My Site, the Create

Blog link will be gone. There is also a Personal Documents document library, which is accessible by the My Site owner and server administrators. The Shared Document library is accessible to other users. My Sites are also populated with five different Web parts. From left-to-right and top-to-bottom, these include: Getting Started with My Site, My Calendar, RSS Viewer, Colleague Tracker, and Share-Point Sites. These Web parts are described in Table 9.2.

TABLE 9.2 DEFAULT WEB PARTS FOR NEW MY SITE

Web Part Name	Description and Content
Getting Started with	Instructions for configuring the My Site, such as Identify.
My Site	The people you know that is hyperlinked to the Add Colleagues Web page for adding new colleagues.
My Calendar	The owner's calendar from Exchange 2003 or later. This will need to be configured with the Outlook Web Access address.
RSS Viewer	Web part to display RSS feeds. This will need to be configured using the Web part's tool pane in edit mode.
Colleague Tracker	This is a very powerful social networking Web part. It displays the user's colleagues based on colleagues added manually, added as part of people search, dynamically added values from the the user profile, and organizational hierarchy. It also alerts the user of changes to colleague's properties.
SharePoint Sites	This Web part shows sites of which the user is a member and any documents for that user on those sites. It also displays a rollup of tasks for the user across the membership sites. This Web part is configurable by the user and updated dynamically.

A user is the owner and administrator of his personal site and as such can further customize his site by adding Web parts, create document libraries and picture libraries, calendars, surveys, tasks, and other SharePoint lists. The owner can create other pages on his personal site and provide links to those pages by using the public home page.

Configuring Colleagues

The Colleague Tracker Web part helps you to keep track of such things as whether your colleagues are in the office, in meetings, or on the telephone. You can also be notified when colleagues' profile properties change, add documents to a SharePoint library, or have an anniversary or birthday. In addition, you can choose who appears on your Colleagues list and organize your Colleagues list by groups. The list of your colleagues is stored in the profile database. During a profile import, the colleague's list is initially populated with a set of "immediate colleagues" that are computed from your profile properties: Manager, Peers, and Direct Reports. Therefore, the Colleagues Tracker Web part should be populated assuming these AD properties are utilized and a successful import has been completed. This Web part is populated several ways, and each option is briefly summarized next.

■ **Manually By Owner.** Colleagues can be added manually using the Colleagues link in the My Profile section on the left-hand side navigation, from the Colleagues Web part on the My Profile page and using the Add To My Colleagues link returned in People search results, as we saw previously.
■ **Immediate Colleagues.** These colleagues are added as part of the profile import and the values of the properties Manager, Peers (others who report to your manager), and Direct Reports.
■ **Suggested by SharePoint.** As you can see in Figure 9.20, there is a link called "See new colleague suggestions." These suggestions are based on: Outlook Sent Items' entries, Office Communication Server contacts if present, and Web sites in which you or others are explicitly included in the "Members" group for the site. This information is collected by a WSS profile synchronization timer job.

Each Colleague is represented by his user name, which is formatted as a hyperlink to his My Site. Colleagues can be organized into groups for easier management, and they can also be added to a special group called "My Workgroup." Colleagues that are members of My Workgroup will have access to any other My Site information made available through this privacy group summarized earlier in Table 9.1.

Figure 9.21 shows a portion of the Colleague Tracker Web part Tool Pane. As can be seen, there are a number of different types of changes that can be tracked, and there are two custom properties. These properties allow you to display all the colleagues or only those with changes. You can also restrict the display to only show colleagues that are members of your workgroup.

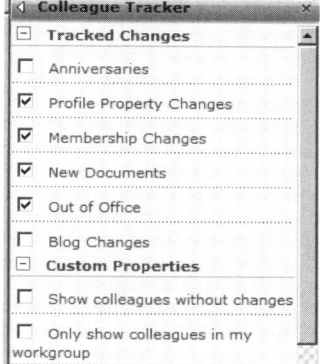

FIGURE 9.21
A portion of the Colleague
Tracker Web part Tool Pane.

Configuring Memberships

Memberships are added manually and created dynamically based on the user's membership to SharePoint sites and distribution lists. Memberships are managed by clicking the Memberships link beneath the My Profile heading on the left-hand side. Membership information drives the display of several Web parts on the My Home and My Profile pages. User membership defines the display of sites shown on the tabbed section of the SharePoint Sites Web part on the My Home page. The Documents Web part on the My Profile page and the distribution lists in the In Common With You Web Part on the My Profile page are also dependent on membership information.

Configuring My Profile

This is the public face of a user's My Site when viewed by a different user. The content of this page will be based on the Web parts configured for display, the user's identity, and the policy control settings established by the My Site owner. A My Profile page is initially created for a user during a profile import so that user's information can be displayed. Upon My Site creation, the My Profile page is completed with the addition of Web parts and filtered views, as shown in Figure 9.22. This figure shows the My Site owner's view. You'll notice in the upper-right corner the enumerated As Seen By drop-down list. This option is great for a site owner because it allows him to view his site as another user would view his site based on the policy settings he established for each of the properties. The individual properties can be configured by clicking the Details link, which displays the Edit Details Web page. Some of the properties are preconfigured by the administrator with a policy of Everyone, and they are not configurable by the My Site owner.

FIGURE 9.22
An example My Profile page upon My Site creation.

A My Site is a central location for viewing and managing personal information, content, and links to other content, as well as a list of colleagues. This provides a personal desktop for improving efficiency, as well as providing a way for other users to learn about you and your areas of expertise, current projects, and colleague relationships. My Sites are an integral part of MOSS' social networking capability and when combined with people search, they provide a very powerful frame for collaboration.

10 Configuring Internet-Accessible Web Sites

In This Chapter

- Introduction
- User Authentication
- Extranet and Intranet Scenario
- Alternate Access Mapping

INTRODUCTION

As we have seen, MOSS includes several major improvements over the previous SharePoint version, SharePoint Portal Server 2003 (SPS), which are highlighted here. Specifically, additional user authentication options enable user access from outside of the corporate environment and expand MOSS use to Internet and extranet Web sites. The previous version required users to authenticate using Windows Integrated Security.

MOSS provides customers with the ability to use other forms of authentication because it utilizes the ASP.NET 2.0 authentication provider model, which allows authentication based on LDAP, SQL Server, or any other data store in general. User authentication can also be done using Active Directory Federated Services (ADFS). This allows each organization to manage their own accounts and utilize a secure trust between organizations to allow authentication. Anonymous access can now be controlled at a more granular level, rather than the virtual server level as in SPS. Several other key advantages of MOSS over SPS are mentioned in the following text.

Web site branding is as much, if not more, important for Internet-accessible Web sites as compared to intranets. MOSS includes template architecture for branding Web pages using ASP.NET 2.0 Master Pages. Now it is much easier to match the look and feel of the extranet to that of the intranet or customize the extranet in a totally different way. Different sites can also be branded in different ways.

MOSS includes Web Content Management (WCM) capability that allows content to be created and copied from one place to another on a schedule. For example, content from an intranet can be published and reused on an externally accessible site. There is also improved multi-lingual support and a technology called "Variations." Variations provide the capability to replicate a site's content to another site or sites so the content can be exposed to other devices or translated into other languages.

Item-level security has been added to MOSS, which provides additional granular control over individual list items and documents. This capability was discussed in Chapter 4, "Securing and Managing Site Content," and will be referred to later in the chapter when we are discussing user access.

MOSS also supports the use of RSS feeds. MOSS still includes the Alert notification, but now includes RSS feeds, which are available on every type of list.

MOSS has support for a larger number of Web browsers, including FireFox, Safari, and Netscape, and includes support for Web pages on mobile devices.

The advantages mentioned previously are not meant to be comprehensive of all the new features, but rather illustrate that MOSS includes a key capability for configuring and managing external access. Access to content from outside the corporate firewall can be categorized into at least three different types of scenarios.

1. Internet Web site that provides both anonymous and secure access capability. Secure access to nonemployees requires that a user database of some type is maintained. Typically, in this scenario, external users register for secure access, which then usually provides them with broader access to more content or some type of special functionality.
2. Remote employee access to the intranet portal using the Internet. This is essentially an extension of the corporate intranet so employees can get access without using a virtual private network.
3. Portal access to customers or partners. Just like in scenario 1, user accounts for the external users must be maintained or some kind of trust must be created between organizations (such as account federation using Active Directory Federated Service).

Scenarios 2 and 3 refer to an extranet environment that represents a private network that is securely extended outside the corporate firewall so that an organization's information can be shared. MOSS provides flexibility for configuring extranet access to Web sites. A subset of sites on a server farm can be exposed to the Internet or all the content can be made available. You can host content inside your corporate network and make it available through an edge firewall, or you can isolate the server farm inside a perimeter network.

In this chapter, we will discuss the administrative requirements and configuration details for establishing a SharePoint Web site that is accessible from outside of the corporate firewall. Our focus will be on the technical details, and we will not discuss any technology or product licensing requirements for implementing such a scenario. We will also not discuss any potential privacy implications that may arise during the process of exposing corporate information. The discussion will begin with the topic of user authentication.

USER AUTHENTICATION

Web site access is governed by user authentication and user authorization. This is true regardless of whether the user is internal or external. User authorization was discussed very thoroughly in Chapter 4 and will not be repeated here. This section will cover anonymous access and user authentication.

ANONYMOUS ACCESS

This type of access is configured in multiple locations to provide a more flexible and granular approach. Anonymous access must first be enabled in Central Administration for the Web application that hosts the sites that are to be exposed and then enabled at the site level.

First, enable anonymous access for a Web application using Central Administration by navigating to the Authentication Providers Web page using the Authentication Providers link within the Application Security section of the Application Management page. The Authentication Providers Web page is shown in Figure 10.1. From this page, select the desired Web application and the zone to be configured. By clicking the hyperlink of the specific zone to be configured, the Edit Authentication page is revealed. A portion of this page is shown in Figure 10.2. Access is enabled by checking the Enable anonymous access check box and clicking Save at the bottom of the page. This enables the Web application for anonymous access and any site hosted by the Web application can be subsequently enabled for anonymous access as well. Keep in mind that you do not have to configure any settings within IIS Manager.

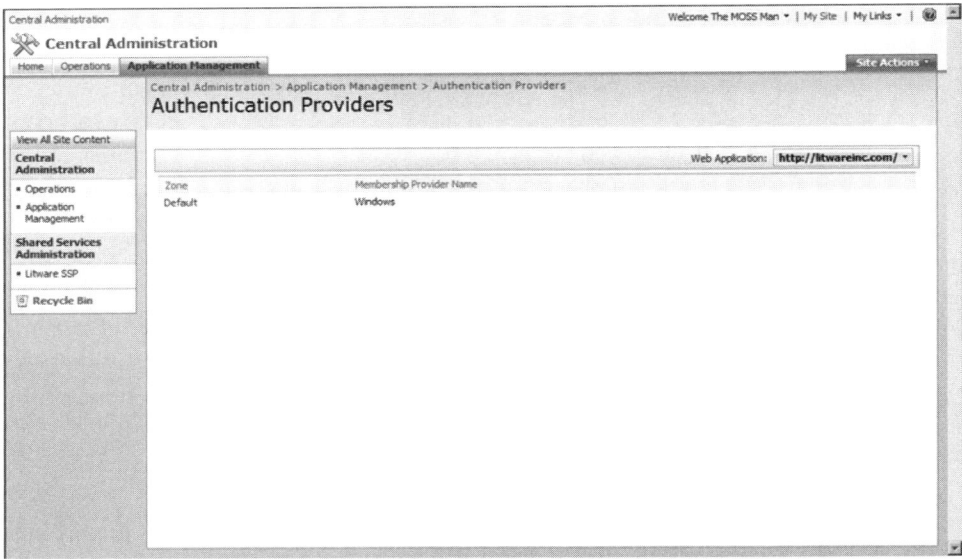

FIGURE 10.1
Authentication Providers Web page.

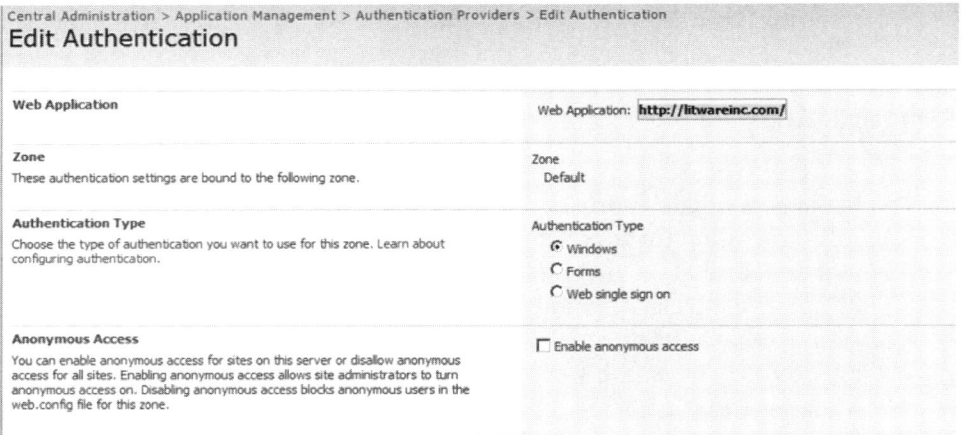

FIGURE 10.2
Edit Authentication Web page for configuring anonymous access.

The second and final step to enabling anonymous access is to turn it on for the specific sites you want enabled. This is accomplished by clicking the Advanced Permissions link from the Site Settings page, which will take you to the Site Permissions page for the specific site. Using the Settings drop-down menu shown in Figure 10.3, click the Anonymous Access option, which will take you to the Change Anonymous Access Settings page shown in Figure 10.4. If the Settings button is not available on the specific site, then it's likely that the current site is inheriting permissions from the parent site, and you will need to break inheritance using the Edit Permissions option from the Actions button. As you can see from Figure 10.4, you can enable the whole Web site or just lists and libraries. Anonymous users will be able to browse the entire site if you enabled the whole Web site. You will notice from Figure 10.4 that anonymous access cannot be set at the item level. These users will have the option to log in using a link provided on the page they are currently viewing.

FIGURE 10.3
Settings drop-down menu used to enable anonymous access.

Use this page to specify what parts of this site anonymous users can access.

Anonymous Access

Specify what parts of your Web site (if any) anonymous users can access. If you select Entire Web site, anonymous users will be able to view all pages in your Web site and view all lists and items which inherit permissions from the Web site. If you select Lists and libraries, anonymous users will be able to view and change items only for those lists and libraries that have enabled permissions for anonymous users.

Anonymous users can access:

○ Entire Web site

○ Lists and libraries

◉ Nothing

[OK]   [Cancel]

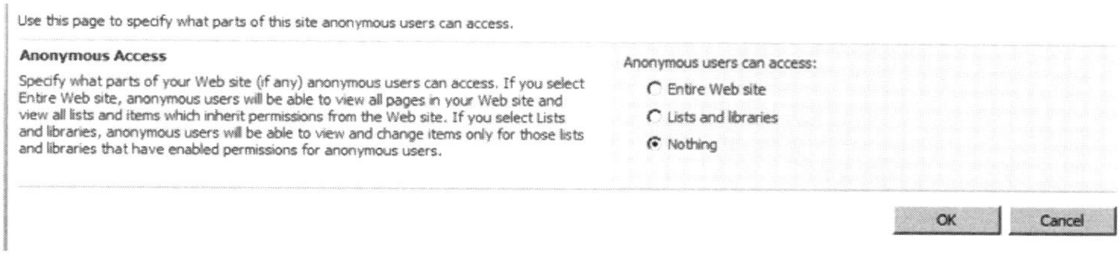

FIGURE 10.4
Change Anonymous Access Settings page.

Therefore, content will be available to enable anonymous access only after you configure at least one zone in the Web application and after the site or site collection is configured to allow anonymous access.

Apply Additional Security

If you are going to enable anonymous access, there are several other precautions that should be taken to help ensure that Central Administration is not accessible, content deployment is disabled if not being used, and you have implemented Lockdown mode.

Central Administration

A few additional security measures should be implemented to help prevent external users from accessing the Central Administration Web site:

■ Ensure that the Central Administration site is not hosted on a Front-end Web server.

■ Access to the Central Administration site should be blocked by placing a firewall between Front-end Web servers and the server that hosts the Central Administration site. The site should also be configured to utilize Secure Sockets Layer (SSL) communication. This ensures secure communication between the internal network and the Central Administration Web site.

Disable Content Deployment

Content deployment should be disabled if not being used to ensure that the server farm is not receiving content from content deployment jobs. This is accomplished from the Content Deployment Settings Web page shown in Figure 10.5, which is accessible from the Operations page using the Content Deployment Settings link and selecting Reject incoming content deployment jobs. If content deployment is being used to deploy content from one server farm to another server farm, ensure that the Central Administration Web site for the receiving server farm is configured to use SSL.

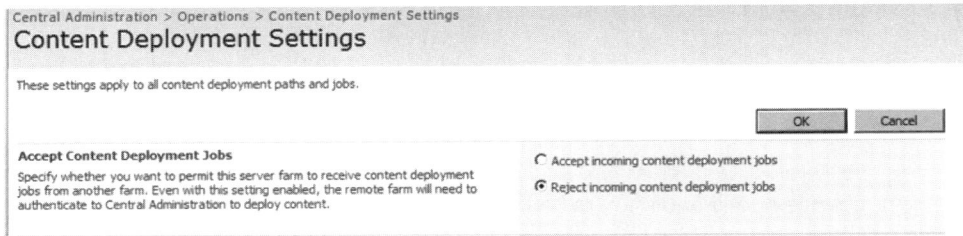

FIGURE 10.5
Content Deployment Settings Web page.

Lockdown Mode

Anonymous users may have access to certain application pages. This occurs because anonymous users are given permissions that are determined by the Limited Access permission level. The default Limited Access permissions are shown in Table 10.1. As you can see from the table, anonymous users have the right to view application pages by default. For example, SharePoint Forms pages (http://SERVER/Pages/Forms/AllItems.aspx) are an example of an application page that may be accessible if you're using the publishing features. There is no way to modify this permission level from the Web browser user interface, but it can be modified programmatically. These default permissions can be changed using a Feature (see Chapter 7, "Managing Site Customization: Templates, Features, and Solution Packages," for a discussion of what constitutes a Feature and how Features are utilized) called the "ViewFormsPagesLockdown Feature," or just the "Lockdown feature," for short. This Feature can be activated using the STSADM Command Line tool:

```
stsadm.exe —o activatefeature —url <site collection url> -filename
ViewFormPagesLockdown\feature.xml
```

Specifically, the Lockdown feature removes the View Application Pages permission and the Use Remote Interfaces permission, as illustrated in Table 10.1. The View Application Pages is the one that allows anonymous users to access the Forms pages. This Feature is activated automatically when the Web site is created using the Publishing Portal template. If your site was created from a different template, you will need to manually activate the Lockdown Feature.

TABLE 10.1 LIMITED ACCESS PERMISSIONS

Permission	Default	Lockdown Mode
View Application Pages	Yes	
Browse User Information	Yes	Yes
Use Remote Interfaces	Yes	
Use Client Integration Features	Yes	Yes
Open	Yes	Yes

Access to Other Applications

Anonymous users will not be able to edit the Web site using SharePoint Designer 2007, and they will not be able to view the site or libraries using My Network Places.

SECURE ACCESS

User authentication for an extranet or Internet-facing portal may require additional configuration compared to the intranet. For the intranet, it is best to utilize Windows Authentication if at all possible. Unfortunately, external users may require a different authentication mechanism. MOSS supports three different authentication types, as seen previously in Figure 10.2: Windows, Forms or Forms-Based Authentication (FBA), and Web Single Sign-On. These types are summarized in Table 10.2.

TABLE 10.2 MOSS AUTHENTICATION MECHANISMS

Method	Description
Windows	Windows authentication, either NTLM or Kerberos. NTLM is selected by default. Users are challenged for their user name and password and then user information is verified using Active Directory. For a discussion of NTLM versus Kerberos, review Chapter 3.
Forms Based	Forms-Based Authentication (FBA) uses the ASP.NET 2.0 authentication provider model. This model eliminates application-specific authentication by providing a common interface that applications can utilize. The specific implementation will reside with the pluggable provider being utilized. MOSS includes providers for Active Directory, LDAP, and SQL Server, but any database system could be utilized with a custom provider.
Web Single Sign-On	MOSS supports the storage and mapping of user credentials so they can be utilized by trusted organizations. ADFS or equivalent Identity Management System integrates with MOSS to provide this capability.

User authentication is configured at the Web application level, as previously discussed and demonstrated in Chapter 3. The authentication provider model actually contains three different individual providers: membership, role, and profile. User authentication and group membership are delivered by the membership and role providers, respectively. The profile provider enables profiles to be created for each user in the user database. The membership and role providers must be specified, the profile is optional. However, if you want each of the FBA users to have a My Site (as discussed in Chapter 9), then you will need a profile provider as well. The following section covers the details for configuring extranet access using FBA.

EXTRANET AND INTRANET SCENARIO

We will consider a scenario where external users are being authenticated using FBA and SQL Server as the database and internal users are being authenticated using Windows Authentication. Both sets of users are accessing the same content. As discussed in Chapter 3, this scenario can best be accomplished by creating a Web application for internal users that represents the default zone and is configured for Windows Authentication. Next, a second Web application is created by extending the first, creating an extranet or Internet zone. An SSP has already been created, and the MOSS Search service has already been started. We will discuss the configuration of this scenario.

CREATING THE SQL DATABASE

We will begin by creating the data store that the FBA provider will use. ASP.NET 2.0 includes a SQL Server authentication provider that will store membership and profile information in a SQL server database. ASP.NET includes a utility that installs the extranet user database for you.

1. Open up a Command Prompt and navigate to the "c:\WINDOWS\ Microsoft.NET\Framework\v2.0.50727\" directory.
2. Launch the aspnet_regsql.exe utility, which will start the ASP.NET SQL Server Setup Wizard. Choose Configure SQL Server for application services (the default choice) on the Select a Setup Option screen and click Next.
3. Specify the SQL Server name that will host the user database (typically the same server that is hosting the MOSS content databases), the database name to create (for example, MOSS_FBA), and Windows Authentication. Click Next. Confirm your settings on the Confirm Your Settings screen and click Next.
4. Click Finish to close the wizard after The database has been created or modified screen appears. Open SQL Server Management Studio and confirm that the database was created successfully. Next, we'll grant a user account access to the database. This will be the identity of the Application Pool running the Web application that will host the portal Web site.
5. Use SQL Server Management Studio to add the Application Pool identity account to the FBA database (MOSS_FBA) and grant it the following roles: db_datareader and db_datawriter. This completes the configuration of the custom database.

CREATING AND CONFIGURING THE WEB APPLICATIONS

For our scenario, we will need to create two Web applications and two zones using the perspective and guidance supplied in Chapter 3 (please review Chapter 3 if you need a refresher). We will be exposing the same content to both our internal users using one URL, http://extranet_internal, and to our extranet users using a different URL, http://extranet. We'll begin by adding hosts file entries.

Adding Hosts File Entries

The next step involves adding some new hosts file entries so that these URLs are accessible from our development environment. Using Notepad or another text editor, open the hosts file from the c:\WINDOWS\system32\drivers\etc location. Add the following two lines to the bottom of the file, right below the localhost entry.

```
127.0.0.1      extranet_internal
127.0.0.1      extranet
```

Web Application Creation

Let's proceed with creating the Web applications. Our process will be as follows. First, we will create a new Web application configured for NTLM Windows Authentication and use the URL http://extranet_internal. This will be the default zone. Second, once the Web application is complete, we will create a new site collection using the Publishing Portal template. Third, we will create a second Web application by extending the http://extranet_internal Web application and use http://extranet as the URL.

1. Click Create or extend Web application under the heading SharePoint Web Application Management on the Application Management Web page.
2. Click Create a new Web application.
3. Select the option to Create a new IIS Web site, enter 80 in the Port textbox, and enter Extranet_internal in the Host Header textbox. Specify the Application Pool account you used previously when you were installing the custom database. Choose to Restart IIS Automatically. Enter a name for the content database so that you can recognize that this database is associated with this Web application. Leave all other options as is and click OK.
4. From the Application Created screen, click the Create Site Collection link. Enter Intranet in the Title textbox. Choose the Publishing Portal template and add the appropriate user as the Primary Site Collection Administrator. Click OK.
5. Open a browser and navigate to the http://extranet_internal Web site. Next, we will create the second Web application that will be configured for authenticating external users.

6. Click Create or extend Web application under SharePoint Web Application Management.
7. Click Extend an existing Web application.
8. In the Web Application section, choose to extend http://Extranet_internal.
9. Choose to Create a new IIS Web site, enter 80 in the Port text box, and enter Extranet in the Host Header text box. In Load Balanced URL section, be sure the Zone is set to Extranet. Click OK.
10. Open a browser and browse to http://Extranet. Note that we have not configured the site for FBA yet.

Creating FBA Providers and New Users

Creating and configuring the membership and role providers is a multi-step process in itself, which can lead to problems when trying to identify an error. To simplify this process, we will create and test the providers using a standard ASP.NET 2.0 Web site independent of MOSS. Once we have the providers configured and working, we can copy the provider information to MOSS. We can also use the ASP.NET Web site to create new users and roles, since the Web site will be connected to the user authentication database in SQL Server. The network or SharePoint administrator may not be familiar with creating an ASP.NET 2.0 Web site so he may need to work with a colleague with .NET development experience.

1. Create a new ASP.NET 2.0 Web site using Visual Studio. Next, we will establish a connection to the SQL database. We will use this connection later when we transfer the provider information to MOSS.
2. Add a new web.config file if one is not already present.
3. Replace the empty <connectionStrings/> element with the following code snippet. This will allow the Web application to connect to the custom FBA database previously created. Make sure to replace the values for the Data Source and Initial Catalog with the values from your installation or else things will not work. Therefore, replace the value of "MOSS" with your SQL Server name and the value of "MOSS_FBA" with that of the name you assigned to your FBA database.

```
<connectionStrings>

    <add name="InsideMOSSAdminConnectionString"

        connectionString="Data Source=MOSS;Initial Catalog=MOSS_FBA;
          Integrated Security=True" />
</connectionStrings>
```

4. Just below the <system.web> element, add the following membership and role provider elements. Save and close the web.config file. We are ready to test the providers. Make sure to update the value of the `connectionStringName` attribute with that which you used for the name in step 3.

```
<!-- membership provider -->
<membership defaultProvider="MOSS_FBASQLMemberProvider">
  <providers>
    <add name="MOSS_FBASQLMemberProvider"
      connectionStringName="InsideMOSSAdminConnectionString"
      enablePasswordRetrieval="false"
      enablePasswordReset="true"
      requiresQuestionAndAnswer="false"
      applicationName="/"
      requiresUniqueEmail="false"
      passwordFormat="Hashed"
      maxInvalidPasswordAttempts="5"
      minRequiredPasswordLength="1"
      minRequiredNonalphanumericCharacters="0"
      passwordAttemptWindow="10"
      passwordStrengthRegularExpression=""

type="System.Web.Security.SqlMembershipProvider,System.Web,Version=2.0.
0.0,Culture=neutral,PublicKeyToken=b03f5f7f11d50a3a" />
  </providers>
</membership>

<!-- role provider -->
<roleManager enabled="true" defaultProvider="MOSS_FBASQLRoleProvider">
  <providers>
    <add
      connectionStringName="InsideMOSSAdminConnectionString"
      applicationName="/"
      name="MOSS_FBASQLRoleProvider"

type="System.Web.Security.SqlRoleProvider,System.Web,Version=2.0.0.0,Cu
lture=neutral,PublicKeyToken=b03f5f7f11d50a3a" />
  </providers>
</roleManager>
```

5. From within Visual Studio, select ASP.NET Configuration under Web site.
6. Switch the Web site from Windows Authentication to FBA by selecting the Security tab and click the Select authentication type link in the Users box on the left.

7. Select the From the Internet radio button and click the Done button in the bottom right-hand corner of the window.
8. Test each of the providers by selecting the Provider tab and then Selecting a Different Provider for Each Feature. Click the Test link next to each provider, the membership and role providers defined in step 4. If there are any errors, return to the markup in step 4 and check for mistakes.
9. Next, we will create a few users that will be valuable when we actually configure MOSS to use FBA. This is done from the Security tab using the Create User within the Users Container. You should create at least two roles and add at least two different users. One role is called "Administrator" and the other is called "User." One user will represent a typical extranet user while the other will have administrative privileges. Make sure to assign the users to the appropriate roles.

This completes the creation and testing of the membership and role providers. The next step is to configure the Extranet Web site with the newly created providers.

Configuring SharePoint to Use the New Providers

There are three different Web applications that may need to communicate with the FBA provider and membership database, but only one Web application, Extranet, will authenticate users with the FBA provider. These three Web applications include the Extranet, Extranet_internal, and Central Administration Web sites. Therefore, all three Web sites will have the capability to communicate with the FBA provider. The next steps involve updating the web.config file for three Web sites, beginning with the Extranet site. First, we need to identify which folders represent the virtual directory for the Extranet site.

1. Open Internet Information Services (IIS) Manager and select the SharePoint-Extranet80 Web site.
2. Right-click the Web site and select Properties.
3. From the Properties dialog, select the Home Directory tab. The string of characters in the Local path text box represents the folder on the file system that contains the web.config for the http://Extranet Web application.
4. Navigate to the folder identified in step 3 and make a backup copy of the web.config file using Windows Explorer.
5. Then copy the connection string markup directly from Visual Studio to minimize any errors. Open the web.config file and replace the empty `<connectionStrings/>` with that from step 3 in the previous section.

6. Add the FBA membership and role providers to the web.config file using the same process as in step 5. Locate the `<system.web>` element and add the `membership` and `roleManager` elements just beneath the `<system.web>` element. Save and close the web.config file.

7. Repeat the earlier process for the Extranet_internal Web application. This site will still use Windows Authentication to authenticate users. Make sure to select the proper Web site in step 1.

8. At this point, both Web applications are configured with the FBA membership and roles providers, giving them access to the membership database. Each is still using Windows Authentication to authenticate users, but in the next section we will configure the Extranet site to use FBA for authenticating users.

9. Repeat steps 1–6 for the Central Administration Web site so that FBA security membership can also be managed from this location. Make sure to select the Central Administration Web site in step 1.

10. One last change is necessary to the web.config for the Central Administration Web site. Change the `defaultProvider` attribute on the `<roleManager>` element to `defaultProvider="AspNetWindowsTokenRoleProvider"`. This is necessary so the Central Administration site will still use Windows Authentication for its role provider.

11. Save and close the web.config file.

Enable FBA for the Extranet Web Application

1. Open Central Administration, click the Application Management tab, and click Authentication providers in the Application Security section.

2. Make sure to select the http://Extranet Web Application in the top right-hand corner of the screen.

3. Two different zones should be listed, a Default zone and an Extranet zone. Click the Extranet zone.

4. On the Edit Authentication page, select Forms in the Authentication Type section. After the page posts back, Membership Provider Name and Role Manager Name text boxes should appear.

5. Enter the appropriate values from the previous section, "Creating FBA Providers and New Users," into the Membership Provider Name text box and the Role Manager Name text box and click Save. Recall we used `MOSS_FBASQLMemberProvider` and `MOSS_FBASQLRoleProvider` as the names of the providers in that section. Your Extranet Web application is now configured to use FBA. However, users will not be able to log in using FBA until they are given permissions for the site.

6. Using the Extranet_internal Web site (default zone), log in with your Windows Authentication credentials and add one of the FBA users previously created to be a member of the Visitors group.

7. Open a browser and browse to http://Extranet. SharePoint should redirect to the FBA login page. Enter the proper credentials and confirm that access to the site is granted.

In step 6, we used our Windows credentials to log into the Extranet_internal Web site and add FBA users as members. There is an alternative approach that will allow you to log in to the Extranet site using FBA and configure FBA users. This is accomplished using Web application policies, which was discussed in Chapter 4.

Navigate to the Central Administration Web site and click Application Management and then click Policy for Web Application. Make sure that you are working on the Extranet Web application. Click Add Users. In the Zones drop-down, select the appropriate zone, which in this case is the Extranet zone, and then click the Next button. Type the name of the FBA user whom you want to have full control for the site in the Users edit box and then click the Resolve link next to the Users edit box. If the Web application's FBA information has been configured correctly, the name will resolve and become underlined. Grant the user Full Control by checking the appropriate box and then click Finish.

Once this is complete, either the Extranet URL or the Extranet_internal URL can be used for configuring FBA users. Irrespective of which entry point you use, you can add, search, and resolve both Windows and FBA users and groups and add them to SharePoint Site Groups.

This completes the configuration of the extranet and intranet scenario. In this scenario, we used host headers to identify the Web site that we were attempting to access. Our scenario had two different zones, each representing a different entry point for the same Web application and a different authentication mechanism. Alternate Access Mapping enables multiple requests for a single Web site to be serviced from different URLs. Even though we didn't configure this approach explicitly, it is important for administrators to know about this capability since it is commonly used in Internet-facing scenarios.

ALTERNATE ACCESS MAPPING

Users type the URL of the Web site they would like to access and that URL is resolved by IIS and it directs the user to the proper Web site. Under certain conditions, it is necessary for multiple URLs to map to a single Web site. For example, an internal URL is used by corporate employees while a different URL is used by external employees. SharePoint addresses this need with the concept of Alternate Access

Mappings (AAM). Each AAM refers to a different zone, and SharePoint allows five different zones to be configured. Therefore, five different entry points for a single site can be configured, each entry point using a different authentication mechanism if desired. At the most basic level, AAM tells SharePoint how to map Web requests to the correct Web application and site so that SharePoint can serve the correct content back to the user making the request.

AAM is needed when the URL of a Web request received by IIS is not the same URL that was submitted by the end user. This occurs most frequently with Internet-exposed sites when a reverse proxy server, such as Internet Security and Acceleration Server (ISA) 2006, is located between the Internet and the Web server and load balancing scenarios with multiple Front-end Web servers.

A reverse proxy server receives all requests that are going to the IIS Web server. Those requests are forwarded to the Web server once the request is analyzed and it passes the necessary security filtering. Reverse proxy servers can also perform off-box SSL termination, which is receiving a Web request over the Internet via SSL (HTTPS), but forward the request to the your Web server via HTTP, and they can also forward the request to a different port number and can even change the HTTP Host header field. Alternate access mappings enable a Web application that receives a request for an internal URL, in one of the five authentication zones, to return pages that contain links to the public URL for the zone. The public URL is the base URL that MOSS uses in the pages that it returns. If the internal URL has been modified by a reverse proxy device, it can differ from the public URL.

The effect of load balancers results in a similar situation, especially if they overwrite the end user's original URL with the URL of the individual Web server that is handling the request. This is solved by adding each individual Web server's URL to AAM as an internal URL and associating all of them to the same zone as the end user's public URL.

Therefore, if your perimeter deployment needs call for the use of a reverse proxy or similar device, or the need of load balanced WFEs, then you will need to configure your AAMs in combination with configuring your reverse proxy server. Or if your needs call for multiple entry points in general, AAM may be what is required for your scenario. AAM is configured from the Central Administration Web site.

11 Optimizing SharePoint Performance

In This Chapter

- Introduction
- IIS
- SQL Server
- Software Boundaries
- Cache
- Other Performance "Gotchas"

INTRODUCTION

In this chapter, you will learn how to optimize SharePoint's performance and take an in-depth look at IIS and SQL Server, as these two products are key to a successful deployment (although for many administrators, they are still unknowns). There is also a section on cache and how MOSS opens the door to granular controls to maximize resources. Finally, you'll learn tidbits of performance knowledge that should enhance your capabilities as an administrator, such as potential causes of slow page loads and guidance on how *not* to overlook the desktop.

IIS can be very deceiving. On the surface, it is easy to start IIS and publish a simple Web page. The problem arises when you want to start fine-tuning those Web sites, and you find that there are more options than you ever thought possible. While there are tremendous numbers of books and resources on everything IIS, most

SharePoint admins don't want that either. They are looking for just the specific components that interact with SharePoint and how they can adjust them. Look no further, because the IIS section of this chapter will do just that.

SQL Server (SQL) is where over 95 percent of all SharePoint data lives so it is easy to see why it is so crucial in the SharePoint performance equation. Disk IO is king when it comes to SQL, and there is no exception. But once you get that part right, then the next piece is making sure to maintain those databases.

While WSS takes advantage of some basic .NET caching capabilities for performance, MOSS adds three more options: output cache, object cache, and blob caching. Each has settings and flexibility that will let you fine-tune them for your specific environment.

The goal of this chapter is to make sure that you are doing everything possible to get the most from your hardware. IIS and SQL administration is a complex topic, but you'll find that just a couple of small tweaks can make drastic changes in your farm performance.

IIS

Internet Information Server 6.0 is a Windows Server 2003 component for serving Web, FTP, and SMTP. While there are entire books dedicated to this topic, the goal of this section is to make sure that you understand the key points for SharePoint.

Since SharePoint is a Web-based tool, it stands to reason that IIS is a key factor in the overall performance of your farm, which can be very daunting to some administrators. While many find it simple to create a basic site within IIS and get things up and running, they find themselves very disheartened at all of the options and configuration settings available. And while the defaults may be perfectly suitable, that is not the goal. To squeeze every ounce of performance out of the machine, you will need to have a strong understanding of the options before you.

Windows Server 2008 introduces IIS 7.0. While this section will concentrate on IIS 6, most of the concepts are still applicable. See Chapter 13, "SharePoint with Windows Server 2008 and SQL Server 2008," for more information on IIS 7.0.

THE WEB APPLICATION

The first key item is a terminology reminder. If you look at Figure 11.1, you will see the different IIS Web sites. The problem here is the nomenclature, as everyone calls these sites something different. They can be called sites, Web sites, virtual sites, virtual servers, and any other random thing you might think of. From a SharePoint perspective, you have learned to call these items Web applications or Web apps. This is a terminology must.

FIGURE 11.1
IIS Manager displaying Web
applications.

Using SharePoint, the Web applications will be created for you, as you have seen in previous chapters. When created, each Web app will be provisioned with default IIS settings. If you have multiple WFEs in your farm, the Web apps will automatically be propagated to the servers. This is key to remember as you start looking at options for manually changing the Web apps. If you make IIS modifications on one WFE, you must manually make those changes on all other WFEs to keep them in sync. Also, if for some reason you start or stop the Windows SharePoint Services Web Application service from Central Admin > Services on Server, this will force the default settings to re-propagate, thereby losing any customizations you have made. So be sure to document any manual changes as part of your overall backup and recovery strategy.

Viewing Web Application Properties

1. From the desktop of your SharePoint WFE server, click Start > All Programs > Administrative Tools > Internet Information Services (IIS) manager. For some users, administrative tools may be on the Start Menu without having to navigate to All Programs.
2. Click the plus to the right of the server name.
3. Click the plus to the right of Web sites.
4. Find your SharePoint Web app in the list, right-click it, and select properties.

The Web Site Tab

On the Web Site tab, you will find settings for configuring the IP Address, Port, and host headers the Web site is listening for. To configure these settings, click the

Advanced button. As discussed in Chapter 10, you need to make sure any changes here are reflected in your Alternate Access Mappings.

The connection timeout setting can be important when uploading large files to SharePoint across slow connections such as the Internet. The default of 120 seconds works well in LAN environments. For more information, see the sidebar "Uploading Large Files."

Uploading Large Files

By default, SharePoint is configured to allow users to upload 50MB at a time. This could be a single file, or if users are uploading multiple files, this would mean the combined size of the files would have to be less than 50MB. For some environments, this boundary is too restrictive so users may want to increase it. The first change to make is in Central Admin. From the Operations tab under SharePoint Web Application Management, select Web application general settings. From this screen, you can change the Maximum Upload Size from 50MB to a maximum of 2048MB. Now the interfaces of SharePoint will permit the larger uploads.

Depending on your environment, this may not be the only required change. The next limiting factor is the connection timeout setting for your Web app in IIS. As discussed in this chapter, the default is 120 seconds. If you find your large uploads timing out, especially in extranet scenarios, increasing this setting is necessary.

In some cases, large uploads will still fail after the previous two changes. This is because the application page, upload.aspx, has a default execution timeout of 360 seconds. To increase this timeout, you will need to modify a special web.config file. This file is located at c:\program files\common files\Microsoft shared\web server extensions\12\template\layouts. Before opening this file, be sure to make a backup copy of it. A corrupt web.config file can completely disable your system.

Open web.config and find the section that looks like this:

```
<location path="upload.aspx">
    <system.web>
      <httpRuntime maxRequestLength="2097151" />
    </system.web>
  </location>
```

You need to update the line <httpRuntime maxRequestLength="2097151" /> and add the executionTimeout like this:

```
<httpRuntime maxRequestLength="2097151"
executionTimeout="999999"/>
```

You can replace 999999 with the number of seconds you would like to use.

By default, your Web app will be generating IIS logs. It is important to note these logs will be stored on the C: drive by default, and they are not purged. You will need to evaluate the proper location for storing these logs, preferably not on the system drive (C:) and possibly even a plan for archiving or deleting them on a schedule so as not to consume unnecessary drive space.

The Home Directory Tab

From this tab, you can discover two key pieces of information: where your configuration files (such as web.config) are being stored and what Application Pool this Web app is using. When you created this Web application from SharePoint, you had the opportunity to specify this information, but sometimes you just need to be able to find it after the fact. The default settings on this tab work well, as this is just an informational tab.

The Directory Security Tab

This tab is generally used for deploying an SSL certificate. You could also potentially change the authentication method from integrated to basic. This is not recommended unless you are using SSL to secure your usernames and passwords. Also, if you make this change, you will need to make sure that you have configured a crawl rule for Search to pass basic authentication or your index process will fail. The one upside to using basic authentication is that you can specify a default domain, so for Internet/extranet scenarios you can keep your users from having to type in the domain to authenticate.

The Other Tabs

The other tabs can be very relevant to the behavior of an IIS site, but they are typically not modified in a SharePoint deployment. For this reason, their settings are better covered in a dedicated IIS book.

Redirecting Web Requests

In some scenarios, administrators find themselves wanting to redirect Web requests from one URL to another. While there are many ways to do this with custom code or third-party tools, such as ISA Server, many overlook the built-in capabilities of IIS. It is possible to create an anonymous Web site to listen for a specified Web request and then for it to redirect the browser to another URL. A good example of this is an SSL scenario.

Perhaps you have set up a SharePoint Web app at https://portal.company.com. But users will typically just type portal.company.com in their browser, which will then default to http://. When they arrive at http://portal.company.com, they will get an error message because the Web app is not configured to accept those requests.

This would be an ideal scenario to set up a redirect site listening for http://portal.
company.com. Follow the steps below for an example of how to create a redirect site.

Creating a Redirect Site

1. Open IIS Manager.
2. Expand the menu by clicking the plus to the right of your server name.
3. Right-click Web Sites and select New > Web Site.
4. Click Next at the Welcome screen.
5. Enter a description and click Next.
6. For this example, specify port 80 and a host header of portal.company.com.
7. Specify a path for storing the files.
8. Select Allow anonymous access to this Web site and click Next.
9. The default permission of Read is all that is required, so click Next.
10. At the successful screen, click Finish.
11. Find your site listed below Web Sites, right-click the site, and choose Properties.
12. Click the Home Directory tab.
13. Choose A redirection to a URL for The content for this resource should come from:
14. For Redirect to, enter https://portal.company.com.
15. Click OK.

The Default Web Site

When you first install IIS on your system, it will come with a site. This site is named Default Web Site. This way if you were to browse the server, you would get a default Under Construction message. The site is set up on port 80 with no host headers. Some administrators are tempted to use this site instead of creating a new Web app when provisioning SharePoint; however, this is not recommended. There are several reasons for this, but the easiest one is to avoid future conflicts. Lots of third-party code that uses IIS will automatically install itself to the default Web site. If SharePoint is on the site, then conflicts and confusion ensue. The way developers accomplish this is by looking for the Web site ID. The Default Web Site is always created with an ID of 1. Future sites are created with a multi-digit ID.

It is recommended that on your SharePoint servers you disable the default Web site to avoid conflicts with SharePoint. Also, if any additional programs attempt to use the Web site, they will not be available until you re-enable the Web site, which gives you a chance to put some thought into the access of the third-party content.

To disable the Default Web Site, find it in the list of Web sites, right-click the site, and choose Stop. This will leave the site inaccessible until you manually start it. It will remain stopped even after rebooting the entire server.

APPLICATION POOLS

An Application Pool (app pool) is a way of isolating your Web apps in IIS from each other. Each app pool is represented by a worker process, w3wp.exe, and can run under a unique account and have its own settings. This allows you to fine-tune each one independently and to keep issues (such as a memory leak, for example) from causing issues in your other app pools. When you create a Web app, you assign it to one and only one app pool, although an app pool can have multiple Web apps associated with it.

Unique app pools also can serve as a security boundary. Each app pool can have a unique identity so if it is compromised, then there is no access to the other content. Remember that because the app pool is what IIS uses to access the content databases, the account is granted database owner access to all databases associated with the app pool. So if two Web apps need to be completely isolated, they should be in separate app pools.

Previously, when examining the home directory tab, you were able to see what app pool your SharePoint Web app was using. To look at the settings for that app pool, follow these steps:

1. Click the plus sign from the right of Application Pools.
2. Find your app pool in the list, right-click it, and choose Properties.

The Recycling Tab

This tab is used to control the recycling of an app pool. Recycling, simply put, means to stop the current w3wp.exe process that is serving up requests and caching information and to start a new one. Often, you will hear people who say to do an IIS reset to clear out your Web site cache. One of the steps in the IIS reset actually stops all of the worker processes so they can be restarted and start caching again. It is possible to manually recycle an individual app pool without having to reset all of IIS. This is much quicker to do and does not take down all of your sites when you are trying to just work with one.

To accomplish this, from IIS Manager right-click the app pool and choose Recycle. This will stop the current worker process from accepting new requests and will start a new process to take future requests. Once the existing process finishes, any active request will be shut down. This is much more graceful than choosing Stop, which terminates the process, and then choosing Start.

There are three options for having the Application Pool recycle on a schedule available for use. The first two are often not used for SharePoint, but would allow you to recycle after so many minutes or after a certain number of transactions. Neither of these options is desirable for SharePoint. The third option, recycling at a specified time, is used and is automatically enabled when SharePoint creates the app pool. This will have the app pool recycle at a specified time each day in the early morning, allowing the app pool to start fresh the next day. In most environments, the default setting is ideal. In some heavy-use environments, where the hardware is approaching its limits, customers have been known to actually perform a recycle shortly before their peak load times of the day. Since applications do not always properly dispose of objects and free up memory as they should, recycling the Application Pool is the only way as an administrator to regain your precious memory resources.

Warm Up SharePoint

You have probably noticed that first thing in the morning, or after an IIS reset, SharePoint can be quite sluggish until "it wakes up." The reason for this is when the app pool is recycled, all of the information that has been cached is discarded. So the first time you request a page, it has to be compiled and loaded into memory before it can be rendered. Depending on the environment, this can take anywhere from five seconds to way too many seconds. For most users, this wait is unacceptable and the cause of many complaints of "the server being slow." In order to avoid these nagging complaints, no matter how brief they are, it is possible to run a warm-up script that will hit any sites you point it at so they can be loaded into memory ahead of time. Now when your users come in, everything is nice and responsive. To read more about the warm script and to download it, go to http://blogs.msdn.com/joelo/archive/2006/08/13/697044.aspx. Once you have the script, modify it with your Web apps and use a scheduled task to run it shortly after your nightly app pool recycle.

Also, if you are developing on SharePoint or find yourself often having to do manual app pool resets, check out this utility from Spence Harbar http://www.harbar.net/articles/APM.aspx. This tool had a small tray tool for performing resets and even doing a warm-up without having to go into IIS. Quite handy!

At the bottom of the Recycling tab, you will see that you can also set the Application Pool to recycle based on the amount of memory consumed. For most SharePoint environments, these settings are ignored, but they are important to understand as they may come in handy. The idea behind each setting is to automatically recycle an app pool when it crosses a certain memory threshold. This can be quite useful if you have an app pool that is trying to consume more memory than your system has to allocate, usually due to either undersized hardware or leaky code. On a 32-bit WFE, the general guidance is not to let an app pool consume more than 1200MB of physical memory. If you are pushing that threshold with your app pool, there is either some really bad code, or your usage is very high. In that case, you should consider switching to a 64-bit WFE so you can scale up to 8GB or more of RAM. On 64-bit WFEs internally at Microsoft, they are seeing app pools still performing well at 2200MB of physical memory and for some environments, they are not setting a maximum memory setting. If you are seeing app pools in this realm, you should be doing performance testing to compare performance levels based on the amount of memory you are consuming and see if you have a drop-off at the upper boundaries. This would be where you should set your limit.

> ### Don't Use the /3GB Switch
>
> The reason for such restrictive memory settings in 32-bit SharePoint is due to the lack of support of greater than 2GB of user mode memory. If you review Microsoft KB 933560, you will see the Windows Server 2003 /3GB switch is not supported with SharePoint. This makes the addition of more memory on your 32-bit WFE servers quite useless. And if you let one of your Application Pools run away with memory consumption, it is very easy to see how stability issues will follow. If you are going to have to scale up SharePoint on the WFE tier, you should be seriously considering 64 bit. Look back to Chapter 2, "Architecture and Capacity Planning," for supporting reasons why 64 bit is the preferred choice.

The Performance Tab

This tab provides you with several options for controlling the resources allocated to the worker process. The first option is the Idle timeout. With this setting, you can have the worker process automatically shut down after a specified period of inactivity. While this is not recommended for your app pools serving user content, it can be used for app pools dedicated to administrator activities, such as the app pool for Central Admin. If your server is sized so that a few hundred MB of RAM can't be spared, then set your central admin app pool to shut down after five or ten minutes of activity. This will not affect SharePoint's performance in any way, but it will cause your admins to have to wait a few seconds when accessing Central Admin while it is reached.

Request Queue Limit and Enable CPU monitoring are typically left to their defaults for SharePoint. There have been some environments where, to be sure, they have never lost a request due to queuing when they have unchecked the box. As a general rule, if more than 1,000 requests are in the queue, something is amiss and should be investigated. The CPU monitoring option will allow you to stop the app pool from using too much CPU. On a SharePoint box, this is counterproductive because you want that processor to hum and serve user requests as fast as possible.

The final setting of Web garden controls the number of worker processes that are in use by a single app pool. It defaults to one, and Microsoft Support highly recommends you only use one due to cache issues. There is quite a bit of debate on this topic as to whether or not there are any performance gains to be had even if it were supported. The recommendation here is make Support happy and stick with one.

The Health Tab

This tab has options for monitoring the health of your Application Pool. Enable pinging is checked by default and should remain so. This is not a normal ping, but instead is an internal IIS function that checks that the app pool is still responding to requests as expected. If the ping fails, the Application Pool will automatically be recycled in an attempt to return it to responsiveness.

Typically, the option for Enable rapid-fail protection is left unchecked. The idea of this setting is that it will monitor the app pool and if there are a certain amount of failures in a specified period, it will shut down the app pool automatically. These could potentially keep the app pool from consuming unnecessary server resources if the app pool were throwing errors and in a loop of constant recycles. While this setting could sound appealing, there are as many horror stories of the setting causing an app pool to be shut down inappropriately as there are of the setting saving the day.

Start-up and shut-down limits set a threshold for the process starting or stopping without generating an error. Typically, if your app pool is exceeding the default of 90 seconds, then something is probably wrong, and an investigation is in order. The good thing is that this threshold only applies to an error being thrown to Event Viewer, and it will not disable the app pool if it were to take 120 seconds to start; it would only flag an error message after 90 seconds.

The Identity Tab

This tab is as straightforward as it sounds. Here you can specify the credentials that the Application Pool runs under. While from a SharePoint standpoint you most likely will not be modifying this setting, it is important to remember that this is the account that your Web app will be using to access resources such as the content database. Random changes to this tab can cause issues and should only be done in extreme situations. The preferred method for changing the identity of an app pool or the password is to use Central Admin. From the Operations tab, under Security Configuration, there is an option for Service accounts. From this screen, you can safely make changes to the Application Pool identity.

Matching App Pools to Their w3wp.exe Processes

As the number of app pools increases, it can be difficult to match a specific w3wp.exe process to its corresponding app pool. This would be very helpful when troubleshooting errors or backtracking to which app pool is consuming too much memory. If each one is set to use its own account, then you could simply open Task Manager, find the w3wp.exe process, check the username for the process, and then compare that to the app pool identity setting. Not an elegant solution, but it will work. Luckily, there is a much more efficient way to proceed by using a built-in administration script, iisapp.vbs. This command will output the worker process PID, which you can then reference against the PID shown in Task Manager. To use this tool, follow these steps.

1. Open a Command Prompt.
2. CD to %SystemRoot%\system32.
3. Type **cscript.exe iisapp.vbs** and press Enter. You will get results similar to those shown in Figure 11.2.

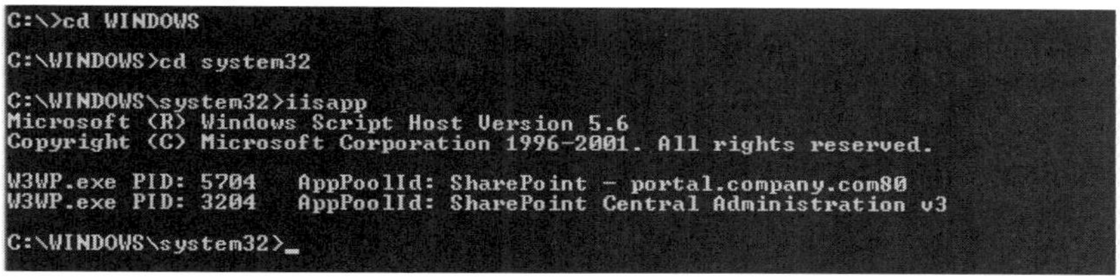

```
C:\>cd WINDOWS

C:\WINDOWS>cd system32

C:\WINDOWS\system32>iisapp
Microsoft (R) Windows Script Host Version 5.6
Copyright (C) Microsoft Corporation 1996-2001. All rights reserved.

W3WP.exe PID: 5704    AppPoolId: SharePoint - portal.company.com80
W3WP.exe PID: 3204    AppPoolId: SharePoint Central Administration v3

C:\WINDOWS\system32>_
```

FIGURE 11.2
Example output from the running iisapp.vbs script.

4. Open Task Manager.
5. Go to the process tab and sort by Image Name.
6. By default, the PID column does not show up. To add it, click View > Select Columns.
7. Check PID (Process Identifier) and click OK. Your results will be similar to Figure 11.3. You will need to check the Show processes from all users box.
8. Now you can match the w3wp.exe PID to the output of iisapp.vbs to get the Application Pool name.

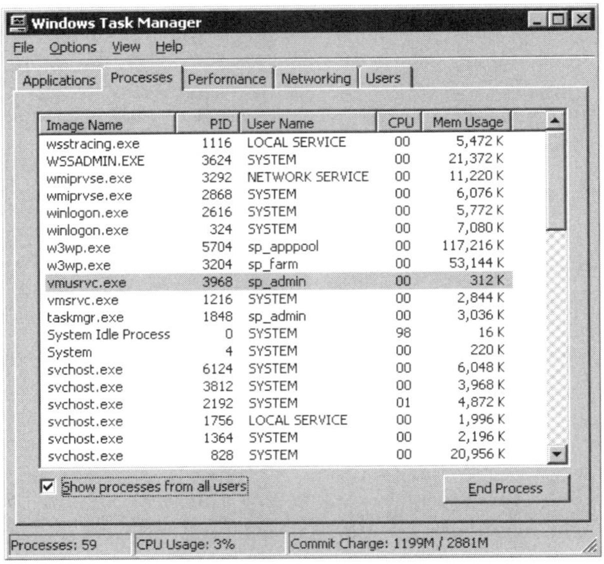

FIGURE 11.3
Example Task Manager processes show the process identifiers.

IIS COMPRESSION

A very powerful, yet seldom mentioned feature of IIS is the ability to do compression. With IIS compression, you can greatly reduce the number of bytes you send across the wire. And since opening a default MOSS collaboration portal home page sends about 800KB of content, it can be a little slow when opening across the Internet. IIS compression offers you the capability to reduce the amount of traffic sent across the wire at the cost of a greater CPU burden on the server and client, and it even works with SSL.

Even more surprising is that SharePoint configures your Web apps to do some compression out of the box, getting that 800KB of content down to around 200K. There are two types of compression in IIS, static and dynamic, and each one can be configured separately. Static compression is used for simple files by default: htm, html, and txt files. When you install MOSS, it adds the file types of js, css, and htc. These files are compressed when accessed the first time, and they are placed in the folder c:\windows\IIS Temporary Compressed. Before digging into that any deeper, let's take a look at how you would find such information by digging into the IIS metabase.

The metabase is where IIS stores all settings, both global and individual. Now before you go exploring the metabase, it is probably a good idea to back it up, since corrupting the metabase can completely disable IIS. Check out this TechNet article for steps on backing up and restoring the metabase: http://www.microsoft.com /technet/prodtechnol/WindowsServer2003/Library/IIS/d40b56ee-90d4-45e1-9b82-4aaea90eb02e.mspx?mfr=true.

Once you have a good backup, it is time to go the command line and learn a new tool.

1. Open a Command Prompt.
2. Cd to c:\inetpub\adminscripts.
3. Type **cscript.exe adsutil.vbs help** and press Enter.

Running that command will present you with a wealth of possibilities. To take a look at what compression settings you are using, run the following command.

```
cscript.exe adsutil.vbs enum /w3svc/filters/compression/parameters
```

This will give you output as shown in Figure 11.4

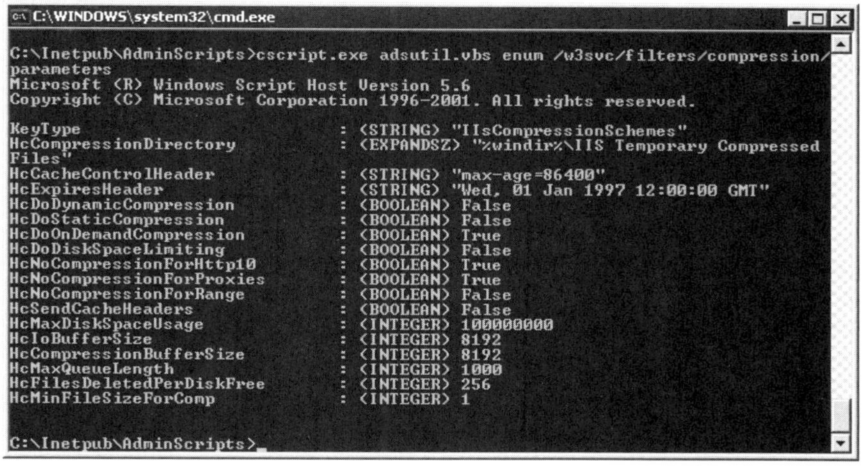

FIGURE 11.4
Example output from the adsutil.vbs script.

From this figure, you can see a couple of things. First, you can see that the Hc-CompressDirectory is set to %windir%\IIS Temporary Compressed Files. This is the location that the compressed version of all static files will be saved to. If you wanted to change this location, you could run the command:

```
Cscript.exe adsutil.vbs set
/w3svc/filters/compression/parameters/HcCompressionDirectory
"d:\compress folder"
```

Keep in mind that for any changes to the metabase to take effect, it requires you to restart the World Wide Web Publishing Service from Administrative Tools > Services or run the command:

```
Net stop w3svc
```

Followed by:

```
Net start w3svc
```

Looking back at the previous figure, you will notice that HcDoDynamic-Compression and HcDoStaticCompression are both set to False. This means that compression is not enabled globally. The next step would be to check the settings for one of your SharePoint Web apps. Unfortunately, this isn't a quick task. The first thing you will need to do is to find the ID for your Web app.

1. Open IIS Administrator.
2. Expand the server name.
3. Click Web Sites.

In the windowpane, you will see a listing of all the Web sites and to the right of each one's description, you will see an Identifier, as shown in Figure 11.5.

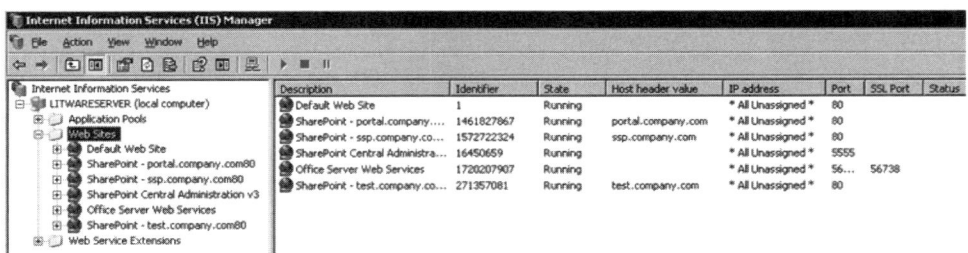

FIGURE 11.5
IIS Admin showing the list of Web sites with their Identifiers.

Armed with this ID number, you can now return to your command line and run a command similar to the following:

```
Cscript.exe adsutil.vbs enum /w3svc/14618278667/root
```

Be sure to replace the sample ID with your own. You will then get a large result set and at the bottom will be the interesting info, as shown in Figure 11.6.

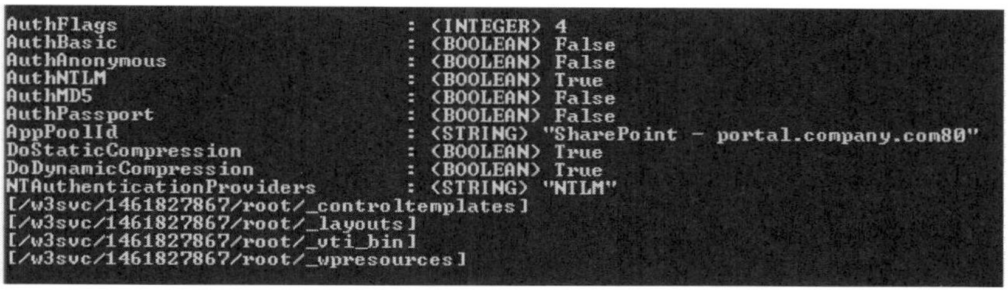

FIGURE 11.6
Example output from the adsutil.vbs script.

Now if you examine DoStaticCompression and DoDynamicCompression, you will see they are set to True, which means that this particular Web site is using compression.

To see what types of files are being compressed and to what extent they are being compressed, run the following command:

```
Cscript.exe adsutil.vbs enum /w3svc/filters/compression/gzip
```

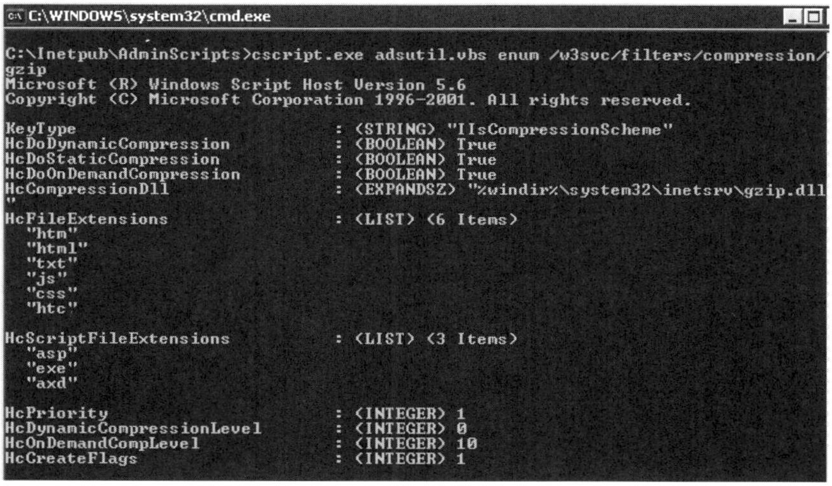

FIGURE 11.7
Example output from the adsutil.vbs script showing the compression settings.

In Figure 11.7, you will see that `HcFileExtensions` shows you the extensions that are used in static compression. `HcScriptFileExtension` shows you the extensions that are dynamically compressed. `HcOnDemandCompLevel` is the level at which static files are compressed; this number can range from 0 to 10. `HcDynamicCompression-Level` is the level at which dynamic files are compressed; this number also ranges from 0 to 10. When considering the range of 0 to 10, it is important to understand the trade-offs. 0 will place very little burden on CPU or memory resources, but it will result in a very small reduction of file size. On the other end, level 10 will greatly reduce the file size, but it will also place a tremendous load on CPU and memory. Ideally, you would do performance testing to find the best setting for your hardware.

When adding file types to the compression list, try to avoid compressed files, such as .jpg or Office 2007 documents. Because these files are already compressed, they will only waste server resources trying to compress them further with very little gain. An ideal candidate for adding to dynamic compression would be ASPX. Be sure if you are going to do this, you run some performance testing to validate your settings.

SQL Server

SQL Server, as you have already learned, is where almost everything for SharePoint is stored. Except for a few files on the file system and some registry settings, SQL is it. What is surprising is that most administrators overlook SQL performance when optimizing their farm. And since SQL disk IO is typically one of the first bottlenecks seen in a SharePoint farm, this is quite an issue.

Keep in mind the wide range of the audience of this chapter. If you are maintaining a small environment with less than 50GB of content, most of the performance madness, such as multiple raid 10 volumes, doesn't pertain to you. At the same time, if you have TBs of data, then you will need to take some of the guidance here to the next level. While all of the guidance here is sound and ideal, be sure to weigh its relevance before going to any extremes.

The Databases

There are several key databases to understand from the SharePoint point of view. The performance of these databases will greatly impact your farm and are always the first place to check for bottlenecks. In this section, there is a discussion of the databases and some maintenance items you can use with the databases.

Tempdb

What is the most important database in your farm for performance? Tempdb. This system database is often ignored when in reality it is key to overall performance. SQL Server uses this db for processing of sorts, storing all temporary tables and procedures, intermediate operations such as work tables, and large objects. As it turns out, SharePoint makes extensive use of the Tempdb. There are a few key changes you can make to really speed up this database and your farm. Keep in mind that tembdb is unique; every time the SQL Server service is started, the database is re-created.

Move the Database

Typically, when SQL Server is installed, the system databases (master, model, msdb, tempdb) are stored on the system drive (C:). Moving tempdb should be your first priority.

When attempting to achieve optimal performance, the tempdb and its data files should be placed on a dedicated raid 10 drive. This provides you with maximum performance and up time.

Use the following instructions to move your tempdb. Keep in mind, these instructions are written assuming the use of SQL Server 2005.

1. Open SQL Management Studio from Start > All Programs > Microsoft SQL Server 2005 > SQL Server Management Studio.
2. If you do not have SQL Server Management Studio listed, then when you installed SQL Server you did not choose the component Management Tools. It is highly recommended that you add these tools, and it will be assumed that you have done so for the remainder of the guidance.
3. At the Connect to server interface, enter your server name and authentication information and click Connect.
4. From the toolbar, click New Query.
5. Find the name and location of the database. Enter the command in the window (see Figure 11.8).

```
use tempdb
go
sp_helpfile
go
```

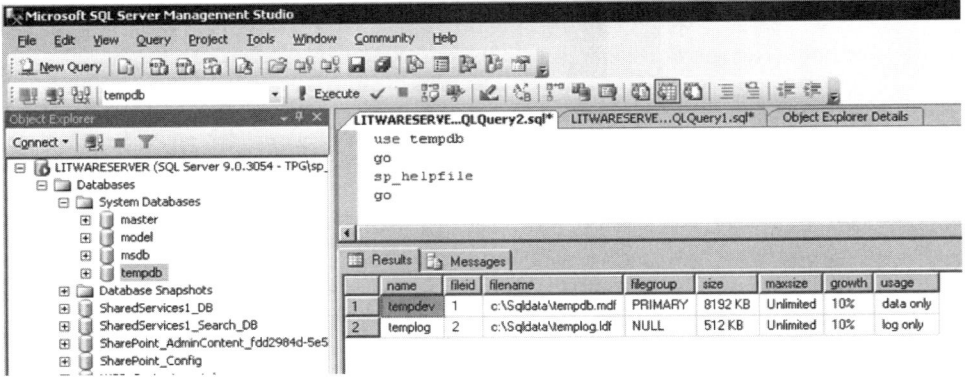

FIGURE 11.8
Microsoft SQL Server Management Studio displaying the output of the `sp_helpfile` query.

6. Now that you know the names, you can run the command

```
use master
go
Alter database tempdb modify file (name = tempdev, filename =
'f:\Sqldata\tempdb.mdf')
go
Alter database tempdb modify file (name = templog, filename =
'f:\Sqldata\templog.ldf')
go
```

Be sure to replace the name or the location as applicable in your environment. If possible, you should also place the log file on a separate disk from the datafile.

The changes to tempdb will take affect next time the SQL Server service is started.

The next change you can make to your environment is to follow the SharePoint Product Team's guidance for creating a separate datafile for your tempdb. You should have the same number of datafiles as your number of CPU cores. So a quad core processer would count as four. Hyperthreaded processors only count as one. Before creating these, you should also determine the size of the data files. To do this, use the formula of (Maximum database size in KB) X .25 / (number of CPU cores) = (data file size in KB) found in the Scaling SharePoint 2007: Storage Architecture paper at http://go.microsoft.com/fwlink/?LinkId=119399&clcid=0x409. Now that you have the number of files and their recommended size, you can return to SQL Management Studio to make the changes. All datafiles should be the same size.

1. From the database list in SQL Management Studio, right-click tempdb and choose Properties.
2. Click Files from the column on the left-hand side labeled Select a page.
3. Click the Add button from the bottom of the window.
4. Set the Logical Name.
5. Set the Initial Size as calculated previously.
6. Change Autogrowth to by 10%. (The hope is that the file will never need to grow, but if it does try to grow and fails, then you will have issues, so enabling this setting is ideal.)
7. Set the Path to the location you want to store the file.
8. After creating all of the necessary files and setting the size of the initial file to the same size, click OK.

From this same screen, you can also optimize the tempdb transaction log. In most environments, the IO is not too heavy on the log. However, it is recommended that you do not allow this database to autogrow. Pregrow the log file to your anticipated size and then monitor it over time, confirming it is not growing. Keep in mind for the SQL file to have to grow is a very expensive (resource intensive) operation and should be avoided if at all possible.

Search Property Store

This database is specified when you first create an SSP. In farms where the search load is moderate or greater, this database can quickly become a bottleneck. The reason is that this database is heavily used while the indexing process is running, and this database also is used to respond to user queries. If you have issues with poor query performance or you are trying to reduce the amount of time your index process runs, look at optimizing this db.

The first consideration for this database is to get it onto its own dedicated raid 10 volume, because it is very disk IO intensive. Determining the size to pregrow the database will be difficult since there isn't an exact formula for calculating size—rather only a few rules of thumb—so take an educated guess at size. Also, instead of pregrowing one big file, you should use file groups, as explained previously, making sure they are of equal size and you have created one per CPU core. Even though you have already grown the database, leave Autogrow on in order to accommodate unanticipated growth. You should monitor the db and if you find the database growing, then pregrow all of the database files again. Also, try to place the transaction log for this database on a different volume, also dedicated, if possible.

The Content Databases

These databases surprisingly are not as performance-driven as one would think. This is not to say that some environments will not be read/write intensive, but the average content database generally has read access. To this end, this database will typically run on a raid 5 volume quite happily. Normal best practices apply to this database. Consider pregrowing your database. How big? A good recommendation is to set the size of the database to its expected size in a year. Try studying your expected churn rate for a month and then plan out for the next year and pregrow to this size. If you don't have enough disk space, then now is the time to have the conversation with the keepers of the hardware budget. Pregrowing the database ensures that you will not have growth problems, and it also reduces the load on SQL Server because it will not have to do expensive growth operations every time a user wants to upload some content. As with the other databases, you can create multiple datafiles in the primary file group. If you do this, each one should be the same size, and you should have one per CPU core.

Using Out-of-the-Box Backups?

While backups are covered in a later chapter, there is something very important to note now. If you set up multiple datafiles for your databases, the out-of-the-box-backup tool can back up the database with no problem. The challenge lies in the fact that the Restore process does not understand how to restore the database to multi-datafiles. For most, this is not a concern because if your farm has reached a level where you are doing multiple datafiles, then you probably are not using the out-of-the-box tools. Instead, try using standard SQL backups, as discussed in a later chapter.

The Other Databases

For the databases such as Config, the SSP db (Not SSP search), SharePoint_admin, and WSS Search Service db, they generally do not need specific tuning performed. Ideally, you would put them all on the same volume and then put their transaction logs on a separate volume.

Database Don'ts

Not surprisingly, Microsoft has some very stringent guidance as to the actions you are allowed to perform on the SharePoint databases. In KB 841057, these are detailed, but to put it simply, you cannot modify the database in any way. If you do make changes, which you shouldn't, Microsoft will not provide you with support. Additionally, it is highly recommended that you do not directly read the database. Reading the database directly can cause SQL locks and performance issues. If you need to get data from the database, you should use one of the included programmatic options, such as the object model or the Web services. Reads and writes of the data through these interfaces are completely supported.

Maintaining the Databases

The database do's, another neglected task, involve database maintenance. Most admins assume since there are such strict rules on database modifications that fact would preclude them from most database maintenance. They hope that Share-Point is taking care of their precious data and don't give it a second thought. While this could be considered partially true, because the timer service does update the database statistics, there are still plenty of things to do.

The easiest way to get started is to create a SQL maintenance plan and work through the options available. To create a maintenance plan, follow these steps:

1. Open SQL Management Studio and log in to your SQL Server.
2. Expand the Server name and then the Management folder.
3. Right-click Maintenance Plans and click Maintenance Plan Wizard.
4. At the first screen, you can set the plan schedule. By default, there is no schedule, so click Change.
5. Make the settings that are necessary and click OK. Typically, you want to schedule the process to run for off hours, as there is a performance impact while these jobs run.

Now you are presented with a screen full of several options, as shown in Figure 11.9. We will discuss the ones that are pertinent to SharePoint and leave the other options for discussions in the dedicated SQL books.

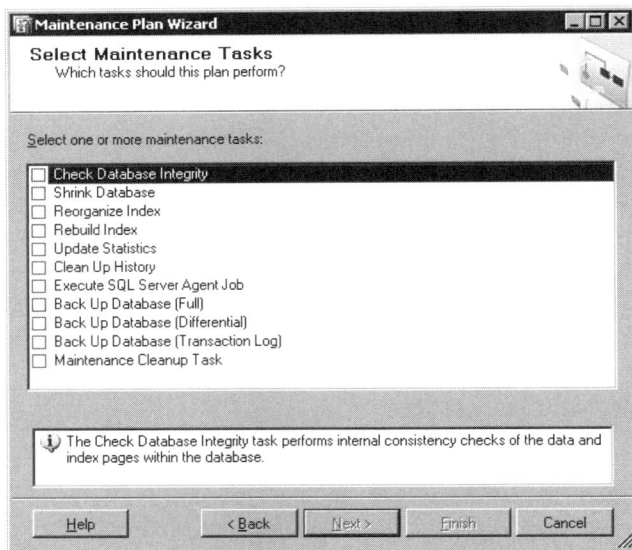

FIGURE 11.9
Available tasks for a database Maintenance Plan in SQL 2005.

Check Database Integrity. This option will perform a check of the internal structure of the database and the data pages for errors. When you select this option, you can have it not only check for errors but also attempt to repair the errors. Typically, errors come from a drive failure or a system crash. Running this check weekly is ideal.

Shrink Database. This option gives you the ability to reduce the size of your database. Hopefully, though, you are following the previous guidance, and you have pregrown your databases, making shrinking them counterproductive. If you don't have pregrown databases, then you could consider using this task on content databases where you have deleted over 50 percent of the data. The other SharePoint databases do not have enough data removed to warrant shrinking.

Reorganize Index. This option will defragment and compact your indexes, helping to increase index performance. This option should not be used in conjunction with Rebuild Index.

Rebuild Index. This option will actually re-create the indexes. When the indexes are re-created, you can specify the Fill factor, setting the amount of space to save for future growth of the index pages and improving performance. The default Fill factor for SQL is 0; for SharePoint databases, it is recommended that you use a Fill factor of 70. If you are running SQL 2005 pre-SP2, there is a bug that will corrupt your indexes after the rebuild. For more information on the symptoms of this issue and how to fix it see http://msmvps.com/blogs/shane/archive/2007/07/23/another-day-another-new-error-message.aspx. This option should not be used in conjunction with Rebuild Index.

Back Up Database. These options will be discussed in detail in Chapter 12, "High Availability, Backups, and Disaster Recovery." Pay close attention to make sure you are accounting for your transaction logs. In environments where they are using out-of-the-box backup tools, it is normal to have a SQL Maintenance job to back up the transaction logs to keep them from consuming excessive disk space.

Maintenance Cleanup Task. This option just tidies up the mess and temp data generated during a maintenance plan.

The following steps outline suggested configuration options for your database maintenance plan.

1. Check the options for Check Database Integrity, Rebuild Index, and Maintenance Cleanup Task.
2. Click Next.
3. At the Select Maintenance Task Order screen, click Next.
4. At the Define Database Check Integrity Task screen, Select All databases, check Include indexes, and click Next.
5. At the Define Rebuild Index Task, choose All databases.
6. There are varying opinions here. While rebuilding your index is ideal from a performance standpoint, there is a performance penalty while it is being run, and although the database remains online while the task runs, there are various locks used. These locks can make access to SharePoint slow or even unavailable until they are released. As the size of your database grows, this will be a longer period of time. So in some environments, this rebuild task is not recommended. If you are not periodically rebuilding your indexes with this task, you should monitor the index fragmentation levels and run the task on demand during your maintenance window.
7. Select the option Change free space per page percentage to 70.
8. Click Next.
9. Accept the clean-up defaults, or customize them as appropriate for your environment and click Next.
10. Make any changes for report options and click Next.
11. At the Complete the Wizard screen, click Finish.
12. The maintenance plan will build. When it completes with success, click Close.
13. Confirm that your SQL Server Agent is enabled, because it is required to run your maintenance plan. You can check for it in SQL Management Studio where it is the last thing listed in the tree view. If it is not started, then right-click it and choose Start.

> **More SQL Server Reading**
>
> While this section has covered the highlights and key recommendations for SQL performance and maintenance, it has only scratched the surface. If you are really looking to dig in and understand the underlying infrastructure, there are some additional papers to consider. Here are a few of them:
>
> "Planning and Monitoring SQL Server Storage for Office SharePoint Server: Performance Recommendations and Best Practices": http://technet.microsoft.com/en-us/library/cc263261.aspx
>
> "Using Microsoft® Office SharePoint® Server to implement a large-scale content storage scenario with rapid search availability": http://technet.microsoft.com/en-us/library/cc262067.aspx
>
> "Database Maintenance for Microsoft® SharePoint® Products and Technologies": http://go.microsoft.com/fwlink/?LinkId=111531&clcid=0x409

SOFTWARE BOUNDARIES

When designing your SharePoint deployment, it is important to take into account the various boundaries in the product. There are two types: hard limits enforced by the product and recommended limits that are tested and supported. Microsoft has an extensive list you should review at http://technet.microsoft.com/en-us/library/cc262787.aspx. As you start to approach some of the boundaries, you will need to plan your hardware accordingly. For example, things like the ability to index 50 million items are a testament to that. SharePoint can support that capacity, but if you don't have a perfectly tuned environment optimized for indexing, it may take you a couple of months to index that many items.

While you are considering the software boundaries, it is an ideal time to think one step lower in the stack—large lists. A large list is typically any list with more than 1,000 items in it. While SharePoint can store millions of items in a list, you need to plan for this and organize you data appropriately. Microsoft has released an extensive white paper "Working with Large Lists in Office SharePoint Server 2007" available at http://go.microsoft.com/fwlink/?LinkId=95450&clcid=0x409. This paper talks not only about scaling lists through the use of folders, but it also shows methods for optimized programmatic access to these large lists.

CACHE

From understanding the infrastructure, you have already seen how many pieces go into making up a simple SharePoint page. There are calls to the file system for the templates in the 12 hive, and there is the pulling of all the data from the databases.

These sources are brought together, and the page is compiled by .NET 2.0 the first time it is accessed. This compiled information is then stored in memory to expedite the rendering on subsequent loads. You can see this at work by watching the w3wp.exe process consuming more and more memory as the day goes on. Both WSS and MOSS use this mechanism to achieve performance automatically. But if you have deployed MOSS and you are using the publishing infrastructure feature (a site collection feature), you get several additional options for fine-tuning the caching process.

OUTPUT CACHING

With this cache, you are able to tune the caching of individual pages and can do so based on whether the page is authenticated (intranet) or anonymous (www). To look at the options available, navigate to a site collection that has the publishing features enabled and log in as a site collection administrator.

1. Click Site Actions > Site Settings > Modify All Site Settings.
2. Under Site Collection Administration, click Site collection cache profiles.
3. Click Intranet.
4. From the menu bar, click Edit Item.

Now you can see all of the options and a nice explanation of each setting. Notice by default, your cache is only valid for 180 seconds, which seems very short. After reviewing the default settings, click OK.

MOSS comes with four profiles by default. Typically, you will want to create your own profile instead of modifying an out-of-the-box profile.

Even though MOSS has provided you with output cache profiles, it is not using any of them by default. To enable a cache profile, use these steps:

1. Return to the Site Settings page.
2. Under Site Collection Administration, click Site collection output cache.
3. Check the box to Enable output cache.
4. From the drop-downs, choose your profiles.
5. For Page Output Cache Policy, you have the ability to specify how granular you can be with cache settings. By default, the entire site collection will use the settings from this page unless you enable control at the site or layout level.
6. You can check Enable debug cache information on pages.
7. This setting will add a line at the bottom of your pages that will tell you if the page was rendered from cache or not and if so which profile and when it was compiled. To see this information, open your page in the browser and choose Page > View Source.

When using output caching on an authenticated site, you should disable caching on the Search Results pages. If not, it is possible that users running the same query could see results they don't have access to. By default, Search trims results, but if caching is enabled, the results may not be trimmed.

OBJECT CACHING

This cache is used to store objects the page works with while rendering a page. Examples are navigation and the Content Query Web Parts (CQWP). To render the page, SharePoint must look to these objects that span across lists and sites to return the proper results. Cross-site queries can be very performance intensive, to the point of slowing down your entire farm. You should be very careful when using the CQWP on high-traffic pages. Luckily, MOSS allows you to use object caching to negate some of this impact.

To access the site collection object cache:

1. Return to the Site Settings page.
2. Under Site Collection Administration, click Site collection object cache.

From this screen, you can make several changes to the cache. The most confusing setting here is the Cross List Query Results Multiplier. This number determines how much data the query will return beyond what is required to render the user results. The idea is that if you are already running the query, it doesn't take much more to grab extra data and cache that also. This way, the next request has a better possibility of coming straight from memory instead of forcing the query to run. If you are using this CQWP on an anonymous site, you should set this number to a low setting, as there is only one set of data to pull versus an intranet site where a higher multiplier will accommodate the different user permissions more efficiently. Also, consider on your anonymous site setting the cache time to a reasonable amount of seconds to reduce the burden even further.

To monitor the object cache, there is a performance monitor object called "SharePoint Publishing Cache." From this object, you can monitor the Publishing cache hit ratio and the Total objects discards counters to help you determine the optimal amount of memory to allocate. If you are seeing a ratio greater than 90 with little churn in the discards, then you have allocated enough memory. Be careful not to set the memory too high, as Application Pool memory is precious and over-allocating it can cause other cache (such as output cache) to be flushed prematurely.

Binary Large Object Cache

Also called "blob" or "disk-based caching," this gives you the ability to cache certain static or slow-to-change types of files that are stored in document libraries, on the local disk of the Web server(s), after their first access instead of constantly retrieving them from the database. By default, this feature is disabled, but it should be enabled. To enable the cache, you must edit the web.config for each Web app you want to use the cache.

To enable blob caching, you need to:

1. Find the web.config for your Web app.
2. Back up the web.config file.
3. Open web.config with notepad.
4. Search the file for blob.

You should get a line that looks like:

```
<BlobCache location="C:\blobCache" path="\.(gif|jpg|png|css|js)$"
maxSize="10" enabled="false" />
```

Change `enabled` to "`true`" (remember the file is case sensitive) and save.

You can see from the line the types of files that will be stored in the cache. `maxSize` is specifying the maximum size in GBs of the cache. By default, items are kept in the cache for 24 hours. You can add `max-age` to the line. This will allow you to specify in seconds the amount of time to keep items in cache. Don't forget that any time you edit the web.config file, .NET will see the change and invalidate your cache, which essentially resets this Web app. Doing this will cause slow loads while everything is re-cached. Try to avoid doing this during production hours to avoid calls to the help desk.

Other Performance "Gotchas"

SharePoint has lots of little things to watch out for or to tweak that don't fit into nice little containers like the previous information. So this section will present those details in no particular order and without rhyme or reason.

Backups and Indexing

These two items are the most intense things that will ever happen in your farm, so plan accordingly. If you read through the Search chapter, you know that the indexing process quite normally runs at 100 percent CPU (assuming it can get content that quickly) for the duration of the crawl. In the case of large environments, this can be for days. But even a small environment can see this process run for hours. You need to plan your schedule around this load. You don't want a full crawl running during peak usage times. Or if you are super-large, you may only want to do one full crawl and then run incremental crawls from then on. The thing to do is to plan your crawl schedule. Maybe you are thinking that you have a dedicated Index server so this isn't a big deal? It still can be. Remember that the crawl process is taxing your database server and has to propagate that index file to your Queries servers. This is causing load in your farm, so proceed with caution.

The backup process also causes strain on the system resources. Another tidbit—if you are using out-of-the-box backup tools, the backup job will pause any active crawls while it runs. So if you try to back up and index at the same time, SharePoint won't let you. Keep that in mind if you are seeing your indexing take longer than it should.

SLOW PAGE LOADS

Slow page loads happen way too often. Everything works fine while the new portal is in development. Page loads are fine, and everyone publishing content is happy. Then 10 minutes after the site goes live, the phone starts ringing. "SharePoint is slow!" "My home page will not open." And so madness ensues. So what are some common reasons for this?

Page bloat is the first reason you'll encounter. Examples of page bloat include too many closed Web parts on the page that are compiled in the background, poorly written Web parts that have improper code, and even graphical additions such as Flash files that are way too big.

When customizing the site to satisfy the request "to make it not look like Share-Point," do so with an understanding of good usability. Pretty Flash intros are cute, but are not practical for the home page of an intranet where 10,000 people have it set as their default page in IE. Branding SharePoint properly can be a challenge, and you should consider training or consulting an outside expert to do it properly.

When editing a page, there are two methods to stop a Web part from showing up: deleting the Web part from the page and closing the Web part. Deleting the Web part is ideal because this actually removes the Web part from the page alto-gether. Closing the Web part can be handy because it will keep your customizations, and you will just set the Web part not to show. The problem is that unknowing page editors will end up with 30 or more closed Web parts on the home page from their "trying things out" phase. The main reason for this is that you can simply click the X in the Web part toolbar to close the Web part. It is easy to assume that since you can't see the Web part anymore, it must be gone. Now you have a home page with 30 Web parts being opened by 30 people at the same time. That is a lot of unnecessary load that you probably did not build into your farm.

To check the page for these closed Web parts, you can do the following:

1. Navigate to the page in question.
2. Click Site Actions > Edit page.
3. Click Add a Web Part (see Figure 11.10).
4. Above the Add/Cancel buttons, click the link for Advanced Web Part gallery and options.
5. In the top of the pain that opened, there is a link for Closed Web Parts; click the link.

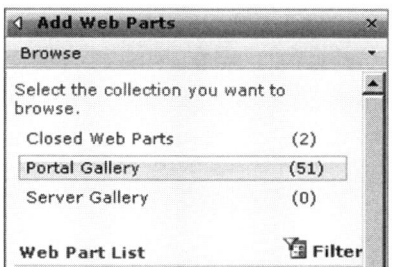

FIGURE 11.10
The Add a Web Part toolbox.

6. Now in the Web Part List, you will see all of the closed Web Parts. You can drag them back into a Web Part Zone on the page and then delete the Web Part from the page.

The final thing to look out for is custom Web parts. Many .NET developers dive headfirst into SharePoint Web parts to add the latest whizbang widget to the home page. This is great, but the challenge is getting them to create the Web Parts properly. This is not a development book, but suffice it to say that there are a lot of poor coding practices that are compounded when that code is deployed to SharePoint. Things like not disposing of objects immediately or too many SQL round trips can really kill the performance of the entire farm. So be sure to performance test any custom or third-party Web parts before deploying them to your farm. Don't get that luxury? Then at least be willing to remove the Web part from the page when you are troubleshooting performance issues. Just because it worked fine on the development server with one person accessing it doesn't mean it will play nicely with 100 people accessing it at the same time.

Another unsuspected culprit in the slow load page times is security trimming. This version of SharePoint is great in that users do not see links or items on the page they don't have access to. The downside to this is that it takes CPU cycles to check all of the security on the page. So if you hit the home page and there are 30 different items and links on the page, and they all have different security, that is 30 checks that SharePoint has to make. The idea here is not to say "don't have links on the home page"; rather, the idea is to plan for the load. Try to inherit security as much as possible, especially on the entry page to your portal. This page will likely be loaded most often because typically it will be the default browser page for the user community. So plan this page accordingly. Do fancy things with custom security on the second page and leave the landing page as efficient as possible.

The content query Web part is worth mentioning again as a possible villain in the slow page load time. While most people understand that this Web part can be very expensive from a performance point of view, they will overlook one of the other CQWP-based Web parts, the Table of Contents Web part. This Web part, depending on its settings, could be iterating through several layers of your site structure to bring back links. And those links are being security trimmed also. Don't get overzealous with either of these Web parts. Instead, try to keep them off the home page or use object caches as much as possible.

Networking Issues

As has been illustrated several times in this book, SharePoint is very network intensive. All of the inter-farm communications alone are enough to bring some environments to their knees. With this in mind, you should deploy all pieces of the SharePoint farm on a gigabit (Gb) network. If your farm isn't using Gb, this is probably the easiest performance enhancement you can make, even if the clients are still connected via slower speeds.

Surprisingly, in the field, there are still lots of environments that are running Gb equipment, and they are still having network issues. This situation usually occurs from mismatched switches and network cards that fail to auto-negotiate properly. And if auto-negotiate fails, then the connection falls back to 10Mbps. SharePoint farms have lots of challenges at that speed. Be sure to confirm your network connections. Also, if your datacenter has gone through a period of growth, be mindful of having the pieces in the farm in the same switch. Some datacenters have been known to have Gb switches linked together through a 100MB switch. In large-scale farms, deploying SharePoint on their own VLAN for inter-farm communications has its advantages. The best situation is to keep all of the chatter between SharePoint off the public network.

END TO END

Finally, the last thing to consider in your deployment is the user desktop. You need to consider not only the bandwidth to the desktop, but also the performance specs and browser versions. A big part of the SharePoint experience comes from a massive java script file named ows.js. This will eat CPU cycles on the client machine. It's nothing to be concerned with if you have modern desktops, but if you are pushing SharePoint to a bunch of undersized desktops, you could add to those help desk calls.

For browsers, SharePoint supports both Level 1 and Level 2 browsers. Level 1 browsers are Internet Explorer 6.x and 7.x. Level 2 browsers are the following:

- Firefox 1.5
- Mozilla 1.7
- Netscape Navigator 7.2
- Netscape Navigator 8.1
- Safari 2.0

For most reading and writing activities, the Level 2 browsers are fully functional; it is only the admin components that sometimes utilize active X controls that require IE. Microsoft has specific information on browser compatibility at http://technet.microsoft.com/en-us/library/cc263526.aspx. Also, you can look at http://www.sharepointcontrols.com for a free add-on to SharePoint that will add some additional functionality for editing rich content to the Level 2 browsers.

12 High Availability, Backups, and Disaster Recovery

In This Chapter

- Introduction
- Content Recovery
- Backup and Disaster Recovery
- High Availability

INTRODUCTION

High availability and backups are like the Rodney Dangerfield of SharePoint administration—*they get no respect.* We all agree how important they are, but they always seem to take a backseat to other administrative tasks. In this chapter, we will address high availability and backups and show a wide variety of ways to address them. We will look at different situations and the methods that address those needs the best. We will cover content recovery, disaster recovery, and high availability scenarios. By the end of this chapter, you will have an arsenal of several techniques that you can employ, depending on the situation you are addressing.

CONTENT RECOVERY

The first scenario we will cover in this chapter is content recovery. By content recovery, we are referring to bringing back content that users have deleted and need to recover. Usually, they need it *immediately*. These techniques will not get back your entire SharePoint farm in the case of a server or facility failure. They will only get back individual content, such as documents and list items—they are very granular.

FIRST DEFENSE, VERSIONING

The first method we will discuss, and the easiest to implement, is versioning. Versioning is not normally considered a disaster recovery device. It is normally used to control exposure to documents. Regular users only see the published or major versions while administrators and contributors work on newer versions. We can use this in our favor to protect against document corruption or unintended edits to the documents. An added benefit is that end users can enable versions, as well as restore versions on their own. There is no need to involve support. It's good for users, and good for IT. The versioning settings are set at the list or library level, so unfortunately IT cannot force their use without touching each and every list or library. Any user or group with the Manage Lists permission can turn versioning on. Out of the box, the Design permission level has this permission. Let's turn versioning on and look at the options we have.

Open up any document library or list, and then go to the Settings menu, as shown in Figure 12.1.

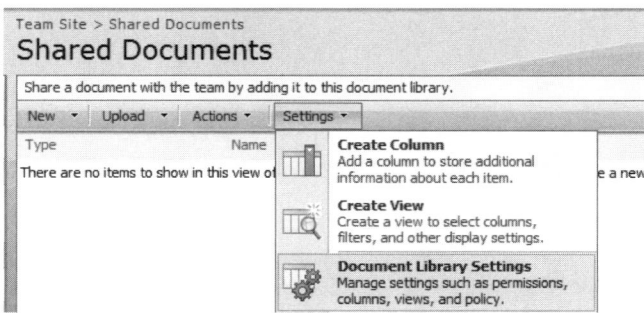

FIGURE 12.1
Document Settings.

Under General Settings, click Versioning settings (see Figure 12.2).

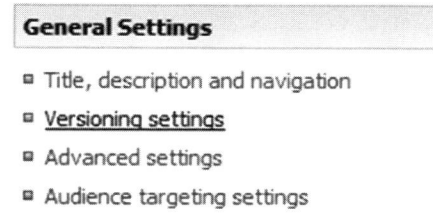

FIGURE 12.2
Choose Versioning settings.

That takes you to the Versioning settings page (see Figure 12.3).

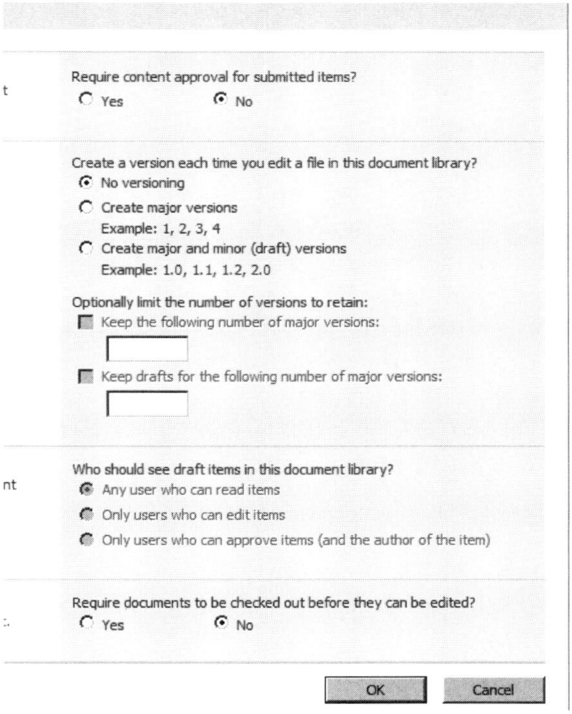

FIGURE 12.3
The Versioning settings page.

This one screen contains all of the settings for versioning. Not much to it. We can leave the first setting, "Require content approval for submitted items?" alone. That does not pertain to what we are using versioning for. The second setting is where it starts getting good. Here we can turn Versioning off, only create major versions, or create major and minor versions. Either of the last two options will work for us.

The next section lets you assign how many major and minor versions are kept. Why would you want to limit this? Since each version counts against your site collection quota, you may want to restrict the number of versions that are kept. Keep in mind that once you exceed the maximum number of versions, older versions will be removed, and they will not go into the Recycle Bin. They are lost and gone forever. The last setting we care about is who can see the draft or minor versions. Since we are not using versions for their intended purpose here, we probably want to allow any user to see the minor versions, which is the default. We can leave the last setting to No. It deals with preventing multiple people from editing the same document at the same time. It is not germane to our discussion.

Now that we have Versioning turned on and configured, let's walk through how a user would work with it and use it to recover content. Make sure that Versioning is turned on and create a new Word document in a document library. Once the document is open, go over to http://www.lipsum.com/ and generate some text. For this example, we will use the default of five paragraphs. Copy that text into your new Word document and save it. After the successful save, go back into the document and delete a few paragraphs and maybe type some unflattering things about Shane Young in there. Really mess it up. Then save it again and close it. To see what our options are, click the white space next to the document to get the Edit arrow and then click it to get your options.

Click Version History from the drop-down like we see in Figure 12.4. That will bring you to a page that shows all the versions that are available to the user.

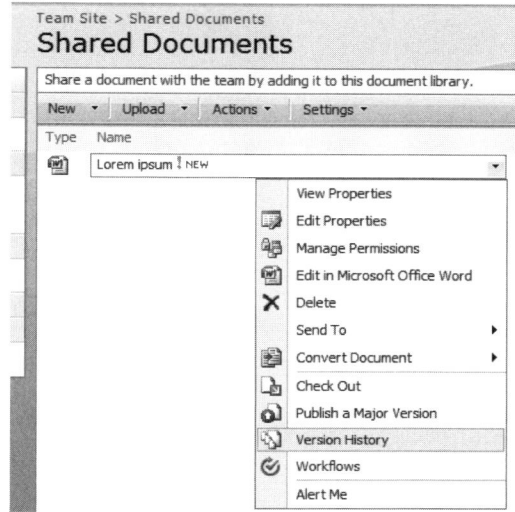

FIGURE 12.4
Document options.

You can see in Figure 12.5 that we have two versions of this document, one for each time we saved it. The newer versions have higher numbers, so 0.2 is the most recent and 0.1 is the first one. We want to restore our document to its original glory, before the paragraphs were deleted and those libelous comments about Shane were made. To do that, click the Edit drop-down for version 0.1 and click Restore, as shown in Figure 12.6.

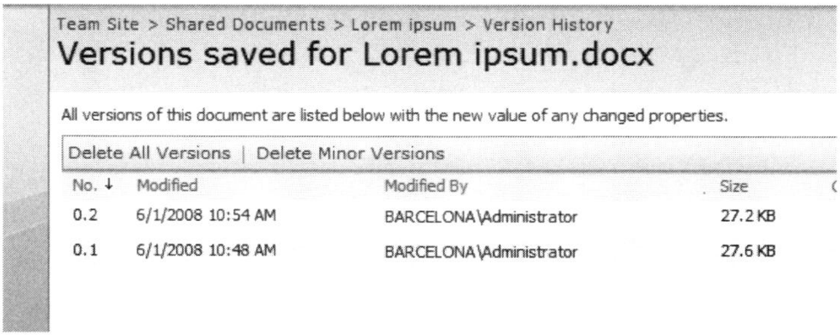

FIGURE 12.5
Document versions.

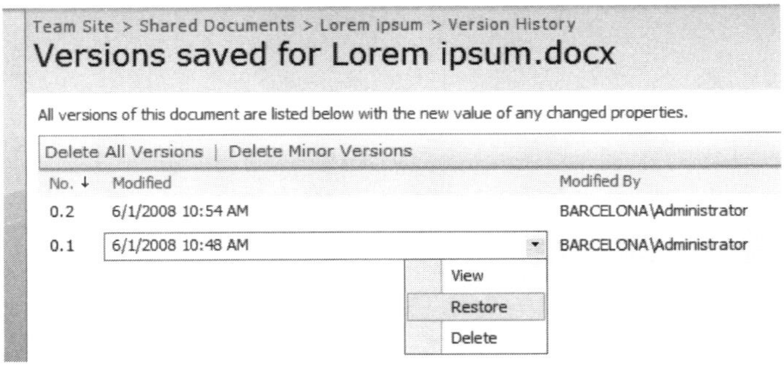

FIGURE 12.6
Restore a document version.

SharePoint is looking out for you, and it will pop open a dialog box telling you that you are going to replace the current version with the existing version. Go ahead and click OK. When the page refreshes, you should see three versions: the two we had before and a new one that SharePoint made when it reverted back to the original. Clicking the modified date and time should open the document for you, and if all went well, it will be the full five paragraphs of Lorem Ipsum. Now if end users make radical, unwanted changes to documents, they can drill down into the Version History and recover their text on their own, without needing to break out the backup tapes. We can all agree this is a good thing.

Second Defense, Recycle Bin

Versioning is a good first step in the defense against having to manually recover content for users, but it has a few shortcomings. Our next weapon is the Recycle Bin. The Recycle Bin is a feature that is new to SharePoint in the 2007 versions of the product, and it was well worth the wait. While Versioning is nice, the Recycle Bin is when we really start looking at a solution that has some power. Unlike Versioning, the Recycle Bin is configured at the Web Application level in Central Administration. That means administrators can force it on, and end users cannot turn it off, unlike Versioning. The Recycle Bin captures all content, so it gets list items, documents, deleted lists, and deleted document libraries as well. Much like the Windows Recycle Bin, items cannot be opened directly out of the Recycle Bin. They must be restored to their original location and opened from there.

First-Stage Recycle Bin

In a very wise move, Microsoft has given the Recycle Bin two stages. The first stage is for users. In the first stage, users can see the items that they have deleted, and they have the option of recovering them. Deleted documents are kept in the first stage for a defined number of days. The default is 30, but that can be changed by a Farm administrator. After they have been in the first stage for the allotted number of days, they are removed for good. Documents in the Recycle Bin do count against the site collection quota. If a site is bumping up against its quota, the Recycle Bins are a good place to look for things that can be trimmed. Users can get to it by clicking the Recycle Bin icon on the left navigation pane shown in Figure 12.7.

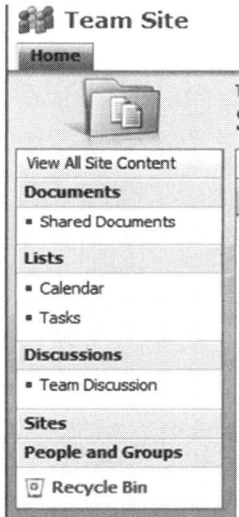

FIGURE 12.7
The left navigation pane.

If you do not see the Recycle Bin, then it has not been enabled for this Web Application, the link was removed with SharePoint Designer, or you do not have permission to use it. A user must be a Contributor or greater to get into the Recycle Bin.

When users go into the first-stage Recycle Bin, they get a list of all of their deleted items in that subsite. It is not all of their deleted documents in the entire Web Application or the site collection, just that subsite.

You can see in Figure 12.8 that they have two options for the documents there. The most important one is the option to Restore Selection. To restore a document, a user just needs to check the box next to the item he wants to restore and click the Restore Selection button. One confirmation dialog and the item is restored. Like Versioning, this is something that users can do without involving IT.

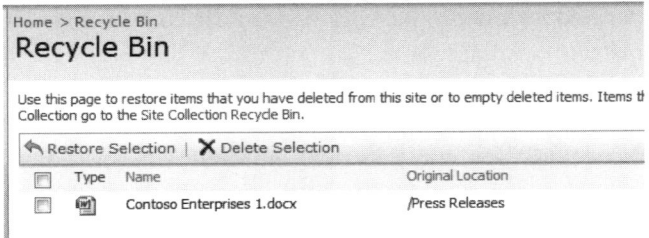

FIGURE 12.8
First-stage Recycle Bin.

The other option in the first-stage Recycle Bin is to delete the selection again. This will remove it completely from the first stage of the Recycle Bin. It does not remove it completely from the system, though, which leads us to our next section, on the second stage of the Recycle Bin.

Second-Stage Recycle Bin

When users delete items from the first stage, they go to the second stage. When I (Todd Klindt) saw how the Recycle Bin was structured in SharePoint, I felt that maybe Microsoft had been looking over my shoulder, it was eerie. Since the Recycle Bin made its way into Windows with Windows 95, I have been misusing it. I'll be honest, every time I delete a document and the Recycle Bin icon on my desktop changes from the empty icon to the "there is something in the Recycle Bin" icon, I want to empty it, immediately. Now I know the whole idea of the Recycle Bin is to leave stuff there in case I want to restore it later. But that icon changing triggers something animal in me. Maybe I am just compulsive, I am not sure. Regardless, it seems that Microsoft took my behavior into account when designing the Recycle Bin for SharePoint. First, no icons change when there are documents in the Recycle Bin. There is nothing to trigger my neurosis. Second, even if I go in and delete all my items again, there is a second stage to protect me from myself. Some places in the SharePoint interface refer to the second stage as the Administrative Recycle Bin or the Site Collection Recycle Bin. All three names refer to the same thing. In Figure 12.8, you can see a link to this second Recycle Bin. If you are logged in as a site collection admin, go ahead and click it. Let's see what this second stage is all about.

The view in Figure 12.9 is similar to the page we saw before, but it has some important differences. It has the old standbys of Restore Selection, Delete Selection, and Empty Recycle Bin, but it expands the scope. This view shows items from the entire Site Collection, and it is not restricted to a single Web. It also shows items deleted by all users, not just the user going there. While this view is nice, it is really just another view of the first stage. It shows the same documents that users would see. The real magic comes when you click the Deleted from end user Recycle Bin link on the left.

FIGURE 12.9
Site Collection Recycle Bin.

The view in Figure 12.10 shows the second stage itself. These are documents that have been deleted and then deleted from the first stage of the Recycle Bin. Again, this is for the whole Site Collection and all users. If you choose to restore an item from here, it will go back to its original spot, not back to the user's first-stage Recycle Bin. This is good because it keeps your users from knowing how easy it really is for you to get their documents back. If they know how easy it is, they will expect very quick results, regardless of what else you have going on.

FIGURE 12.10
The Second-stage Recycle Bin.

Now that you are excited about the second stage, let's cover some of the specifics of it. As mentioned previously, items do not expire out of the first stage into the second stage. We mention that twice because it is a common misconception and the question is asked a lot. Items only show up in the second stage if the user manually deleted them out of the first stage. While the first stage's retention is assigned by days, the second stage's is assigned as a percentage of the site collection quota. By default, the setting is 50 percent. That is above and beyond the regular site quota. If your site collection has a quota of 1GB, and the second stage is set to the default of 50 percent, that site collection and its second stage could conceivably take up 1.5GB of space. This can be a blessing or a curse. You will have to make sure and consider the second stage when planning for database growth. When the second stage hits its allotted size, SharePoint makes space by removing the oldest items. The second stage also brings with it a potentially sticky legal situation. Items do not expire until it reaches its quota by space. Because of that, items can stay in there for an indeterminate amount of time.

Because of legal discovery, some legal departments want to know exactly how long something can be made available. Because of this, some companies only use the first stage of the Recycle Bin, since items expire there by a predetermined amount of time. They are configured separately, so that is an option.

Since we mentioned configuration, let's look at the configuration for the Recycle Bin. Since this is scoped at the Web Application level, the settings are in Central Admin on the Application Management tab. There is not much to the Recycle Bin configuration, as you can see in Figure 12.11. So it gets lumped into the Web Application General Settings (/_admin/vsgeneralsettings.aspx) page. When you get to the settings page, make sure that the correct Web Application is selected. Then scroll to the bottom of the page. The Recycle Bin settings are the last group on the page.

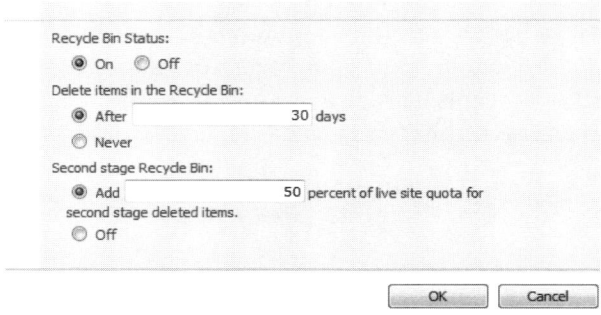

FIGURE 12.11
Recycle Bin settings.

The first radio box allows you to choose whether you want to use the Recycle Bin at all. When you check the On button, the rest of the options light up. First, you choose how many days that deleted items stay in the first stage. The default is 30 days, but you can increase or decrease that if you would like. You also have the option of leaving things in their Recycle Bin forever by setting the expiration to Never. While this gives your users the most protection, it also takes the most space and the first stage does count against the site collection quota. This is something to keep in mind with your planning.

While the settings for the first stage are pretty simple, the second stage is even easier. You basically just have an on and off switch and a percentage to choose. If you wanted to use only the first stage, here is where you disable the second stage by choosing Off. Otherwise, choose how much of a site collection's quota you want to add for the second stage. When planning for growth, consider making both Recycle Bins as large as you can. After you have it all configured, press the OK button to save the changes. One thing to keep in mind is that if you shut off the Recycle Bin, it will be flushed immediately. Both stages.

Using STSADM to Configure the Recycle Bin

While configuring the Recycle Bin in Central Admin is just fine, it can also be done with the Command Line tool, STSADM (for more information on STSADM, see Chapter 5, "Command Line Administration with STSADM"). STSADM exposes the Recycle Bin settings through the `getproperty` and `setproperty` operations. There are five properties that pertain to the Recycle Bin.

`recycle-bin-retention-period`: This property is the same as the first-stage retention settings. You can view the current settings using the following command:

```
stsadm -o getproperty -pn recycle-bin-retention-period -url
http://webapplication
```

The output will look like Figure 12.12:

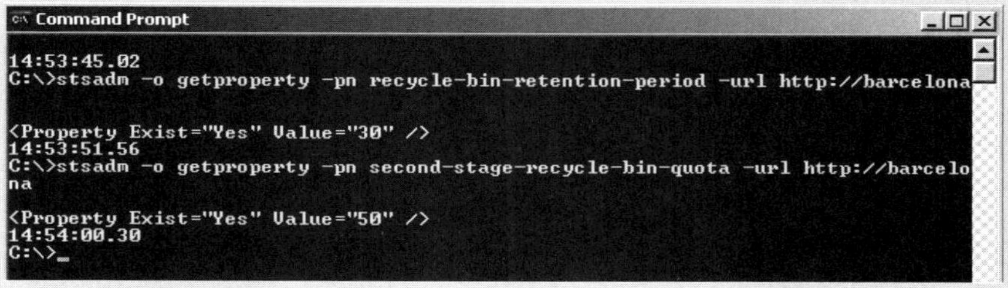

FIGURE 12.12
Recycle Bin settings via STSADM.

The property exists, and it is set to 30. For the first stage, that is the number of days. That screenshot also shows the second stage setting is 50, which equates to 50 percent in Central Admin.

To turn the Recycle Bin completely on or off, you can use the `recycle-bin-enabled` property.

While STSADM has all the functionality, it has two options that are not available in the UI. You can disable the Recycle Bin cleanup without removing your settings with the `recycle-bin-cleanup-enabled` property. If you set that property value to Off, the Recycle Bins will continue to collect items, but those items will never time out, regardless of the day or quota restrictions set on them. You can also use STSADM to determine when the cleanup activity happens, when it is enabled, with the `job-recycle-bin-cleanup` property. Simply set it to the time of day when you want the cleanup to happen, as in Figure 12.13.

continued

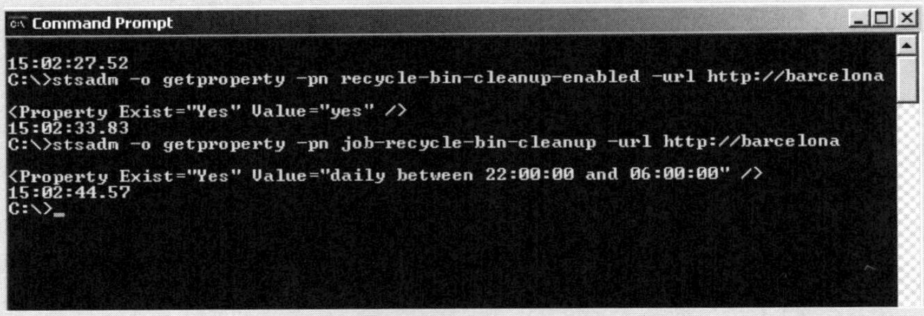

FIGURE 12.13
Cleanup settings.

Knowing the STSADM commands to change the Recycle Bin settings is especially handy if you do any scripting of your environments. Knowing that you can run a script and have it set all your Recycle Bin settings exactly how you want is very powerful.

Third Defense, Web Backups

So far we have covered two methods you can use to recover content without needing to do a full recovery of SharePoint. The third method we are going to cover is backing up the Webs themselves. Fortunately, there are many ways to accomplish that, and we will cover a couple of them here. Like the other solutions we have covered, the one that is right for you really depends on your situation.

SharePoint Designer

We can hear a collective groan from all the readers of this book when we mention SharePoint Designer (SPD). Come on, folks, it's not that bad. We know, you were hurt by FrontPage and you are holding a grudge. We are here to tell you that your fears are unfounded. SPD is a huge improvement and even a joy to use in most cases. One of the ways you can use SPD is to back up Webs and site collections. Like the other options we have discussed so far, this is something that end users can do for themselves, without involving IT, if they have SPD installed.

To back up a site collection or Web with SPD, open SPD and open the site you want to back up (see Figure 12.14).

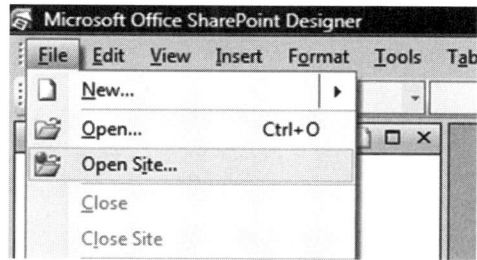

FIGURE 12.14
Opening a site in SharePoint Designer.

Once it is open, click Site > Administration > Backup Web Site (see Figure 12.15).

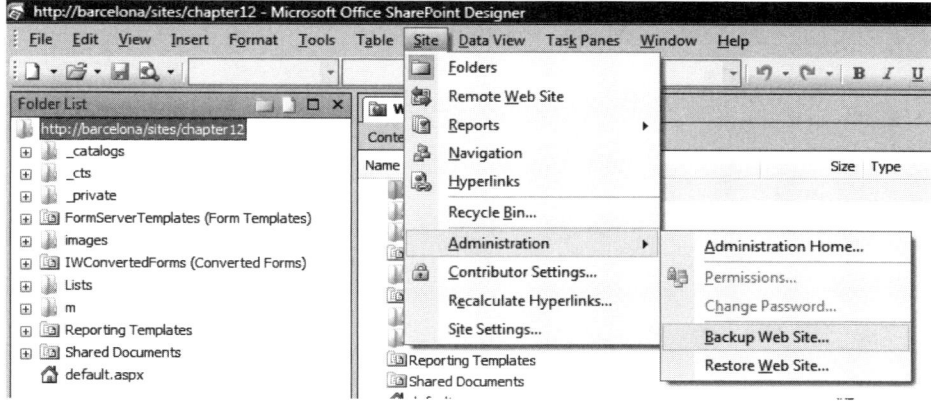

FIGURE 12.15
Backing up a Web.

You will get a dialog box asking if you want to include subsites in the archive you create. If you click Advanced, you will get a dialog box asking for a temporary location to store temp files (see Figure 12.16). When SPD does a backup of your site, it is doing a backup using the Content Deployment APIs, and it needs a place to store the files while it is creating them. If your site collection is near its quota limit, there may not be space to store those files before they are downloaded to your computer. SPD gives you an option of saving those files somewhere else in SharePoint before you download them. If you have space concerns, put in an alternate location.

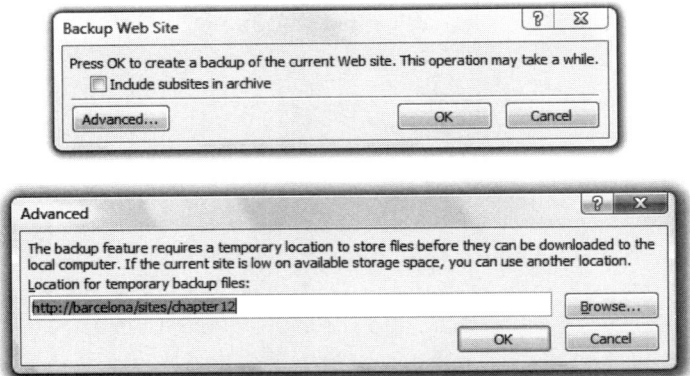

FIGURE 12.16
The Advanced options.

After you fill that in, press OK. You will be prompted for a location to save the CMP (Content Management Package) file. SPD will trigger the backup and save the file to your file system. The user can later use that CMP file to restore his Web, or if he is really fancy, he can use the method outlined in Chapter 5 and extract individual files out of them. Since these CMP files are just CAB files, you can put a .CAB extension on the file and open them up in Explorer. Also, since the files were made with the content deployment API, its focus is on content. It does not save out things like workflows, alerts, and some properties.

We mentioned before what an improvement SPD is over FrontPage, and we meant it. However, it is not without its faults. The default size of a CMP package is 25MB. If you are backing up a Web that is larger than 25MB, there is a chance that SPD may not save all of it back to your local file system. If you do a backup with SPD and it is obviously too small, check the Recycle Bin for your site. SPD creates the CMP files, saves them to your computer, and then deletes them. If it does not copy them all to your computer before it deletes them, you can restore them and copy them back manually. When you restore them from the Recycle Bin, they are returned to the root of the Web site. You can use SPD to move them from there to a document library where they can easily be downloaded with a Web browser. We know—the process has some flaws. Give it a chance, though. It may work fine for you.

Backing Up Webs and Sites with STSADM

We have exhausted all of the options that we can put in the hands of end users. We now have moved to the options that only administrators can use. In the last section we talked about making backups with SharePoint Designer. As an administrator, you can make the same backups without SPD on the server using STSADM. The

STSADM operation export uses the same content deployment APIs to export Webs out. The output is CMP files, like the output that SPD creates. Because of that, the two backups are compatible with each other, since they are the same format. Like the SPD backups, you have granular control of which Webs you back up and to what extent you back them up. Figure 12.17 shows the usage:

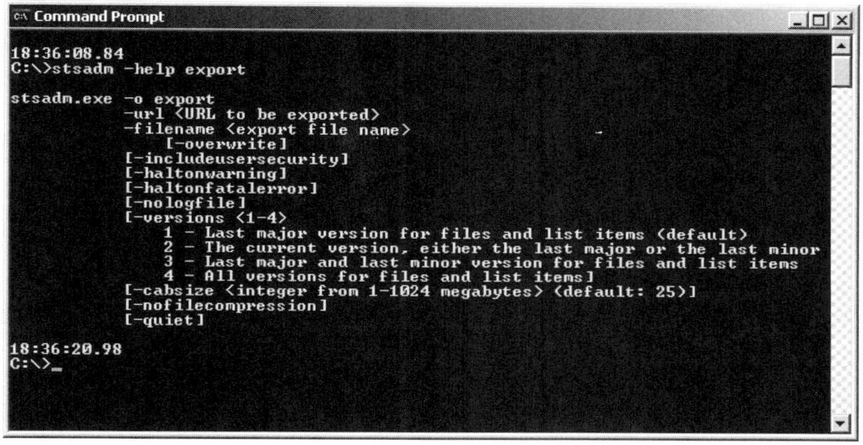

```
18:36:08.84
C:\>stsadm -help export

stsadm.exe -o export
            -url <URL to be exported>
            -filename <export file name>
                [-overwrite]
            [-includeusersecurity]
            [-haltonwarning]
            [-haltonfatalerror]
            [-nologfile]
            [-versions <1-4>
                1 - Last major version for files and list items <default>
                2 - The current version, either the last major or the last minor
                3 - Last major and last minor version for files and list items
                4 - All versions for files and list items]
            [-cabsize <integer from 1-1024 megabytes> <default: 25>]
            [-nofilecompression]
            [-quiet]

18:36:20.98
C:\>_
```

FIGURE 12.17
Export usage.

The –url parameter must be the location to a Web, which can also be the rootweb of a site collection. You cannot point it at an individual list or library, though. You can choose whether you want the security included or not. If you plan to use this for content recovery, you probably want to include it. If you were moving the content to another farm, the security information would not be valid, so it makes no sense to include it. Your next granular setting is how many versions to include. Since we are talking about this in the context of content recovery, you probably want all of the versions, so you would use the –versions 4 parameter. Again, if you were moving this content to another farm for publication, the last major version would be sufficient. Your last options have to do with how the backup is written. The first, –cabsize, lets you choose how large of chunks the back files are. For our purposes, it makes sense to make them as large as possible, using –cabsize 1024. The option is there because if you are moving these files to another farm across a slow link, you may want smaller files that are easier to restart if there are failures. The last option, –nofilecompression, allows you to have STSADM dump the backup into a directory instead of a CMP file. If you do that, provide a directory name for –filename instead of a filename.

Since it runs from a command line, you can schedule this to run at periodic intervals. This is handy if you have a Web that is particularly important or is more prone to accidental deletions than others. We all know a few Webs that meet this description. Simply put the STSADM command in a CMD file and use Windows' Task Scheduler to have it run at whatever interval you would like. The script file would look like Figure 12.18.

```
stsadm -o export -url http://barcelona/sites/chapter12
-includeusersecurity -versions 4 -cabsize 1024 -quiet
-filename barcelona.cmp
```

FIGURE 12.18
Export script.

If you would like to build the date into the file name, you can do it by parsing the %date% variable. You could use the following for your filenames to make them sort well in the file system (see Figure 12.19).

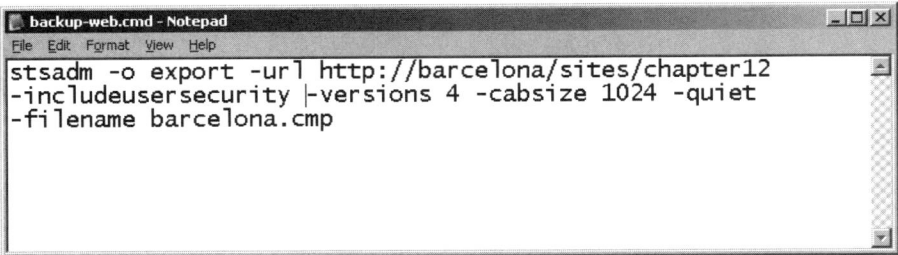

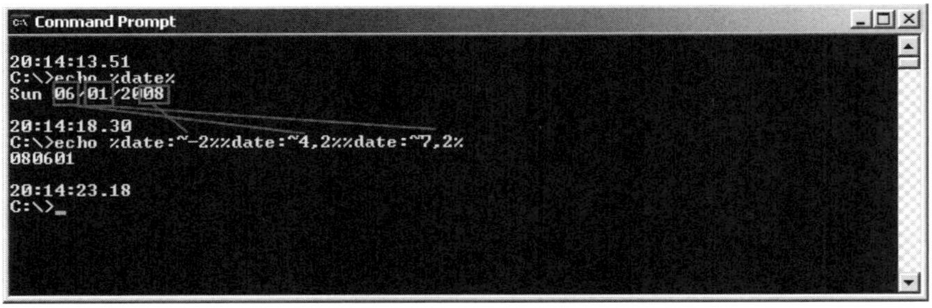

FIGURE 12.19
The Date variable.

You can pull out individual chunks of the %date% variable to get the string you need. The format YYMMDD works well because the files will sort in order. The script in Figure 12.20 saves your backups in that format.

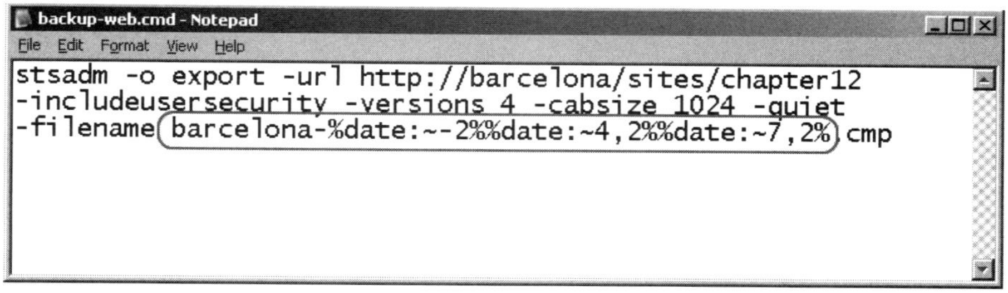

```
backup-web.cmd - Notepad                                    _ □ ×
File  Edit  Format  View  Help
stsadm -o export -url http://barcelona/sites/chapter12
-includeusersecurity -versions 4 -cabsize 1024 -quiet
-filename barcelona-%date:~-2%%date:~4,2%%date:~7,2% cmp
```

FIGURE 12.20
Backup script.

That will create a unique file based on the date. If you are worried about building up too many backup files, you could use the `forfiles` command to delete files older than a certain date. The following command removes all of the CMP files that are older than seven days.

```
forfiles /d -7 /m *.CMP /c "cmd /c del @file"
```

You could add that at the end of your backup script to clean up stale backup files.

Keeping Up to Date

While you have the `-overwrite` option with STSADM, what do you do if you want to keep multiple backups of the same Web? Like we demonstrated, you can use the `%date%` variable to save each backup with a different name. But how did we come up with that seemingly random string of characters? Turns out the secret lies in the `set` command. We stumbled onto the capability while looking for something else a few years ago. If you type `set /?` at a Command Prompt, you get a couple of pages of usage for `set`. The part we care about is the substitution. Here is the relevant part:

```
        May also specify substrings for an expansion.
            %PATH:~10,5%
        would expand the PATH environment variable, and then use
        only the 5 characters that begin at the 11th (offset 10)
        character of the expanded result. If the length is not
        specified, then it defaults to the remainder of the
        variable value. If either number (offset or length) is
        negative, then the number used is the length of the
        environment variable value added to the offset or length
        specified.
```

continued

```
        %PATH:~-10%

would extract the last 10 characters of the PATH variable.

        %PATH:~0,-2%

would extract all but the last 2 characters of the PATH
variable.
```

Using that formula, we dissected the `%date%` variable. First, we took the final two characters to get the year. Then we took the two characters after position four to get the two digits of the month. We end the string with two characters following the seventh character, which gives us the two digits for the date. That's all there is to it. Obviously, this works for anything, not just STSADM exports. You could use it with STSADM backups or any other Command Prompt command.

Backups made with STSADM export are portable, so they can be restored back to their original location, a different location in the same farm, or a completely different farm entirely. In order to restore to a different farm, both farms must be at the same SharePoint build number. This is worth doing, though. When you need to recover content, being able to do it without overwriting your production data is incredibly valuable. A best practice is having a warm SharePoint environment ready for recoveries when you need them. Then you can just import the CMP file backups into your recovery environment and pull out the content you need to recover. It is common to have a recovery environment virtualized. Due to its low usage, a virtualized environment is perfect. It also saves money on hardware and software licenses. This eases some of the pain of the recovery environment and makes it an easier sell when budgets are being planned.

Getting these Web-based backups into SharePoint is as easy as using the import operation with STSADM. The usage is pretty self-explanatory:

```
stsadm.exe -o import
            -url <URL to import to>
            -filename <import file name>
            [-includeusersecurity]
            [-haltonwarning]
            [-haltonfatalerror]
            [-nologfile]
            [-updateversions <1-3>
                1 - Add new versions to the current file (default)
                2 - Overwrite the file and all its versions (delete then insert)
```

```
        3 - Ignore the file if it exists on the destination]
[-nofilecompression]
[-quiet]
```

Essentially, you need to provide a filename and a URL to import the Web. The import operation is covered in more detail in Chapter 5.

STSADM has another operation that can be used for content recovery, and that is backup. Unlike export, backup only works at the site collection level, and it does not allow the granular control that export does. However, it is a more full fidelity backup than export allows. It does not use the Content Deployment API, so its focus is not solely on content. With backup, you will maintain things you lose with export, such as alerts and workflows. Let's take a quick look at the usage in Figure 12.21.

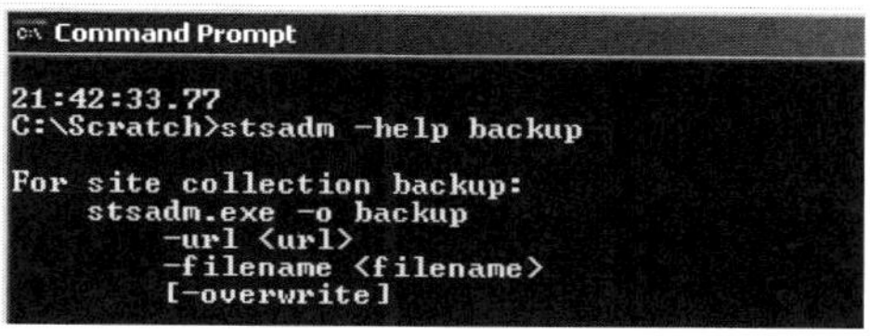

```
Command Prompt

21:42:33.77
C:\Scratch>stsadm -help backup

For site collection backup:
    stsadm.exe  -o backup
            -url <url>
            -filename <filename>
            [-overwrite]
```

FIGURE 12.21
Backup operation usage.

All STSADM backup needs is a URL and a filename. Like export, it can also be scripted if you want periodic backups, and you can use the same techniques to keep multiple copies of backup files. Also, like the export operation, the backups made with the backup operation are portable and can be restored to other SharePoint farms.

Dynamic Backups

If you have a small- to medium-sized environment, using STSADM backup might be a good way to go. One potential issue is that any script you will use to leverage STSADM will be static and will not automatically pick up any newly created site collections. Fortunately, several individuals have written VBS scripts that parse the output of stsadm −o enumsites and runs stsadm −o backup against the entire site collections list. You can find one written by Michael Noel at this blog entry, http://www.toddklindt.com/blog/Lists/Posts/Post.aspx?ID=46. He was kind enough to share it with us. Thanks, Michael.

If you decide to use STSADM backup, there are a few caveats you should know. They all revolve around the same problem: it does not scale very well. Microsoft does not recommend that it be used for site collections larger than 10 to 15GB, and we agree with them. The process is very slow. Of course, the performance depends a lot on the hardware you use, but generally you can expect a throughput of around 12GB an hour. For large environments, that runs afoul with prescribed backup windows. Also, under some circumstances an STSADM backup can lock the content database that contains the site collection being backed up. This is not nearly as likely of an issue with recent releases of SharePoint, but it is still a possibility.

You should also lock site collections before backing it up with STSADM –o backup. If not, it is possible that your backup file will not restore. Two things can cause this, and they both also relate to scale. If anyone is changing the site collection while it is being backed up, it may result in an inconsistent backup. Also, if anyone tries to access the site collection while it is being restored, it may prevent the backup from restoring successfully. This can happen even if they are viewing it read only. When a user accesses a site, a row is created for that user in the UserInfo table in the content database. If that happens before the restore process has written the restored UserInfo table to that database, it may encounter a row that collides with one it is trying to write. That will make the restore fail. To prevent these issues, set your site collection's lock status to "no access" with this STSADM command:

```
Stsadm –o setsitelock –url http://server/sites/sitecollection -lock noaccess
```

Then after the backup is complete, turn off the site lock with this command:

```
Stsadm –o setsitelock –url http://server/sites/sitecollection -lock none
```

Locking your site collections will greatly decrease the possibility of a restore operation failing. When you do need to restore a site collection, use the STSADM operation restore. Here is the usage:

```
For site collection restore:
    stsadm.exe -o restore
        -url <url>
        -filename <filename>
        [-hostheaderwebapplicationurl <web application url>]
        [-overwrite]
```

Like import, you need to provide a filename and a URL. If there is currently a site at the URL specified, use the –overwrite parameter to overwrite it.

The backup and restore operations are covered in more detail in Chapter 5.

Third-and-a-Half Defense, Site Delete Capture

This tool is kind of a combination between the last two topics covered. Our second defense against a full recovery was the Recycle Bin. This works great for lists and libraries, but it does not work for sites. Our third defense was STSADM. It handles sites and Webs, but it does not work dynamically like the Recycle Bin does. If only there were a way to combine the best of both worlds. Now there is. On Codeplex there is a project called the MS IT Site Delete Capture Utility. This project bridges the gap between the Recycle Bin and STSADM. It will capture any Webs or sites that users or administrators have deleted and save them to disk before they are deleted. It does this by installing an event receiver that hooks into the Web Delete and Site Delete events. The backups are saved to a location in the file system that you specify. Those backup files can be easily moved to tape if you choose, and they are easily restored via STSADM if content needs to be restored. Optionally, emails can be sent to users when their site is deleted letting them know it was backed up successfully or not.

Are you convinced that this utility is the greatest thing since sliced bread? Good, because it is. The only downside is that the install could use a little polish. It is a little more manual than you are used to. But, the product is free, so we really cannot complain. First, you will need to download it from http://www.codeplex.com/governance. Microsoft has graciously made several tools available for free there, but the only one we care about right now is Microsoft IT Site Delete Capture 1.0. Download the .zip file to your local hard drive and extract the files. In the zip file you will find a Word document outlining the install steps. Those are the steps we will follow here.

The first step is to copy the four folders in the install to the Template\Features folder of the 12 Hive. This makes the features available to SharePoint. If you have multiple Web front-ends, you will need to do this on all of them. Next, you need to install the MS.IT.SiteDeleteCapture.dll DLL into the Global Assembly Cache (GAC). To do this, copy MS.IT.SiteDelectCapture.dll in Explorer. Then open C:\windows\assembly in Explorer and paste the file in. Next copy the Messages.xml file to the C:\Program Files\Common Files\Microsoft Shared\web server extensions\12\TEMPLATE\LAYOUTS\1033 directory on each of your Web front ends. The 1033 directory is the U.S. English locale. If you have other languages installed, you will need to copy the messages.xml file there, too.

The next step is easy. Run install.bat to install the Features we copied over. After that has finished, you need to decide where the backups will be stored. Open C:\Program Files\Common Files\Microsoft Shared\web server extensions\12\TEMPLATE\Features\ MSITDeleteFeature\ConfigurationForReceiverDLL.xml and put your location in the backupFolder node. The value can be a local path like D:\Backup, or it can be a UNC path like \\server\backups. If you have multiple Web front-ends, a UNC path to a central server makes the most sense.

The heavy lifting of the install is finished at this point. Now you just need to do a couple more steps to configure it. The application uses a SharePoint site and list to store its configuration. The location of /sites/CaptureConfiguration is specified in the Messages.xml. You can use that or any other location. If you use another location, you will need to edit Messages.xml appropriately. We are going to install it in the default site to keep things easy. We used the following command to create the Site Collection:

```
stsadm -o createsite -url http://barcelona/sites/CaptureConfiguration
  -ownerlogin administrator -owneremail admin@barcelona -sitetemplate STS#0
```

You will want to replace our Web application URL (http://barcelona) with your own, as well as the admin information. The -sitetemplate parameter at the end, STS#0, tells STSADM to create a Team Site. Now you need to upload the custom list the Feature uses to the Site Collection. Open up the site collection you created and go to the Site Settings. Under Galleries, click List templates. You need to upload the configuration list template to the gallery, so click Upload. On the Upload Template screen, browse to the directory where you unzipped the file and select AppConfig.stp. Click Open and OK. Click OK again on the summary screen. Now you need to create an instance of the list. Click Site Actions and then Create. Under Custom Lists, click AppConfig. Use AppConfig as the name of the new list. You can see in Figure 12.22 that the list has some values prepopulated, but you will want to change them to fit your environment. Open the AppConfig list, select the AppConfig list item, and click Edit Item in the drop-down.

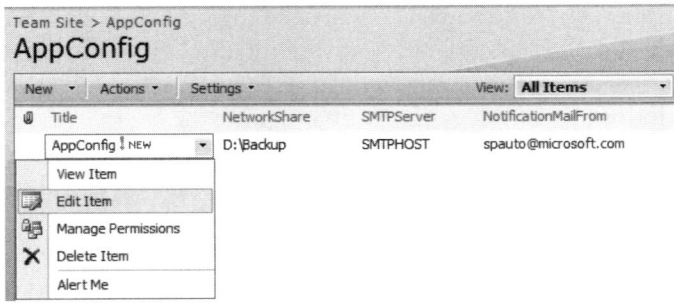

FIGURE 12.22
Edit the AppConfig list properties.

Replace the NetworkShare with the location where the backups should be placed. Put your SMTP server name in the SMTPServer value and the address you want the mail to come from in the NotificationMailFrom value. That's it—it's all configured.

All that is left is to activate the Feature. Go into Central Admin > Application Management> Manage Web Application Features. Click Activate for the Microsoft IT Site Delete Capture Feature 1.1. Now your sites and Webs are protected from deletion. Go ahead and create a sacrificial Web or site. Upload a couple of documents to the site to give it some bulk. Now delete the Web or site. The delete process should look exactly the same. There is no indication that anything special is going on. Now look in the folder you specified when you configured the Feature. You should see a BAK file that matches the name of the Web or site you deleted. There is also a Log directly that contains CaptureLog.txt. When the Feature captures a site deletion, it logs it here.

Figure 12.23 shows how the backups are saved. The file system mirrors your SharePoint-managed paths. The files in the Site folder are Site Collections that were in the Site's Managed Path. The Site Collection http://barcelona/sites/DeleteSite was captured as c:\backups\sites\DeleteSite.bak. When we deleted the Web at http://barcelona/sites/CaptureSite/DeletedWeb, it was saved to c:\backups\sites\ CaptureSite\DeletedWeb.bak.

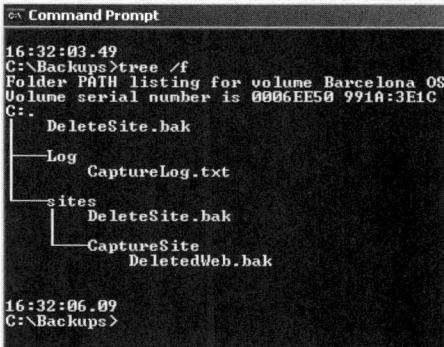

FIGURE 12.23
Screenshot of capture directory.

All that functionality and all it costs you was a little time. Not too shabby. To get the Web or sites back, use the `import` or `restore` STSADM operations respectively. Specify the filename and the URL where you would like it to be restored. Remember, you do not have to restore them to the same location where they were backed up. You can restore them somewhere else to pull documents or items out without overwriting the entire Web or site.

Backup and Disaster Recovery

We have covered what you can do to minimize the impact of accidental file deletion, but what happens if your entire server crashes? This could be due to a massive hardware failure or a location failure like fire or flood. In this part of the chapter, we will cover techniques you can use to protect yourself against such catastrophic failures.

Unfortunately, the backup story for catastrophic failures is not great in SharePoint. There is not just one place to back up to get everything you would need to do a full recovery. Because of that, you have to use several tools in concert to get everything you need. Since you have to use many tools, the size of your SharePoint farm and the budget you have will figure in to how you will back up SharePoint.

What Are You Backing Up?

Before we get into how you are going to back SharePoint up, we need to cover what you need to back up. SharePoint information is scattered hither and yon about your WFEs and database servers. From a high level, the information you are backing up falls under the category of content, configuration, and software you have installed on top of SharePoint. That further breaks down between SharePoint configuration and other configurations. Microsoft has done a great job building SharePoint on top of other technologies, so these technologies must be backed up as well. First, we will cover where each of those components is, and then we will cover your options for backing each of them up.

SharePoint Content

We will cover content first, because it is arguably the most important. When we talk about content we mean anything that users add to SharePoint. This includes Microsoft Office documents that are being collaborated on, surveys that have been filled out, contacts added to a Contact list, everything. If we do not get the SharePoint configuration backed up, well, we have to redo everything. If we do not get the content backed up correctly, there is no recourse. Not to mention how upset the users will be. Fortunately, the content is one thing that is easy to back up and is not spread out as much as the configuration. All content in SharePoint exists in content databases. (There is an API that allows remote blob storage. If you are using a product that uses remote blob storage, consult with them on the best way to back up your content.) These databases can be backed up a number of ways, and they are portable. Content Databases can be attached to other farms if necessary, or the content itself could be extracted out of the database directly. The moral of this story is that as long as you have your Content Databases, you can get your content back.

SharePoint Configuration

Here is where things start to get dicey. The phrase "SharePoint Configuration" covers a variety of things, and therefore is stored in a variety of places.

Configuration Database

The mother of all SharePoint configurations is the Configuration Database, or the ConfigDB to its friends. The ConfigDB is the heart of your SharePoint farm. It all starts with the ConfigDB. Like the name suggests, it is a database on your SQL server, so it can be backed up in the same manner as your content databases. However, the restoration is different. Unlike the content databases, the ConfigDB is not portable, and it cannot be restored to another environment. It must be restored in the same place with the same machine names. In the case of a disaster, it is quite likely that you would end up reinstalling SharePoint and building a new farm before restoring your content. Because of this, many SharePoint disaster recovery plans tell you to not even back up your ConfigDB. While you likely cannot restore your ConfigDB, it is great to have it in the form of documentation. If you know how the ConfigDB is laid out, it can answer questions about how your farm was configured, increasing your chances of replicating it, should you need to do so. The Objects table is a wealth of information about your farm.

The Objects table has hundreds of rows, one for each object in your farm's configuration, and it details much of your farm's environment. Each type of object has its own `ClassId`. There is a `ClassId` for Content Databases, SQL servers, Alternate Access Mappings, and so on. Using the following SQL query, we found 120 different `ClassIds` in our `ConfigDB`:

```
use SharePoint_Config
select distinct [ClassId]
from objects
```

We will not cover what each of the `ClassIds` are, but we will cover some that are of interest. By knowing some of the key `ClassIds` to look for, you can see how to recreate your new farm. Here are a few `ClassIds` that pertain to disaster recovery:

TABLE 12.1 OBJECTS AND THEIR CLASSIDS

Object	ClassId
Content Database	3D4F5451-1735-48BB-B920-76C1EC240B1D
Server	E77AAF47-3CAC-4001-BC6B-5BCCB6486318
AAMs	9920F486-2FF4-4D10-9532-E01979826585
Incoming email address	1F503A44-EA73-498E-B002-F6037E004D84
Outgoing email	FF859B31-F963-4683-A9E8-7CAE97A867B8
Persisted File	8DB85FC9-F090-4762-93AA-022E2BA0CC55
Solution Files	9425ad4c-e595-42f9-92bf-b33ae4ef3c68

Each of those objects has value when trying to re-create your SharePoint farm in the case of a catastrophe. If you have your ConfigDB backed up, you can run simple SQL queries against it when rebuilding. For instance, to get a list of all of the Content Databases you had, execute the following SQL query:

```
Use SharePoint_Config_old
select * from objects
where classid = '3D4F5451-1735-48BB-B920-76C1EC240B1D'
```

You will need to change the database named in the Use statement to match whatever you restored your ConfigDB as, or choose it from the Available Databases drop-down. When you execute that query, it will list all the Content Databases that were in your failed farm. You can use that to verify you get them all reattached when rebuilding.

Alternate Access Mappings (AAM) are tough to back up and restore. You can use this same method to retrieve the AAMs, as they are stored in the ConfigDB as well. Replace the ClassID in the previous query with the one for AAMs and execute it. You will get one row back for each Web Application that was in your farm. The Properties column is an XML blob that enumerates all the AAMs for that Web App, as well as when they were changed last and by whom. This is a great way to document your AAMs

The last ClassId in Table 12.1 is for Solution files. This one can be used to see which Solutions were installed in your farm. As you are rebuilding things, you do not have to worry about content not rendering correctly because a needed solution was not installed. Replace the ClassId in the SQL query with the Solution file ClassId to get a list of Solutions that are installed in your farm. When new WFEs are brought into your farm, Solutions that are installed in your farm are automatically pushed out to them. For that to work, the Solutions must be stored someplace common. That place is referred to as the Solution Store and is in the ConfigDB. They are stored as persisted files in the ConfigDB Binaries table. Persisted files are files that SharePoint uses for Administration and Deployment purposes. To see what persisted files are in your ConfigDB, use their ClassId in the SQL query. Once we know their ID in the Objects table, we can query for them in the Binaries table. You can also run the following query that returns all the rows in the Objects database that have corresponding entries in the Binaries database.

```
SELECT      Objects.Name, Binaries.FileImage, Objects.Id
FROM        Objects INNER JOIN
                Binaries ON Objects.Id = Binaries.ObjectId
```

This query finds all the objects in the Objects table that have entries in the Binaries table and displays their name, their ID, and the first part of the file blob. That in and of itself is not helpful, but you could write a program that would extract those Solution files and other persisted files out of the database in the case of a disaster. This is just another way that backing up your ConfigDB can be helpful, even if you never restore it.

Solutions Are the Only Way to Go

Now seems like a great time to cover Solutions and how important they are to you, as the SharePoint administrator. If you are working with developers that developed for SharePoint 2003, they had all kinds of wacky ways to bolt onto SharePoint. In the SharePoint 2003 days, there was not any great way to add functionality to SharePoint, so sometimes it had to be done in creative ways. In SharePoint 2007, that has all been fixed with the advent of Solutions and Features. As a SharePoint administrator, do not add any software to your SharePoint farm that does not come to you in a Solution file, which are either WSP or CAB files. Your developers may be tempted to give you DLL files and manual web.config changes, as that is what they have done in the past. Force them to package it as a Solution. For you, the benefits are many. First, you do not need to keep track of all of the files needed or the instructions on how to install them. A Solution contains all that in a single file. You also do not need to worry about updating versions or keeping your WFEs in sync. You install a Solution in one place, and it is distributed to all the SharePoint servers automatically. There is even a facility for upgrading Solutions built into the framework. Finally, if something should go wrong, removing a Solution is only a few clicks of a mouse or an STSADM command away.

Solutions make for a much better administrative experience. Do not install any software on your SharePoint servers by hand—demand Solutions.

Alternate Access Mappings

One of the first hard lessons you learn when you start using SharePoint 2007 is about Alternate Access Mappings. They are not implemented in an intuitive way, and if they are not configured exactly right, you will experience all kinds of weird behavior. We covered in the last section how AAMs are stored in the ConfigDB. Since we will likely not be restoring the ConfigDB, how do we back them up in such a way that we can re-create them easily? The bad news is that there is no good way to restore them, but the good news is that they are very easy to document and re-create. First, let's start with how to document them. STSADM includes an operation, `enumalternatedomains`, that enumerates all the AAMs in your farm. It creates nice, easy-to-read XML output, as shown in Figure 12.24.

FIGURE 12.24
Output of `stsadm —o enumalternatedomains`.

To save this, simply pipe the output to a file with this command:

```
stsadm -o enumalternatedomains > aam.xml
```

Now just make sure that file is someplace in the file system that gets backed up. There is no way to import that file, unfortunately, but you can automate the creation of AAMs. The STSADM operation `addalternatedomain` creates AAMs. You can quickly re-create your AAMs with it by referencing the aam.xml file you created. A best practice is to script the creation of AAMs. If you create them initially with a script, you can use that same script to reproduce them in the case of a disaster.

SSP Databases

Like the Content and Config databases, the SSP databases can be backed up with regular database backup tools. The exception is the search database. It must be backed up with a SharePoint aware tool. Search is comprised of two pieces: a database in SQL and an index file that exists on the Index and Query servers. These two components must be exactly in sync. If you restore them and they are not in sync, you must rebuild them by initiating a full crawl of your content.

SharePoint Customizations

SharePoint seems to be infinitely customizable. From a disaster recovery standpoint, this can be a curse since all the customizations are not stored in the same place. Most of them are stored in the file system of the WFEs with the majority of them being in the 12 Hive. Here is a short list of some of the customizations that are stored there:

- Features
- Master Pages
- Spthemes.xml and Custom Theme files
- Webtemp.xml
- Docicon.xml and file icons
- Custom site definitions

These are just a few of the customizations we have to be concerned about backing up. Since they are just files, though, they can be backed up and restored with any backup software that does files.

Installed Software

As we mentioned in the sidebar, all software that is installed into your SharePoint environment should come in a Solution file. Not only is it the correct thing to do, but it also makes backup and recovery very easy. Just back up the WSP files. Since they are just files, they can be backed up with any file-aware backup software. If you are in doubt as to which Solutions you have deployed, you can look in Central Admin > Operations, or if SharePoint is offline, query your ConfigDB. Some things, like iFilters, which are not SharePoint specific, may not offer a Solution installation. Make sure you back up the installation for that software as well.

Some software will add .NET assemblies to the Global Assembly Cache. You can back these up by backing up the c:\windows\assembly directory.

IIS

Since SharePoint relies so heavily on IIS, it only makes sense that to do a proper restore you need to back up items in IIS. While SharePoint does a good job of making the necessary changes to IIS, it does not do a good job of backing them up. Here are a few IIS components that SharePoint needs to function properly, but does not back up on its own.

- Host headers
- SSL Certificates
- Application Pool settings
- Web site settings
- Web.config changes

Each of these is very important, but it is easy for the first two to get away from you. Likely any changes you have made to your web.config were made by software installations, and they would be re-created. The host headers and SSL certs are not, and must be taken care of by hand. Host headers, and all your other IIS settings, can be backed up with the iisback.vbs script that is included with IIS. It makes backups of IIS's two most important configuration files, metabase.xml and MBSchema.xml, and stores them in %systemroot%\system32\inetsrv\MetaBack. The usage is pretty simple:

```
iisback.vbs /backup /b SharePointBackup
```

That will back up your IIS configuration and name the backup created "Share-PointBackup." Iisback can keep multiple versions of a backup, so do not be afraid to use the name more than once. You can see what backups are available by running iisback.vbs /list. Once you have run iisback.vbs to back up your IIS configuration, you can use any backup software to write those files to tape, or whatever your long-term solution is. Do not to forget to include your SSL certificates in that backup.

Another location you will want to back up is your Inetpub directory. There's a directory in Inetpub for every Web application you have in SharePoint. These directories could have customized web.config files or assemblies that have been installed into that Web Application's Bin directory. The directories are small, so you should add them to your list of file system folders that you back up.

MOSS Only

There is one location in the file system that you only need to worry about if you are running MOSS, C:\ProgramFiles\Microsoft Office Servers\12.0. MOSS keeps a few things in here like both Office Search and WSS Help Search files, the Index file, and the binaries for the Web services it uses. If you did a Basic install, that directory also contains your SQL Express files. If you have MOSS installed, consider adding this directory to any file level backups you do. Keep an eye on your index file, though, as it is included in that directory. If it gets large, it will make your backups large.

HOW WILL YOU BACK IT ALL UP?

Now that we have covered what you need to back up in order to recover from a disaster, we need to figure out how you are going to get it all backed up. Much like the questions "How much is a new car?" or "How long is a string?" the answer depends. Several things factor in.

- Do you have an existing disaster recovery plan in place?
- How much SharePoint data do you have to back up?
- How business critical is your SharePoint content?
- Can you afford to lose any data?
- What is your level of expertise with SharePoint?
- What is your budget?

Each of these factors weighs in on your decision on how to back up your Share-Point farm. The methods we discuss here will be in order of scale, essentially. We will start with built-in options that work well with small environments and finish with more expensive third-party solutions. Combining the information we learned in the last section, with your options in this section, you should be able to determine which method or methods will work best for you.

SharePoint Central Admin

The first and most obvious backup method is built right into SharePoint. Microsoft has included farm-level backup in the Central Admin Web site. For small- to medium-sized environments, this is a great option. To use it, fire up Central Admin and navigate to the Operations tab. There is a Backup and Restore heading that houses all of the links you need (see Figure 12.25).

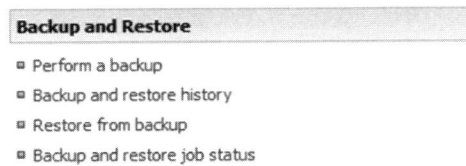

FIGURE 12.25
Backup and Restore options in Central Admin.

You can see in Figure 12.25 that there are four links that pertain to backups. To get started, click Perform a backup. From this screen, you can see your components start with farm and get more granular from there. You can see in Figure 12.26 all the different components of the farm that can be backed up.

Select	Component	Type	Description
☐	Farm	Farm	Content and configuration data for the entire server farm.
	SharePoint_Config_5deead6d-5d40-4ec7-ab2e-ac3e66e4fe80	Configuration Database	Configuration data for the entire server farm.
☐	Windows SharePoint Services Web Application	Windows SharePoint Services Web Application	Collection of Web Applications
☐	SharePoint - 80	Web Application	Content and configuration data for this Web application.
☐	WSS_Content	Content Database	Content for the Web Application.
☐	WSS_Content2	Content Database	Content for the Web Application.
☐	WSS_Content_Move	Content Database	Content for the Web Application.
☐	WSS_Content3	Content Database	Content for the Web Application.
☐	WSS_Content_d1922aff200b48c2a0868a55068c8665	Content Database	Content for the Web Application.
☐	SharePoint - extranet80	Web Application	Content and configuration data for this Web application.
☐	WSS_Content_Extranet	Content Database	Content for the Web Application.
	WSS_Administration	Central Administration	Collection of Web Applications
	Web Application	Web Application	Content and configuration data for this Web application.
☐	SharePoint_AdminContent_33b9c499-f1ed-4a56-8a1d-b940908abf68	Content Database	Content for the Web Application.
☐	SharedServices1	Shared Services Provider	Database and Configuration Settings for this Shared Services Provider
	SharePoint - 15843	Web Application	Content and configuration data for this Web application.
☐	SharedServicesContent_95827fde-2007-425f-99e5-13333938c5db	Content Database	Content for the Web Application.
	SharedServices1_DB_abb922fd-29a6-48ea-a464-b8e421feb4c6	Shared Service Provider Database	Stores Configuration Settings for this Shared Services Provider
	UserProfileApplication	User Profile Application	User Profile Application
	SessionStateSharedApplication	Session State	Session State
	Shared Search Index	Search index files for SharedServices1	Search index file for the Shared Services Provider
	SharedServices1_Search_DB_0e7a632d-2bdc-4073-baf0-3800377e1e2b	Search database for SharedServices1	Search database containing the property store and the crawler history
☐	Global Search Settings	Search object in configuration database	Crawler impact rules for the farm
☐	Windows SharePoint Services Search	Index files and Databases	Search instances for Windows SharePoint Services
	Search instance	Index files on BARCELONA	Search index files on the search server
	WSS_Search_BARCELONA	Search database for BARCELONA	Search database for the search server

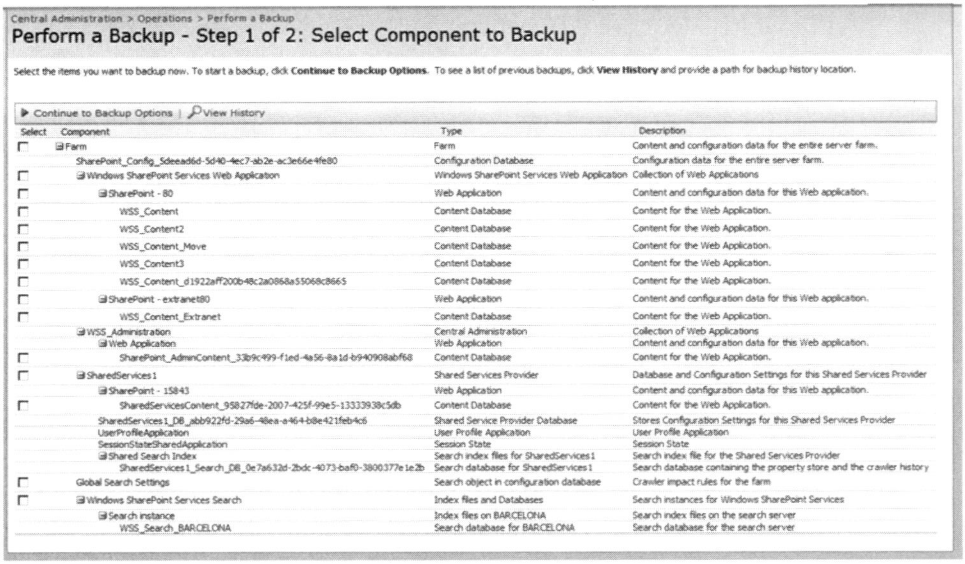

FIGURE 12.26
Backup components.

Some items cannot be backed up on their own. They can only be backed up as part of a group. The Search components are a great example. You cannot back up the Search database or index files individually. They have to be in sync, so they have to be backed up at the same time to be able to be restored. If a backup is started while a crawl is running, SharePoint will pause the crawl long enough to get a snapshot of the Search database and index files.

Now select the entire farm and click Continue to Backup Options.

Figure 12.27 shows the final options you have for your backup. If you decide not to back up the entire farm, you can click the Farm drop-down and be taken back to the previous screen. You can also choose between a Full and Differential backup. The last thing to fill out is the Backup location. You can see both the example in the UI and the entry in Figure 12.27 are UNCs. This is important. In the interest of performance, the backups run from here are broken into pieces, and these pieces can be run by different servers. If you put a local path in this box instead of a UNC, that path will only work for one of the machines involved. One example of this is SQL. Part of the Central Admin backup is a backup of the databases selected. To improve performance, this backup is performed on the SQL server itself, not the machine Central Admin is running. If SQL is not running on the same machine as Central Admin, it could not access a local backup directory. This is why using a UNC is so important.

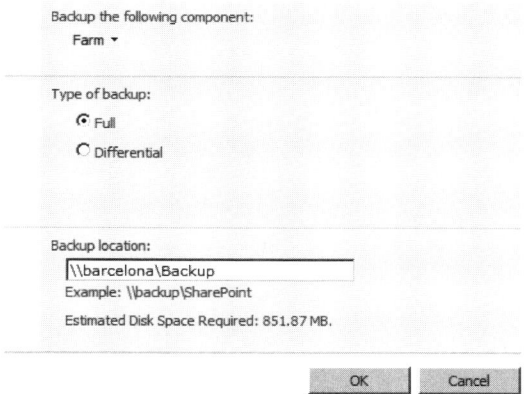

FIGURE 12.27
Backup options in Central Admin.

It is also important to make sure that the necessary accounts have permission to this share. For starters, the Central Admin App Pool account will need read-write access. This account is the ringleader for the backup process. It creates the Timer Job that kicks off the backup. After the job starts, it also creates the entry for the backup in the SPBRTOC.XML file and creates the directory for the backup files. The service account that SQL is running will also need read-write permission to this share. The database backups are SQL database backups and performed directly on the SQL server itself, by the SQL service account. This is very good for performance, as it cuts out the middleman. If you back up a site collection with STSADM –o backup -filename and save it to a different machine, the network traffic looks Figure 12.28.

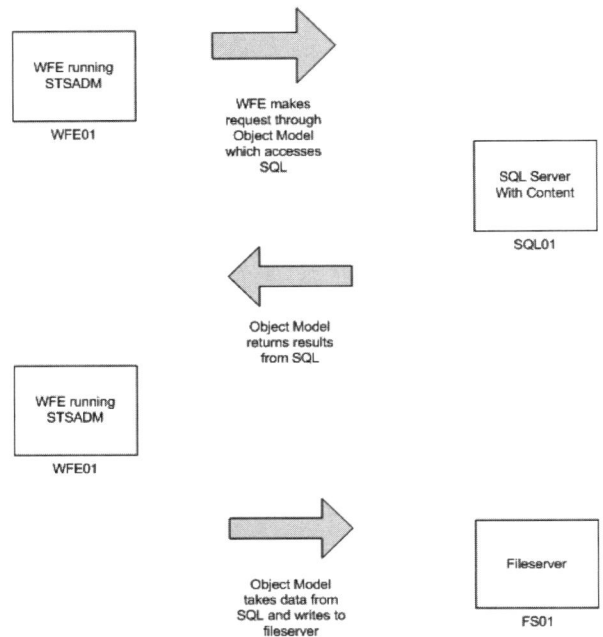

FIGURE 12.28
Network traffic used during site collection backup.

This pattern is not very efficient for a couple of reasons. First, the Object Model (OM) has to touch the content several times and package it. This adds extra steps and requires processing on the WFE. Second, this process requires that the same data go across the wire twice, once from the SQL server to the WFE and then from the WFE to the storage location. The backups done by Central Admin are more efficient. It uses the process in Figure 12.29.

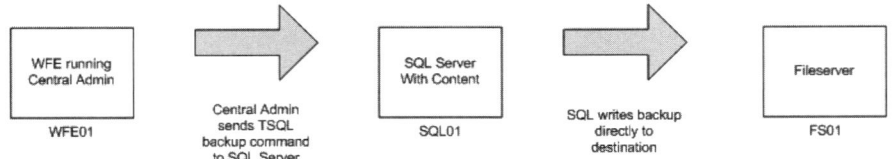

FIGURE 12.29
Central Admin backups.

This process results in faster backups, but requires the SQL server and SQL Service account have direct access to the archive location. Another benefit of this is that SharePoint is not required to restore these databases, since they are simply SQL backups. Let's finish our walkthrough of the backup process.

After you have entered the UNC path of the backup location, press the OK button to start the backup. If all the accounts have permission and all the machines involved can access your backup directory, you will be taken to the Backup and Restore status page. You can keep an eye on the backup process by refreshing the page.

After the job is finished, open up My Computer and browse to your backup directory. It should look like Figure 12.30.

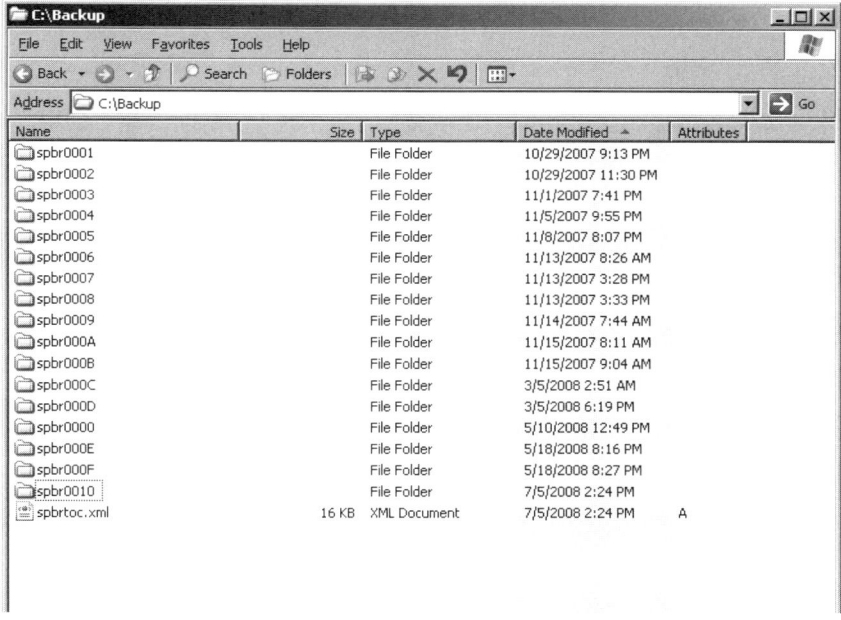

FIGURE 12.30
SharePoint backup directory.

This directory is pretty basic. It consists of a single file, SPBRTOC.XML, and a folder for each backup you have created. The file, the SharePoint Backup Restore Table of Contents, contains an entry for each backup and restore job that has been executed. Let's open it up and take a look at it. Just double-click the file, and it should open in Internet Explorer.

Figure 12.31 shows the first few lines of the SPBRTOC.XML file. Each Backup or Restore operation is recorded there. The newest operations are on the top. Walking through the first operation, you can figure out what each line means. Table 12.2 describes each line.

```xml
<?xml version="1.0" encoding="utf-8" ?>
- <SPBackupRestoreHistory>
  - <SPHistoryObject>
      <SPId>93bb8032-2718-4e15-91e3-0731cf4e0abc</SPId>
      <SPRequestedBy>BARCELONA\Administrator</SPRequestedBy>
      <SPBackupMethod>Full</SPBackupMethod>
      <SPRestoreMethod>None</SPRestoreMethod>
      <SPStartTime>07/05/2008 19:20:46</SPStartTime>
      <SPFinishTime>07/05/2008 19:24:06</SPFinishTime>
      <SPIsBackup>True</SPIsBackup>
      <SPBackupDirectory>\\barcelona\backup\spbr0010\</SPBackupDirectory>
      <SPDirectoryName>spbr0010</SPDirectoryName>
      <SPDirectoryNumber>16</SPDirectoryNumber>
      <SPTopComponent>Farm</SPTopComponent>
      <SPTopComponentId>abda9cce-1b77-4984-a518-70bf8689d598</SPTopComponentId>
      <SPWarningCount>0</SPWarningCount>
      <SPErrorCount>0</SPErrorCount>
    </SPHistoryObject>
  - <SPHistoryObject>
      <SPId>46f21208-e804-4169-b72f-8a121546ce99</SPId>
      <SPRequestedBy>BARCELONA\Administrator</SPRequestedBy>
      <SPBackupMethod>Full</SPBackupMethod>
      <SPRestoreMethod>None</SPRestoreMethod>
      <SPStartTime>05/19/2008 01:27:07</SPStartTime>
      <SPFinishTime>05/19/2008 01:27:12</SPFinishTime>
      <SPIsBackup>True</SPIsBackup>
      <SPBackupDirectory>c:\Backup\spbr000F\</SPBackupDirectory>
      <SPDirectoryName>spbr000F</SPDirectoryName>
      <SPDirectoryNumber>15</SPDirectoryNumber>
      <SPTopComponent>Farm\Windows SharePoint Services Web Application\SharePoint - 80\WSS_Content_Move</SPTopComponent>
      <SPTopComponentId>018702f9-6108-42c0-83c0-6289fc322670</SPTopComponentId>
      <SPWarningCount>0</SPWarningCount>
      <SPErrorCount>0</SPErrorCount>
    </SPHistoryObject>
  - <SPHistoryObject>
      <SPId>2d9dbbc2-0b88-43cf-b407-70c21ef34981</SPId>
      <SPRestoreId>35948a09-f3ff-48cb-b26d-49da6b69f33e</SPRestoreId>
      <SPRequestedBy>BARCELONA\Administrator</SPRequestedBy>
      <SPBackupMethod>Full</SPBackupMethod>
      <SPRestoreMethod>Overwrite</SPRestoreMethod>
      <SPStartTime>05/19/2008 01:15:57</SPStartTime>
      <SPFinishTime>05/19/2008 01:16:49</SPFinishTime>
      <SPIsBackup>False</SPIsBackup>
      <SPBackupDirectory>c:\Backup\spbr000E\</SPBackupDirectory>
      <SPDirectoryName />
      <SPTopComponent>Farm\Windows SharePoint Services Web Application\SharePoint - 80\WSS_Content</SPTopComponent>
      <SPTopComponentId>9cff3e25-ffdd-4477-afaf-6ae6a27538b4</SPTopComponentId>
      <SPWarningCount>0</SPWarningCount>
      <SPErrorCount>0</SPErrorCount>
    </SPHistoryObject>
  - <SPHistoryObject>
```

FIGURE 12.31
Contents of SPBRTOC.XML.

TABLE 12.2 DESCRIPTION OF OBJECTS IN SPBRTOC.XML FILE

Object	Description
SPId	A unique GUID that is generated for each job.
SPRequestdBy	The user that executed the operation.
SPBackupMethod	The method that was used for the backup. The value is either Full or Differential.
SPRestoreMethod	Will be none if the operation was a Backup, overwrite if the Restore operation was restored to its original location, or new if the Restore was written to a new location.
SPStartTime	Start time of the operation in UTC.
SPFinishTime	End time of the operation in UTC.
SPIsBackup	Set to True for Backup operations and False for Restore operations.
SPBackupDirectory	Location and name of the directory used for the Backup or Restore operation.
SPDirectoryName	Name of the directory.
SPDirectoryNumber	Number in Base 10 of the directory.
SPTopComponent	The level clicked when starting the backup. If you back up the whole farm, this will be farm. If you back up a single Web App, this will be Farm\web app name.
SPTopComponentID	The GUID for the previous entry.
SPWarningCount	Number of warnings generated during the operation.
SPErrorCount	Number of errors generated during the operation.

The information in this file is what Central Admin uses when you click the Backup and Restore History link in operations, or when you use the STSADM operation `backuphistory`.

The Table of Contents is no good without the contents. Open up the folder that the first backup was written to in Explorer. The directory will look like Figure 12.32.

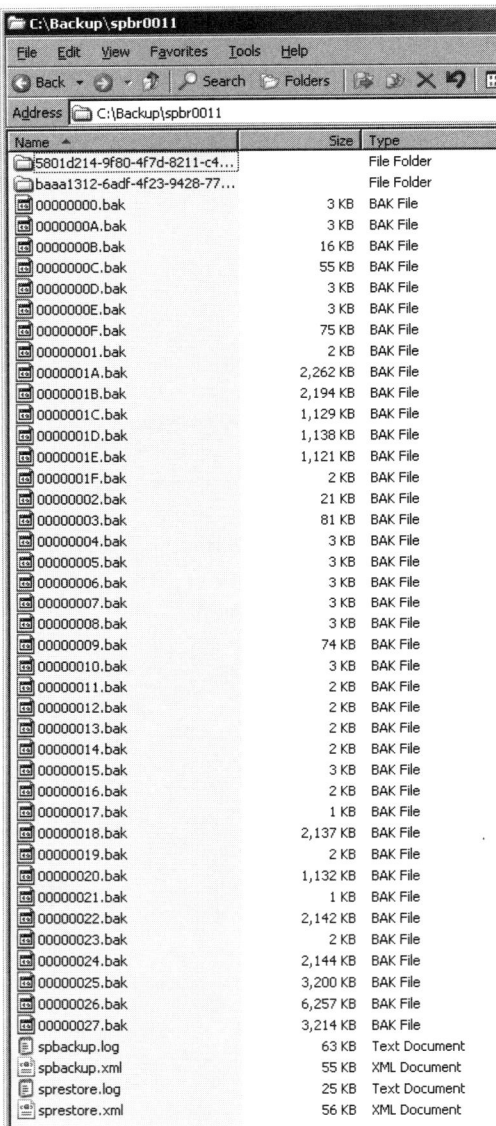

FIGURE 12.32
Contents of backup directory.

All your backups will be similar to Figure 12.32. There are four basic types of files and folders. The first are log files. This directory has two: spbackup.log and sprestore.log. They are created by backup and restore activities. They are standard text files, and they log each object that is backed up or restored, and any warnings or errors that are generated. Many of the backup operations are SQL commands, as mentioned earlier. These commands are in the LOG files, so you can see exactly how the backup process is backing up or restoring your databases. The next type of file is the XML files. Again, they are generated for both backup and restore operations. These files contain all the information about each element that was backed up and saved to the BAK files, the third type of file in the directory. The BAK files are XML or SQL BAK files, so they can be restored or interrogated without involving SharePoint. The spbackup.xml provides the key to the contents of each BAK file. The BAK files containing XML can be viewed in a standard text viewer like Notepad. The BAK files containing SQL backups can be restored directly into SQL from SQL Management Studio. Figure 12.33 shows the entry for a typical database.

```xml
- <SPBackupNode>
 - <SPBackupObject Name="WSS_Content2">
     <SPBackupRestoreClass>Microsoft.SharePoint.Administration.SPContentDatabase, Microsoft.SharePoint, Version=12.0.0.0, Culture=neutral,
       PublicKeyToken=71e9bce111e9429c</SPBackupRestoreClass>
     <SPBackupSelectable>True</SPBackupSelectable>
     <SPRestoreSelectable>True</SPRestoreSelectable>
     <SPName>WSS_Content2</SPName>
     <SPId>e4801db2-b1cc-4fe4-95bd-1cf131cd821b</SPId>
     <SPCanBackup>True</SPCanBackup>
     <SPCanRestore>True</SPCanRestore>
     <SPCurrentProgress>100</SPCurrentProgress>
     <SPLastUpdate>07/05/2008 20:15:51</SPLastUpdate>
     <SPCurrentPhase>Done</SPCurrentPhase>
   - <SPParameters>
     - <SPParameter Key="MaximumSiteCount">
         <![CDATA[ 3 ]]>
       </SPParameter>
     - <SPParameter Key="SPLocation">
         <![CDATA[ c:\Program Files\Microsoft Office Servers\12.0\Data\MSSQL.1\MSSQL\DATA\ ]]>
       </SPParameter>
     - <SPParameter Key="e4801db2-b1cc-4fe4-95bd-1cf131cd821bSTATE.xml">
         <![CDATA[ 00000005.bak ]]>
       </SPParameter>
     - <SPParameter Key="SPTimeout">
         <![CDATA[ 60000 ]]>
       </SPParameter>
     - <SPParameter Key="SPDiskSize">
         <![CDATA[ 51183616 ]]>
       </SPParameter>
     - <SPParameter Key="BARCELONA\OfficeServers:WSS_Content2.dat">
         <![CDATA[ 0000001B.bak ]]>
       </SPParameter>
     - <SPParameter Key="SPSqlPreviousPosition">
         <![CDATA[ 1 ]]>
       </SPParameter>
     - <SPParameter Key="SPDescription">
         <![CDATA[ Content for the Web Application. ]]>
       </SPParameter>
     - <SPParameter Key="ServerId">
         <![CDATA[ 27a4425f-1376-48e4-adea-1490016dd1d6 ]]>
       </SPParameter>
     - <SPParameter Key="SPServer">
         <![CDATA[ BARCELONA\OfficeServers ]]>
       </SPParameter>
     - <SPParameter Key="InstanceId">
         <![CDATA[ f358982c-4625-498b-9547-e49f4af933f3 ]]>
       </SPParameter>
     - <SPParameter Key="SPName">
         <![CDATA[ WSS_Content2 ]]>
       </SPParameter>
     - <SPParameter Key="WarningSiteCount">
         <![CDATA[ 0 ]]>
       </SPParameter>
     - <SPParameter Key="Url">
         <![CDATA[ http://barcelona/ ]]>
       </SPParameter>
     - <SPParameter Key="SPSqlFullLocation">
         <![CDATA[ \\barcelona\backup\spbr0010\0000001B.bak ]]>
       </SPParameter>
```

FIGURE 12.33
Content Database entry in SPBackup.xml.

The `SPBackupObject Name` is the name of the object being described in this node. In this case, it is `WSS_Content2`. The `SPBackupRestoreClass` type tells us it is a `SPContentDatabase`. By looking through the XML, you can see all the information about that database. The entry for `<SPParameter Key="SPSqlFullLocation">` is the gem we are looking for. This line defines which of the BAK files is the SQL backup for the database. We know from looking at the spbackup.log file that the BAK file was created with a SQL backup command. We can use a similar command, or the SQL Management Studio UI, to restore it back into SQL. If we want to reproduce the settings for the database, they are in that node as well. This method is very handy when restoring content out of band. There are ways to extract documents directly out of SQL without getting SharePoint involved. Being able to get to the database itself makes this all very quick and simple. You may also just want to query the database to see how something was set up. Not needing to attach the database to SharePoint can be the easiest way sometimes.

The fourth type of file in the backup directory is not really a file at all, but folders. You will notice two folders in Figure 12.32. These are where components of the Search system are stored. One such object is noise words. If you add more noise words to the noise words file for your language, that gets backed up into this directory.

Central Admin backups bring a lot to the table. The graphical interface is very easy to use. It is also included for free on every SharePoint farm, so your expertise with it is universal. It backs up all of your content and a majority of the SharePoint configuration components that you need to do a catastrophic restore. It uses native SQL dumps for performance and portability, and it supports restoration to different farms.

With all this going for it, why would anyone use anything else? It does have some drawbacks. Primarily, it does not get everything you need to do a catastrophic restore. Namely, it will not restore the configuration database to a different environment, and it does not get all the file system–level items you need. Also, it cannot be scheduled, though we will show a workaround for that later in this chapter. If there is a problem with a backup or restore, it will not run again until a timer job is manually removed. Finally, these backups can take a lot of space, and there is no way out of the box to prune out old backups. You have two options to mitigate that problem. You can use multiple directories for your backups. Keep a certain number of backups in one folder and then move on to another one. After all of the backups in the first directory have aged out, you can delete it. It is not perfect, but it is usable. You do have another option. Microsoft has created a script to prune out backup folders and their entries in the `SPBRTOC.XML` file. You can download it at http://support.microsoft.com/kb/941330. The script seems to work, but it is not tolerant of errors at all. If your `SPBRTOC.XML` file references a directory that does not exist, the script errors out, for instance. If you are worried about your backup directory getting too large, this script is a good starting point, but it is probably not ready to go right off the page.

STSADM Catastrophic Backups

A close cousin of the Central Admin backups are the catastrophic backups you can do with STSADM. We covered earlier in this chapter how the STSADM operation backup could make single file backups of individual site collections and how they could be restored with the restore operation. Consider this functionality their secret identities. They also have a superhero identity. Backup and restore can also do catastrophic, or farm-level backups. Figures 12.34 and 12.35 show their catastrophic usage.

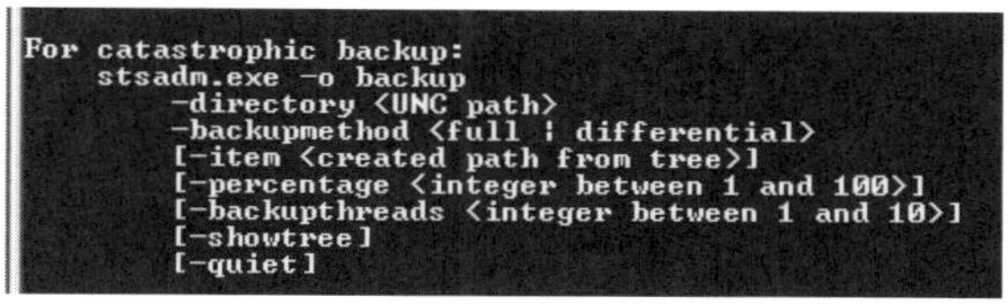

```
For catastrophic backup:
    stsadm.exe -o backup
        -directory <UNC path>
        -backupmethod <full | differential>
        [-item <created path from tree>]
        [-percentage <integer between 1 and 100>]
        [-backupthreads <integer between 1 and 10>]
        [-showtree]
        [-quiet]
```

FIGURE 12.34
Backup usage.

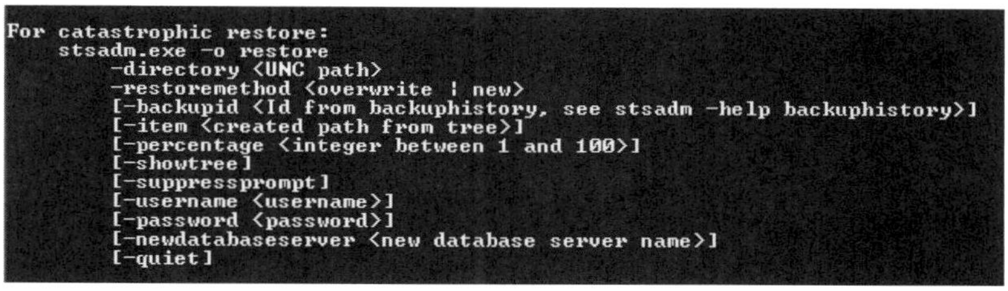

```
For catastrophic restore:
    stsadm.exe -o restore
        -directory <UNC path>
        -restoremethod <overwrite | new>
        [-backupid <Id from backuphistory, see stsadm -help backuphistory>]
        [-item <created path from tree>]
        [-percentage <integer between 1 and 100>]
        [-showtree]
        [-suppressprompt]
        [-username <username>]
        [-password <password>]
        [-newdatabaseserver <new database server name>]
        [-quiet]
```

FIGURE 12.35
Restore usage.

The options from STSADM are the same that you have if you create the backup from Central Admin. You can choose the directory the backups will go into, whether they are full or differential, which items to back up, and so on. If you do not want to back up the whole farm, use the -showtree parameter to see which other items you can specify. Figure 12.36 shows the output.

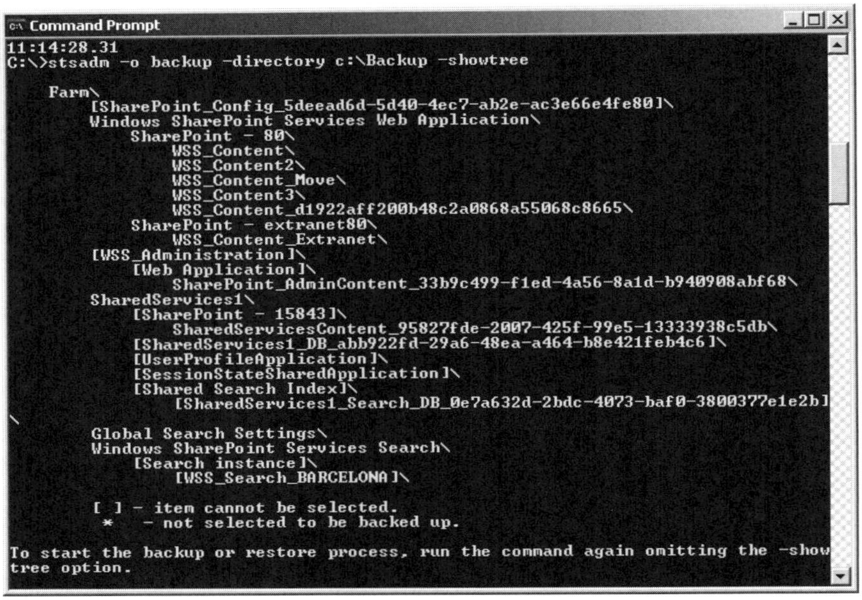

FIGURE 12.36
Showtree usage.

Once again, you have the same options as Central Admin. If you want to use STSADM to back up the Search Settings, you would use the following command:

```
stsadm -o backup -directory \\server\Backup -backupmethod full -item
"Global Search Settings"
```

You must be a local administrator on the box you run STSADM, and you must be dbowner on the Config and Content databases. Since you are not running this through Central Admin, the SharePoint portion does not run as the Central Admin app pool identity, like it does when you run the backup through the UI. Instead, it uses the identity of the account running STSADM. You will have to verify that the user has access to SharePoint, as well as the backup location. The backup that is created is exactly the same as one created in Central Admin. They are interchangeable. You can create a backup with STSADM and restore it with Central Admin, or vice versa. Just make sure you put them in the same directory. One of the downsides of the Central Admin backups is that they cannot be scheduled. Now that you know STSADM makes compatible backups, you have a way around that. You can schedule an STSADM script to make your backups, and then use Central Admin should you need to restore anything. STSADM is a great tool in your admin tool belt. Like

Central Admin, this functionality is built into SharePoint so there is nothing to install. It also can create an entire farm backup and supports restoring to different environments. Its main downsides are that it is tougher to use than Central Admin and that unlike Central Admin, it may have an impact on performance for the end users when it is running.

Restoring with Central Admin and STSADM

Backing up your data is only half of the equation, and the smaller half, if that is possible. Being able to restore your content when you need to is what is really important. Having your data backed up does not do any good if you cannot restore it when you need to. In Figure 12.25, where we found the link to Perform a Backup, you can also find a link to start a restore operation. On the first screen, you enter the location of your backup directory, as shown in Figure 12.37.

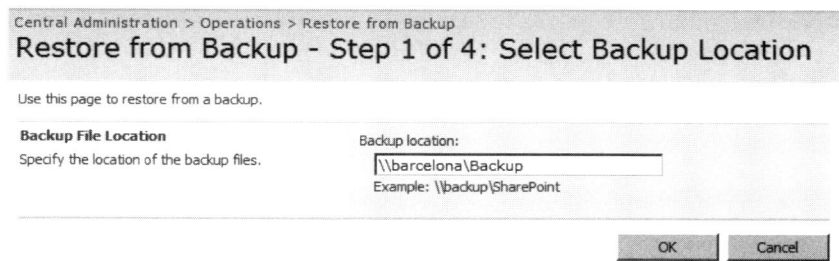

FIGURE 12.37
First Restore screen.

It has not been explicitly spelled out, but SharePoint does not keep track of where it does backups. When you enter a location in this box, SharePoint looks for a SPBRTOC.XML file there. From there, it gets a list of the backups available. The full directory is stored in the SPBRTOC.XML file, so when you execute the backup to c:\backup that is where SharePoint will look for it when it tries to recover it. You can see this in the directory column of Figure 12.38.

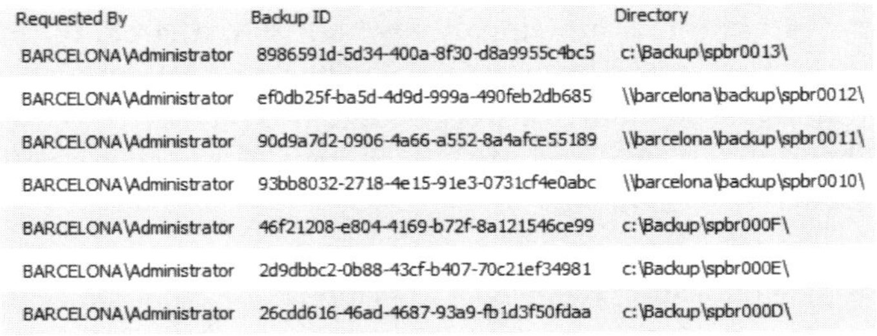

Requested By	Backup ID	Directory
BARCELONA\Administrator	8986591d-5d34-400a-8f30-d8a9955c4bc5	c:\Backup\spbr0013\
BARCELONA\Administrator	ef0db25f-ba5d-4d9d-999a-490feb2db685	\\barcelona\backup\spbr0012\
BARCELONA\Administrator	90d9a7d2-0906-4a66-a552-8a4afce55189	\\barcelona\backup\spbr0011\
BARCELONA\Administrator	93bb8032-2718-4e15-91e3-0731cf4e0abc	\\barcelona\backup\spbr0010\
BARCELONA\Administrator	46f21208-e804-4169-b72f-8a121546ce99	c:\Backup\spbr000F\
BARCELONA\Administrator	2d9dbbc2-0b88-43cf-b407-70c21ef34981	c:\Backup\spbr000E\
BARCELONA\Administrator	26cdd616-46ad-4687-93a9-fb1d3f50fdaa	c:\Backup\spbr000D\

FIGURE 12.38
Second Restore screen.

This is another good reason to use UNCs instead of local paths. If you are doing your restores with STSADM, use the operation `backuphistory` to get the same information. After you have looked over your available backups, choose the one you would like to restore and click Continue Restore Process. If you do not find the backup set you are looking for, click the Change Directory link and point Central Admin at a different location. Figure 12.39 shows you the elements of the backup set you have chosen and lets you choose which of them you would like to restore.

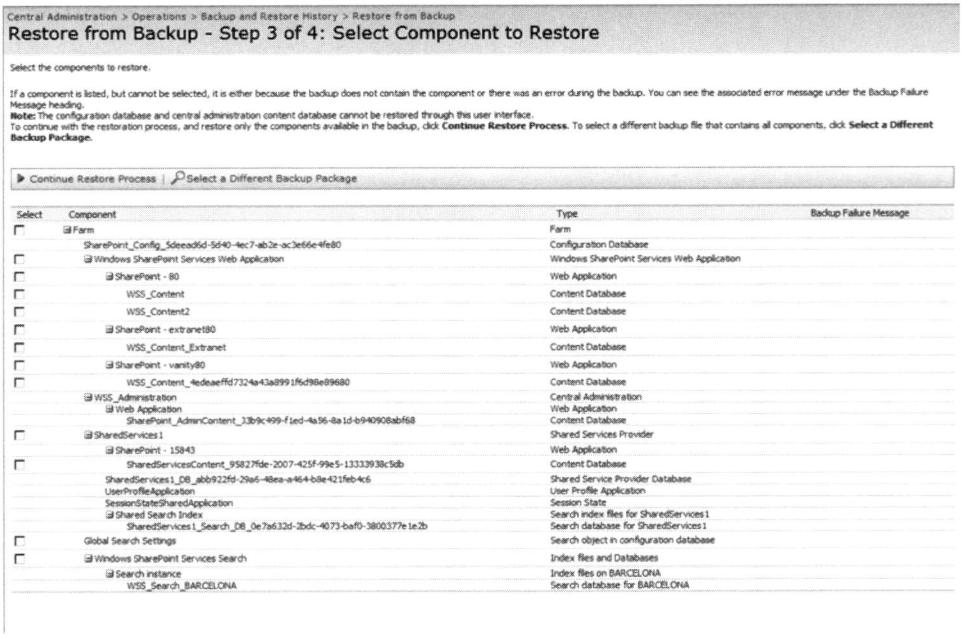

FIGURE 12.39
Third Restore screen.

This was a full backup, so everything is available. Had you chosen a backup that was only a backup of a single site collection, only those items would have had check boxes next to them. Check the boxes next to components you want to restore and click Continue Restore Process. If you cannot restore the component you want, click the Select a Different Backup Package link to choose another backup set.

Figure 12.40 shows your options. If you click the first link and select the Change Backup Component to Restore menu, then you will be taken back to the previous screen of components. The next option lets you choose whether to restore this content back to its original location or a new location. If you choose New configuration, the screen with all the settings on the bottom will open up, and you will be able to enter new database names and URL names as appropriate. Once you have everything set correctly, press OK at the bottom of the page to restore the content. You have the same options with the STSADM `restore` operation. You can choose a new restore method, and there is a `newdatabaseserver` parameter. Both options are very flexible and allow you to restore as much or as little as you need.

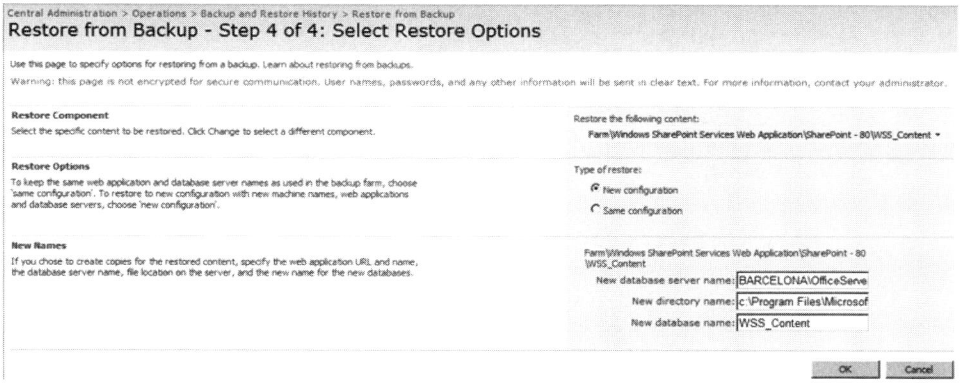

FIGURE 12.40
The Final Restore screen.

Restoring SharePoint Content Without SharePoint

You might be wondering what good your content databases are if they are not attached to SharePoint. They are just databases, so any tool that can access databases can extract data from them. A friend of mine, Keith Richie, was kind enough to write up a blog post with some sample code. His program will take a recovered Content Database and copy out all of the documents in it. You probably would not want to do this in production, but it serves as a good example of what is possible. This code was not designed to be run on databases that are attached to SharePoint. As it is written, it will surely cause database locks that will prevent your users from accessing your SharePoint environment.

You can find the code and his writeup here, http://blog.krichie.com/2008/07/06/exporting-site-content-from-a-sharepoint-content-database-for-recovery-purposes/. Thanks, Keith.

Native SQL Backups

If your environment already has SQL Server installed, it is possible that there is already a disaster recovery process in place. It only makes sense to leverage that for SharePoint. You may also want to do your backups in SQL if you want to write directly to tape, or if your organization has outgrown the built-in SharePoint backups. In this section, we will talk about native SQL backups and the considerations that come along with them.

If you use the native SQL Management studio with SQL 2005 or 2008, it is very easy to use, and it is included with most versions. You are probably familiar with it if you do any administrative work in SQL. If the version of SQL you are using does not come with Management Studio, you may be able to download it from Microsoft. SQL 2005 Express does not include it, but it can be downloaded from http://www.microsoft.com/downloads/details.aspx?FamilyID=c243a5ae-4bd1-4e3d-94b8-5a0f62bf7796&displaylang=en and installed. SQL offers more flexibility than native SharePoint backups because it supports writing directly to tape. It also allows better management of versions. You can choose to keep a certain number of backups, or only keep backups for a certain length of time. If you are doing your backups on the SQL Server, there is a reduced impact on the SharePoint server itself. Both processes are accessing the same SQL databases, but you have removed the backup overhead from your SharePoint server. Depending on which other SharePoint roles the server running Central Admin also has, the impact to your end users will vary. You also have the option of using third-party backup suites if your organization is already using them. This allows you to roll your SharePoint backups under a central umbrella if one exists. This simplifies management and lets you spend your time on other activities.

If you choose to use native SQL backups, there are a few things to be aware of. The first is that not all of your SharePoint environment is in SQL, so this is not a full fidelity backup. You will need to augment it with some of the other techniques described in this chapter. Since you will not be backing up your index file with your Search database, you will always need to execute a full crawl if you have to restore your Search databases. If you are using SQL Express, you will not be able to schedule SQL backups, even with the downloaded Management Studio. It does not include the SQL agent, which is the process that executes scheduled SQL jobs. Finally, if you do restore a SharePoint content database in SQL, you will need to detach it from SharePoint and reattach it. SharePoint keeps details about the Content Databases in the Config Database. If the Content Database changes without SharePoint knowing, that information gets out of sync, and you will see strange behavior like sites not rendering. When you reattach the Content Database, SharePoint does an inventory of it and gets everything back in sync.

Now that you know the pros and cons of doing native SQL backups, let's walk through setting up a database backup job. Go to your SQL server and open up SQL Management Studio. If the SQL Server Agent is not already running, start it. It will be the last item at the bottom of the Object Explorer. Now that it is running, open up the Management node. Right-click Maintenance Plans and click Maintenance Plan Wizard. This will walk you through the process of creating a Maintenance Plan to back up your databases. Click Next on the Welcome screen. Give the task a name you will remember, like SharePoint Database Backup. If you want to schedule the plan, click the Change button on the bottom. We will not walk through that here. After you have typed in a name, click Next. The next screen lets you choose which tasks will be performed on your databases. For this example, we will only be choosing a full backup, as in Figure 12.41, but you may want to investigate the other tasks when planning your SQL maintenance.

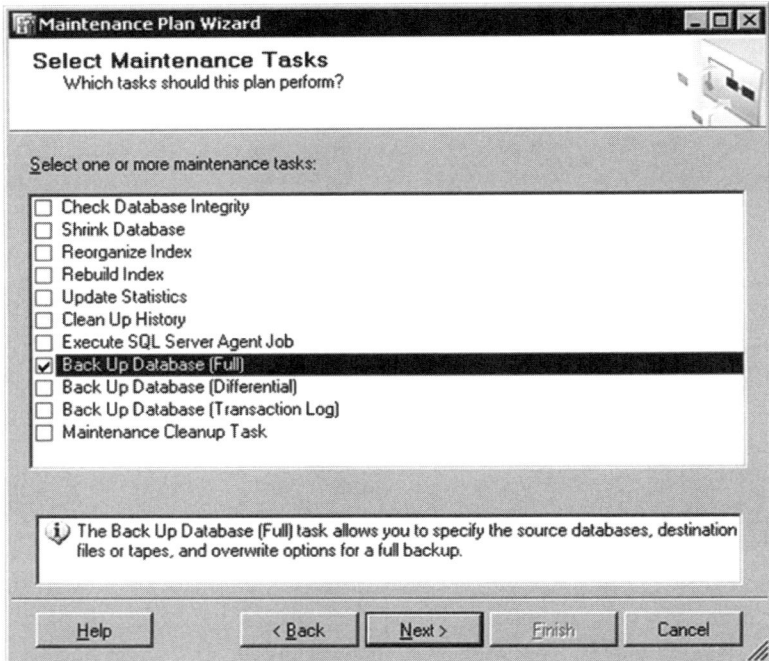

FIGURE 12.41
Planning a full backup.

Click Next. Since we are only executing one task, there is nothing to configure on the next screen. If we were going to do multiple tasks in this one job, like a database integrity check, we would put that before the backup task on this screen. Click Next to move on. This screen lets us choose which databases to back up. Of course, we want all of the SharePoint database, but don't forget about the system databases. They do not take up much space and provide invaluable information should you need to recover from a SQL failure. We would recommend choosing all databases, as shown in Figure 12.42.

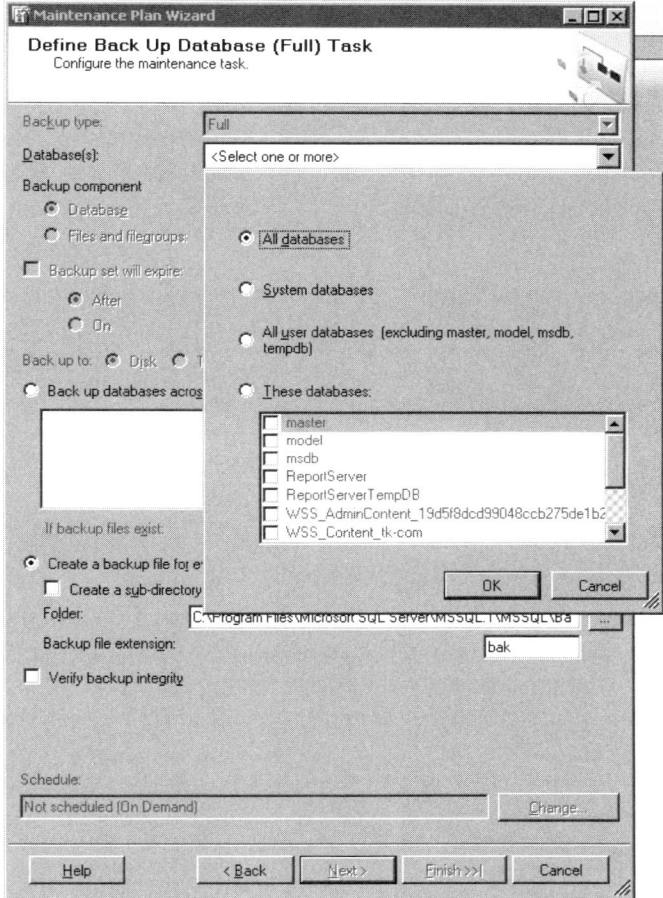

FIGURE 12.42
Backing up all databases.

Select Disk or Tape, whichever is appropriate for your environment, and click Next. The next tab sets the report options. Having the report written to a text file and emailed to you or your Operations is a good idea. You want to know as soon as possible if there is a problem. Click Next and then Finish. That is all there is to it.

Backing up your databases in SQL is a good approach, as long as you supplement that with other methods, like Ntbackup.exe.

Using NTBackup.exe to Back Up SharePoint

Included with Windows 2003 is the old standby, NTBackup.exe. You can use this to augment other backup processes you use with SharePoint. In the beginning of this chapter, we demonstrated several places on the file system that SharePoint keeps settings. NTBackup.exe is one way to make sure they get included in your backup plan. Like many of the other options presented, NTbackup.exe has a nice, easy-to-use graphical interface, and it is included with Windows 2003. It can also be scheduled. Unfortunately, it cannot get any SharePoint content, only configuration data, so you must augment its usage with other products, such as the Central Admin backups or SQL backups.

> ### Windows 2008 Backup
>
> NTBackup.exe is not available in Windows 2008. It was removed and replaced with a new backup utility, based on the backup utility in Vista. It utilizes Volume Shadow Services (VSS) for faster backups and better support for applications. Unfortunately, you lose the ability to back up specific files or folders. You can only back up full volumes. You can still use this to back up your SharePoint server, but you just do not have the granular control you did in Windows 2003.

Other Options

In this chapter, we have covered several options for backing up SharePoint. We have focused mainly on included solutions. There are many fabulous third-party solutions. If you have an enterprise backup solution already in place, there is a good chance they have a SharePoint plug-in. If you have looked at the solutions presented earlier in this chapter, and think your organization is too large for them, here are a few third-party solutions to look at. These are in no particular order, nor should you consider this any kind of endorsement for any product.

Avepoint

Avepoint makes some great SharePoint administrative software. Their product, DocAve, covers many areas of administration and backup and recovery is part of that. You can download a full-featured evaluation of DocAve at http://www.avepoint.com.

Commvault

Commvault makes backup and archive software for many platforms, including SharePoint. You can find more information at http://www.commvault.com.

Idera

Like Avepoint, Idera makes a suite of SharePoint administrative tools that include incredible back and recovery support. You can read more about it at http://www.idera.com/Products/SharePointToolset/default.aspx.

Microsoft

Data Protection Manager (DPM) is Microsoft's backup and recovery. It allows many options, including disk-to-disk-to-tape archiving. You can get information about it at http://www.microsoft.com/dpm.

Symantec

Venerable backup software, Backup Exec is now a part of the Symantec suite of products. Backup Exec can handle most of your backup needs. You can download a trial version at http://www.symantec.com/business/products/family.jsp?familyid =backupexec.

High Availability

The third leg of the fault tolerance stool is High Availability. High availability can be thought of as how to keep your application continuously available, regardless of what happens. In the Windows world, this is a fairly new development, and not very many enterprise applications have good support for it. SharePoint is no different. In this section, we will discuss your options.

Web Front-Ends

The front-facing part of SharePoint is the WFEs. SharePoint has support out of the box for multiple WFEs, which is your first defense against downtime. Putting your multiple WFEs behind load-balancing software, like Windows' Network Load Balancing Service (NLBS), gives you tolerance to the failure of a WFE. Your users can access SharePoint via a virtual IP address that is distributed to your WFEs. If a WFE goes offline, the load-balancing software will simply route users to another WFE that is online. This allows your farm to continue serving users while you replace or repair the failed WFE. If you find NLBS does not scale well enough for you, there are hardware-based load balancers that scale better and have more features. Both Cisco and F5 make popular hardware load balancers.

Application Servers

Several SharePoint roles fall under the category of Application servers. Many of these roles are load-balanced automatically by SharePoint, so as long as you have more than one you are covered. The Query role and Excel Services roles fall under this category. If you have two Query servers in your farm and one fails, SharePoint will automatically route users to a Query server that is online (likewise, with Excel Calculation Services). One role that cannot be redundant is the Index role. Each SSP can only have a single Index server so there is no facility for fault tolerance. The good news is that if your Index server fails, your users will not be affected. They only query the Query servers. The only impact will be that new content will not be discoverable in searches until a new Index server is built and a full crawl is executed, or your Search database and index files are restored.

DATABASE SERVERS

SQL is the weak link in SharePoint high availability. As we know, all SharePoint content, and your SharePoint Configuration database reside in SQL. SQL 2005 has three options for SharePoint high availability: clustering, mirroring, and log shipping. Each has its benefits and drawbacks. We will cover each.

SQL Clustering

Your first consideration for making SQL, and therefore SharePoint, highly available is SQL Clustering. Clustering requires more than one SQL server using the same storage. In the case of a server failure, the other server in the cluster will take over the cluster automatically and respond to requests. You can also leverage clustering for machine maintenance. Apply patches to the passive node of the cluster, then fail the cluster over and do your maintenance on the other node. Clustering is easier to set up and maintain than mirroring, which is why you should consider it first. Figure 12.43 shows a simple SQL cluster.

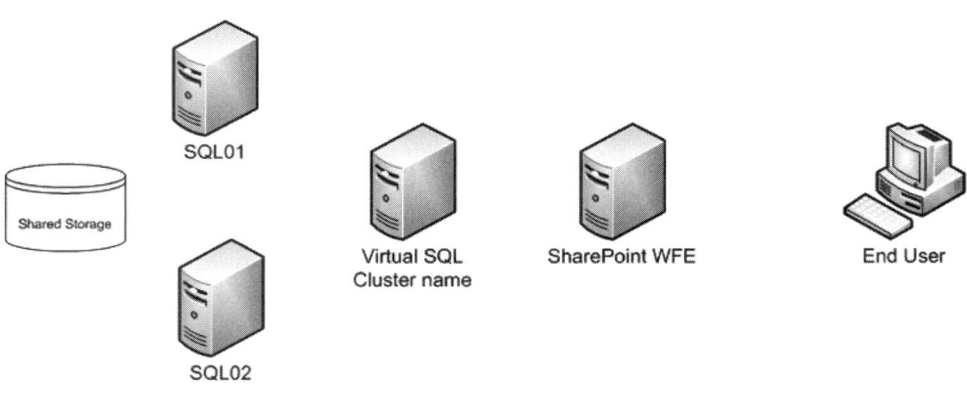

FIGURE 12.43
A simple SQL cluster.

In this figure, the end user is on the right. Their requests are handled by the SharePoint WFE. The content that WFE is serving is stored in SQL. SharePoint references SQL via a virtual name that references the SQL cluster. SharePoint does not know that SQL01 or SQL02 even exist. The cluster software in Windows and SQL handles which server is the active node and which one is passive. If the active server fails, the cluster software promotes the passive server to the active role and requests continue to get handled. Clustering gives you tolerance against a single SQL Server failure, but does not help against a storage or facility failure. That is where Database Mirroring comes in.

Database Mirroring

Database mirroring is clustering's big brother. It protects against a server failure like clustering, but it also protects against storage failure and facility failure. With a cluster, if your SAN fails, you are not protected. If your facility loses power or is the victim of a natural disaster, you are also taken offline. Mirroring allows tolerance of these faults. Figure 12.44 shows a basic Mirroring scenario.

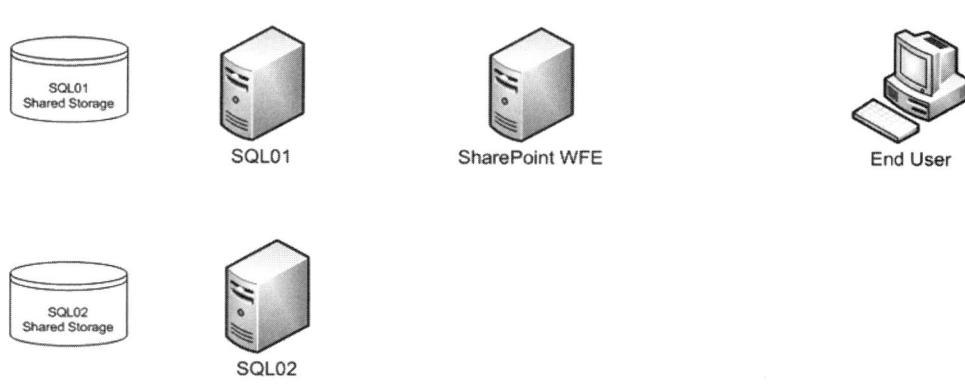

FIGURE 12.44
A simple database mirror.

In this example, your users access SharePoint via the WFE, but the WFE does not access a SQL cluster, it accesses SQL01 directly. During normal operations, SQL01 is mirroring all of its transactions to SQL02 and its storage. Should SQL01 or any of its components fail, everything is replicated to SQL02. The biggest "gotcha" with mirroring is that SharePoint does not support failing over automatically. You will need to use the SQL client to remap the SQL server being used, or use STSADM –o renameserver to get SharePoint up and going after a member of the mirror fails. The changes that need to be made for SharePoint can be scripted, but the solution is less than ideal.

Database mirroring is very complicated and is not quite up to its potential in SQL 2005. Its complication means you probably need a dedicated SQL administrator to configure and monitor it, whereas clustering is much easier to set up and maintain. Database mirroring also is very rough on resources. Each database that is mirrored requires two threads to maintain, as well as memory. This limits the number of databases that can be mirrored before performance is impacted. Its network needs also make it unusable for some environments. It has very strict requirements for latency. Our recommendation would be to wait for SQL 2008 before evaluating database mirroring. It promises to have improvements that may make mirroring a more viable option.

Microsoft has a great white paper on how they implemented mirroring for their internal SharePoint environment. You can download it here, http://go.microsoft.com/fwlink/?LinkId=83725&clcid=0x409.

Log Shipping

Not necessarily a high availability option, Log Shipping deserves some discussion here as well. Log shipping allows you to replicate databases between SQL environments like mirroring, but without the complication or strict requirements. In a log shipping environment, the transaction logs from one environment are copied over to a file share on another server. Those transactions are then played against the databases in the backup environment to keep them in sync. Unlike mirroring, the transactions can be minutes or even hours behind. As the administrator, you have complete control over how often the transactions are copied over.

Log shipping has the advantage of being very easy to set up and maintain. It has the drawbacks of the potential of data loss if the source server fails before the logs are copied over. Like mirroring, it also requires manual intervention to have Share-Point use the backup environment, should the primary one fail.

13 SharePoint with Windows Server 2008 and SQL Server 2008

In This Chapter

- Introduction
- Windows Server 2008
- SQL Server 2008

INTRODUCTION

SharePoint cannot take credit for all of its success. It is built on top of some pretty impressive building blocks: Windows and SQL Server. Since the release of SharePoint 2007, both Windows and SQL have had new releases come out. In this chapter, we will cover a bit about these new versions and what advantages they have for you as the SharePoint administrator.

WINDOWS SERVER 2008

When Windows 2008 hit the street in February of 2008, SharePoint 2007 was ready for it. SP1 for SharePoint had been released four months earlier, and Microsoft had quietly added support for Windows 2008 to it. That is all you need to install Share-Point 2007 on Windows 2008—SP1 slipstreamed into the install. If you try to install on Windows 2008 without SP1, you will get a friendly error message telling you the install failed. The first improvement you will notice is that if you did not already have IIS on Windows, the SharePoint install will install it for you. It will also make the necessary configurations, such as enabling IIS 6 Management Compatibility. We would walk through the install in this chapter, but there is nothing different about it from installing on Windows 2003.

Now that we have convinced you to install SharePoint on Windows 2008, what benefits will you see? Windows 2008 introduces improvements in three main areas: Management, Security, and Performance. We will cover each of these areas in the sections that follow.

MANAGEMENT IMPROVEMENTS

The first improvements you will notice in Windows Server 2008 are the management improvements. Of the three areas of improvement, this one is the most obvious, as it deals with how you will interact with Windows and SharePoint on a day-to-day basis. These improvements come in many forms. The following sections walk through some of the main management improvements in Windows Server 2008.

Server Manager

After missing from Windows 2000 and 2003, Server Manager is back in Windows 2008. It bears little resemblance to the tool of the same name from Windows NT, though. Windows 2008 introduces the concept of Roles and Features. Server Manager is your window into that functionality. Roles are large blocks of functionality that can be turned on and off. There are 16 Roles available out of the box. Some of the Roles available are Active Directory Domain Services, DHCP Server, and IIS. Features are smaller blocks of functionality. They include things like Desktop Experience, .NET Framework, and PowerShell. There are 35 Features available. One of Server Manager's functions is the management of Roles and Features. You can see in Figure 13.1 the overview that Server Manager provides when you log into Windows, or when you open it up from Administrative Tools.

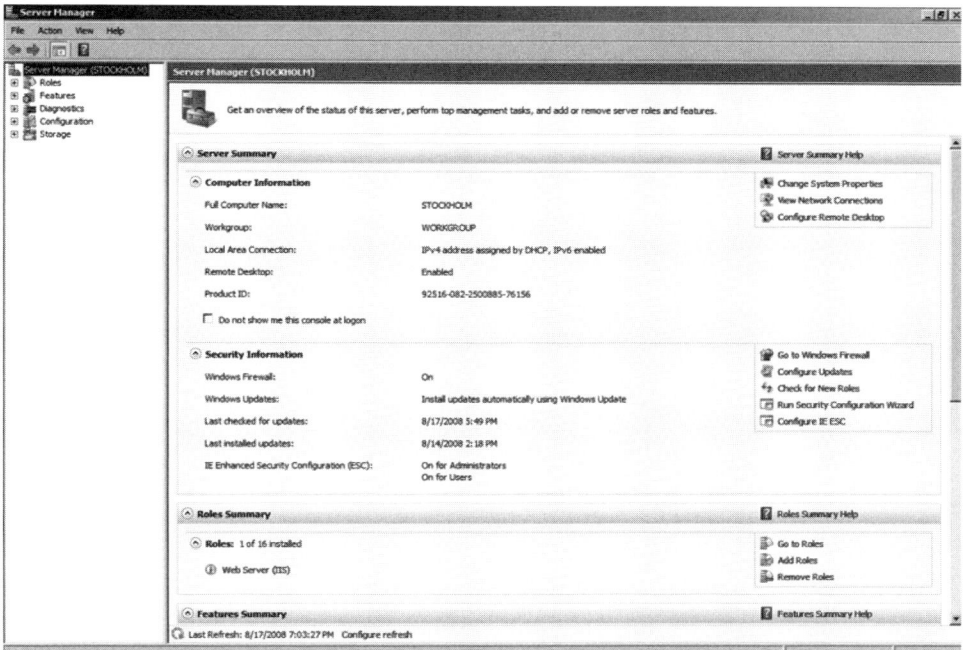

FIGURE 13.1
Server Manager.

The top two nodes of Server Manager are the Roles and Features nodes. Clicking either will give you a summary of the Roles or Features installed. Figure 13.2 shows what the Roles screen looks like if you have the IIS Role installed.

The top pane shows the Roles that have been installed, and it allows you to add or remove Roles. The next pane lets you manage the Roles that are installed.

If you keep walking the tree, you can click the Role that is installed and see more details about it, as in Figure 13.3.

Here you can see the Events related to this Role, as well as any Services associated with it. On the right are links that you can use to manage the services or drill down into the Events more. If you expand the tree a final time, you get the management interface for IIS (see Figure 13.4).

This pane is exactly the same interface you get if you open up IIS Manager from Administrative Tools. This is just another way to drill down to it. If you want to add Roles to Windows Server 2008, click the Add Roles link in Figure 13.2. This brings up the wizard that walks you through the process. Figure 13.5 shows the first screen.

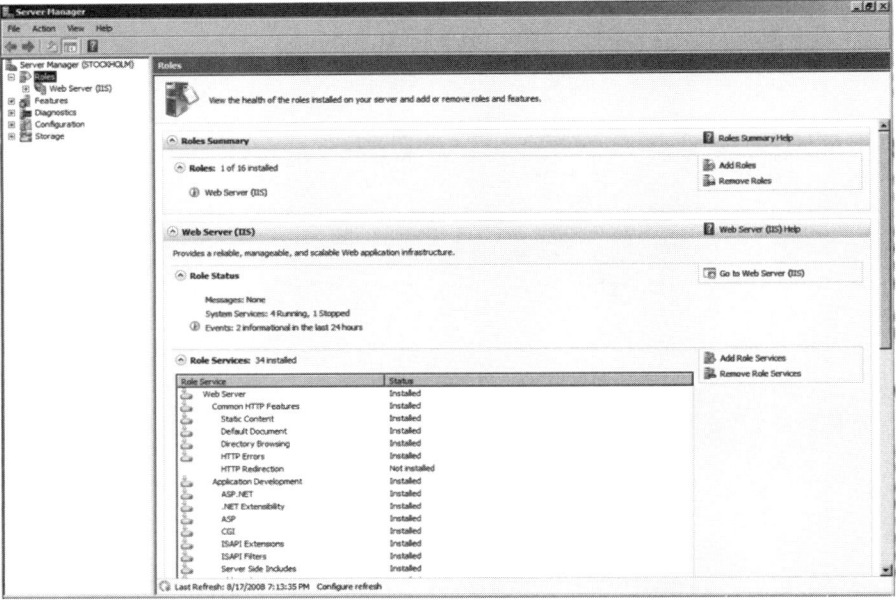

FIGURE 13.2
Roles expanded.

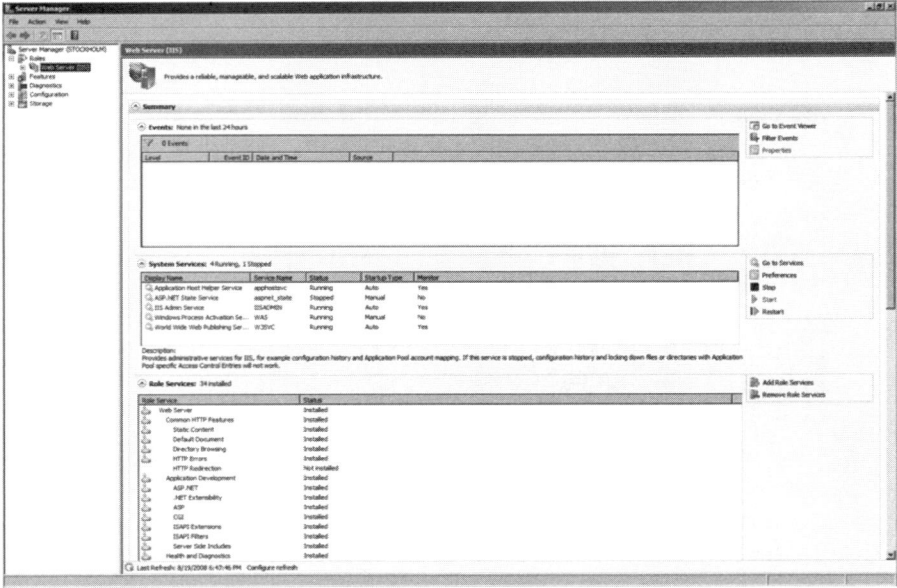

FIGURE 13.3
Web Server Role information.

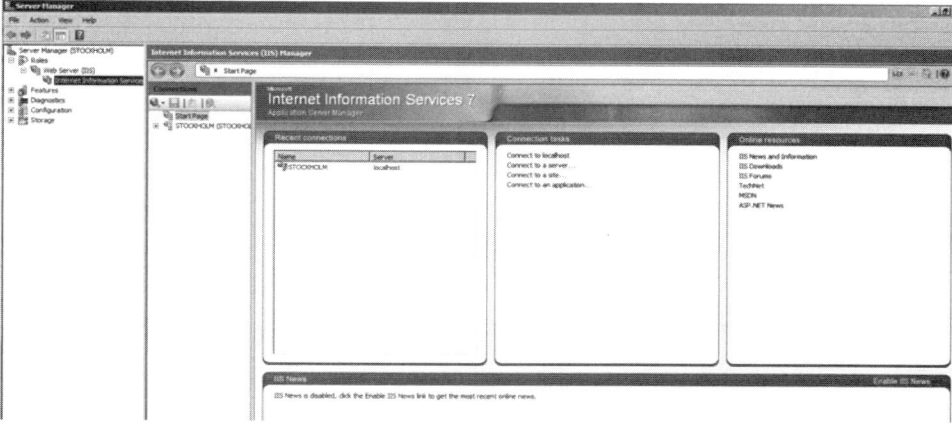

FIGURE 13.4
IIS Manager.

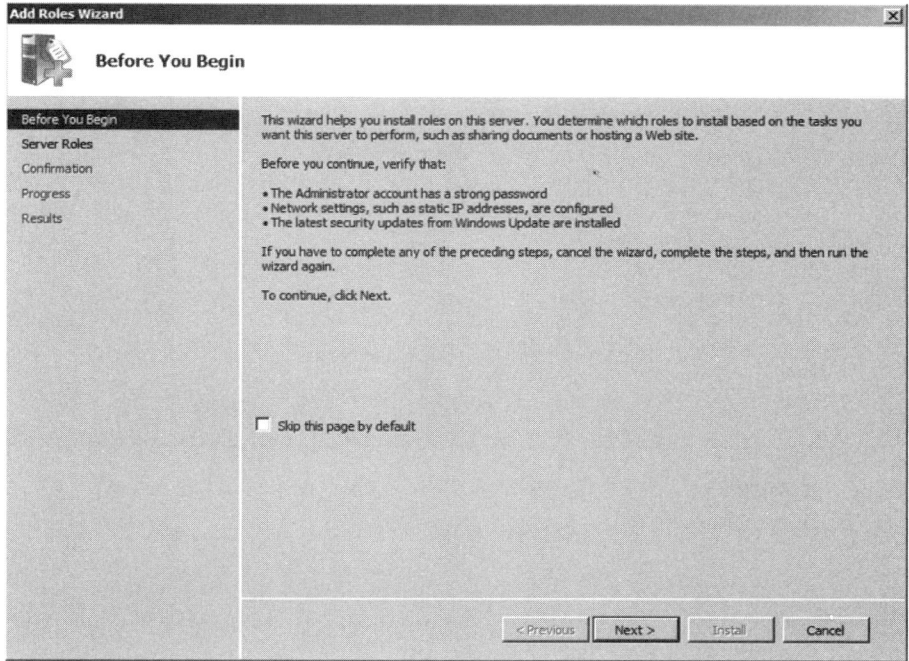

FIGURE 13.5
Add Roles Wizard.

If you have been wondering why Windows adopted this modular Roles-based architecture, the opening screen explains why. Before you install any Roles, you should make sure your Administrator account has a strong password, your network settings are correct, and you have all the latest security updates installed. This makes it pretty clear that Roles are being used to reduce the exposure of Windows Server 2008. Each Role you install adds a potential attack vector, so Windows defaults to the most secure option of no Roles installed.

Clicking Next takes you to the list of Roles that can be installed on your server. You will notice in Figure 13.6 that IIS is grayed out because it is already installed.

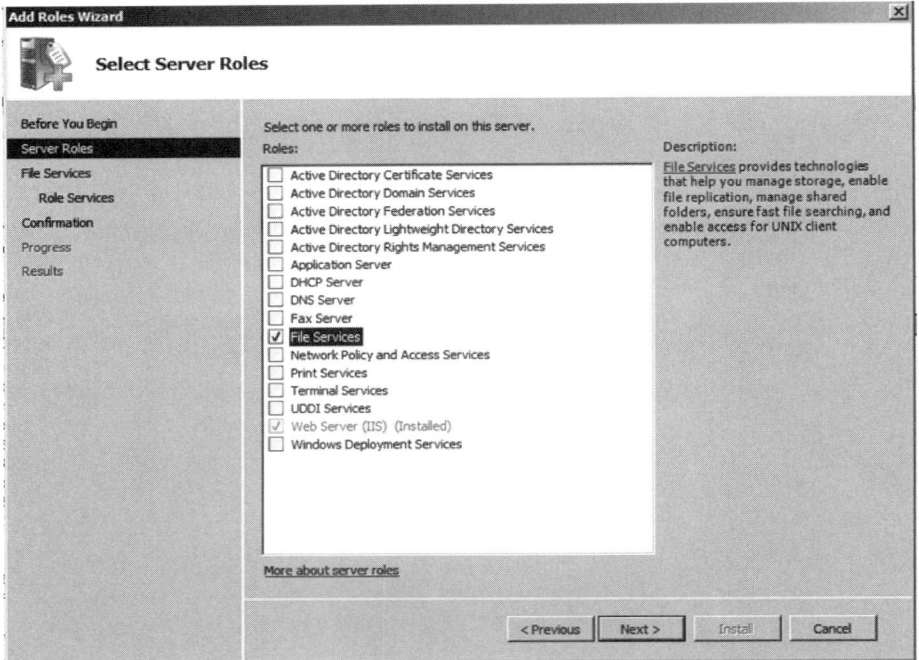

FIGURE 13.6
Select Server Roles.

Since IIS is already installed, you will install the File Services Role to show the wizard in its entirety. You do have the option of installing multiple Roles at a time, if you would like. Figure 13.7 shows the Introduction screen for the Role.

Clicking Next takes you to a screen where you can further control which services get installed. Again, Windows defaults to the smallest footprint, so everything in Figure 13.8 is disabled except the core service. For each service there is a description on the right side and a link to the help file that explains each service.

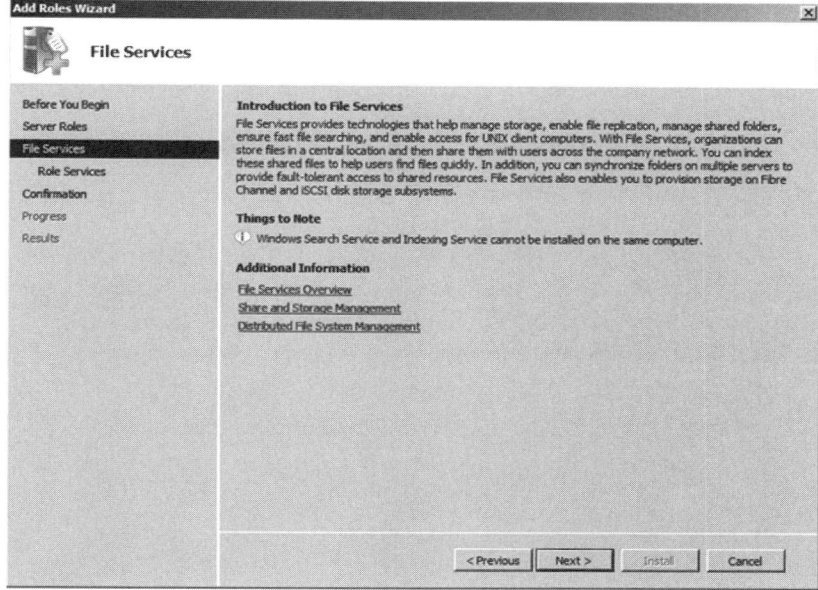

FIGURE 13.7
File Services overview.

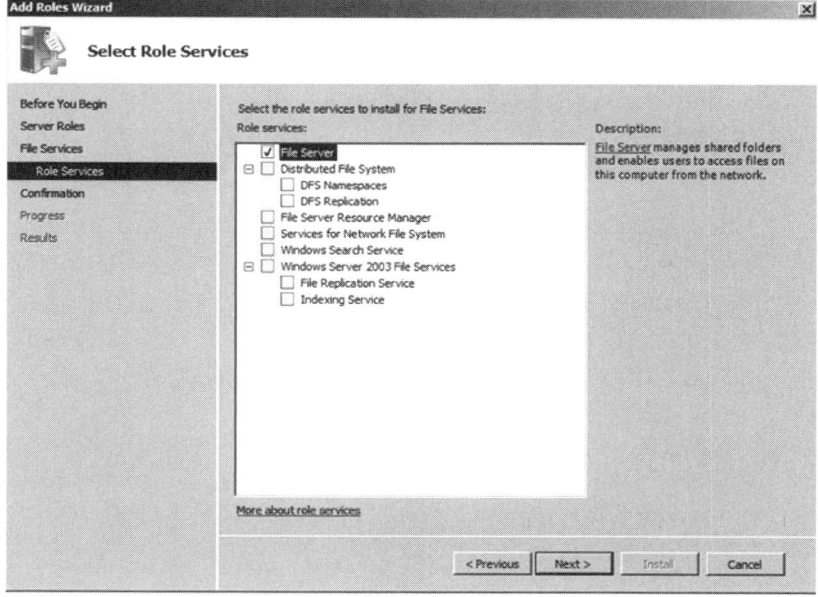

FIGURE 13.8
Select Role Services.

Now, let's leave the default and click Next. Figure 13.9 shows the final screen. For change control purposes, you have the option to save, print, or email the summary. If you click that link, the summary will open in Internet Explorer.

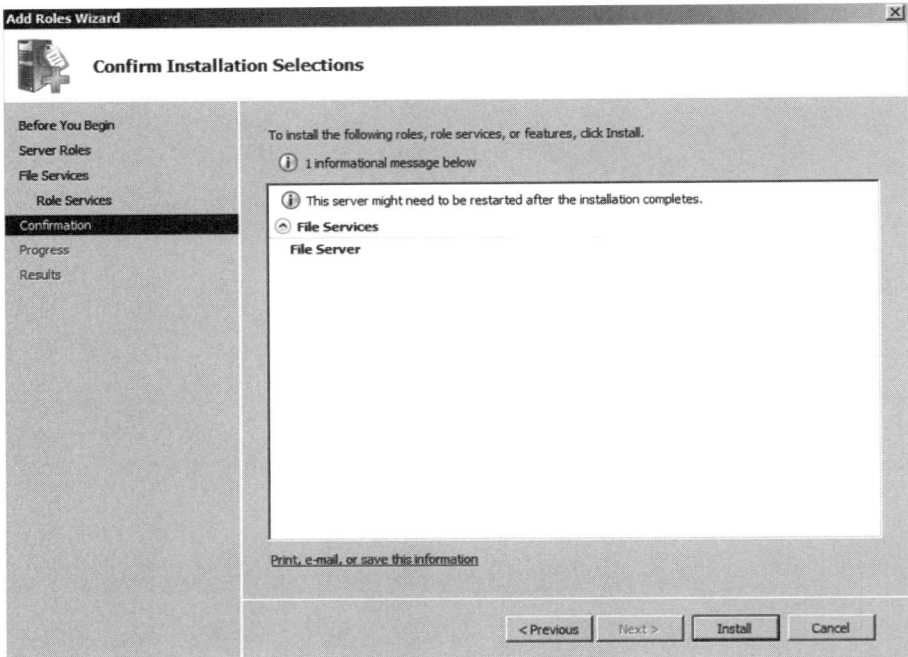

FIGURE 13.9
Confirming Installation.

Clicking Install starts the install process. Once the Role is installed, you will get a screen similar to Figure 13.10. Again, you have the option of saving the installation report. Now the Roles overview shows two Roles: IIS and File Services. Figure 13.11 shows both Roles under the Roles Summary.

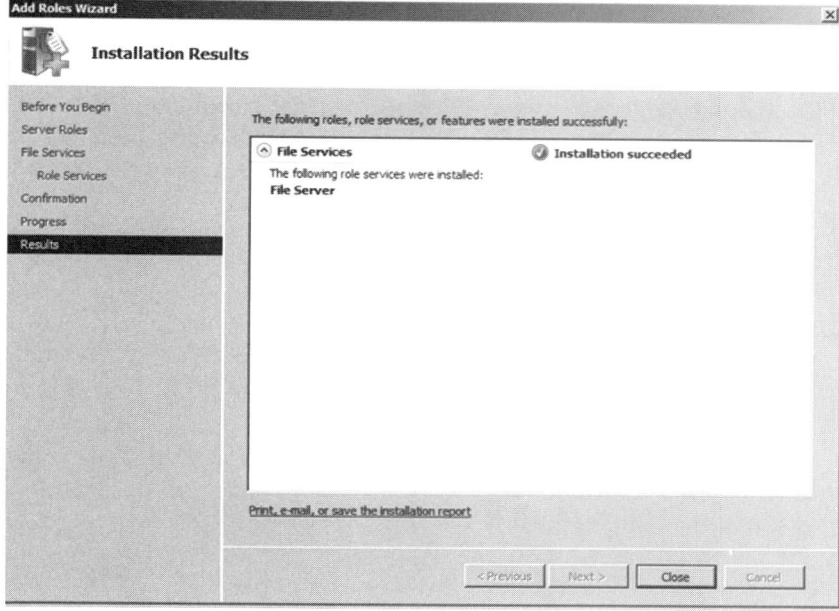

FIGURE 13.10
Installation finished.

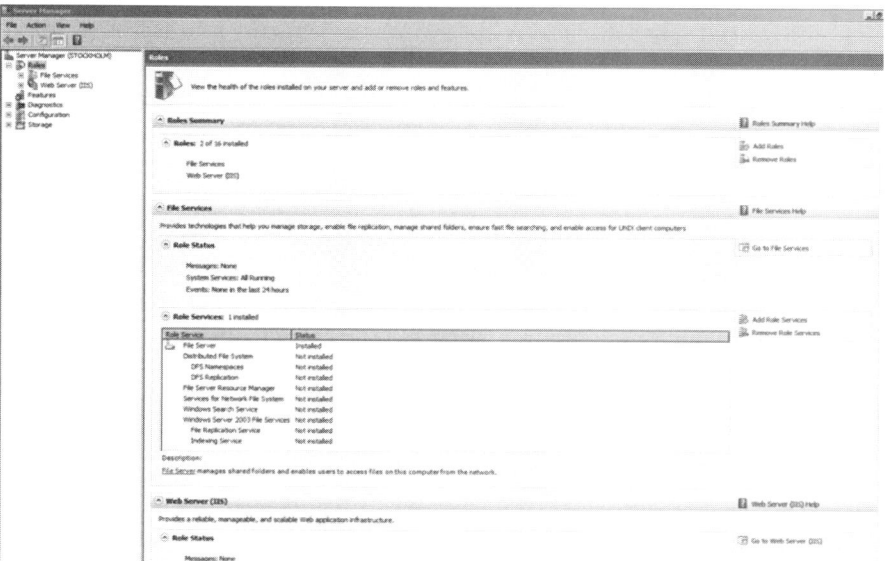

FIGURE 13.11
Both Roles installed.

From the Command Line

As with each successive version of Windows, the command line experience in Windows Server 2008 is better than it was with Windows Server 2003. If you prefer to script your installs, or are just more comfortable managing your servers from the command line, you can use Command Line tools to manage your Roles and Features. `ServerManagerCmd.exe` is nearly a direct replacement for the Server Manager UI. Executing `ServerManagerCmd.exe /?` at a Command Prompt will show you the usage. It is extensive. You can pass it answer files or specify the parameters explicitly. Both the input and output files that `ServerManagerCmd.exe` uses are XML, which makes them very portable and easy to use. You can also use it to query the Roles, Role services, and Features that are installed with the following command:

```
ServerManagerCmd.exe —query
```

It also supports the `—whatif` parameter that allows a user to test a change without modifying the system. You should use it instead of `pkgmgr` and `ocsetup` for manipulating Roles and Features, even though they both can also be used.

PowerShell

Unless you have been living under a rock, you know that Microsoft released Windows PowerShell in 2006. It is a new command line shell and scripting language designed primarily for administrative tasks. It is an evolution of Windows CMD scripts and VBScript. It takes VBScript's ability to be extended via COM one step further by integrating directly with the .NET Framework. This allows PowerShell to instantiate .NET objects. PowerShell also uses cmdlets (pronounced "commandlets"), which are specialized .NET classes that have specific functionality. PowerShell scripts are collections of cmdlets, instantiated .NET classes, and external executables. PowerShell uses providers to access data in data stores like the Registry or the file system. Other products, such as Exchange 2007, can provide their own cmdlets for PowerShell and utilize it for administration. While SharePoint 2007 does not include any cmdlets, since PowerShell can instantiate .NET objects, you can use it to access the SharePoint Object Model. Using this approach, PowerShell can be quite powerful in day-to-day operations. We also expect the next version of SharePoint will heavily leverage PowerShell cmdlets, much like the latest versions of Exchange and SQL Server do.

If PowerShell is something you would like to add to your SharePoint arsenal, you are in luck, because it is included with Windows 2008. To use it, simply install the PowerShell Feature in Server Manager. After you have PowerShell installed on your Windows Server 2008 machine, turn to Chapter 14, "Administrating SharePoint 2007 with PowerShell." We have devoted an entire chapter to PowerShell and how you can use it with SharePoint.

Installing PowerShell the Easy Way

Of course you can install PowerShell through the Server Manager UI, but that almost seems sacrilegious. Installing a powerful new scripting language with a UI? For shame! In the previous section, we covered using ServerManagerCMD.exe to manage roles and features. It seems apropos to install PowerShell with it. To install Power-Shell from the command line, use the following command:

```
servermanagercmd -install PowerShell
```

This will install the PowerShell Feature for you in one line and lets you know whether it was successful. Pretty slick, aye?

IIS 7

One of the biggest improvements in Windows Server 2008, with regard to Share-Point, is IIS 7. IIS is one of the building blocks that SharePoint builds on heavily. While SharePoint 2007 cannot leverage all of the new capabilities that IIS 7 brings, you as the SharePoint administrator can take advantage of many management improvements. One improvement you can take advantage of right away is that Share-Point will install IIS 7 for you if it is not already installed. We recommend this approach, as it lets SharePoint install all the bits it needs. There is no guesswork on your part, no forgetting to enable the .NET framework—you just install Share-Point, and IIS 7 comes along. You will also notice that all the management objects are laid out in one view—no more tabs, no more right-clicking to find things. It is all laid out for you.

IIS Manager is right where you are used to seeing it, in the Administrative Tools folder under Programs. Unlike its predecessor, it has a start page when you open it, shown in Figure 13.12.

There is so much new functionality that it is tough to know where to begin. For those with multiple IIS servers, you can see the new interface is geared more toward easy management of them. There is a single-click option for connecting to additional servers, as well as a list of the recent list of servers to which you have connected.

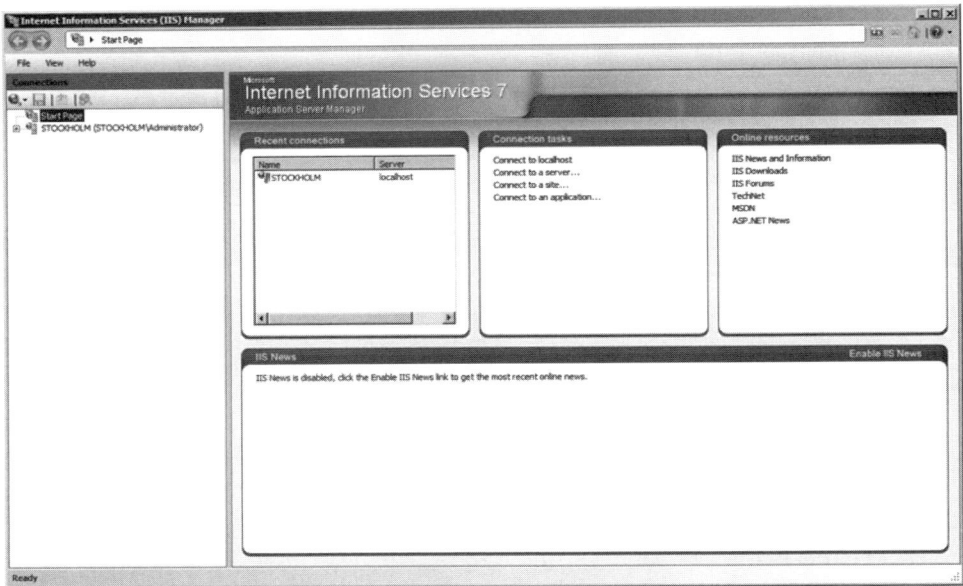

FIGURE 13.12
IIS Manager in Windows 2008.

After seeing how easy it is to manage multiple IIS servers, you might be tempted to try to connect to your IIS 7 servers right away. If you do so, you will likely be disappointed. Once again, the security consciousness of Windows Server 2008 comes out. Before you can manage an IIS 7 installation remotely, you must install the Management Service and enable it. You can do it through the Server Manager UI. Click Add Role Services from the Roles page. When the Select Role Services dialog box appears, scroll to the bottom of the Web Server Role Services until you find the Management Tools section. In order to manage this IIS 7 instance remotely, you will need to install the Management Service Role Services, as shown in Figure 13.13. If you have not installed the .NET Environment yet, you will be prompted to install it, too. Click Next and Install to finish it out. Alternatively, you can use the command `Server-managercmd.exe —install Web-Mgmt-Service` to install the Management Service.

We are not finished quite yet. After we install the service, we need to configure it and start it before we can connect remotely. To do that, open up the IIS Manager. Click the name of your server, which will take you to the management for your server. Toward the bottom, under the Management heading, find the link for Management Service and click it. Click Enable remote connections to enable the service. You have several other configuration options, so tweak them as appropriate. After you have made your changes, click Apply in the right pane, as seen in Figure 13.14 and then click Start to start the service.

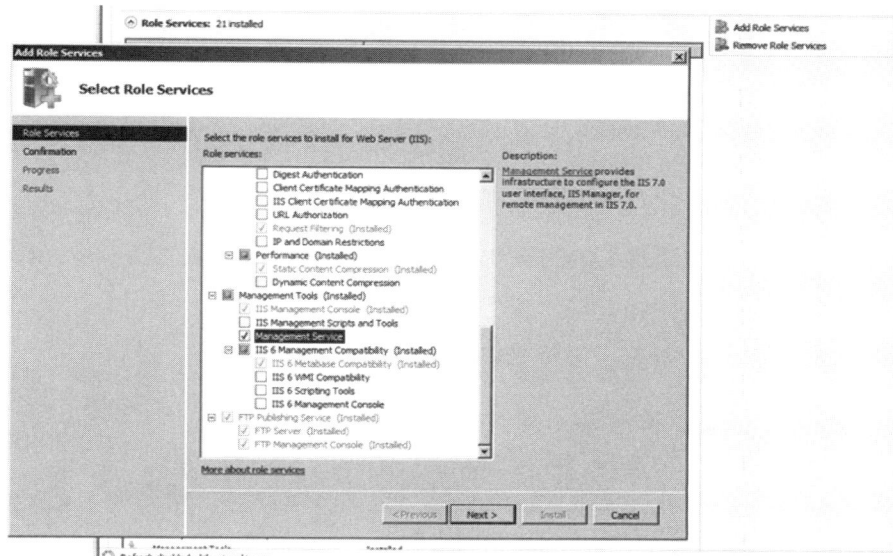

FIGURE 13.13
Install the IIS Management Service.

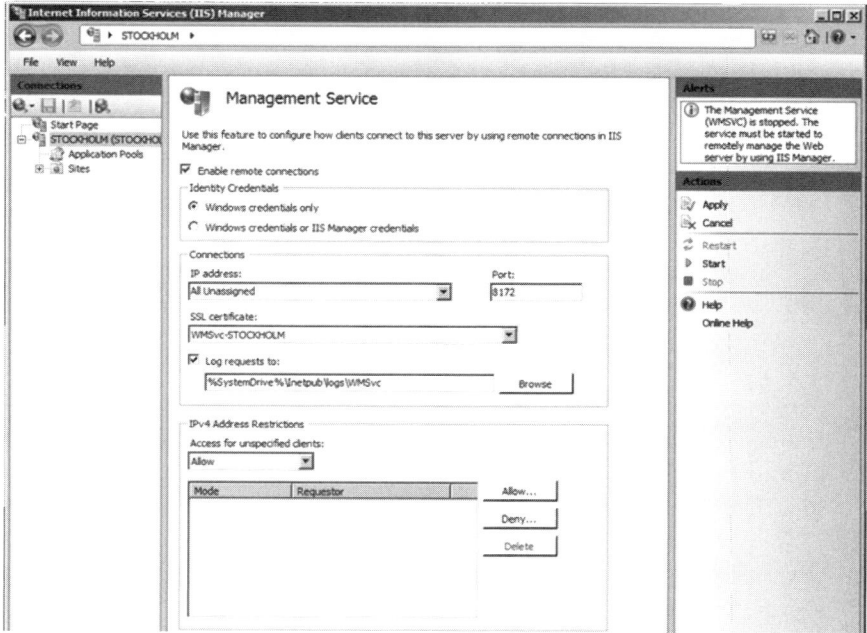

FIGURE 13.14
Configure the IIS Management Service.

After the service is started, you can go to another Windows Server 2008 server, or a Vista client running the Remote Server Administration Tools (RSAT), and connect to this server. From the start page, click Connect to Server. This brings up the Connect to Server dialog box. On the first screen, enter the name of the remote server you want to connect to. In Figure 13.15, we are on the server Stockholm connecting to the server orlando2.

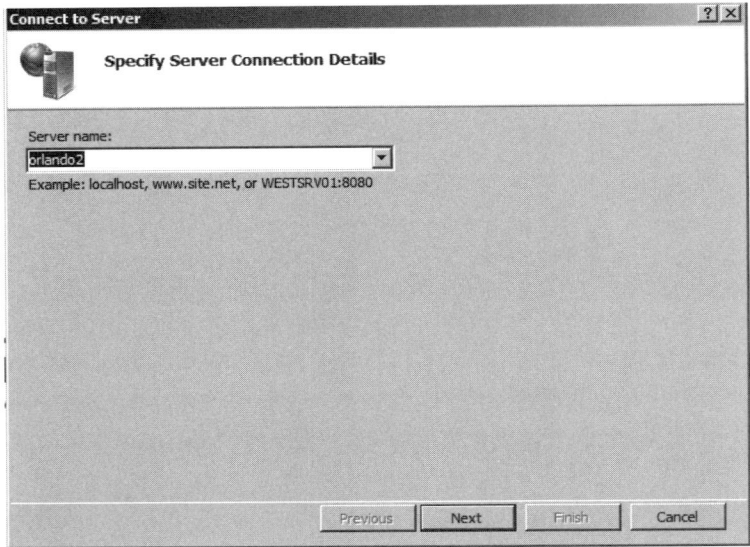

FIGURE 13.15
Connect to a remote IIS server.

After you have typed the server name in, click Next. In the next screen, enter the username and password you want to use to connect to the remote server. When we were configuring the Remote Service, we had the option of using Windows authentication only, or Windows and IIS Manager Credentials. If we had chosen the latter option, we could create users in IIS 7 itself that could be used for management. This allows for IIS management, without giving someone a domain account or a local account on the server. In Figure 13.16, we are connecting as the local administrator account.

After you have entered the username and password, click Next. Another configuration option we had in Figure 13.14 was which SSL certificate to use. Each server generates its own, if there is not a domain certificate server to get one from. That is what the servers we are using have done. Since their certificate store is not trusted by the remote server, we get the message in Figure 13.17 asking if we want to connect anyway, since the non-trusted certificate might be a security problem.

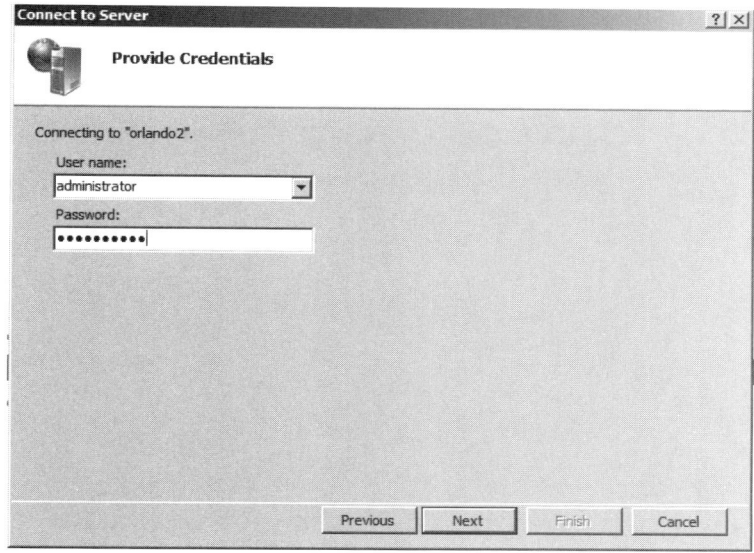

FIGURE 13.16
Provide credentials.

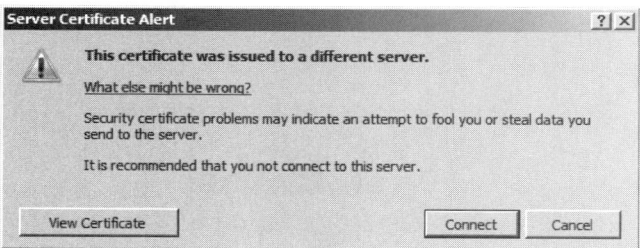

FIGURE 13.17
Certificate alert message.

Since we trust the server, go ahead and click Connect. Your last step is to give the Connection a friendly name. We will leave it as the remote server name, orlando2, as in Figure 13.18.

Click Finish to get connected. If everything went well, you should have both servers in your left pane like we do in Figure 13.19. These will also be reflected in the Start page now as well.

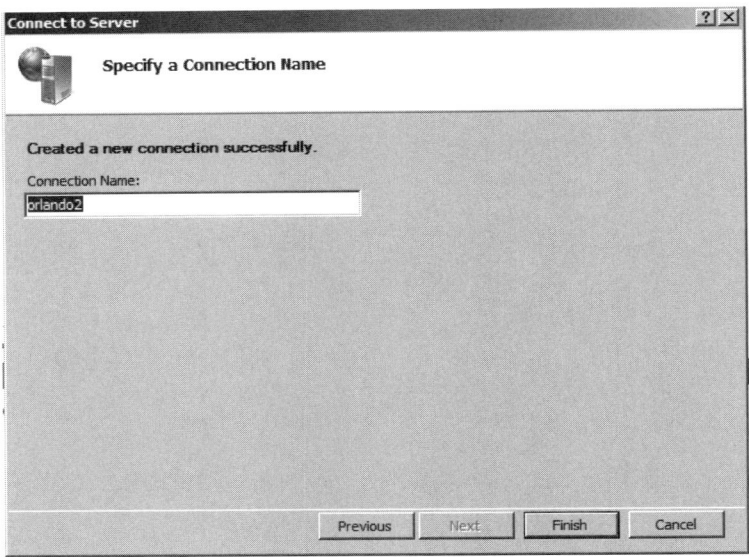

FIGURE 13.18
Specify a Connection Name.

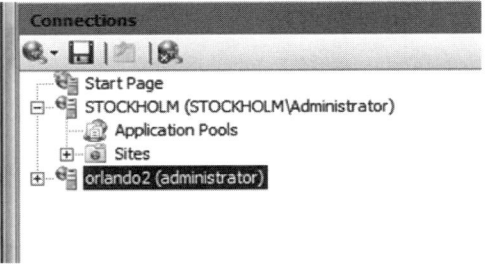

FIGURE 13.19
Multiple servers.

Connecting to remote servers easily is not the only improvement to IIS 7. It also makes it easier to keep tabs on what your server is doing. One way it does that is Failed Request Tracing. Just like the name suggests, this allows you to track failed requests. You create rules about the type of failure you want to track and IIS will log each time they occur. If you do not see a link for Failed Request Tracing Rules under the IIS heading in IIS Manager, you may need to install the Role Service. You can do this under Roles in the Server Manager UI or with the command `servermanagercmd.exe -install Web-Http-Tracing`. If you have IIS Manager open when you run that command, you may need to close it and open it back up for the Failed Request Tracing Rules link to appear.

After Tracing is installed, go to the Site you want to enable it on in IIS Manager and double-click Failed Request Tracing Rules. Figure 13.20 shows where to find it.

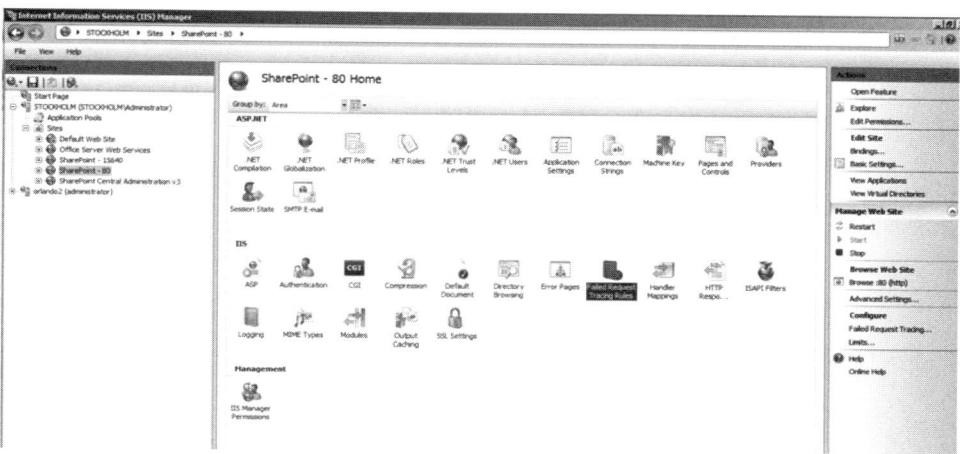

FIGURE 13.20
Failed Request Tracing.

The first time you go in you will get an error message stating that Failed Request Tracing is not configured. Before IIS can trace the failed requests, you need to tell it where to save the logs. Click the link shown in Figure 13.21 to choose where to save the logs and enable Tracing.

After you have configured the log directory and enabled the Tracing, you need to create a rule for IIS to trigger on. Do that by clicking the Add link under Actions. The first page of the wizard asks you what content you would like to trace. Since we are mainly concerned with SharePoint, we will limit our traces to just aspx files. Figure 13.22 shows the content options you have with aspx selected. After you have selected .aspx files, click Next. This page is the important one, as this is where you define what IIS is looking for. For our example, we will trace 404 Page Not Found errors. You might use this to keep an eye on dead links that might crop up. Figure 13.23 shows how to configure it to look for 404 errors.

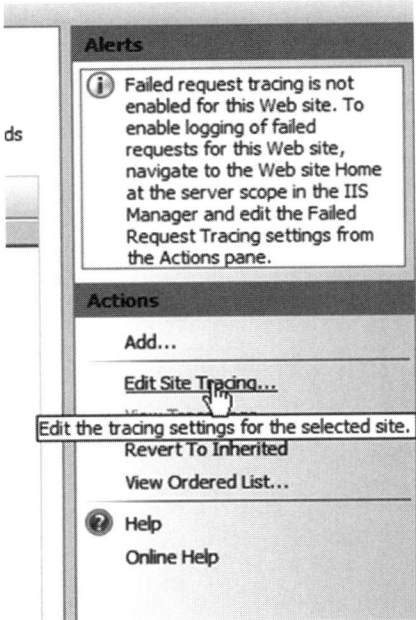

FIGURE 13.21
Log directory.

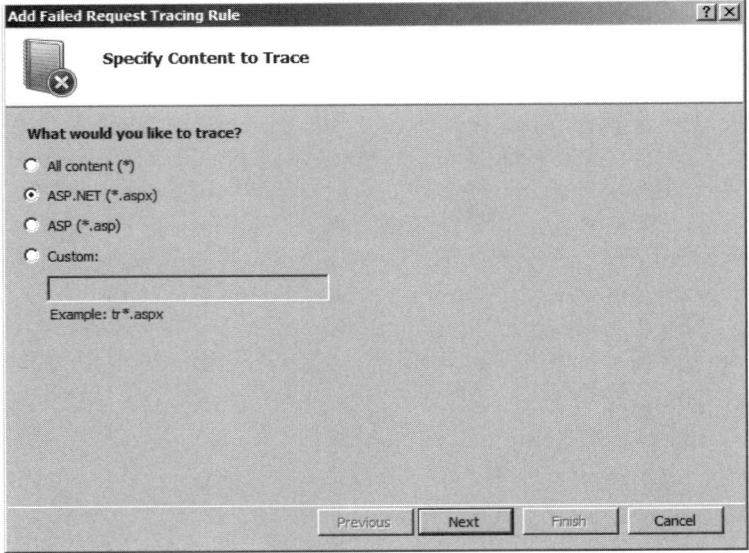

FIGURE 13.22
Looking for .aspx files.

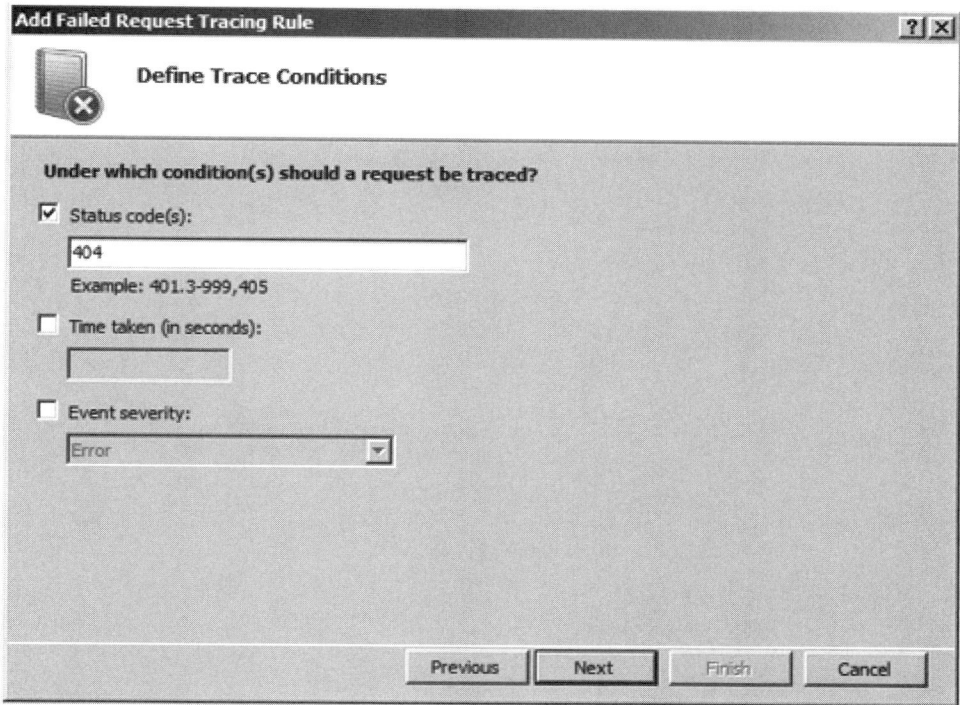

FIGURE 13.23
Looking for 404s.

Another good use for Tracing would be to keep track of slow-loading Web pages. The second option in Figure 13.23 lets you set a time in seconds to trace. If users are complaining of slow pages, you could use this to get all the slow pages logged. This would let you know exactly which pages are slow, how slow they are, and when they are failing.

After you have entered 404, then click Next. The final page allows you to narrow down providers. In Figure 13.24, we left it at the default, which means that all four providers are checked.

Now that the trace is configured, you can test it. Since it is on the lookout for 404 errors, all you need to do is request an .aspx page that does not exist. To test it, we tried to browse to http://stockholm/default2.aspx. Figure 13.25 shows the 404 page the user gets, as well as the log that was created by the Tracing.

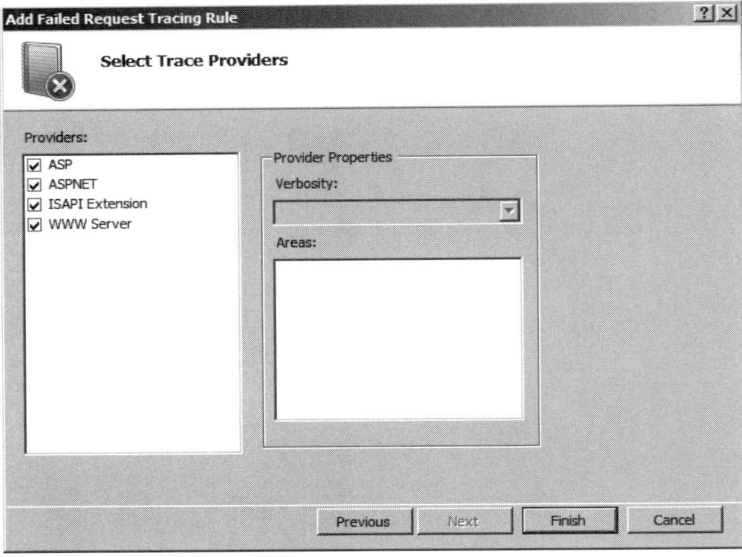

FIGURE 13.24
Choose providers.

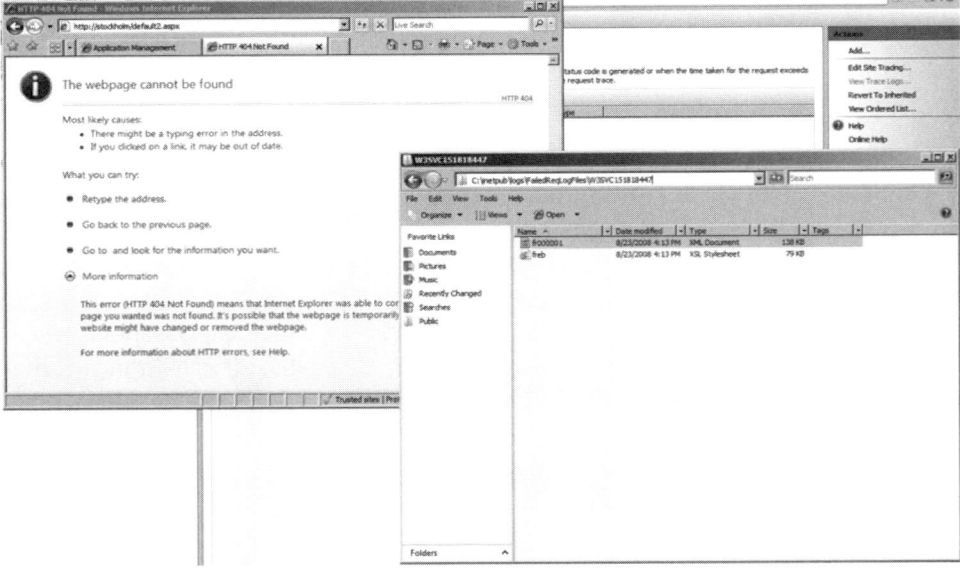

FIGURE 13.25
404 Error and trace log.

The failed request generated two files: an XML file and the stylesheet for it. If you double-click the XML file, you can see the actual log file that was generated. Figure 13.26 shows the XML file rendered in IE. The information is quite extensive, and the page has tabs across the top allowing you to see more detailed information about the request.

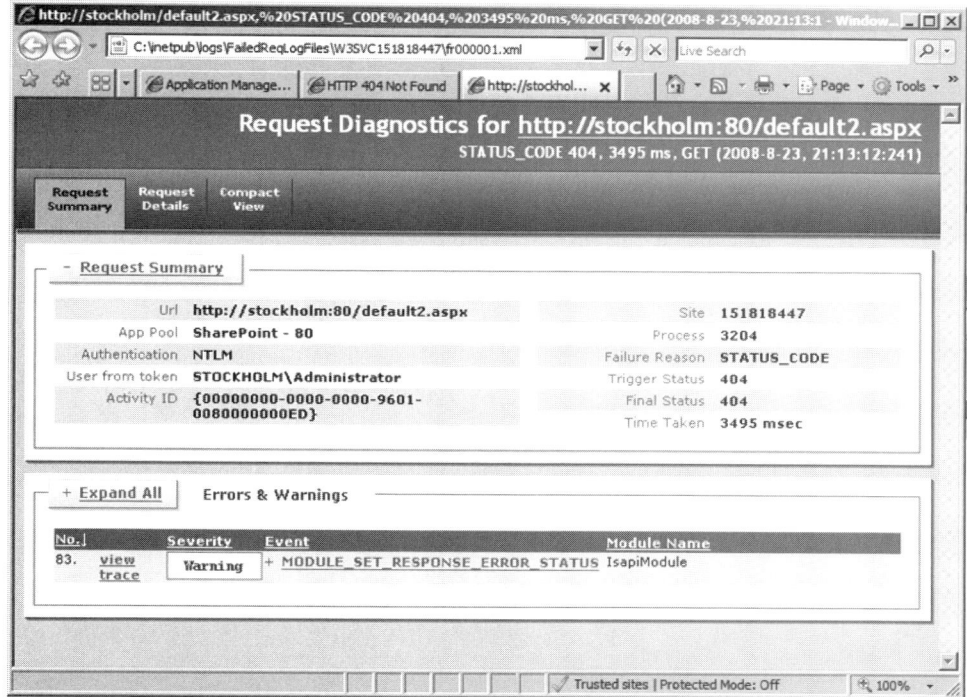

FIGURE 13.26
Failed request.

This has many potential uses when it comes to troubleshooting. We recommend not enabling it unless you are actively looking for an error, since it does take some resources.

These are just a couple of the management improvements in IIS 7 that SharePoint administrators should know about. The new interface is very easy to use, and we recommend you do some exploring. Jump in there and get your hands dirty. We think you will like what you find.

Reliability and Performance Monitor

Windows Server 2008 and Vista share quite a bit of code and functionality, and this is good news for administrators. One great piece of functionality that Windows Server 2008 and Vista share is the Reliability and Performance Monitor. This is almost one-stop shopping when it comes to determining what is going on with your server. Let's start by opening it up. You can find a link to it under Administrative Tools. The starting screen is very similar to Task Manager in that it gives you an overview of what is going on with your server. It goes one step further, though. It shows you CPU, Network, and Memory usage like Task Manager, but it also shows you Disk utilization.

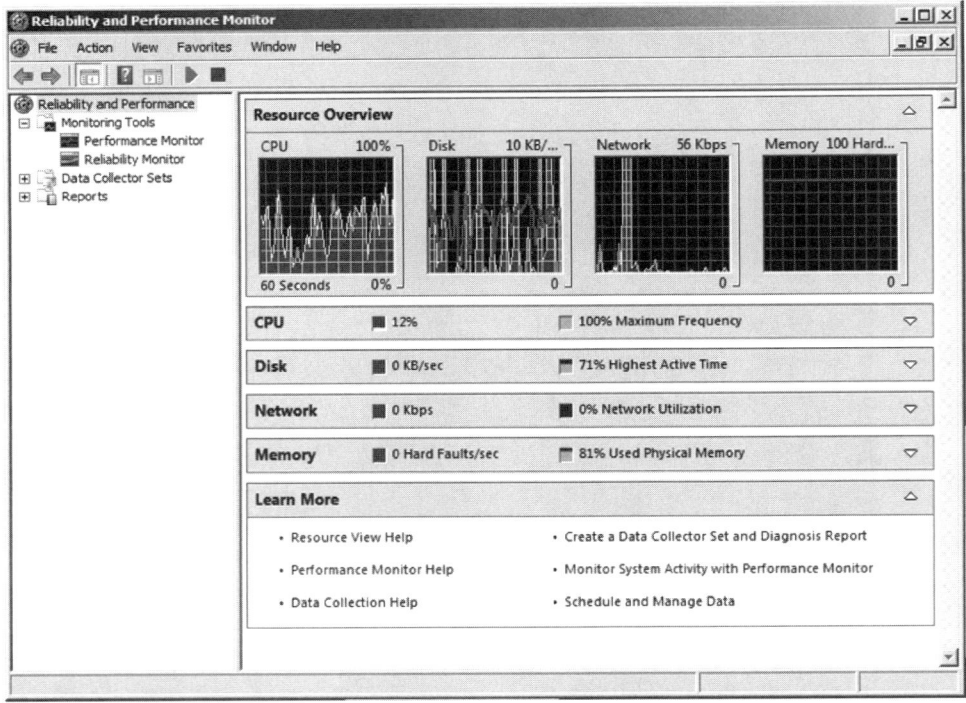

FIGURE 13.27
Reliability and Performance Monitor.

Figure 13.27 shows that the server is experiencing some heavy disk usage. Knowing that a performance issue is based on disk usage is nice, but not horribly helpful. Fortunately, the Monitor lets us drill down into each of the four areas and see exactly what is going on. Figure 13.28 shows the Disk resource expanded and sorted by the Write column.

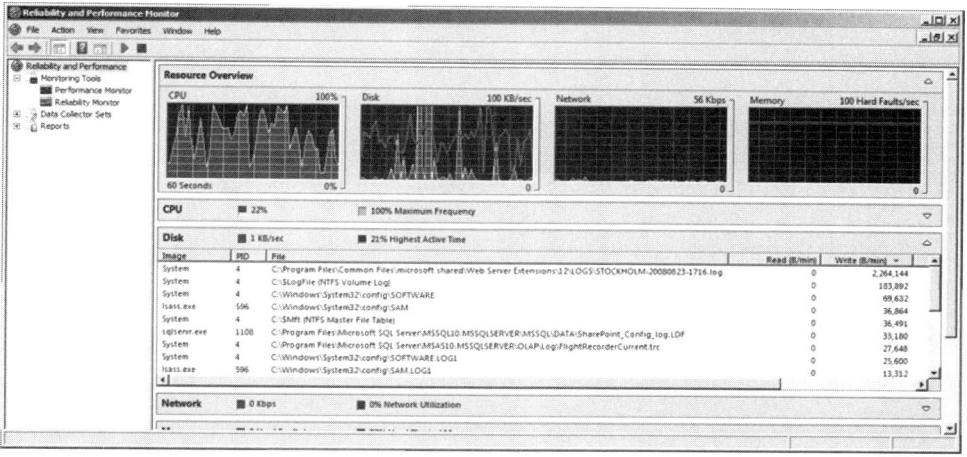

FIGURE 13.28
Disk usage sorted by Write.

You can see that the ULS log is getting the most use at this point. This view can be very handy if you are seeing high disk usage, and you are not sure what process is causing all of the thrashing. You have the same view with CPU, Network, and Memory, which makes narrowing down resource hogs a breeze.

The Reliability and Performance Monitor's usefulness does not end here. The name of this tool may sound familiar, and that is because it replaces the Performance Monitor from previous versions of Windows. This means it has all the same functionality of Performance Monitor as well. You can monitor specific objects on the local machine or remote machines with it.

Now we have the Reliability Monitor coupled with it. Clicking Reliability Monitor in the left pane opens it. This is new with Vista and Windows Server 2008. It shows your system stability and matches it up with events that may impact your system's performance.

In this view, you are seeing all of the events that the system has. Each day where an event occurred that may impact stability, an icon is placed on that date in the appropriate column: Software (Un)Installs, Application Failures, Hardware Failures, Windows Failures, or Miscellaneous Failures. Figure 13.29 shows several informational icons and one warning. If you click the warning, the Report in the bottom pane will open up the report for that day so that you can review it and see what happened. This is very useful if you can pinpoint a point where performance started to degrade or your server became unstable.

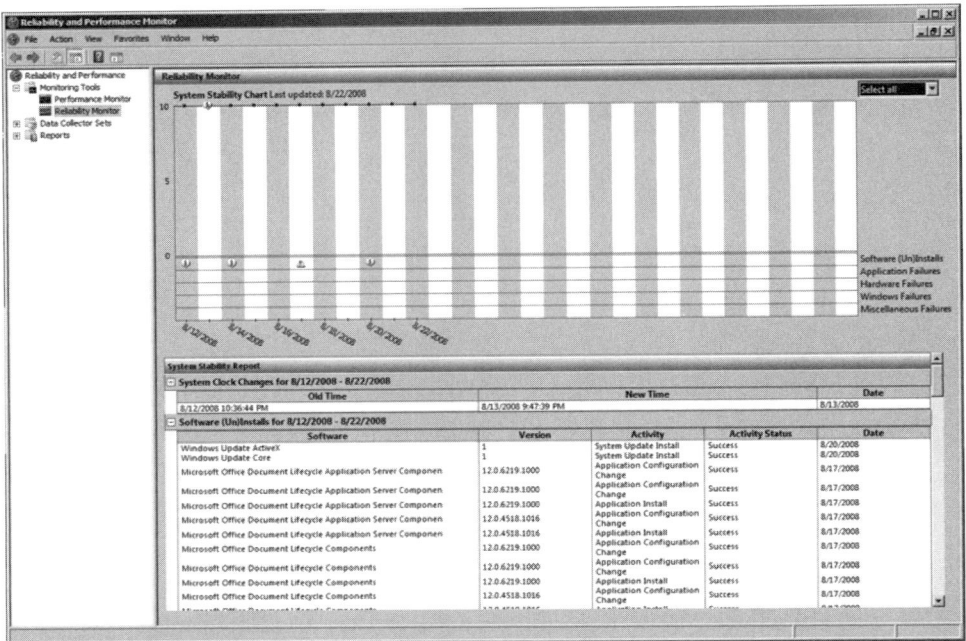

FIGURE 13.29
Reliability Monitor.

Event Viewer

Again, thanks to the shared lineage of Windows Server 2008 and Vista, Event Viewer received some modest upgrades. It is a major overhaul from Windows 2003 and a lot of functionality has been added. Like many things these days, it supports XML. When you save a log out, you have the option of using the Event View–specific EVTX file or an industry standard XML file, as well as TXT and CSV. These XML files can be rendered in any tool that can handle XML. In Windows Server 2003, you have the option of filtering one of the existing logs for specific events based on type, source, and so on. Windows Server 2008 takes this a step farther. Now instead of filtering an existing log, your filter becomes a Custom View. This allows you to have many different filter sets defined without having to reconfigure each one when you want to use it. It also lets you aggregate events from different logs instead of just a single one. You also have the option of exporting the Custom View so that you do not need to configure it on each of your servers. Windows also creates Custom Views for each Role you have installed, so that you can drill down to events specific to that Role.

If you have multiple servers that you want to keep track of, you can use another of Event Viewer's new features, Subscriptions. Subscriptions allow you to collect events from remote computers and store them locally. You have the option of pushing or pulling the events. This can be done with machines that are in a domain or in a workgroup, although the configuration and options are different for the latter. Subscriptions can be optimized for WAN links, so it is well suited for branch offices. The setup is complicated, so we will not walk through it in this book. The steps are outlined in the help file, if you want to investigate it further.

Before Windows Server 2008, if you wanted to look out for specific events in your logs, you either needed to create some solution using scripts that scraped event logs and took action on them, or you had to pay for monitoring software like System Center Operations Manager. Not only are both of those solutions complicated and time consuming, but the latter may be too expensive for your budget. With Windows Server 2008, you now have a third option, one of the most exciting additions to Event Viewer, which is the ability to attach a task to an Event. Now, without third-party software, you can choose an event in the log, and Windows will perform any number of tasks when that event happens again. Let's walk through it.

Open up Event Viewer and find the event you would like to act on. In the Action pane on the right, click Attach Task To This Event, as shown in Figure 13.30. If the Action pane is not visible, you can also right-click the event and select the same option.

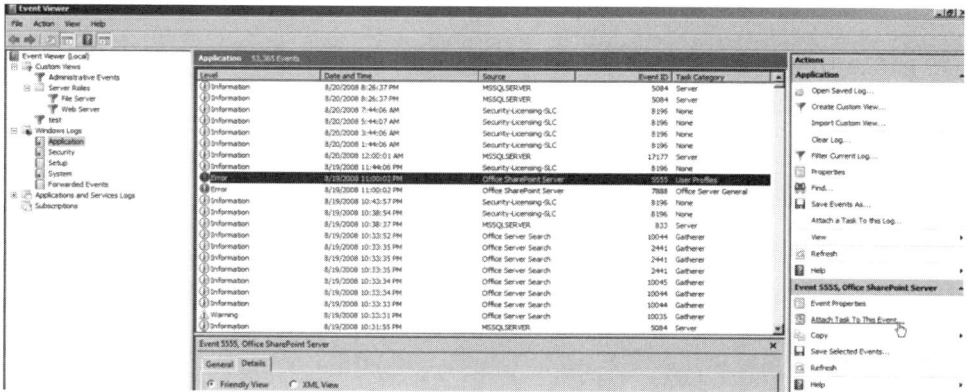

FIGURE 13.30
Attaching a Task to an Event.

This starts the Create Basic Task Wizard, which actually shows improvements in two areas of Windows Server: Event Viewer and Task Scheduler. You have similar task options outside of Event Viewer as well. In the first dialog, you need to give a Name and Description to your new task. In Figure 13.31, we've left the defaults. After you have entered a name, click Next.

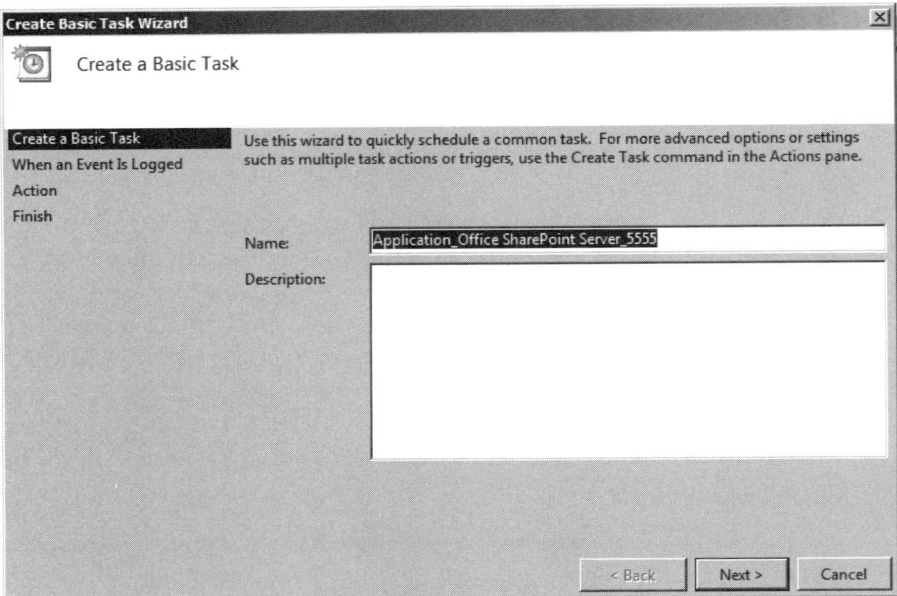

FIGURE 13.31
Create a Basic Task.

The next dialog, shown in Figure 13.32, is already filled out for you, so there is nothing to do. It shows the event you are binding to. Go ahead and click Next.

The third dialog is where things get fun. Figure 13.33 shows the three options: Start a program, Send an e-mail, or Display a message. The first option lets you run a program or script with optional parameters when the event fires. The third option sends a Messenger-style pop-up to the desktop. In Figure 13.33, we use the second option: Send an e-mail.

The fourth dialog is where you can configure the email. In Figure 13.34, we have set the To and From address the same and put a short message in. You do have the option of attaching a file if you would like, and you get to specify an SMTP server to use.

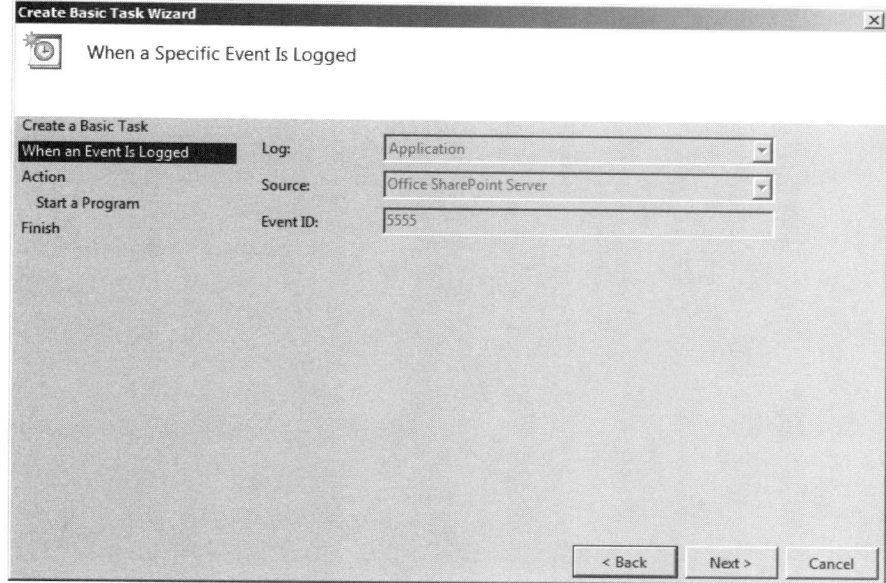

FIGURE 13.32
The event that is being logged.

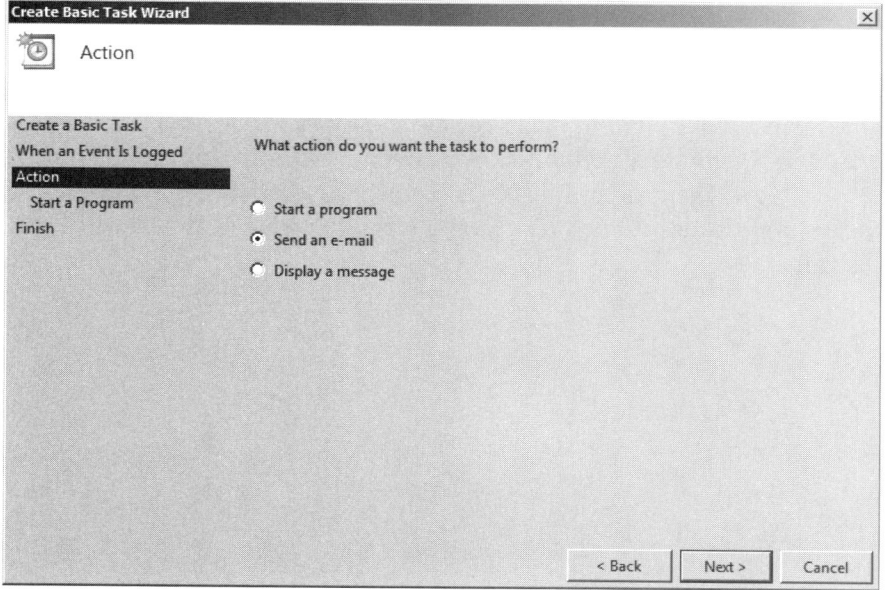

FIGURE 13.33
Send an e-mail.

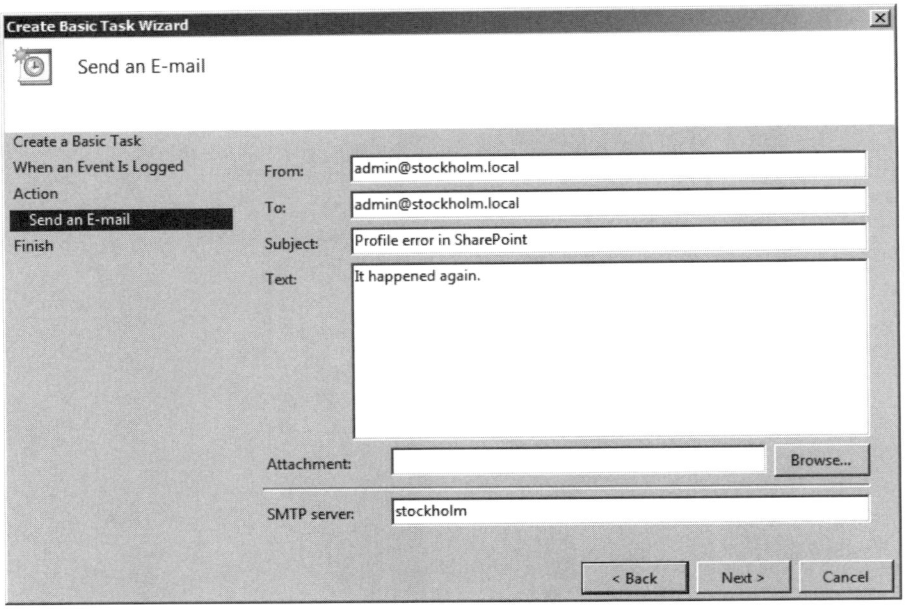

FIGURE 13.34
Configure an email.

Clicking Next takes you to the Finish screen, which is just a recap of what we have entered so far. You also have the option of opening the Properties dialog for the task if you want to tweak it some more. In Figure 13.35 we left that unchecked and just clicked Finish. If you decide later that you want to modify this task, you can do so by editing it in the Task Scheduler under Administrative Tools.

Now when the profile error you tagged happens, you will get an email. This example leads into the next area of improvements in Windows Server 2008: Task Scheduler.

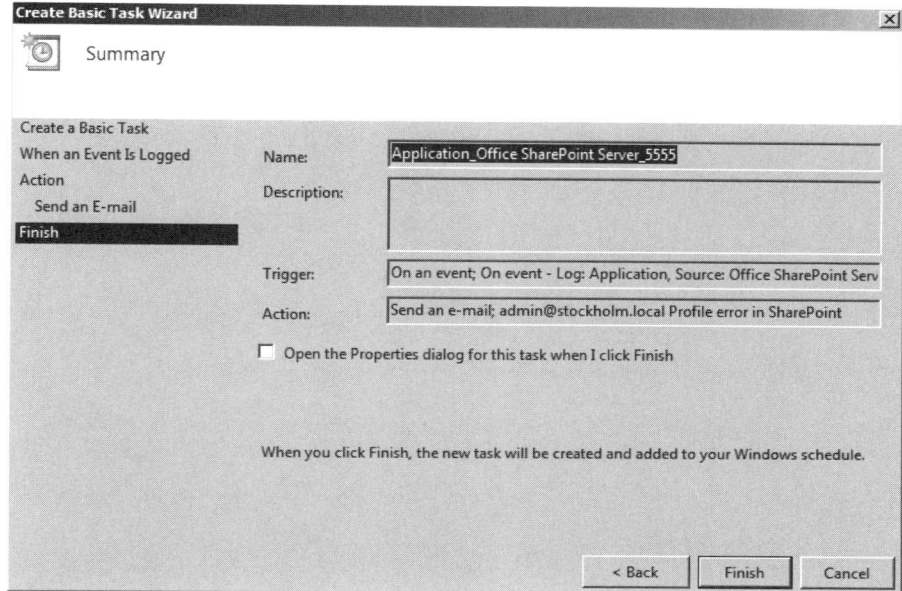

FIGURE 13.35
Task recap.

Task Scheduler

Like Event Viewer, Task Scheduler has benefited from a major overhaul in Windows Server 2008. In the previous section, we looked at some of its new capabilities. That gave us a glimpse of what the new Task Scheduler can do. Let's start our tour by opening up its interface. The first change you will notice is that it moved. In Window Server 2003, you managed tasks by going to Control Panel > Scheduled Tasks. In Windows Server 2008, it has a new address: Administrative Tools > Task Scheduler. This is a good indication that scheduled tasks have gotten an upgrade. Figure 13.36 shows the new Task Scheduler interface has the familiar three-pane MMC interface that Microsoft has adopted.

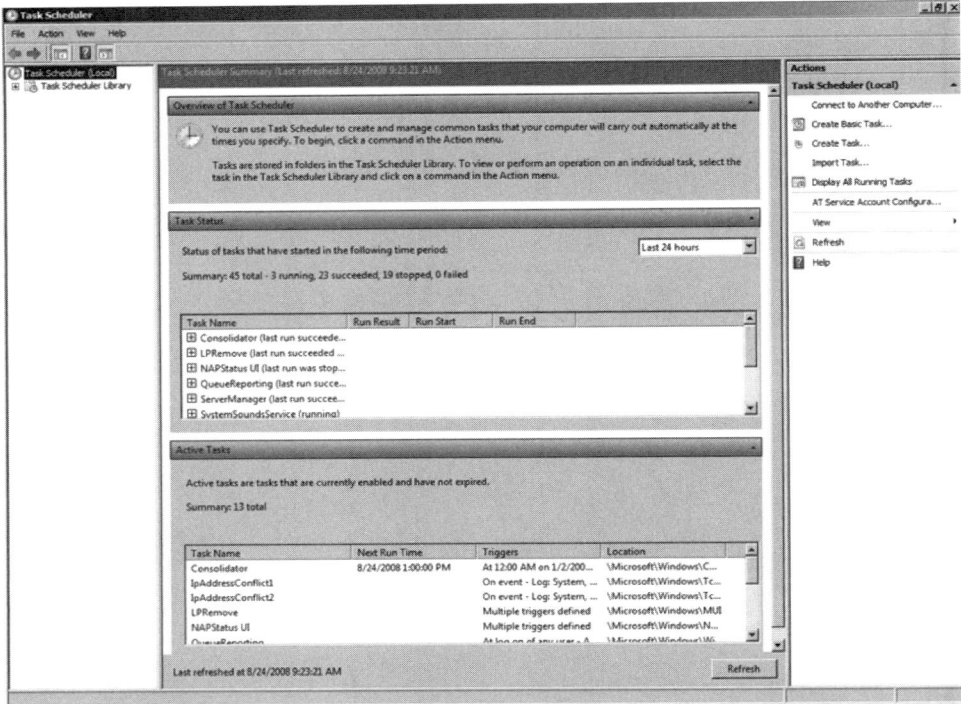

FIGURE 13.36
The new Task Scheduler.

Figure 13.36 shows the Task Scheduler from a fairly fresh install. Another change is that the Task Scheduler is not just for batch files anymore. Since tasks are no longer just time based, Windows now uses them for a variety of management tasks. This is very similar to how SharePoint uses Timer Jobs. A Scheduled Task is used to start Server Manager when a user logs in, for instance. It uses the "At log on of any user" trigger to accomplish this. Figure 13.37 shows all the tasks that are created automatically by Windows and how the Server Manager task triggers off of log on.

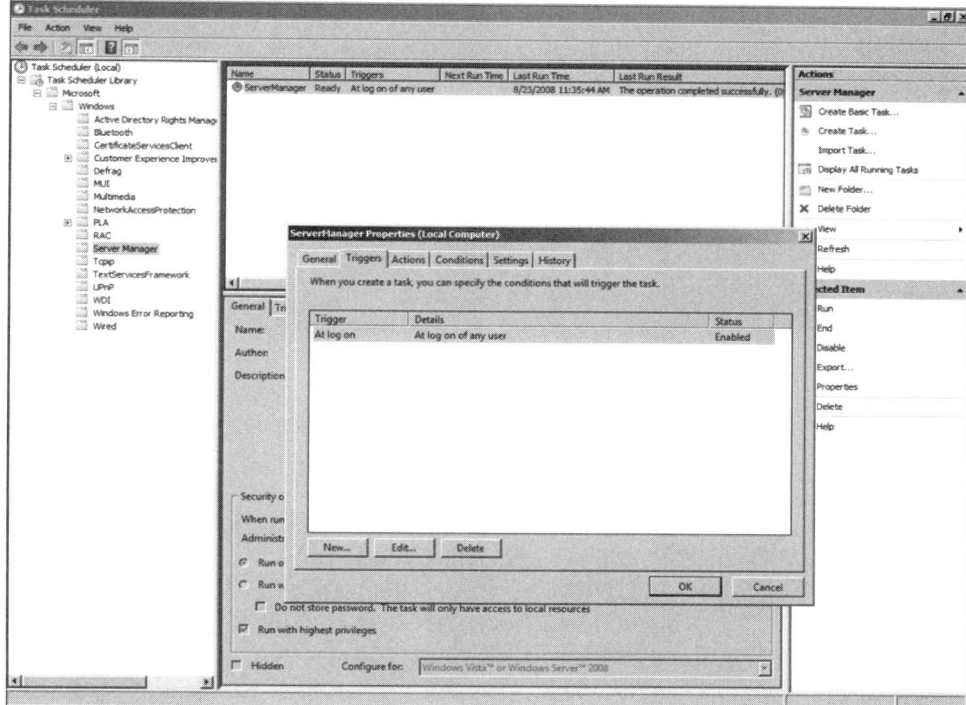

FIGURE 13.37
Server Manager task.

Since tasks are used more, Task Scheduler has improved their management. For one, you can create folders to manage your tasks. In the previous section, we created a task based on an Application Event. When that task was saved, it was created in an Event Viewer Tasks folder. That keeps the number of tasks in one view from getting overwhelming, and it also keeps tasks from getting lost in the crowd. Also, as you leverage tasks more, you can now export them for import to other servers. This keeps you from having to re-create your work. You can import tasks from the Action pane of the UI, or you can automate the process by using schtasks from the command line and import them that way. Exported tasks are saved out as XML files. To import them into a new system, use the following syntax:

```
schtasks /create /XML <xmlfile> /TN <taskname>
```

The Create parameter has many options. `Schtasks /create /?` will show all of them. It can be used to create tasks from scratch, as well as to import them. Task Scheduler has also added another very important bit of functionality—it tells you if you enter a bad password. If you entered a bad password for the user executing a task in previous versions of Windows, for example, the Task Scheduler would happily take it, and then your task would inexplicably fail to run. In Windows Server 2008, the Task Scheduler tries your password when you assign it and lets you know if it is incorrect. That alone is worth the upgrade to Windows Server 2008.

WinRM and WinRS

The last two management improvements we want to cover are WinRM and WinRS. WinRM is shorthand for Windows Remote Management. WinRM is an interface to WMI, much like VBScript. WinRM is a Web service, allowing access to WMI through Web clients over port 80 or 443. This capability allows for a wider variety of clients that can be used, and makes it firewall friendly, which strikes a good balance between network security and functionality. WinRM uses XML data that makes it easy to consume by a variety of clients. As an end user, you probably will not interact with WinRM itself, but you may use clients that take advantage of it. You can use the `winrm.exe` command line executable to configure aspects of WinRM. `Winrm /?` used at a Command Prompt will show you what options you can configure. WinRM is installed, but not enabled by default in Windows Server 2008. From a security standpoint, this is a good idea. To see if WinRM is enabled on your server, execute `winrm enumerate winrm/config/listener` at a Command Prompt. If nothing is returned, a listener is not configured. You can use `winrm quickconfig` to enable WinRM. Figure 13.38 shows how things look before and after you enable WinRM.

Now WinRM is ready to accept requests from remote clients.

WinRS is one of the WinRM clients you may find yourself using. If you have ever used Sysinternals' PSExec, you are already familiar with the concept. WinRS stands for Windows Remote Shell and can be used to execute commands on remote machines. You will need WinRM enabled and configured on both the client and the server to use WinRS. If both machines are in the same domain, WinRS will be able to connect. If the machines are in a workgroup, you will need to add them to each other's trusted clients list. This is done with the following `winrm` command:

```
winrm set winrm/config/client @{TrustedHosts="stockholm"}
```

This was run on the orlando2 server. A similar command was run on the Stockholm server trusting orlando2. Once that is configured, you can use WinRS run commands remotely. While you can run individual commands, you can also just open up a Command Prompt on the remote machine. Figure 13.39 shows a remote Command Prompt on orlando2 from Stockholm using WinRS.

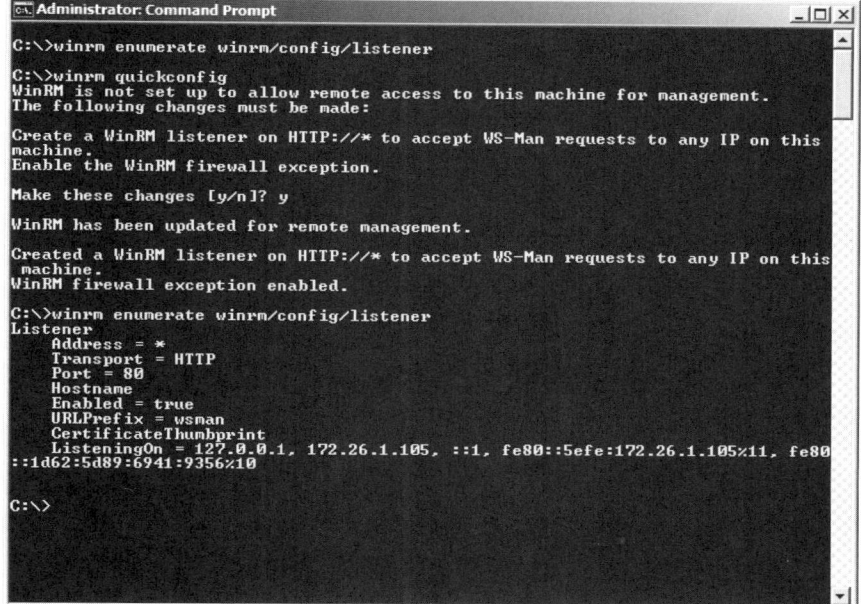

FIGURE 13.38
Enable WinRM.

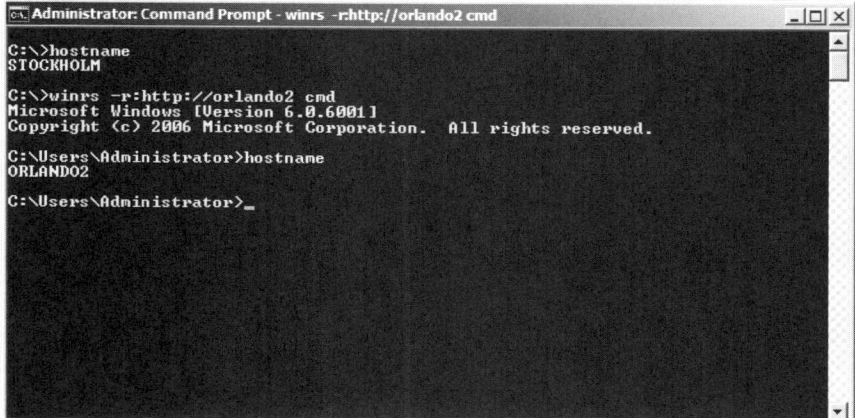

FIGURE 13.39
Remote Command Prompt.

From here, you can install new Roles with `Servermanagercmd.exe` or manipulate tasks with `schtasks.exe`. As this chapter has shown, Windows Server 2008 has added even more command line support, making tools like WinRS more useful than ever before and a great management tool.

SECURITY IMPROVEMENTS

Each successive version of Windows makes security improvements, and Windows Server 2008 is no exception. While there are numerous security improvements to mention, there are two that are of particular interest to SharePoint administrators: IIS and the improved firewall.

IIS

Earlier in this chapter we walked through some of the management improvements in IIS. That is not the only area where IIS was improved. IIS also benefitted from Microsoft's commitment to improving security. In this section, we will cover some of the security improvements made to IIS.

Minimal Install

In previous sections, we have covered various aspects of Windows Server 2008's improved security model. Microsoft has definitely changed its stance from "easy to use" to "painfully secure." A minimal amount of services are installed and enabled in Windows Server 2008, removing as many attack vectors as possible. IIS benefits from this as well. IIS 7 introduces a new modular design that allows administrators to only turn on the functionality they want to use. As your functionality needs change, you can add and remove modules as necessary. This is done through our old friend Server Manager or its slimmer counterpart, `servermanagercmd.exe`. You can add to IIS's functionality by adding or removing Role Services from the Web Server Role. In the case of SharePoint, it is best to let SharePoint install and configure IIS because it will install all the Role Services it needs.

If you did want to add additional Role Services, simply open up Server Manager and select the Web Server Role. The bottom of the middle pane shows the Role Services that are currently installed. Click the Add Role Services link in the right pane to add additional functionality. Alternately, you can use `servermanagercmd.exe` to install new Role Services. Use `servermanagercmd.exe` –q to query the Role Services and to see which ones are installed. Each Role Service has a shortened name that can be used at the Command Prompt. This name is shown in brackets after the full name. You can see it when installing new Role Services with `servermanagercmd.exe`. You can use the following command to install the Basic Authentication Role Service:

```
servermanagercmd -install Web-Basic-Auth
```

This modular design allows you to only expose what you need in IIS.

URLScan

URLScan is also built into IIS 7, which lets you filter requests before they get to the rendering engine and cause trouble. In the past if you wanted to take advantage of this functionality, you had to download URLScan separately. In IIS 7 the functionality is built in as the Request Filtering Role Service. To configure how URLs are filtered, use IIS 7's command line administrative tool `appcmd.exe`, found in the `%windir%\system32\inetsrv` directory. As with most Command Line tools, passing `appcmd.exe /?` will give you its usage. It is used to configure many aspects of IIS, so much of it is not germane to Request Filtering. To see the current settings, run `appcmd.exe list config`. That output is quite verbose, so we recommend piping it to an XML file and reading it that way. If you do that you can search for the `requestFiltering` section and see what the current settings are. If you want to change them, use the `set` command along with the `config` object. To disable high-bit characters in URLs, you would use the following command:

```
appcmd set config /section:requestfiltering
/allowhighbitcharacters:false
```

The change takes place immediately. This gives you a great deal of control if an exploit comes out.

Windows Firewall

The Windows Firewall has also been improved in Windows Server 2008. It has been improved enough that Microsoft gave it a new name: Windows Firewall with Advanced Security. What does this mean for the SharePoint administrator? First, the UI is improved. It uses the standard three-pane MMC format that we have all grown to know and love. This means it is easier to use. Microsoft has also combined the Firewall with the configuration for IPSec into this interface. In earlier versions of Windows, these were in different tools, which made it difficult to know which tool to use for which purpose. Now it is all together. The Firewall is also bidirectional now. Previous versions of the Windows Firewall only protected against inbound traffic. In Windows 2008, you can now also filter outgoing traffic. Finally, the rule set is much more flexible and will automatically create rules when you add new Roles and Features. If you are using the Windows Firewall, it will automatically open up the appropriate ports when you install IIS and SharePoint.

As you are designing the security policies for your SharePoint servers, investigate whether adding the new Windows Firewall to your servers makes sense.

PERFORMANCE

Microsoft has made more improvements to the network stack in Windows Server 2008. The ones that are of interest to SharePoint administrators fall into two categories: improvements to TCP/IP and SMB.

TCP/IP Optimization

As your clients are requesting Web pages from SharePoint on a Windows Server 2008 server, their network traffic is getting a shot in the arm from one of Windows' new network optimizations, called "CTCP" (Compound TCP) or the "TCP/IP Sliding Window." In TCP/IP, the Window is the number of packets a host can send before getting an acknowledgement from the client. Normally, a host sends a number of packets, waits for an acknowledgment, and then sends more packets. Both Windows Vista and Windows Server 2008 support sliding windows through CTCP. This means that they can adjust the number of packets sent before an acknowledgement. They make this adjustment on the fly based on the network speed and latency. It allows them to make more efficient use of available network bandwidth. Since this is at the TCP/IP level, HTTP and HTTP's traffic is able to take advantage of it, so long as it is enabled on both the client and the server. CTCP is turned on by default in Windows Server 2008, but not in Windows Vista. To enable CTCP, run this command:

```
netsh interface tcp set global congestionprovider=ctcp
```

To disable it, run this command:

```
netsh interface tcp set global congestionprovider=none
```

You may be asking yourself, "If this is so great, why would you want to disable it?" Some routers and firewalls do not play nicely when you modify the TCP Window size, so you may need to disable it at the request of your network staff.

Windows Server 2008 also supports offloading some TCP handling to hardware cards. If you have a high-traffic server, this could be used to improve performance since it takes some load off your CPU.

SMB 2.0

SMB has also gotten an upgrade in Windows Server 2008. SMB 2.0 boasts the following improvements over SMB 1.0:

- Support for multiple SMB commands in a single packet, reducing the number of packets sent between a client and server
- Larger buffer support than SMB 1.0
- Support for symbolic links
- Support for durable handles that are more tolerant of network interruptions
- Limits have been raised, including the number of concurrent connections a server can have open at once

SMB also now supports offloading requests to multiple processors. Previous versions of SMB could only use one processor to handle the incoming requests. With multiple processor machines commonplace, this is an easy way to gain some performance. This first debuted in Windows 2003, but it did not work very well. It is ready for prime time in Windows Server 2008.

While none of these help SharePoint's core business of serving up Web pages, they do help in management and tasks like moving index files around. Every little bit helps.

OTHER CHANGES IN WINDOWS SERVER 2008

While there have been many great additions in Windows Server 2008, we must also say good-bye to some old friends that did not make the cut. The biggest exclusion is Windows Backup. The `ntbackup.exe` that has existed in Windows since the days of NT is gone. It is replaced by a Vista-style backup tool. It has a few limitations that are worth noting. It does not support specifying individual files or folders. It only does full disk backups. It also does not support any tape devices; it only writes to file systems. It is also not Exchange Server aware, so it cannot be used to back up any Exchange objects. To get all this functionality back, you will need to purchase another backup solution. Microsoft's Data Protection Manager (DPM) fills in these gaps and is SharePoint aware.

The POP3 server that existed in Windows Server 2003 is also gone. There is no replacement for it. The SMTP server has been moved out of IIS and is now its own Feature.

WHAT IF I HAVE WINDOWS SERVER 2003?

There is a supported upgrade path from Windows Server 2003. You will need to be running SP1 for Windows Server 2003. If you have any databases running on Windows Server 2003, like SQL Embedded, you should make sure they are also patched to a level that supports Windows Server 2008. Once that is all taken care of, run the Windows Server 2008 install and choose the upgrade. We also recommend making very good backups. The upgrade procedure is solid, but as with any change, you should have backups.

WINDOWS SERVER 2008 RESOURCES

Windows Server 2008 is a big change from Windows Server 2003, and it deserves diligent research before you roll it out. Microsoft has a SharePoint on Windows Server 2008 Resource Center that is a good starting point. You can find it at http://technet.microsoft.com/en-us/office/sharepointserver/bb735844.aspx. It is full of resources, and it has an excellent case study from AMD. It also covers upgrading to 64 bit, which is something all SharePoint 2007 environments should be working toward. Check it out before you roll Windows Server 2008 out in production.

SQL Server 2008

Most of this chapter has been on Windows Server 2008 and the improvements it has that pertain to SharePoint administrators. Windows was not the only platform to benefit from a major upgrade in 2008. Microsoft released SQL Server 2008 as well. Like Windows Server, SQL Server is one of the building blocks of SharePoint, and its new version has a few features that should be of interest to SharePoint administrators. We will spend a few pages showing a couple of them.

MANAGEMENT

SQL Server saw improvements in many areas, management being one of them. Many of these improvements can be used by SharePoint administrators.

Mirroring

Database mirroring is a common approach to SharePoint disaster recovery. It keeps a frequently updated copy of your databases on another server. If you should experience a server or facility failure, your databases are safe and sound on a different server. Database mirroring works very well in SQL Server 2005, and it works even better in SQL Server 2008. One of the biggest improvements is the compression of the log files by the principal as they are sent to the mirror. This reduces network utilization and the time it takes for the logs to get to their destination. Mirror pairs can also recover from some types of data corruption by requesting fresh copies of the corrupted pages. Much like the sliding TCP windows mentioned previously, mirroring now supports asynchronous log file writes. This shortens the time it takes for log files to be written because it allows the principal to send log files without waiting for an acknowledgment from the mirrors. Finally, 10 additional Performance Counters have been added that deal with mirroring. They allow for easier troubleshooting when problems do arise.

Compressed Backups

As mentioned in the "Mirroring" section, SQL now supports native compression. This compression can be used for logs in mirroring or for regular backups. Before you get too excited, this feature is only available in the Enterprise version of SQL Server 2008. If you have the Enterprise SKU, you can choose to compress your databases or transaction logs when they are backed up. The amount of compression you will see depends on the type of objects you have in your databases. Your SharePoint ConfigDB will probably not compress much. If it is large, that is probably from the Solution store, which is already compressed. Your ContentDBs will compress well, depending on the type of documents your users have uploaded. If you have documents that compress well, like text files, your databases will compress well. If you have documents that are already compressed, like Office 2007 documents, you might not see as dramatic of gains.

You can specify whether a particular backup is compressed when you define it. Figure 13.40 shows how you compress a backup in the UI.

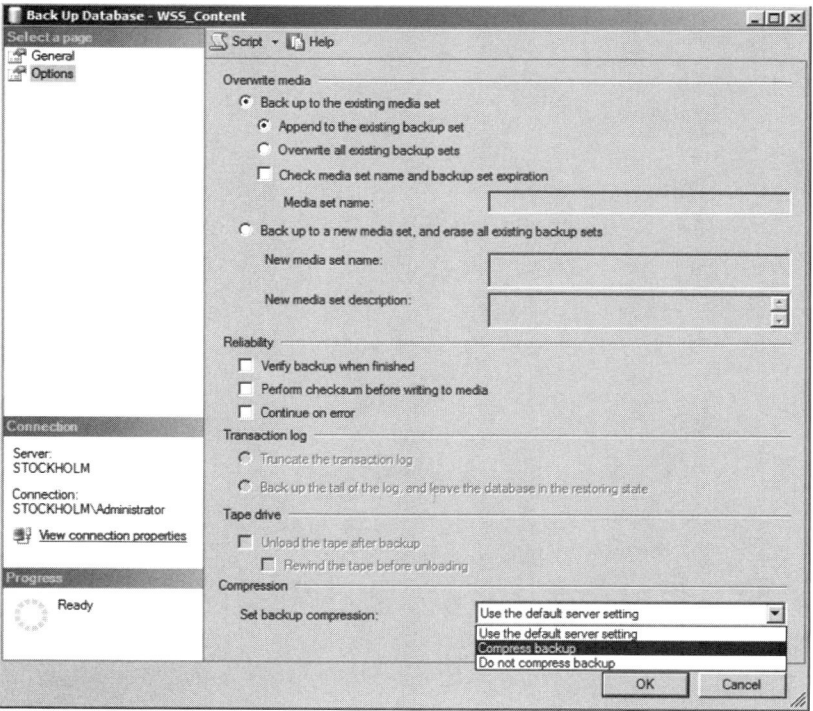

FIGURE 13.40
Compress a backup in the UI.

If you choose to do your backups in Transact-SQL, you can use the COMPRESSION keyword to compress the backup. Here is the TSQL script to do the same backup in Figure 13.40.

```
BACKUP DATABASE [WSS_Content] TO DISK = N'C:\Program Files\Microsoft
SQL Server\MSSQL10.MSSQLSERVER\MSSQL\Backup\WSS_Content.bak' WITH
NOFORMAT, NOINIT,  NAME = N'WSS_Content-Full Database Backup', SKIP,
NOREWIND, NOUNLOAD, COMPRESSION, STATS = 10
```

This will back up the database and compress it. That is all there is to it. If you would like, you can also set the server default to compress backups. This is set on the server's properties. In Management Studio, right-click the server and select Properties. On the Properties page, go to the Database Settings page. Check the Compress backup check box, as shown in Figure 13.41.

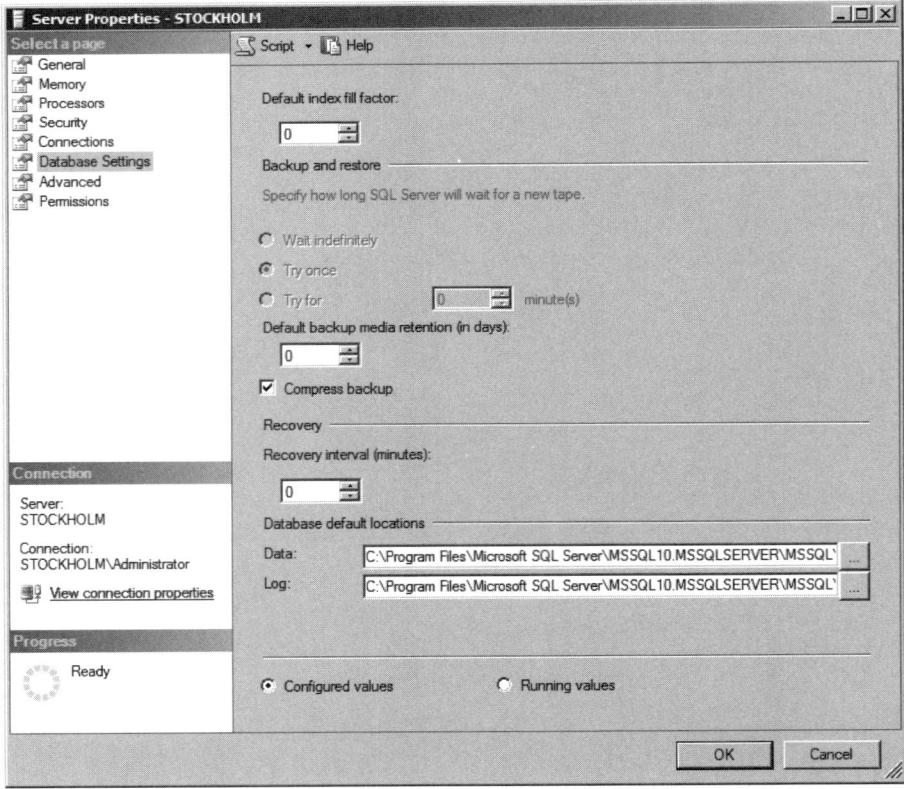

FIGURE 13.41
Set compression at the Server level.

By default, a backup job uses the server's compression setting, so this setting can save you a lot of time. There is another benefit to using this for SharePoint administrators. One part of the farm-level backups done in Central Admin is dumps of all of the databases. These are done by executing backups on the SQL server itself. If you set the server default to use compression, then your SharePoint backups automatically get compressed as well. It is a pretty nice feature if you already have Enterprise. If you do not have the Enterprise SKU, there are several third parties that offer the same functionality for the other versions of SQL.

The benefits to compressing your backups are twofold. The first is obvious: your backup files will take up less space. The second is less obvious: your backups will use less I/O because the file sizes are smaller. This could remove a bottleneck from your system if I/O is the problem.

Resource Governor

On the heels of compression is the Resource Governor. This is a new feature of SQL that allows for the restriction of the amount of RAM or CPU that a given procedure can use. This could be used to make sure that compression of the database backups does not negatively impact your server. The process for configuring the Resource Governor is lengthy, so we will not walk through it here. From a high level, there are three steps involved. First, you need to create a Resource Pool. A Resource Pool is how you define the CPU and memory limits for a given process. SQL creates two when it is installed, internal and default, but you can also define your own. After your Resource Pools are defined, you need to define Workload Groups. Workload groups are the bridge between your process and the Resource Pool. They act as containers for the processes, and they are assigned to Resource Pools. Again, SQL creates two Workload Groups when it is installed, internal and default, but you are allowed to create your own. Workload Groups that are user-assigned can be moved from one Resource Pool to another as needed.

The final piece of this puzzle is Classifications. Classifications are the criteria SQL uses to determine in which Workload Group to place the process. The classification is done by a user-defined classifier function that is included in the query being run. The return value of this function is how SQL determines which Workload Group is correct.

This may sound complicated, and it is. Fortunately, the SQL Server 2008 help files have a walk-through for creating all the necessary code to put compressed backup jobs into their own Resource Group. You can use that as a foundation for writing your own queries and processes.

PowerShell

The final management addition to SQL Server 2008 that we want to cover is PowerShell. SQL Server 2008 includes full integration with PowerShell. You can use PowerShell cmdlets to work with SQL objects in Management Studio or PowerShell itself. A SQL PowerShell provider exposes the SQL hierarchy to PowerShell, allowing access to it similar to the Windows File System with the SQL: drive. Right-clicking an object like a database or security object includes a PowerShell option that opens that object in PowerShell. You can use PowerShell for regular SQL queries, as well as jobs run by the SQL Agent. This allows you to leverage your PowerShell skills in SQL scripts, as well as in SharePoint and Windows.

TRANSPARENT DATA ENCRYPTION

There are many security improvements to SQL Server 2008, but one is of particular interest to SharePoint administrators. Transparent Data Encryption (TDE) allows for the encryption of your SQL database files and logs on the physical media. This can protect your data in the case of stolen drives. It uses an encryption key to encrypt and decrypt the MDF and LDF files, which allows usage of the databases while SQL is running, but renders them useless if the drives are removed from the machine. SQL can use a domain certificate if one exists, or it can generate its own. The encryption is done at the database engine level, so the data files, transaction logs, snapshots, and backups are all protected. In the case of snapshots and backups, the certificate must be in place before they can be restored. Existing transaction logs will not be rewritten encrypted, and new transactions will not be encrypted until a new virtual log file (VLF) is created. When that is done, a new header is written and subsequent logs will be encrypted. Since it is used for temporary transactions if any database on the server is encrypted, tempdb gets encrypted as well.

SQL decrypts the individual data pages as it reads them into memory. This means the data exists in the clear in the server's memory. Subsequently, it may exist unencrypted in the pagefile, or a hibernation file, if hibernation is enabled on your server. You can disable pagefile creation in the OS. That will protect your data from being written in the clear, but you will suffer a performance penalty because Windows will not be able to page out unused information.

Encrypting a database is done through Management Studio. Right-click the database and choose Tasks, Manage Database Encryption, as shown in Figure 13.42.

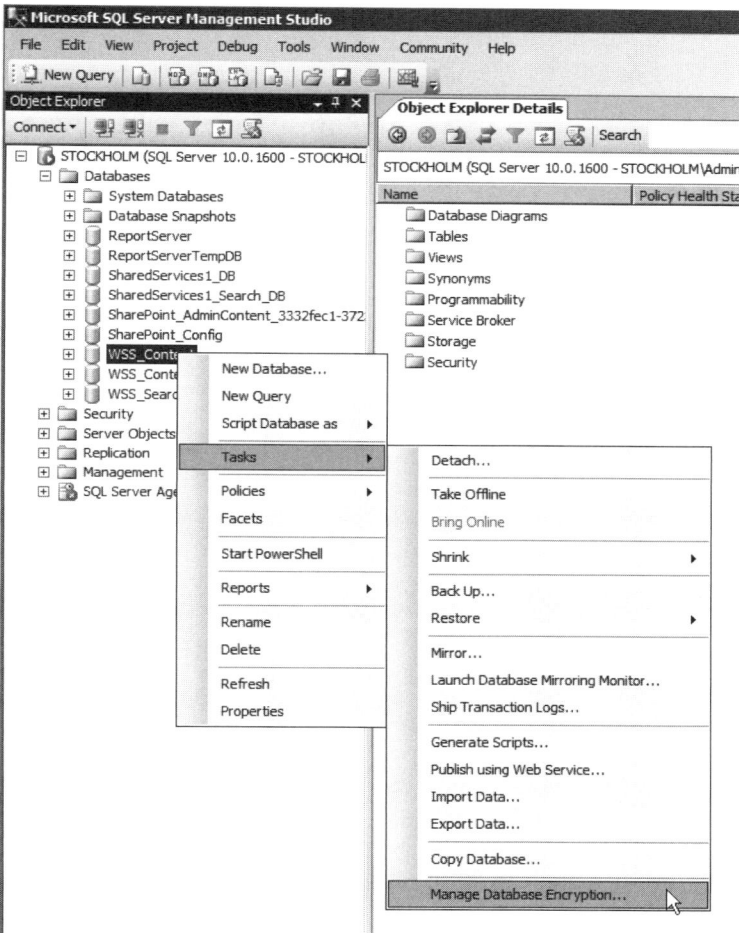

FIGURE 13.42
Encrypt a database.

Clicking that opens up the Manage Database Encryption dialog box. There really is not a lot to configure. Choose an algorithm, a certificate, and turn encryption on. Figure 13.43 shows a SQL certificate being used to encrypt a database.

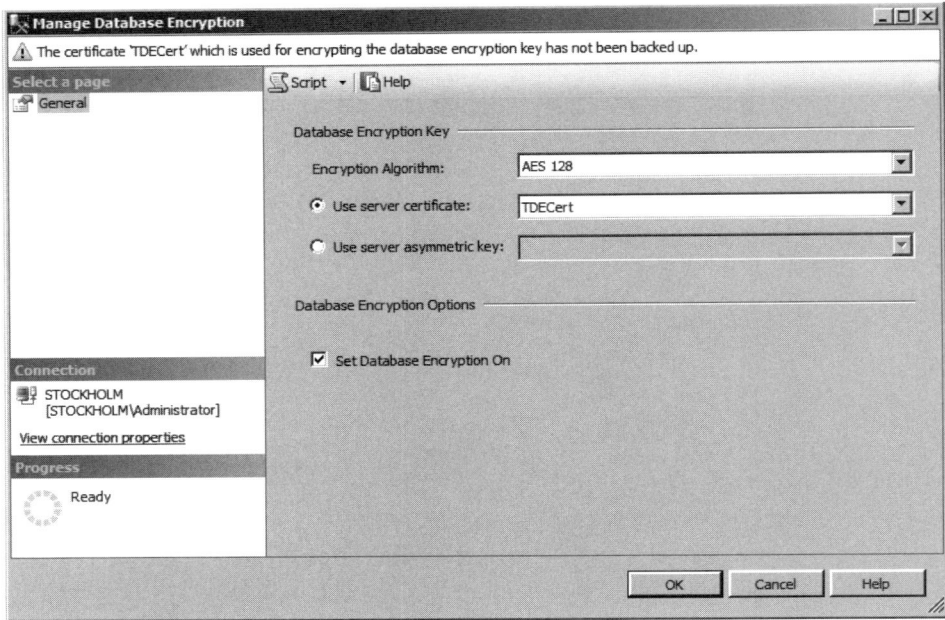

FIGURE 13.43
Assign a certificate.

Click OK, that is all there is to it. SQL will encrypt your database in the background while you work.

Since this encryption and decryption is done at the database engine level, applications like SharePoint are completely unaware of it. That means there are no configuration changes that need to be done in SharePoint if you want to take advantage of it.

About That SQL Certificate

If you do not have a certificate authority in your domain, how can you take advantage of TDE? You can create a certificate in SQL Server itself and use that, as we did in Figure 13.43. Creating that certificate was a two-step process. First, we created a Master Key, which is used to create the certificates. We used the following query to create it:

```
USE master;
CREATE MASTER KEY
ENCRYPTION BY PASSWORD = 'Pass@word1';
GO
```

After the Master Key is created, we can create a certificate off it. We used this query to do that:

```
USE master;
CREATE CERTIFICATE TDECert
WITH SUBJECT = 'SharePoint Certificate'
GO
```

After that is finished, the TDECert will show up in the Master database under Security > Certificates. It can now be used for TDE. Of course, this method should only be used in test environments. If you want to use TDE in production, you should use stronger certificates.

While TDE is pretty amazing, it does have a few drawbacks. For one, it is only offered in the Enterprise SQL Server SKU. Also, since the encryption and decryption is going in real time, it does take CPU cycles and there is a performance penalty. Microsoft estimates that penalty to be 3–5 percent.

Another thing to keep in mind is that TDE is not used to control access. Anyone who has access to the database before TDE is enabled will have access to it afterward. Finally, if databases take advantage of the Filestream datatype, those files will not be encrypted, since they are not part of the database itself.

14

Administrating SharePoint 2007 with PowerShell

In This Chapter

- Introduction to PowerShell
- Installing PowerShell
- PowerShell Commands
- Using PowerShell Cmdlets
- PowerShell Scripts
- PowerShell and SharePoint

INTRODUCTION TO POWERSHELL

STSADM is the hard-core administrator's Command Line tool for SharePoint. As we showed in the previous chapter, there are too many STSADM operations to demonstrate in a single chapter, and PowerShell will be no different. Administrators feel comfortable with the STSADM utility because it is similar to batch file scripting. We use STSADM to script out many of the repeatable tasks we have to do as administrators. At times we find that STSADM does not provide the operation we need. Sometimes we want to chain many of these commands together to form a larger repeatable process. For this we reach for Microsoft's newest command-line scripting environment, PowerShell. This chapter will introduce Microsoft PowerShell and how you can create reusable scripts to administer your SharePoint environment. PowerShell is much bigger than a single chapter in a book and to be very honest, PowerShell and SharePoint is a new concept. This chapter cannot possibly be an all-inclusive overview of PowerShell and SharePoint, but we can certainly get you started in the right direction. If you want to really impress your neighbors and friends and have some really great party conversation starters, read on!

PowerShell is Microsoft's newest command-line scripting environment. You are probably wondering why we need another Command Line tool. PowerShell is different from STSADM—way different. STSADM has a large but finite list of supplied operations. It can be extended with new operations, but that requires a developer to write them. Why rely on those developers when you can take matters into your own hands?

PowerShell is different. PowerShell is a generic scripting and command-line environment tightly integrated with Microsoft's .NET Framework and relying heavily on objects. Objects are normally the tools of developers, but administrators have been using them for a long time whether they realize it or not. ADSI, WMI, VBScript, and CScript all make use of objects.

For SharePoint administrators, the reliance on objects can be good or bad. It is good or even great for administrators because PowerShell, the .Net Framework and objects, and more specifically the SharePoint object provide practically unlimited scripting access to SharePoint without requiring compiled code. It is bad for administrators for similar reasons. We need to start working with another scripting language and a new object model. PowerShell shipped after MOSS 2007 and WSS 3 were well into development, so therefore there is no out-of-the-box SharePoint functionality. Since PowerShell can access and use .Net objects, PowerShell can easily access SharePoint objects.

The last bit of information you need to know is that PowerShell does not come installed. You must install it before the first use and when working with SharePoint Object Model, you must install PowerShell on the SharePoint server. The current version of PowerShell (version 1.0) and SharePoint APIs do not remote. This means that we cannot run our SharePoint/PowerShell scripts on a client; we must run them on the SharePoint server itself, like STSADM. Using SharePoint Web services with PowerShell would be one way around this, but that is outside the scope of this book.

INSTALLING POWERSHELL

You need to install PowerShell before you can start to create and use scripts. STSADM is included with SharePoint, but PowerShell is not. And to make it more interesting, the version for PowerShell and how you install PowerShell really depend on which platform you will be installing PowerShell on (XP, Vista, Windows Server 2003, and Windows Server 2008). It is a simple install once you have the correct package for the operating system you are using. Since we are planning on accessing the SharePoint object model, we will only be interested in Windows Server 2003 or Windows Server 2008.

To install PowerShell on Windows Server 2003, you will need to download and run the correct PowerShell install file. The install file can be found in the Microsoft Download Center by searching for PowerShell. Make sure that you download the correct install file for Windows Server 2003, because there are downloads for x86 and x64, as well as different languages. After you have the correct install file on the SharePoint server, it is a simple install, and you should be ready to go.

Installing PowerShell on Windows Server 2008 is slightly different; there is no installation file to download. Windows Server 2008 includes PowerShell as an installable Windows Server 2008 Feature. This means that you can install it from the Server Manager Screen. It does not install by default. To install PowerShell as a Windows Server 2008 Feature, navigate to the Server Manager utility and install it, as shown in Figure 14.1.

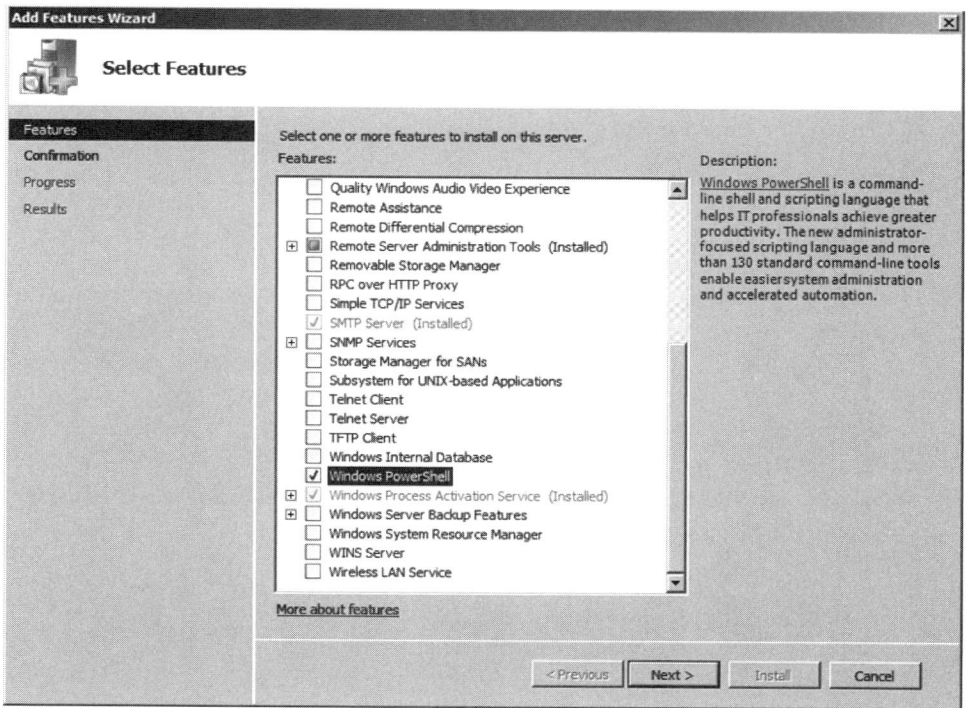

FIGURE 14.1

Install PowerShell on Windows Server 2008.

From this point on, it should not matter if you are using PowerShell on Windows Server 2003 or Windows Server 2008, other than the fact that Windows Server 2008 is newer and cooler.

PowerShell Commands

PowerShell is powered by commands. Commands get things done. There are four basic types of commands. They are cmdlets, functions, scripts, and native. You do not have to really know the differences between the command types to work with PowerShell, but it does not hurt either. For someone just starting out with PowerShell, you can find a wealth of general information at http://www.microsoft.com/powershell.

Cmdlets

Cmdlets (pronounced command-lets) are compiled commands that are registered with PowerShell. Cmdlets have a very predictable naming convention. All cmdlets are named using the format: verb-noun. Generally the verb portion of the name is a well-known verb such as Get, Set, or Remove. An example of a cmdlet is `Get-Process`. Figure 14.2 shows its output. There is also a `Stop-Process`. Notice the verb-noun naming convention. These cmdlets are installed and registered with PowerShell when you install PowerShell. You can create custom cmdlets and register them with PowerShell, but that is the realm of developers in the organization, so we will not be covering custom cmdlet development.

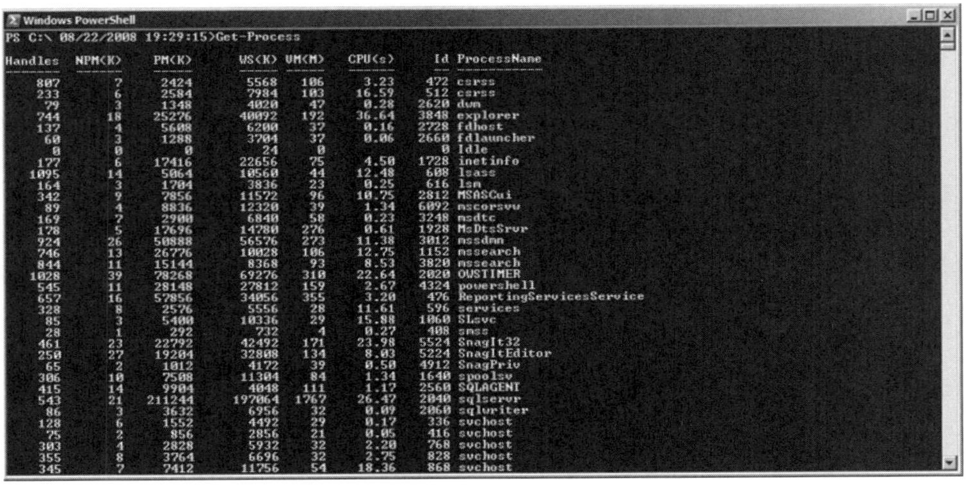

```
Windows PowerShell
PS C:\ 08/22/2008 19:29:15>Get-Process

Handles  NPM(K)    PM(K)      WS(K) VM(M)   CPU(s)     Id ProcessName
-------  ------    -----      ----- -----   ------     -- -----------
    807       7     2424       5568   106     3.23    472 csrss
    233       6     2584       7984   103    16.59    512 csrss
     79       3     1348       4020    47     0.28   2620 dwm
    744      18    25276      40092   192    36.64   3848 explorer
    137       4     5608       6200    37     0.16   2728 fdhost
     60       3     1288       3704    37     0.06   2660 fdlauncher
      0       0        0         24     0               0 Idle
    177       6    17416      22656    75     4.50   1728 inetinfo
   1095      14     5064      10560    44    12.48    608 lsass
    164       3     1704       3836    23     0.25    616 lsm
    342       9     7856      11572    96    10.75   2812 MSASCui
     89       4     8836      12320    39     1.34   6092 mscorsvw
    169       7     2900       6840    58     0.23   3248 msdtc
    178       5    17696      14780   276     0.61   1928 MsDtsSrvr
    924      26    50888      56576   273    11.38   3012 mssdmn
    746      13    26776      10028   106    12.75   1152 mssearch
    844      11    15144       8368    93     8.53   3820 mssearch
   1028      39    78268      69276   310    22.64   2020 OWSTIMER
    545      11    28148      27812   159     2.67   4324 powershell
    657      16    57856      34056   355     3.20    476 ReportingServicesService
    328       8     2576       5556    28    11.61    596 services
     85       3     5400      10336    29    15.88   1060 SLsvc
     28       1      292        732     4     0.27    408 smss
    461      23    22792      42492   171    23.98   5524 SnagIt32
    250      27    19204      32808   134     8.03   5224 SnagItEditor
     65       2     1012       4172    39     0.50   4912 SnagPriv
    306      10     7508      11304    84     1.34   1640 spoolsv
    415      14     9904       4048   111     1.17   2560 SQLAGENT
    543      21   211244     197064  1767    26.47   2040 sqlservr
     86       3     3632       6956    32     0.09   2060 sqlwriter
    128       6     1552       4492    29     0.17    336 svchost
     75       2      856       2856    21     0.05    416 svchost
    303       4     2828       5932    32     2.20    768 svchost
    355       8     3764       6696    32     2.75    828 svchost
    345       7     7412      11756    54    18.36    868 svchost
```

FIGURE 14.2
`Get-Process` example.

FUNCTIONS

Functions contain one or more commands and can accept parameters that allow us to create reusable code. Functions can encapsulate multiple commands to accomplish tasks. Functions are typed into PowerShell and can be reused for the lifetime of the PowerShell session. Unless you add your functions to your profile, which will load during the PowerShell startup, the functions will be gone once you shut down PowerShell. A large, complex function lost at shutdown? Consider yourself warned to save the function to a profile or a text file so you can copy and paste next time. We will not worry much about functions in this book. Functions have their place in PowerShell, but in a single chapter about SharePoint administration, we will not have space to cover them. The function in Figure 14.3 demonstrates customizing the PowerShell Prompt.

FIGURE 14.3
Function example.

SCRIPTS

Scripts are what we are most interested in. Scripts are simply one or more commands that are saved to the file system and can be called from the PowerShell application. There is no big secret behind scripts; create these in your favorite text editor (Notepad, for example) and save them to the file system with a .PS1 extension. Later you can run the script by typing in the filename. In contrast to other commands, such as some cmdlets and functions, these commands survive the PowerShell shutdown and can easily be called and reused. Built-in cmdlets survive, but custom cmdlets do not unless they are included in a profile. The great benefit of the script is a script library. Once a script is created and tested, it can be saved there.

> **Stay Safe**
>
> For security reasons, the PowerShell application is not associated with .PS1 files. The default application associated with PowerShell is Notepad. Double-clicking a .PS1 file will result in it opening in Notepad. While you can change the file associations, you do run the risk of inadvertently running a malicious script.

NATIVE

Native commands are commands that run outside of the PowerShell process. An example of a native command is invoking Notepad to view a file. SharePoint administrators should learn to love native commands because one key native command is STSADM. You can leverage all that you learned about STSADM while working with PowerShell.

USING POWERSHELL CMDLETS

Now that you have an understanding of the components it uses, let's run a few simple examples to demonstrate basic PowerShell. We will start with the Get-Process cmdlet. It is by far the most common PowerShell example and is a good place to start.

Start up PowerShell on your SharePoint server. It will be under Start > Programs > Windows PowerShell 1.0. Notice how similar it looks to a cmd.exe console. Type Get-Process and press Enter. If you spelled the cmdlets correctly, PowerShell will display a list of processes running on your server, similar to those shown in Figure 14.2.

Anything You Can Do I Can Do Better

You may have noticed that we changed the prompt for PowerShell to be similar to the prompt we used in the command window for the STSADM chapter. Changing the PowerShell prompt is simple. Enter the following function in the PowerShell window:

```
Function prompt{ 'PS ' + $(Get-Location) + ' ' + $(Get-Date) + $(if
($nestedpromptlevel —gt 1) {'>>'} ) + '>'}
```

As mentioned earlier, the function will expire when you close your PowerShell window. If you want the change to be permanent, you will need to add it to your PowerShell profile.

Let us take a brief second to explain what happened. Get-Process is a PowerShell command, a cmdlet to be exact. It has the standard verb-noun syntax of a cmdlet. PowerShell executed the command and generated a list of process information. That in and of itself is not very impressive. Many of the interesting features included in PowerShell are practically transparent to the user. What really happened is that PowerShell executed the command, and a collection of process objects were created—one process object for each process and then the collection was passed to the next command. Because there was no other command, PowerShell sent the collection though a default format command and displayed the process information on the screen.

We mentioned multiple commands. Objects that are the resultant output of one command can be input for another command. In PowerShell terminology, these objects are "piped" from one command to another though the pipeline. To pipe objects to another command, simply use the pipe character "|". Figure 14.4 shows PowerShell executing Get-Process | Format-List ProcessName, ID. The `Format-List` command will display a list with the ProcessName and ID fields.

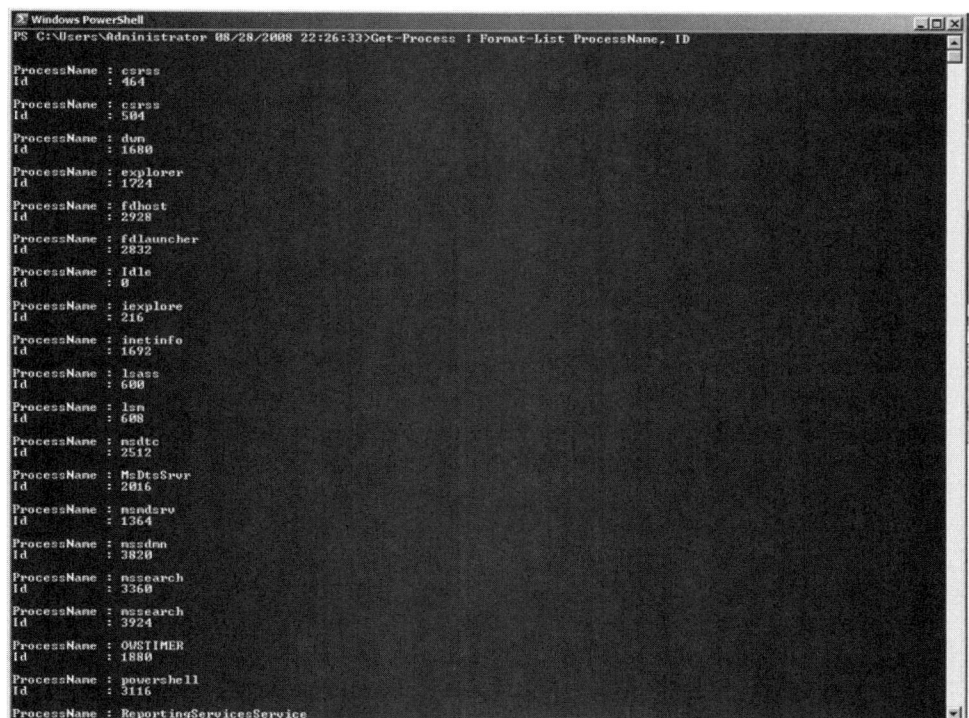

FIGURE 14.4
Pipe `Get-Process` through `Format-List`.

We can use three commands if we would like. Figure 14.5 adds the `Sort-Object` command to the mix.

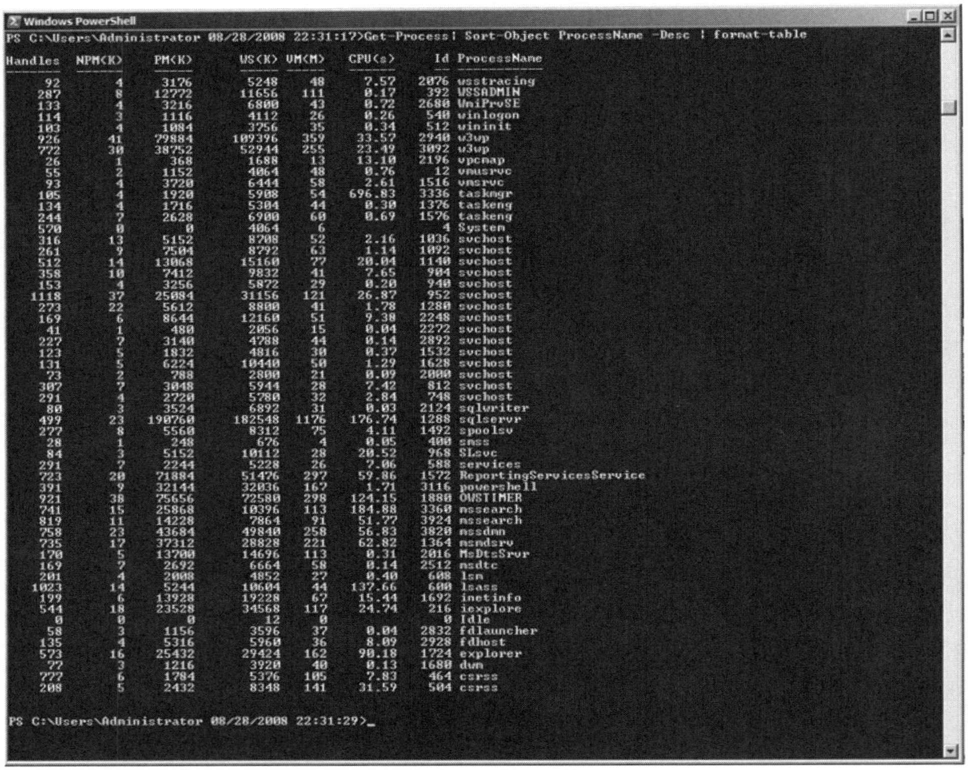

FIGURE 14.5
Pipe `Get-Process` through `Sort-Object` and `Format-List`.

> **Help!!!**
>
> Similar to the Help operation in STSADM, PowerShell cmdlets will display help information. Executing `Get-Help` will return a list of PowerShell commands (among other constructs) for us to look at. Executing `Get-Help Process` will display a list of commands with the word `Process` in the command. `Get-Help Get-Process` will display the specific help information for `Get-Process`, including syntax, parameters, and usage information.

POWERSHELL SCRIPTS

We might not be PowerShell experts just yet, but we do have a basic understanding of running one or more PowerShell commands. We can now turn our attention to another tool in our toolkit, Scripts. Scripts are simple—we can create, test, and save a set of commands and then rerun them as needed. There is nothing magical about scripts. We can take any of the previous examples and create a script.

We can easily create a script by simply opening Notepad and adding the following, like we did in Figure 14.6.

FIGURE 14.6
Create a PowerShell script in Notepad.

This script will return only those process objects that have a process name starting with win. The `Sort-Object` command will order the process objects by `ProcessName` in descending order. The token `$_` represents the current object in the pipeline, in this case, the current process object. The `Where-Object` is inspecting the ProcessName property of the current object to determine if it should continue on or be dropped from the pipeline. This script is a simple pattern that can be used with PowerShell to list various SharePoint objects. For example, it could be used to list all Webs where the port number is equal to 8088.

To use the script, save the file with a useful filename with the .PS1 extension. You will have to change the default extension in the Save dialog box to All Files, as we've done in Figure 14.7, or surround the filename with double-quotes to prevent Notepad from saving the file as a .txt file. This is also a good time to suggest a single folder that will contain all of your scripts. We generally create a folder under the root drive named PSScripts, although any folder will work.

All you have to do now is run the script. There is one minor problem: PowerShell does not run scripts by default. That seems strange except when you think about malicious scripts. As we mentioned many times in Chapter 13, Microsoft is tightening down on more things in the name of security. Loosening up the security policy to run PS1 files is pretty simple. PowerShell provides cmdlets to Get and Set the Execution-Policy. To check the current execution policy, execute the `Get-ExecutionPolicy` command. By default, it will return "Restricted," which means that you will not be allowed to execute your scripts without signing them first. To set the execution policy to be a little forgiving, use the following command: `Set-ExecutionPolicy RemoteSigned`. This will allow local scripts to be executed. Don't forget to use `Get-Help ExecutionPolicy` or `Get-Help Set-ExecutionPolicy` to learn more about these commands.

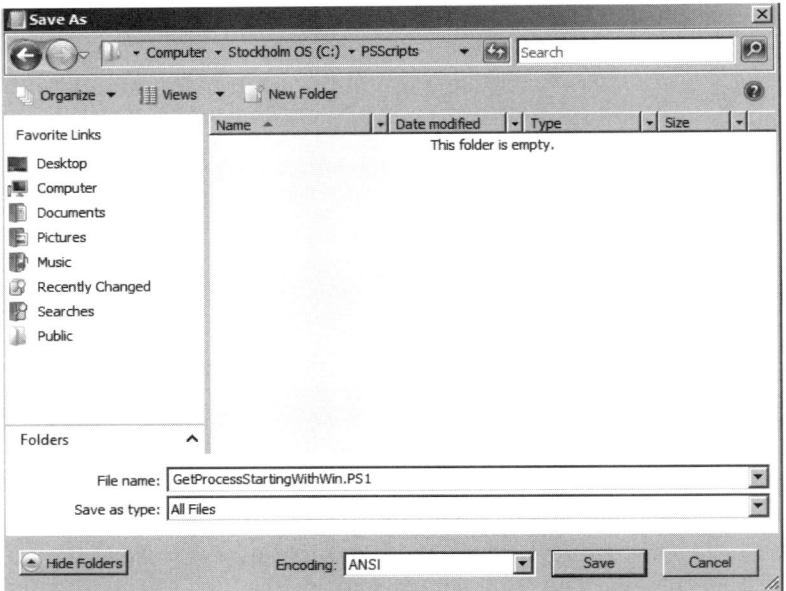

FIGURE 14.7
Save a PowerShell script.

Too Restricted to Reduce Restriction?

If PowerShell does not allow you to change your execution policy, try running Power-Shell as the administrator in Vista and Windows Server 2008. To run PowerShell as an administrator, right-click the PowerShell application icon on the Start button and select Run As Administrator.

The final part you need to run your scripts is to provide the full path to the script or to use the .\ token. Even if PowerShell is in the same directory as the scripts, PowerShell requires the use of the token before it will run the script. This is another security feature. It keeps you from accidentally running a PS1 file if it exists in the folder you are in. For instance, if there were a malicious script named cd.PS1, you would execute it instead of the built-in CD command if PowerShell did not require the .\ token. If the script is located in the PSScripts folder within the C drive and you named it `GetProcessesStartingWithWin.PS1`, then use the command `c:\PSScripts\GetProcessStartingWithWin.PS1`, like we did in Figure 14.8, to execute it.

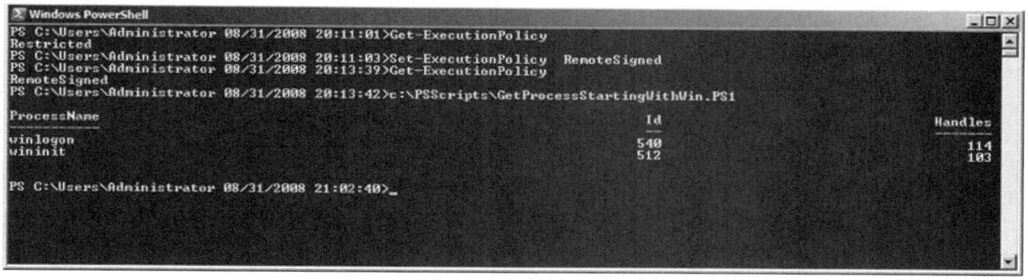

FIGURE 14.8
Run a PS1 script.

Now set your location to the PSScripts directory and try to run `Get-ProcessStartingWithWin.PS1`. To change to the PSScripts directory, use `Set-Location C:\PSScripts`. Attempting to run the `GetProcessStartingWithWin` script will fail, like it did in Figure 14.9. PowerShell will return an error message telling you that `Get-ProcessStartingWithWin` is not recognized as a cmdlet, function, operable program, or script file. The PowerShell team really covered their options with that message. Now use the .\ token before the script filename, and you should see the script run.

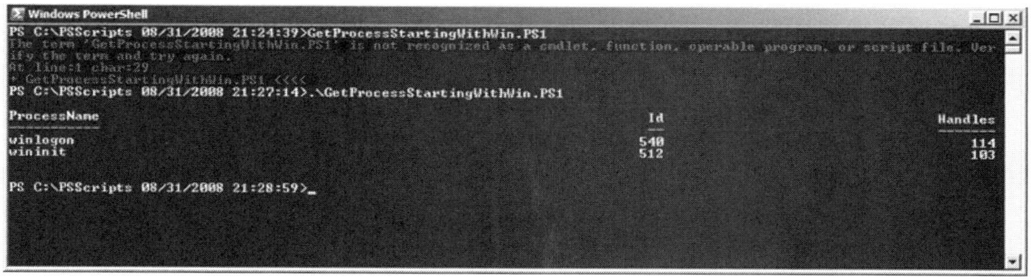

FIGURE 14.9
Run a PS1 script without ./.

That was a whirlwind PowerShell primer, but you did not buy this book to learn PowerShell. Instead of going further in depth with PowerShell, we are just going to jump in and create some SharePoint PowerShell scripts. As we do that, we will explain some key SharePoint and PowerShell points to help you get started.

POWERSHELL AND SHAREPOINT

Finally, the section that you really were interested in reading: How to work with SharePoint using PowerShell. This is a very wide-open topic and practically anything in SharePoint can be scripted. By anything, we mean anything that is accessible via the SharePoint Object model. This single chapter cannot possibly cover all areas of PowerShell and SharePoint integration, but we do plan on providing a good foundation for you to build on. In this section, we will show some basic scripts and SharePoint administrative functions using PowerShell.

POWERSHELL SETUP FOR SHAREPOINT

To script against the SharePoint Object Model, you need to do a little housekeeping first. PowerShell does not know about SharePoint. You need to make sure that PowerShell knows where to find the SharePoint objects so it can do all of your heavy work. Basically, you need to register the SharePoint assemblies (fancy developer names for DLLs) so that PowerShell can access them. The basic assembly that we will be using for this chapter is the Microsoft.SharePoint assembly.

There are many other SharePoint assemblies, depending on what you need to do. The SharePoint Software Development Kits (SDKs) is the best place to determine what assemblies contain which objects you are interested in. As a matter of fact, the SDKs contain a lot of demo code that you can use for your scripts. You can download the most recent SDK from the Microsoft Download Center. Since most of the objects we are interested in are included in the Microsoft.SharePoint assembly, we will stick with it. To register the Microsoft.SharePoint assembly with PowerShell, execute the following in PowerShell:

```
[Reflection.Assembly]::Load("Microsoft.SharePoint, Version=12.0.0.0,
Culture=neutral, PublicKeyToken=71e9bce111e9429c")
```

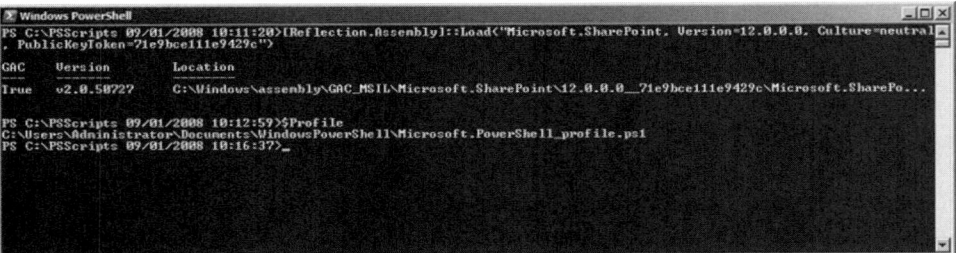

FIGURE 14.10
Load the SharePoint assemblies.

As in Figure 14.10, PowerShell will acknowledge that the assembly has been loaded, which means its objects are available for scripting by PowerShell. Every time you start PowerShell, you will need to register these assemblies if you plan on scripting with SharePoint. To save time and typing, we recommend placing that command in a PowerShell profile. Once in the profile, the command is executed when PowerShell starts. The quickest way to find your profile is to type $Profile into PowerShell. The $ character denotes a variable and $Profile variable contains the path to the current user's PowerShell profile. Simply create the PS1 file at the profile location, add the commands to load your library, and save. Restart Power-Shell, and the assemblies should be registered. If you choose not to include this command in your profile, you must remember to register the assembly each time you restart PowerShell.

WORKING WITH THE FARM

The farm is the top-most SharePoint administrator object and contains key properties and collections associated with the SharePoint Farm. The term "farm" can be confusing, especially in single-server environments. Do you need multiple servers to have a farm? You do not. In SharePoint parlance, a farm is any group of servers that all share the same Config database. Because of this, the farm object can provide the administrator with key information, such as the space needed for a backup, version, installed features, Web applications, servers, services and solutions, and upgrade status. Many administration scripts will use the farm object as a starting point to access other administration objects.

To access the farm, you must have the Microsoft.SharePoint assembly loaded already, and the commands or scripts must be run locally on the SharePoint server. There is no real need to create a script. We will use PowerShell in interactive mode. We type, it works. Here is the first joint PowerShell and SharePoint command:

```
[Microsoft.SharePoint.Administration.SPFarm]::Local
```

After you press the Enter key, you should see some text fly by on the screen. As you can see by the output, PowerShell found the local Farm object, SPFarm, and re-turned the farm object to the screen. Since this pipeline only had a single command, PowerShell formatted some of the properties to be displayed for the user. If you look closely at the farm information, you can see collections such as Services and Features Definitions and Solutions. You can also see properties such as the Build Version, Id, Name, and Status.

We can put the results into a variable for use later. $Farm seems like an obvious choice. Modify the command to look like this:

```
$Farm = [Microsoft.SharePoint.Administration.SPFarm]::Local
```

You might notice there is no screen dump of the farm object. That is because it was captured into a variable instead of going by default to the screen. The SPFarm object did not hit the end of the pipeline, and the default formatter was not used. Any PowerShell gurus reading this know that this is a simplistic explanation of the pipeline, but it will work for this chapter. Once we have it populated, we can dump the `$Farm` variable to the screen by simply typing the variable name into PowerShell and pressing the Enter key.

```
$Farm
```

If everything went well, the output should be the same as the output of the farm object itself. Figure 14.11 shows each of those commands and their output.

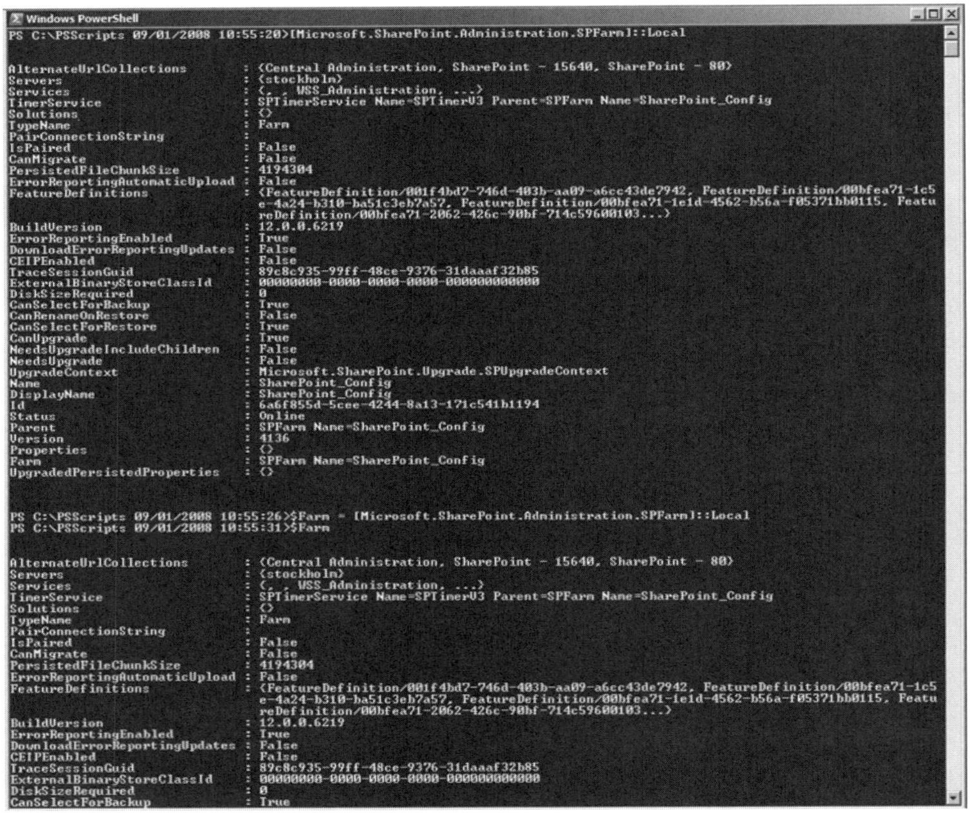

```
Windows PowerShell
PS C:\PSScripts 09/01/2008 10:55:20>[Microsoft.SharePoint.Administration.SPFarm]::Local

AlternateUrlCollections        : {Central Administration, SharePoint - 15640, SharePoint - 80}
Servers                        : {stockholm}
Services                       : {, , WSS_Administration, ...}
TimerService                   : SPTimerService Name=SPTimerV3 Parent=SPFarm Name=SharePoint_Config
Solutions                      : {}
TypeName                       : Farm
PairConnectionString           :
IsPaired                       : False
CanMigrate                     : False
PersistedFileChunkSize         : 4194304
ErrorReportingAutomaticUpload  : False
FeatureDefinitions             : {FeatureDefinition/001f4bd7-746d-403b-aa09-a6cc43de7942, FeatureDefinition/00bfea71-1c5
                                 e-4a24-b310-ba51c3eb7a57, FeatureDefinition/00bfea71-1e1d-4562-b56a-f05371bb0115, Featu
                                 reDefinition/00bfea71-2062-426c-90bf-714c59600103...}
BuildVersion                   : 12.0.0.6219
ErrorReportingEnabled          : True
DownloadErrorReportingUpdates  : False
CEIPEnabled                    : False
TraceSessionGuid               : 89c8c935-99ff-48ce-9376-31daaaf32b85
ExternalBinaryStoreClassId     : 00000000-0000-0000-0000-000000000000
DiskSizeRequired               : 0
CanSelectForBackup             : True
CanRenameOnRestore             : False
CanSelectForRestore            : True
CanUpgrade                     : True
NeedsUpgradeIncludeChildren    : False
NeedsUpgrade                   : False
UpgradeContext                 : Microsoft.SharePoint.Upgrade.SPUpgradeContext
Name                           : SharePoint_Config
DisplayName                    : SharePoint_Config
Id                             : 6a6f855d-5cee-4244-8a13-171c541b1194
Status                         : Online
Parent                         : SPFarm Name=SharePoint_Config
Version                        : 4136
Properties                     : {}
Farm                           : SPFarm Name=SharePoint_Config
UpgradedPersistedProperties    : {}


PS C:\PSScripts 09/01/2008 10:55:26>$Farm = [Microsoft.SharePoint.Administration.SPFarm]::Local
PS C:\PSScripts 09/01/2008 10:55:31>$Farm

AlternateUrlCollections        : {Central Administration, SharePoint - 15640, SharePoint - 80}
Servers                        : {stockholm}
Services                       : {, , WSS_Administration, ...}
TimerService                   : SPTimerService Name=SPTimerV3 Parent=SPFarm Name=SharePoint_Config
Solutions                      : {}
TypeName                       : Farm
PairConnectionString           :
IsPaired                       : False
CanMigrate                     : False
PersistedFileChunkSize         : 4194304
ErrorReportingAutomaticUpload  : False
FeatureDefinitions             : {FeatureDefinition/001f4bd7-746d-403b-aa09-a6cc43de7942, FeatureDefinition/00bfea71-1c5
                                 e-4a24-b310-ba51c3eb7a57, FeatureDefinition/00bfea71-1e1d-4562-b56a-f05371bb0115, Featu
                                 reDefinition/00bfea71-2062-426c-90bf-714c59600103...}
BuildVersion                   : 12.0.0.6219
ErrorReportingEnabled          : True
DownloadErrorReportingUpdates  : False
CEIPEnabled                    : False
TraceSessionGuid               : 89c8c935-99ff-48ce-9376-31daaaf32b85
ExternalBinaryStoreClassId     : 00000000-0000-0000-0000-000000000000
DiskSizeRequired               : 0
CanSelectForBackup             : True
```

FIGURE 14.11
Access `farm` properties with PowerShell.

As you can see in Figure 14.11, the farm object has many properties. You can access a single property by using dot notation. For instance, if you only wanted to see the `BuildVersion` property of the farm, you would execute the following command:

```
$Farm.BuildVersion
```

Figure 14.12 shows it in action.

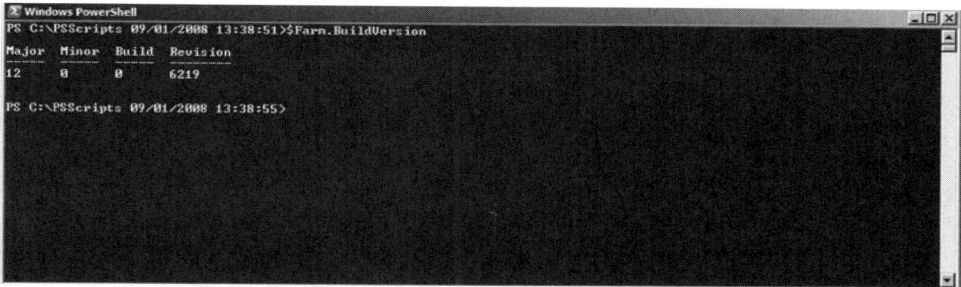

FIGURE 14.12
The `farm BuildVersion` property.

If your command was successful, you should have seen only the build version sent to the screen. We have just accessed the `SPFarm` object's `buildversion` property. We are practically thumbing our noses at all the compiled code developers out there. We can do that for all the properties of the `SPFarm` object. In the following sections, you will see us using the farm object's properties to list various SharePoint objects.

There are some methods on the `SPFarm` object that might be of interest to advanced users, but in general most scripts will get the local farm object to access other more interesting objects. Basically, we use this object as a parameter to get to other interesting SharePoint objects, such as Solutions and Feature definitions.

Moving Around

As you move around in PowerShell, you will find there are new ways to do things, and that is part of the learning curve of PowerShell. It uses the verb-noun approach, and does not have the 8.3 naming limitation that had been held over from the DOS days. To clear the screen in DOS, you used the `CLS` command. In PowerShell, the command is `Clear-Host`. Changing directories is different in PowerShell, too. PowerShell uses the command `Set-Location`, whereas DOS uses `CD`. These are just a couple of examples.

Take heart, though, some of the old ways still work, too. In the preceding examples, PowerShell will happily accept either `CD` or `CLS`, so you have some time to get accustomed to PowerShell and its wordiness.

WORKING WITH WEB APPLICATIONS

Every SharePoint site collection is associated with a Web Application. `SPWeb-Application` is the SharePoint object that we will use in scripting to get access to them. Probably the most common reason to use the `SPWebApplication` in a script is to list Web Applications and their properties. We can also create new Web Applications using the `SPWebApplicationBuilder` object. Why would you want to do that? This is a great way to script the creation of test environments or even production.

First, we should list all the Web Applications on the farm. The SharePoint object model contains many collections. To list all of the Web Applications, we need to get a list or collection of all the Web Services that run on SharePoint. These are not the same Web services that we associate with end points for developers. These are special services that SharePoint runs. The SharePoint object model contains many collections within collections, and there just happens to be a `SPWebServiceCollection`. We need the local farm variable to retrieve the collection of Web services. We can create a new SharePoint `SPWebServiceCollection` object and pass in the local `$Farm` variable. Once we have all the `SPWebServices` in a variable, we can simply look at each `SPWebService` and get all Web Applications. Here are the commands you would use to list the all Web applications in your farm:

```
$WebServices = New-Object
Microsoft.SharePoint.Administration.SPWebServiceCollection($Farm)
$WebApps = $WebServices | ForEach-Object{$_.WebApplications}
```

Feel free to let PowerShell format the Web Applications to the screen or catch it in a variable like we did.

We now have a collection of `SPWebApplication` objects in the `$WebApps` variable. Once we have them in a collection, we have a lot of options. If you want to see how many Web Application objects you have in your collection, you can use the following command:

```
$WebApps.Count
```

Figure 14.13 shows how to format this in a table to view what was returned from this command:

```
$WebApps | Format-Table ID, DisplayName, Status, DefaultServerComment,
RightsMaskt —auto
```

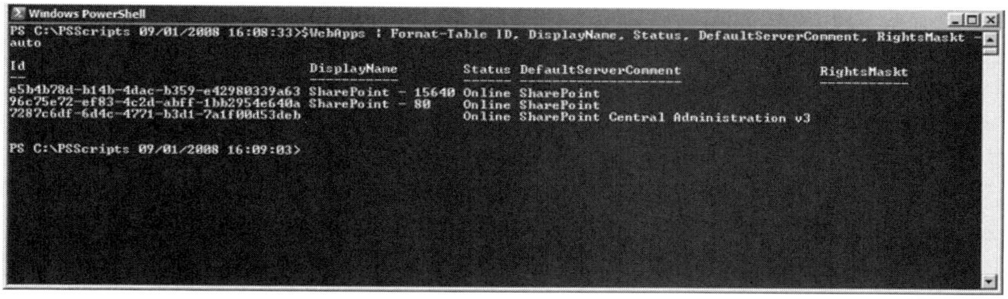

FIGURE 14.13
Format the output of the $WepApps variable.

If you want to know what kind of object a variable is storing, you can use the .NET Get-Type method. To use it with our existing variable do this:

```
$WebApps[0].GetType()
```

The output should tell you that the type name is SPWebApplication. The brackets and the 0 value denote the first object in the $WebApps collection. Another command to keep close by is Get-Member. Get-Member will display all the properties and functions of an object. To see all of the Methods and Properties of the first object in the $WebApps collection, use this command:

```
$WebApps[0] | Get-Member
```

The output of this command will probably cover more than a screen, as there are many Methods and Properties.

While we can see all of the Web Applications associated with a single farm, it would be useful to see which Web Application is associated with a specific URL. The following commands drill down to that.

```
$URI = New-Object  URI('http://localhost')
$SPWebApp =
[Microsoft.SharePoint.Administration.SPWebApplication]::LookUp($URI)
$SPWebApp
```

This series of commands creates a new URI, assigns it the value "http://localhost," looks for it in the Web Application collection, and assigns the related Web Application to the $SPWebApp variable. Then we output that variable.

We know how to deal with existing Web Applications, but what about creating new ones? This is also very easy with PowerShell. There is an object, `SPWebApplication-Builder`, which exists for just such an occasion. Here are the commands you would use to create a new Web Application with PowerShell.

```
$WebApplicationBuilder = New-Object
Microsoft.SharePoint.Administration.SPWebApplicationBuilder($Farm)
$WebApplicationBuilder.DataBaseName = 'TestDataBaseName'
$WebApplicationBuilder.CreateNewDataBase = $True
$WebApplicationBuilder.Port=8099
$WebApplicationBuilder.RootDirectory=
'c:\inetpub\wwwroot\WSS\VirtualDirectories\DemoSiteOnPort8099'
$WebApp = $WebApplicationBuilder.Create()
$WebApp.Provision()
```

We did not add any error checking, but assuming that you have the correct permissions, you will have created and provisioned a new Web application. If you have not noticed, you also ended up with the new `SPWebApp` in a variable and can perform further actions on it, such as create a site collection, which leads us to our next section.

WORKING WITH SITES

In Chapter 5, "Command Line Administration with STSADM," we looked at sites. Sites or site collections contain all the Web and subweb objects. In object model terms, sites collections are equivalent to `SPSite` objects. You can use PowerShell to list, create, and delete site collections. Along the way, you can edit and change site-level properties, and you can add new Webs to the site collection.

Let's start working with sites by listing all the site or site collections we have on the farm. To do this, we need to build on the examples we have already seen by getting a collection of Web applications and listing the sites that are contained in the Sites property. Here are the commands to list all sites (`SPSites`):

```
$Farm = [Microsoft.SharePoint.Administration.SPFarm]::Local
$WebServices = New-Object
Microsoft.SharePoint.Administration.SPWebServiceCollection($Farm)
$WebApps = $WebServices | ForEach-Object{$_.WebApplications}
$WebApps |ForEach-Object {$_.Sites} | Format-Table ID, URL, Owner
```

In this example, we need to integrate over various collections to get a complete list of sites on the farm. The `ForEach-Object` command will loop through each collection and execute the commands between the braces. The code surrounded by the braces is called a "script block." We are using the `$_` token, which represents the current object in the pipeline. The third command in this example captures the Web Applications from each Web Services object. It is accessing each Web Service object from the `$WebServices` variable and returning the WebApplications object. The fourth line in this example is retrieving the Site Collections (`SPSiteCollec-tion`), which contains all the site's objects from each Web application object.

Since we are working with PowerShell, we have the option to capture the results as objects in a variable or display our text on the screen. In this case, we are using `Format-Table` to list the ID, URL, and Owner information to the screen, as seen in Figure 14.14.

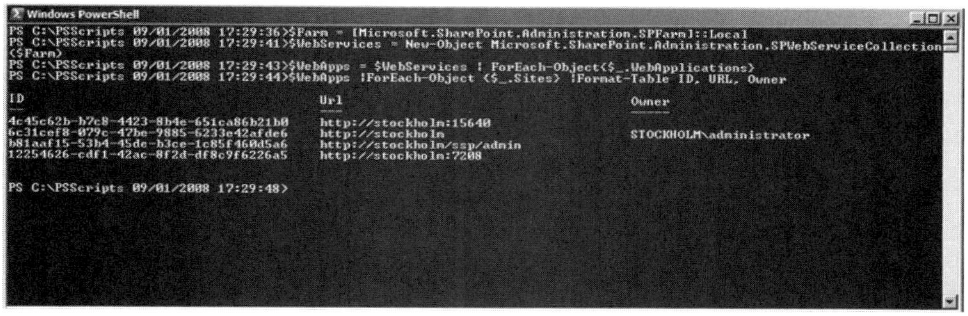

FIGURE 14.14
List Site Collections.

If you want to work with a single site and not list all sites, you have a few options. You can extend the previous set of commands to include a `Where-Object` command before you send the information to the screen. The `Where-Object` command will only pass objects through the pipeline if they meet the supplied criteria. To learn more about the `Where-Object` command, view the help function by using the `Get-Help Where-Object` command.

There is a second and more common method of accessing a specific site object when the site's URL is known. This method is cleaner, and it requires less typing.

```
$Site = New-Object Microsoft.SharePoint.SPSite('http://localhost')
```

A Cautionary Note

When working with objects, there is a concept called "disposing" that we need to be aware of with SPSite and SPWeb objects. Objects, particularly SPSite and SPWeb, are leaky. That is a developer term that means if not properly taken care of, these objects will not return all of the memory they are using to the OS when they are finished. Opening and not properly closing or disposing of these objects can cause errors or memory leaks. This does become somewhat complicated in PowerShell. Since PowerShell has a pipeline and objects may be used elsewhere, you cannot just dispose or close the objects without risking closing the object before it is done being used. If you are not passing the object back as a result into the pipeline, you should be safe in disposing SPSite or SPWeb. Microsoft has a white paper titled "Best Practices: Using Disposable Windows SharePoint Services Objects." It discusses leaky SharePoint objects and how to handle them. It can be found at http://msdn.microsoft.com/en-us/library/aa973248.aspx.

The $Site variable contains the SPSite object and can be used to change properties. Later in this chapter, we will demonstrate how to enumerate and add Features to a site using the SPSite object. To dispose of this SPSite object, simply call the Dispose method:

```
$Site.Dispose()
```

Like the STSADM utility, you can create a new site or delete an existing site. To create or delete a site, you need the SPSiteCollection object. This can be confusing as this is not a "Site Collection" but a collection of SPSite objects. Let's create a script to create new sites. To create the script, copy the commands into Notepad and save the file as CreateSite.PS1 to the PSScripts directory.

```
Param( [String]$WebAppURL= $(throw "Web App URI is a required parameter"),
             [String]$ServerRelSiteURL= $(throw " ServerRelSiteURL is a
required parameter"),
[String]$OwnerLogIn= $(throw " OwnerLogin is a required parameter"),
[String]$OwnerEmail= $(throw " OwnerEmail is a required parameter")
)
$URI = New-Object  URI($WebAppURL)
$SPWebApp =
[Microsoft.SharePoint.Administration.SPWebApplication]::LookUp($URI)
$Site =  $SPWebApp.Sites.Add($ServerRelSiteUrl,  $OwnerLogin, $OwnerEmail)
$Site
```

This script starts with required parameters so you can reuse this script and simply change the parameters. To run the script from the PSScripts location, use the following command:

```
.\CreateSite.PS1 http://stockholm sites/testsite stockholm\administrator
admin@stockholm
```

The last line of the script returns the $Site variable, which contains a new SPSite object. Since we did not catch the output, it will be formatted and sent to the screen, as shown in Figure 14.15. We could have easily caught the output from the script with the following command:

```
$newSite =.\CreateSite.PS1 http://stockholm sites/testsite
stockholm\administrator admin@stockholm
```

With the new site object captured, we can then work on the new site, something we will do in a later section. This is where disposing the SPSite object is not simple. The script returns a SPSite object, but the script author has no idea when the SPSite should be disposed. The person running the script will need to be responsible to dispose of the SPSite object when he is done working with it.

You can navigate to the site to make sure it was created. The SharePoint SDK provides other constructors that accept more parameters, such as the Web Template, LCID, and database.

Deleting a site is easier and more dangerous than creating a site. Remember we are deleting a site, which includes all the Webs and subwebs, lists, and libraries. Deleting a site is easy, because you simply need to change the method from Add to Delete. Often, when a user assures you that a site is no longer being used, he really means "I have no idea whether I'm using that or not, and I reserve the right to change my answer at any time."

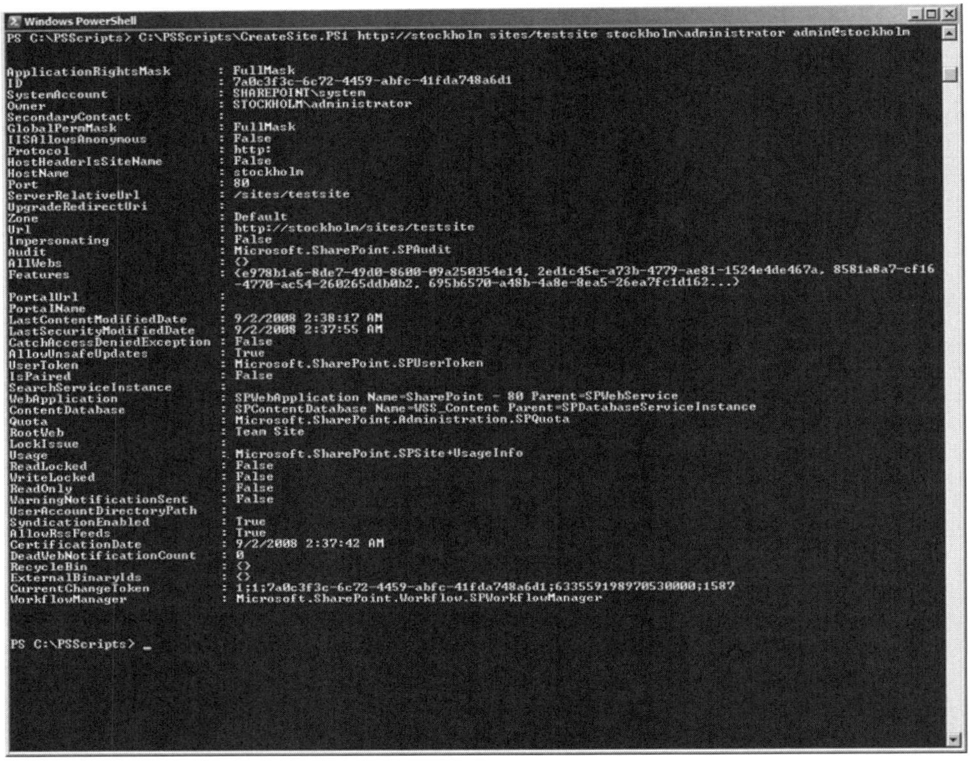

FIGURE 14.15
Create a Site Collection with PowerShell.

We can create a delete script fairly easily, but we are getting ahead of ourselves. We should create a backup script first. This is just good insurance. Here is a script that just does the job:

```
Param( [String]$WebAppURL= $(throw "Web App URI is a required parameter"),
[String]$ServerRelSiteURL= $(throw " ServerRelSiteURL is a required
parameter"),
[String]$BackupFilePathAndName= $(throw " BackupFilePathAndName is a
required parameter"),
[Bool]$Overwrite= $False
)
$URI = New-Object  URI($WebAppURL)
$SPWebApp =
[Microsoft.SharePoint.Administration.SPWebApplication]::LookUp($URI)
$SPWebApp.Sites.Backup($ServerRelSiteUrl,  $BackupFilePathAndName,
$Overwrite)
```

```
If(Test-Path $BackupFilePathAndName)
{
$SPWebApp.Sites.Delete($ServerRelSiteUrl)
}
```

Let's walk through this script and explain it. We use $False, which is the Boolean value of false for PowerShell. This script also introduces the use of the IF statement and the Test-Path command. The IF block evaluates the statement in parentheses and if it evaluates true, it executes the code in the braces. The Test-Path cmdlet returns True if the file exists. This script does not do any real error checking. The backup method does not return a true/false value. There is a simple check that the backup file exists before the delete happens. More robust error handling should be considered before the site is deleted. Also keep in mind that locking, backing up, and deleting sites require administrator privileges.

WORKING WITH WEBS

Sites contain Webs, SPWeb from the object model point of view. Like the object types we have looked at, we can list, add, and delete Webs. You will probably work more with SPWeb than any other object. The SPWeb contains many of the objects the end users work with, such as lists and libraries. The first script we'll create will be a script that creates Webs.

Creating a Web is similar to creating the site. The parent site object has collections of SPWeb objects in an SPWebCollection. Adding a new Web is accomplished by calling the Add method of the SPWebCollection object.

```
Param( [String]$ParentWebUrl= $(throw " ParentWebUrl  is a required
parameter"),
[String]$WebRelUrl= $(throw " WebRelUrl is a required parameter"),
 [String]$Title="Demo Web",
 [String]$Description= "",
  [Int32]$LCID= 1033,
  [String]$WebTemplate="STS#1",
 [Bool]$UseUniquePerms=$FALSE
)
$site = New-Object Microsoft.SharePoint.SPSite $ParentWebUrl
$site.AllWebs.Add($WebRelUrl, $Title, $Description, $LCID,
$WebTemplate, $UseUniquePerms, $FALSE)
```

Save this as CreateWeb.PS1, and once you run the script with your parameters, a new Web will be available.

Now that we have a few Webs, we might be interested in listing them. We have already seen how to create a Web, and listing Webs is even simpler. This script will list all Webs for a site collection.

```
Param(
[String]$SiteUrl= $(throw "SiteUrl is a required parameter")
)
$site = New-Object Microsoft.SharePoint.SPSite  $SiteUrl
$site.AllWebs
```

Save this script as ListWebs.PS1. This will return all of the SPWeb objects for the site collection. Unless you want to watch a large amount of text fly by on the screen, you might consider capturing the objects in a variable or sending the output to a Format-Table.

Like other commands, PowerShell scripts can be piped through other commands, as we can see in Figure 14.16. In that figure, we piped the output through Format-Table. We could also combine it with the Sort-Object command to further refine our results.

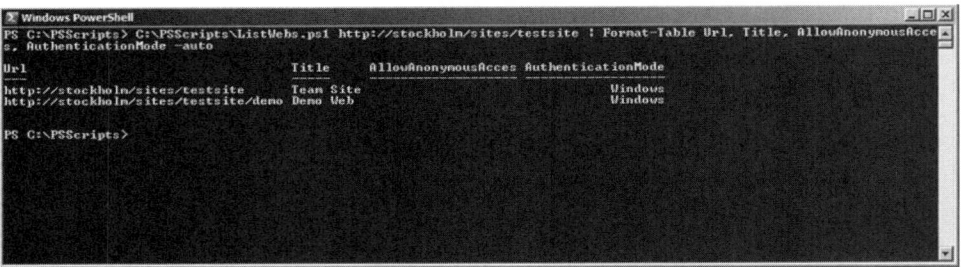

FIGURE 14.16
List Webs and formatting.

In Figure 14.17, the order of the Webs is the opposite of Figure 14.16 because we added items to the Rootweb after we added them to the Demo Web.

You can also filter the list results using the Where-Object command. For example, you can filter the Webs using Where-Object{$_.IsRootWeb}. This will only allow Webs to pass through the pipeline that are RootWebs of the site. The command would look like this:

```
.\PSScripts\ListWebs.ps1 http://stockholm/sites/testsite | Where-
Object{$_.IsRootWeb} | Format-Table Url, Title, AllowAnonymousAcces,
AuthenticationMode -auto
```

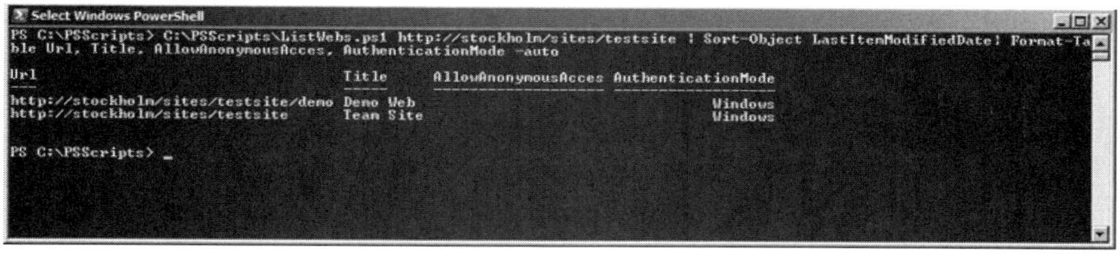

FIGURE 14.17
Sort by `LastItemModifiedDate`.

If you want to target a single Web, and you know its URL, then you can get to it more directly with these commands:

```
$Site = New-Object Microsoft.SharePoint.SPSite http://localhost/sites/top
$Site.OpenWeb()
$Site.Dispose()
```

Finally, we get to the point where you might want to delete a Web. In the site section of this chapter, we did a backup of the site before we deleted it. We could do the same thing here and back up, but this time we will simply delete the Web. Here are the commands to save as a script file.

```
Param( [String]$WebUrlToDelete= $(throw "WebUrlToDelete is a required
parameter")
$SPSite = New-Object Microsoft.SharePoint.SPSite
http://localhost/sites/top
$SPSite.AllWebs[$WebUrlToDelete].Delete()
$SPSite.Dispose()
```

Notice that we used a slightly different way to access the SPSite. We used the AllWebs property on the site object. This will return the SPWeb if it exists.

WORKING WITH SOLUTIONS

The STSADM chapter (Chapter 5) discussed Solutions and their use for deploying Features and other artifacts. Solutions contain one or more Features, files, assemblies, and other artifacts for a packaged deployment. It is a farm-level operation to install and deploy a Solution and has two separate steps. STSADM uses the addsolution operation to install a Solution into the Solution Store. We could create a script to do this, but since STSADM already has the operation, this is probably a good time to show how to use a native command. Remember, from the very beginning of this chapter we discussed the different types of commands. A native command is a command that runs outside of the PowerShell process. STSADM can be used as a native command. For this example, we use the interactive mode of the PowerShell environment instead of creating a script. To follow along, simply enter these commands into PowerShell:

```
$STSADM = "C:\Program Files\Common Files\Microsoft Shared\Web Server
Extensions\12\Bin\STSADM.Exe"
$STSADM
& $STSADM —o enumsolutions
```

You should get the same results as if you had used STSADM.exe with the command console. You should see your Farm Solutions on the screen as XML. How did we come up with these commands? First, we created a variable $STSADM and gave it the value of the path and name of STSADM.exe. The second line dumps the variable by executing the $STSADM variable. You should have seen the path and name of STSADM.exe returned to the screen. For all practical purposes, the variable only contains a string representation of the path to STSADM.exe.

Keeping STSADM Around

Using STSADM can be handy, but setting the variable every time you fire up Power-Shell can be a pain. This is a good place to use your PowerShell profile. Setting the $STSADM variable in the profile will mean that the $STSADM variable will be ready whenever you need it.

On the third and last line of this example, we use the & character, the call operator, to tell PowerShell to execute the next string as though it were a command. PowerShell executed STSADM.exe with the enumsolutions operation. Any STSADM operation can be called or included in a script using this technique.

You can redirect the results to a file just like using the command console. To redirect the results to a file, use the following command:

```
& $STSADM —o enumsolutions > EnumSolutionsOutput.xml
```

You will not see the XML scroll on the screen, as they were sent to the file.

This is nice, but you have no control over the output, nor can you make it nice and readable. We demonstrated how to use STSADM.Exe and enumsolutions to show that you can still use STSADM from PowerShell. There is no need to reinvent the wheel, if the wheel works. Here is a great one-liner to enumerate Solutions that you can use in interactive mode or save to a script file.

```
[Microsoft.SharePoint.Administration.SPFarm]::Local.Solutions
```

Your screen should be full of information about the Solutions installed in your farm. We should pipe the results to `Format-Table` to make them easier to consume.

```
[Microsoft.SharePoint.Administration.SPFarm]::Local.Solutions | Format-
Table SolutionId, DisplayName, Deployed
```

Figure 14.18 shows how it looks:

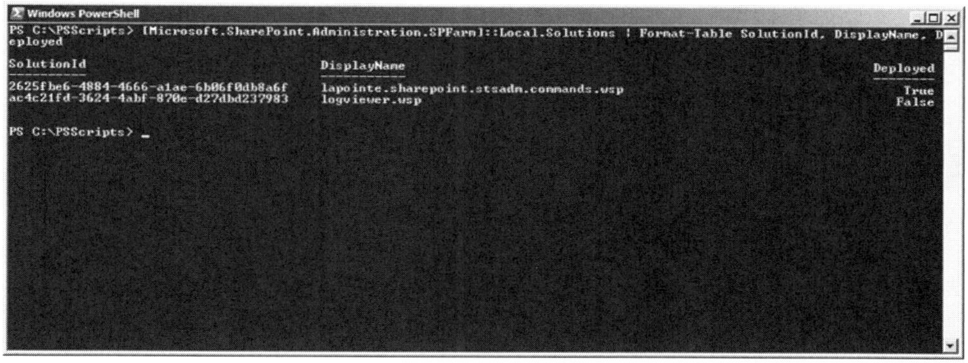

FIGURE 14.18
Enumerate Solutions with PowerShell.

We know that we can use a `Where-Object` command to limit the output. The following command will output only the Solutions that have not been deployed:

```
[Microsoft.SharePoint.Administration.SPFarm]::Local.Solutions | Where-
Object{$_.Deployed –eq $FALSE} | Format-Table SolutionId, DisplayName,
Deployed
```

We see from the output of `enumsolutions` operation and our PowerShell commands that we have two Solutions added: `lapointe.sharepoint.stsadm.commands.wsp` and `logviewer.wsp`. Logviewer.wsp, which, has not been deployed. Let's use STSADM and PowerShell to install it into the Solution Store. First, we need to see what parameters the `deploysolution` operation needs. To do this, let's ask the operation for help.

```
& $STSADM –help deploysolution
```

Now that we know the parameters that the `deplysolution` operation needs, we can use the following command:

```
& $STSADM –o deploysolution –name logviewer.wsp –immediate
```

Figure 14.19 shows the Solution will now be deployed via Timer Job.

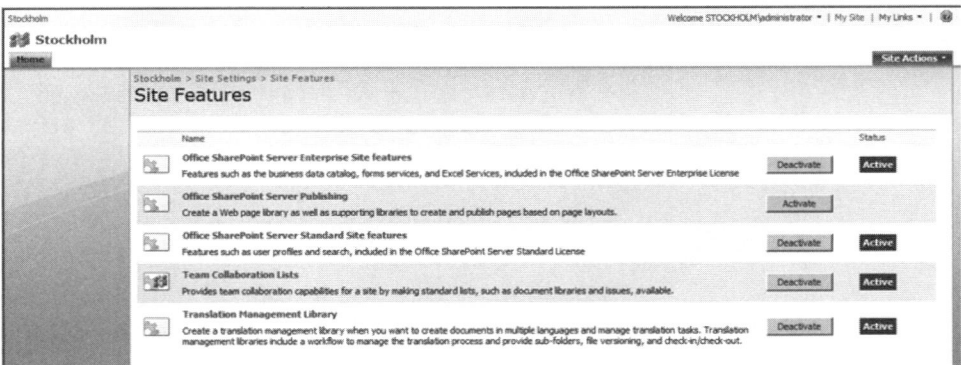

FIGURE 14.19
Deploy a Solution with PowerShell.

WORKING WITH FEATURES

Features are a key piece of the modular deployment process for the current version of SharePoint. As a matter of fact, much of the basic functionality of SharePoint is based on Features. This allows administrators the ability to easily turn on or off key sets of functionality at various levels or scopes. For example, the standard lists and libraries, such as document libraries and task lists, are made available to a team site from a Feature, the Team Collaboration Lists Feature to be exact. It is scoped at the Web level. This means that each Web or subweb can have this Feature activated or deactivated. Figure 14.20 shows the Site Feature page for a team site.

FIGURE 14.20
Site Features.

STSADM already has the commands to install and remove Features. But if you were closely reading the Solutions section, you already know that you should be using Solutions to deploy your Features. The Solution deployment will install the

Feature for you. If you, for some reason, are not using Solutions, you can easily install a Feature and activate it using STSADM with PowerShell by using the technique shown in the Solution section.

Before we jump in and start listing Features, there are a few things to know about them. All Features that have been installed have a Feature definition at the farm level. A Feature definition, represented by the SPFeatureDefinition object, contains basic information about the Feature, including the name, display name, scope, id, and dependencies. Features can be scoped at one of four levels: farm, Web Application, Site (site collection), or Web. Like most other SharePoint objects, SPFeatureDefinitions are contained in a collection. The local farm object contains a collection named FeatureDefinitions, which is of type SPFeatureDefinitionCollection. We can very easily get a listing of all Features that are installed on the farm by displaying all the Feature definitions. We can create a ListFeature script using this command:

```
[Microsoft.SharePoint.Administration.SPFarm]::Local.FeatureDefinitions
```

Remember that you can create a file, add this command, and save it with a PS1 file, and you now have a script. You can also use PowerShell in the interactive mode and simply type this command and execute it. Either way, script or interactive, there will be a lot of text on the screen. There are a lot of Features that have been installed in the farm. Remember, we are viewing Feature Definitions: these are Features that are installed on the farm and may or may not be activated.

Features and Feature Definitions are worth a few minutes of our time. There are a lot of Features that have been installed on the farm. How many? We can find out in interactive mode with the following command:

```
$FeatureDefs =
[Microsoft.SharePoint.Administration.SPFarm]::Local.FeatureDefinitions
$FeatureDefs.Count
```

Out of the box, there are 136 or so Features. To get a better look at the Features that are installed on the farm, let's sort them by scope and format the output to make it easier to read.

```
$FeatureDefs | Sort-Object  Scope | Format-Table ID, DisplayName,
Scope, Hidden —Auto
```

Here is one place where PowerShell really shines compared to STSADM. There is no easy way to get a list of all of the Features in your farm without coding something. PowerShell makes that possible. We can take it even further, because we can show only those Features installed on the farm that are hidden. We would do that with this command:

```
$FeatureDefs | Where-Object {$_.Hidden —eq $TRUE} | Sort-Object  Scope
| Format-Table ID, DisplayName,  Scope, Hidden —Auto
```

That is still a pretty long list. We can use the .Count property to see exactly how many.

```
($FeatureDefs | Where-Object {$_.Hidden —eq $TRUE}).Count
```

Figure 14.21 shows that 112 out of 136 Features are hidden by default.

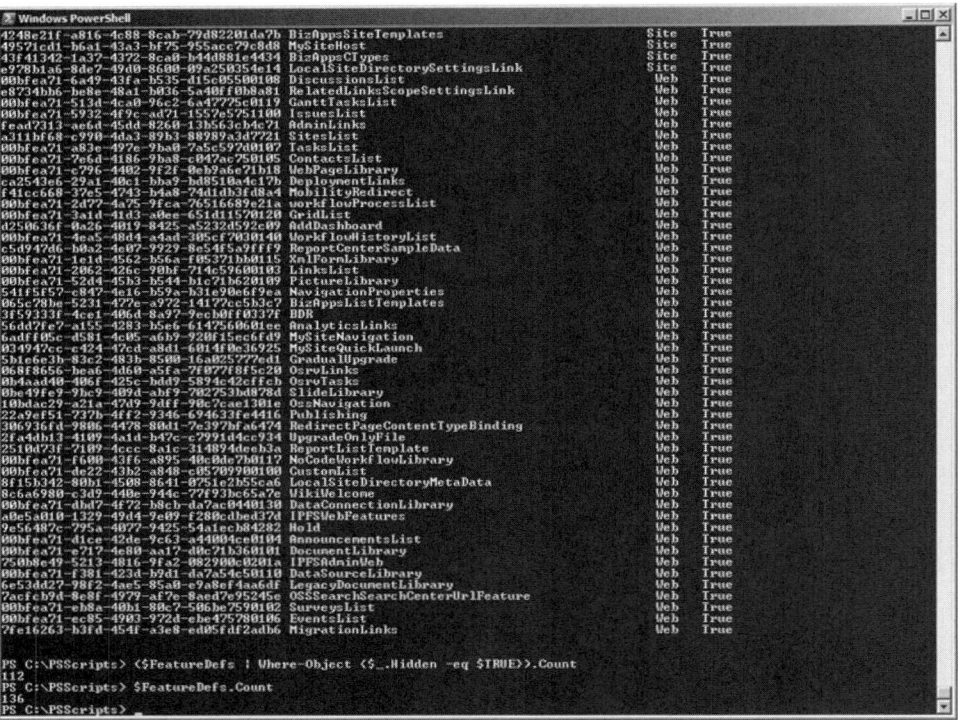

FIGURE 14.21
Show Features with PowerShell.

You can filter on practically any field used by the SPFeatureDefinition object. Ever come across a Feature ID and wonder what Feature that was associated with? You can get all Feature IDs and filter by one particular Feature. Here is a Feature ID 00BFEA71-4EA5-48D4-A4AD-7EA5C011ABE5—wonder which Feature this is? By running the command in Figure 14.22, you can see it is the TeamCollab Feature, which matches the Team Collaboration Lists Feature we saw in Figure 14.20.

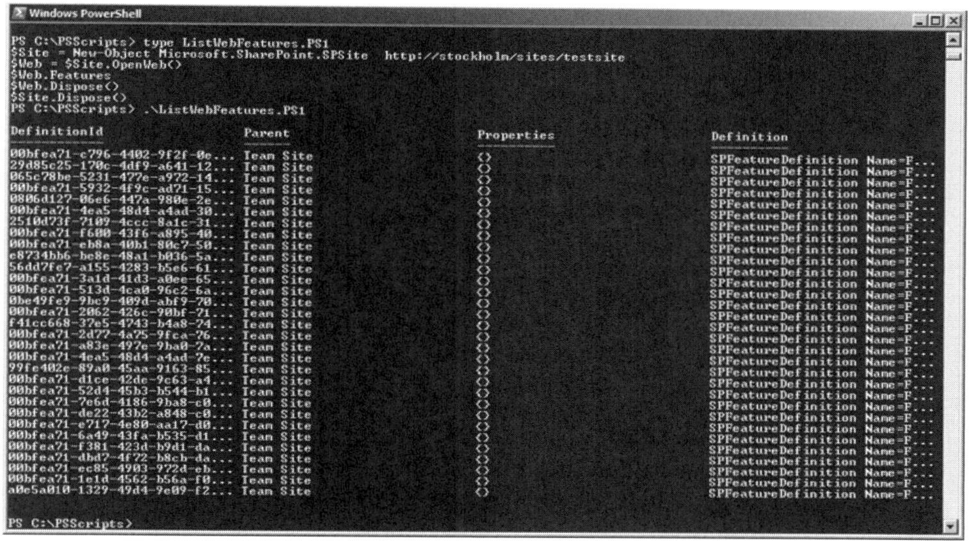

FIGURE 14.22
Find a Feature by ID.

You now know about Feature definitions and how you can list and filter them. Feature Definitions are installed Features on the farm and not necessarily activated Features. How do you activate or deactivate a Feature with PowerShell? Web Applications (SPWebApplication), Sites (SPSites), and Webs (SPWebs) all have a Features property. This is a collection of Features. More specifically, this is a collection of activated Features. If the Feature ID is in the SPFeatureCollection for a particular Web application, site, or Web, it is active for that scope. If it is not in the collection, it is not active at the scope. To see all the Features activated at a particular Web, get the SPWeb object and dump the Feature collection. Here are the commands based on our previous Web examples. Create this as a script named ListWebFeatures.ps1.

```
$Site = New-Object Microsoft.SharePoint.SPSite  http://localhost/sites/top
$Web = $Site.OpenWeb()
$Web.Features
$Web.Dispose()
$Site.Dispose()
```

The output should look like Figure 14.21.

You may notice that the output is not very readable. The SPFeature object does not have all the nice fields that the SPFeatureDefinition has. But through the magic of PowerShell, we can fix that. There are many ways to clean this up so it is usable, and here is one way to update ListWebFeatures.ps1

```
$FeatureDefs =
[Microsoft.SharePoint.Administration.SPFarm]::Local.FeatureDefinitions
$Site = New-Object Microsoft.SharePoint.SPSite
http://stockholm/sites/testsite
$Web = $Site.OpenWeb()
$Web.Features | foreach-object{$FeatureDefs[$_.DefinitionId]}
$Web.Dispose()
$Site.Dispose()
```

Figure 14.23 shows the output when we apply the Format-Table command.

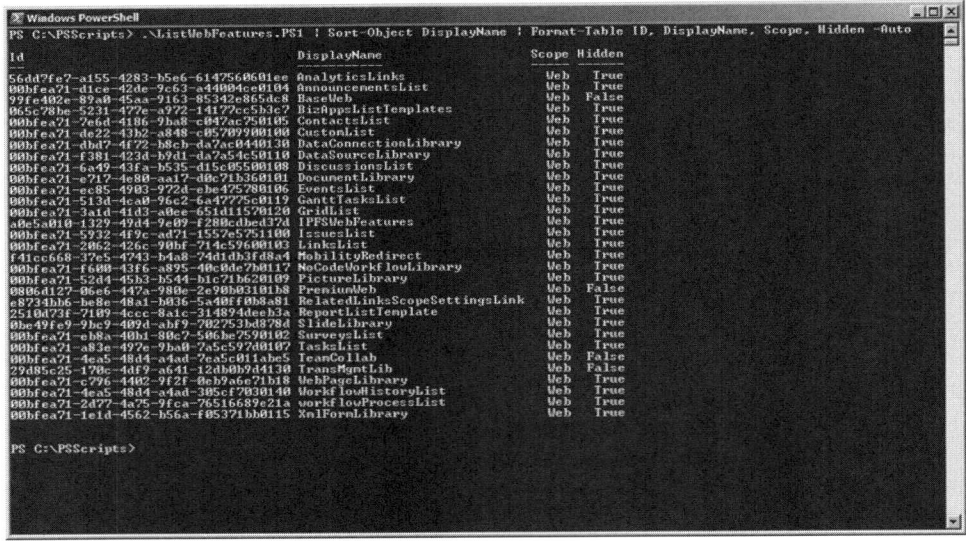

FIGURE 14.23
Improved listing of Web Features.

Index

$Site variable, 472–473
$WebApps variable, 468–469
12 Hive, 130
32 bit SharePoint, 23–27
32 bit Windows, 11–12
32-bit MOSS version, 231
/3GB switch, 329
64 bit SharePoint, 23–27
64 bit Windows, 11–12
64-bit MOSS version, 231

A

AAMs. *see* Alternate Access Mappings
access, Web site
    anonymous access, 307–311
    overview, 307
    secure access, 312
access control lists (ACLs), 237–238
accounts, install, 54–57
Actions menu, Site Permissions Web page,
    118–119
Activate Feature STSADM command, **161,** 221–222
ActivationDependencies element, 220
Active Directory account creation mode, WSS, 54
Active Directory (AD)
    groups, 115–117, 122
    importing from, 276
    user profiles, 274
Active Directory Federated Services (ADFS), 305
Add a Web Part toolbox, 349
Add and Customize Pages permission, 97
Add Colleagues Web page, 294–295
Add Crawl Rule Web page, 256, 257
Add Crawler Impact Rule Web page, 243

Add Heading button, Navigation Editing and
    Sorting section, Site Navigation Settings, 189
Add Items permission, 95
Add Link button, Navigation Editing and Sorting
    section, Site Navigation Settings, 189
Add Content Source Web page, 250
Add Roles Wizard, 411
Add Scope Rule Web page, 268
Add User Profile Properties page, 284
Add Users Web page, 123, 126–127
addcontentdb operation, 162–163
addpath operation, 167
addpermissionpolicy operation, 170
Add/Remove Personal Web parts permission, 98
addsolution operation, 160, 477
addtemplate operation, 162
adduser operation, 146
ADF (application definition files), 251
ADFS (Active Directory Federated Services), 305
administration
    MOSS model
        Farm Administrators, 90
        overview, 88–90
        Site Collection Administrators, 90–93
        site collection, 69–70, 84
Administrative Recycle Bin, 360
administrators, 282
Adobe PDF iFilters, 25
adsutil.vbs script, 333, 335
Advanced install, 52–54
Advanced option, Backup Web Site dialog box,
    365–366
Advanced Search Web page, 262

alerts
email, 13
search, 259–260
Alias check box, Add User Profile Property page, 286
All Content rule type, 268
All Sites scope, 265
All Sites tab, Search Center with Tabs Web site, 289
AllWebs property, 477
Alternate Access Mappings (AAMs)
backing up, 380–381
ClassId for, 378
overview, 319–320
scripts for, 167
versus server name mappings, 271
analyze operation, 165
anonymous access, 116, 307–311
APIs (application programming interfaces), 239
app pools (Application Pools), IIS, 327–332
appcmd.exe command line tool, 441
application definition files (ADF), 251
Application Management tab, Central Admin,
63–64, 125
Application Pool accounts, 56, 76
Application Pools (app pools), IIS, 327–332
application programming interfaces (APIs), 239
Application Security section, Application Management page, 63, 95
Application servers, 33–34, 227, 403
applications, Web. *see* Web applications
Apply Style Sheets permission, 97
Apply Themes and Borders permission, 97
Approve Items permission, 96
Approve permission level, 100
architecture, 17–47
mixed, 27
overview, 17
planning for hardware throughput
32 bit versus 64 bit, 23–27
network considerations, 23
overview, 22–30
virtualization considerations, 27–30
planning for software boundaries, 18–22
planning for SQL limits, 30–32
scaling options
important considerations, 42–47
server roles, 32–42

ASP.NET Web site
creating FBA providers and new users, 315
creating SQL database, 313
assigning permissions
overall permission management guidance, 122–123
overview, 122
to users and groups, 123–124
Audience field, Navigation Heading dialog box,
189–190
auditing, site, 199–200
Authenticated Users group, 109–110
authentication
Kerberos or NTLM, 57–60
user
anonymous access, 307–311
overview, 307
secure access, 312
authentication mechanisms, MOSS, 312
Authentication Providers Web page, 307–308
Authoring farms, 42
authoritative pages, 270
authorization. *see* site and content authorization
autogrowth, 31
availability, 192. *see also* high availability
Avepoint DocAve software, 402

B
Back Up Database option, SQL Server Maintenance Plan Wizard, 343
backup and disaster recovery, 376–403. *see also*
content recovery
backup methods
Central Admin, 383–392
native SQL backups, 398–401
NTBackup.exe, 401–402
other options, 402–403
overview, 383
restoring with Central Admin and STSADM,
395–398
STSADM Catastrophic Backups, 393–395
compressing in UI, 445
controlling downtime, 192
optimizing performance, 347–348
out-of-the-box, 340
overview, 353, 376

SharePoint configuration
  Alternate Access Mappings, 380–381
  Configuration Database, 377–379
  IIS, 382–383
  installed software, 381–382
  MOSS only, 383
  overview, 377
  SharePoint customizations, 381
  SSP databases, 381
SharePoint content, 376
SQL compressed, 445–447
STSADM
  farm level, 155–159
  overview, 149
  site collection level, 152–154
  Web level, 149–152
Webs backup
  overview, 364
  SharePoint Designer, 364–366
  STSADM, 366–372
**Backup and Restore section, Operations tab,
Central Admin,** 62, 384–385
backup directory, 387, 390
Backup Exec software, 403
backup operation, STSADM, 152–154, 393
backup scripts, 369, 474–475
–backupthreads parameter, 158
BAK files, 391
BaseSiteStapling feature, 212
Basic install, 35, 51–52
BDC (Business Data Catalog)
  content sources, 246, 251
  LOB applications, 274
  overview, 9
  permissions, 67
  SSP and, 228
binary large object cache, 347
blob caching, 347
blocked file types, 194
Blog template, 4
boundaries
  hardware
    32 bit versus 64 bit, 23–27
    network considerations, 23
    overview, 22–30
    virtualization considerations, 27–30
  software, 18–22, 344
  SQL, 30–32

bread crumbs
  current, 183
  global, 179–180
Browse Directories permission, 97
Browse User Information permission, 97, 311
Burns, Cory, 192–193
Business Data Catalog. *see* BDC
business systems, 9

C
.CAB files, 150
-cabsize parameter, 367
cache, 344–347
CAL. *see* client access license
**CAML (Collaborative Application Markup
Language),** 207
capacity planning, 17–47
  hardware
    32 bit versus 64 bit, 23–27
    network considerations, 23
    overview, 22–30
    virtualization considerations, 27–30
  overview, 17
  scaling options
    important considerations, 42–47
    server roles, 32–42
  software boundaries, 18–22
  SQL limits, 30–32
Capacity Planning Tool, 44–47
catastrophic backups, STSADM, 393–395
Central Administration v3 (Central Admin)
  adding Index server, 232
  anonymous access, 307
  Application Management page, 63–64
  backups, 157–158, 383–392
  enterprise search administration
    crawler impact rules, 242–245
    Farm-Level Search Settings, 240–242
    overview, 239–240
  FBA providers, 317
  Operations page, 62–63
  overview, 61
  permissions mapping between STSADM and,
    169–170
  restoring with, 395–398
  security, 310
  service configuration, 76–77
  solution packages, 225

Certificate alert message, 421
certificates, SQL, 451
Change Anonymous Access Settings page, 309
Change Group Settings page, 112, 114
Change Log, 252
changepermissionpolicy operation, 170
Check Database Integrity option, SQL Server
    Maintenance Plan Wizard, 342
Check Out permission, 95
churn rate, 31
ClassIds, 377–378
classifications, SQL Resource Governor, 447
Clear-Host command, 467
client access license (CAL)
    Microsoft Office Forms Server 2007, 10
    MOSS, 5
    MOSS FIS, 10
    WSS, 2
cluster properties, 171–172
cmdlets, 416, 456, 458–460
CMP (Content Management Package) files, 366
Collaboration Portal, 7, 212–213, 261
Collaboration templates, 6
collaboration traffic, 43
Collaborative Application Markup Language
    (CAML), 207
Colleague Tracker Web part, My Site, 285, 301–303
column limits for software, 22
columns, indexed, 18–21
command line administration. *see* STSADM
Command Prompt window, 134, 139
communication, IT governance, 200
Commvault software, 402
Complete install, 35, 53
Compound TCP (CTCP), 442
compression
    Internet Information Services, 332–336
    SQL Server, 445–447
ConfigDB (Configuration Database), 377–379
ConfigDB Binaries table, 379
configuration, 49–86. *see also* Internet accessible
    Web sites
    avoiding DCOM errors, 75–76
    backing up
        Alternate Access Mappings, 380–381
        Configuration Database, 377–379
        IIS, 382–383
        installed software, 381–382

        MOSS only, 383
        overview, 377
        SharePoint customizations, 381
        SSP databases, 381
    Central Administration
        Application Management page, 63–64
        Operations page, 62–63
        overview, 61
    Configuration Wizard, 60–61
    content sources, 246–251
    enabling usages analysis processing, 79–80
    infrastructure update, 85
    installing
        on additional servers, 74–75
        choosing install accounts, 54–57
        MOSS, 72–74
        overview, 50–54
    Kerberos or NTLM authentication, 57–60
    managed properties, 263–265
    My Sites, 302–304
    outgoing email, 79
    overview, 49–50
    Shared Service Provider
        advantage of, 66
        choosing quantity of, 65
        creating first, 80–84
        overview, 64
        setting security, 66–67
    site collections, 69–72
    site definition, 214–215
    site definition information, 211–212
    slipstreaming service pack 1, 84–85
    starting services, 76–79
    to use new providers, 317–318
    user profile
        import connections, 276–280
        overview, 275
        profile properties and mappings, 280–287
    Web applications, 68–69
Configuration Database (ConfigDB), 377–379
Configuration Wizard, 55, 60–61, 73–74
Configure My Site for Microsoft Office dialog box,
    300
Configure Search Settings page, 246–247, 269
Contact E-mail Address option, Manage
    Farm-Level Search Settings Web page, 241
content, backing up, 376. *see also* site and content
    authorization

Content Access Account, 235
content databases
    backing up, 376
    growth management, 193–194
    overview, 70–72
    SQL Server, 340
    STSADM management of, 162–166
content deployment, disabling, 310
Content Deployment section, Operations tab,
    Central Admin, 63
Content Deployment Settings Web page, 310
content index, 231
Content Management Package (CMP) files, 366
content properties, 263
Content Query Web Parts (CQWP), 72, 346
content recovery, 354–375
    overview, 354
    Recycle Bin, 358–364
    Site Delete Capture, 373–375
    STSADM, 149
    versioning, 354–358
    Webs backup
        overview, 364
        SharePoint Designer, 364–366
        STSADM, 366–372
Content Source scope rule type, 268
content sources
    configuring, 246–251
    defined, 245
    Index server role, 229
continuous propagation, 231–232
Contribute permission level, 100
cookies, 258
.Count property, 482
CQWP (Content Query Web Parts), 72, 346
Crawl complex URLs option, Add Crawl Rule Web
    page, 257
crawl log, 254–256
crawl rules, 231, 256–258
crawl schedules
    configuring, 253–254
    defined, 230
    full and incremental, 252–253
    overview, 251–252
Crawl Settings section, Edit Content Source Web
    page, 249
Crawl SharePoint content as Http pages option,
    Add Crawl Rule Web page, 257

crawled properties, 236, 263
crawler account, 230
crawler impact rules, 242–245
crawling, 37–40, 126
Create a new group radio button, Visitors to this
    Site section, Set Up Groups for this Site page, 112
Create Alerts permission, 96
Create Basic Task Wizard, 432
Create Groups permission, 97, 109
Create parameter, 438
create personal site permission, 67, 298
Create Site Collection Web page, 208
Create Subsites permission, 97
Create View page, 20
createsite operation, 136–137
createsiteinnewdb operation, 142–143
createweb operation, 145
"Creating a Custom Feature in Office SharePoint
    Server 2007" white paper, 221–222
CRM (customer relationship management)
    systems, 9
Cross List Query Results Multiplier, 346
CTCP (Compound TCP), 442
current bread crumbs, 183
Custom option, Add Content Source Web page, 251
custom site templates
    composition of, 204
    versus custom site definitions, 215–216
    defined, 201–202
    global use of, 208–209
    overview, 204
    saving, 205–207
    site definition dependency, 205
customer relationship management (CRM)
    systems, 9
customizations, backing up, 381. *see also* site
    customization

D
dashboards, 9
.DAT files, 150
Data Configuration section, Operations tab,
    Central Admin, 62
Data Protection Manager (DPM), 402, 443
Data View Web Part (DVWP), 144–145
database migration upgrades, 15
database mirroring, 405–406, 444

database servers
  high availability, 404–406
  overview, 227
  searches, 238
databaserepair operation, 154, 174
databases
  backing up SSP, 381
  encrypting, 449
  offline, 143, 192
  placement of, 30–31
  pregrowing, 339–340
  site collections, 70–72
  size of, 31–32, 51, 193
  specification for Web applications, 68–69
  SQL Server
    maintaining, 341–344
    overview, 336–341
datacenters, 350
date variable, 368
days-to-show-new-icon property, 173
DCOM errors, 75–76
Deactivate Feature STSADM command, 162,
  221–222
dedicated Web Front-end servers, 234
default Limited Access permissions, 310–311
default scopes, 266
Default Web Site, 326
definitions. *see* site definitions
delegation settings, 58–59
Delete Items permission, 96
Delete Versions permission, 96
deletecontentdb operation, 163
–deletecorruption parameter, 174
deleted documents, 358
deletepath operation, 167
deletepermissionpolicy operation, 170
deletesite operation, 141–142
deletesolution operation, 161
deletetemplate operation, 162
deleteuser operation, 146
deleteweb operation, 145–146
deleting sites, 473
DeliverPoint: Permissions tool, 124
Deny All permission, 127
Deny Write permission, 127
dependency
  Features, 220–221
  site definition, 205

deployment, Features, 221–222
deploysolution operation, 160
Description box, Navigation Heading dialog box, 189
Design permission level, 100
development environments, virtualized, 28–29
Development farms, 42
differential backup, 156
directory Search dialog box, 291
Directory Security tab, IIS, 325
disabling
  content deployment, 310
  My Site creation, 297–299
disaster recovery. *see* backup and disaster recovery
disaster recovery environments, virtualized, 30
Disk resource, Reliability and Performance
  Monitor, 428–429
disk-based caching, 347
display names, alternative, 284
displaysolution operation, 161
disposal, object, 472
DocAve software, 402
Document Center site template, 6
Document Conversion Services servers, 34
Document Conversions Launcher Service, 78
Document Library Settings option, Settings menu, 19
documents
  deleted, 358–359
  software limits for, 22
double-hop problem, 57–58
downtime
  controlling, 192–193
  SLA requirements, 43
DPM (Data Protection Manager), 402, 443
dual-homing servers, 23
DVWP (Data View Web Part), 144–145
dynamic backups, 371

E
ECS (Excel Calculation Services), 9, 33, 77
Edit Authentication Web page, 308
Edit Connection page, 279
Edit Content Source Web page, 248–249
Edit Group Quick Launch page, 111
Edit Items permission, 96
Edit Personal User Information permission, 98
Edit User Profile page, 280
Element files, 219–220

email
  configuring outgoing, 79
  sending and configuring, 433–434
  server, 13–14
Enable CPU monitoring option, Performance tab,
  Application Pools, 329
Enable rapid-fail protection option, Health tab,
  Application Pools, 330
encrypting databases, 449
enterprise client access license, 5
enterprise search, 227–271
  Central Administration Web site
    crawler impact rules, 242–245
    Farm-Level Search Settings, 240–242
    overview, 239–240
  overview, 227–228
  Shared Service Provider architecture
    Database server role, 238
    Index server role, 229–236
    overview, 228
    Query Server role, 236–238
    Web server role, 239
  SSP-level administration
    authoritative pages, 270
    configuring content source, 246–251
    configuring indexing, 251–260
    federated locations, 271
    managed properties, 263–265
    overview, 245–246
    search centers, 261–263
    search scopes, 265–270
    server name mappings, 271
Enterprise site templates, 6
Enterprise version, MOSS, 8–9
enumcontentdbs operation, 163
Enumerate Permissions permission, 97
enumgroups operation, 146
enumroles operation, 146
enumsites operation, 132, 144
enumsolutions operation, 161, 478
enumtemplates operation, 162
enumusers operation, 146–147
enumwebs operation, 145
"Estimate performance and capacity requirements
  for Internet environments" white paper, 44
"Estimate performance and capacity requirements
  for portal collaboration environments" white
  paper, 44

Ethernet connections, 23
Event Viewer, 430–435
Event Viewer Tasks folder, 437
Everyone setting, Default Privacy Setting menu,
  Add User Profile Property page, 285
Excel Calculation Services (ECS), 9, 33, 77
Excel Services
  application servers, 403
  defined, 9
  double-hop problem, 57–58
  SSP and, 228
Exchange Server, Microsoft, 14
export operation, STSADM, 149–152, 367–370
exported tasks, Task Scheduler, 437
extending STSADM, 175
External Service Connections section, Application
  Management tab, Central Admin, 63
Extranet Web site, 317
Extranet_internal Web site, 317
extranets
  creating and configuring Web applications,
    314–319
  creating SQL database, 313
  overview, 313

F
Failed Request Tracing, 422–427
Farm Administrators, 89–90
Farm BuildVersion property, 467
Farm Search Service Account, 77
farms
  Configuration Wizard, 60–61
  scaling with, 41–42
  search administration on level of
    crawler impact rules, 242–245
    Farm-Level Search Settings, 240–242
    overview, 240
  STSADM backup and disaster recovery, 155–159
  working with PowerShell, 465–467
Fastrup, Lars, 251
FBA. *see* Forms Based Authentication
Feature Office SharePoint Server Publishing
  Infrastructure, 187–188
Features
  creating new, 222–223
  dependency, 220–221
  deployment, 221–222
  description and Feature.xml, 217–220

folder hierarchy, 217
importance of, 160
managing third-party code, 198
overview, 217
Server Manager, 408
site definitions, 203–204, 214–215
STSADM management of, 161–162
working with PowerShell, 480–484
Feature.xml file, 217–220
federated locations, 271
field types, 22
file propagation, 237
File Services, Add Roles Wizard, 413
file shares, 194
file types, 194, 224, 258–259
filegroups, SQL, 31
filtering Web parts, 9
filters, Crawl Log, 254
find command, 133
Firewall, Windows, 441
flyouts, 191
folder hierarchy
Features, 217
site definitions, 209–211
folders, 18
FOR command, 140–141
forcedeletelist operation, 174
ForEach-Object command, 470
forfiles command, 369
forms, InfoPath, 8
Forms Based Authentication (FBA)
crawl rules, 258
enabling for extranet Web application, 318–319
overview, 312
providers, 315–318
Forms Server 2007, 10
Forms Services, 8–9, 228
Foxit PDF iFilter, 25
FQDN (Fully Qualified Domain Name), 37–39
fragmented files, 31
Full Control permission level, 99–100
full crawl schedules, 252–253
full-text catalog, 231
Fully Qualified Domain Name (FQDN), 37–39
functions, PowerShell, 457

G
GAC (Global Assembly Cache), 373, 382

Gb switches, 350
Get-Process cmdlet, 456, 458
getproperty operation, 170, 363
getsitelock operation, 145
Getting Started with Web part, My Site, 301
geturlzone operation, 167
ghosted pages, 203
gigabit Ethernet connections, 23
Global Assembly Cache (GAC), 373, 382
global bread crumbs, 179–180
**Global Configuration section, Operations tab,
Central Admin,** 62
global navigation, 180–181
global use of custom site templates, 208–209
governance. *see* IT governance
gradual upgrades, 14–15, 25
group permission levels, 108–109
groups
assigning permissions to, 123–124
defined, 93
permission levels, 101
SharePoint versus Active Directory, 115–117
site
enabling Publishing Site, 107–108
key points, 108–110
managing groups, 110–114
overview, 106–107
working with STSADM, 148–149
growth management, 193–194
guids, 81

H
hardware
32 bit versus 64 bit, 23–27
network considerations, 23
overview, 22–30
SQL, 30–32
virtualization considerations, 27–30
HcCompressDirectory, 334
HcDoDynamic Compression, 334
HcDoStatic Compression, 334
HcDynamicCompression Level, 336
HcFileExtensions, 336
HcOnDemandCompLevel, 336
HcScriptFileExtension, 336
headings, 186, 189
Health tab, IIS Manager, 330
Help operation, PowerShell, 460

–help parameter, 131–132
high availability
  application servers, 403
  database servers, 404–406
  overview, 353, 403
  web front ends, 403
Home Directory tab, IIS, 325
Home screen, Capacity Planning Tool, 44–45
host headers, 68, 80, 382
hosts files, 38–40, 314
HP SharePoint sizing tool, 47
Hyper-V, 28

I

Identity tab, IIS Manager, 330
Idera software, 402
Idle timeout setting, 329
IF statement, 475
iFilters, 25, 230, 259
IIS (Internet Information Services)
  Application Pools, 327–332
  backing up, 382–383
  compression, 332–336
  overview, 321–322
  security improvements, 440–441
  version 7, 417–427
  Web applications, 322–326
  and Windows Server, 11
iisapp.vbs script, 331
iisback.vbs script, 382
iisresets, 327–328
Immediate Colleagues option, Colleague Tracker Web Part, 302
–immediate parameter, 161
import connections, 276–280
import operation, 149–152
imported tasks, 437
incoming email, 13–14
incremental crawl schedules, 252–253
index management, 237
index propagation, 231–232
Index servers
  adding, 232–236
  content index, 231
  content source, 229
  identifying, 77–78
  index propagation, 231–232
  indexing process, 229–231

  in medium farms, 36–38
  overview, 227–229
  scaling, 33
  single role per SSP, 229
  upgrades, 26–27
  virtualization of, 29–30
indexed columns, 18–21
Indexer Performance setting, Configure Office SharePoint Server Search Service Settings Web page, 233
indexing
  configuring, 251–260
  Index server role, 229–231
  Lotus Notes content, 229
  optimizing performance, 347–348
Indexing Schedule, 78
InfoPath 2007, 8
InfoPath Forms Services section, Application Management tab, Central Admin, 64
infrastructure update, 85, 228
inheritance, 117–122
  access rights, 100
  breaking, 118–122
  defined, 93
  and group permissions, 109
  key points, 117–118
  navigation, 190
  overview, 117
in-place upgrades, 14
install accounts, 54–57
Install Feature STSADM command, 221–222
installation
  on additional servers, 74–75
  Advanced installs, 52–54
  Basic install, 35, 51–52
  choosing install accounts, 54–57
  MOSS, 72–74
  overview, 50
  WSS-only option, 54
installed software, backing up, 381–382
installfeature operation, 161
Internet accessible Web sites, 305–320
  Alternate Access Mapping, 319–320
  extranet and intranet scenario
    creating and configuring Web applications, 314–319
    creating SQL database, 313
    overview, 313

overview, 305–307
user authentication
anonymous access, 307–311
overview, 307
secure access, 312
Internet Information Services. *see* IIS
Internet Security and Acceleration Server (ISA) 2006, 320
Internet sites, MOSS for, 10
intranets
creating and configuring Web applications, 314–319
creating SQL database, 313
overview, 313
I/O performance, 30
ISA (Internet Security and Acceleration Server) 2006, 320
IT governance, 191–200
communication, 200
controlling downtime, 192–193
controlling site proliferation, 198–199
managing growth
blocked file types, 194
content databases, 193–194
overview, 193
quotas, 193
managing third-party code, 198
overview, 177–178, 191–192
quotas, 197–198
resources, 200
security and site auditing, 199–200
usage reporting, 195–197
items, list, 18, 21–22

J
job-immediate-alerts property, 173
job-recycle-bin-cleanup property, 363

K
Kerberos authentication, 57–60

L
Lapointe, Gary, 175
large farms, 40–41
large lists, 344
LDAP (Lightweight Directory Access Protocol) database, 274
least privileged administration, 54–55, 57

licensing
Foxit PDF iFilter, 25
Microsoft Office Forms Server 2007, 10
Microsoft virtualization technology, 28
MOSS, 5
Search Server 2008, 10
WSS, 2–3
Lightweight Directory Access Protocol (LDAP) database, 274
Limit Page Depth option, Add Content Source Web page, 251
Limit Server Hops option, Add Content Source Web page, 251
Limited Access permission level, 99, 101
line-of-business (LOB) applications, 274
lists, 18, 22, 209, 344
ListWebFeatures.ps1 script, 483–484
LOB (line-of-business) applications, 274
Local Administrators, 89–90
–local parameter, 161
Lockdown mode, 310–311
locked site collections, 153–154
log, crawl, 254–256
log directory, 423–424
LOG files, 391
Log Shipping, 406
Logging and Reporting section, Operations tab, Central Admin, 62, 79
Lotus Notes content, 229

M
Maintenance Cleanup Task option, SQL Server Maintenance Plan Wizard, 343–344
Maintenance Plan Wizard, SQL Server, 340, 342–344, 399
major versions, 356
MAKECAB tool, 224
Manage Alerts permission, 98
manage audiences permission, 67
Manage Content Sources Web page, 246–247
Manage Database Encryption dialog box, 449
Manage Farm-Level Search Settings Web page, 240–241
Manage Hierarchy permission, 100
Manage Lists permission, 95
Manage Permissions permission, 67, 96
Manage Permissions: Shared Service Rights Web page, 298

Manage Personal Views permission, 98
Manage Search Service Web page, 240
Manage Usage Analytics permission, 67
Manage User Profiles permission, 66
Manage Web Site permission, 97
managed paths, 22, 167
managed properties, 236, 238, 263–265
management
    growth, 193–194
    improvements in Windows Server 2008
        Event Viewer, 430–435
        IIS 7, 417–427
        overview, 408
        Power Shell, 416–417
        Reliability And Performance Monitor, 428–430
        Server Manager, 408–416
        Task Scheduler, 435–438
        WinRM and WinRS, 438–440
    permission
        inheritance, 117–122
        overall guidance, 122–123
        overview, 114–115
        SharePoint versus Active Directory groups,
            115–117
    SQL Server 2008, 445–448
    STSADM
        content database, 162–166
        Feature, 161–162
        managed paths and zones, 167
        Solution Store, 159–161
        template, 162
        Web application policies, 168–170
    of third-party code, 198
    user profile
        import connections, 276–280
        overview, 275
        profile properties and mappings, 280–287
Management Service, IIS, 418–419
managepermissionpolicylevel operation, 168
manifest.XML file, 151, 224
Manually By Owner option, Colleague Tracker
    Web Part, 302
Mapped Attribute, 282
mappings. see also Alternate Access Mappings
server name, 271
user profile, 280–287
Mappings to Crawled Properties section, New
    Managed Property page, 264

Master Key, 451
max-template-document-size property, 173
medium farms, 36–37
Meeting site templates, 6
meeting workspaces, 3–4, 186–187
Members group, 122
memberships, My Sites, 303
memory support, 23–24
mergecontentdbs operation, 163–166
Messages.xml file, 374
metabase, ISS, 333
metadata, 263
Metadata Property Mappings Web page, 263–264
Microsoft Data Protection Manager, 402, 443
Microsoft Exchange Server, 14
Microsoft Office Forms Server 2007, 10
Microsoft Office SharePoint Server 2007. see MOSS
Microsoft virtualization technology, 27–28
Microsoft white papers
    "Creating a Custom Feature in Office SharePoint
        Server 2007", 222
    "Estimate performance and capacity require-
        ments for Internet environments", 44
    "Estimate performance and capacity requirements
        for portal collaboration environments", 44
    "Plan for software boundaries", 21
    "Predeployment I/O Best Practices", 30
migrateuser operation, 147–148
minimal install, IIS, 440
minor versions, 356
mirroring, database, 405–406, 444
mixed architecture, 27
Model Summary, Capacity Planning Tool, 45–47
Modify Permissions: Shared Service Rights Web
    page, 299
MOSS (Microsoft Office SharePoint Server 2007).
    see also enterprise search; Internet accessible Web
    sites; personalization
    backing up, 383
    Enterprise version, 8–9
    installation, 72–74
    for Internet sites, 10
    Microsoft Office Forms Server 2007, 10
    MOSS Search Account, 56
    navigation, 187–191
    overview, 5
    Search Server 2008, 10–11
    site groups, 107

Standard version, 5–8
tips for choosing SharePoint version, 11
MOSS FIS (Office SharePoint Server 2007 for Internet Server), 10
MS IT Site Delete Capture Utility, 373
multiple farms, 42
Multiple Query servers, 237
My Calendar Web part, My Site, 301
My Colleagues setting, Default Privacy Setting menu, Add User Profile Property page, 285
My Home tab, My Site, 296
My Manager setting, Default Privacy Setting menu, Add User Profile Property page, 285
My Profile pages, My Site, 296–297, 303–304
My Site Host site template, 7
My Site Web part, My Site, 301
My Sites
creation of site, 297–299
overview, 273–274, 296
people search, 293–296
SSP and, 81–83, 228
use of, 299–304
My Workgroup setting, Default Privacy Setting menu, Add User Profile Property page, 285

N
native commands, 458, 477
native SQL backups, 398–401
navigation, 177–191
current bread crumb, 183
global bread crumbs, 179–180
global navigation, 180–181
MOSS, 187–191
overview, 177–178
Quick Launch bar, 181–182
security trimming, 183
WSS
maintaining, 184–185
meeting workspaces, 186–187
overview, 183–184
Quick Launch bar, 186
top link bar, 185
Navigation Editing and Sorting section, Site Navigation Settings, 188–189
Navigation Heading dialog box, 189–190
.NET assemblies, 382
.NET Framework 3.0, 11
Network Load Balancing Service (NLBS), 33, 403

networking issues, 350
networks, planning for hardware, 23
New Crawl Rule button, 256
New Managed Property Web page, 265
New Scope button, 266
New Scopes Web page, 267
newdatabaseserver parameter, 397
NLBS (Network Load Balancing Service), 33, 403
Noel, Michael, 371
-nofilecompression parameter, 367
noise words, 230
Notepad, PowerShell script in, 461
NTBackup.exe, 401–402, 443
NTLM authentication, 57–60

O
object caching, 346
Object Model (OM), 386
objects
ClassIds and, 377–378
description of in SPBRTOC.XML file, 389
Objects table, 377
Office SharePoint Server 2007 for Internet Server (MOSS FIS), 10
Office SharePoint Server Search Service Settings Web page, 233
Office SharePoint Server Shared Services section, Application Management tab, Central Admin, 63
offline databases, 72, 143, 192
Oleson, Joel, 194
OM (Object Model), 386
ONET.XML file, 214
Only Me setting, Default Privacy Setting menu, Add User Profile Property page, 285
Open Items permission, 96
Open permission, 98, 311
Operations tab
Central Admin, 62–63, 76–77
SharePoint Web Application Management, 324
optimizing performance, 321–351
backups and indexing, 347–348
cache, 344–347
end to end, 351
Internet Information Services
Application Pools, 327–332
compression, 332–336
overview, 321–322

Web applications, 322–326
networking issues, 350
overview, 321–322
slow page loads, 348–350
software boundaries, 344
SQL Server
databases, 336–341
maintaining databases, 341–344
overview, 336
organizational units (OUs), 54
outgoing email, 13, 79
output caching, 345–346
Override permission, 95
-overwrite parameter, 369
Owners group, 122–123
ownership, site collection, 69–70
ows_FullName(Text) property, 263

P
PAE (Physical Address Extension), 24
page bloat, 348
Pages library, 7
Pages toolbar, 186–187
PDF iFilters, 25
People and Groups: All Groups page, 110–111, 123
People and Groups: Members page, 112–113
People Picker dialog box, 123
people search, 287–296
People tab, Search Center with Tabs Web site, 262, 289
people.aspx Web page, 289
–percentage parameter, 158
performance, 442–443. *see also* optimizing performance
Performance tab, IIS Manager, 329–330
permission levels
creating and modifying, 104–106
Full Control, 98–99
for groups, 108–109
inheritance of, 117–118
key points, 100–101
new, 103–104
overview, 88, 93, 99–100
viewing permissions for, 102–103
permissions
assigning
overall permission management guidance, 122–123

overview, 122
to users and groups, 123–124
inheritance of, 117–118
key points, 98–99
management
inheritance, 117–122
overall guidance, 122–123
overview, 114–115
SharePoint versus Active Directory groups, 115–117
mapping between STSADM and Central Administration, 169–170
overview, 88, 93, 94
for permission levels, 102–103
setting, 66–67
viewing, 95–98
Permissions Levels Web page, 102–106
Persisted Files, 379
Personal Documents document library, 301
personalization, 273–304
My Sites
creation of site, 297–299
overview, 296
use of, 299–304
overview, 273–274
people search, 287–296
user profiles
import connections, 276–280
overview, 274–275
profile management overview, 275
profile properties and mappings, 280–287
Personalization Site template, 7
PH (protocol handler), 230
Physical Address Extension (PAE), 24
pinging, 330
"Plan for software boundaries" white paper, Microsoft, 21
policies
site-use, 200
Web application, 124–128
Policy for Web Application Web page, 125–126
port numbers, 61, 68
Portal site connections, 179–180
posters, STSADM, 135
PowerShell, 453–484
commands, 456–458
installing, 417, 454–456
overview, 416–417, 453–454

scripts, 460–463
   overview, 457
and SharePoint
   farm, 465–467
   Features, 480–484
   overview, 463–464
   setup, 464–465
   sites, 470–475
   Solutions, 477–480
   Web applications, 468–470
   Webs, 475–477
   SQL Server 2008, 448
   using cmdlets, 458–460
"Predeployment I/O Best Practices" white paper,
   Microsoft, 30
Premier support, Microsoft, 27–28
prescan tool, 15
presizing databases, 31
privacy policies, 284–285
process isolation, 54
production environments, virtualized, 29–30
Production farms, 42
proliferation, site, 198–199
propagation, index, 231–232
properties
   cluster, 171–172
   content, 263
   crawled, 236, 263
   displaying, 285
   managed, 236, 238, 263–265
   modifying, 281
   user profile, 280–287
   virtual server, 172–173
   Web application, 323
   working with STSADM, 170–173
Property Import Mapping section, Add User
   Profile Property page, 286
Property Picker, Advanced Search page, 263
Property Query rule type, 268
property stores, 230
protocol handler (PH), 230
providers, Forms Based Authentication, 315–318
ProvisionAssembly attribute, 213
ProvisionClass attribute, 213
ProvisionData attribute, 213
provisioning process, 202
proxy servers, 241
.PS1 files, 457

PSScripts directory, 463
Publishing farms, 42
publishing features, site collection, 261
Publishing Portal site template, 7
Publishing Sites, 107–108, 206
Publishing templates, 6–8
publishing traffic, 44
PublishingSite Feature, 220

Q
Query Server Default File Location section,
   Configure Office SharePoint Server Search
   Service Settings page, 238
Query servers
   adding, 237–238
   application servers, 403
   identifying, 77
   index management, 237
   index propagation and, 231
   in medium farms, 36–37
   multiple, 237
   overview, 227–228
   scaling, 33
   virtualization of, 29–30
Quick Launch bar, 181–182, 184–186
quotas
   growth management, 193
   in IT governance, 197–198
   storage, 70, 196

R
RAID 5, 10, 31
Read permission level, 100
Rebuild Index option, SQL Server Maintenance
   Plan Wizard, 342–343
Receiver element, 219–220
Records Center site template, 6
recovery. *see also* backup and disaster recovery;
   content recovery
   controlling downtime, 192
   SLA time requirements, 43
Recycle Bin, 358–364
recycle-bin-cleanup-enabled property, 363
recycle-bin-enabled property, 173
recycle-bin-retention-period property, 173, 363
Recycling tab, IIS Manager, 327–329
redirecting Web requests, 325–326

registration, site definition, 211–213
Reinstall Feature STSADM command, 221–222
Reliability and Performance Monitor, 428–430
Remote Command Prompt, 439
Remote Server Administration Tools (RSAT), 420
renamesite operation, 145
renameweb operation, 145
renaming permission levels, 103
Reorganize Index option, SQL Server Maintenance Plan Wizard, 342
Replicable check box, Add User Profile Property page, 285
Report Center site template, 9
reports, usage, 195–197
Request Queue Limit option, Application Pool Performance tab, 329
Reset Crawled Content Web page, 259
Resource Governor, 447
Resource Pools, 447
resources
    IT governance, 200
    Windows Server 2008, 444
restore operation, STSADM, 152–154, 393
Restore Selection option, Recycle Bin, 359
–restoremethod parameter, 158
restoring
    with Central Admin and STSADM, 395–398
    SharePoint content without SharePoint, 398
Restricted Read permission level, 100
results page, people search, 292–296
retractionsolution operation, 161, 225
Richie, Keith, 398
roles, 148–149, 408
RSAT (Remote Server Administration Tools), 420
RSS Viewer Web part, My Site, 301
rules, crawl, 256–258

S
Save site as template option, Site Settings page, 205–206
Save Site as Template Web page, 207
saving custom site templates, 205–207
scaling
    capability in installations, 52
    important considerations
        traffic types, 43–47
        usage, 42–43
    of objects, 21–22

server roles
    application servers, 33–34
    farm roles, 41–42
    topologies, 34–41
    Web Front Ends, 32–33
scanforfeatures operation, 161
scopes
    feature, 218–219
    search, 265–270
scripts
    backup, 369, 474–475
    PowerShell
        overview, 457
        use of, 460–463
    warm-up, 328
SDKs (Software Development Kits), 464
Search Administration Web page, 260
search alerts, 259–260
Search Center, 7, 246, 261–263, 288–296
Search Center Lite, 261
Search Center with Tabs, 7, 261, 289
Search Crawling Accounts, 125–126
Search Pages Web page, 292
Search Property Store database, SQL Server, 339
search request process, 239. *see also* enterprise search
search scopes, 265–270
Search section, Application Management tab, Central Admin, 64
Search Server 2008, 10–11
Search Server Express, 11
searches, 228. *see also* enterprise search
second-stage-recycle-bin-quota property, 173
securable objects, 93
secure access, 312
Secure Sockets Layer (SSL), 258, 310, 382
security, 87–128. *see also* site and content authorization; user authentication
    import schedule, 279
    improvements in Windows Server 2008, 440–441
    IT governance, 199–200
    overview, 87–88
    .PS1 files and, 457
    Shared Service Provider, 66–67
    site collections, 69
    Web Application Policies, 124–128
Security Configuration section, Operations tab, Central Admin, 62, 90

security trimming, 183, 237, 239
Select Role Services dialog box, 418
Server Manager, 408–416
server name mappings, 271
server roles
    application servers, 33–34
    farm roles, 41–42
    topologies, 34–41
    Web Front Ends, 32–33
Server Web page, 232
ServerManagerCmd.exe, 416, 440
Service Account option, Configure Windows
    SharePoint Services Search Service Settings on
    server Web page, 235
Service Administrators, 89
Service Level Agreement (SLA), 43
service pack 1 (SP1), slipstreaming, 84–85
service principal names (SPNs), 58–60
services, starting, 76–79
Set As Default My Site tab, My Site, 300
Set Up Groups for this Site page, 111–112
setproperty operation, 162, 170, 363
setsitelock operation, 145
SetSPN.exe support tool, 58–59
Settings menu
    Members Web page, 113, 118–119
    Site Permissions Web page, 119–120
    versioning and, 354
Shared Document library, 301
shared scopes, 266
Shared Services Administration, Central Admin, 80
Shared Services Provider (SSP)
    Administrators, 89
    advantage of, 66
    Application Pool Account, 56
    backing up databases, 381
    choosing quantity of, 65
    creating first, 80–84
    Database server role, 238
    defined, 5
    example Web site, 277
    Index server role
        adding, 232–236
        content index, 231
        content source, 229
        index propagation, 231–232
        indexing process, 229–231
        overview, 229
        single role per SSP, 229
    overview, 64
    Query Server role
        adding, 237–238
        Index management, 237
        multiple, 237
        overview, 236–237
    search administration
        authoritative pages, 270
        configuring content source, 246–251
        configuring indexing, 251–260
        federated locations, 271
        managed properties, 263–265
        overview, 245–246
        search centers, 261–263
        search scopes, 265–270
        server name mappings, 271
    Service Account, 56
    setting security, 66–67
    Web server role, 239
SharePoint 2007, 1–15
    choosing version
        MOSS, 5–11
        overview, 2
        WSS, 2–4
    overview, 1–2
    supporting technologies
        email server, 13–14
        SQL Server, 12–13
        Windows Server, 11–12
    upgrading options, 14–15
SharePoint Admin Account, 55
SharePoint Administration Toolkit, 174
SharePoint Designer (SPD), 364–366
SharePoint Farm Account, 55
SharePoint Site Management section, Application
    Management tab, Central Admin, 63, 90–91
SharePoint Sites Web part, My Site, 301
SharePoint Web Application Management section,
    Application Management tab, Central Admin,
    63, 83–84
SharePoint_admin database, 340
sharing, site collection, 72
–showtree parameter, 393–394
Shrink Database option, SQL Server Maintenance
    Plan Wizard, 342

shut-down limits, 330
Simple Mail Transfer Protocol (SMTP), 11, 13
single file installation, 223
single server install, 34–35
Site Actions menu, 186
site and content authorization
    administration model and levels
        Farm Administrators, 90
        overview, 88–90
        Site Collection Administrators, 90–93
    overview, 88
    permission assignment
        assigning to users and groups, 123–124
        overall permission management guidance,
            122–123
        overview, 122
    permission levels
        creating and modifying, 104–106
        key points, 100–101
        new permission levels, 103–104
        overview, 99–100
        viewing permissions for, 102–103
    permission management
        inheritance, 117–122
        overview, 114–115
        SharePoint versus Active Directory groups,
            115–117
    permissions
        key points, 98–99
        overview, 94
        viewing, 95–98
    security terminology, 93–94
    site groups
        enabling Publishing Site, 107–108
        key points, 108–110
        managing groups, 110–114
        overview, 106–107
Site Collection Administrators, 89–93
Site Collection Features Web page, 107
Site Collection Recycle Bin, 360–361
site collections, 21, 69–72, 83–84, 152–154
site customization, 201–225
    custom site templates
        composition of, 204
        versus custom site definitions, 215–216
        global use of, 208–209
        overview, 204

        saving, 205–207
        site definition dependency, 205
    Features
        creating new, 222–223
        dependency, 220–221
        deployment, 221–222
        description and Feature.xml, 217–220
        folder hierarchy, 217
        overview, 217
    overview, 201–202
    site creation and, 202–204
    site definitions
        configuration, 214–215
        custom site templates versus custom, 215–216
        description and registration, 211–213
        folder hierarchy, 209–211
        overview, 209
    solution packages, 223–225
site definitions
    configuration, 214–215
    custom site template dependency on, 205
    custom site templates versus custom, 215–216
    description and registration, 211–213
    folder hierarchy, 209–211
    overview, 202–204, 209
Site Delete Capture, 373–375
Site Directory site template, 7
site groups
    defined, 93
    enabling Publishing Site, 107–108
    key points, 108–110
    managing groups, 110–114
    overview, 106–107
Site Owners, 89–90
Site Permissions Web page, 118–119
Site Settings page, 185, 205–206
Site Template Gallery, 207–208
site templates. *see also* custom site templates
    compared to site definitions, 211
    MOSS, 6–9
    quota, 197–198
    size of, 162, 207
    STSADM management of, 162
    in STSADM site collections, 137–138
    WSS, 3–4
Site Undelete tool, 200
site usage summary report, 196–197

sites. *see also* Internet accessible Web sites
    auditing, 199–200
    controlling proliferation, 198–199
    creation of, 202–204
    navigation settings, 188–189
    redirect, 326
    working with in STSADM
        groups and roles, 148–149
        overview, 135–145
        users, 146–148
        Webs, 145–146
    working with PowerShell, 470–475
sizing tool, 44–47
SLA (Service Level Agreement), 43
SlideLibrary Feature directory, 217–219
slipstreaming service pack 1, 84–85
slow page loads, 348–350
small farms, 36
Smart Client Authoring feature, 78
SMB 2.0, 442–443
SMIGRATE.exe tool, 149
SMTP (Simple Mail Transfer Protocol), 11, 13
software
    backing up installed, 381–382
    boundaries, 344
    planning for boundaries, 18–22
    third-party, 24–25
Software Development Kits (SDKs), 464
solution packages
    key points, 223–225
    managing third-party code, 198
    overview, 223
Solution Store, 159–161
Solutions
    ClassIds, 378–379
    importance of, 160–161
    working with PowerShell, 477–480
Sorting section, Site Navigation Settings page, 188
sp_helpfile query, 338
SP1 (service pack 1), slipstreaming, 84–85
SPBackupDirectory object, 389
spbackup.log file, 390–391
SPBackupMethod object, 389
SPBackupObject object, 392
spbackup.xml file, 391
SPBRTOC.XML file, 385, 387–389, 392, 395
SPD (SharePoint Designer), 364–366
SPDirectoryName object, 389

SPDirectoryNumber object, 389
SPErrorCount object, 389
SPFarm object, 465–467
SPFeatureDefinition object, 481–482
SPFinishTime object, 389
SPId object, 389
SPIsBackup object, 389
SPNs (service principal names), 58–60
SPP Application Pool account, 56
SPRequestdBy object, 389
sprestore.log file, 390–391
SPRestoreMethod object, 389
SPSite objects, 470, 472
SPStartTime object, 389
SPTopComponent object, 389
SPTopComponentID object, 389
SPWarningCount object, 389
SPWeb objects, 472, 475
SPWebApplication object, 468
SPWebApplicationBuilder object, 468, 470
SPWebServiceCollection object, 468
SQL Express 2005, 13, 51
SQL Server
    32 bit versus 64 bit SharePoint versions, 26
    additional reading, 344
    BAK files, 391
    certificates, 451
    clustering, 404
    creating database for intranets, 313
    databases
        maintaining, 341–344
        overview, 336–341
    improvements in 2008 version
        management, 445–448
        overview, 407, 444
        Transparent Data Encryption, 448–451
    native backups, 398–401
    overview, 12–13, 336
    planning for hardware limits, 30–32
    scaling, 34
    SharePoint performance, 322
SSL (Secure Sockets Layer), 258, 310, 382
SSP. *see* Shared Services Provider
Stand-Alone install, 35, 54
standard client access license, 5
Standard version, MOSS, 5–8
Standard View option, Create View page, 20–21
stapling, Feature, 222–223

start-up limits, 330
static compression, 332
Stop Inheriting Links button, Top link bar, 185
storage space allocation report, 195–196
storage units, site collection, 70–71
STSADM, 129–175
  advanced management
    content database, 162–166
    Feature, 161–162
    managed paths and zones, 167
    Solution Store, 159–161
    template, 162
    Web application policies, 168–170
  backup and disaster recovery
    farm level, 155–159
    overview, 149
    site collection level, 152–154
    Web level, 149–152
  catastrophic backups, 393–395
  exclusive functionality of
    extending STSADM, 175
    other STSADM-only operations, 174–175
    working with properties, 170–173
  Features management, 221
  overview, 129–135
  versus PowerShell, 453
  Recycle Bin and, 363–364
  restoring with, 395–398
  setting up Kerberos for Excel Services, 60
  Solutions and, 477–478
  Web backups, 366–372
  working with sites
    groups and roles, 148–149
    overview, 135–145
    users, 146–148
    Webs, 145–146
subscriptions, 431
subsites, 21, 117, 190. *see also* site collections
subWebs, 151–152. *see also* site collections
Suggested by SharePoint option, Colleague Tracker
  Web Part, 302
supporting technologies
  email server, 13–14
  SQL Server, 12–13
  Windows Server, 11–12
Symantec software, 403
syncsolution operation, 161
System Status, Search Administration Web page, 260

T
targeting links, 189–190
Task Scheduler, 435–438
TCP/IP optimization, Windows Server 2008, 442
TDE (Transparent Data Encryption), 448–451
Team Collaboration Lists Feature, 480
Team Site templates, 3–4
Temp directory, 153
Tempdb database, SQL Server, 337
templatename='global' property, 212
templates. *see* custom site templates; site templates
test environments, virtualized, 29
Test farms, 42
Test-Path command, 475
third-party code, 198–199
third-party software, 24–25
three-tier administrative model, 88–91
thunking, 25
Tisseghem, Patrick, 251, 271, 287
top link bar, 185
topologies, 34–41
Topology and Services section, Operations tab,
  Central Admin, 62, 76–77, 79
tracing failed requests, 422–427
traffic types, scaling, 43–47
Transparent Data Encryption (TDE), 448–451
tree view control, 181–182
trial versions, 11, 73
trimming, security, 183, 237, 239

U
UI (user interface), compressing backups in, 445
uncustomized pages, 203–204
Uninstall Feature STSADM command, 162,
  221–222
Update Personal Web Parts permission, 98
Update Schedule option, Scopes section, Configure
  Search Settings page, 269
updatealert operation, 174–175
updates, 85, 192–193, 228
Upgrade and Migration section, Operations tab,
  Central Admin, 62
upgrades, 14–15, 192–193
upgradesolution operation, 161
uploading large files, 324
–url parameter, 367
URL summary page, Crawl Log, 255
URLs, crawler impact rules and, 242

URLScan, IIS, 441
usage reports, 195–197
usages analysis processing, 79–80
Use a dedicated Web front-end for crawling option,
    Configure Office SharePoint Server Search
    Service Settings Web page, 234
Use all Web front-end computers for crawling
    option, Configure Office SharePoint Server
    Search Service Settings Web page, 234
Use Client Integration Features permission, 98, 311
Use cookie for crawling option, Add Crawl Rule
    Web page, 258
Use Links from Parent button, Top link bar, 185
Use Personal Features permission, 67, 298
Use Remote Interfaces permission, 98, 311
Use Self-Service Site Creation permission, 97
user authentication
    anonymous access, 307–311
    overview, 307
    secure access, 312
user interface (UI), compressing backups in, 445
user profiles
    overview, 274–275
    profile management and configuration
    import connections, 276–280
    overview, 275
    profile properties and mappings, 280–287
    SSP and, 228
User Profiles and Properties Web page, 278, 280–281
user Web applications, 83–84
UserGroup.xml file, 151
userrole operation, 148–149
users
    assigning permissions to, 123–124
    creating FBA providers and new, 315–317
    defined, 93
    SSPs, 65–66
    working with STSADM, 146–148

V
Variations technology, 306
versioning, 354–358
Versioning settings page, 355
versions, SharePoint
    MOSS, 5–11
    overview, 2
    WSS, 2–4

–versions 4 option, 367
View Application Pages permission, 96, 311
View by Relevance link, search results page, 293
View Items permission, 96
View Only permission level, 99
View Pages permission, 97
View Profile Properties page, 282
View Scopes Web page, 267, 269–270
View Usage Data permission, 96
View Versions permission, 96
virtual log file (VLF), 448
virtual server properties, 172–173
virtualization
    development environment, 28–29
    disaster recovery environments, 30
    overview, 27–28
    production environment, 29–30
    test environment, 29
Visio diagrams, 46–47
Visitors group, 122
VLF (virtual log file), 448
VMware, 28
Volume Shadow Services (VSS), 402

W
W2k3 (Windows Server 2003), 11–12, 443
W2k8. *see* Windows Server 2008
w3wp.exe processes, 331–332
warm-up script, 328
WCM (Web Content Management) capability, 306
Web 2.0 site templates, 3–4
Web Address scope rules, 268
Web Application permissions, 94
Web application policies
    overview, 124
    policy management, 125–128
    STSADM management of, 168–170
Web applications
    creating and configuring, 314–319
    creating first user, 83–84
    Internet Information Services, 322–326
    overview, 68–69
    working with PowerShell, 468–470
Web Content Management (WCM) capability, 306
Web Front Ends (WFEs)
    high availability, 403
    installation, 35, 53

in medium farms, 36–40
overview, 32–33
upgrades, 27
virtualization of, 29–30
Web parts
CQWP, 72, 346
filtering, 9
limits on, 22
Web server role, 227, 239
Web Single Sign-On authentication, 312
Web Site tab, IIS, 323–325
Web sites. *see* Internet accessible Web sites; sites
Webs. *see also* site collections
backups
overview, 364
SharePoint Designer, 364–366
STSADM, 366–372
STSADM backup and disaster recovery, 149–152
working with PowerShell, 475–477
working with STSADM, 145–146
WEBTEMP files, 211
WFEs. *see* Web Front Ends
–whatif parameter, 416
Where-Object command, 471, 476, 479
white papers, Microsoft. *see* Microsoft white papers
Wiki Site templates, 4
wildcard characters for crawl rules, 243
Windows 32 bit, 11–12
Windows 64 bit, 11–12
Windows authentication, 312
Windows External Connector License, 2
Windows Firewall, 441
Windows Internal Database, 13, 51
Windows Remote Management (WinRM), 438–440
Windows Remote Shell (WinRS), 438–440
Windows security groups, 106–107, 115–116
Windows Server 2003 (W2k3), 11–12, 443
Windows Server 2008 (W2k8), 407–444
management improvements
Event Viewer, 430–435
IIS 7, 417–427
overview, 408
Power Shell, 416–417

Reliability And Performance Monitor, 428–430
Server Manager, 408–416
Task Scheduler, 435–438
WinRM and WinRS, 438–440
other changes in, 443
overview, 11–12, 407
performance, 442–443
resources, 444
security improvements, 440–441
Windows Server 2003, 443
Windows SharePoint Services Search Service Settings Web page, 235
Windows SharePoint Services v3. *see* WSS
WinRM (Windows Remote Management), 438–440
WinRS (Windows Remote Shell), 438–440
Workflow Management section, Application Management tab, Central Admin, 63
Workload Groups, 447
workspaces, meeting, 186–187
World Wide Web service, 11
WSPs. *see* solution packages
WSS (Windows SharePoint Services v3)
navigation
maintaining, 184–185
meeting workspaces, 186–187
overview, 183–184
Quick Launch bar, 186
top link bar, 185
overview, 2–4
search, 78
site groups, 107
WSS-only installation option, 54
WSS Crawl Account, 56
WSS Search Account, 56

X
XML files
backup directory, 391
Event Viewer, 430
failed requests, 427

Z
zones, STSADM management of, 167